eturned on or b
bel

PRIMO LEVI

PRIMO LEVI

TRAGEDY OF AN OPTIMIST

MYRIAM ANISSIMOV

TRANSLATED BY STEVE COX

AURUM PRESS

First published in Great Britain
1998 by Aurum Press Ltd
25 Bedford Avenue, London WC1B 3AT

First published as *Primo Levi ou la tragédie d'un optimiste*

Copyright © 1996, éditions Jean-Claude Lattès

English translation copyright © 1998 by Steve Cox

A catalogue record for this book is available from the British Library.

ISBN 1 85410 503 5

10 9 8 7 6 5 4 3 2 1
2002 2001 2000 1999 1998

Printed and bound in Great Britain
by MPG Books, Bodmin

To Samuel Frocht Ydl, Khyl and Israël Frydman,
my uncles, and Dinah and Moshe Frydman,
my grandparents, murdered by the Nazis.

Picture Acknowledgements

Page 1: Giansanti/Sygma. Page 2: (top) Jewish Library, Turin (below) *La Gazzetta del Popolo*, 28 October 1933 and 28 October 1937.
Page 3 (top) F. Antonicelli, Ricordi Photographic; (below) Myriam Anissimov; drawing: E.G. Tedeschi.
Page 4: (top) Archives of Jewish Documentation Centre, Paris; (below) Panstowowe Museum, Auschwitz.
Page 5: (top) Paola Agosti; (centre) Fondazione Bellonci, Rome; (below) Agnese Incisa.
Page 6 (top left) Giorgina Levi; others: All Rights Reserved.
Page 7 (middle) Ferdinando Camon; others: All Rights Reserved.
Page 8: (top) Renato Portese; (below) *La Stampa*.

Text Acknowledgements

The author and publishers wish to thank the following for their kind permission to reproduce the works quoted in this book:
Cesare Cases for his review of *If Not Now, When?* from *L'Indice*;
Corriere della Sera, Milan, for an interview with Primo Levi;
Editions Ramsay, Paris, for *Chroniques d'ailleurs* by Paul Steinberg;
Giulio Einaudi Editore, Turin, for *La ricerca delle radici*, Primo Levi's preface to the stage version of *Se questo è un uomo*, and letters from Italo Calvino to Primo Levi;
Faber and Faber, London, for *Collected Poems* by Primo Levi;
The London Review of Books for Philip Roth's interview with Primo Levi;
Michael Joseph, London, for *The Drowned and the Saved* by Primo Levi;
Risa Sodi for her interview with Primo Levi from the *Partisan Review*;
Bruno Vasari for Primo Levi's speech "The Camp and Memory."

Every year, at the moment of telling how a third of our people disappeared in smoke, and how this was later denied, we feel helpless and discouraged, as were our ancestors who survived, and who dedicated all their strength and time to bearing witness, and to passing on an experience both impossible to pass on, and impossible to forget.

Liliane Atlan, *An Opera for Theresienstadt*

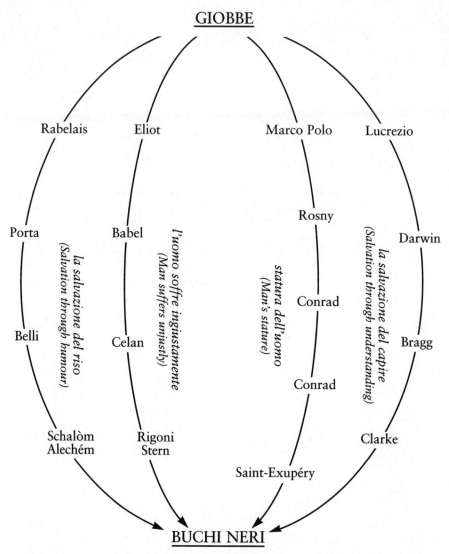

GIOBBE

Rabelais   Eliot   Marco Polo   Lucrezio

Porta   Babel   Rosny   Darwin

la salvazione del riso
(Salvation through humour)

l'uomo soffre ingiustamente
(Man suffers unjustly)

statura dell'uomo
(Man's stature)

la salvazione del capire
(Salvation through understanding)

Belli   Celan   Conrad   Bragg

Conrad

Schalòm
Alechém   Rigoni
Stern   Clarke

Saint-Exupéry

BUCHI NERI

The bipolar spheroid drawn by Levi to preface his anthology of some books that had influenced his life, *La ricerca delle radici* ("The quest for roots"). At the north pole is Job ("Giobbe"), at the south pole are the "*buchi neri*," black holes, including Auschwitz. See p. 182.

CONTENTS

PRIMO LEVI'S WORKS

This section sets out Primo Levi's major works and their translations published in English. Bibliographic details of Levi's less major works are given in the footnotes to the text. All references to Levi's major works are given using shortened forms of the titles, as set out below. Where two sets of figures are given for page numbers, the first (in *italic*) is for the US edition of a translated work and the second (in roman) for the UK edition. Details of the specific translations quoted are given in the Notes, starting on p. 417.

The major works
   Se questo è un uomo, 1958, second edition, Einaudi, Turin.
   La tregua, 1963, Einaudi, Turin.
   Storie naturali, 1966, Einaudi, Turin.
   Vizio di forma, 1971, Einaudi, Turin.
   Il sistema periodico, 1975, Einaudi, Turin.
   La chiave a stella, 1978, Einaudi, Turin.
   Lilit e altri racconti, 1981, 1985, Einaudi, Turin.
   La ricerca delle radici, 1981, Einaudi, Turin.
   Se non ora, quando?, 1982, Einaudi, Turin.
   L'altrui mestiere, 1985, Einaudi, Turin.
   I sommersi e i salvati, 1986, Einaudi, Turin.
   Racconti e saggi, 1986, Editrice La Stampa, Turin.

Complete works
The works of Primo Levi are available in three volumes, published by Einaudi, as follows:
Volume I, 1987: *Se questo è un uomo*; *La tregua*; *Il sistema periodico*; *I sommersi e i salvati*;
Volume II, 1988: *La chiave a stella*; *Se non ora, quando?*; *Ad ora incerta*;
Volume III, 1990: *Storie naturali*; *Vizio di forma*; *Lilit e altri racconti*; *L'altrui mestiere*; *Racconti e saggi*.

Poetry
L'osteria di Brema, 1975, Scheiwiller, Milan.
Ad ora incerta, 1984, Garzanti, Turin.

Works in English Translation
Se questo è un uomo: translated by Stuart Woolf as *Survival In Auschwitz* (US) and *If This Is A Man* (UK), Orion Press, New York, 1960: The Bodley Head, London, 1965. The title is abbreviated to *Man*.

La tregua: translated by Stuart Woolf as *The Reawakening* (US) and as *The Truce* (UK), Little, Brown and Co., Boston, 1965; The Bodley Head, London, 1965. The title is abbreviated to *Truce*.

Storie naturali and *Vizio di forma*: translated by Raymond Rosenthal as *The Sixth Day*, 1990, Summit Books, New York; Michael Joseph, London.

Il sistema periodico: translated by Raymond Rosenthal as *The Periodic Table*, Schocken Books, New York, 1984; Michael Joseph, London 1985. The title is abbreviated to *Table*.

La chiave a stella: translated by William Weaver as *The Monkey's Wrench* (US) and *The Wrench* (UK), Summit Books, New York, 1986; Michael Joseph, London, 1987. The title is abbreviated to *Wrench*.

Lilit e altri racconti: translated by Ruth Feldman as *Moments of Reprieve*, Summit Books, New York, 1979; Michael Joseph, London, 1986. The title is abbreviated to *Reprieve*.

Se non ora, quando?: translated by William Weaver as *If Not Now, When?*, Summit Books, New York, 1985; Michael Joseph, London, 1986. The title is abbreviated to *INNW*.

L'altrui mestiere: translated by Raymond Rosenthal as *Other People's Trades*, 1989, Summit Books, New York; Michael Joseph, London. The title is abbreviated to *Trades*.

I sommersi e i salvati: translated by Raymond Rosenthal as *The Drowned and the Saved*, 1988, Summit Books, New York, 1988; Michael Joseph, London. The title is abbreviated to *DS*.

Racconti e saggi: translated by Raymond Rosenthal and included in *The Mirror Maker*, Schocken, New York, 1989; Methuen, London, 1990.

Ad ora incerta: translated by Ruth Feldman and Brian Swann as *Complete Poems*, Faber and Faber, London, 1988. References to this title are taken from the new 1992 edition.

Introduction

On 11 April 1987 Primo Levi plunged down the stairwell of the house where he was born and had always lived; the house where he was born now became the scene of his death.

Before him, Stefan Zweig and Walter Benjamin, hunted by the Nazis or by the Vichy Government of France, had killed themselves. Other writers, whose families had been swallowed up in genocide or who had themselves experienced the ghettos or the hell of the concentration camps, have committed suicide — among them Tadeusz Borowski, Paul Celan, Bruno Bettelheim, and Piotr Rawicz, as well as Jean Améry, whose gesture Primo Levi had attempted to interpret.

At least in his public statements, Levi gave the impression that he had come to terms with the experience of Auschwitz. In 1979, for example, he wrote "I lived through happy years after the camp because I was lucky. My time there did not destroy me physically or morally, as was the case with other people. I did not lose my family, my country, or my home. I would probably never have written had I not had that experience to write about...."

This gentle, reserved and unassuming man, whose fame had spread worldwide, chose a violent and dramatic death. Yet he had written that suicide was "a meditated act, a non-instinctive, unnatural choice," and went on to say that

> in the majority of cases, suicide is born from a feeling of guilt that no punishment has attenuated; now, the harshness of imprisonment was perceived as punishment, and the feeling of guilt (if there is punishment, there must have been guilt) was relegated to the background only to re-emerge after the liberation, in other words, there was no need to punish oneself by suicide because of a (true or presumed) guilt, one was already expiating it by one's daily suffering.[1]

Primo Levi had an innate and intuitive faith in mankind. He had been a practising chemist for thirty years. As he saw it, the actions of a chemist in his laboratory were sacred gestures that belonged to mankind's long experience on its march towards civilization. There were many who wondered why, if his suicide was indeed premeditated, he had not prepared some lethal substance that would have ensured a painless death. A few days previously, he had written to Ferdinando Camon[2] that the existence of Auschwitz meant there could be no God. But the emptiness of Heaven was no new discovery for this child of the Enlightenment and heir to Italian Jacobinism.

In a last interview published on 26 April 1987 he asked the questioning journalist not to consider him as a prophet: "Prophets are the plague of today,

1

and perhaps of all time, because it is impossible to tell a true prophet from a false one."

A storm of sudden violence tore through the careful reserve of Primo Levi on the morning he went out on to the landing and threw himself down from the third floor. At about 10 a.m., "*Dottore* Levi" had affably opened the door to Jolanda Gasperi, the concierge, when she brought up his morning post as she did every day. He thanked her, and she noticed nothing unusual about his behaviour before she walked downstairs again. A few minutes later she heard the sound of a heavy impact. She looked through the windows of her lodge and rushed towards the body that lay on the stone floor behind the lift cage. The face was covered in blood, but Signora Gasperi knew who it was immediately.

Primo Levi's senile mother lay in her bedroom upstairs. His thirty-two year old son, who lived on the same landing, had heard nothing. Levi's wife Lucia had gone out shopping. A few minutes after the concierge, she in her turn discovered her husband's bleeding, broken body, sprawled in the lobby of the apartment block where three generations of Levis had lived.

The news of Levi's suicide raced across Turin. A few of his close friends hurried to the scene, while the forensic pathologist made out the death certificate and an ambulance carried the body to the Medical–Legal Institute.

The world of politics responded with emotion. The president of the Republic, Francesco Cossiga, sent a telegram of condolence to the family of "the writer, who has so tragically departed." The many other messages included telegrams from the president of the Senate, Amintore Fanfani, and from the president of the Chamber of Deputies, Nilde Jotti, who wrote:

> The tragic death of Primo Levi must be viewed as the ultimate reminder of Nazi genocide, the unforgettable crime against mankind and human civilization. Only now do we understand the pain and difficulty which his books and his words — so full of faith in humanity and in reason — must have caused Primo Levi; the utterly human resistance they represent is not now broken, but transmuted into our grief in the face of his final message.

The secretary of the Republican Party, Giovanni Spadolini, expressed his sorrow for "the interpreter and witness of the greatest tragedy ever to have befallen mankind ... Let us all beware of the rebirth of antisemitism .... His death impoverishes the landscape of our culture and gives us greater cause to reflect on the future of humanity."

As a writer, Levi the chemist had succeeded in transmuting the memory of the year he spent in Auschwitz, and the grief that burned inside him, into thought and meditation. In death, the author of *The Periodic Table*,[3] which derived from Mendeleev's table of the elements, the metaphor that illuminated one of his finest books, now returned to the great chain of life, the cycle of matter, that he had described in his concluding chapter, "Carbon."

Primo Levi's funeral, solemn and silent, took place on the eve of the Jewish festival of Passover. The walnut coffin was covered in flowers — red roses, white irises, pink orchids. There was no funeral oration, and no speeches (Jews do not read funeral addresses on the eve of holy days), but a large and respectful crowd filled the streets.

The body was laid in its coffin at the Medical–Legal Institute in the Via Chiabrera at 1:30 in the afternoon of 13 April, in the presence of Lucia Levi, his wife, Anna Maria, his sister, and Renzo and Lisa, his children.

In front of the Institute building on the bank of the River Po stood representatives of the Jewish communities of Turin, Milan, and Rome, ex-deportees, writers, former members of the partisan movement Giustizia e Libertà ("Justice and Liberty"), and politicians of all parties. Many of his friends were in the crowd, among them Professor Mario Sacerdote, the judge and historian Alessandro Galante Garrone, the philosopher and life senator Norberto Bobbio, the astrophysicist Tullio Regge, the writers Nuto Revelli and Corrado Stajano, Professor Massimo Mila, his publisher Giulio Einaudi, the critic Cesare Cases, Lorenzo Mondo, editor-in-chief of La Stampa, Bruno Vasari, vice-president of the Association of Ex-Deportee-Internees of Mauthausen, Nella Bellinzona, ex-internee of Ravensbrück, and Federico Silla Accati, founder and owner of the SIVA company (Società Industriale Vernici e Affini) where Levi had worked for twenty-eight years.

At 2 p.m., in the mortuary, the chief rabbi of Turin, Emanuele Artom, read out Psalm 91: "He that dwelleth in the secret place of the most High shall abide under the shadow of the Almighty. I will say of the Lord, He is my refuge and my fortress, my God; in him will I trust."

The coffin, followed by the family, was carried to the hearse by survivors of the camps, and the funeral procession made its way to the Jewish cemetery in the Corso Regio Parco, where the burial took place according to custom, in the presence of five hundred people. The ceremony ended with the recitation of the Kaddish, followed by El Melech Rachamim and then Psalm 103, verses 13–14: "Like as a father pitieth his children, so the Lord pitieth them that fear Him. For He knoweth our frame; He remembereth that we are dust." Lastly the rabbi spoke verse 19 of Genesis, chapter 3: "In the sweat of thy face shalt thou eat bread, till thou return unto the ground; for out of it wast thou taken, for dust thou art, and unto dust shalt thou return."

Late that afternoon, the lawyer Bianca Guidetti Serra, mayor of Turin and a close friend of Primo Levi, paid tribute to him in the town hall, in the presence of the family. She recalled how the little group of young men and women to whom she and Primo Levi had belonged in 1938 had gone underground to fight against Fascism. The members of the group remained in touch throughout their lives; for forty years it was their regular custom to meet on chosen Sundays.

In November 1987, seven months after his death, Primo Levi's literary reputation was at last confirmed in his own country, when the Accademia Nazionale dei Lincei posthumously awarded him the Antonio Feltrinelli prize. His works had been translated into seventeen languages in eighteen countries.

3

On his grave, which lies next to that of his mother, who died five years later, his family laid a slab of plain black marble carved with his name, the dates of his birth and death, and the number 174517, which the Nazis had tattooed on his arm in Auschwitz. On either side of the gravestone they planted a Japanese maple with slender, dark red leaves which today have spread all over the Jewish cemetery.

Prologue

Today the work of Primo Levi holds a central place in the extensive literature of testimony to the extermination of the Jews of Europe and to the world of the camps, the "concentrationary world." Yet in Italy Levi was long recognized solely as the author of *If This Is a Man* and *The Truce*,[1] which deal with the eleven months he spent in Auschwitz and the further nine months of his travels through a devastated Europe after his liberation. Not until the American publication of *The Periodic Table* in 1984, which Saul Bellow praised as a masterpiece, did the literary world finally take notice, and a larger number of readers begin to discover his other books.

This modest man, who was not really taken for a writer in his own country because he was known as a chemist, found fame two years before his death, but since then his readership has grown and continues to grow. Yet he brought us no information about the world of the camps that was not available elsewhere. The testimony offered to the reader in his first book, *If This Is A Man*, made no claim to be exhaustive. Levi, who had retained almost total recall of his captivity in Auschwitz, was selective in conveying what he had lived through. Moreover, he deliberately omitted some episodes, which he recounted two decades later in the form of articles in *La Stampa*. Although he devoted his life to his mission as a witness, he avoided recounting his experiences too frequently, because, he said, the story tended to set into a crystallized form that displaced the raw memory. His originality lay in the way he wrote, a style he had acquired in the laboratory, where accuracy and concision were insisted upon, and lyricism and passion excluded.

In Primo Levi the world discovered a moralist with a subtle mind and subtle sense of humour. He was a Jew who had returned to his roots, not a believer, but a great reader of the Bible, the Talmud and the Shulchan Aruch.[2] He was also an optimist, a follower of the Enlightenment and of Italian Jacobinism, opposed to suicide — and yet it was this man who on an April morning, after a period of dreadful depression, suddenly "exited life by the window", in the words of the Italian critic Cesare Cases, who attempted, two years after Levi's death to analyse the contradictions that closed in upon his friend:

> He was condemned to speak about Auschwitz, to be the guardian of its memory, and he was compelled to acknowledge that that memory was fading. He was shocked first of all by the revisionism of Faurisson,[3] and later by that of the rightist German historians. The excellent article that he wrote about them in *La Stampa* showed some weariness, the weariness of a man who kept on having to repeat the same thing. His private

life was shrinking, the outside world widening enormously, and the spirit of the time was completely different from what he had hoped. He must have been crushed by these contradictions.

Levi had written that "suicide invites a host of explanations," arguing that no one has ever returned to tell of their own death. He left no message, so it would be mere speculation to list the possible reasons he may have had for choosing death, and that particular death.

Primo Levi was born in Turin, the capital of Piedmont, in the heart of a very ancient Jewish community, recently emancipated, which had rapidly integrated and assimilated. Although it was still proud of its identity, its sense of heritage was dissolving, and the community retained only a few of its rites, the meaning of which seemed to have been forgotten in the span of two generations.

The same process of assimilation was overtaking the entire Jewish community of Italy, which, while small, was the oldest in Europe, its origins dating back to the Second Temple. Primo Levi himself delved into the history of the Jews of Piedmont when in 1984 the Jewish community of Turin put on an exhibition to celebrate the centenary of the inauguration of its great synagogue built in the Via Pio Quinto (Pius V was a pope and grand inquisitor particularly cruel towards the Jews).[4] On this occasion the Hebrew Library published a handsome illustrated volume, *Ebrei a Torino* ("The Jews of Turin"),[5] and Primo Levi wrote the preface, which begins as follows:[6]

> On the occasion of the centenary of our synagogue ... we, the Jews of Turin, have decided just this once to abandon our traditional twofold reserve. The Piedmontese reserve, rooted in its specific geography and history, is well known; because of it there are some who see in us the least Italianate of Italians. And subject to the age-old reticence of the Jews of the diaspora, we have always had to live in silence and suspicion, to listen a lot and talk a little, to avoid attention, because "you never know."
>
> We have never been numerous: just over four thousand in the thirties, and that was the greatest number we have ever reached; just over a thousand today. And yet we do not feel that we exaggerate if we say that we have counted for something, and still do count for something, in the life of this town ....
>
> When our fathers (for the most part not Turinese, but mainly dwelling in the small community of Piedmont) came to live in the town towards the end of the last century, they brought with them the great strength — undoubtedly unique, and a specific gift — that history has bequeathed to the Jews: literacy, religious and secular culture understood as a duty, a right, a necessity, one of life's delights; ...

Levi's preface celebrates both the contribution of the Jews to Italian society as well as the way in which Italy, and most specifically Turin, was able to accept and integrate its Jewish communities. The text testifies to Levi's double commitment — to his Jewish origins and to the region and city of his birth — seen not as a conflict of allegiance but as a positive integration of diverse influences. Thus he honours men such as Umberto Terracini, Leone Ginzburg, and Emanuele and Ennio Artom, among many others, for their specifically Jewish contribution in the fight against Fascism. For Levi, the exhibition was a vital record of the valuable contribution of his Jewish Turinese community which, he feared, was bound, in the end, to disappear.

Part One

1   Corso Re Umberto

The Corso Re Umberto is one of the broad avenues that criss-cross the elegant La Crocetta quarter in Turin. There are only a few shops, and the heavy gates of *palazzi* with austere façades often open on to hallways as spacious and sonorous as crypts. Passers-by are rare. Amid the dense foliage of the chestnut trees, the tramcars glide on rails covered in weeds.

One Saturday morning in April 1987, a tragedy disrupted the peace and quiet of the Corso Re Umberto. Primo Levi had taken his own life.

He left no farewell note to family or friends to account for the reasons that made him choose to die. Two days before, he had phoned the office of the Jewish community of Turin to ask whether the *matzah*, the unleavened Passover bread, had arrived. The previous day, on the last afternoon he was to spend in his study in Turin, he had phoned his cousin Giulia Diena, and Giovanni Tesio, a literary critic with whom he had begun an authorized biography which had been interrupted by his prostate operation.

He was going through a phase of deep depression — not the first — as he struggled to recover from the after-effects of the operation, which had affected him severely. He was constantly occupied with his ninety-one year old mother, who was paralyzed, tyrannical and senile, and with his blind mother-in-law who was four years older. Primo Levi had a strong sense of duty, and had taken it upon himself to keep them both inside the family circle. Nevertheless, between them the two old ladies were a heavy responsibility and a source of tension for himself and his wife Lucia.

In the public sphere, he had been deeply offended by the arguments denying the Holocaust which had received broad coverage in the press, and had replied to the French revisionist Holocaust denier Robert Faurisson and Ernst Nolte, the German apologist for the Nazi regime,[1] in an article called "The Black Hole of Auschwitz," published shortly before his death in *La Stampa*, the newspaper to which he had been a contributor for twenty-seven years.

Some people have claimed that Primo Levi committed suicide, like the writer Jean Améry, because of the Holocaust. Yet when writing about his deportation to Auschwitz he had stated: "Auschwitz left its mark on me, but it did not remove my desire to live. On the contrary, that experience increased my desire, it gave my life a purpose, to bear witness, so that such a thing should never occur again."[2]

Levi had argued against suicide several times in his books, and he had conducted a kind of posthumous argument with Jean Améry after the latter's suicide on 17 October 1978. He had replied to Améry in a chapter of his last book, *The Drowned and the Saved*, entitled "The Intellectual in Auschwitz,"

11

in which he also defended himself against being the "forgiver" that Améry had claimed to have unearthed in him, in a book called *Jenseits von Schuld und Sühne*.[3]

Nine years after Améry, Levi too chose suicide. But Améry had premeditated and organized his death, whereas Levi, despite the period of dreadful depression he was suffering, appears to have succumbed to a sudden violent impulse. It is worth noting that his paternal grandfather also committed suicide — because of his wife's infidelity — and that the adolescent Primo Levi had mentioned the possibility of taking his own life to Alberto Salmoni, one of his close friends. The reasons that made him think about killing himself at the age of seventeen were tied up with the torments of a painfully shy young man born into an assimilated middle-class Jewish family. Referring to his sense of inferiority in the presence of girls, and uncontrollable terror at the idea of approaching them in spite of his longing to do so, he explained that this inhibition was undoubtedly linked to the feeling of being Jewish and circumcised. The truth is that his identity was still unformed, and his sense of belonging — or not — was imposed at first by his Christian classmates, who were the chief reminders of his difference. A Jew, he wrote in *The Periodic Table*, is someone who is circumcised, who does not celebrate Christmas, and does not eat pork. By likening circumcision to castration, his classmates intensified his feeling of being both odd and inferior. The racial laws which came into force in Italy in October 1938 made him aware of his Jewishness. At the time he was studying chemistry and was able to take his doctorate, even though he was an "impure Jew," only thanks to the protection of an anti-Fascist teacher, the astrophysicist Nicola Dallaporta.

When a journalist once asked him whether, after surviving Auschwitz, he still had trust in mankind, Primo Levi replied:

> I have always had it intuitively from birth. The camp did not manage to destroy it. That doesn't mean that it is necessary to have trust in all men, nor that one should not totally distrust some of them .... It is better to begin with a feeling of trust, at the risk of being mistaken. I prefer that in principle to despair and pessimism. That is a gamble. Optimism too is a gamble. It seems to me that optimism, although irrational, is the way to start out on the right foot, even it if turns out that one was mistaken.[4]

2   A Jewish childhood under Fascism

Primo Levi was away from his apartment on the Corso Re Umberto only on rare occasions and for brief periods, except for the year he spent in the concentration camp of Monowitz-Buna (Auschwitz III), and the long months of being shunted around through Eastern Europe and Byelorussia before his return to Turin on 19 October 1945.

He described his apartment in an article published in *La Stampa*, to which he regularly contributed essays, articles, notes, and poems.[1] This nest, this "territory," was situated in a brick-built apartment block, in keeping with the other buildings on the avenue, and clad in a stucco that had turned dark grey in the course of almost a century. Perhaps it looked more sober than the rest, rather more austere in appearance, with no elaborate friezes above the high windows. On the other hand, when you pushed open the heavy entrance door, it came as a surprise to discover a hall and then a handsome flight of stairs, painted a creamy white, with a glazed lift of the kind manufactured at the turn of the century, and cast-iron banisters of Art Nouveau design.

Nothing could have induced Primo Levi to move out of the apartment he was born in. He never preferred a more modern, luxurious or comfortable home, because he loved the place where his father and grandfather had lived. Every nook and cranny in the corridor was dear to him, including the wardrobe where as a child he had cut his knee on a splinter of glass while playing hide-and-seek. He never dreamed of leaving the solid walls that shut out the noises from the avenue, which during his childhood still had a village air about it, where the glazier and rag-and-bone man passed by, as well as the "collector of hair-combings," and the street singers with their barrel organs, who would catch the coins thrown out of windows, wrapped in a scrap of paper. Only close friends crossed the threshold of that quiet apartment.

Agnese Incisa, a young editor from the publishing house Einaudi, who had a very friendly and trusting relationship with Primo Levi, describes a visit she paid him in November 1986, when his bedridden mother kept summoning her son to her room. Incisa remembers a dark passageway and the tidy hush of the austere apartment. The living-room had a flowered settee, late nineteenth-century furniture and lace mats. She noticed two bookcases — one of them completely devoted to the Holocaust, with books in Yiddish and Hebrew — a computer, a big table used as a writing desk, the shutters drawn over the two windows, and the cloistered atmosphere permeating the whole apartment. During her visit, the old lady called her son several times to ask him to fetch a glass of water, or tell her the time, or account for what he was doing. Levi told Agnese Incisa that each day at lunchtime it was his duty to spoon-feed his mother, even though she always had a nurse by her side.

After meeting him the previous spring in London, the writer Philip Roth came to visit Primo Levi in Turin in September 1986. He spent "a long weekend" in his company, conducting a series of interviews.[2] Roth explained that

> The Levis' large apartment is still shared, as it has been since they met and married after the war, with Primo Levi's mother. She is 91. Levi's 95-year-old mother-in-law lives not far away, in the apartment imme-diately next door lives his 28-year-old son, a physicist, and a few streets off is his 38-year-old daughter, a botanist. I don't personally know of another contemporary writer who has voluntarily remained, over so many decades, intimately entangled and in such direct, unbroken contact with his immediate family, his birthplace, his region, the world of his forebears and, particularly, with the local working environment which, in Turin, the home of Fiat, is largely industrial ....

Roth writes about

> the lively, wide-ranging conversation we conducted, in English ... mostly behind the door of the quiet study off the entrance foyer to the Levis' apartment. Levi's study is a large, simply furnished room. There is an old flowered sofa and a comfortable easy chair; on the desk is a shrouded word-processor; perfectly shelved behind the desk are Levi's variously coloured notebooks; on shelves all round the room are books in Italian, German and English. The most evocative object is one of the smallest, an unobtrusively hung sketch of a half-destroyed wire fence at Auschwitz. Displayed more prominently on the walls are playful constructions skilfully twisted into shape by Levi himself out of insu-lated copper wire — that is, wire coated with the varnish developed for that purpose in his own laboratory. There is a big wire butterfly, a wire owl, a tiny wire bug, and high on the wall behind the desk are two of the largest constructions — one the wire figure of a bird-warrior armed with a knitting needle, and the other, as Levi explained when I couldn't make out what the figure was meant to represent, "a man playing with his nose." "A Jew," I suggested. "Yes, yes," he said, laughing, "a Jew, of course."

According to family tradition, Primo Levi was born in the room that was later to become his study, on 31 July 1919, the year when the National Socialist Party was founded in Germany and when Benito Mussolini created the *Fasci italiani di combattimento*. (It was also the year Antonio Gramsci, Angelo Tasca, Palmiro Togliatti and Umberto Terracini launched the Communist weekly *L'Ordine nuovo*, in Turin.)

Primo's father, Cesare, was forty years old when his son was born. He himself was born into a well-to-do family in 1878, in Bene Vagienna, a small highland locality in Piedmont, in the province of Cuneo. Levi's paternal grand-father, a civil engineer, who had a small estate and also owned a bank that went bankrupt, died there around 1885. Cesare had studied electrical engi-neering in 1901, then had lived in France and worked in Belgium. After that he had been taken on as a designer by a big firm in Hungary, where he became a terrified witness of the revolution and subsequent Red Terror led by Béla Kun in Budapest in 1919 during his many journeys there. In the course of the inter-views he granted to Ferdinando Camon, Primo Levi explained that his father had been appalled for several reasons: on the one hand because Béla Kun, who was Jewish and did not conceal it, had published a Soviet constitution in 1919; and furthermore because he feared Communism, feared the reaction to Communism, and dreaded the reaction to Jewish Communism. In 1918 Cesare Levi married Ester Luzzati, born in 1895, and nicknamed Esterina.

Primo Levi's ancestors, according to the details collected in *The Periodic Table*,[3] were descended from ancient Jewish communities of Spanish origin who arrived in Italy by way of the Comtat Venaissin, in Provence, around 1550, half a century after the expulsion of the Jews from Spain.

In Bene Vagienna, the village where he was born, Levi's father suffered the taunts of his schoolmates after school, when they chanted "Pig's ear, donkey's ear, give 'em to the Jew that's here" and imitated a donkey's ear by screwing up the tails of their jackets in one hand. In *The Periodic Table*, Levi explains this gesture as follows:

> The allusion to the ear is arbitrary, and the gesture was originally the sacrilegious parody of the greeting that pious Jews would exchange in synagogue when called up to read the Torah, showing each other the hem of the prayer shawl whose tassels, minutely prescribed by ritual as to number, length, and form, are replete with mystical and religious significance. But by now those kids were unaware of the origin of their gesture. (*Table* 5)

The uncles (*barbe*) and aunts (*magne*), only distantly related to the author, and proud of belonging to "the people of Israel," spoke the Piedmont dialect, inter-spersed with words of Hebrew origin, some of them now absorbed into present-day Italian. Levi tells how his remote ancestors would acquire the title *barba* and *magna* when they reached a venerable age. He lists the names of some of those odd characters who caught the attention of their descendants: Barbaiòtô (Uncle Elijah); Barbasachin (Uncle Isaac); Magnaiéta (Aunt Maria); Barbamôisin (Uncle Moses); Barbasmelín (Uncle Samuel); Magnavigaia (Aunt Abigail), who according to family legend came from Carmagnola to Saluzzo as a bride, riding on a white mule; Magnafôriña (Aunt Zepora, "from the Hebrew *Tsippora* which means 'bird'"); Nònô (Grandfather) Jacob; and Barbapartín (Uncle Bonaparte), so named, like many Jews, in memory of the brief emanci-pation granted by Napoleon, and "fallen from his rank as uncle because the Lord, blessed be He, had given him so unbearable a wife that he had had

himself baptized, became a monk, and left to work as a missionary in China."
Then there was Nona (Grandmother) Bimba, the beautiful owner of an ostrich
feather boa, and ennobled together with all the members of her family for
having lent money (*manòd*) to Napoleon, and Barbarônín (Uncle Aaron), who
came from Fossano and was taken on by the Teatro Carignano as an extra in
Don Carlos. Having invited his parents, Uncle Nathan and Aunt Allegra, to
come to the opening night, he was shocked to hear his mother shout down
from the gallery when the curtain rose and she saw him "armed like a
Philistine": "Aaron, what are you doing? Put down that sword!" (*Table*, 6–7).

Among these distant ancestors were the Della Torres (more correctly the
Vitale Della Torres), who came from the aristocratic communities of
Alessandria and Chieri. They were related through Levi's maternal line, which
he did not know. He compared them to the noble and rare gas Argon (the
Inactive) because, as they were isolated and few in number — like this gas,
which is present in tiny amounts in the atmosphere and does not combine with
its other component gases — the Jews of Piedmont's rural communities did not
merge into Italian society. Notable Della Torres include Natale Della Torre,
who in 1881 published a popular newspaper, *La Miseria*, the writer Carlo Levi
and the historian Giovanni Levi.

Primo Levi belonged to a Sacerdote family through the paternal line.
Barbamiclín or Piantabibini (the "Turkey-planter"), who came from Aqui,
became legendary for his stupidity. Uncle Pacifico reared a turkey-hen at home
which disturbed Signor Lattès, a musician by profession. Uncle Gabriele, the
rabbi, was called Barba Moréno, "Uncle Our Teacher." Gnôr Grassiadiô of
Moncalvo, ashamed of being born a Jew, had married a *goyà* called Magna
Ausilia, who was unfaithful to him.

"Noble, inert and rare," according to the analogy drawn by Levi between
the noble gases and his ancestors, these characters peppered the Piedmontese
dialect with numerous "crippled" Hebrew words so as not to be intelligible to
the *goyim*, the gentiles, and to be able, for example, to talk about them, curse
or insult them without their knowledge. Primo Levi was fascinated by etymology from childhood, and in the first chapter of *The Periodic Table* he examines
in detail the traces of Hebrew in the dialect of the Jews of Piedmont. In particular, he shows how the hieratic language of the Bible became, in that dialect,
colloquial and sometimes comic. Thus he quotes a remark by Aunt Regina to
Uncle David as they sat in the Café Florio on Via Po: "*Davidin, bat la cana,
c'as sento nen le rukhôd!*" ("David, thump your cane, so they don't hear your
winds!")

Later came Barbaricô, an unusual character who gave up his career as
ship's doctor on board a transatlantic liner because "there was too much
noise." After settling in Turin he lived on the Borgo Vanchiglia "with a big
vulgar *goyà*," Magna Morfina, and dabbled in medicine but hardly ever
charged his poor patients. There was also Grandmother Fina of Carmagnola,
who once gave the rabbi of Moncalvo a pork cutlet to eat without his knowing.

She had a brother, Barbaraflín (Uncle Raphael), "the son of the Moses of Celin," as rich as he was shy, who had fallen in love with Dolce Valabrega. He wrote her love letters that he never sent, and wrote himself equally passionate replies. Another legendary family figure was Marchín, who worked as a clerk for Susanna, and nursed deep feelings for her. When Susanna, who had a secret recipe for goose sausage, repulsed Marchín's advances, he avenged himself by selling the recipe to a *goy*.

Barbabramín of Chieri, the son of Aunt Milca (the Queen), fell in love with a *havertà*, a maidservant, endowed with "splendid *khlaviòd*" (breasts). When he informed his parents that he intended to marry this *goyà*, only to receive their categorical refusal, he decided to spend his time in bed, which he left only to play billiards at night in the café below. Needless to say, as soon as his parents died he married his *havertà*.

Levi devoted several pages of the same chapter to his paternal grandmother, who was called "the Heartbreaker." It seems that the first husband of this irresistible creature, the writer's grandfather, committed suicide because she was unfaithful to him. She had three sons by him, including Cesare, Primo's father, brought them up without much affection, and made them study. In her old age she married a taciturn Christian doctor who may have been a freemason. After living extravagantly in her youth, with age she had grown terribly miserly. Apparently incapable of feeling the slightest tenderness for anyone, she lived with her aged husband, whom she forced to wear a patched-up overcoat even though he owned eight brand-new ones, mothballed away, that his heirs found hanging at the back of a cupboard. In her gloomy apartment on the Via Po, Grandmother Malia, who threw nothing away — not even cheese rinds — lived in squalor and was torn between Judaism and Catholicism, so much so that she sometimes attended the synagogue, sometimes the parish church of Sant' Ottavio, where she went to confession. Levi relates that she died of uraemia in 1928, surrounded by ancient neighbours, among them a Madame Scilimberg whom she kept an eye on till her dying breath, fearing that she would filch the key hidden under the mattress and make off with her money and jewels — which were all fakes.

In paying homage to his ancestors, Levi told the story as his family's traditions had preserved it. Even if he was not certain whether all the anecdotes were completely reliable, they belonged to the saga, to the way the family saw itself. If Aunt Abigail did not really cross the frozen River Po on a white mule to meet her future husband, that was how she told the tale to her descendants. Levi said that he would have loved to know more, and to become his family's chronicler, but that he had neither added nor subtracted anything, and unfortunately the material was exhausted.

Primo Levi revealed very little about his childhood in his books, including *The Periodic Table*. On the other hand, in his exchanges with Tullio Regge, no doubt prompted by his interviewer's ready interest, he talked about his father's influence on his later choices. Cesare Levi had studied engineering in Liège,

17

then before the First World War had found work with the Ganz company in Budapest, and studied German there. Apart from the episode of Béla Kun's bloody revolution, he enjoyed his time in Hungary, and made many friends. In the Ganz factory German was spoken, but Cesare also learned Hungarian. When the First World War broke out, the Hungarian authorities expelled him with regret, and paid for his journey home, although he continued to travel frequently between the two countries. He remained the Ganz representative for Piedmont and Liguria until 1942. The company's director used to send him a card at Christmas time with a chess problem of his own devising printed on the back, which the recipient was invited to solve.

Cesare returned to Turin with a deep-felt fear of Communism. In 1917 he married Ester Luzzati, the daughter of Adelina and Cesare Luzzati, who was seventeen years his junior, loved literature and music, and still spoke the Judaeo-Piedmontese dialect. Ester came from a family of six children, four sisters and two brothers.

Adelina, Ester's mother and Primo's grandmother, was the daughter of Salomone Della Torre and Ester Sacerdote. Salomone Della Torre had six brothers. He was the son of Leone Vitale Della Torre, from Alessandria, and "Aunt" Milca, the one whose *goyà* maid her son Barbabramín fell in love with and married after his parents' death. He himself died in 1883.

In her old age, Primo's mother continued to speak a dialect that contained Hebrew loanwords often twisted and transformed to suit Italian pronunciation. In Chapter 1 of *The Periodic Table*, Levi compares the "hybrid language" of his family roots — "that minor, Mediterranean, less illustrious Yiddish"[4] — with the dialect of the Jews of Eastern Europe.

Although he had studied for a degree, Cesare Levi had the self-taught man's special love for books. In one of the villages where they used to spend their holidays, he bought a whole crateful for his son, which contained, among others, works by Camille Flammarion and Voltaire. His interest in the sciences seems to have outweighed all the rest. As Primo Levi reports, humorously borrowing from Deuteronomy, chapter 6, verse 7:

> he read in his house and when he went out, and when he lay down and when he rose up. He had big deep pockets sewn, which could each hold a book. He had two brothers, equally avid indiscriminate readers. The three of them — an engineer, a doctor and a stockbroker — were fond of each other, but they were forever wrangling over books in the bookshops.

Always in competition with his two brothers, Cesare scoured the bookshops of Turin for all sorts of rare and unusual books, such as the "Little Library of Science" published by the brothers Bocca, a collection in which his friend Cesare Lombroso had published some of his lectures under the title

18

Antisemitism and the Social Sciences. Lombroso, who was a socialist, wrote about Jewish neuroses, portraying the religious factor as a hereditary defect. He approached Judaism only in the narrowest sense of the word, and was disapproved of by his conservative coreligionists.

As a child, Levi read popular science books such as *The Microbe Hunters* and *The Architecture of Things* by William Bragg, *Man the Unknown* by Alexis Carrell, and *Introduction to the History of Human Stupidity* by Wilkins. Chemistry and astronomy became and remained his favourite subjects, because he found in his reading some of the answers to the questions he asked himself about the apparent chaos of the world.

> I read a lot because I belonged to a family in which reading was an inno-
> cent and traditional vice, a rewarding habit, a mental exercise, and an
> obligatory and compulsive way to fill in spare time. A kind of Fata
> Morgana, destiny in the way of wisdom .... I went through my youth
> in an atmosphere saturated with printed pages, and in which textbooks
> were in the minority.[5]

In his conversations with Ferdinando Camon, Levi states that his father was hostile to Fascism, but he does not trace this rejection to any deep political convictions, and describes its causes as "superficial" — "The play-acting, the parading, the lack of seriousness, put him off."

Levi goes on to make a very revealing remark: he tells Camon that his father had no foreboding of the tragic events that were to follow during the War, and that his death from stomach cancer in 1942 was a blessing in disguise, because he could never have stood "what happened afterwards" — better to die of disease than of sorrow. At the same time, he admits that because of the gap between their ages he rarely spoke at length with his father whom he could not imagine confronting the despair of genocide. Yet he cherishes the memory of a man who was above all a townsman, "in love with the centre of Turin," with a loathing for nature. Cesare used to take his son on strolls through the streets of the town when Primo's head was full of mountain scenery. The horror of straying from the quiet Corso Re Umberto — which had its own view of the fields in any case — and facing all those insects, dust, and country heat! When his family twisted Cesare's arm and he agreed to go for a walk out of town, he would take several books along, and once they had reached their destination he would sit on a newspaper to keep his clothes from getting dirty, and plunge straight into his reading without once looking up at the landscape.

Cesare was a Jew who went to synagogue for Yom Kippur and ate ham in secret, while cursing his own weakness. He was an Italian Jew, and Italian Jewry was highly assimilated — Primo Levi said that it was the most assimi-lated in the world. Cesare Levi believed in the Enlightenment, and was a keen reader of Herlitzka, Angelo Mosso and Cesare Lombroso. This same Lombroso, the criminal anthropologist from Turin, who read Fontenelle, Flammarion, and Annie Besant, was a very influential figure who used to organize spiritualist seances and boasted of his table-turning powers. In his work, Lambroso looked for signs of criminal propensities in the minorities. He claimed that criminality depended on genetic inheritance and that the body, with its deformities, became "a mirror of the soul." Citing Aristotle, he stated that the wild beast, nature, and the criminal body are evil, and that the soul they harbour is criminal by nature. Could it have been possible that Cesare Levi, who was a peaceful man, self-educated, a book-lover and a keen believer in scientific progress, shared some of his friend Lambroso's ideas?

Although he had not forgotten his origins, Cesare Levi regularly broke the Mosaic law in the presence of his son, and when that happened he would seek a kind of collusion in his eyes. This little scene was played out on Sunday mornings, when Levi, the engineer, his pockets stuffed with books, set out on foot with Primo to visit his grandmother in her gloomy apartment on the Via Po. On the way there, he used to stroke all the cats, "sniff at all the truffles," and look in on a pork butcher's to buy a slice of the ham he loved to eat. He paid after checking the butcher's tally with his slide-rule, then consumed the forbidden food with a mixture of shame and voracity. In a conversation with Stefano Jesurum,[6] the writer remembered that his father

> was a fundamentally secular man, but nevertheless attached to certain customs. Out of a kind of superstitious fear, he did not eat pork, yet he adored ham. He ate it. I blamed him. He put on a guilty expression that was as if to say "I sin because the flesh is weak, but you, don't give in, behave yourself."

The visit to Grandmother Malia always followed the same pattern. After ringing the bell, his father would call out "He's first in his class!" Not that his grandmother cared; she took no pleasure in her guests, and it seems that the two visitors unsettled her. She would lead them through the labyrinth of her vast and dusty apartment, which contained the office of the old doctor who was never there, and whom little Primo feared because he had heard tell that he used scissors to cut the frænum linguæ, the web beneath the tongue, of children who stuttered. Grandmother Malia would delve into a cupboard for the same old box of mouldy chocolates, and her grandson would hurriedly take one and shove it to the bottom of his pocket.

During the school holidays Cesare Levi would resign himself to letting the sprawling country spoil his happy urban life. In winter he and his wife would set out into the valleys near Turin in search of a place to rent in summer. As the Levis did not own a car — in those days hardly anybody could afford one — they would look for a house near a railway station, because this hardworking father, who gave himself only three days off in August, caught the train every night to rejoin his wife and two children — Levi's sister Anna Maria was born on 27 January 1921 — in localities like Cogne, Torre Péllice, Meana or Bardonècchia.

Every evening, the whole family would wait for Cesare at the station, and early next morning the poor man would leave in time to reach his office on the Corso San Martino by eight o'clock. It is not surprising that at this rate he quickly fell ill. Nevertheless, every June, Ester Levi would start to pack impressive amounts of luggage: suitcases, bags, and three wicker baskets weighing "nearly a quintal each," containing the linen, sets of pots and pans, toys, books, provisions, clothing for all weathers, shoes, remedies and accessories, "as if we were leaving for Atlantis."[7]

Friends and members of the family used to choose the same place, so as to be together in the country. Later on, the Levis owned a house on a hillside in Piossasco, not far from Turin, and sometimes the entire family would gather there in late summer. In those days, the homeward journey took them through the countryside; nowadays the train runs through built-up areas, and the house, which still exists, no longer belongs to the family.

Primo Levi recalled the three months of summer holiday as quiet and boring, but with occasional diversions. His holiday homework felt like a cruel burden, but he delighted in the afternoons spent by the side of a mountain stream, exploring nature and discovering animals, while his mother knitted in the shade of a willow tree. When he was ten, the sight of tadpoles in a stream was a marvel, and his attempts to rear them an instructive failure: later he drew an almost biblical conclusion from it. When the few tadpoles that survived the treatment he inflicted on them turned into tiny frogs and scattered into the garden looking for non-existent water, a robin swooped on one of them, and in turn was pounced on by the white household cat, who, having caught the bird, took it into a corner to play with before eating it. This series of destinies ruthlessly cut short by death in a savage world recalled the *Chad Gadiah*, the song sung at the end of the *Seder*, the Passover meal. It tells how, because of a lamb bought by the narrator's father, a great many animals perish, driven by their natural urges or as victims of the elements, until the Angel of Death in person intervenes to finish what has been begun.

One night, in his bedroom in the country, Primo had one of his worst childhood scares when up above his head, rasping on the peeling, curling wallpaper, he heard "a ticking sound" which was gradually coming closer. He switched on the light and saw a spider crawling down on to his bedside table "with the uncertain and inexorable step of Death" (*Trades* 153/141). This childish fear of spiders was later to develop into a revulsion, and a supply of metaphors. He often commented on the fact that certain female spiders consume the male after or during mating. A few days before his death he published a story in *La Stampa* in which a female spider is interviewed by a timid, cautious journalist. Levi knew the source of his phobia. It went back to his childhood, when he saw Gustave Doré's etching of Arachne in Canto XII of Dante's *Purgatory*. In the illustration the girl punished by a dreadful metamorphosis is "almost half a spider." She is portrayed with full breasts and a back from which grow "six legs, knotty, hairy, painful six legs which, together with human arms that writhe desperately, add up to eight. On his knees, before the new monster,

Dante seems to be contemplating its crotches, half disgusted, half voyeur" (*Trades 157/145*).

His cousin Giulia recalls that one of Primo's favourite games was playing schoolteacher and correcting his cousins' homework with all the proper gravity. He also used to bring the telescope his father had given him, and spend his nights on the roof terrace, observing the stars and constellations. He knew their names and courses. In the house in Torre Péllice there was a large kitchen with a set of copper saucepans. Paolo Avigdor, Primo's first cousin, remembers what noisy drums they made.

Primo used to organize charades which he played with his female cousins and his cousin Giovanni, the son of one of his mother's sisters. Giovanni Levi, who owes his surname to the fact that his grandmother married a Levi not related to Cesare, recalls how Primo would enter the room where the audience of children was gathered, then perform a mime, and the children had to guess the saying or character it stood for. One day, Primo imitated the Discus Thrower by striking the famous statue's stance. He posed, then went straight out again to pee. The phrase they had to guess was "I'll be right back"!

In fact, Primo Levi did not play much, except for chess, which his father had taught him with pieces passed down in the family for generations. Carla Ovazza, a descendant of the wealthy Ovazza family — to which Alexander Stille (né Kamenetzki), an American Jewish writer of Italian ancestry, devotes a chapter of his book *Benevolence and Betrayal: Five Italian Families under Fascism* — still recalls how she introduced her friend Primo to the art of skating. Fifty years later, Primo dedicated his last book to her with the words "For Carla, my skating teacher."

Levi's books tell us very little about his relationship with his mother, his sister, to whom he remained deeply attached all his life, and his extended family, which teemed with cousins. Giulia, his mother's sister's daughter, has clear recollections of the tribe of Levis, who all lived close to one another in the fashionable district of Crocetta.

Giulia, whose mother was only one year younger than her sister "Esterina," lived on the Via Alfonso Lamarmora, parallel to Corso Re Umberto. Both sisters lived to a great age and died only two days apart. Ester Levi survived her son for five years. She was not informed about his suicide, but told that he had died of a heart attack, although it seems that, in spite of her senescence, she had had her doubts about this version.

Giulia was born in 1921, a month after Anna Maria, Primo's younger sister. They attended the same district school, the Felice Rignon, at 40 Via Massena, and played together with the same friends in the same places.

Giulia's and Primo's maternal grandmother, who had eleven grandchildren, lived not far from there, on the Corso Vittorio Emanuele II. Giulia recalls how the children of the family — numbering no fewer than eleven — used to visit her for tea after school. There was a veranda, a stool, and a table where little Primo, who had finished the first year, taught his female cousins to read and count. When the lesson was over, teacher and pupils piled into an armchair turned motor car. With Primo at the wheel and his cousins behind him, they would explore the big wide world.

One day, Giulia and Primo, who were suffering from a very violent and contagious cough, were playing together in a park. A very pretty little girl who was all alone and looked rather sad came up to them and said "I'm on my own, would you like to play with me?" "Yes, but we've both got donkeys' cough [whooping cough]" the cousins chorused in reply, and the little girl turned and ran. "All we saw was her behind!" Despite his seriousness, Giulia remembers that Primo enjoyed doing gymnastics. His little sister Anna Maria, who was a very lively girl, used to jump on the armchairs and furniture, to the fury of the woman downstairs.

All the cousins were good friends. Primo, Anna Maria, and Giulia were the eldest. Paolo Avigdor, born in 1925, the son of a younger sister of Ester, also belonged to their merry band until his parents left for Genoa when he was ten years old. Primo's and Avigdor's fathers, both electrical engineers, often went off for a walk together on the Corso Re Umberto. Primo was considered the cleverest of the family's children, an example to be followed in every area, and although he remained very good-natured and never tried to boss the rest around, Paolo felt a sense of inferiority towards him. So in order to gain their attention and respect he boasted to Primo and Anna Maria that he never washed his hands or his ears, which earned him some lessons on cleanliness.

Grandmother Adelina had her own way of observing the Jewish festivals. She fasted for Yom Kippur, and as this meant that the kitchen was free she took the opportunity to make her tomato purée at leisure. In her view, not working meant not knitting or sewing. The Passover Seder was also held at Primo's maternal grandparents' house. Grandfather Luzzati sat at the head of the table. As the family was vast, on Seder night no fewer than forty young children would throng around their grandparents while consuming the Passover *matzah* and meal. Giulia sat next to Primo, because they were the eldest. Primo would recite a few pages of the *Haggadah*, the story of the Exodus, together with his father, and Giulia's father and grandfather. She says today: "Primo did not really know what he was reading, but he read. It was not exactly a proper *Seder*. Our fathers came in from the office feeling tired, and they read at high speed."[8]

Primo was a serious little boy, very thin, with straight fair hair. Giulia recalls that when she was six and Primo eight years old, a primary teacher from the Jewish school used to give them lessons in Hebrew and biblical history in a classroom in a state school. She came on Mondays from four till five, after class. Although her cousin was as shy as she was, Giulia used to wait for Primo to take her by the hand before they both went in. This shyness was not unique to them; in those days, that kind of reticent behaviour was fostered by their upbringing.

Ester Luzzati's father, who died in 1941, kept a store that sold fabrics on the Via Roma, whose ancient buildings were torn down by order of Mussolini's architects to make way for sinister, arrogant concrete blocks, squatting on ugly arcades, which appear all the more appalling when the street emerges at last into the Piazza San Carlo, which the vandals left intact. Grandfather Levi's shop looked nothing like the showy boutiques lining the Via Roma today. It was a long and shadowy semi-basement, whose entrance was down a short flight of steps. Not far away was a café-bar decorated to look like a cave full of stalactites, the ceiling studded with crudely plastered scraps of broken mirror glass that were also set along the bottom of the counter, so that the reflections made the passers-by sprout multiple legs. Levi wrote that the children used to ask "to be taken to the Via Roma just for this."

Grandfather Luzzati had bought his business from a Monsù Ugotti, and his customers called him by the same name, which even spread to other family members and eventually included Primo Levi himself. In an article entitled "Grandfather's Store," first published in *La Stampa* and then collected in *Other People's Trades*, Levi paints a portrait of this imposing patriarch — laconic, ironic, uneducated, but a *maestro* of his trade. Calm and commanding, he brought the same authority into the kitchen at home, on the special occasions when he cooked there, as he did into his store, which was staffed by eccentric employees like Tota Gina, whose real name was Savina, the cashier with the mighty bosom and teeth of gold and silver. Anchored to her cash-desk, larger than life, she handed out Leone pastilles to the children. Signor Luzzati–Ugotti sold his fabrics alongside his two sons, who spoke a jargon intelligible only to the salesmen, so as to work surreptitiously on the customers.

The Via Roma had other textile stores belonging to competitors, some of them distant relatives of the grandfather's. They all spent their time spying on one another and called each other "Signor Thief" and "Signor Crook." As a paternalist employer, Monsù Ugotti treated his staff now and then at the Boringhieri brasserie. Levi also describes how his grandfather used to send a young salesman to the nearby Portanuova station to intercept engaged couples from the provinces as they alighted from the train to do their shopping in the big city. Once they had made their purchases at the Luzzati–Ugotti store he would steer them to the other merchants' premises.

The high point of the year was the carnival, when Grandfather Luzzati would invite his grandchildren to watch the procession of decorated floats from the balcony of the store. On this occasion Grandmother Luzzati, usually kept out of sight in Levi's stories, would also emerge onto the balcony. He describes her as "a fragile little woman ... the mother of many children," who came from an extensive family of twenty-one children, one of whom had been eaten in his cradle by a pig.

From the age of six to eleven (1925–30), Primo Levi attended the primary school in the Via Massena, just at the back of his house. He appears in a family photo album, a slender figure with straight fair hair, wearing the black shirt that schoolboys were obliged to wear during the Fascist period.

When he was eleven, during the three months' endless summer holidays in the country, Primo fell in love with a nine-year-old girl named Lidia, but was too shy to say so. In the hope of winning favour, he gave her stamps for her collection, which he had encouraged her to start, and also helped with her holiday homework. Lidia was not pretty, and she loved to tell the story of her tonsil operation, which gave Primo the shivers.

With hindsight, when writing about her in 1984,[9] Levi wryly describes his sweetheart as "polite, homely, sickly, and not all that bright." So why fall in love with her? The boy was enchanted because Lidia had a special affinity with animals. She alone was able to stroke a ferocious German shepherd dog, and she only had to call and the hens and chicks would come flocking from the nearby farmyard and eat out of her hand. Of course, Primo did not dream of making the slightest advance towards her, but he did notice that Lidia favoured a boy named Carlo, who was bigger and stronger than he was. Indifferent to Lidia's advances, Carlo played football, tussled with the other village children, and play-acted at driving the wreck of a truck abandoned in a meadow. To grasp the full scale of this drama, one should add that Carlo was Primo's best friend at the time, and that they played with Meccano together, combining the pieces in both of their boxes to build larger constructions. In all their ventures, Carlo was the brawn and Primo the brains. Loving both Lidia and Meccano led Primo to the obvious conclusion that he had to woo Lidia by means of Meccano.

On the pretext that it would soon be Lidia's name-day, he persuaded Carlo, "the bolt tightener," to build a machine of Primo's own devising that was bound to impress his beloved and make her realize the strength of the feelings she inspired. What he had in mind was a clock, though not a conventional clock, given the materials available. Primo's clock only had a cardboard face and a single hand, and it did not tell the time — the hand went "round once in twenty or twenty-one minutes." On Saint Lidia's day, the ungrateful girl glanced for a moment at this outlandish object, asked "What's it for?," and then went into raptures over Carlo's present: a cellophane envelope containing a collection of stamps from Nicaragua.

That is how the primitive, less sensitive rival won against the pure, noble, thoughtful lover. No doubt that is also how the solitary child from the Corso Re Umberto came to feel a shyness towards women that he never overcame.

The bourgeois and puritan families of Turin's small Jewish community often lived in the smart district of La Crocetta,[10] while the rich also owned villas set in spacious estates in the hills, or in Montacaliere, a green locality lying very close to the town, along the banks of the Po. It was on these luxurious properties that the children would gather in the summer months to play tennis, all dressed in white. In winter they would also go to the skating rink, together with non-Jewish children, because there was no reluctance on either side to spend time with each other.

In the course of two generations the Jews had become invisible. The Risorgimento, which had recognized all citizens as equal under the law, had lured the Jews of Italy into secularism, and the traditions piously sustained throughout centuries of segregation and humiliation were discarded and forgotten. They did not call for the right of separate identity, as they do today, but for equality. And the facts appeared to justify their choice: many Jews had become important and prosperous figures.

At the age of thirteen, Primo became *bar mitzvah*.[11] While religion was not deeply important to him, the *bar mitzvah* was a custom in the family along with a few rites which had been preserved such as the festivals of Rosh Hashanah and Purim.[12] Primo Levi learned enough Hebrew at the Talmud Torah (Torah study class) on Thursday afternoons to celebrate his *bar mitzvah*, but because this was counted as a pure formality, by the time he was eighteen he had forgotten it all. It took the racial laws of 1938, and above all the shock of encountering the Jews of Eastern Europe in the camp of Monowitz-Buna, to turn him back to the Hebrew language again.

Giorgio Bassani describes how the Jews of Italy experienced their Judaism at this time in his *Garden of the Finzi-Continis*:

> The fact that we were Jews, ... inscribed in the registers of the same Jewish community, in our case hardly counted. Because what on earth did the word "Jew" mean? What meaning could terms like "community" or "Israelite universality" have *for us*, since they took no account of the existence of that more basic intimacy — a secret intimacy that can be properly appreciated only by those who have had it — derived from the fact that our ... families, not from choice, but through a tradition older than any possible memory, belonged to the same religious rite, or rather to the same "school"?[13]

In view of his fragile state of health, Primo's parents arranged for him to take lessons at home for a year after primary school, to prepare him to enter the Liceo Massimo d'Azeglio. This was a famous school in the Via Parini where the brightest young pupils from Turin's middle classes came to study under secular liberal teachers such as Cesare Pavese, Massimo Mila, Augusto Monti, Franco Antonicelli, Umberto Cosmo, Zino Zini, and Norberto Bobbio. When Primo Levi arrived, the Fascists had already purged the school of those teachers who had refused to sign the oath of loyalty to Fascism in 1931, and he bitterly resented being force-fed the diet marketed by the servants of the regime. Grudgingly and without the least conviction, his own father had joined the

Fascist Party in the hope of continuing to enjoy a quiet bourgeois life, which meant that *Ingegnere* Levi too could be seen on election days despondently wearing his black shirt so as not to call attention to himself.

The social climate was very much like the one described in *The Garden of the Finzi-Continis*. Many fathers who had recently been "agnostics or opponents" resigned themselves to enrolling in the *Fascio*. When Primo Levi joined the Massimo d'Azeglio classical secondary school, the peaceful mood prevailing in the city and the school gave no hint of the dark times that lay ahead. Certainly, the regime that Mussolini himself described as totalitarian had clamped down on the teaching profession and on intellectuals in general, but the days of open repression still lay ahead. Levi soon grew wary of the type of teaching devised for the edification of Italian youth by the Fascist ideologue, the Sicilian philosopher Giovanni Gentile, even though he was a disciple of the intellectual mentor of Italy's liberal middle classes, Benedetto Croce.

When Primo entered the Liceo d'Azeglio, the Fascists had already been in power in Italy for twelve years. He was born four months after the founding of the *Fasci italiani di combattimento* in Milan. On 23 March 1919 about a hundred war veterans had met in a hall on Piazza San Sepolcro lent by the Circle of Industrial and Commercial Interests, at the invitation of Benito Mussolini, editor of the newspaper *Popolo d'Italia*. (In those days the word *fascio* — "bundle," hence also league, or alliance — belonged to the political vocabulary of the far left.) Their programme was Irredentist, antiparliamentary, antisocialist and anticlerical. In the sphere of foreign policy, the founders of the *Fasci italiani di combattimento* advocated war as a means of settling every problem. Among the troupe of malcontents who took part in this rowdy meeting was the poet Filippo Tommaso Marinetti, whose *Technical Manifesto of Futurist Literature* had been published in Paris in 1912, and who quickly showed his sympathy for Fascism, which had a lot in common with his futurist ideas.

As Dan Vittorio Segre records so well in his *Memoirs of a Fortunate Jew*, for a child there was nothing particularly remarkable about the early years of the Fascist regime. Primo Levi, like Segre, did not "enter" Fascism: he was more or less born inside it. Segre goes so far as to write that when he was a boy, Fascism was "the only natural form of existence." He continues: "I was not aware of its specific character because I had no means of comparing it with other political systems."

Fascist youth organizations such as the *Balilla* and the *Avanguardia* had been integrated into the school system. Segre recalls that they used to arrange "the gym display at the end of the year," and it was easy to get oneself excused from attendance. In their childhood, neither Levi nor Segre had to suffer taunts from their schoolmates because they were Jews. Their difference was felt as a "label of quality" by Segre and "a small amusing anomaly" by Levi.

Levi was born in the year when the high cost of living provoked a series of violent strikes, followed by the looting of hundreds of food stores and warehouses. In Florence there was even a short-lived republic of Soviets that lasted for three days. The troubles resumed and intensified in 1920, when a great many factories were occupied. In response to this agitation, the propertied classes organized, and founded the industrial and agricultural confederations *Confindustria* and *Confagricoltura*. They did not hesitate to call on the Fascists to oppose the workers and the peasants. The Fascist *squadre*, paramilitary "action squads," imposed a reign of terror in the countryside: there were lynchings and murders. Violence and arson then spread into the many towns invaded by the *squadristi*, when the workers declared a general strike. In 1921, the year Fascism constituted itself as a formal political entity, the National Fascist Party, thirty-five Fascists were elected to parliament, including Mussolini, who published his political programme on 21 June.

Born in 1883 in the Romagna, not far from Forlì, into a very humble family, Mussolini was close to revolutionary syndicalism until 1914, a left-wing interventionist between 1915 and 1918, and a nationalist from 1919 onwards. Having edited the socialist daily *Avanti!* in 1913, he quickly left it to found his own newspaper, *Popolo d'Italia*, during the First World War.

In October 1922, King Victor Emmanuel III and the state caved in to the violence of the *ras*,[14] and allowed Mussolini to seize power after the March on Rome, when some 26,000 poorly-armed Fascists set out to conquer the capital. They faced a garrison of 28,000 which did not intervene because the prime minister, Luigi Facta, resigned, and Mussolini, supported by *Confindustria* and *Confagricoltura*, was invited to form a cabinet. Fascism replaced the crippled state.

In 1926, Mussolini created an official institution of Fascist culture, the *Accademia d'Italia*, to oppose the *Accademia dei Lincei*, which had not accepted his ideas. Benedetto Croce refused to take a seat there, but Pirandello, Marinetti, Gioacchino Volpe, and Marconi did not share his scruples. Gentile, the regime's official ideologist, embraced a doctrine he called "actual idealism," and declared himself opposed to positivism, aestheticism, and "decadent" intellectualism. This is his view of state authority:

> State and individual are identical, and the art of government is the art of according and uniting these two terms so well that a maximum of liberty harmonizes with a maximum of public order, not only in the external sense but also and above all in the sovereignty devolved to the law and its necessary organs. For the maximum of liberty always coincides with the maximum of state power.[15]

Gentile, who became minister of public education in Mussolini's first government, laid the foundations of a reform derived from a plan that Croce had not had time to develop during his spell as education minister in Giovanni Giolitti's cabinet in 1920–21. The aim of this legislation, deemed by Mussolini "the most

Fascist of reforms," was to promote the traditional disciplines of the very conservative Italian school system by emphasizing its elitist and selective aspects. But Gentile did not leave it at that; he wanted to outdo the other less famous but more Fascist theoreticians of the regime, men such as Luigi Federzoni, the minister of the interior, and Alfredo Rocco, the minister of justice, both of them nationalists who had rallied to the Mussolini cause.

In 1925, Gentile became the leader of a movement of intellectuals sympathetic to the regime, after a cultural conference held in Bologna, and published a "Manifesto of Intellectuals for Fascism" for the attention of "intellectuals of all nations." Among the signatories were Luigi Barzani, Francesco Coppola, Ardengo Soffici, Enrico Prampolini, Marinetti, and Pirandello. This manifesto caused a split with the liberal intellectuals who a few days later published a counter-manifesto in the daily *Il Mondo*, organized by Croce and signed by, among others, Giovanni Amendola, Luigi Albertini, Gaetano Salvemini, Luigi Salvatorelli, A.C. Jemolo, Gaetano Mosca, Luigi Einaudi, and Arturo Labriola.

This counter-manifesto, a statement of divorce from Fascism, reminded all writers that their duty lay in "raising all men and all elected parties to the highest spiritual level." It also advised all intellectuals to go back to their desks and to steer clear of politics. Croce, from now on a declared anti-Fascist, suffered violence and harassment from the regime: his mail was censored, his associates spied on, and his house looted by *squadristi*. As for Gentile, Mussolini appointed him editor-in-chief of the *Enciclopedia italiana*, where in 1932 he published Mussolini's article on "The Doctrine of Fascism," which paid tribute to the one who inspired it, Gentile, now enthroned in the Fascist "Grand Council" with other pillars of the regime. Yet these favours did not last, since Gentile, the most moderate of the Fascist intellectuals, fell into disgrace after appealing to the Duce for greater freedom of the press. He was eventually shot by partisans of the Resistance in 1944.

It was Giovanni Gentile who became the bane of the young and frail Primo Levi who entered the Liceo d'Azeglio in 1932:

> I had a curious sensation: that there was a plot at my expense, that family and school kept something hidden from me, which I went looking for in the places that were reserved for me: for example, chemistry or also astronomy ... In my time the conspiracy was acclaimed. It was the Gentile conspiracy. I too had an excellent relationship with my Italian teacher, but when she publicly said that literary subjects have a formative value and scientific subjects have only an informative value, my hair stood on end. This confirmed in me the idea that the conspiracy existed. You young Fascist, you young Crocean, you young men grown up in this Italy must not approach the sources of scientific knowledge because they are dangerous. I never read Croce on this subject, but apparently he considered them pseudosciences, technical matters, useful for life but not for the understanding of the world.[16]

This passionate interest in the sciences had been prompted by his father, whose trawling of the second-hand bookstalls had dredged up wonders by Camille Flammarion on astronomy and the stars, by Ghersi on mathematics, and the *Nuovo Ricettario Industriale* (the "New Industrial Recipe Book"), whose author provided "genuine recipes for the utilization of materials such as glue, glass or tin, but in which he also explained how to prepare oneself spiritually and physically so as to promote the spirit of invention."

Cesare Levi allowed his son free access to his library, and it seems that only Emilio Salgari, an author generally regarded as journalistic, hence too frivolous and vulgar, fell victim to his censorship. In his conversations with Tullio Regge, Levi recalled that he had enjoyed the privilege of discovering in *The Architecture of Things* "a treatise on genetics, which was then in its infancy." "My own reading was just as random and unsystematic, in line with the custom of the house, and I must have retained a certain and excessive faith in the nobility and necessity of the printed word as deriving from a certain ear, a certain flair."[17]

Primo Levi was a shy and studious pupil, but his achievements never earned praise from his teachers, who in any case were second-rate, appointed by the Fascist regime which had purged the most brilliant of the staff. Although Cesare Pavese taught him Italian literature in his penultimate year, Levi was a mediocre pupil in this subject, and seems to have kept no lasting memory of Pavese's readings of his own works during lessons. He took more interest in linguistics than in literature, but he acquired a thorough knowledge of the standard classical authors such as Dante, Ariosto, Manzoni, and Leopardi. Even so, in order to pass the *Matura*, the advanced level exam, he had to resit the Italian paper in the October exams of 1937, having failed with the low mark of 3 from Professor Pasero. It has to be said that the subject, which was about the war in Spain, had paralyzed him to the point that he handed in a more or less blank paper, because even in that special instance he refused to adopt the rhetoric in vogue. Classical secondary schooling in its Fascist phase shocked and annoyed him, and he could not accept that the sciences were to be considered less part of the cultural heritage than literature, Greek, and Latin. Primo Levi bitterly regretted the breach between the arts and the sciences, feeling that, for men of his generation, the gap between the two cultures was truly dramatic.

With his passion for etymology and philology, Primo was not at all averse to the study of ancient languages, but even the Latin syllabus did not cover authors that interested him, namely Lucretius, Vitruvius, or Aulus Cornelius Celsus, whose writings explained in great detail how tonsils were removed early in the first century AD. He was convinced that truth lay in the sciences, that they "smelled good," whereas history and literary criticism "smelled foul," as he put it in his talks with Tullio Regge.

At the age of fourteen, Primo decided that he was going to be a chemist. *Ingegnere* Levi most certainly wanted his son to follow a scientific career, and in this field at least he was a happy father. In chemistry, Primo not only sought the key to unlock the universe — "the why of things," as he told Tullio Regge. He thought of the science of matter as a poetic discipline, from which in his teenage years he seems to have derived more meaning than from literary works, although these gave him a grounding in classical culture that imbued his future writing with a wealth of images and quotations. For Levi, chemistry contained at least as much poetry as *The Divine Comedy*; indeed it was his study of Dante that had shown him that there was also great poetry among the science books his father collected. Yet in the lowest moments of his existence, even in Auschwitz, Dante Alighieri remained a support, a benchmark, and an infinite resource.

"I was substantially a romantic, and also in chemistry it was the romantic aspect that interested me. I hoped to go very far, to the point of possessing the universe, to understanding the why of things."[18]

In fact, he had refused very early on to accept that his high school's classical ethos in the age of Mussolini should speak in terms of two cultures: for him, it was always clear that culture was indivisible. He pointed out in an interview that Kant had studied astronomy, and that Galileo had become a great writer in the process of describing what he had discovered. Did he already foresee that science would provide a mine of raw material for the future writer? In any case, his father's deliberate introduction of science books into the house, "step by step, imperceptibly, without abusing his authority," proved decisive.

A small book his father bought in the Via Cernaia when Primo was fifteen years old engrossed him even more than the rest. It was a handsomely bound volume published in London in 1846 under the title *Thoughts on Animalcules, or A Glimpse of the Invisible World*, by G.A. Mantell, Esq., LL.D., F.R.S., and dedicated "To the most Noble Marchioness of Northampton." In those days, Levi did not speak a word of English, but, delighted by the illustrations, he bought a dictionary and soon got the hang of the text. He found in the epigraph

an electrifying dictum hovering between the scientific and the visionary: "In the leaves of every forest, in the flowers of every garden, in the waters of every brook, there are worlds pullulating with life, as innumerable as the glories of the firmament."... Sudden and painful as a stomach cramp there grew in me the need for a microscope, and I told my father. (*Trades* 59/48)

Though Cesare Levi regretted not having followed a career in science himself, he was surprised to find his teenage son so absorbed, but he bought the microscope which had a magnification of × 250. Driven by his new craze, Primo examined everything that would fit on a slide: his hair, the skin of his fingers, flies' wings, their eyes, their legs, pollen from flowers, salt from the kitchen, copper sulphate, potassium bichromate, water from the torrent at Sangone and from a flower vase, in which he recognized Mantell's promised "animalcules" and saw them swarming. He would have liked to examine a drop of his blood, but was afraid to prick himself, and Anna Maria flatly refused either to prick him or to let herself be pricked. Cesare Levi also bought his son a Pathé-Baby projector that Primo often produced to entertain his schoolmates when they visited; in his Pathé-Baby projector, instead of film, he would arrange a slide spread with crystals in a solution of alum, then his guests would marvel at the sight of the salts springing up on the screen.

A year after acquiring the microscope, he conducted his first experiment, working with a classmate, called Enrico in *The Periodic Table*. Enrico, whose brother was a chemistry student and had the use of a laboratory, was a quiet, determined, down-to-earth boy. Faced with this placid adolescent, Levi recalled his fears of a "brutal realization of an inferiority which each time seemed eternal, definitive."

At first, their secret venture had no set purpose. All that the two boys intended was to enter the holy of holies unknown to Enrico's brother, who had forbidden him access, and then to contrive an experiment. Stealing the key to the laboratory and gaining entrance was a feat in itself. Levi saw himself as making contact with the alchemists who sought to penetrate the secrets of matter and who had the intuition that it was possible to proceed from the one element to another, as Mendeleev discovered.

After ages spent heating and bending glass tubes, Primo and Enrico decided to make nitrous oxide, also known as laughing gas. The laboratory filled with toxic white smoke produced by boiling a mixture of ammonia and nitric acid. Primo then spotted a dry battery and decided to impress his friend by carrying out the electrolysis of water. The procedure succeeded, but not to Enrico's satisfaction, and his scepticism so offended Primo that to prove to his accomplice that they really did have oxygen and hydrogen present, he "lifted the cathode jar" and held a burning match to it. Needless to say, the jar exploded into flying shards, which by good fortune did not harm the sorcerer's apprentices. Levi was glad all the same, and proud to have "unleashed a force of nature." "It was indeed hydrogen," he wrote, "the same element that burns in the sun and stars, and from whose condensation the universes are formed in eternal silence."

Nothing could divert the young Primo from his passion for the sciences, just as nothing could curb his urgency when he begged his father for an etymological dictionary, which proved a lot harder to secure than a technical or scientific book, and which became his lifelong bedside companion — "To know the depth of history that lies behind each word seemed important to me."

Cesare Levi was an open-minded man who enjoyed life and advised his newly adolescent son to drink, smoke, and run after girls. As far as could be, Primo seems to have been a docile, cooperative son. He did not drink, did not smoke, and although attracted to girls, he was much too shy to dare to flirt. For the moment, all he thought about was escaping from town to explore the nearby mountains with a friend from school. His father wondered how his son could bear to wear objects as dangerous as skis, and reluctantly accepted tennis, a more urban sport. Primo used to go and play at Carla and Franca Ovazza's house in Moncalieri, and at the farm in Rivoli, close to Turin, which belonged to the mother of Vittorio Segre, who was to emigrate to Palestine in 1939. Hiking and climbing were common leisure activities among Turin's young middle classes. The mountains were no more than an hour or two by bicycle from town. Generally it was only the boys who spent the night at some climbers' hut high in the mountains, while the girls went back to sleep at home, obedient to the morals of the time. As Levi's cousin Giulia says today, they were traditionally "old-fashioned," and Primo chaperoned the young ladies of the family.

Primo's first contact with mountaineering was a mortifying failure. The family was on holiday in Bardonècchia, a town perched 1,312 metres above sea level, right next to the French frontier, where Primo and his friends played mixed doubles in tennis. One day, together with a friend his own age and another boy of sixteen who claimed to be a guide, he decided to walk to Valle Stretta by way of Catena dei Magi. They set out in the afternoon, without having eaten, and it was after nightfall when they reached the summit. The three scared boys saw the light of a mountain rescue hut in the dark and started to call for help. Eventually a group of climbers came to their assistance, with shouts of "*Son mac dei gagno brodos!*,"[19] then roped them together like a string of sausages and took them down to the village by the light of their lanterns.

The indignity did not deter him. Levi did not give up climbing and hill-walking on Saturdays and Sundays with his oldest friends until the moment of his fall into the deepest depression. The mountains were his first source of inspiration when as a teenager he attempted to write a short story, which he never finished nor published.

When he reached his classical school's penultimate year, most of whose forty-one members he considered apathetic, Levi reckoned that he and another five classmates were the elite. Many years later he judged this arrogance to have been mistaken, but in those days he thought that "studying was a necessary evil, to be accepted with the patience of the strong." The six had devised a hierarchy in the subjects they were taught. First came philosophy and the natural sciences. Greek, Latin, mathematics, and physics were tolerated as giving access to the first two disciplines; Italian and history were viewed with indifference; and, at the foot of the ladder, considered as "pure affliction," lurked art history and physical education. Those who endorsed this view of things belonged to a club whose members also shared a coarse and contemptuous attitude to girls. Another hierarchy had been worked out in the sporting field. Swimming and fencing were OK, skiing reluctantly tolerated. Football was out, no doubt because it was considered too popular in this hothouse for the sons of the middle class. Athletics came top of the scale and brought automatic access to the club. As for tennis, it was strictly for upper-class girls.

But tennis was the summer game that Primo played in Bardonècchia, concealing it from the rest of the club, who in fact made room for him only on sufferance, on the strength of his being an excellent Latinist and always ready to let the others crib his work. His Italian they considered too refined.

In Bardonècchia Primo sighed in secret for a girl named Vera Marconi. As soon as he heard her name spoken, and each time they were together, he blushed to the tips of his ears, and his friends deliberately kept mentioning her for the pleasure of watching the display. In a small photo with deckled edges taken in 1935, which Vera preserved in an album tied with ribbon, he appears, racket in hand, thin, fair-haired, and dressed in white, next to his cousin Guilia and his sister Anna Maria, gazing at his beloved. Vera Marconi still lives in Turin and remembers Primo as a walking companion and doubles partner, but not as an admirer. In another photo taken on the same day at a small hotel called The Seven Springs in Valle Stretta, Primo, who is wearing climbing boots and is still standing next to Vera, is masking his face behind the strings of his racket.

Vera's and Primo's parents were friends, and lived in the same district. Their mothers used to meet when they went shopping in the Corso Sommeiller, Via Massena, Via Goberti, and Via San Secondo. Their children — Vera had a sister eight years younger — attended the same primary and secondary schools, and it was this family in particular that the Levis used to join in summer in Bardonècchia, in the Val de Susa. Like other friends of the Levis, the Marconis were Christians, and in 1935, only three years before the promulgation of the racial laws by Mussolini, there were no tensions between Christians and Jews.

In 1932, as Levi recalls in an essay called "A Long Duel," published in *Other People's Trades*, Beccali had won the 1,500 metres in Los Angeles, and the club members dreamed of similar triumphs. They organized their own competitions in a stadium that no longer exists, opened in 1915 and already gone to seed by the mid-1930s, its giant scale a prototype of Mussolinian architecture. (The architects appointed by the Duce to reorganize the centre of Turin had also demolished and rebuilt the old Via Roma between the Piazza San Marco and Piazza Carlo Felice, so that the splendours of the main shopping street of the city of Fiat should match the pharaonic pomp of the regime.)

When Levi and his classmates used it, unofficially, the stadium's track and terraces were falling apart. Primo's slender build did not equip him for putting the shot (a lump of concrete) or throwing the makeshift javelin. He and his friend Guido Bonfiliol ran the 800 metres. Guido was a handsome teenager from a modest background, well built, and successful with girls. A less gifted student than Primo, he envied Primo's scholastic successes. Each envying the other, the two were inseparable rivals. The first of the contests they invented was holding their breath for as long as possible, pushing themselves almost to the point of passing out. "We competed in turns, each holding the second hand in front of the increasingly bulging, glazed eyes of the other" (*Trades* 65/54).

After that came a more perverse and aggressive game — invented by Guido, of course. The slapping game consisted of smacking the opponent hard in the face, only on the cheeks, and by surprise. In this contest Primo came out on top, because he was small and light and had fast hands. After the slapping came the striptease, not yet known anywhere by that name, a game at which Primo was too modest ever to get past removing his shoes. This number was performed in the natural science lessons, in front of a short-sighted teacher who was either absent-minded or chose to ignore what went on below the rostrum. The only boy in the class who managed to take off all his clothes, and even stood up naked on his desk (at the back of the class) at the risk of being called up to the blackboard, was, naturally, Guido, the rogue who fascinated the well-behaved Primo.

With Guido determined to prove his supremacy in every field, their rivalry finally came to running race. The first time, they ran neck and neck until they were exhausted, with Primo collapsing only moments before his friend. After that they ran against the stopwatch, one following the other by bike, and timing his performance. When it was Primo's turn to run, Guido used to exploit his friend's shyness by telling dirty jokes to make him laugh and put him off his stride. The only contest where Primo came first was in agility, when the stadium coffee bar from which they had gained access to the track closed down, and he managed to wriggle through the bars of the gate, which were sixteen centimetres apart.

Looking back on his relationship with Guido, his masculine, lusty, impudent friend, Levi, a puritanical introvert who felt inferior because of his small size and slender build, recognized ambivalent feelings on both sides: admiration, envy, rivalry, and even hatred on the stadium track.

Despite being included in the "sporty" club, the studious Levi had to suffer jeers from classmates who kept insisting that circumcision amounted to castration. So he felt the distinctiveness of being Jewish as a sort of anomaly. Even though he seems not to have felt it too strongly at first, later on a sense of inferiority linked to his consciousness of being Jewish came to inhibit his relations with girls. He hardly dared approach them. He wrote in *The Periodic Table*:

Within myself, and in my contacts with my Christian friends, I had always considered my origin as an almost negligible but curious fact, a small amusing anomaly, like having a crooked nose or freckles; a Jew is somebody who at Christmas does not have a tree, who should not eat salami but eats it all the same, who has learned a bit of Hebrew at thirteen and then has forgotten it. (*Table* 35–6)

Levi speaks of anomalies inherent in being Jewish, and cites as examples the look of one's nose or skin. The most disabling handicap — castration — is not mentioned in this context, but this fantasy, fuelled by the taunts of his Christian fellow pupils at the Liceo d'Azeglio, spoiled his affections. At the time of the Treaty of Alliance between Italy and Germany, and the Fascist regime's adoption of the racial laws in 1938, his inhibitions tangled with a hostile reality that forbade all relations between Jews and Christians. Thus, when in 1942 he gave a lift on his bike to Gabriella Garda Aliverti, who loved somebody else, he felt hatred for his rival:

> A *goy*, and she was a *goyà*, according to my atavistic terminology: and they could have got married. I felt growing within me, perhaps for the first time, a nauseating sensation of emptiness: so this is what it meant to be different, this was the price for being the salt of the earth. To carry on your crossbar a girl you desire and be so far from her as not to be able even to fall in love with her: to carry her on the crossbar along Viale Gorizia to help her belong to someone else, and vanish from my life. (*Table* 124–5)

The idea of assimilation — at the cost of discarding age-old cultural traditions and particularisms — as universal panacea against all the evils suffered down the centuries, even after the emancipation of the Jews, proved illusory. The equality proclaimed had not been gained in practice. Even emancipated — "regenerated" as the Abbé Grégoire used to say[20] — the Jew was not a person like other people. His difference was ingrained in flesh and blood. Primo Levi was considered part of "the Jewish street," with which he was unfamiliar, yet he embraced — though also toned down — the clichés of anti-Semitism. The notional anomaly he found amusing, not monstrous.

Until then, in that most Catholic of countries, Italian Jews had felt at home in Italy, so much so that some of them supported the Fascist regime in its early days. Even though the first indications of the developments in Germany had already begun to arrive, the growing threat remained a distant rumbling. The Italian Jews felt safe, even while Zionist-inspired magazines in Germany — including one that was translated by Anna Maria Levi — were printing items about the many Jews who had fled Nazi Germany to seek refuge in Italy.

In 1937, at the age of eighteen, Primo Levi was preparing to leave school and enter university. Yet the young man, who was to become one of the essential writers of this century, first had to resit the literature paper in the October exams before enrolling. On top of having to suffer this first academic setback, he received a fright: a few days before the exam, an official turned up at his home to check his papers and military situation, and complained at his lack of enthusiasm for conscription. The visit was an error, caused by a mistaken address, but Levi's nerves were utterly on edge. Nevertheless, although he had a poor record in Italian, with his thorough knowledge of Dante, he was typical of Italian classical culture in the 1930s. He passed the resit without difficulty, and — free at last from the classical high school in its Fascist heyday — went on to enrol in the Chemical Institute he had been longing to enter for so many years.

3   The Chemical Institute

In 1937 Primo Levi started his first year at the Chemical Institute with a feeling of release. For his generation the study of the science of chemistry meant

> a haven of reason against the madness of Fascism. Fascism triumphant clouded reason. Our Fascist history and philosophy books signified peaks of discouragement for independent reason. Each of us in our own way, some in mathematics, some in geometry, some in chemistry, we found a patch of solid ground to stand on.[1]

The first classes he attended, given by Professor Ponzio, delighted him for various reasons: the information provided by Dr Ponzio was "clear, precise, verifiable" and expressed in "a well-defined language that [came] straight to the point." Later on, clarity, precision, and conciseness were to be key aspects of Levi's professed faith in his stylistic expression.

Professor Ponzio, a declared anti-Fascist, was a sarcastic, very clever, occasionally cruel old man, notorious for his hostility to women, nuns, priests, and anyone in uniform. This surly eccentric, and his technical assistant, Caselli, gave rise to all kinds of more or less truthful tales among the students, featuring Ponzio's quirks of character and the mixture of fear and respect that he inspired. In any event, Levi took to him because he dared make a mockery of the compulsory Fascist black shirt by replacing it with a ridiculously tiny black dickey on examination days. Students, for Professor Ponzio, were a collection of idiots whom he treated with scathing contempt.

The laboratory where the apprentice chemists spent five hours of every day was an equal source of wonder. Contact with matter was described as "returning to origins," and as a final verdict on the teachers at the Liceo Massimo d'Azeglio, Levi adds: "The hand is a noble organ, but the school, obsessed with the brain, left it out of account."[2]

The young Levi worked in a team with fellow students such as Alberto Salmoni, a young Jew from Naples who had been living in Turin for a year. The two became and remained close friends until the end of Levi's life. Salmoni made a deep impression on Levi. He was a handsome, athletic, outgoing young man, who was not overawed by the conventions of Turin, and used to turn up at the Chemical Institute on roller skates. Girls could not resist him. Primo, who wanted to be like him, hardly left his side, but according to Alberto the bond that united them "above all" in those days was their love of the mountains. They shared a common passion for nature, etymology, and linguistics. Primo was already a practised climber, and started to take his friend on walks in the hills, at first just the two of them, but soon the group admitted new members such as Sandro Delmastro, Bianca Guidetti Serra, who was engaged to be married to Alberto, and Eugenio Gentili Tedeschi, who lived two streets away from the Levis in the Corso Galileo Ferraris.

Once, when Alberto and Primo were hiking by themselves, a starving dog followed them all the way up to the peaks, then suddenly collapsed, and seemed too exhausted to stand up again. The two friends delved into their supplies and gave it something to eat, which so revived the animal that it got up and followed them down to the next village, where it left them to continue their walk.

During these long expeditions, Primo spoke to Alberto openly about his most intimate concerns. He confided that his shyness with women, and his inability to communicate with them, caused him so much torment and despair that thoughts of suicide had crossed his mind.

Bianca Guidetti Serra, who was part of the group, was studying law. She remembers Primo Levi as a small, thin young man who would tie himself in knots trying to strike up conversation with the female students in his year. In *The Periodic Table* he describes how, after trying and trying to master his sense of inferiority, he set his heart on a solitary girl whom for reasons of tact he calls Rita. He tells how, "very thin, pale, sad, and sure of herself," she "discouraged all contact" (*Table* 34–5). In other words, the brightest and most inhibited male student of his year had picked on the gloomiest girl for his first encounter. The young man, who believed that he might be banished for ever from the company of women, bravely dismissed his fears and spoke to Rita because he had recognized the book, Thomas Mann's *The Magic Mountain*, sticking out of her bag. Levi had read it and jumped at the chance to debate the novel's "political, theological and metaphysical discussions" with Rita. As it turned out, she was a lot more interested in the romantic plot line that runs through the book. Levi might have deduced an interest in love, or at any rate in flirting. One of the characters in the novel is Jewish, and it entered Primo's mind to make use of that fact, even though in the time of *La difeza della razza* ("The Defence of the Race"), the anti-Semitic monthly created by Mussolini to provide a theoretical basis for his racial laws, Jews were considered to be impure, stingy, and cunning. All the same, he offered to walk Rita home, and while a torrent of words poured out of him, "trembling with emotion" he ventured, unthinkably, to slip his arm under hers. Although it appears that the episode was confined to this one evening walk and simple gesture, for Levi it was an exhilarating victory over the ordeals that life had in store.

The first steps in qualitative analysis, which consisted in identifying the composition of a given unknown substance, were hard work but exciting. At the end of the 1930s, laboratory equipment was scarce and expensive. Unskilled students could easily injure themselves when they pushed a pierced plug over a bent glass tube, which often broke as they turned it. The sharp glass stump then skewered the palm of the hand, and a scar there was one of the painful badges that future chemists had to earn. It was a rite of passage. All wore while lab coats, and carried spatulas in their pockets, to spread the preparations. The glassware was fragile, each issue carefully recorded, and the supervising store-keeper had to be paid for any breakages. If the damaged article was salvageable it was resold for a few lire, perhaps to someone who had bungled an experiment. The area around the enormous sink was always busy: "One went there to smoke, to chat, and also to court the girls" (Trades 99/88).

Qualitative analysis called for patience, judgement, and imagination, but these did not cover the novice against mistakes and disappointments. "Sometimes you found chrome when there was not the slightest grain of it, sometimes it was bismuth and you couldn't recognize it." To fail an oral exam was annoying, but tacitly accepted. "To botch an analysis was worse: perhaps because unconsciously one realized that the judgement of men (in this case the professors) is arbitrary and debatable, while the judgement of things is always inexorable and just."[3]

After five months, their professor made a selection from his eighty first-year students, and only twenty — fourteen young men and young women — were admitted to the preparation laboratory, where a crude kind of initiation ritual took place. To break the strain of the five hours a day spent in the rigour of the laboratory, the students treated themselves to tea at five o'clock, made in the glassware used for analyses. Sometimes the tea was served with tiny experimental rusks, made of starch and diastase and baked in the small oven used to dry precipitates.

For Levi, quantitative and qualitative analysis provided a new experience in which individual rankings could be turned upside-down. Those at the top of the class, who readily absorbed chemical theory, were not necessarily the most dexterous. The lab demanded nimble fingers, good eyesight and hearing, a keen sense of smell, and an obstinate refusal to be thwarted.

According to Levi's sketch of his teacher in *The Periodic Table*, Professor Ponzio's approach resembled that of a Zen master who trained his disciples by firing off a series of short, sharp, disconcerting messages, both negative and cryptic, which amounted to announcing that those who lacked both the will and the ability to submit to his guidance were welcome to remove themselves. Sixty of them left without completing the course. Those who remained, including Levi, then spent five hours a day in their master's laboratory, under the gaze of his henchman and vassal, the laboratory assistant Caselli. In his pungent account of the relationship that bound the two together, Levi wrote:

Caselli was a modest, taciturn man, in whose sad but proud eyes could be read
— he is a great scientist, and as his "famulus" I too am a little great;
— I, though humble, know things that he does not know;
— I know him better than he knows himself; I foresee his acts;

— I have power over him; I defend and protect him;

— I can say bad things about him because I love him; that is not granted to you;

— his principles are right, but he applies them laxly, and "it wasn't like this in my day ... " If I weren't here ....

In Professor Ponzio's laboratory, Primo Levi, the apprentice chemist, pondered over his first encounter with "Matter." He writes it with a capital letter and also calls it by its Greek name, *hyle*, the opponent of Spirit, also capitalized. On that day, Levi received a few granules of zinc from Caselli's hand. Describing its characteristics, he observes that this metal behaves differently in the presence of acids, according to its state of purity: pure zinc is highly resistant to acids. This property leads him to make two observations:

the praise of purity, which protects from evil like a coat of mail; the praise of impurity, which gives rise to changes, in other words, to life. I discarded the first, disgustingly moralistic, and I lingered to consider the second, which I found more congenial. In order for the wheel to turn, for life to be lived, impurities are needed, and the impurities of impurities in the soil, too, as is known, if it is to be fertile.

(*Table* 34)

It was 1937. Mussolini in power wanted his citizens to be identical, pure Fascists, and Levi was not. Soon, publication of a pamphlet entitled the "Manifesto of Racist Scientists" would officially class him as impure, because he was a Jew.

———

As a student in 1937, Levi already had a deep hatred of Fascism, but had not yet made contact with the anti-Fascist movement, of which Turin was one of the centres. In fact it was there that the followers of Piero Gobetti founded the movement *Giustizia e Libertà* ("Justice and Liberty"). Gobetti was a young socialist who in the 1920s had set up *Rivoluzione Liberale* ("Liberal Revolution") groups in all the main towns, and had edited a newspaper of the same name. He died in exile in Paris in 1925, from the effects of injuries suffered during an attack by Fascist thugs.

The resistance to Fascism in Italy sprang up immediately before and after the March on Rome. Members of the opposition to Mussolini quickly became the targets of punitive raids mounted by the *squadristi*. After the victory of Fascism, many were banished and many more forced into exile. The anti-Fascist movement was therefore literally divided into two groups, which sometimes fell out: the activists at home, and those abroad — the *fuorusciti*, exiles — who for twenty years provided the nucleus of the forces hostile to Fascism. The mass exodus was chiefly bound for France, where a great many Italian workers had been seeking jobs in industry and agriculture ever since the late nineteenth century, and were fairly well organized. They gave generous assistance to the activists, and then to the leaders of the political opposition. Paris in the mid-1920s became the capital of the *fuorusciti*, because successive French governments encouraged the opposition to settle there, to the fury of the Italian authorities who considered creating *fasci* abroad to fight the anti-Fascists. The vigilance of the French police deterred them from going into action, but the émigrés took the threat seriously, and in March 1924 they shot dead the secretary of the Italian *Fascio* in Paris, on a café terrace. But émigré circles were riddled with spies and *agents provocateurs*, and when one of their French-based plots came to light, the *fuorusciti* started to operate more cautiously.

An anti-Fascist press developed in France, and in April 1927 at the Nérac conference a political organization was created. In Nérac, the formation of an "Anti-Fascist Concentration" was planned which would enrol members independently from their political parties. The exact opposite happened: the Concentration eventually became a coalition of parties. It published a newspaper, *Libertà*, whose first issue appeared on May Day 1927, but the émigrés' contacts with the "Italian masses" were very rare.

After 1922, the most effective movement against Fascism was the Partito comunista italiano (PCI), the Italian Communist Party, which went underground in 1924. Its Third Congress met in Lyons in 1926, the year all political groups were banned. In addition to underground activity in Italy, an external directorate was headed by Palmiro Togliatti, in Paris. It was very well organized in the north of Italy, and secretly distributed a number of publications, including the party daily *L'Unità* and the journal *Battaglie Sindacali*. The dissolved *Confederazione Generale del Lavoro* (CGL) (the "General Confederation of Labour") was reconstituted, and in a ferment of strikes and agitation the movement prepared its activists for an insurrection against Fascism. The Communists refused to ally with the Socialist Party, which they described as a "negative element of the situation, which must be eliminated," and also condemned the bourgeois and allegedly masonic allegiances of the anti-Fascist Concentration in Paris. The Fascist police arrested all the members of the PCI's internal leadership, then extended the repression to the other opponents of the regime. The anti-Fascists were tried by a special tribunal. Only Carlo Rosselli, the founder and theoretician of the *Giustizia e Libertà* movement, was brought before the regular court in Savona, after Filippo Turati, the director of the theoretical weekly *Critica sociale*, had escaped from the Lipari Islands where the Fascists confined their political prisoners.

The political mentor of the group of young anti-Fascist intellectuals whose leader, Nello Rosselli, had also escaped from the Lipari Islands where he was under house arrest, was Piero Gobetti. Theirs was a non-party group, left-leaning but firmly anti-Marxist, whose members advocated "La Rivoluzione Liberale," which combined party pluralism with the social and economic aims of socialism. The membership included many Jews, among them the Rosselli brothers, Carlo Levi, Leone Ginzburg, Sion Segre Amar, Hugo Sacerdote, and Emanuele Artom. Carlo Rosselli and Carlo Levi were on the editorial staff of the underground journal *Non Mollare!* ("Don't give in!"), published by Gaetano Salvemini. Ernesto Rossi, a professor of political economy since 1926, formed a group in Milan in 1928 with the founders of the journal *Il Caffè*, Ricardo Bauer and Ferrucio Parri, who had been released from the Lipari Islands.

Carlo Rosselli, the real political leader of *Giustizia e Libertà*, had escaped from the Lipari Islands in 1928 with Emilio Lussu and Frances Fausto Nitti, and reached Paris by way of Tunisia and Marseilles. The following year, more political detainees escaped and went to Paris, where they helped to lay the foundations of the new republican organization, also called *Giustizia e Libertà*, which was not a party coalition and whose members joined as individuals. In 1929 it published the manifesto of a programme of government that aimed to replace the Fascist regime by gathering all anti-Fascists together in a revolutionary, non-party movement — it suggested that its members should destroy their party cards. Italy would be re-created on the basis of liberty, the republic, and social justice. Carlo Rosselli believed that only a revolutionary process could achieve this goal, and several lines of action unfolded.

In July 1930 Giovanni Bassanesi, one of the leaders of the Italian League for Human Rights, dropped pamphlets from an aeroplane over Milan in broad daylight. A second attempt went wrong when the plane had to make a forced landing and Bassanesi was arrested and put on trial in Lugano.

The activists in the Milan region received money and weapons from Paris, to support a general uprising. Rossi and Bauer published a tract called "Tactical Advice" which advocated passive resistance — withholding taxes to cause a financial crisis — and revolutionary agitation. Plans to dynamite the tax offices in Italy's seven main towns came to nothing. The members of *Giustizia e Libertà* launched individual attacks, as when Ferdinando De Rosa fired shots at the Prince of Piedmont in Brussels on 4 October 1929. This was followed by numerous attacks on official representatives of the regime abroad, and on Fascist emigrant workers. The authors of plans to assassinate the Duce himself were executed by firing squad in 1930.

Both the passive campaigns and the plans for violent action ended in defeat. On 30 October 1930 police arrested the twenty-four leaders of the movement in Milan, Bergamo, Trento, Florence, and Rome. The organization was smashed, and its leaders given heavy prison sentences in May 1931; Bauer and Rossi got twenty years. Only the members of the Turin group, all of them intellectuals, centred on Carlo Levi, escaped the dragnet. But the arrests did not prevent the groups from rising again out of their own ashes, especially in Turin, which became the capital of anti-Fascism, with Benedetto Croce as a spiritual guide in his role of editor of the journal *La Critica*.

The anti-Fascist Concentration and *Giustizia e Libertà* had many fierce debates, which focused in particular on a pamphlet published by Carlo Rosselli in 1930 under the title "Liberal Socialism," in which he criticized Marxism and insisted on the necessity for socialism to uphold the principle of political liberty. In the end, the two movements joined forces. Rosselli accepted the merger only for tactical reasons. In 1932 he founded an ideological review, entitled *I Quaderni di Giustizia e Libertà*, which reiterated its founder's hostility to political parties and expressed the movement's revolutionary, republican, and leftist commitment. It caused resignations both in the anti-Fascist Concentration and in the *Giustizia e Libertà* movement, but Rosselli's programme was adopted in the Pact of November 1932. Thus *Giustizia e Libertà* became a restricted organization, made up of intellectuals sympathetic to Carlo Rosselli, who thought that Fascism had emerged from the old liberal democratic model on whose ruins he dreamed of building a new world.

In 1935, Italian anti-Fascism, which was deeply divided, suffered harsh repression. When the Spanish Civil War broke out, Rosselli issued the slogan "Today in Spain, tomorrow in Italy!," which was opposed by both the Communists and the Socialists. Allying himself with anarchists and independent socialists, he collected arms and funds and recruited volunteers for Spain. The unit he formed, the Italian Column, was the first Italian anti-Fascist group to reach Spain. In August 1936 Rosselli was seriously injured in Monte Pelato, near Huesca, and was sent back to France to convalesce.

On 9 June 1937, the Rosselli brothers left their hotel in Bagnôles-de-l'Orne in Normandy to go for a walk. They stopped to help a motorist whose car had broken down, and were killed — as the price for two hundred rifles — by agents of the Cagoule (the extreme right-wing French "Secret Committee for Revolutionary Action") on behalf of the Italian secret service. More than two hundred thousand people followed their coffins to the Père-Lachaise cemetery in Paris. Franco Antonicelli, who was later to become Primo Levi's first publisher, then became president of the movement.

On 11 March 1934, Sion Segre Amar, a native of Turin and soon to become a comrade of Primo Levi, was caught in the frontier town of Ponte Tresa in the act of smuggling anti-Fascist literature into Italy from Switzerland. He was working with Gino and Mario Levi — young Jewish anti-Fascists. Mario managed to escape by plunging into a mountain torrent and making for the frontier, where Swiss customs officers sent out a boat to rescue him from drowning. Giuseppe Levi, Mario's father (a famous professor of anatomy at Turin University and also the father of Natalia Ginzburg), who had found a hiding place for Turati and helped him to escape from Italy, was also briefly jailed in Turin.

Following Sion Segre Amar's arrest, his father, who also taught at Turin University, was arrested, along with sixteen key members of *Giustizia e Libertà*, including Leone Ginzburg and Carlo Levi. Others arrested were Gino and Albert Levi, Mario's brothers, Cesare Pavese, Giulio Einaudi, and the editors of *La Cultura*, an anti-Fascist literary review published in Turin and managed by Franco Neri. Gino was released after two months, and his father was proud to spend three weeks in jail. Since seventeen of the accused were Jewish, for the first time the case was presented as a Jewish conspiracy against Italy. *Giustizia e Libertà* was not a Zionist organization, but a liberal socialist movement with both Jews and non-Jews as members. Carlo Rosselli, for example, summed up his Jewishness as follows:

> I call myself a Jew because the idea of monotheism is firmly rooted in my mind, because I loathe all forms of idolatry, because I look on the mystery of the hereafter with a thoroughly Jewish severity, because I love all men, as Judaism commands ... and therefore I have ideas about society that seem to me to flow from our best traditions.[4]

The Fascist press launched an anti-Zionist campaign which ranted "Anti-Fascist equals antipatriot, equals Zionist, equals Jew." The 31 March 1934 issue of the paper *Il Tevere* ran the headline "Next year in Jerusalem, this year in the Special Tribunal!" Roberto Farinacci wrote in his paper *Il Regime fascista*: "Anyone who calls himself a Zionist has no right to honours or profits in our country." Yet on 17 February 1934 Mussolini had received Professor Weizmann, the future first president of the State of Israel, in the Palazzo Venezia.

Their conversation touched first on the situation of the ten thousand German Jews who had found refuge in Palestine under the British mandate. Chaim Weizmann tried to draw the Duce's attention to the state of affairs in Austria and the plight of Chancellor Dollfuss. Mussolini claimed that he was ready to support Dollfuss, and added "What threatens us is more than war, it is the total destruction of European civilization. The collapse may happen, even without a war, through the victory of barbarism."

When the question of Palestine came up, Mussolini declared:

> In order to return to Palestine, you must create a Jewish State. I have already spoken to the Arabs. I believe that an agreement can be reached. The difficulty may arise from the question of Jerusalem. The Arabs say that the Jews should have their capital in Tel Aviv.

Weizmann replied:

> It is a very great idea that you have just formulated. As I see it, the State, even if it is small, is the fulcrum of Archimedes.

Mussolini:

> The importance of a State consists in its being recognized by others. Nations (which are not crystallized into sovereign States) are born and die because others do or do not do certain things. For the existence of a nation, it is therefore its recognition as a State that is decisively important. But what do you think about Jerusalem?

Weizmann:

> One thing is absolutely clear: if Jerusalem does not become a Jewish
> capital it cannot in any case become an Arab capital, because there is
> the Christian world to consider. Jerusalem is the confluence of three
> religions. But it must be noted that the sanctity of Jerusalem for
> Muslims is something of a recent invention, whereas for Jews Jerusalem
> is the city of David, and for Christians it is the centre of the holy places.[5]

To Nahum Goldmann, whom he received on 13 November 1934 in the
presence of the chief rabbi of Rome, Mussolini declared again: "You must
create a Jewish State ... You must have a proper State, and not that ridiculous
national home that the English have offered you. I will help you to create the
Jewish State."[6] As he took his leave of them, he told them in his usual theatrical manner that Hitler was just an idiot, made a few more promises about the
Saarland, Poland, and Austria, and even agreed to make public the audience
that he had just granted them.

Hitler had become the chancellor of Germany on 30 January 1933, and
Mussolini felt proud that his "protégé" had supervened to prove the decadence
of liberal democracy. That said, he did not welcome Hitler's taking an interest
in the German minorities in the north of Italy and in Austria, which he looked
on as his own sphere of influence — so much so that when Chancellor
Engelbert Dollfuss was murdered by Austrian Nazis on 25 July 1934,
Mussolini mobilized his troops against the Germans in the Brenner Pass.

It was precisely at that moment that he abandoned the anti-Semitic
campaign he had launched and sought a *rapprochement* with France and
Britain to obtain their good will towards his military campaign in Ethiopia. In
a sudden change of tack, he wrote:

> Thirty centuries of history enable us to view with supreme disdain the
> doctrines brought into fashion across the Alps by the descendants of
> peoples who could not write, and owned not a single document about
> their history, in the time when Rome had Caesar, Virgil and Augustus.[7]

A side-effect of this development was that when they went on trial, the accused
at Ponte Tresa were largely forgotten. Only three were condemned, without
publicity, to short sentences.

At that point, Mussolini therefore chose to look on the Italian Zionists as
democrats and socialists who professed a dual allegiance, even though he still
felt more liking for the Zionist revisionist leader Vladimir Jabotinsky — who
made no secret of his admiration for the Duce — to the point of allowing
members of his organization to study at the Naval School in Civitavecchia.
Although Mussolini believed that the power of the Jews reached far and wide
and could help him to maintain his influence in the Mediterranean, he was also

keen not to antagonize the Arabs. Nevertheless, finding himself isolated after his land-grab in Ethiopia, he intervened in the Spanish Civil War, and he and his son-in-law, Count Galeazzo Ciano, took the decision to ally themselves with Germany. Anti-Semitism was stoked up again, and scurrilous lampoons reappeared in the newspapers. Thus Farinacci, writing in *Il Regime fascista*, accused the Jews of putting Judaism before Fascism and country. In the same year, anti-Semitic graffiti appeared on the walls of Jewish homes in Ferrara. In April 1937 Paolo Orano published his book "The Jews in Italy." Elsewhere the Catholic right-wing, the Church, and papers like *La Civiltà cattolica* and *Vita e pensiero*, the periodical of the Catholic University of Milan, which saw Jews in the same light as Bolsheviks, published articles hostile to the Jews. Yet Ciano did not give his support to the anti-Semitic campaign launched by Giovanni Preziosi in *La vita italiana*, and while talking with his father-in-law on 6 February 1938 he stated that he favoured a "solution which will not raise a problem which fortunately does not exist here."[8]

On 3 June 1938, Mussolini criticized Farinacci, a member of the Fascist Grand Council and leader of the anti-Semitic movement in Italy, for employing a Jewish secretary, Jole Foa. It was things like that, wrote Ciano, — who, when it came down to it was a man of politics not of principle — "which foreigners see as proof of a lack of seriousness in many Italians."[9] So it was by a calculated decision that Mussolini chose to run an anti-Semitic policy in 1938. The racial laws are not attributable either to the anti-Semitic campaign waged by the Catholic right-wing and the Church, nor to the domestic Fascist ideology. Mussolini switched his line because he wanted to consolidate his alliance with Germany, and to give credibility to the "Rome–Berlin Axis." Various omens had pointed to the Duce's sudden U-turn. Count Ciano had backed the idea of going along with the German theories. For another thing, when Hitler came to Rome in May 1938, five hundred foreigners — among them many German Jews and persecuted Austrians who had fled or had been banished by the Nazis when Italy was not yet aligned with the Axis — were arrested as a security precaution, despite not being involved in any political activity. In June, an official delegation of the German government's Race Policy Office, which was run by Doctor Gross, arrived in Italy.

The adoption of the racial laws was preceded by a press campaign designed to mobilize public opinion. A new publication, *La difesa de la razza* ("The Defence of the Race"), was founded by Telesio Interlandi to promote the state's official anti-Semitism. It did not close down until 1943, with the fall of Mussolini. In this journal, the Jews, accused of being foreigners and responsible for all the ills of Italy, were considered pro-British and shown to be on the side of the Republicans in the war in Spain. Their contribution to intellectual life was presented in a totally negative light. Yet despite the anti-Semitic lectures and radio broadcasts organized for students by the National Fascist Institute of Culture, the people of Italy did not welcome this tide of propaganda.

On 14 July 1938, the *Manifesto degli scienziati razzisti* (the "Manifesto of Racist Scientists") was published. Mussolini had unearthed a handful of "men of science" able to assert that "the population of present-day Italy is of Aryan origin. There exists a pure Italian race. Jews do not belong to it." Mussolini declared: "I am Nordic, my daughter is married to an Etruscan, my son to a Lombard, and I myself feel affinities with the English and the Germans."

The ten "expert" signatories to this manifesto were young lecturers vulnerable to pressures exerted at the start of their careers. At first the manifesto was published without signatures, and it was not till a few days later that the names of the ten "men of science" who had written it were published. Mussolini claimed that his racial laws were different in kind from the Nazis' Nuremberg laws. The Italian Fascists argued that their legislation — whose aim, they said, was to pick out and isolate the Jews from the rest of society, not to persecute them — was of a spiritual, not a biological nature.

On 18 September 1938, speaking in Trieste, Mussolini declared:

> The racial problem was not stumbled upon unexpectedly, as think those who are startled by a sudden reveille because they are used to long lazy dreams. It is related to the conquest of the empire. Because history teaches that empires are won by force of arms but are maintained by prestige. For prestige requires a clear, stern racial awareness that establishes itself not only in differences but in highly distinct superiority ....
> As regards domestic policy, the burning question is the racial problem. Even in this domain, we will adopt the necessary solutions.[10]

The Duce therefore made himself responsible for the anti-Semitic campaign and the race laws, along with a few fanatics like Farinacci, Starace, Buffarini-Guidi and Giuseppe Bottai, the minister of national education present at the session of the Grand Council that launched the campaign. During the month of July 1938, the interior minister announced that the Central Office of Demography was to become the Office of Demography and Race. A census of Italy's Jews was planned for August of the following year.

At the time of their adoption, the measures directed against the Jews met with no opposition from the Vatican, just as the anti-Semitic publications issued by men of the Church had not been condemned by Rome. Although the Holy See was traditionally hostile to the Jews — the liturgy, anti-Jewish prejudice and political motives continued to blame them as a deicidal people — Pope Pius XI had spoken his mind in private about anti-Semitism, and published a homily strongly condemning racism; and *L'Osservatore Romano* kept quiet. The pope's words had annoyed the Fascist hierarchy, and Ciano summoned the papal nuncio Borgongini-Duca to remind him that the Duce took the racial question very seriously. "I spoke very frankly and explained the reasons and aims of our racism," he wrote in his diary. "He seemed to me very convinced. And I must say that, personally, he has turned out to be very anti-Semitic. Tomorrow I will speak with the Holy Father."[11] Following the pope's public condemnation of racism, Mussolini asked his son-in-law to have all Jews removed from the diplomatic corps.

The *Anschluss* in Austria in March 1938 and *Kristallnacht* in Germany in November brought a new exodus of Jews towards an Italy now practising state anti-Semitism. Renzo De Felice[12] estimates that eleven thousand Jews arrived in Italy between the promulgation of the anti-Semitic laws and the country's entry into the war in June 1940.

In this connection it is worth recalling that a number of Jews deprived of their civic rights by the racial laws wrote to Mussolini asking for permission to fight in defence of their country. Of course, they were refused the privilege of dying for Italy, with the one exception of Umberto Pugliese, who had resigned from his post as inspector-general of the navy at the age of fifty-eight. In November 1940 the Duce's government realized that Pugliese was the only man capable of refloating the Italian fleet sunk by British torpedo planes in Taranto harbour. When envoys were sent to ask him how much he wanted to be paid for the job (given that Jews loved money most of all), Pugliese replied that the only payment he wanted was his return ticket, and to be allowed to wear his uniform and decorations while he worked. His wish was granted. After that, he went into retirement.[13]

The papal encyclical *Mit brennender Sorge*, condemning racism, had been published in 1937, but the Church continued to make use of anti-Semitism against freemasonry and the secular currents in the country. On 16 September 1938 Pius XI received a Belgian pilgrim, and, after reading a few passages from the Mass, told him, in a voice choked with emotion:

> Be careful, Abraham really is our patriarch, our ancestor. Anti-Semitism is not compatible with the sublime reality alluded to in this text. Anti-Semitism is an odious movement that we Christians must have nothing to do with. Anti-Semitism is intolerable. All of us are spiritually Semites.

During a visit from the students of the Urban Pontifical College of the Propagation of the Faith, the pope, in a clear allusion to the "Manifesto of Racist Scientists," published a few days previously, had made overt remarks rejecting racism. His death in February 1939 prevented him from issuing an encyclical, hostile to Fascism and to the anti-Jewish policy, which he had instructed three Jesuits to draft in June 1938. To this day it has still not been published by the Vatican.[14] All this presents a striking contrast with the silence of his successor, Pius XII, during whose pontificate vicious attacks on the "deicidal people" by Father Agostino Gemelli were published in the magazine *Vita e pensiero*. The Vatican, which favoured the racial laws, gave individual assistance to Jews wishing to emigrate. Paradoxically, it also sometimes gave work in its offices to Jews laid off from their jobs, and later on it admitted

Jewish students into the Pontificum Institutum Ustriusque Juris when they were excluded from the universities. The lower clergy displayed great humanity, and usually did their best to help persecuted and fugitive Jews.

In September 1938, as commanded by the Duce, the interior ministry drew up an anti-Jewish statute. On 6 October Marshals Italo Balbo and Emilio De Bono, together with the president of the Senate, Federzoni, spoke out in favour of the Jews at a meeting where the education minister, Giuseppe Bottai, defended the decree. "They will hate us," he declared, "because we have driven them out. They will despise us if we let them return." Speaking to Ciano at the same meeting, Mussolini confided that for the moment he was being conciliatory, but soon he would get tough. Yet on 10 November, at a meeting of the Council of Ministers, when Lieutenant-General Achille Starace, speaking as the general secretary of the Fascist Party, proposed that Jews should be expelled from the party, Mussolini refused.

In November 1938, the first round of the anti-Jewish legislation was ready (the second was to come in June 1939). It reflected the influences at work in the country in those days: racialism, xenophobia, clericalism, and bureaucratic paternalism.[15] On 17 November 1938, the government announced that Jews were forbidden to study or teach in the universities. However, those who had already begun their studies — among them Primo Levi — would be allowed to complete them. In primary schools with more than ten Jewish pupils, a separate section was to be formed. If the Jewish pupils were excluded from secondary schooling, their teachers might open their own schools, as happened in Turin, where a Hebrew school, which still exists, was started.

In August 1938 ten thousand Jews of foreign origin were living in Italy. On 2 and 3 September, the government announced that foreign Jews were no longer allowed to live in Italy, Libya, or the islands. Those already settled in the country had six months to get out. Jews naturalized after 1919 became foreigners again. Marriages between Jews and Christians were forbidden. In 1938 it was estimated that nearly 7,500 mixed marriages had produced 2,000 Jewish and 7,000 Catholic children. Mussolini's "experts," having discovered the superiority of the "Italian race" and promulgated the racial laws, were suddenly wondering what constituted Jewishness — to whom did the laws apply? Finding answers to this urgent question did not overtax their ingenuity. Unlike the Nuremberg laws of 15 September 1935, the Italian legislation recognized no intermediate categories between Jews and non-Jews. It identified as Jewish

> children of Jewish parents, even if they had converted to another
>   religion:
> children of a single Jewish parent;
> children of a Jewish mother and an unknown father;
> children of mixed marriages with more than 50 per cent of Jewish
>   blood;
> children belonging to the Jewish community, or practising Judaism.

For children of mixed marriages born between 1 October 1938 and 1 October 1939, their parents had the option of baptizing them. Those born after 1 October 1939 had to be baptized within ten days. Jews baptized before October 1938, but married to a Jew, found themselves in a confusing situation.[16]

This definition was succeeded by a series of decrees that barred Jews from the armed forces, the public services, and of course from the Fascist Party. Marriages between Jews and non-Jews were forbidden, except if performed on the point of death or to legitimize a child. Jews were forbidden to adopt or foster a non-Jewish child. One clause deprived a Jewish parent of his or her Christian child if the child was not receiving an education consistent with Christianity and with the national objectives.[17]

The later decrees provided for the expulsion of Jews from state schools, the annulment of changes of name and removal from the civil lists. The law of 17 November 1938 cancelled any naturalization granted to Jews after 1 January 1919 and stipulated that all foreign and all denaturalized Jews, with the exception of those who were over sixty-five years old or were married to a non-Jewish spouse, must remove themselves from Italy and its dependent territories by 12 March 1939. Those who married an Italian citizen by that date could remain on Italian soil. Nine hundred and thirty-three were permitted to stay, and 6,480 were forced to leave Italy, which enforced the complete closure of its frontiers to Jews from Poland, Hungary, and Romania in August 1939. However the frontier guards were often sympathetic, and would turn a blind eye. In the month of October 1941, 7,000 foreign Jews, including 3,000 recent arrivals, all of them destitute, were put under house arrest or interned in camps.

It was forbidden for Jews to own companies that produced or marketed military equipment. They were forbidden to employ more than a hundred workers or to own factories worth more than a given amount. They could not own personal estate worth more than 20,000 lire, or arable land worth more than 5,000. They could not employ non-Jewish servants, or work in banks, insurance companies, or the municipal or national administration. These clauses had grave implications, because a good many Jews were farmers or public servants.

Certain categories of Jews could be exempted from the terms of the racial laws. Those who enjoyed this privilege were the families of Jews killed, wounded, or decorated during the war in Libya, the Great War, the Ethiopian campaign or the war in Spain; Jews who had taken part in the seizure of Fiume by an Italian free corps led by Gabriele D'Annunzio in 1919; and Jews who had joined the Fascist Party between 1919 and 1922, or during the second half of 1924 — after the assassination by the Fascists of the Socialist deputy Giacomo Matteotti. These exemptions, which were subject to limitations and monitored by a committee of the interior ministry, were not granted automatically. Those who applied had to grease palms, then wait for months for an arbitrary response. The exemptions, which did not cover the full spread of the racial laws, might affect one member of a family but not another, and could be withdrawn for no reason and with no explanation provided. In fact, on 13 June 1939 the government decided to Aryanize whomever it pleased. A Jew could be declared non-Jewish; the Aryanized enjoyed greater privileges than the exempt. By 15 January 1943, the Ministry of Demography and Race, which had examined 5,870 applications, had accepted 2,486 and turned down 3,384.

In 1939, more bans were announced. On 29 June Jews learned that they no longer had the right to be lawyers, and only the exempt could practise the professions of journalist, doctor, pharmacist, veterinarian, judge, engineer, architect, chemist, agronomist, mathematician, or accountant. The non-exempt could practise only on behalf of other Jews. It was forbidden for Aryans to provide any service to Jews. "There are those who speak up for the Jews — they'd better watch out," huffed Starace, the secretary of the Fascist Party. Fully applied, the racial laws forbade Italian Jews to own a radio, have a death notice printed in a newspaper, publish a book, deliver a lecture, have their name in the telephone directory, or visit a holiday resort. Those Jews who were affected by this last measure, as of 29 June 1939, had to return home. In certain towns, the local bylaws went further than the national legislation. In Rome, for example, the Jewish second-hand clothes' dealers had to shut up shop.

Over a thousand members of the Fascist Party were expelled for "pietism" — in other words, being soft on Jews. A population which had accepted the slurs on Zionism and insults against foreign Jews took much less kindly to the persecution of home-grown Jews, and started to help them. Some Fascist officials either refused to apply the racial laws, or found ways round them. Others tipped Jews off that they were about to be arrested, and advised them to go into hiding. Customs officials sometimes helped them to cross over into Switzerland. However, there is also no denying the shameful and cowardly behaviour of certain blinkered or fanatical bureaucrats and officials who applied the laws with zeal and enthusiasm. Some of them cashed in on the desperate situation faced by Jews who were compelled to abandon their businesses.

As will be seen later, paradoxically, the Italians protected Jews abroad in the zones they controlled or occupied.

The chairs of racial studies that were to have been inaugurated after the passage of the racial laws never saw the light of day. From now on, the members of every local branch of the Fascist Party were supposed to look into the "Jewish question." Out of a countrywide membership of 400,000, only 864 took part. In Milan, of the party's 10,000 members, 65 took an interest in the Jews. Of course, a minority were glad to humiliate them, and to see the racial laws applied to the letter.

After the adoption of the racial laws, nearly 4,000 people lost their jobs. Some obtained a kind of retirement; others, whose properties were confiscated, were partially indemnified. Two hundred university students, 4,400 primary and 1,000 secondary school pupils were affected by the laws. Jewish children and students were only allowed inside the state schools to sit examinations, and in this case they were kept separate from the "Aryan" children.

Jewish teachers were given permission to teach in the Jewish schools that opened in Florence, Trieste, Milan, Venice, and Turin. These absorbed the cream of all the disbarred teachers, especially in Turin, where rivalry was wonderfully intense, because pupils and teachers, discovering that they were now to be regarded as Jews, resolved to be proud of the fact.

The adoption of the racial laws had a particularly harsh impact on the Italian Jewish community because it had taken its emancipation for granted. The citizens, so well-integrated into Italian society, were stunned and bewildered. Six thousand Jews converted to Christianity, 6,000 emigrated, and some committed suicide. On 29 November 1938, Angelo Fortunato Formiggini, writer and anti-Fascist editor, threw himself from the top of the Ghirlandina tower in Modena, after writing to his wife, who had begged him not to go through with his plan — "I can't forsake what I consider to be my duty. I have to demonstrate the wicked absurdity of the racial laws."

The last editorial of the magazine *Israel* (on 22 September 1938), published by Dante Lattes before the promulgation of the anti-Jewish laws, was entitled "In the Time of Trial." This is an extract:

> A great and profound sense of being Italian exists among all Italian Jews. It does not come out of the blue nor from the history of this land, but was given to us with our mothers' milk, our lullabies, the history of our grandparents, and with our maternal tongue, the Italian language. For us, it is a great and tragic sorrow that it is possible to throw doubt on the reality and grandeur of this feeling, and to misjudge the sincerity of the mettle shown by centuries of Jews living in Italy, taking part with heart and mind, like all other Italians, in the life of this land.

For his own part, despite his public statements, Ciano wrote in his diary as early as 3 September 1937:

> The Jews bombard me with offensive anonymous letters in which they accuse me of having promised Hitler to persecute them. That is untrue. The Germans have never raised this question with us. Nor do I believe that we should set off an anti-Semitic campaign in Italy. The problem does not exist here. There are not many Jews, and apart from a few exceptions they do no harm.[18]

In the ranks of the Christian intellectuals, Benedetto Croce expressed his solidarity with the Jews, but at the same time advised them to melt more fully into the Italian crowd by trying to discard the distinctions they had preserved for centuries. He thought that their uniqueness had encouraged persecutions in the past and could give rise to new ones in the future.

Dante Lattes replied to Croce that he would not have offered this kind of advice to any follower of any other religion, or to any other ethnic or national group. Why reserve it for the Jews, then? Arnaldo Momigliano also censured Croce's good advice: "Only the lack of all contact with Jewish culture can explain why, in the end, Benedetto Croce fails to understand that Italian Jews have the right, which may subjectively be a duty, to remain Jews."[19]

Priests were inconsistent in their attitudes. Some readily dispensed certificates of baptism, others spread false rumours to spur conversions, while still others refused to provide certificates of baptism if the conversion was not genuine. If Jews expected little from the Church, they did on the other hand expect help from the royal House of Savoy. They had venerated the royal House so deeply that many Jewish households and shops owned a framed portrait of King Victor Emmanuel III, although he made not the slightest public objection when the racial laws were issued in his name. Yet the king, who had no liking for the Jews, was not an anti-Semite. When he had to sign the anti-Jewish decrees he told Mussolini three times that he felt "infinite pity for the Jews." The fuming Duce informed the king that there were twenty thousand people in his kingdom who were sorry for the fate of the Jews. In private, the king made no secret of his view that it would have been better not to venture upon the kind of persecutions that were being forecast before the promulgation of the laws.

In the armed forces, five generals and five admirals were forced to resign. When Colonel Segre, who was directing exercises in Vercelli, received a letter informing him that he was being retired as a Jew, he ordered his troops to assemble, then shot himself dead with his pistol before their eyes.

The writer Giorgio Bassani had to break off his engagement to a Catholic girl. The future Nobel prize winner Rita Levi Montalcini, one of Primo Levi's closest friends, who had taken her doctorate at the faculty of medicine in Turin, was dismissed from the institute where she worked and had to pursue her research at home.

At the start of the academic year in 1938, a few months before the promulgation of the "Manifesto of Racist Scientists," after passing a series of exams, Primo Levi and about thirty other second-year students had been admitted to the Qualitative Analysis laboratory.

Hitler had entered Prague unopposed, Franco had defeated the republicans, and Mussolini had occupied Albania.

In Turin, the laboratory of the Chemical Institute felt to Levi like a refuge against the "night" that was falling over Europe. Cut off from the reality of the world by the Fascist censorship, he confronted "Mother-Matter," which was also "our hostile mother." This struggle did not only express itself in the passion that drove him when he performed qualitative analysis experiments in the Institute laboratory. It was a duel:

Two unequal opponents: on one side, putting the questions, the unfledged, unarmed chemist, at his elbow the text by Autenrieth as his sole ally ... on the other side, responding with enigmas, stood Matter, with her sly passivity, ancient as the All and portentously rich in deceptions, as solemn and subtle as the Sphinx. (*Table* 38–9)

At home, Primo's father was not unduly worried, and kept on repeating in an effort to reassure himself: "Ah, but in Italy, as long as the Church and the Vatican are here, they wouldn't dare start anything against us." And then he would say, "We are not German subjects, and they will treat us accordingly."[20]

In his spare time, Levi went climbing in the nearby Alps with a classmate he admired. Sandro Delmastro was not Jewish. He was a wiry, laconic young man, the son of a Piedmontese family from Serra d'Ivrea, and made few contacts with his classmates. Levi, isolated by the passage of the racial laws, realized that he was gradually being shunned by his fellow students. Neither teachers nor pupils ever spoke a hostile word, but the looks of suspicion they exchanged with the young Jew caused him to retreat into solitude. Sandro's extensive knowledge of nature and animals commanded Primo's great respect.

Primo earnestly explained to Sandro that he had chosen to study chemistry in order to continue the noble struggle against matter which man had been fighting since the dawn of time. He wanted to probe the secrets of the universe, and Mendeleev's Periodic Table, which they were just starting to discover, seemed to him to be infinitely more poetic than all of the literature they were required to read in school.

Dmitri Ivanovich Mendeleev saw nature as forming a whole, and discovered the linkages between its phenomena. By comparing the atomic weights of the elements with their properties, and "choosing analogous elements and similar atomic weights," he discovered that "the properties of the elements are in a periodic dependence related to their atomic weight." This discovery enabled him to group the vast accumulation of scientific facts into a single harmonious system, and to predict the existence of new elements and their properties.

No doubt Sandro Delmastro did not see all the poetry that his classmate perceived in Mendeleev's table of the elements, but he saw it in their climbing expeditions, often made in the company of Alberto Salmoni, who was also affected by the racial laws. Sandro was anti-Fascist above all, and searched for the truths in nature in order to elude the lies in the Fascist newspapers. Primo enlarged Sandro's reading, Sandro brought Primo to see that "Matter" was not just, "for lack of something better," their "political school" (*Table* 42), neither was it merely the little heaps of powder or granules shared out for analysis in the Institute's laboratory — it was also the nearby Alps. Sandro knew how to live at altitude, in Spartan conditions. Primo saw him as the man of iron — Sandro's ancestors had been tinkers and blacksmiths — because in the depth of winter he would cycle off penniless, taking nothing but an artichoke, lettuce leaves, a hunk of bread, and a pocket knife, and sleep in barns, withstand storms, and return famished but fulfilled.

Sandro owned a small sandy mongrel dog that he used to take with him and would rope up for climbing with him in the summer. He was rude about guide-books, avoided the recommended routes, and climbed in his own way, with hunger in his belly. He skied, but never in the usual resorts, which he thoroughly despised. "What mattered was to know his limitations, to test and improve himself; more obscurely, he felt the need to prepare himself (and to prepare me) for an iron future, drawing closer month by month" (*Table* 45).

As he watched Sandro tackle the mountains of the Canavese, close to Turin, Primo forgot the racial laws, and the war, and communed with the universe. Emerging at dawn from the Martinotti mountain hut in the Gran Paradiso national park, they looked up and admired the snow-capped summits. On other trips they tackled the Straw Stack Pinnacles, the Wolkmann Tower, the Teeth of Cuminia, Patanüa Rock, the Plô, and the Sbarüa, which only a handful of enthusiasts knew about.

During this period, climbing became the key to everything for Primo Levi: he was learning vital lessons in patience, strength of purpose, and endurance. Delmastro often led him on very dangerous adventures, and when they seemed to go wrong, he gave this deliberate taking of great risks a name: he called it "tasting bear meat." Levi also learned to endure fatigue, thirst, and hunger. "When you are roped together," he wrote in *La Stampa* on 27 November 1982,

> you win victories that last a whole lifetime ... I think that without that unconscious training in the mountains my generation would have lived much less well through the war and the Resistance. And no doubt I would not have survived. We truly learned a few of the basic virtues: resistance, endurance, not losing faith, being prepared for danger and the unexpected.

Massimo Mila, a Resistance fighter and climber, reports that after 8 September 1943, when the Italian government surrendered and Hitler's forces took over in Italy, "going to the mountains" meant "joining the Resistance." The two expressions had become synonymous: the anti-Fascist was a mountaineer. Sandro, a partisan in the Piedmontese military command of the Resistance, and a member of the *Partito d'Azione* (the "Party of Action"), which was its political branch, tasted that "bear meat" to his death, the circumstances of which have been related by his nephew, who was fifteen years old when Sandro was killed on 3 April 1944:

> Sandro was born on 7 September 1917 in Turin. He was the fourth son of Maria Peracelione and Enrico Delmastro, a building contractor who built blocks of civilian flats and came from Zubiena, in the province of Vercelli. The first child of that marriage was Adela, my mother, who

was born in 1906 and died in 1987. I bear the same name, Delmastro, as Sandro because my father's family also comes from Zubiena.

Sandro Delmastro went underground a few days after the armistice of 8 September 1943, as the founder and coordinator of the *Formazioni Partigiane Giustizia e Libertà* ["Justice and Liberty Partisan Formations"] in Turin and in the mountains and valleys of Piedmont. That commitment was a logical consequence of the upbringing he had received, in a family where the love of freedom reigned.

In the 1930s he studied at the Vittorio Alfieri classical high school in Turin, then at the Chemical Institute at Turin University. It was during those years, in the context of their mutual passion for the mountains, that the personal and political friendship between Primo and Sandro developed.

Sandro was arrested in Cuneo during one of his frequent shuttle trips from Turin to the mountains, no doubt as the result of a tip-off to the Fascist Nazi police. He tried to escape by using his great athletic ability. He made a run for it in the Corso del Quattro Novembre in Cuneo. Sadly, he was shot down by a burst of automatic fire just a few metres from the corner of the street. Sandro's body rests in the little cemetery in Zubiena, facing the Pre-Alps of Biella, where he so loved to go training.[21]

In the chapter of *The Periodic Table* devoted to Sandro, Primo Levi records that Sandro tried to escape from the Fascist Party headquarters in Cuneo. It was a young Fascist of fifteen who killed him with a tommy-gun burst in the back of the neck. His body was left lying in the middle of the avenue for a long time, because the Fascists had forbidden its burial. So the man who helped Primo to become "the master of his destiny" died while Primo himself was also in Fascist hands, and in Auschwitz.

Bianca Guidetti Serra, who had never made any distinction between her Jewish and her Christian friends, often partnered Primo, Alberto, and Sandro on their mountain excursions. She was close to Primo's sister Anna Maria, and to their mother, Ester, and also knew their father Cesare.

Some of the young Jews of Turin who were affected by the racial laws also used to visit a farm in Rivoli belonging to Dan Vittorio Segre's mother, which could be reached by tramcar. They included Primo Levi and the two anti-Fascist activists, Emanuele and Ennio Artom.

After the early shock wave and confusion caused when the racial laws were introduced in September 1938, the Jewish communities very quickly made arrangements for alternative higher education. Until then, the Jews of Turin had possessed only a small primary school. The first-class teachers who were now barred from the state system were eager to involve themselves, and

Benvenuto Terracini wrote the following letter to the Jews of Turin:

> Dearest friends, so it has finally happened ... Possibly worse than we
> expected. It is not a matter of withstanding the blows, taking as few as
> possible, and thinking of what will be necessary. For the children, I
> think it very likely that it is not necessary to resort to teaching them at
> home, because I have no doubt that in Turin we will be able to organize
> a [...] school for them.[22]

As victims of expulsion, the students were exceptionally highly motivated, and
their marks matched their commitment. On top of that, their forced re-entry
into the Jewish world developed an interest in the historical and cultural
origins of Italian Jewry.

To begin with, the principal of the Hebrew School of Turin, which opened
its doors on 7 November 1938 and was closed by the Nazis on 20 May 1943,
observed some caution towards the Fascist authorities. For example, he
ordered an anti-Fascist composition to be rewritten, for fear of an inspection.

The first principal of the school, Giacomo Tedesco, who taught history,
economics, and philosophy, and who was to die of a heart attack in the middle
of a lesson, organized a schedule of six days a week, five and three-quarter hours
a day. Pupils were allowed to come half an hour late if there had been an air-raid
alert after midnight. No portraits of Mussolini appeared on the classroom walls,
but there were portraits of the king and queen. The Jews had kept faith with the
House of Savoy, in spite of its palpable silence about the racial laws.

"Devotion to Italy runs in our veins," wrote the historian Arnaldo
Momigliano in ironic recollection:

> My grandmother wept each time she heard the *Marcia Reale*, and if you
> can weep for music as awful as that, you can weep for anything. Shut
> out of the state schools through no fault of their own, these teachers and
> these students were all, every last one, fired by a burning flame of
> Italianness, and joined with all their heart in the patriotic fervour of
> their Aryan compatriots in those hard and heroic times of war.

In the Hebrew School in Turin, first situated in the Via Giorgio Bidone, then in
the Via Sant'Anselmo, religious teaching was reduced to a bare minimum. This
is how Momigliano accounts for his rejection of Jewish law:

> It seems to me that the reasons lost in the darkness of the centuries for
> which the Jew has abstained from eating certain animals no longer have
> any meaning for me. No doubt I should abstain .... This was probably
> the pretext that the ancients offered to the prophets to excuse their idol-
> atry. But neither Isaiah nor Jeremiah believed them. I reason this way,
> and yet I wonder, and cannot answer, whether this reasoning is genuine
> or whether it does not rather represent the ultimate Jewish explanation
> for my forsaking Judaism.[23]

The studies were the responsibility of a kind of committee chaired by Professor Emanuele Montalcini, president of the community, Raimondo Foa, Giulio Segre, Riccardo Levi, and Eugenio Norzi, the last leader of the community before the catastrophe. Cesare Pavese was invited to join, but he failed to reply.

Mario Sacerdote succeeded Giacomo Tedesco as principal. Marco Levi, a teacher dismissed from the Liceo Gioberti, taught Latin and Greek. Other experienced teachers were Salvatore Foa, Bonaparte Colombo, Quinza and Bianca Amar, Tirsa Levi, Aldo Melli, Lia Corinaldi, who was shot dead in 1943, Marisetta Treves, Marussia Ginzburg, Leone's sister, Amelia Allan Civita, and Bemporad, ex-director of the Astronomical Observatory of the Sciences. Giuseppe Morpurgo, who had taught literature at the Liceo d'Azeglio, now taught at the Hebrew School of Turin, whose principal he became after Sacerdote. His two daughters — one of whom, Lucia, was to marry Primo Levi after his return from Auschwitz — and Primo's sister Anna Maria were among his pupils.

Aldo Fernex, a goldsmith turned school janitor, joined the Resistance. He was arrested, and died under torture, as did Emanuele Artom, professor of ancient history and Jewish culture, who used to explain to his pupils that the emancipation of the Jews was a feature of the Italian Risorgimento, whose sources lay in the French Revolution, and which had been achieved through national unity and independence. Thus, he wrote,

> little by little one grows convinced that the Italian people and the Jewish people are oppressed by the same system, the same men ... that the freedom of the former and of the latter are one and the same, and that we must fight on behalf of them both against absolutism and intolerance.[24]

At the same time as working for the Resistance after 8 September 1943, Emanuele Artom also wrote a number of books. One of them, *Euterpe e l'Egitto* ("Euterpe and Egypt"), was not published by Einaudi until 1946, because each of Artom's manuscripts was rejected in turn by Cesare Pavese, who remained indifferent to the tragedy suffered by the Jews during the war. Pavese took an interest in Ernst Jünger, but none at all in Emanuele Artom, and even refused to offer help. Artom exerted a profound influence over his pupils, and some of them followed him into the mountains to fight the Germans after the announcement of Marshal Badoglio's surrender to the Allies, and the subsequent declaration of war on Germany on 13 October 1943, by the marshal, now Mussolini's successor.

Signor Morpurgo and his teachers turned the Hebrew School into a model of its kind. The hundred pupils, divided into five classes, were unusually intelligent, and their teachers wanted to make them good, decent, thoughtful citizens whom Italy could take pride in. It is clear that, despite the racial laws, the cult of Italian patriotism practised by Morpurgo, who described the racial laws as an "unexpected and personally undeserved misfortune," remained intact, and expressed itself in the teaching of Italian literature. The cornerstone was Dante — each class had to study him for an hour a week. Other key figures were Petrarch, Ariosto, Machiavelli, Alfieri, Foscolo, Leopardi, Manzoni, Carducci, Pascoli, and the inevitable Gabriele D'Annunzio.

Primo's cousin Giulia and the twin sister of his future wife, Lucia, sang in the teachers' and pupils' choir which was directed by Vittore Veneziani, the choirmaster dismissed from La Scala in Milan because he was Jewish. The choir's piano accompanist was Guido Bachi, a young man who some months later was to play a very important role in Primo Levi's life.

The following is the programme of a concert given in the Hebrew School on 28 June 1942:

Part One

Marcello — *Salmo 27e*

Peri — *Gioite al canto mio — Aria dall' "Euridice"*

Palestrina — *Ahi! che quest'occhi miei — Canzonetta*

— Vedrassi prima senza luce il sole

— Canzonetta

Donato — *Villota*

Azzaiolo — *2 Villotte dei fiore*

Part Two

Cinque canti popolari ebraici

Sinigalia — *Sepoltura di bimba*

— Cansone d'inverno

Verdi — *Va penserio sull'ali dorate —* dal *"Nabucco"*

— O signore che dal letto natio

— da *"I Lombardi"*

Rossini — *Dal tuo stellato soglio — Preghiera,* dal *"Mosè"*[25]

The Jews who had become outcasts in Italy nevertheless continued to revere its culture and its music much of which drew upon Hebrew sources. The Hebrew Slaves' chorus from *Nabucco* is particularly ironic.

It was in Courmayeur, near Mont Blanc, where the Artom family owned a house, that Hugo Sacerdote, who belonged to the climbers' group, had met Primo Levi in 1937. The Artom brothers' father had prepared Sacerdote for his *bar mitzvah*. In the afternoons, the house in Courmayeur was full of young people who met there to talk. After the promulgation of the racial laws, the meetings took place in the library of the Turin synagogue, which in those days was just a little storeroom filled with books.

The students, among them Primo and Anna Maria Levi, prepared lectures for the Jewish festivals, and talked about their strength in overcoming the problems they now had to face.

60

The names of those involved with the resistance to Fascism — Giulio Einaudi, Leone Ginzburg, Vittorio Foa, Zini, Carlo Levi, Augusto Monti — were known to Primo Levi and his friends, but at that point they were either in exile, or prisoners of the Fascists, or somewhere under house arrest, powerless to act. A gap had opened between the two generations.

Leone Ginzburg, who was arrested for the second time in 1940, and whose Italian citizenship had been removed, was under house arrest in Pizzoli, with his wife Natalia and their two children. The director of the publishing house of Einaudi, founded in 1943, he stayed in the Abruzzi till the fall of Mussolini, then made his way to Rome, where he resumed his Resistance activities with the *Giustizia e Libertà* movement, while his family stayed in Pizzoli. The Germans occupied northern and central Italy after the armistice (by then the Allies had taken Sicily and the south), and Leone Ginzburg was arrested again in November. He died, like Emanuele Artom, as the result of the torture he suffered in February 1944.

Primo Levi was much younger than Ginzburg and his friends Sion Segre Amar and Mario Levi. While he was feeling his way towards resistance, he had no idea that Mario Levi also lived on the Corso Re Umberto and was pacing its back streets with Ginzburg, making plans against Fascism.

When they celebrated Passover, the young Jews of Turin talked about freedom and compared their situation with the flight from Egypt, because the Bible seemed to offer precedents and "certainty."

> We gathered in the gym of the Talmud Torah — in the School of the Law, as the very old Hebrew primary school was proudly called — and taught each other to find again in the Bible justice and injustice and the strength that overcomes injustice; to recognize the new oppressors in Ahasuerus and Nebuchadnezzar. But where was Kadosh Barukhú, "the Saint, Blessed be He" who breaks the slaves' chains and submerges the Egyptians' chariots? He who dictated the Law to Moses, and inspired the liberators Ezra and Nehemiah, no longer inspired anyone; the sky above us was silent and empty. He allowed the Polish ghettos to be exterminated, and slowly, confusedly, the idea was making headway in us that we were alone, that we had no allies we could count on, neither on earth nor in heaven, that we would have to find in ourselves the strength to resist. (*Table 52*)

It was an "impulse" that drove Levi and his friends Sandro Delmastro, Alberto Salmoni, Silvio Ortoni, and Bianca Guidetti Serra to deliberately face hunger, cold, and fatigue in the mountains near Turin. They cycled all the way to the French frontier, and strove to imagine the struggle against Fascism, the possible alternatives. Leaving for the mountains was a form of rebellion: "You, Fascist, you discriminate against me, you isolate me, you claim that I am inferior. I'm proving that's not so. I've promoted myself to first on the rope, with no experience and no training.'[26]

They did not go to Sestriere, because the resort was equipped with a funicular railway, which the young rebels disapproved of. Anna Maria had given her brother a pair of karabiners, three pitons and a hammer, but he did not have new boots or a well-filled saddlebag. The official guidebook helped them to do exactly the opposite of what it advised. One night, Delmastro, Salmoni, and Levi set out on foot from Bard to Champorcher. The next day they were skiing with thirty-kilo packs on their backs. Delmastro wanted to cross the Finestra de Champorcher, which is 2,826 metres high, then go down to Piantonetto and head for the Gran Paradiso. Primo Levi gave up, exhausted, in Cogne.

> My passion for the mountains colluded with the passion I felt for chemistry, because there I found the elements in the Periodic Table embedded in the rocks, prisoners of the ice, and through them I tried to find the nature of the mountain, its structure, the why of the shape of a channel, the history of the architecture of a serac. Once, on the Pic du Pagliaio, Sandro pulled at a crystalline rock spike and it came away in his hands. He showed it to me and said "It split at 001," which is the terminology of stereographic operations. Crystals are identified by the way they split.[27]

The mountains offered a substitute for impossible journeys, those journeys described in the books by Melville, Conrad, Kipling, and London that Levi loved to read: "The equivalent of those journeys for us was Mount Herbetet."[28]

Emanuele Artom had gone underground again on 8 September 1943. He organized political activity in the *Giustizia e Libertà* partisan groups. These included a number of Jews, such as Franco Momigliano and Bruno and Alberto Salmoni. Artom, the political commissar of the *Partito d'Azione*, was later captured by the Germans and other captured partisans saw him in Turin jail, where he suffered dreadful tortures without spilling a single name. He died on 7 April 1944, and no one knows where his body was buried. His father, in hiding in Turin hospital, suffered a stroke and lost the use of speech when he learned about the dreadful death of his second son. His mother, who survived, was to become the headmistress of the Emanuele Artom Jewish primary school after the war. In April 1984, Primo Levi announced in *La Stampa* a commemoration of the fortieth anniversary of the murder of Emanuele Artom, in the street in Turin which is called after him. Quoting Fichte, he concluded his article "From man, it is not wisdom alone that is required, but also virtue which is the highest degree of morality."

Primo Levi thus began to develop a political awareness through contact with Resistance figures of the calibre of Emanuele Artom, who was four years his senior. Yet his political education was not as thorough as Artom's, and this may explain why, when the time came, his will to fight was not strong enough to lead him to one of the valleys of the Valdesi, where groups better armed and organized than his own were preparing for underground warfare, even though they too lacked both military experience and the taste for violence.

———

Levi had started his course at the Chemical Institute before the introduction of the racial laws, so he was entitled to complete it. During his meetings with the young Jewish intellectuals of Turin in the library of the Hebrew School, he had heard it said that the Nazis were exterminating the Jews of Europe. This news had been spread by fugitives from Poland and France, and a British White Book published in Palestine recorded similar stories. The crimes committed seemed so enormous, so monstrous, that Levi and his comrades discounted half of them.

Levi was reading *The Oppenheim Brothers* by Leo Feuchtwanger, and he refused, in January 1940, to imagine that the same mortal danger was stalking the Jews of Italy. He had vague notions of getting out to one of the few countries that had kept their borders open, such as British Honduras or Madagascar, while various members of his family were choosing emigration. Thus, a cousin of his mother's, who had become an ardent Zionist in Turin in the 1920s, had considered leaving Italy for Palestine in 1934. He shelved his plans so as to organize assistance for the Jews who had fled from Nazi Germany to seek refuge in Italy, then left for Palestine in November 1939.

No one in Levi's immediate circle seems to have had the energy or the means necessary to attempt such an emigration. And in fact the situation had not yet become disastrous. The vast majority of Italians displayed no hostility to the Jews, and often provided assistance.

———

Did Levi — "the impurity," "the grain of salt or mustard," as he described himself in *The Periodic Table* — feel Italian? In an interview with Philip Roth,[29] he gave this answer:

> I see no contradiction between "rootedness" and being (or feeling) "a grain of mustard." To feel oneself a catalyst, a spur to one's cultural environment, a something or a somebody that confers taste and sense to life, you don't need racial laws or anti-Semitism or racism in general: however, it is an advantage to belong to a (not necessarily racial) minority. In other words, it can prove useful not to be pure. If I may return to the question: don't you feel yourself, you Philip Roth, "rooted" in your country, and at the same time "a mustard grain"? In your books I perceive a sharp mustard flavour.

(Roth had quoted a remark made by Arnaldo Momigliano, who said that "the Jews were less a part of Italian life than they thought they were.") Levi continued:

> I think this is the meaning of your quotation .... Italian Jews (but the same can be said of the Jews of many other nations) made an important

contribution to their country's cultural and political life without renouncing their identity, in fact by keeping faith with their cultural tradition. To possess two traditions, as happens to Jews but not only to Jews, is a richness: for writers but not only for writers .... Yes, sure, I am a part of Italian life.

The harsh and dreaded professor of the Chemical Institute gave Primo Levi the top mark of 30 when he passed the "exhausting" quantitative analysis examination in 1940. He attributed his success not to merit but to his own cunning, demonstrated when he found a pretext for entering "the secret room where the practical quizzes were prepared" and found — as he had suspected — the burette used by the professor to measure out the dosage to be analysed, "a long vertical tube calipered and graded, assigning to each a whole number of centimetres of solution," full of a sky-blue preparation (*Trades 100/89*). Levi deduced that all he had to do was to perform the analysis and then round off his findings to fit a table he had prepared by correlating results already obtained by some of his fellow students. He passed on his discovery to his two closest friends, who received the same marks as himself. This trick, which worked only for a substance measured out for the sake of convenience by the disciplinarian professor, using the same burette, enabled Levi to claim, with characteristic modesty, "an ambiguous merit."

There was a moment when Levi, now in his fourth year in chemistry, had doubts about that discipline, as he considered its inglorious origins in "the dens of the alchemists." On reflection, perhaps he preferred the logic of physics, whose clarity and rigour had come down from Euclid and Archimedes. He developed this fondness for physics while taking a course taught at the Institute of Experimental Physics by a young lecturer called Nicola Dallaporta, whose behaviour surprised the students, because unlike his colleagues he seemed to doubt the subject he was teaching. Levi, who describes him as "thin, tall, a bit hunched over, polite, and extraordinarily shy," adds that all the girls he taught fell in love with him. So Dallaporta's aura seemed to glow, for Levi too was shy, but he was a young Jew, slight, and lacking in glamour, and he suffered agonies from the isolation to which his inhibitions, sharpened by the racial laws, appeared to condemn him.

His despair had other causes than his self-image. For months he had been looking in vain for a professor who would agree to supervise his thesis. Ponzio and Perucca refused. Professor Milon, a notorious Fascist with a mission to expel every Jew from the university, callously dismissed him. Too cautious to risk compromising themselves, they all turned him down with contempt, either citing the racial laws or invoking some transparent excuse. His classmates had started to avoid him, but no one mentioned his race, even though most of them were members of the *Gioventù Universitaria Fascista* (GUF), the Fascist student movement.

One freezing winter night, as he was cycling home, he thought he spotted Nicola Dallaporta, clad in a long black overcoat, walking bare-headed through the mist that was drifting out of the nearby Valentino Park and into the Via Valpergo Calusa. Discouraged by his teachers' rejections, and paralyzed by fear of another snub, Levi looked at the lecturer who was walking in his direction without seeing him. He passed him by without daring to approach him, then changed his mind, turned round, but still hung back. Finally quelling his fear of being rebuffed by a man he knew nothing about, he at last went up to him and asked point-blank to be admitted to his institute to do experimental work, even though physics was a subsidiary subject for the chemists. After hearing him out with some surprise, Dallaporta "replied with two words from the Gospel: 'Follow me.'"

Nicola Dallaporta remembers his meeting in the mist with Primo Levi very clearly. According to him, what he told Primo was "Listen, do your thesis — who gives a damn about the laws?" He remembers feeling pleased, and even delighted, to accommodate this young student (he calls him a "cool enthusiast") whose sheer intelligence had caught his attention, but the words from the Gospel do not strike a chord with him.

> I got to know Primo Levi in 1941. The questions he asked and the way he went into things put him at a quite exceptional level compared with other students. When he passed the exam we gave him an exceptional mark. I took an immediate liking to him. With intelligent people, you're very glad to see them. The following year he had to produce his thesis, and at the Chemical Institute he was running into trouble. The professors were hedging, refusing to commit themselves.[30]

Most of the teachers at the Institute of Experimental Physics who were opposed to Fascism listened to the BBC, although the director and the technicians were in fact Fascist sympathizers. All the same, Nicola Dallaporta was obliged to put in an occasional appearance at Mussolini's public speeches, so as not to draw attention to himself, and suffer the consequences. The racial laws shocked him, because during his student days most of his friends had been Jews, so it came quite naturally to him to lend Levi the necessary books now that he was no longer allowed to use the public libraries, and to give him access to the physics institute's laboratory. What made things even simpler was that the director did not check on what went on there. "I said to him: 'Look for what interests you, and what you can do to research a subject I've been working on: the study of the electrical dipoles of certain chemical compounds in solution, and the interactions that may occur between them.'"

The work involved verifying theories, and adapting a chemical subject for the purposes of physics. It was necessary to know the properties of certain components and to carry out a kind of physical analysis, which called for measuring electrical interactions. Levi prepared a thesis that contained a compilation of some twenty pages of chemistry, and an experimental subthesis in physics, the first an excuse for the second.

So for Levi, half rejected by his university, and forced to obtain his degree by discontinuing his chemical studies in favour of marginal studies in physics, the door was swinging shut. After the war, and his return from Auschwitz, he would have to earn a living, and that meant giving up the studies he had dreamed of, and for which both his abilities and his exceptional intelligence were naturally suited.

From that moment on, the lecturer and his protégé spent a lot of time together, and became close friends. Dallaporta, who had just got married, arranged for Levi to occupy his room — really a sort of boxroom, which he had no use for. They shared a community of tastes, and literary sympathies. Inside the high walls of the Institute, its long corridors lined with glass cabinets full of apparatus, they could talk in safety about politics and philosophy.

The young astrophysicist, who came from a Catholic family, followed a religion of his own devising, related to Hindu wisdom, and tried to interest Levi in metaphysics. While the student aspired to be a man of the Enlightenment, Dallaporta sought to convince him that Hinduism, a portion of the universal wisdom, was concerned with the nature of God, whereas science simply described the states of matter, making connections between things more or less on the same level.

The lecturer also explained that Hindu wisdom considers that life does not end here, that there is a whole series of lives, so that on the evidence of a single life it is impossible to reach a judgement. The man of science told his pupil that in his eyes, science has no bearing on what lies beyond its scope, and that science is limited by its assumptions, and studies things within the terms of those very assumptions, which are experience. Positivism, he claimed, is essentially based on determinism, which depends on the fact that the basic equations of mechanics seem to be such that the future depends wholly on the past. But that is not so. The laws of physics are presented in the simplest way, in those cases in which they are very roughly verified. French mathematicians have discovered that, in certain instances, by changing the initial conditions very little, the eventual alteration snowballs hugely. Determinist approximations apply to extremely simple problems. In the end, the world is not predictable, and the cases where it is are exceptions. That is what he wanted Levi to take on board, Levi, who had chosen science precisely because he wanted to get to grips with matter, and extract its solid truths.

To say that on the other side of matter there is only a vast black void is a great limitation, Dallaporta continued, adding that there is a realm of the spirit that expresses itself through man. Levi, the young man whose passionate hopes lay in the comprehensible world conceived by Darwin and by the neopositivists of Turin, heard the man of science grant that world a fairly humble place in the scheme of knowledge.

Dallaporta also believed that "the brain is an essential instrument for translating the realm of the spirit into a rational form, but a form of spirit exists outside it. That state is completely unimaginable, and the essence that is in us is eternal."

For Levi, who gave Dallaporta a courteous hearing, the "Truth," the "Reality," was the advance of the Nazi forces in Yugoslavia, Crete, and Greece. He defended his thesis before eleven examiners — but in the absence of Dallaporta, who was ill — in one of the institutes on the Corso Massimo d'Azeglio, which extend along Valentino Park.

In 1942, Nicola Dallaporta left for Padua, where he had been appointed as head of department the previous year, while pursuing his work at the university of Turin. Throughout the university year of 1940–41 he commuted between the two towns once a week, leaving Turin at seven in the morning to arrive in Padua at three in the afternoon. When he returned he had to stand all the way, because the train arrived chock-full, and it often had to halt along the way because of air raids. Since dividing his time between Turin and Padua, the lecturer and his pupil had exchanged letters.

Although Levi had not yet chosen to fight, he sensed that tragic events loomed ahead, and he dreaded their intervention in his life. At the same time, he marvelled at the process of distillation in which he was engaged in the laboratory put at his disposal by Nicola Dallaporta:

> Distilling is beautiful. First of all, because it is a slow, philosophic, and silent occupation, which keeps you busy but gives you time to think of other things, somewhat like riding a bike. Then, because it involves a metamorphosis from liquid to vapor (invisible), and from this once again to liquid; but in this double journey, up and down, purity is attained, an ambiguous and fascinating condition, which starts with chemistry and goes very far. And finally, when you set about distilling, you acquire the consciousness of repeating a ritual consecrated by the centuries, almost a religious act, in which from imperfect material you obtain the essence, the *usia*, the spirit, and in the first place alcohol, which gladdens the spirit and warms the heart. (*Table 57–8*)

The work done in the laboratories of the Institute of Experimental Physics and the conclusions it suggested to Primo Levi enabled him to receive his doctorate in Chemistry, *summa cum laude*, in the month of July 1941. The "illuminated parchment" given to the brilliant young doctor specified that its holder was "of the Jewish race."

It seemed to Levi as if nothing was happening in Italy, and it is true that the situation cannot be compared to the tragedy visited on France, Holland, Norway, Poland, Yugoslavia, the Baltic States, and Russia. In the footsteps of the invading German army in Soviet-held territory, the *Einsatzgruppen*,[31] the mobile killing squads, were methodically exterminating the Jews of every area they passed through — the Balkan States, Byelorussia, eastern Galicia, the

Ukraine, and the Crimea — using firing squads to shoot them by the sides of mass burial pits that the victims first had to dig with their own hands.

In Turin, Primo Levi was searching unsuccessfully for a job, while his father, stricken by a cancer of the stomach, was suffering and slowly dying. The family was in dire need of money. Who would agree to employ a young Jewish chemist, when the racial laws forbade it?

His rescuer was a young man in military uniform who rang on the doorbell one day. Levi's name, and his *summa cum laude* degree, had been mentioned to him by Caselli, assistant to the cantankerous chemistry professor. The would-be employer could not fail to be aware that a man called Levi was Jewish. Nevertheless, he had a mysterious job to offer him "in some place" unnamed. It turned out that this involved working in a mine that contained 2 per cent of asbestos and 98 per cent of sterile material bearing a minute quantity of nickel. Nickel was now so expensive that the man who was working the mine — this was Levi's visitor, a lieutenant in the army — had decided to try to extract it. As he could not spare time from his military duties, he wanted to hire Levi to conduct a series of feasibility tests in his laboratory.

The mine's young owner gave his host the strong impression that although he wore uniform he was no supporter of Fascism, and even condemned it, though without being ready to oppose it. He would employ his new chemist under a false name. From now on, he told him, you are no longer Levi, you're — let's see — Michele. At last he revealed the location of his almost undercover operation. The mine was in Balangero, not far from Lanzo Torinese, a small medieval town about thirty kilometres north-west of Turin.

The lieutenant and the chemist agreed to meet the next day at Turin's central station, Porta Nuova. Levi took only some clothes and a few books. Board and lodging and a warm laboratory awaited him in Balangero. The engineer who managed the mine had obviously been informed of the newcomer's situation, and kept the formalities to a minimum. Levi was taken straight to the laboratory, to meet his assistant, Alida, a lanky girl with red hair and green eyes. Invited to take his first meal in the office buildings, he heard on the radio the news of the attack on the American fleet in Pearl Harbor by the Japanese air force: Japan was now at war with the United States. At that moment the lieutenant, who was sitting with some clerks, darted a knowing look in his direction.

Levi's fascination with the mine was linked to the legends born in "the bowels of the earth," where precious and worthless minerals lie side by side, and some metals take their names from imaginary subterranean creatures. The manager took him on a tour of the various working sites, from the extraction, crushing, and grinding of the raw material to sifting out the 2 per cent of asbestos and dumping the rest — "thousands of tons a day" (*Table 65*). These masses of crushed ore, mixed with asbestos, crept slowly down towards the valley, each year causing buildings below them to slide a few centimetres more. It was in one of these buildings, nicknamed "the submarine," that Levi stayed.

In *The Periodic Table*, he describes how the fine asbestos dust pervaded the site, both in and out of doors. While in the valley and in Lanzo Torinese, five kilometres away, there was rationing and black marketeering, at the mine the fifty workers who lived on the spot reared poultry and cultivated their own vegetable plots.

Levi met no prejudice from any of the local people. On the contrary, although they knew nothing about him they readily told him all sorts of very intimate and juicy stories about the legendary depravities of their tiny republic. It was not long before everybody knew about *Dottore* Levi, and how on no account must his true name be mentioned.

His and Alida's job was to run quantitative analyses of the various underground lodes that made up the mine, looking for traces of nickel. It was a repetitive task, but at long last he was seeing the barren, monotonous routines learned at the Chemical Institute applied for a practical purpose. It was a kind of feat to squeeze the secrets out of matter, another way of measuring himself against it, as he had during his climbs with Salmoni, Delmastro, and Ortona.

Once a week, the lieutenant travelled up from his barracks in Turin to check on the findings of his new chemist, who had ascertained that the average nickel content in the rock of the quarry was 0.2 per cent. This was a trifling amount, compared with the yield of the ores mined in Canada or New Zealand, but the lieutenant wanted to know what chance there might be of enriching the ore.

Because, for obvious reasons, he could not show his face in the valley, Levi killed time by reading in the bareness of his room, working extra hours in the laboratory, or walking around the quarry on moonlit nights. He also started writing two stories. "Lead" and "Mercury," which now appear in *The Periodic Table*. The first was a work of imagination, inspired by his research into nickel. The second was based on his reading about the adventures of Tristão da Cunha, the Portuguese navigator who discovered the group of islands named after him in 1506.

The first tale, "Lead," has close connections to Levi's experiences at the mine in Balangero. His hero, a solitary character named Rodmund, who comes from a small Germanic tribe with blue teeth, has wandered southward, teaching the secrets of smelting and working lead in return for gold. The narrator–protagonist tells his story with simplicity and realism, but in all his adventures a tinge of fantasy permeates the atmosphere. The story takes place in a bygone age which is not explicitly located, but clues are provided, as in a treasure hunt — the kinds of tools used, the building materials, dwelling places, means of locomotion, knowledge or ignorance of certain techniques. The traveller makes his way through Europe, visits towns, reaches a port and sees ships there, and sailors fighting over women with knives made of bronze. In a quiet, laconic tone, Rodmund relates his voyage southward, in a ship rowed by wild-eyed galley slaves, to a land where lead has not yet been discovered, but there are rich deposits. When he arrives, he observes that the stories told in the north about the peoples of the south are mostly untrue, and totally distorted by the imagination of the teller.

When Rodmund grows old, he decides to settle in this land where he has been accepted. He takes a wife to carry on his line, almost forgets his language — German — and adopts a Latin dialect into which he translates the name of the village he has founded and where his son Rodmund will be born: Bak der Binnen, "Brook of the Bees," becomes Bacu Apis. The story's happy ending derives from Rodmund's success in harnessing and marketing his secrets about the extraction and the use of lead. Even though he is a foreigner, he can at last settle in the quiet, secluded place where he has decided to end his wandering days.

In the second tale, "Mercury," Primo Levi adopts a dry tone, later to become a familiar one, to tell two stories set in the wilderness of Desolation Island, appropriately named. It lies more than a thousand miles from the nearest land, the island of St Helena, where according to the author "an important and dangerous person ... a renegade, an adulterer, a Papist, rabble-rouser, and braggart" (*Table* 96–7) had been exiled. When Napoleon — who is never named — died, the garrison on this island, posted there as a precaution, went home to Wales and Surrey. All except one, Corporal Abrahams, who because of unpaid debts chose to remain and raise pigs with his wife, Maggie.

Levi provides the reader with a map of Desolation Island, which contains a headland, a volcano, a cave, and a "Weeping Forest." The tiny neighbouring Seal Island and the two Egg Islands make up the couple's universe. Seagulls lay their eggs, seals birth their pups, the corporal and Maggie, a strange woman who hears voices, look after their pigs. It is Maggie who names the cave "Holywell Cave." For several years, the two live entirely on their own, except when Captain Burton's whaler pays its annual visit, bringing news and provisions and buying the smoked pork produced by the Abrahamses, until the day the ship puts two Dutchmen ashore. One is young and shy; the other is older, and asks for sanctuary on the island so as to avoid the gallows at home, where he claims to have killed a man in a brawl.

Some months later, the corporal discovers two shipwrecked Italians on one of the Egg Islands. There are too many men for a single woman, as the corporal sensibly points out, while the wayward Maggie commits adultery with the older Dutchman, who calls himself an alchemist. For good measure, the volcano erupts. Lava pours out of the crater. Inside the cave, mercury comes oozing out of the crevices. Abrahams is obviously an easy-going man, but when he finally understands what's going on as the Dutchman turns to Maggie and openly invites her "to make the beast with two backs" he pulls out his knife and puts it to the Dutchman's throat.

However, Abrahams is a sensible, even if not a quick-witted man, and he asks Captain Burton to bring four women when next he comes sailing in these waters, to be bartered in exchange for forty jars of purified mercury. Some months later the four women arrive, and are quickly paired off. Our man suddenly realizes that the skinny girl with two children, who answers to the sweet name of Rebecca Johnson, would really suit him better than Maggie, who is definitely too old to have children.

"'Do you wish, Corporal Daniel K. Abrahams, to take as your wife the here present Rebecca Johnson?' and I answered myself yes, and since the girl too was agreed, we got married."

It is not very hard to understand how ideas like this might appeal to the mind of a man confined to the mine, prevented by the racial laws from going down to Lanzo, and in any case so shy that even if there had been a girl within reach, he would never have dared to approach her. In his painful solitude, the young man — who possibly saw himself as a castaway — had never yet had an affair with a woman, and dreamed of adventures on a desolate island where anything was possible. Despite his sadness, his humour never left him. He imagined situations that never recur in his work, where love stories hardly ever appear. Corporal Abrahams who readily gives up his wife to the Dutchman in order to marry a younger woman with two children of her own, simple-minded though he is, looks like someone a thousand times more free in his love life than his author would ever become.

At that point, in the midst of wartime, having just written his first two tales, but cut off from everything else on this territory of the mine, Levi realized that the experiments he had begun with such enthusiasm were leading nowhere. In June 1942 he raised the question with the lieutenant and the manager, and all three agreed that the time had come for him to look for work elsewhere.

By 1942 the Nazis had decided that they needed faster and more effective methods than mass shootings to exterminate the Jews of Europe, and were stepping up their efforts to enforce the final solution in the mobile gas chambers of Chelmno and the static gas chambers of Majdanek, Sobibor, Treblinka, and Auschwitz. Their armies had reached the Crimea and were laying siege to Leningrad. They were preparing — so they thought — to capture Stalingrad, and knocking on the gates of Moscow, while the Japanese were invading southeast Asia.

In 1942, Cesare Levi died of his gastric cancer, and the young doctor of chemistry was learning by experience how hard it was for a Jew to find work in Italy. On 6 May of that year, all Jews aged between eighteen and fifty-five — including those exempted — were supposed to register for forced labour. Shortly after the fall of Mussolini, an official report stated that 15,517 people had complied, 2,410 received temporary exemption certificates, and 1,301 permanent certificates. Of the 11,806 people who remained, only 2,038 actually had to work. That was the situation, but still no one dreamed that death was so imminent a threat.

One morning, quite unexpectedly, Primo Levi was called to the phone at the mine. A student friend named Gabriella Garda Aliverti, referred to in *The Periodic Table* by the pseudonym "Giulia Vineis,"[32] had warmly recommended him to the director of the pharmaceutical firm, Wander. A man with a peremptory voice, *Dottore* Martini, made an appointment to meet him the following Sunday in Milan, in the foyer of the Hotel Suisse, a wealthy, old-fashioned establishment, with walls draped in velvet. When he gave his name to the doorman, Levi was informed that the *dottore* should also be addressed as *"commendatore,"* an honorific title awarded by the Italian state. His host appeared: "He was a thickset man of about sixty, of medium height, tanned, almost bald; his face had heavy features, but his eyes were small and astute, and his mouth, a trifle twisted to the left as in a grimace of contempt, was thin as a cut" (*Table* 110).

The *commendatore* adopted an attitude towards Levi that reminded him of the mine-owner's when he took him on: polite and "no-nonsense." He saw this behaviour, which avoided any personal interchange, as the response of an "Aryan" to dealing with a Jew. With a Jew, one did not incur the risk of having to show "understanding and compassion." Nevertheless, after he had put a few brief questions of his own, and evaded Levi's, *Dottore* Martini hired him there and then. He was Swiss, as was the Wander factory, a subsidiary of Nestlé, so he did not feel bound by the anti-Jewish laws. The salary he offered exceeded Levi's most optimistic hopes. The director and owner informed his new employee that he manufactured hormonal extracts in his factory, which was on the outskirts of Milan, and that Levi's job was to conduct research into a new cure for diabetes. Did he have any insights into this illness? Very little, Levi replied, except for some family memories about uncles who ate too much pasta, hence too little sugar, and who had suffered the disease in their old age, and a maternal grandfather who had died of it. This went down well, and when Levi looked back on the episode it struck him that Martini might have seen his new chemist as a possible human guinea-pig. In any event, the conditions of work were superb, the salary likely to rise, the factory had a library of ten thousand books, and the friend who had recommended him was already working in the laboratory.

Levi had two weeks' grace before giving his reply. He could hardly believe his luck, particularly because he had a ready-made home available in Milan. His cousin, Ada Della Torre, was living alone in her parents' flat since they had left town to escape from the bombing. The next day, Levi returned to the mine to hand in his notice and pack his few belongings: "my bike, Rabelais, the *Macaronaeae, Moby Dick* translated by Pavese, a few other books, my pickax, climbing rope, logarithmic ruler, and recorder" (*Table* 111).

72

4   The Era of the Racial Laws and the Nazi Occupation

Living in Milan put an end to loneliness and helpless isolation, for Primo Levi was not the only young Jew from Turin to come and work there. Several of his friends who had woken up one morning to find themselves Jewish with the promulgation of the racial laws had already made their choice to move to this great city where it was that much easier to find a job and pass unnoticed.

Ada Della Torre worked for the publisher Corbaccio. Although her small circle of Jewish friends — which included her future husband, Silvio Ortona — saw themselves as hostile to Fascism, with hindsight Levi described them as more "cynical" than active and determined. Every night they met for dinner, then moved on to the big sitting-room in Ada's ground-floor apartment at 7 Via San Martino, a late nineteenth-century building in a fashionable district. The seven were: Primo Levi; Ada Della Torre, also called "the bi-doctor" (she had two degrees) by Silvio Ortona, who had a degree in law, was writing a philosophical treatise, and worked for a shipping company; Emilio Diena; Eugenio Gentili Tedeschi, a young architect who nicknamed Ada *cousimo* (cousin of Primo), and whose dream was to rebuild Milan; Carla Consonni; and Vanda Maestro, a feminist, later to be arrested with Levi, interned like him in the transit camp of Fossoli di Carpi near Modena, and deported in the same convoy to Auschwitz, where she died of exhaustion. Vanda Maestro, whom Tedeschi had met in Turin when they were still at high school, was a chemist like Levi, but could not find work in Milan.

For a while, the evenings at Ada's apartment were cheerful, in spite of the rationing, the lack of coal, and nightly bombings by the British. It was not unusual for the friends to go to the theatre or a concert, which was often interrupted by air-raid sirens. Sometimes they stayed at home and talked about the plays of Eugene O'Neill and Thornton Wilder. In Ada's flat, the seven friends used to entertain themselves by organizing spiritualist seances. They all wrote compulsively, either poetry, or journals, or philosophy, and they sang mountain songs from Valle d'Aosta. Primo tended to feel out of place, and often spent his weekends in Turin with his family. He would announce his arrival to Alberto Salmoni by sending him postcards whose mood shows that these young people were facing their plight with good humour, at least for the moment:

> I hear you're working in Grugliasco — is it true? I'm writing this at
> Silvio's [who lived at 3 Via Solferino], who's in bed and shaking with

fever. He'd like to write to you, but doesn't feel like getting up. He wants you to buy him a very big rucksack, with a frame, or else get one made for him. You can go to Ravelli's, or "Bottega Artigiana" on the Corso Re Umberto, on the corner of the Via Montevecchio, the odd-numbered side. (If you go to Ravelli's, ask him for me if he has any size 12 crampons.) Here in Milan they cost 700 (!) lire. If they're cheaper in Turin, tell him not to hesitate to buy them — he won't be sorry. And what about you, can you be free on the first of August? We're busy arranging the trip. Thanks, goodbye. Abandon sloth.

Silvio adds a few last typewritten words: "Dear Alberto, so we're expecting you on Friday to go to the mountains, probably with my new rucksack and Primo's crampons. *Ciào.*"
Primo recommends Alberto to one of his friends:

Dear Eucardio, the bearer of this letter is my friend Doctor Alberto Salmoni, whom I've mentioned before. He's in Milan to get in touch with the Officine Farmacolgiche Lombarde S.A. about the possibility of working for them; if you can offer him some advice on the subject, or better still, give him any kind of help, I would be very glad. Thank you ....

Another card, sent by four women friends, shows that while Primo might fret about his shyness, Alberto was a different character altogether: "There's a young lady here who wants to send her kindest regards to Alberto. Me too." Signed Adele, Maria Olivetti, Ada Beltrami, Fausta Beltrami.
Here is another letter, posted by Levi to Salmoni from Milan:

Dear Alberto, I enclose a letter for my mother; if she is not in Turin, I'd be grateful if you would leave it with the concierge. I also enclose a card that concerns you; I don't dare to insist that you should come to Allassio, but I've just received a letter from my cousin and she insists we should be there, as well as Silvio, Anna Maria, etc. The address is: Villa Levi, Regione Costa 10, Allassio ....

Eugenio Gentili Tedeschi, who dreamed of demolishing Milan and rebuilding the town as he wanted, drew sketches of the happy band, for which Ada provided rhyming captions: "Anna Maria, Primo's sister, came to Milan one snowy December night; Silvio Ortona crossing the Piazza della Scala; Ada bringing Silvio a cup of coffee; Primo, portrayed with two wings." And Ada adds the commentary: "Primo arrives on wings of summer, the evenings start to lengthen." On each wing is written: "Ovomaltina, formitrol, crescenzol, lactomellin, nestogen." One hands holds an ice-axe, the other some laboratory glassware. Other sketches show Ortona juggling with a pile of plates during an air raid; the whole gang at the table, drinking wine and tucking into a pie, next to a stove that gives off hardly any heat; the same bunch again on bicycles; the same again, spending an evening with Anna Cases, Cesare's sister, who nurtured fond feelings for Primo, which she never expressed. Whether or not Primo realized it remains a mystery. He himself, a very correct young Jew, brought up like his friends in a middle-class, puritan family, would never have dreamed of making the slightest move. Another sketch shows the tall Silvio, followed by a diminutive Primo, each with his rucksack and ice-axe, at the foot of "Disgratia Mons" — Monte Disgrazia — in July 1942. In their spare time, in fact, the young men often went off on cross-country ski treks, or scaled quite difficult mountains near Turin, while the women waited in the mountain hut: "The mountains enabled us to find pleasures that made up for all the ones we were forbidden, and to feel equal to the boys of our age whose blood was less culpable."[1]

According to Tedeschi, mountaineering was a cultural affair: "We received a very rigid, repressive upbringing. We were terribly shy with girls. Mountaineering was a kind of sublimation. We were the ones who did not look at girls and didn't go out dancing. We were the mountain men."[2]

One Saturday, Silvio and Primo left for the Val Malenco by train. That night they arrived in Chiesa, near the Swiss frontier, and put up at a modest hotel where they handed over their identity cards and had dinner. Just as they were about to go to bed, because they needed an early start, they heard a knock on the door. A frightened woman muttered that the *carabinieri* were waiting downstairs, where a brigadier flourishing the *Gazzetta Ufficiale* informed them that they were breaking the law, because their identity cards were inscribed "of Jewish race." As it was forbidden for Jews to visit frontier regions, he explained, they must leave.

"Leave for where?" Silvio broke in. "At this hour, there are no more coaches running. If need be, we could go down on foot to Turin, which is outside the ten-kilometre limit."

The brigadier pondered and said: "But who's to say that you'll really take the valley road? I have no men to escort you, and with the curfew, you could cross over with no one the wiser. What's to be done?"

Levi and Ortona amused themselves by thinking up petty objections, while the brigadier floundered. Of course, they did not reveal the purpose of their visit — to climb the Disgrazia — and simply told him that they had come for the fresh mountain air. The hotel owner, who had been paid in advance, tended to side with his customers, and spoke up for them. Surely his guests were not to be made to spend the whole night crammed into the village's one small cell, in the company of a smuggler?

After racking his brains, the brigadier came to his decision. He suggested that the hotelier should keep the two travellers on his premises, under detention. Ortona, who was enjoying watching the brigadier squirm, objected that if they were to be detained then the *carabiniere* ought to reimburse them for the cost of the room — and why shouldn't they also pay for any meals consumed while in detention? This put the brigadier in a jam: in order to reimburse them, he would have to file a report. So to resolve the problem, the hotel-keeper, who was a kindly man, gave Silvio and Primo their money back, while the brigadier cooled down and promised to send one of his men to make sure that they caught the coach the next morning at eleven.

Years afterwards, Levi wrote that two photographs had been taken of this episode in which two young Jews were forbidden to climb a mountain because they were "stamped as biologically inferior."[3] Silvio Ortona photographed Primo at the window of their hotel. In one of the two snaps, his face is half shrouded in a towel, and his wide, sharp, startled eyes stare out of the darkness of the room.

Ortona and Levi did not let their failure deter them, and the following month they reached the Disgrazia by way of a different valley, the Val Mazino.

Tedeschi also belonged to the band of hikers who spent their Sundays tackling steep slopes, and slept in mountain huts. He went climbing with Primo in the difficult mountains of the Gran Paradiso and in the Pre-Alps. "The mountains were men's business. We were already twenty-three years old." "The little commune," as Levi called it, was trying to have fun, to go off into the mountains without worrying too much about the future. At the same time, Tedeschi, despite feeling that he too was a victim of the puritanism that afflicted the bourgeois Jewish families, had a girlfriend called Lina, and was even sleeping with her, as Levi reports in *The Periodic Table*.

During one of their climbs, Levi and Tedeschi were roped on a rock face with Eugenio twelve metres in the lead, when the rope that joined them caught against a rock that suddenly broke loose and struck Primo on the head. He did not fall off, but clung on, injured and bleeding profusely, while Eugenio made his way down to him. They abandoned the climb. Fifty years later, Eugenio recalled that once they were down, Primo had told him that when he saw the rock start to fall he told himself: "I'm dead." Eugenio saw this accident as a kind of premonition. "Sometimes the fear of the deep is mingled with a kind of fascination. I think of that expression, 'a suicide waiting to happen.' Even in a mind as rational as his, there was a tiny irrational corner."

Tedeschi had started his architectural studies before the racial laws came into force, and he was therefore able to complete them and receive his diploma, but he was not then allowed to practise his profession. When he came to Turin in 1940 he met a well-known architect, Gio Ponti, who, knowing his situation, nevertheless invited him to work in his office. Primo and Eugenio lived close to each other — Eugenio lived in the Corso Galileo Ferraris — and had met two years earlier, on climbing trips. Like Primo, Eugenio had studied Hebrew and the customary prayers with the rabbi of Turin, before his *bar mitzvah* and had then left his Jewish background behind. "We were laymen till the moment when the racial laws were proclaimed; we weren't interested in Judaism. Then one morning we woke up Jews, and we weren't politically ready. We didn't know what to do." Eugenio, whose father, a university professor, found himself jobless overnight, thought about emigrating to the United States, but had to give up the idea because no one there could vouch for him.

Levi was half thrilled and half chilled by the Wander laboratory. Everything in it was in perfect Swiss order, spotlessly clean. The *commendatore* was an autocrat, slightly unhinged, and obsessed with secrecy. He was worried that the work he had in mind for the chemist he had just engaged might attract industrial espionage, and in this field *Dottore* Martini trusted no one. The spy could just as easily come from inside the firm as from outside, so Levi had orders to speak to no one about his research. In order to minimize the risks, working hours were staggered and the employees arrived and left according to a preset schedule at roughly five-minute intervals. Any infringement was punished by a fine. The same obsession dictated that the last hour at work must be spent dismantling the equipment, so that anyone who broke into the lab would find no clue as to what went on there. Each day's work had to be summarized in a sealed report, for submission either to the boss himself or to his secretary, Signora Loredana. The *commendatore* suggested that Doctor Levi have lunch in the laboratory: if he brought the food, one of the workers would prepare it for him.

The library with the ten thousand volumes was hard to get into. The librarian was Signorina Paglietta, pathetically ugly, and a stickler for rules, who guarded the entrance and had instructions to scrutinize each book, page by page, once it had been consulted. The book had to be spotless when returned: no bookmark, no dog-eared pages, and no annotations. The slightest mark, and the book would be instantly destroyed, and replaced with a new one at the tamperer's expense. Of course, the books could only be consulted on the spot. The library and all the laboratories were locked by key at night, and the keys deposited with the caretaker. Only *Dottore* Martini had a master key.

Fortunately, in the laboratory Primo found Gabriella Garda Aliverti, the classmate from Turin who had recommended him to the *commendatore*. She was a Catholic, sharp, resourceful, and inquisitive, and knew all about the owner and his mistress–secretary, "La Loredana," a mature, attractive woman who went sailing with him on the lake. Gabriella's solution to the *Dottore's* bans and edicts was to totally ignore them. She talked to everybody in the factory, worked in a notional kind of way, assembled her trousseau, and wrote to her fiancé. Varisco, the woman who prepared Primo's meals, was devoted to Gabriella. In this era of rationing, she cooked her special meals, using cuts from the laboratory animals.

The first urgent task set by the *commendatore* was for Primo to read a study of diabetes written in German by a Doctor Kerrn. Martini's own reading of Kerrn had given him ideas, and he asked his chemist to perform two sets of experiments:

> The first idea concerned anthocyanins. Anthocyanins, as you know very well, are the pigments of red and blue flowers: they are substances easy to oxidize and deoxidize, as also is glucose, and diabetes is an anomaly in the oxidizing of glucose: "hence," with the anthocyanins one could try to reestablish a normal oxidizing of glucose. The petals of the cornflower are very rich in anthocyanins; in view of the problem, he had put a whole field under cultivation with cornflowers and had the petals harvested and dried in the sun: I should try to make extracts from them, administer them to rabbits, and check their glycemia. (*Table* 116)

The *commendatore*'s second idea involved the role of phosphoric acid in the metabolism of carbohydrates. Following the ideas of Doctor Kerrn, he theorized that a small dose of vegetal phosphorus, taken internally, should restore the disrupted metabolism of the diabetic to normal. When Levi tried raising objections, Martini changed his tune and instructed his employee to choose those plants that were richest in organic phosphorus, make up extracts from them, and inject them into the laboratory rabbits. When Primo passed this news on to Gabriella, she flared up and told him that if he had had a girlfriend, he would not have bothered with anthocyanins, and would not have thrown himself into the lion's mouth. How could he be so stupid as to waste his time on messing about with rabbits in the lab?

Gabriella was pretty, slim, and dark, and tended to fall out with her fiancé. Primo was in love with her, but would never have dared to admit it, even if she had not been engaged. She claimed that she could read palms, and talked about introducing him to a cousin of hers who was as shy as he was.

Once, Primo took Gabriella to the cinema to see *Quai des Brumes*. No doubt this could have been his moment, because they were both enchanted by the film. She identified with Michèle Morgan, and Primo longed to be like Jean Gabin, "a fascinator and a tough guy, killed dead — ridiculous, and besides, those two loved each other and we didn't, right?" (*Table* 118)

Nothing much frightened Gabriella, but she was terrified of spiders, and when she found one on her work bench one day, she had to call Primo for help. Another time, when a violent thunder storm broke, she rushed over to him for protection. The gesture overjoyed him, but it mortified him too, because he could not make the slightest response. More than thirty years later, his regrets had still not faded when he confessed: "I felt the warmth of her body against mine, dizzying and new, familiar in dreams, but I did not return her embrace; if I had done so, perhaps her destiny and mine would have gone with a crash off the rails, towards a common, completely unpredictable future" (*Table* 118).

When Primo Levi first visited her library, Signorina Paglietta demanded his identity card, made him sign a register, questioned him about his reasons for consulting Kerrn's book, and finally, reluctantly, handed it over. Kerrn's arrogant style spurred Levi's immediate "resentful distrust." In any event, the *commendatore* soon gave up on cornflowers and their anthocyanins and ordered Levi to focus his efforts on phosphorus. Every morning he would find plants left on his bench, and set about measuring their phosphorus content, while Gabriella clattered glassware in the room next door.

It was not long before they noticed that the owner had been visiting the labs at night. Gabriella claimed that it was here that he made love to La Loredana.

After two disheartening months of meticulous analyses for what he saw as a futile project, Levi had established that sage, celandine, and parsley were the plants with the highest phosphorus content. He proposed to isolate this, but *Dottore* Martini ordered him to introduce the concentrated extracts into the rabbits' oesophaguses, and then measure their glycemia. Levi's problem was that he detested rabbits: like certain human beings, they had nothing in their heads but food and sex. Except for a cat or two in Bardonècchia, he had never touched an animal. Nor had he ever touched a woman. The physical contact he found both repulsive and alluring was almost impossible for him.

Nevertheless, he had to insert a gastric probe into the rabbits' stomachs, prick their ears to collect a drop of blood, and even operate on one of them — it died — which had developed a large tumour on its neck. The irony was that the rabbits lived in segregated chastity, with the males and females kept in separate cages, until an air raid damaged some of the cages and an orgy broke out. As it was now impossible to identify individual rabbits, the trials were disrupted.

Perhaps unwittingly, Gabriella offered her friend Primo one last chance. He was in love, but had no thoughts of making himself more attractive and attached no importance to the way he dressed, though according to Tedeschi he was "very tidy and clean in his person." One day when she was in a special hurry, and knowing that he came to work by bike, she asked him to give her a ride to Porta Genova to save her from having to change trams three times. Primo left first, as the Martini drill required, and waited round the corner for Gabriella, who arrived ten minutes later. This was wartime, and it was common for cyclists to carry a passenger on the crossbar. Sometimes a stranger might ask for a lift in exchange for a few lire. Gabriella was talkative and fidgety, and as she delivered a stream of confidences to Primo, she kept on waving her arms and shifting her position, while the wobbling bicycle wove its way from the Via Imbonati to Porta Genova, then along the Largo Cairoli. All this was because Gabriella was furious with her boyfriend's parents, who objected to her because they thought she wasn't good-looking enough. Primo ventured a compliment — she looked pretty enough to him.

"If you're trying to court me now, I'll knock you down."
"You'll fall too."
"You're a fool. Go on, keep pedaling, it's getting late." (*Table* 124)

Her soldier fiancé couldn't seem to make up his mind. And what was Levi thinking as they neared number 40 Viale Gorizia, with Gabriella wobbling on the crossbar? That she was a *goyà*, as was his rival; they could marry, while he, "the salt of the earth," impure by definition, he who longed for her, would never possess her. He watched her dart through the doorway of the house, and then sat down on a bench and gave in to sombre thoughts. No, he told himself, more than the racial laws were to blame. Though full of regret and bitterness, he had to admit his own "inability to approach a woman," and he feared that this inhibition would pursue him all his life. It was only a few years before that he had confided his thoughts of suicide to Alberto Salmoni.

Two hours later, when Gabriella emerged jubilant and victorious, she found her friend still sitting on the bench. Seeing that he was upset, she asked him "What were you thinking about?"

"Phosphorus," he told her.

Gabriella married her fiancé a few months later, and left the laboratory, after briefing her friend Varisco about keeping Primo fed. She had many children, and she and Primo remained friends. Thirty years after these events, they would meet now and then in Milan. "We both have a curious and not unpleasant impression (which we have both described to each other several times) that a veil, a breath, a throw of the dice deflected us onto two divergent paths, which were not ours" (*Table* 126).

After Gabriella's marriage, a despondent Primo started going back to Turin every week. Bombings were a daily threat. Many buildings were damaged, and the family regrouped for a while in the house where Primo's grandfather and his cousin Giulia lived. Primo reoccupied his bed, which was borrowed by a refugee during daylight hours. He daydreamed about writing the story of an atom of carbon, and thirty years later he did so. The atom's adventures after its long imprisonment in limestone and through the cycles of photosynthesis provide the final chapter of *The Periodic Table*.

All the members of the group except Emilio Diena spent time writing poetry, a fact not quite so startling as it might first appear. As yet, they knew nothing about the destruction of European Jewry, and though outcasts from society, they had not yet made serious contact with the active opponents of Fascism. So in the evening they sang songs taught them by Silvio Ortona, or wrote, or made up parlour games, and thought that the never-ending war was the business of the "Aryans" alone, who had shut them out. But were they, in truth, so thoroughly ignorant of the atrocities that the Nazis were perpetrating all over occupied Europe? Did they have no information at all about the spread of genocide? They did hear stories, through Italian soldiers returning home on leave from Greece or Russia, about the staging of mass executions on the eastern front, but they did not believe them, or preferred not to believe them.

Meanwhile Operation Torch, the successful Allied landings in north-west Africa, had started on 8 November 1942, and the Soviet counter-offensive in Stalingrad, launched on 19 November, had forced Field Marshal von Paulus to surrender the remainder of his shattered Sixth Army on 2 February 1943.

As Eugenio Gentili Tedeschi remarked during our interview, the group of young Jews bound together and isolated by the anti-Jewish laws had been drifting, not knowing what to do. When they realized that the war was coming to Italy, it was as if they suddenly grew up. Now, finally, they made contact with the ill-equipped underground groups who had already been resisting Fascism for a long time:

> and we recognized in them our teachers, those for whom we had futilely searched until then in the Bible's doctrine, in chemistry, and on the mountains. Fascism had reduced them to silence for twenty years, and they explained to us that Fascism was not only a clownish and improvident misrule but the negator of justice; it had not only dragged Italy into an unjust and ill-omened war, but it had arisen and consolidated itself as the custodian of a detestable legality and order, based on the coercion of those who work, on the unchecked profits of those who exploit the labour of others, on the silence imposed on those who think and do not want to be slaves, and on systematic and calculated lies. They told us that our mocking, ironic intolerance was not enough; it should turn into anger, and the anger should be channelled into a well-organized and timely revolt, but they did not teach us how to make bombs or shoot a rifle. (*Table* 130)

What had become of the Italian anti-Fascist movement since the murder of the Rosselli brothers? Emilio Lussu had taken over a leadership position in *Giustizia e Libertà*, and Umberto Terracini had resigned. On the eve of the war the group had dwindled to become a leadership of exiles who had been away from their country for twelve or fifteen years.

They had founded the *Partito d'Azione* in 1941. Its members were Mario Levi, Norberto Bobbio, imprisoned by Mussolini's puppet Republic of Salò in 1943, Leone Ginzburg, who was to die under torture in the Regina Coeli prison in Rome, his wife Natalia, and Carlo Levi, whose exile under house arrest to the southern province of Lucania in the 1930s inspired his classic novel *Christ Stopped at Eboli*.[4] Carlo Levi joined the armed Resistance in 1943, and edited an underground newspaper. He took part in the street fighting in Florence in 1944. Vittorio Foa, who also belonged to the secret group in Turin, became its leader after Ginzburg's arrest. Foa had been arrested in 1935, and sentenced to fifteen years in prison by a special tribunal. Released by Badoglio in 1943, he joined the *Partito d'Azione*, whose members were the heart of the armed Resistance in the years 1944–45.

In *The Periodic Table*, Primo Levi wrote that he finally heard mention of Gramsci, Salvemini, Gobetti, and the Rosselli brothers in 1943, yet his connection with the intellectual circle based at the Hebrew School in Turin, before he left to work in the Balangero mine, had put him in touch with Hugo Sacerdote and Emanuele Artom, active anti-Fascists who shared the same apartment after the bombing raids on Turin. The only conclusion is that the two of them kept their Resistance work separate, and did not attempt to recruit comrades in arms, even among the young men and women of the Jewish community. After the German occupation of Italy, Sacerdote became Artom's political commissar in the valley of Torre Pèllice, where *Giustizia e Libertà* partisan groups were in action.

Certainly the political maturity of the seven friends in Turin had been a long time in coming, for soon after the shock of the racial laws they had already seen racist graffiti scrawled on the walls of buildings near the synagogue, which had been the target of an arson attack on 14 October 1941. A few days afterwards, leaflets had been circulated in Turin giving the names and addresses of local Jews and calling for them to be killed. Even so, on the eve of the Anglo-American landings in Sicily and the ousting of Mussolini, the seven — some of whom were to play important roles in the struggle against the Nazi takeover of northern Italy — had still not gone into action.

In addition to its chief rabbi, Zolli, who was to convert to Catholicism in 1944 — he was one of the six thousand Italian Jews who converted under pressure — in liberated Rome, Italian Jewry had two leading organizations: the *Giunta*, headed by Ugo Foa, a former judge, and the *Unione delle comunità*, the "Union of Jewish Communities," which had been created by the terms of the law of 1930 regulating the Jewish community, and to which all Jews who practised a profession were supposed to belong. In 1943, the president of the *Unione* was Dante Almansi, who before 1938 had been a member of the Fascist Party, and a high-ranking police official. The *Unione* ran a relief service, *Delasem — Delegazione assistenza emigranti ebrei —* on behalf of the nine thousand Jewish refugees from abroad who were being held under house arrest with no means of support, or in internment camps. It provided them with clothing, medicines, books, toys, and money, collected from within the Italian Jewish community or by an American organization, the Joint Distribution Committee. Many young Jews worked for *Delasem*, which had opened offices in Rome and Genoa, with the permission of the authorities. Its president was Renzo Levi, and its secretary Settimio Sorani.

The organization, which continued to function under the German occupation, carried messages to and from the remotest of hiding places, and helped Jews to escape to Spain, Portugal, America, China, Tangiers, England, France, Argentina, Cuba, Paraguay, and Palestine. *Delasem* also took charge of children brought to Italy after their parents had been murdered in occupied countries. One group of young children and adolescents housed in the Villa Emma, near Modena, were reported by the Fascists to the Nazis when they took over. Local people removed and hid them, and had false papers made for them. Not one of the children was captured.

On 12 May 1943 the last Axis forces in North Africa surrendered. On 10 July the Allied forces landed in Sicily and were welcomed by the people. On 19 July an Allied bombing raid on Rome killed 1,500 people, with the threat of more to come, and on 25 July at 10:45 p.m. Mussolini was deposed, and then imprisoned by the Grand Council. Marshal Badoglio was appointed prime minister. Jubilant crowds opened the doors of the prisons in Rome and Turin (freeing Leone Ginzburg and Mario Finzi), smashed the windows of Fascist committee rooms, and tore down Fascist emblems from the façades of public buildings. Young men last seen in public bellowing *"Duce! Duce!"* took to the streets to call for Mussolini's execution. In the aftermath of the collapse of Fascism, the Party was dissolved, the Fascist militia merged with the army, and a number of Fascist chiefs were arrested. Among these was the director of the Office of Demography and Race, who was interned in the Regina Coeli prison on 27 July, but the Office itself was not dismantled.

During the forty-five days of his ministry, Badoglio, who with King Victor Emmanuel III was involved in secret negotiations with the Allies while playing for time with the Germans, did nothing to help the Jews. The racial laws and forced labour still operated, and so did the standing orders issued to the regional prefects. In spite of Jewish requests, the files were not destroyed, nor were the lists of members of the *Unione* and the *Giunta*, and they fell into Nazi hands after Italy's surrender on 8 September 1943.

Nevertheless in August 1943 the seven friends went on holiday in the mountains

> not caring too much about the future. Upon that future, I believed that I could not exert any influence. Towards Fascist Italy, we felt a shadow of bitter resentment and revenge. Italy had expelled us. Well then, let it pursue its fate, whatever that might be, but not with us. Besides, we had talked with anti-Fascist friends more knowledgeable than we were, and they had reassured us ....
>
> Even if Italy had signed the armistice with the Allies, the Germans could not enter, and those who had stayed in Italy would stay as prisoners. Never fear. There would be a separate peace, and the Allies would reach the Alps in the blink of an eye. We left Milan during a heavy air raid and went on holiday with the clear conscience of fatalists. On 8 September we were already back in town. The news of the armistice filled us with a stupid joy. There we were, peace had come, and with it a return to just laws, equality, fraternity .... So the war was bound to end, and with the war, Fascism and Nazism, discrimination, humiliation, and bondage would disappear. We felt in the same state of mind as our distant ancestors after the flight from Egypt, when the waters of the Red Sea closed over Pharaoh's chariots.[5]

Italy's surrender was signed on 3 September and made public on 8 September. The king and Badoglio fled to Brindisi, leaving the armed forces leaderless. Italian servicemen were disarmed by the Germans, captured in their hundreds of thousands and deported to Germany. While Montgomery was landing in Calabria and Clark in Salerno, the Germans occupied the north and then the centre of the country. On 12 September SS commandos freed Mussolini from his imprisonment at Gran Sasso, and Hitler quickly set him up as leader of the new Fascist Italian Social Republic, which became known as the Republic of Salò because its propaganda ministry was based there, on Lake Garda. During this period the Italian troops who had occupied the south of France came flooding back to Italy in total disarray, followed by a large number of Jewish refugees who had been living more or less under their protection on the Riviera and in the hinterland of Nice.

Primo Levi relates that the returning Italian soldiers thought only of exchanging their uniforms for civilian clothes. They avoided the railways and valley roads, and were so famished that they had to go begging for polenta, bread, and milk.

"[A]nd then came the eighth of September, the gray-green serpent of Nazi divisions on the streets of Milan and Turin, the brutal reawakening: the comedy was over, Italy was an occupied country, like Poland, Yugoslavia, and Norway." (*Table* 130)

Guido Bachi, a good friend of the Via San Martino group, who was ten years older than Primo Levi, had moved in *Giustizia e Libertà* circles while he was living in Turin, and had met Franco Antonicelli several times. His father ran an insurance company, the Adriatica, and, intending to follow in this father's footsteps, he had taken up a work placement in a firm in Milan. When he started to hear talk about race, rather then be thrown out he resigned, and earned his living working on the black market with one of his cousins, who owned a wholesale business.

At this time, through his father-in-law, who was an intellectual from Trieste and close to Benedetto Croce, Bachi was put in touch with Giulio Einaudi, Franco Antonicelli, Massimo Mila, and Leone Ginzburg, leaders of *Giustizia e Libertà* and of the *Partito d'Azione*, which was only just beginning to emerge from hiding. The youth group in Turin included some Jews. Guido Bachi recalls today that until 1943 the group was all theory: its members met in order to deliberate about what it might be possible to do.

Then, when Mussolini was dismissed by the Fascist Grand Council on 25 July 1943, Bachi and a few of his friends called at the German consulate, rang the doorbell, and said that they had come to empty out the desk drawers. This they did, and, as a result, found themselves on the wanted list. In 1943, in the days of the air raids, Bachi went to live in a friend's house in Moncalieri, where on the night of 8–9 September they saw a regiment arrive in town and pitch its tents in the park. These were elements of the Fifth Army who were returning to Italy after the armistice. By morning, all the officers had deserted and gone home.

The very next day, Bachi decided that he could no longer sit and wait for the arrival of the Germans, whose troops he had seen after the armistice punching through the Brenner Pass towards Genoa and southern Italy. The time had come for Primo Levi and all his friends to move from rhetoric to action. Each one of them chose the same road: the mountains, and partisan warfare. "It had been by no means easy to flee into the mountains and to help set up what, both in my opinion and in that of friends little more experienced than myself, should have become a partisan band affiliated with the Resistance movement *Guistizia e Libertà*."[6]

The first groups formed haphazardly, through connections among friends, as was the case of the one formed by Guido Bachi, which Primo Levi soon joined. The friends dispersed into different valleys, although some of them stayed together. Primo Levi, Vanda Maestro, and Luciana Nissim — a young doctor friend of Vanda Maestro — joined Bachi, who was an officer, and familiar with the Valle d'Aosta and the medieval village of Brusson, which lies close to the French frontier at 1,338 metres above sea level. In the past, he had stayed at the Hotel Aquila with his father, who ran summer camps using trucks lent by the Olivetti company to ferry the children about.

A number of Jews from Turin had joined other partisan bands of *Giustizia e Libertà* in Piedmont. Emanuele Artom's band, organized by Hugo Sacerdote, who was its political commissar, also included Franco Momigliano and Bruno Salmoni. Bruno Salmoni's brother Alberto — who later married Bianca Guidetti Serra — also joined the Resistance. Eugenio Gentile Tedeschi was away from Milan on 8 September 1943. At first he headed for the Valle d'Aosta, where his parents had fled, to help them find a hiding place. Then he made contact with a group of partisans in another valley in Piedmont.

Primo Levi had joined Guido with Vanda Maestro in Saint-Vincent after locating his family, who had taken refuge in the hills near Turin. He now sent Vanda as a courier to inform Eugenio that they belonged to a small group of partisans recently set up, and that they had made contacts among the population. He invited Eugenio to come and join them. When I interviewed Eugenio, he told me

> I answered that I wasn't coming. "You're being very careless," I told them. "Watch your step. Change your location at once. Organize in a different way — you mustn't have that sort of contact with the people. You have no military organization, no weapons, and no experience. This kind of work must be done in a different way." Everybody knew they were looking for weapons, and that they were getting woollen socks knitted for them by the local women, because winter was on its way.

Since each group was confined to its own valley, none of them knew what was going on in the valley beyond. Bianca Guidetti Serra, whose parents used to invite Primo Levi's mother and his sister Anna Maria to their house in the country, joined the Communist Party in 1943, and then went underground with *Giustizia e Libertà*. According to her, total confusion reigned in the first days after the armistice. The soldiers who had ditched their uniforms deserted with their weapons, workers began to form groups, and the parties that had existed before the advent of Fascism started to reorganize.

Bianca worked in the Resistance in the mountains for twenty-three months, in a well-trained group which was divided into sectors. She was in charge of the women's sector, which played a key role: 70,000 women in northern Italy helped Resistance members in prison or in the mountains, and collected money and information.

In the Col de Joux, near Saint-Vincent, Guido Bachi had formed a group that grew from its original five or six members to eleven. Of these, only two, Bachi and Aldo Piacenza, had held a gun before: "My experience as a conspirator and soldier was non-existent. To fight and kill. I was not ready to fight and kill. No one had taught me. These notions were very far removed from all that I had thought or done till then."[7]

Vanda Maestro had come with Luciana Nissim, a young Jew from Biella, who had studied medicine at Turin University, and had met Primo Levi in the Hebrew Library after the passage of the anti-Jewish laws.

According to Guido Bachi, the first members of the network were sent to him through Camillo Reynaud, a lawyer in Turin and a friend of his brother. Among these first recruits was Aldo Piacenza, a doctor and officer from Turin who knew Anna Maria Levi when she was a student. The group was split in two, one half in Saint-Vincent, the other in Amay, a small nearby village above the Dora valley, 1,429 metres above sea level. The group had very few weapons and no petrol. Guido Bachi, whose policy was not to start fighting straightaway, owned a small revolver. So did Primo Levi: "[I]t was tiny, all inlaid with mother of pearl, the kind used in movies by ladies desperately intent on committing suicide" (*Table* 131).

Guido lived alone in his headquarters, an isolated *baïta*,[8] or chalet. The other young men were billeted, like Piacenza, on farms in the Col de Joux.

The group started scouting for weapons. The young men new an old socialist who owned a barn in the village of Nus where he kept some submachine guns hidden beneath the straw. They decided to go in search of them, and set out on foot in the middle of the night. They found the barn around midnight, but discovered that the ammunition consisted of wooden bullets used for training purposes. Out of politeness, they put everything back in place under the straw before returning to the valley.

The commander of the Committee of National Liberation (CLN) — one of whose leaders, Aurelio Peccei, an acquaintance of Bachi, had founded the group — paid him a visit. Bachi had asked to have two officers sent to help him, because two of his men, ex-members of the Italian army from Turin, were causing him problems, in particular by helping themselves to chickens from the neighbourhood farms without paying for them. Bachi had sold his family jewels to keep himself going, and he wanted no stealing by his men. The local people knew about the group, and were not hostile, and he wanted to keep it that way. Bachi recalled that after his request for officers he was sent three men, who arrived on the day of Peccei's visit and introduced themselves as deserters from the Fifth Army. During the meeting, Bachi stated that he wanted to set up a training centre, and would take no action until he received orders. Today he believes that these words — testifying to the fact that he had as yet taken no action — saved his life, because the three "officers" were in fact informers who had infiltrated the group, and one of them appeared as an interrogator after the group's arrest. How had the network been so easily infiltrated? Bachi blames the other Resistance group, "*Inceza*," which had failed to observe the security regulations issued by the CLN command in Turin that each time a newcomer arrived, he was to be closely interrogated to make sure of his credentials. The three supposed soldiers from Turin had introduced themselves to the *Inceza* group and been accepted straightaway. They had then been passed on to Bachi — who in fact carried false papers in the name of Bianchi, and had had others produced for his sister-in-law and her daughter, who were hiding in a house in Brusson.

Primo Levi had reached Bachi by way of a mule trail from Saint-Vincent, with Vanda Maestro and Luciana Nissim. To begin with, they had simply been lying low in this village, which Levi knew well because he had spent several holidays there and made climbing trips in the region. But when they realized that there was a Resistance group five hundred metres away, they went to see Guido and offered him their services.

Both girls were very brave. Bachi related how they used to go down to Saint-Vincent and dance with Germans to pump them for information. Posing as refugees — the area was full of deserters, Jews, refugees, and Fascists — Primo and the two girls had rented a pretty little house and rooms between Saint-Vincent and the Col de Joux. (Luciana Nissim, who had come there with her family, described Primo Levi and the young Jewish intellectuals of Turin as extremely clever, brilliant boys, and yet very few affairs went on among the members of the group, because by the standards of masculine beauty at the time, Primo Levi and Ennio and Emanuele Artom were not at all handsome. "Marvellous heads on poor bodies. It wasn't the full flush of manhood. I thought they were terribly ugly.")

In late November, Luciana, Vanda, and Primo moved into a small hotel in Amay. How did the two young women pass the time, when they were not going down to Saint-Vincent to fish for information? They knitted and made compresses. The eleven unarmed, untrained partisans spent very little time together. As well as Guido, Primo, Vanda, and Luciana, there was another young Jew; the rest were demobilized soldiers. When they did meet it was to plan the actions to be carried out once the CLN had given the green light. On this point, Guido was very strict, because he felt that no one should take needless risks.

Despite his orders, it seems that Vanda was a dare-devil. On one occasion she went down to Ivrea to prospect for weapons, and took prisoner an old Fascist in uniform, then didn't know what to do with him and wanted to kill him. Guido was against it. He explained to Vanda that there was no call to kill a man of over forty, "someone the Fascists had grabbed just to put a uniform on him."

In *The Periodic Table*, Primo Levi writes in enigmatic terms about the liquidation of two of their comrades:

> in each of our minds, weighed an ugly secret: the same secret that had exposed us to capture, extinguishing in us, a few days before, all will to resist, indeed to live. We had been forced by our consciences to carry out a sentence, and had carried it out, but we had come out of it destroyed, destitute, waiting for everything to finish and to be finished ourselves; but also wanting to see each other, to talk, to help each other exorcize that so recent memory. (*Table* 132)

According to Guido Bachi, who still has a clear recollection of the facts, these two men — the two who had been poaching chickens from the local peasants — had made up their minds to kill him because he rejected their urging to go straight on to the offensive without waiting for orders from the CLN. A few days later, Aldo Piacenza, who had got wind of the affair, told Guido that "those two, who would rather be bandits than partisans," had been taken down a footpath by members of the group from the Col de Joux, and then shot. So before ever managing to mount an operation against the Nazis, the partisans experienced death within their own group.

On the day after the arrival of the three bogus officers, the Turin CLN had paid the group another visit. The meeting, which was attended by Peccei and Passoni, took place in the Col de Joux. A few days later, Bachi offered to get the spies a pair of mountain boots, because of the harsh winter. The next day, on 12 December, he gave "Vinticelli," apparently the nicest of them, the boots, a blanket, and a few other items. The arrest, by 297 militiamen, came early the next morning. This is Primo Levi's account:

> We were cold and hungry, we were the most disarmed partisans in the Piedmont, and probably also the most unprepared. We thought we were safe because we had not yet moved out of our refuge buried under three feet of snow but somebody betrayed us, and on the dawn of December 13, 1943, we woke surrounded by the Fascist Republic: they were three hundred and we eleven, equipped with a tommy gun without bullets and a few pistols. Eight of us managed to escape and scattered among the mountains: three of us did not get away: the militiamen captured Aldo, Guido, and myself, still half asleep. As they came in I managed to hide in the stove's ashes the revolver I kept under my pillow, and which in any case I was not sure I knew how to use ... Aldo, who was a doctor, stood up, stoically lit a cigarette, and said: "Too bad for my chromosomes." (*Table* 130-1)

Guido Bachi recalls the episode slightly differently:

> I left my little house, where I lived on my own, and walked out into the snow. I found myself facing forty militiamen, an officer, and a centurion

[militia officer], who arrested me at once. I produced my papers; they told me they knew who I was. The three traitors weren't there. Primo, Vanda and Luciana had been taken in the house. They were sitting on the ground. I was the last. The militiamen had come up from Saint-Vincent to scour the area. Among the eight partisans who lived further up the pass, and who managed to get away because a peasant gave them a warning, there was a Jew, Cesare Vitta. They stayed in hiding for several days, and then they left to join other groups. The centurion stood me in front of a firing squad. When a man has seen death, he is no longer afraid. Then suddenly the centurion, whose name was Ferro, instead of having me shot, said that I was to be taken away with his men.[9]

Luciana Nissim is more terse:

The Resistance began in the mountains. They arrested us on 13 December 1943. We were in Brusson, near the Col de Joux, which links Brusson to the other side. Someone had come to us posing as a partisan. He probably informed on us, but it was never quite clear. On the morning of 13 December, Primo, Vanda and I were staying in a little hotel in Amay. We'd heard dogs barking all night long. The militiamen arrested five of us.[10]

Primo Levi had a clumsily faked identity card, which had him down as born in Battipaglia. The militiaman who had captured him happened to come from there. They gave their prisoners a moderate beating, and one of the militiamen told Levi: "If you're a partisan we'll put you up against a wall. If you're a Jew, we'll send you to Carpi."[11] They warned them not to try to escape, and promised them an intensive interrogation, followed by the firing squad.

The walk down to Brusson took them several hours. Levi used the time to tear up and swallow his identity card, bit by bit, and to bury in the snow a notebook that contained the addresses of several of his friends, that could have got them arrested. The militiamen were not very vigilant guards: they sang, took pot-shots at hares, and threw grenades into streams to kill trout, instead of keeping a sharp watch on their prisoners. A number of buses were waiting in the valley below, and Levi found himself sitting behind a militiaman who had a German hand grenade dangling from his belt. If he had had the courage, he knew that he could have made a grab for the grenade, pulled the cord, and killed both himself and some of his captors. He did not try, and the militiamen took them back to their barracks outside Aosta, on the road to Courmayeur.

This is the report of the arrest, a wild fabrication, compiled on 11 January 1944 by Carnazzi, the head of the province of Aosta, in an obvious attempt to curry favour in high places:

Memorandum, for the attention of His Excellency Dolfin, Private Secretary to the Duce. In accordance with the orders given to me on the

evening of 13 December, the Legionaries of the XIth Battalion of the
Armed Militia — survivors from Greece — the Legionaries of the XIIth
"Mont Blanc" Legion, and the Militiamen of the Centuria Confinaria,
respectively under the command of Seniore Da Philippi, Commander of
the Legion, and of Centurion Ferro, Commander of the Centuria
Confinaria of Aosta, executed and successfully completed an action
against the rebel groups dispersed in the Brusson valley. The men (a
total of 297) were divided into two columns. The first column set off for
Arcesa, the second for the Amay area. At 8 hours 40 on the 13th, the
column went into action. The whole Arcesa group was rounded up, and
a rebel-occupied building taken by storm after a grenade attack. The
rebel Carreri Giuseppe was killed, and two others wounded. One
legionary was slightly wounded. Four insurgents were taken prisoner,
among them an Austrian and five other individuals, presumed to be in
league with the enemy. — Booty: one bus — one small truck — two Fiat
500s, provisions, ammunition, and clothing.

The column dispatched to Amay attacked and destroyed the group
of rebels settled there. The camp was burned down. In the action, six
rebels were killed. Various wounded. Among the latter, two threw
themselves into a deep ravine, and are presumed dead. The prisoners
captured amount to five, among them three Jews. — Booty: seven rifles,
two pistols, ammunition for the rifles, eight hand grenades, provisions,
valuables, and money. Five persons suspected of collusion with the
enemy were arrested.

The group was wiped out. We hold in our hands the clue to the
subversive organization in Piedmont.

Chief of Province Carnazzi — Prefecture of Aosta

Guido Bachi has made it clear that "no house was burned, and the equipment
amounted to some bags and two rifles. There weren't any vehicles. Prefect
Carnazzi's understanding is as dim as he was. He conducted the interrogations
with the three spies: Edilio Cagni, Enrico Di Ceglie, and Bianchi, all three ex-
intelligence officers of the Fifth Army in full retreat from France."

Ferro, the commander of the Centuria Confinaria, locked up the captives,
one to a cell, in the cellars of the barracks. They slept on camp beds, used
wooden slop pails, took soup at eleven, and were granted one hour's exercise
a day. They were forbidden to communicate with each other.

Luciana Nissim, who was not ill-treated, remembers that Ferro fell in love
with her and asked her to run away with him. "With a Fascist, never!" was her
reply. When her sixteen-year-old sister came looking for her at the barracks, on
the day she had been moved to the transit camp of Fossoli di Carpi,
Commander Ferro told her: "I couldn't do anything for your sister — but you
and your family, you get away." In fact the Nissim family went into hiding in
Brusson, thanks to the protection of a priest who later moved them to Milan,

where a Catholic organization managed to ferry them to Switzerland.

Guido Bachi's memories of his stay in the cellars of the Aosta barracks are not too painful:

> The militiamen, who were all fairly old, weren't bad fellows. In the evening, when the lights went on, they let us out of our cells for an hour to warm ourselves near the central heating boiler. In the cell, it was very cold, and dark; outside, in the only opening, there was snow. During the interrogations, I was never ill-treated or beaten. I suffered no violence and no torture.

During the long hours he spent alone in his cell, Levi feared he would be sentenced to death and shot as a partisan by the special tribunal. He fretted about not having had the time to write his history of a carbon atom. During the interrogations, Ferro, who was a stupid man, did not even ask Levi whether he was Jewish. The Fascists had told him, if he admitted to being Jewish: "We'll send you to a concentration camp, and you'll stay there for the rest of the war, in Italy we don't hand anyone over to the Germans."[12]

Guido Bachi was interrogated by Ferro, who had him brought up to his office one day to tell him: "You are to appear before the special tribunal." This meant the firing squad. Yet, after asking him whether he had any family, Ferro began: "You know, I had a visit from a gentleman...". This was Vanda Maestro's brother, who had dared to come and ask for news about her under a false name. Ferro had identified him, but had then let him go. After that act of kindness, Ferro was later to behave with brutality and was executed after the war.

Levi was also interrogated by one of the spies responsible for their capture. He refers to "the spy" in *The Periodic Table*, although according to Bachi there were three. In the book his interrogator is called Cagni, and described as a sadist, with ties to the Gestapo. Levi writes that he had also infiltrated a partisan formation in a valley next to theirs. He talked them into doing firing practice with real bullets, so as to use up their ammunition, and then came to arrest them all, at the head of his militiamen. When he conducted his detailed, endless interrogations, he made a show of putting his Luger on his desk, and threatened his prisoners with torture or the firing squad.

It was Cagni who told Levi that he knew he was a Jew; if he admitted it then he would him to the Fossoli transit camp, if he were a partisan, he would end up with a bullet through the chest. In *The Periodic Table*, Levi states that Cagni was bluffing when he claimed to be so certain of Levi's background, and that he only admitted it "partly because I was tired, partly out of an irrational digging in of pride" (*Table* 134).

Aldo, Primo, Guido, Vanda, and Luciana spent a month in their cells in Aosta. Levi, who had asked to have his watch taken away from him because he would rather not be reminded of the passage of time, did a lot of reading, in spite of the faint light shed by the one dim bulb that stayed on day and night.

He managed to communicate with Guido by exchanging the books that they were allowed to read, marking particular letters with tiny dots on pages whose numbers they would whisper as they sat around the boiler in the evening.

In his ice-cold cell, which he shared with a rat that gnawed his bread, Primo Levi thought sadly about his loss of freedom. His guard was the militiaman who had struck him at the time of his arrest, but when he found out that his prisoner was a "*dottore*" he came to apologize, and brought blankets for him and his comrades, and it was he who arranged for them to be able to sit a while by the central heating boiler before lights-out. Here Levi met a boozy smuggler who said he knew where gold was to be found, in a small river called the Dora. His freebooting account of himself has several parallels with the story entitled "Lead" in *The Periodic Table*, and the smuggler–prospector from Aosta is not unlike Rodmund, its hero.

One night the militiaman guarding them dozed off, and the submachine gun leaning between his thighs slid to the ground. The smuggler and Levi jumped to their feet in unison, without a word, but it was too late: the guard picked up his gun and took them back to their cells. As he passed Guido and Aldo in the corridor, on their way to the boiler room with another guard, Levi's mind turned to what he had in store: the cold, his memories of the past, and the prospect of a sombre future.

After their series of interrogations in the Aosta barracks, the fate of Guido Bachi, who admitted at once that he was a Jew, took a very different turn from those of Primo Levi, Vanda Maestro, and Luciana Nissim, who were taken by train to the transit camp at Fossoli di Carpi, near Modena. Bachi was remanded to the town prison, pending his trial before the special tribunal of Turin as a group leader, political commissar, and member of the CLN. When Ferro gave him the bad news, he told him that on the other hand his friends were in luck, they would see the war out in the Fossoli camp — which shows how much the Italian militia knew about the fate in store for Jewish internees. Bachi replied that, for him, death would be quick, whereas he could not tell what his comrades in the camps had coming to them.

In the end it was his fate that proved kinder. He was taken to prison by two militiamen, and thrown into a cellar occupied by a cautious, tight-lipped Englishman, captured after an escape. There was nothing else in the cell except a bucket to relieve themselves in. Next morning they took Bachi to the administration block, where all his possessions were removed, even his diary, where he had written a kind of will. Hearing him protest at the top of his voice, the assistant governor of the prison, who unusually was a Piedmontese, came to investigate the din. Bachi was then put into a cell that contained a murderer, a thief, and other common-law prisoners, who gave him a friendly reception. The food was so foul that he could not eat it. The next day, the governor sent for him and said:

"You're a doctor of commercial science, and you're Jewish. Could you do book-keeping?"

"Possibly," said Guido.

"The man who keeps the books gets his sentence reduced."

As soon as he set to work, Bachi realized that he was dealing with a thief. The prison governor held the keys to the canteen, and each time he took out twenty bottles, he filled in ten and sold the rest. When Bachi had been working for a month, the accounts went off to be examined in Turin. The furious governor yelled at Bachi: "Go back to your cell, you don't understand. Your sums are all wrong. It seems I've earned three hundred lire!"

The guard asked Bachi how the governor could have earned three hundred lire when he only received thirty, and from then onwards he saw his prisoner as a hero. He put him on his own in a heated cell, invited him to his house, and asked him to give French lessons to his children. The prosecutor also took a liking to him. He was a royalist, and no great Fascist. He reassured his prisoner: "You needn't worry, nothing's going to happen to you." In Bachi's own words, the judge was "half-and-half." Through a member of her family who belonged to the Verona militia, his wife arranged for Bachi's dossier to stay at the bottom of the pile. In those days of uncertainty, the prison guard had two irons in the fire. His son ran messages for the Resistance, and warned them when the militia was about to stage a raid.

Towards the end of the war, the defeated Germans were still there, and the prisoners were afraid of being taken hostage and shot. The guard's son, in touch with a partisan group, made detailed plans for an escape, with the governor and guards in collusion. The chief of the militiamen used to stand watch in the evening and took his meal with the guards. That night they got him drunk, then posed as militiamen themselves. This was the moment.

Bachi crossed several valleys, sleeping in the open, and took to the mountains. When he tried to enter Switzerland in April 1945, the soldiers refused to let him pass because the German Swiss officer on guard had questioned him and knew that he was wanted. Bachi stayed close to the frontier for some days, then made his way down to the partisans in Saint-Vincent, then on to Ivrea.

5 From the Mountains to Fossoli di Carpi

Primo Levi, Vanda Maestro, and Luciana Nissim were less fortunate than Guido Bachi. As soon as Levi's friends, one of whom was Silvio Ortona, heard the news of his arrest, they cooked up a plan to capture a local Fascist leader, with support from a partisan group in Biella, in the hope of exchanging him for Levi. They failed, being unable to get in touch with the group. The two young women, who had lost contact with their comrades during their detention, were reunited with Levi on board the train that was taking them to Fossoli, on 20 January 1944. When the train reached Chivasso, at sunset, he could make out the Mole Antonelliana, Turin's huge unfinished synagogue which became the symbol of the Piedmontese capital when given to the municipality by the Jewish community. "That moment of separation, that farewell, pierced my heart."[1] Levi took advantage of the journey to scribble a letter and throw it out on to the railway track. It was addressed to his gentile friend, Bianca Guidetti Serra, because that way it stood more chance of reaching its intended destination, and that is exactly what happened. The letter was picked up, and posted by an anonymous hand. Bianca took it to Levi's mother and to his sister, who was working as a courier for the Resistance in the valleys of Piedmont. Today the letter is displayed in the Museum of the Resistance in Milan.

The camp at Fossoli di Carpi, north of Modena, which in those days held only a few detainees, most of them Jews, had been run, Italian-style, by officers of the Public Security Service, before passing under German command in the early spring of 1944.[2] The Italians commanding the camp swore to the Jews "on their word as Fascists"[3] that they would be kept there till the end of the war. The German commander of the Fossoli camp was *Untersturmführer* — an SS rank equivalent to second lieutenant — Karl Tito. Before his arrival, the regime was fairly relaxed: the inmates were allowed to receive mail, and parcels of food and clothing. The Italian policemen who guarded the perimeter never behaved brutally and sometimes gave the prisoners bread. As for the previous camp commander, a Neapolitan, and very easily bribed, not only did he give the girls — Vanda Maestro and Luciana Nissim — permission to leave the camp, but he would escort them to the nearby town, where they could visit the public baths and the hairdresser. This Neapolitan also used to organize friendly boxing matches with the prisoners, and would readily enter the ring himself.

In Fossoli, Primo Levi met a young doctor, Leonardo De Benedetti, interned there with his wife when Swiss soldiers turned them away after they had managed to reach the frontier. That day, the Swiss had admitted only old people, children, and their parents. All others had been escorted to the Italian frontier and handed back to the Fascists and the Germans. This is how Levi described Leonardo: "He was not handsome, but had an intriguing ugliness that he was cheerfully aware of, and that he used in the way a comic actor uses a mask. He had a large crooked nose, big, blond, bushy eyebrows, and between them a pair of shining blue eyes, never melancholic, almost childlike."[4]

However, even if the management of the camp was fairly lax, this was the first time that Primo Levi had found himself immersed — by force, and under stressful circumstances — in an exclusively Jewish world. He felt his Jewish identity confirmed like a sentence of tragic exile, of a kind he had hitherto associated with biblical stories. "I lived through the surprise and the pride of an identity." But although it was felt and embraced with real pride, the return to Jewish roots took place in desperate circumstances.

The camp had been created by the Italians in December 1943, in the heart of German-occupied northern Italy, and a total of 6,746 Jews were confined there before they were deported to the extermination camps. In September 1943, after the fall of Mussolini, it had first been intended for American and British prisoners of war, then converted to receive Jews and political prisoners. When Guido Buffarini-Guidi, the interior minister from 1938 until 1945, ordered all Jews to be interned, the camp was empty, but in working order. Ten huts were added to accommodate the Jews, the rest being for political prisoners and ordinary criminals. The two groups were kept separate. Whole Jewish families had been shipped there. Some prisoners had been denounced and arrested; others had given themselves up because they were tired of hiding or had run out of living resources, or else because some other member of their family had been captured. Lastly, a legalistic minority, failing to foresee the possible consequences, had made this fatal choice so as "to be in conformity with the law." When Primo Levi arrived, in addition to the 150 Italian Jews in Fossoli there were also 100 Yugoslav soldiers and some foreigners considered dangerous by the Fascists. In a few weeks the number of Jews arrested and brought to the camp came to over 600. They wore a yellow triangle on their shirts.

The camp, which was two kilometres long and a kilometre wide, contained a long series of huts, each divided into thirty cells, with two rows of bunk beds, and a canteen. Some huts intended for 80 or 100 prisoners received as many as 200. It was cold, and there was little food. The perimeter was lined with barbed wire and watchtowers. Internees with money were allowed to buy provisions from the peasants in the area. The Jewish children used to crawl underneath barbed wire to beg for bread from the non-Jewish detainees. At night, people played cards, studied, read books and wrote letters — Levi sent a letter to Nicola Dallaporta, who sent him a reply. He remembered that, because the mail was censored, these letters were full of commonplaces and their tone was completely bland.

Gradually, the conditions worsened, each stage creating a new normality until the moment when the Germans took total control of the camp. All at once, the parcels and letters dried up. The overlord was Hans Haage, a fanatical Nazi and sadist, who frequently murdered Jews with his own hands. He was assisted by an Italian major and an adjutant, who were subject to his orders. He divided the Jews into two categories: the "pure Jews," liable for prompt extermination, and the "*Mischlinge*,"[5] who remained in Fossoli, working within the administration and organizing the deportation of the first category.

Primo Levi, Vanda Maestro, and Luciana Nissim had no illusions about their probable fate once the Germans took over the camp from the Italian Public Security Service. They had spoken at length with Polish and Croatian Jews who talked about events in Eastern Europe. In Aosta, Luciana had got to know a Jewish refugee from Yugoslavia, who described how the Germans loaded Jews into trucks and took them away to be shot. So they knew what to expect when an SS detachment arrived in the camp, even though their fellow inmates closed their eyes to the future, so much so that they were surprised when the day of deportation was announced.

In this context, there is no denying the Nazis were past masters of the art of duping their victims and lulling their fears, even as the decision to proceed with their murder was made. Cunning and reassurance always preceded the switch to all-out violence and cruelty. Thus on 20 February, two days before the deportation of all the Jews in Fossoli, the Germans put on a charade of inspecting the camp and rebuking the Italian commissar for his poor management of the kitchens and the shortage of firewood. They even promised that an infirmary was to be opened for the inmates, who learned the next morning that every Jew without exception was to be deported on 22 February. "For every person missing at the roll-call, ten would be shot" (*Man 14/*20). The deportees were ordered to prepare for a fortnight's travel, and the SS gave cynical advice to "bring along gold and jewels, and above all woollen clothing and furs, because you're going to work in a cold country" (*DS 110/*87–8).

On the last day, as they waited to leave — for their deaths: there was no doubt in Levi's mind — the camp continued to operate as usual. The teachers taught in their little school, the cooks prepared meals, those on the duty roster scrubbed and cleaned. One of the most deeply moving passages in all of Primo Levi's work is his account, biblical in its resonance, of the Jews' last night in Fossoli di Carpi, the night of 21 February 1944:

> And night came, and it was such a night that one knew that human eyes would not witness it and survive. Everyone felt this: not one of the guards, neither Italian nor German, had the courage to come and see what men do when they know they have to die.
>
> All took leave from life in the manner which most suited them. Some praying, some deliberately drunk, others lustfully intoxicated for the

last time. But the mothers stayed up to prepare the food for the journey with tender care, and washed their children and packed their luggage; and at dawn the barbed wire was full of children's washing hung out in the wind to dry. Nor did they forget the diapers, the toys, the cushions and the hundred other small things which mothers remember and which children always need. Would you not do the same? If you and your child were going to be killed tomorrow, would you not give him to eat today? (*Man 15/21*)

Levi — the honest witness, the prosecutor calm in his precision, who appeals to each reader to demand recognition of the crimes that were committed, and their punishment, no more and no less (although no punishment exists that can match the crime committed) — relates that in hut 6A there was a whole clan of Jews, Gattegno by name, who had come from Libya with all their belongings, including their musical instruments. When everything was ready for the final journey, the women observed the ceremony of mourning:

When all was ready, the food cooked, the bundles tied together, they unloosened their hair, took off their shoes, placed the Yahrzeit candles on the ground and lit them according to the customs of their fathers, and sat on the bare soil in a circle for the lamentations, praying and weeping all the night. We collected in a group in front of their door, and we experienced within ourselves a grief that was new for us, the ancient grief of the people that has no land, the grief without hope of the exodus which is renewed every century. (*Man 16/22*)

For the first time, during that terrible night, Primo Levi felt a sense of belonging to the Jewish people. This was no longer "a small amusing anomaly," or the angry pride of declaring himself "impure" because the racial laws had made him a pariah. This time the feeling dawned in him that he shared the fate of a very ancient people that for centuries had met nothing but exile and persecution. It was at the end of that tragic, sleepless night that Levi began to become a Jew, not by religious conviction, but in the grief he endured and shared with the hundreds of Jews who were on their way to board the sealed wagons bound for the largest extermination camp in Eastern Europe. He took upon himself the whole past history of the Jews, starting with the stories told in the Bible.

Daybreak came, and the Germans took the roll-call. The first step was taken into the methodical dehumanization of the concentrationary universe when, after finishing his count, the corporal shouted to his officer that 650 "*Stücken*," "items," were ready to be shipped.

The 650 Jews, the first convoy to set out from Fossoli di Carpi boarded their buses and were taken to the railway station where twelve goods wagons and an escort of soldiers stood waiting. The soldiers clubbed and struck these men, women, and children who were going to be reduced to ashes in a few days' time, adding a vein of pointless brutality to the martyrdom inflicted. Why such cruelty, since they were going to die?

Primo Levi pondered this question at length in his last book, *The Drowned and the Saved*. At the end of the chapter devoted to "useless violence," he quotes from Gitta Sereny's book, *Into That Darkness*,[6] which deals with the Nazi war criminal Franz Stangl, the commander of the extermination camps of Sobibor and Treblinka, where 250,000 and 750,000 Jews respectively were murdered. Together with Rudolf Höss, of Auschwitz, Stangl was the only commandant of a Nazi extermination camp to be brought to justice for his actions. Gitta Sereny wanted to understand and explain "the personality of at least one of the people who had been intimately associated with this total evil."[7]

One day, as Stangl was giving some particularly hideous details about the acts of barbarism inflicted on Jews as they flocked naked down "the tube," the fenced-off path that led to the gas chambers, Gitta Sereny asked him:

"Could you not have changed that? ... In your position, could you not have stopped the nakedness, the whips, the horror of the cattle pens?"
"No, no, no. This was the system. Wirth had invented it. It worked. And because it worked, it was irreversible."[8]

Another time, she asked:

"Why ... if they were going to kill them anyway, what was the point of all the humiliation, why the cruelty?"
"To condition those who actually had to carry out the policies .... To make it possible for them to do what they did."[9]

The head of the Jews in Fossoli, who was included in the convoy, had arranged to take food supplies, but he did not think of bringing water, taking its presence on the train for granted. No one brought any receptacle that might have contained some, nor did anybody think about latrines. The Germans left no buckets in the wagons: it was part of the procedure for humiliating their victims, eroding their dignity and will to resist, to prove they were no longer human beings.

Into the small wagon occupied by Primo Levi, Vanda Maestro, Luciana Nissim, and their friend, the handsome Franco Sacerdoti, the SS packed a total of forty-five people before they bolted it shut from the outside. When they reached the station, Levi had noticed signs marked "Auschwitz" on the wagons. The name told him nothing at all: Auschwitz meant an unknown place, the end of the journey.

With 650 Jews crammed into its twelve sealed wagons, the convoy stood all day long on the track at Fossoli di Carpi, before setting off, from morning till night.

When they were liberated by the Russians, Primo Levi and his fellow survivor Leonardo De Benedetti were asked to draft a report on the hygienic and sanitary conditions in the Monowitz camp, part of the Auschwitz complex.

Back in Turin, he and De Benedetti, who was a doctor, published a detailed account in the medical journal *Minerva Medica*, adding some general observations. This evidence was later republished in 1993 by Franco Angeli on behalf of the General Council of Piedmont and the ANED (National Association of Ex-Deportees to the Nazi extermination camps).

In particular, Levi and De Benedetti described their journey from Fossoli di Carpi to Auschwitz: "The oldest was over eighty, the youngest a baby of three months. Many were ill, some of them seriously: an old man of seventy who had suffered a cerebral haemorrhage some days before the departure was also loaded on to the train and died during the journey."

Nearly all of the deportees who thronged the wagons had brought plenty of luggage with them, because a German officer in the Fossoli camp had advised them to bring "woollens, blankets and furs." "He added, with a kindly smile and an ironic wink, that if anybody had hidden money or jewelry away, they had better bring those as well, because there they too would come in useful."[10]

What with the number of suitcases and packages that littered the soaking wet floor of the wagon, where no one had troubled to spread straw, there was no room for everyone to lie full-length to sleep, so many of the starving, thirsty deportees had to stand or squat, jammed up against each other, during the four-day journey from Fossoli to Auschwitz.

The task of shipping Jews from all over Europe to the place of their destruction was performed by the Reichsbahn, attached to the transport ministry. The railways of the Reich employed 500,000 clerical and 900,000 operating staff.

In *The Destruction of the European Jews*, Raul Hilberg writes

The Traffic Division set priorities and rates, the Operations Division was concerned with train formation and schedules, and Group L (*Landesverteidigung* [Defence of the Territory]) worked with OKH/Transport ... in the dispatch of trains carrying troops and munitions.[11]

[...]

Territorially the railroad structure was composed of three regional *Generalbetriebsleitungen* [general managements], a larger number of subregional *Reichsbahndirektionen* [railway managements], and many local railway stations. Of the three *Generalbetriebsleitungen*, the eastern was preeminent. It was from here that the stream of traffic to the eastern front as well as to the death camps was directed.[12]

Transported and crammed into cattle trucks, the Jews were counted as passengers by the officials who worked out the Reichsbahn's budget. "The basic rate for a third-class seat was 4 pfennigs per kilometre of track. Children under ten travelled at half fare, those under four travelled free."[13]

The group rate was charged when four hundred people travelled together. "The invoice was addressed to the body which had requisitioned the convoy."

The RSHA (*Reichssicherheitshauptamt*: "Reich Main Security Office") bought a single ticket for the Jews, a return ticket for the soldier escort. The payment for transports like this sometimes passed through the hands of clerks in the official travel services. In short, the Jews were shipped to the death camps like goods in bulk, but in the eyes of the German railway service they remained passengers who had chosen to travel economy class. The Reichsbahn had 850,000 wagons running in the countries that Germany occupied and looted. Often, trainloads of Jews for extermination were given priority over goods shipments, and rated just as urgent as "armed forces trains." It was Eichmann, assisted by a host of civil servants making phone calls and sending telegrams, who decided on the urgency of each Jewish *Sonderzug* ("special train"). When the lines were congested or jammed, Bureau 33 arranged for these convoys to be squeezed in between the movements of other trains, when the track was clear.[14] Finally, and even if he had to spend several days without food or water in an overcrowded wagon, no Jew was to escape his lawful fate. It was imperative to unload him at the place where his death had been decreed. In *If This Is A Man*, Levi relates that the train moved slowly, and sometimes made long, nerve-racking halts in sidings. Hilberg's account provides the explanation.

Luciana Nissim survived her deportation, and when she returned she wrote a memoir for the information of her friends.[15] At the time of the Liberation, she was one of four survivors from her wagon, and Levi points out that this was the highest survival rate in the entire convoy.

The daily food for the Jews from Fossoli di Carpi consisted of "bread, cheese and jam. It got everywhere: hands, blankets, luggage. Everything was smeared with jam, and we suffered terribly from thirst. The weather was cold. The people in the wagon were very anxious, very nervous. The children had no grasp of what was happening, and actually they didn't feel too bad."

Luciana Nissim recalls that the adults were always quarrelling, and Levi, in *Minerva Medica*, refers to these disputes, which erupted late at night, in darkness, when the exhausted deportees who lay in a tangle on the floor fought and insulted one another in an effort to win a few square centimetres of extra space in the stifling air.[16]

In every wagon, crude latrines were devised using makeshift receptacles and a blanket strung across a corner between nails prised from the wooden walls. Luciana Nissim explains:

> That is why we waited impatiently for the moment when we could go outside and find more space, if not more peace and quiet, to relieve ourselves. It was truly dreadful to witness the spectacle of these distinguished gentlemen and elegant women defecating to each side of the train. The German soldiers pointed out the excrement lying on the snow with gestures of disgust, and took photos of Jews with their trousers unbuttoned.

The train passed Verona, Trento, and Bolzano, and then came to the Brenner Pass. The deportees peered out at the world through small slits in the sides of the cattle truck.

> People stopped and stared at this train that kept its "cargo" locked in. We would shout out: "Look, this convoy is full of children, women, old men, sick people. These are the people the Nazis are deporting!" From time to time we dropped messages outside for our families.

After they passed through the Brenner, the signs of life gave out. The deportees rolled on into the void, and no one in Italy knew any more about them. In the words of Luciana Nissim: "The whole train and its cargo disappeared."

In the wagons, some fell ill, others lost their minds, and others died. Those who survived were hungry, thirsty and exhausted.

The train reached the valley of the Inn, then the fine sunlit mountains around Innsbruck. Luciana thought about the free men who would be skiing there. The convoy left Salzberg and Vienna behind, crossed the Czech border, and passed through Ostrava into Poland. It was freezing cold, thick snow covered the pine forests, and the railway track was now a branch line, with just a few deserted stations.

Luciana, Vanda, and Primo watched their companions, nearly all of whom were soon to be turned into ashes, for of the 650 Jews in the convoy, 23 came home. Among those deported was little Emilia, the daughter of Aldo Levi, and engineer from Milan. She was five or six years old. She had boarded the train with her elder brother and her parents, who achieved the feat of giving her a bath along the way in a zinc basin "with tepid water which the degenerate German engineer" (here Levi is being ironic) "had allowed them to draw from the engine that was dragging us all to death" (*Man 20/26*).

Giorgina Levi, a cousin of little Emilia Levi, who during the war found asylum with her husband in Brazil (which had agreed to house a few Jewish doctors in some of its most underprivileged regions), lives in Turin today. A history teacher and Communist deputy, in her old age she has grown closer to the Jewish community, to the point of making it a gift of her apartment after her husband's death, and moving into a simple room in the retirement home near the synagogue. She still writes frequent articles, particularly in the magazine published by the Jews of Turin.

Enriquetta Levi Viterbo, Giorgina's sister, was a cousin by marriage of little Emilia's parents. The family's papers and some documents deposited at the Centre for Contemporary Jewish Documentation in Milan were found by the two sisters. *Il libro della memoria — ebrei deportati dal Italia 1943–1945* ("The Book of Memory of the Jews Deported from Italy between 1943 and 1945") by Liliana Pittocto Fargiorne, mentions only the birth dates of the two Levi children, born in 1931 and 1938, who were killed on arrival in Auschwitz.

In the wagon, Luciana, Vanda, and Primo listened to their companions saying things like: "Whatever is coming, anything's better than this awful journey. Good God, when are we going to arrive?" By contrast, the three friends would have preferred that the journey should never end. It was the arrival that frightened them. The train made another long halt in open country, in utter silence, then it chugged off very slowly once again, before it drew to a stop, on 26 February 1944, around nine o'clock at night, on a dark plain. "On both sides of the track rows of red and white lights appeared as far as the eye could see; but there was none of that confusion of sounds which betrays inhabited places even from a distance" (*Man 18/24*).

Auschwitz, and journey's end. Luciana Nissim remembered the families in the wagon who had brought along mattresses, sheets, suitcases, furs, money, precious stones and jewels sewn into the lining of overcoats. Luciana, Vanda Maestro, and Primo Levi harboured no illusions about their fate.

In *If This Is A Man*, Levi wrote:

> Next to me, crushed against me for the whole journey, there had been a woman. We had known each other for many years, and the misfortune had struck us together, but we knew little of each other. Now, in the hour of decision, we said to each other things that are never said among the living. We said farewell and it was short; everybody said farewell to life through his neighbour. We had no more fear. (*Man 19/25*)

Primo Levi survived. Vanda Maestro died.

Before the doors were opened by German soldiers, Luciana Nissim looked out through the small slit in the wagon. In the pitch-darkness, floodlights illuminated a vast expanse of huts, surrounded by barbed wire. "Is this the camp?" she wondered.

Chapter 6

Auschwitz (Part I)

The doors of the train were flung open and the cattle trucks rapidly cleared by squads of SS men armed with pistols and wielding clubs, who bellowed orders along a vast floodlit platform — the Auschwitz ramp. Luciana Nissim described her arrival in Auschwitz in her "Memories of the House of the Dead":[1]

A few metres away from us stands a long line of waiting lorries. We take courage again. There is a camp, and they've come to collect us with lorries. Then it won't be too hard. Finally, they make us dismount. We unload our baggage, which we have to leave by the train. We're told it will follow us. I am with Franco, Vanda, and Primo. We've decided to claim we're related, so as to try to stay together in the same camp. Suddenly an SS man comes up. He brutally separates off the adolescents and herds them into another group, where all the men are gathered. We have no time to say a word to each other. In their group, Franco and Primo look at us with infinitely sad eyes. I know they are thinking that if harm comes to the women, they won't be beside us to help. We are in the big group with the women and children. I don't speak German and I have no idea what is happening. Next to me is an Austrian woman who had taken refuge in Italy and then been deported with us, and she translates what is being said around us. Those who are tired can board the lorries — the old, the sick, the children. Vanda has hurt her arm. I suggest that she should board a lorry, but myself, after several days' travelling I would rather walk instead. From now on I am all she has left in the world, and we ought to stay together, she replies. She clings on, and grips my arm very tightly. An SS man comes over to us again. As he chooses, he inspects the women closely. Some he sends to the left, others to the right. Vanda and I are sent to the left-hand group, which is smaller than the other. We're walking, we're strong and healthy, aren't we? The others, with the children, climb into the lorries. They line us up five abreast. The count us. There are twenty-nine of us. The same choice has been made among the men. Franco and Primo are gone. Where are you, my dear friends? What will become of us all?

By means of this triage, quickly performed, the SS men were able to determine who could still be useful as workers for the Reich, in the light of their present requirements. From the transport newly arrived that night, after selecting twenty-nine women the SS picked ninety-six men. The rest were gassed within forty-eight hours. Levi adds that later on the selection was even more arbitrary

103

between those who were to die at once and those whose death was postponed for a few days or weeks or months. The SS would open the doors on both sides of the train instead of one, allow the deportees to get down as chance dictated, and then decree the lucky side at random. The rest went straight to the gas chamber.

Among the Jews gassed that night were Leonardo De Benedetti's wife, little Emilia Levi, and her brother Italo, who was around fourteen years old. Their mother also died in Auschwitz, although according to Giorgina Levi, it seems that their father Aldo was still in Monowitz-Buna in January 1945. The whole family had been given away by their hairdresser, who received 7,000 lire per Jew betrayed and arrested. Later he was killed by partisans.

Luciana and Vanda marched in ranks of five abreast, escorted by armed SS men.

> I am very excited. I confide to Vanda that all I am feeling is great curiosity. Now, we are going to see with our own eyes what goes on in these mysterious concentration camps in Poland. We pass through a gateway. We walk along a road which has rows and rows of huts on either side. They warn us that the wire that surrounds them is electrified. Touch them and you die. We are inspected again by some more SS men, in a small Block post. We pass another gate. Now we have arrived in the camp. They stop us in front of a hut. From the station to here, we have walked for about half an hour.

Primo Levi, Leonardo De Benedetti, and Franco Sacerdoti, who remained on the platform with the men selected for work, saw for the first time the kind of men that they too would become in a few hours' time — *Häftlinge*.[2] "They walked in squads, in rows of three, with an odd, embarrassed step, head dangling in front, arms rigid. On their heads they wore comic berets and they were all dressed in long striped overcoats, which even by night and from a distance looked filthy and in rags" (*Man 20/26*).

These were the men of the Auschwitz *Aufraumungskommando an der Rampe* ("clearing Kommando on the ramp"),[3] whose job was to clean out the wagons and collect the baggage left behind on the platform, to be transferred to "Canada" — the Auschwitz jargon for a specialized area of the camp made up of thirty huts. "The Polish inmates had given the nickname Canada to the huts where the sorting and storage of Jewish belongings were carried out, this name standing as a symbol of fabulous wealth for them. The crew that worked there, the Canada Kommando, therefore had the best opportunities to "organize."[4] This enormous mass of goods — clothing, baggage, money, jewelry, precious stones — was meticulously sorted by a special crew of *Häftlinge*, and shipped in whole trainloads to the Reich. Canada operated with two sorting crews, a day shift and a night shift. Each hut had its speciality — children's clothing, women's clothing, boots and shoes, men's clothing, gold, valuables, jewelry, foodstuffs. The quantities of food brought with them by the deportees and stored in the huts were so great that they rotted where they lay, while in the camp the inmates were deliberately allowed to die of hunger. The women's clothing had to be carefully folded and tied in bundles of twelve items. Each sorter and packer had to produce a set number of packages in a given time. Then the packages were stored in another hut, to be forwarded to Germany. One survivor, Kitty Hart, recalled how she preferred to use banknotes as toilet paper, in peril of her life, rather than hand them in to the Germans. She and her companions buried boxes filled with gold and precious things in order to pass them on later to the Polish Resistance on the outside, which used them to buy arms for a possible uprising.[5]

The SS men who helped themselves in Canada to cigarettes, perfumes, expensive tinned foods, luxury underwear, and jewelry were part of an immense black market trade.

Primo Levi had no doubt that he would soon be like these shuffling men in striped pyjamas who bustled in silence around the empty wagons.

The *Kalendarium*, the Auschwitz log-book, for 26 February 1944 preserved a trace of the arrival of a transport of Jews, "men, women, and children," shipped by the RSHA from Fossoli. Following the selection, ninety-five men were tattooed. They received numbers 174471 to 174565.[6] The twenty-nine women who survived the selection carried the numbers 75669 to 75697. All were interned in the camp as detainees; 536 people were gassed. Primo Levi received the number 174517. The ninety-five selected men were taken away in a covered truck guarded by a soldier who asked them whether by any chance they wanted to give him their money or their watches, since from now on they wouldn't be needing them.

Twenty minutes later, the truck unloaded its human cargo in front of a big illuminated gateway surmounted by the motto "*Arbeit macht frei*," "Work sets free."

Primo Levi had arrived in Auschwitz III Monowitz, a gigantic chemical complex known in the camp slang as the Buna, because the intention was to produce synthetic rubber and petrol there. It had been built by the I.G. Farben dye trust, the most powerful European transnational company of its time, in order to take advantage of cheap slave labour. The name Buna, from the two ingredients of synthetic rubber, *bu*tadiene and *na*trium, was a trademark of I.G. Farbenindustrie.

The Nazis kept some prisoners alive for a while in order to use them as slave labour in factories that were mainly located in Auschwitz. While the Jews were being exterminated in the camps of Eastern Europe, SS *Obergruppenführer* (Lieutenant-General) Oswald Pohl, head of the SS *Wirtschafts–Verwaltungshauptamt* (*WVHA*), the Economic–Administrative

Main Office, gave Himmler an account of "the present situation in the concentration camps":

1 The war has brought visible structural changes in the concentration camps, and has radically altered their tasks as regards the utilization of detainees. Detention for the sole purposes of educational or preventive security is no longer the priority. The centre of gravity has shifted towards the economic side. The mobilization of the whole detainee work force for military tasks (increasing war production), and at a future date for peacetime reconstruction, is coming more and more to the forefront.

2 From this observation follow the measures necessary to make the concentration camps abandon their old, unilaterally political form, and to give them an organization suited to their economic tasks.

3 This is why on 23 and 24 April 1942 I assembled all the inspectors and commandants of the concentration camps, and personally informed them of the new development. The main points, whose application has priority, so that the completion of construction work for the armaments industry should suffer no delay, I have summarized in the regulations enclosed ....

Here are some extracts from Pohl's regulations:

The camp commandant is solely responsible for the labour force. Its exploitation must be exhaustive in the true sense of the word, so that the work may achieve maximum efficiency.

The duration of the work is unlimited. This duration depends upon the structure and nature of the work; it is set by the commandant alone.

All circumstances that may limit the duration of the work (meals, roll-calls, etc.) are therefore to be reduced to a bare minimum. Long marches and breaks for midday meals are forbidden....[7]

Pohl also decreed that: "Employable Jews who are to be resettled in the East will have to interrupt their journey and work in the war industry."[8]

In other words, the extermination of the Jews in the camps is simply postponed in the case of the strongest. Those who are not usable to the absolute limits of their strength are gassed on arrival. But the men of the SS, who had their hearts set on completing the "Final Solution to the Jewish question in Europe," did not always observe these instructions, and sent the majority of the transports straight to the gas chambers.

Despite the reluctance of the SS to make Jews available to the war industry, private companies attracted by a work force that cost them next to nothing (one Reichsmark per prisoner per day at the start) appeared in the camps.

In 1935, representatives of I.G. Farben had visited Dachau, but to no avail, because the camp was considered too small for the enormous investment projected. However, it was I.G. Farben that became the first company to seize the opportunity in a big way. Auschwitz became a dual-purpose camp — work and death. I.G. Farben was not just Germany's most important industrial chemical empire, it also played a key role in the business of exterminating Jews, because it manufactured the Zyklon B gas used in the gas chambers of Auschwitz. Raul Hilberg made a detailed analysis of the structure of this giant enterprise, which was headed by a board of directors and an elected management committee. Naturally, the shareholders ratified all the decisions taken by the management of the company, with its very complex organization. Hilberg describes three strata of the hierarchy, "the top echelon, the plants, and the central services."[9]

The group consisted of fifty-six factories, "arranged into three divisions according to production specialization, and into work combines, grouped territorially."[10] The administration of the industrial empire was shared between offices in Berlin and Frankfurt. Doctor Max Ilgner, in Berlin, was in charge of personnel, protocol, legal problems, exports, and economics. The commercial services — central accounts department, central insurance services, and customer files — were managed in Frankfurt.

The I.G. Farben policy towards the workers it employed was straightforward: "The Spartacists and Bolsheviks of the Red State must be eliminated." The slogan "*Arbeit macht frei*" displayed above the main gate of all the camps, and in particular in Auschwitz, where the conglomerate set up a gigantic factory, was by no means an invention of the SS. It was plastered all over I.G. Farben's factories, as part of the campaign to dissuade its workers from joining a trade union.

There was no single leader at the head of the group, no real boss, and even though the company produced and sold the lethal gas to the Auschwitz commandants, it cannot be said that the trust reserved any special hatred for Jews. Its main concern was to put its synthetic rubber, Buna, into production. As far back as 1937, all members of its board of directors who were not already Nazis had joined the party. During the war its factories worked round the clock, producing synthetic fuel, dyes, and other by-products of coal, synthetic rubber, explosives, methanol, magnesium, nickel, and all sorts of other products, as well as Zyklon B.[11]

Before it launched its Monowitz operation, I.G. Farben had opened two Buna plants, one in Schkopau in 1936, the other in Hüls in 1938, but with the Anschluss it had taken over the largest Austrian chemical enterprise, the Skoda Werke Wetzler. It was at the request of Under-Secretary of State Hermann von Hanneken, of the Reich economy ministry, that representatives of the company had agreed to make urgent efforts to increase the production of synthetic rubber. They built a third plant in Ludwigshafen, but its output was reckoned too low to reach the overall target of 60,000 metric tons, so plans were made to launch a fourth production unit with a capacity of 25,000 tons, either in Norway or in Auschwitz. Von Hanneken had preferred the Auschwitz site, which was part of the territories incorporated into the Reich. On 11 December 1940 a decree offered fiscal exemptions to companies that built factories in these territories. After the occupation of the Sudetenland in October 1938, the chairman of the board sent the following telegram to Adolf Hitler: "I am deeply impressed by the return of the Sudetenland to the Third Reich, which you, my Führer, have achieved. I.G. Farbenindustrie puts the sum of half a million Reichsmarks at your disposal to be used in the Sudetenland." Gradually, I.G. Farben became totally integrated into the highest realms of power. After 1939, the firm expanded into Luxembourg, Denmark, Belgium, and Poland.

In the course of three meetings held at governmental level on 6 February 1941, it was unanimously agreed — in particular by Karl Krauch, the chairman of the board — that the Auschwitz site was the more profitable option. It was more accessible, and there were adequate supplies of water, coal, and lime. The lack of skilled labour to build the plant was resolved as follows: on Himmler's order, the population of the town of Auschwitz was to be totally evacuated, to make room for I.G. Farben's building workers. Only those Poles capable of playing some useful part in the project would be allowed to remain. Every prisoner in Auschwitz would be put at the firm's disposal, according to their competence. On 19 and 24 April 1941 it was decided to construct two plants in Auschwitz — one for synthetic rubber (Buna IV) and the other for acetic acid. The group's management confirmed the decision the next day. The stake in the plant's construction was enormous — 700 million Reichsmarks.

Roads were laid out, buildings for the plant and huts for the *Häftlinge* constructed in the new camp of Auschwitz-Monowitz, situated 8 kilometres from the main camp, and then the camp, which covered a rectangular area of about 35 square kilometres, was surrounded by barbed wire. The I.G. Farben staff were lodged in the town of Auschwitz, and in addition two workers' estates were laid out. Building the Buna works was designated a priority. I.G. Farben bought two mines — the Fürstengrube and the Janinagrube — to be worked by Jewish deportees. On this vast site, the SS and I.G. Farben collaborated at every level. The SS provided the guards, who were supplemented by a works police force. Any slave labourer who broke the rules was liable to penalties inflicted by the SS. The management of the Auschwitz camp issued food rations, slightly augmented by the Buna, in order to keep up the level of production. The Buna director and his wife were on cordial terms with Höss, the camp commandant.

I.G. Farben's ten thousand inmates were dying of exhaustion, like those in the other Kommandos of the thirty-eight camps attached to the main Auschwitz camp. The life expectancy of a Jewish prisoner was three to four months in the Buna, and one month in the coal mines that supplied it. Thirty-five thousand prisoners worked in the Buna, and at least 25,000 died there. Apart from the Jews from all across Europe who made up the lowest category, a small minority consisted of German and Polish criminals, Polish "politicals," and "saboteurs." There were also 40,000 prisoners of war — British, French, and Russian — plus German, Italian, and Polish civilian workers, volunteers, or conscripts. The Monowitz camp was peopled entirely by Jews, who in theory provided the unskilled labour force — in theory, because there was a shortage of skilled German labour (the men were at the front) and at a certain point the Buna managers started to scan the slaves for specialists. A kind of registry office was established to classify incoming prisoners. Their profession, level of studies, and qualifications were recorded and filed.

In 1944, when Primo Levi arrived in Monowitz-Buna, the daily rate for an inmate had risen from 1.5 to 5 Reichsmarks. (The upkeep cost per inmate, originally put at somewhere between 0.30 and 0.70 marks a day, had risen to about 1.30.) By then, the death camps and the *Einsatzkommandos* had more than fulfilled their task. Very few Jews were left who had the skills to keep the factories going for the German Reich, which was facing imminent defeat on every front. The manpower which had once seemed inexhaustible was running out, and the transports arriving from Hungary contained many women and children. Pohl asked Himmler whether the women could be used. Himmler's view was clear. "My dear Pohl! Of course, the Jewish women are to be employed. One will have to worry only about good nourishment. Here the important thing is a supply of raw vegetables. So don't forget to import plenty of garlic from Hungary."[12]

The manpower expert Fritz Schmelter saw the situation in a less favourable light:

> "Until now," he said in the *Jägerstab* [fighter headquarters] meeting of May 26, "two transports have arrived in the SS camp Auschwitz. What was offered for the [fighter aircraft] constructions were children, women, and old men with whom very little can be done. If the next transports do not contain some men in the proper age group ... the whole Aktion will fall through."[13]

What struck Primo Levi particularly forcibly was that to consume the strength of prisoners of "inferior race" to the point of total exhaustion, and then to reduce them into ashes, was not only an ethical atrocity but also a redundant, exaggerated act. The immense output of "useless violence" seemed monstrous. For all its elaborate organization, the Buna system never sent a single gram of synthetic rubber into the world outside, as he repeated several times in *If This Is A Man*. In saying this, he was not so very different from the Polish Jews who have sometimes been criticized for not having grasped the intentions of the Germans. Jews did believe themselves safe from "evacuation to the East" when they were working inside the ghettos in companies that were producing goods for the Wehrmacht, and the Nazis played along with that illusion until the very last moment, the final liquidation of the ghettos. But they did not understand things in the same way as the Jews. They preferred to kill as many Jews as possible, even if the Russians were only a few kilometres away; to keep the trains running to the death camps, even if there was a shortage of rolling stock for the routed soldiers of the Wehrmacht, straggling back across the vast Russian plains. Better to see their soldiers die of cold, than to spare the life of a single Jewish child. How understandable is that?

Shut up by themselves in a big empty room, still without food or water, Primo Levi and his comrades waited until an SS man came in and ordered them to remove all their clothes, sort out anything woollen into a separate pile, and make two bundles of them. All watches, papers, and articles of value were also to be handed over. The ninety-five pairs of shoes formed a heap that was swept outside the hut by an inmate equipped with a broom. The SS man pushed the door wide open, to enjoy the spectacle of his naked captives shivering in the icy wind.

The following account of the arrival in Monowitz-Buna was written by Paul Steinberg, whom Levi calls "Henri" in *If This Is A Man*:

> Once out of the showers, we filed past the storekeepers, who issued us with a pair of long underpants, a shirt, striped trousers, jacket and cap — the stripes in blue and white — and a pair of big boots with heavy wooden soles. They had the gaze of tailors, which most of them had been in civilian life. Somehow we found ourselves with gear our size. By the luck of the draw, some inherited sets of patched-up rags, others fairly clean clothes, out of the camp workshops. Having no belts, clinging to our trousers, driven forward by the shouting of the men who, as we were to learn, held our fate in their hands — the Kapos, Block leaders, *Stubendienste* and other assistants of the SS — we came out into the barber's shop.[14]
>
> Standing behind a row of stools, the local Figaros waited with their clippers. It took an average of two minutes to crop our skulls bare.[15]

Paul Steinberg obviously takes quite a different tone from Primo Levi, whose verdict on Steinberg in his book is one of fascination and severity. Paul Steinberg was seventeen years old when he was deported. His survival was due only partly — given the vital role of luck — to his ready grasp of situations, his ability to make quick decisions and adapt himself, even in Auschwitz, and also to his capacity to distance himself from the events that he witnessed, in other words to protect the most vulnerable part of himself. His evidence has the oddest possible ring, because the tone he adopts is occasionally cynical. He never appeals to the compassion or collusion of the reader.

The healthy *Häftlinge* dressed in striped trousers and jackets, with a number sewn on to the chest, who were shaving the newcomers' heads and pubic areas at top speed, were privileged inmates. The men would be shaved like this every week. A door now opened to reveal an unheated shower room with neither towels nor soap. Aldo Levi, the father of little Emilia and Italo, was worried above them, wondering whether his wife and children were having to suffer the same ordeals as himself.

For Levi, the fatal outcome was never in doubt. But before they died, the Jews first had to be humiliated, as Franz Stangl explained to Gitta Sereny. The SS man who had just come in demanded silence, because, he said, the camp was not "a rabbinical school" (*Man 24/30*).

After a while, a *Häftling* who spoke pidgin Italian sneaked in to speak to the new arrivals in secret. (He turned out to be a Hungarian doctor who was working in the camp as a dentist.) He told them the name of the camp they had come to "Monowitz, near Auschwitz, in Upper Silesia" (*Man 25/31*). Ten thousand prisoners worked here in the synthetic rubber plant, the Buna Werke.

Later they were herded into the shower room, and they were still there when the rest of the camp woke up in the early morning.

> Tired, hungry, thirsty, sleepy, stunned by what they had seen already and anxious about their immediate future, but above all anxious about the fate of the loved ones from whom they had been suddenly and brutally separated a few hours before, their minds tormented by dark and anguished forebodings, they had to spend the whole night standing up with their feet in water that trickled from the shower heads and pooled inches deep on the floor. Finally, around six the following morning, they underwent a general rub down with a disinfectant solution, and then a hot shower.[16]

After that, they were ordered to another hut which they had to reach by leaving the shower hut naked and still wet, and running across the snow. There they finally received the revoltingly dirty striped uniform that consisted of a shirt, a pair of canvas underpants, a pair of footcloths, a pullover, a jacket, a pair of trousers, a beret, a woollen coat, and a pair of shoes with wooden soles. Many of the footcloths and underpants had been cut and sewn out of the talliths, prayer shawls, found in the luggage of the deportees and used for this purpose as a sign of contempt.

Häftlinge were strictly forbidden to possess a change of outer clothes or underclothes, and it was impossible to wash the shirts or underpants, which were changed every six weeks according to availability and without picking and choosing. Though stained by every kind of filth, none of the clothing was washed, but merely disinfected with steam, because there was no laundry in the Monowitz camp. Shirts and underclothes were often reduced to tatters, and to replace them the men would sometimes be issued with women's underwear. All these small items came from the shabbiest of the clothing stolen from the deportees who came flooding into Auschwitz. It was forbidden to own a handkerchief, or any other piece of cloth.

The boots were made in a special camp workshop. Wooden soles were nailed on to leather or imitation leather uppers salvaged from the most dilapidated shoes recovered from the transports. When, by chance, they happened to be in good condition they offered some small protection against the cold and damp, but they were totally useless for even the shortest march. They caused festering sores that turned into abscesses that led to tetanus and death. One boot was too small, the other too large; one had a heel, the other did not. "When they were damaged, they were mended innumerable times — beyond any sensible limit — so that one rarely saw new boots, and none of those issued lasted more than a week."[17] No laces were provided, and the inmates made do with bits of string or electrical wire, if they were able to get hold of them.

> Death begins with the shoes; for most of us, they show themselves to be instruments of torture, which after a few hours of marching cause painful sores which become fatally infected. Whoever has them is forced to walk as if he was dragging a convict's chain (this explains the strange gait of the army which returns every evening on parade); he arrives last everywhere, and everywhere he receives blows. (*Man 34–5/40–1*)

Those who reported to the hospital with swollen feet were turned away — it was too common a complaint. They were then sent straight to the gas chamber.

The surviving men from the Fossoli transport entered the labour camp. The Hungarian, who was not a Jew, offered a few tips for gaining advantages. Levi could not bring himself to believe a word of what he said. The bell sounded reveille, the man disappeared, hot water gushed from the shower heads, and then the earlier "barbers" rushed in to jostle and abuse them, driving them naked over the frozen snow towards a hut a hundred metres away, where they put on the striped rags that were tossed to them. In just a few hours, the SS had robbed them of their names, all their possessions, however intimate or humble, and the hair on their heads and bodies. Already, by having deprived the Jews in the transports of the most elementary articles of hygiene, and then having forced them to relieve themselves by the railway tracks when the train stopped and the doors were opened, the Nazis had set out to prove that they were not human being but "swine" that deserved their fate. The Nazis considered that it was natural either to use as beasts of burden, or else to exterminate like vermin, the beings they had stripped of dignity, the creatures they deemed unworthy to live.

The nature of the "offence" suffered by the deportees made them victims for ever.[18] The rare survivors remain incurable, and those who have been offended, tortured, will never regain peace of mind. In this context, Primo Levi cites the Austrian-born philosopher Jean Améry:

> Anyone who has been tortured remains tortured.... Anyone who has suffered torture never again will be able to be at ease in the world, the

abomination of the annihilation is never extinguished. Faith in humanity, already cracked by the first slap in the face, then demolished by
torture, is never acquired again.[19]

Levi, who recalls in *The Drowned and the Saved* that "the offence to
modesty represented, at least in the beginning, an important part of the global
suffering" (*DS 112/89*), received, like an animal bound for the slaughterhouse,
a serial number tattooed on his left forearm by an inmate official, the *Schreiber*
— "scribe" — in the camp slang. (Mosaic law forbids tattooing — see
Leviticus, chapter 19, verse 28.) This number, 174517, had to be sewn onto his
jacket, his trousers, and on his winter coat. Men were tattooed on the outside
of the forearm, women on the inside.

Children — even newborn Polish babies, who arrived in the camp after the
Warsaw uprising, and who were not gassed on arrival — were likewise
tattooed. Only the non-Jewish German prisoners escaped tattooing.

At the end of the first day, the Germans made a quick survey of the new
arrivals' civil status and noted each *Häftling*'s educational and professional
background. This turned out to be a stroke of luck for Primo Levi, who told
them that he was a chemist, not knowing that he was on the site of a chemical
plant. Leonardo De Benedetti stated that he was a doctor, but because he did
not speak German he was assigned to a Kommando of unskilled labourers who
toiled all day in mud and snow, pushing truckloads of coal or earth.

No one could receive his ration of soup or ersatz coffee without first
quickly displaying his serial number to the inmate orderly in charge, who
would smack or punch whoever moved too slowly. Three daily meals were
provided, but the portions were inadequate and the quality rotten. In the
morning, just after reveille, the prisoners received 350 grams of bread four
times a week, and 700 grams the other three days — officially a daily average
of 500 grams. This quantity might have sufficed had it always been issued and
had it not often been adulterated with ingredients such as sawdust. In addition
to this bread came an official 25 grams of margarine and 20 grams of sausage,
or else a spoonful of jam. The margarine was issued only six days a week, and
gradually the rate fell to three days. At noon the prisoners received a litre of
cabbage or turnip soup, quite tasteless because of the lack of seasoning. In the
evening, after work, a further, slightly thicker litre of soup might contain a few
potatoes, or sometimes green peas or chickpeas. Neither soup ration contained
a trace of fat, although very rarely some shred of meat would make an appearance. At morning and evening time there was also an issue of half a litre of
"coffee," without sugar, which on Sundays was sweetened with saccharine. In
Monowitz there was a shortage of drinking water; the water in the washrooms
could only be used for external purposes. Pumped straight from a river, it
reached the camp neither filtered nor sterilized, and was highly suspect. At first
sight it looked clear, but closer inspection in a container revealed that it had a
yellowish colour. It tasted of metal and sulphur.[20]

According to the scientific report drawn up for the Soviet authorities by Levi and De Benedetti, many illnesses suffered by the prisoners were due to the nature of the diet. Quantitatively it fell well short of the necessary minimum. Qualitatively it lacked two essential elements, namely fats and animal proteins — except for the paltry 25 grams of sausage doled out three times a week. It was also short of vitamins. These dietary deficiencies caused the troubles that affected nearly all of the prisoners from the very first week of their arrival. They all lost weight very fast, and most of them suffered from cutaneous oedemas located mainly at the lower limb joints. Facial oedemas were not unusual. The prisoners also caught all sorts of chronic skin infections. Their feet were blistered and gouged by the crippling boots, whose size, shape, and texture all caused damage. The very numerous boils, phlegmons, leg ulcers, and abscesses resisted the application of silver nitrate, failed to heal, and turned into gnawing, suppurating sores. Nearly all the prisoners suffered from dysentery, caused by the consistency and quality of the food. Thus their strength dwindled fast, because the running down of the fatty tissues was accompanied by extensive atrophy of the muscular tissues. The diseases of vitamin B and C deficiencies were also rife

The *Häftling* newcomer had to learn to recognize his number pronounced in German, and to speak it in that language. For Levi's 174517 this makes *Hundert vier und siebzig fünf hundert siebzehn.*

A year before he died, Levi wrote in *The Drowned and the Saved* that his tattoo had become "a part of my body." He continued:

> I show it unwillingly to those who ask out of pure curiosity; readily, and with anger, to those who say they are incredulous. Often young people ask me why I don't have it erased, and this surprises me: why should I? There are not many of us in the world to bear this witness. (*DS* 119–20/95)

According to the Austrian political prisoner Hermann Langbein: "Unlike many concentration camps, in Auschwitz the numbers were not reissued after the death or transfer of the bearer, so that they indicated at first glance the date of arrival in the camp."[21]

The bearers of low numbers (from 30,000 to 80,000), marking deportees who had arrived early in the career of the camp, were the most respected and also the fewest: only a few hundred of them remained. These Yiddish-speaking Polish Jews were the last representatives of an age-old culture annihilated in less than five years, rare survivors of the liquidated ghettos of Eastern Europe. In the eyes of Levi, an assimilated Jew, these were the real Jews. Their memory stayed with him, and to them he dedicated his only novel, *Se non ora, quando?*[22]

The forty-odd Jews from Salonica bore numbers between 116,000 and 117,000. These men had survived the annihilation of their whole community in the gas chambers of Treblinka and Auschwitz-Birkenau (the latter also known as Auschwitz II, as the Monowitz camp became Auschwitz III). The bearers of high numbers, like Levi and his companions, were conspicuous novices who got scant sympathy from their seniors. Some had not lost weight, and more than that, they were backward enough to know nothing of the ways of the camp, its volumes of unwritten rules. Instead of helping them, the veterans played dangerous, potentially lethal jokes on the newcomers, which earned them beatings, humiliations, or the loss of their rations. Integration came about at the cost of these thousand cuts and scratches that made their victims a constant laughing-stock to hard-bitten older hands. When Levi reached out of a window and broke off a fat icicle to quench his thirst, a guard snatched it out of his hands. "*Warum?*" asked Levi — "Why?" "*Hier ist kein warum,*" came the answer — "Here there's no why."

Primo Levi spent the first day in a vacant hut, where it was forbidden to go near the bunks, and there was no other furniture. That evening the newcomers were taken in columns of five to the *Appellplatz*, the main square and parade ground, where roll-call was held. There they stood motionless for an hour, waiting for the return of the labour Kommandos, who came at last, marching stiffly and all in step, to the rhythm of a band that played a popular song called "Rosamunda" and a repertoire of German marches.

In Auschwitz, Primo Levi observed and recorded. Nothing escaped him. He scanned the most ordinary conduct, the most seemingly insignificant reactions, and found in them the depths of human behaviour. The man placed in an extreme situation is still capable of doing good or evil. Auschwitz was the place of absolute evil, a world without God. Although he did not doubt the final outcome, Levi drew upon all his mental energy to memorize each detail, in case he should survive, in order to tell the story, to bear witness, and to call for justice, for he still believed in humanity and in justice. As he told Philip Roth, his vigilance was perfect, even though forty years later he wrote in *The Drowned and the Saved* that the prisoners in the Nazi camps were no longer capable of thinking.

> I remember having lived my Auschwitz year in a condition of exceptional spiritedness. I don't know if this depended on my professional background, or an unsuspected stamina, or on a sound instinct. I never stopped recording the world and people around me, so much that I still have an unbelievably detailed image of them. I had an intense wish to understand, I was constantly pervaded by a curiosity that somebody afterwards did, in fact, deem nothing less than cynical the curiosity of the naturalist who finds himself transplanted into an environment that is monstrous, but new, monstrously new.[23]

It was not only the behaviour of the victims that Levi observed, but also the behaviour of their torturers and killers. He analysed the actions of the Nazis who conceived and sustained the concentrationary world. He examined those who suffered and died there, according to plan. Despite the beatings, hunger, cold, incessant danger, constant exhaustion, he watched the operation of the machine for dehumanizing human beings and compelling them to live and die in indignity, in degradation. In so extreme a situation, his curiosity and capacity to understand were so keen that after his return he could say — borrowing the expression from his friend Lidia Rolfi, who was deported to Ravensbrück for having given shelter to a partisan — that the *Lager*, the camp, had been his university.

Some escaped the indignity that the SS wanted shared by all their victims. Thus, after the first roll-call Levi was approached by a teenage Jew whose name he renders as "Schlome," Shlomo, who was amazed that an Italian could be Jewish, and not speak Yiddish. Schlome, instinctively brotherly, spoke words of advice and then hugged him. This very young man, who had entered the camp as a child, was Levi's first contact with Polish Jewry and with the whole Yiddish world that was to make such a deep impression on him, so that for him it came to personify true Jewry, if not its entirety. The shy young man had nothing to say when, having asked him why he did not pray, he learned that Levi was not a believer. For Schlome, a Jew was a believer by definition.

Soon after his return to Italy, Levi wrote a poem, "Ostjuden," dated 7 February 1946, on the East European Jews whom he had discovered in Auschwitz and who had been destroyed:

> Our fathers of this earth,
> Merchants of multiple skills,
> Shrewd sages of the numerous progeny
> God sowed across the world
> As mad Ulysses sowed salt in the furrows
> I've found you everywhere,
> Countless as the sea's sands,
> You stiff-necked ones,
> Poor tenacious human seed.[24]

These Jews were not only the members of a vanished people, for whom the Yiddish word "*yid*" meant both a Jew and a man, they were human beings who were slaughtered solely for the crime of having been born; they were the ones who, certain of dying, and armed only with a few rifles, pistols, and Molotov cocktails, took on the German army that was liquidating the Warsaw ghetto in April 1943; and they too were the ones who formed or joined partisan bands in the forests of Byelorussia.

116

Monowitz was one of the thirty-eight satellite camps of the central Auschwitz camp. The *Lager* measured about 600 metres square, and was surrounded by two barbed-wire fences, the inner fence carrying a high-tension current. The ten thousand *Häftlinge* were housed in about sixty wooden huts, called Blocks, and the camp also contained an experimental farm worked by privileged prisoners, plus shower and latrine huts, "one for each group of six or eight Blocks" (*Man 31/37*). In their report, Levi and De Benedetti gave a detailed description of the inner regime of the Monowitz Blocks. The floors were neatly swept and washed down each morning. In the three-tier bunks derisively baptized as "castles," the beds had to be made and the blankets smoothed out over the pallets. But all this was a mere sham; into Blocks that would normally have housed 150 to 170 prisoners, 200 and sometimes as many as 250 were crammed. Each bed was shared by two people. In such conditions, the air was stifling. The movable planks of each bunk supported a kind of pallet, loosely stuffed with wood shavings reduced almost to dust by prolonged used, and two blankets. These were never changed, and only in exceptional circumstances were they disinfected. They were threadbare, torn, and stained. Only the most visible bunks — the lower bunks, closest to the entrance — were equipped with better blankets that were almost clean and sometimes even presentable. Naturally, these bunks were awarded to the higher echelons of the inmate hierarchy, Block leaders' or Kapos' subordinates, *Stubendienste*, or just friends of these powerful figures. (The Block leaders and Kapos themselves had quarters of their own.)

This explains the impression of cleanliness and hygiene that the Blocks might convey to any casual visitor who entered them for the first time and spared them half an eye. In fact, the bunks, planks, and supporting beams crawled with fleas and lice whose ferment kept the prisoners from sleeping. The disinfection routines that were staged every three or four months were unable to get rid of these vermin, which continued to proliferate.[25]

Spartan as they were, the presence of shower huts amounted to an immense privilege for the prisoners, compared with the situation in Birkenau, where they were non-existent. These showers had been installed by the management of I.G. Farben, who did not want their staff from Germany contaminated by unclean *Häftlinge*. The threat of epidemics exercised their minds. In Birkenau, of course, Jews and Gypsies were intended for instant extermination.

The prisoners had access to the showers once or twice a week, but that did not mean that they kept clean, because soap was issued once a month in the grudging form of a single rectangular 50-gram bar of the cheapest quality, rock-hard, low in fats or oils, and high in grit. It did not lather, and it fell apart after one or two uses. There were no towels, and when they left the shower hut, no matter what the season the men always had to run naked back to the Block where they had left their clothes.

In addition to the showers and the latrines, one end of the camp also contained eight Blocks assigned to the infirmary and dispensary. Levi and De Benedetti described the Blocks occupied by the "hospital," or *KB*, pronounced *Ka-Bé* (*Krankenbau*) in their extremely detailed report. Many of the elements of this report do not appear in *If This Is A Man*.

The Monowitz camp hospital was created at the end of February 1944. Before that, there had been no medical service, and the sick, compelled to work to the point of total exhaustion, had no hope of treatment. Death was established by an unusual procedure: two prisoners armed with clubs had to beat the subject for some minutes. If he did not react, he was deemed to be dead and his body was taken straight to the crematorium. If he moved, he had to start working again.

The first nucleus of a medical service to repair the Buna Werke's "economically useful Jews" appeared with the creation of a doctor's surgery where anyone could go who felt ill. The punishment for suspected malingering was a severe beating from the SS. If the doctors diagnosed a disabling illness likely to make a man unfit for work, they would allow a few days' rest. Later, a number of Blocks were assigned to the infirmary, which then expanded to make room for new departments. During the captivity of De Benedetti and Levi, the following clinics operated in the Monowitz camp: general medicine, general surgery, ear, nose and throat, ophthalmology, odontology (which provided the most basic fillings and dental work), and septic surgery. The general medical ward contained a section for nervous and mental illnesses, with equipment for electrotherapy. There was also a clinic reserved for infectious diseases and diarrhoea; a recuperation ward, or *Schonungsblock*, which housed men suffering from dystrophy and oedemas, as well as some convalescents; two rooms equipped for infrared and ultraviolet treatment; and lastly a lab responsible for chemical, bacteriological, and serological research. If a radiological examination was required, the patient was sent to the main camp, Auschwitz I, which had good X-ray equipment.

On the face of this account, it might appear that Monowitz had a proper small hospital. In fact it was hopelessly inadequate, and lacked the most basic necessities. It had no medicines, no proper dressings, and not even a waiting-room for the sick, who had to linger outside in all weathers. Applicants were allowed to be admitted only after all the outside labour squads had returned to the camp, and after the subsequent roll-call. Before reporting sick, they all had to remove their boots, which meant being forced to walk barefoot over a floor that in the case of the surgical department was littered with dressings soiled with blood and pus. In the wards, there was a dire shortage of beds. Each bunk had to hold two patients, whatever the nature and gravity of the occupants' ailments. Hence contagion was rife, and aggravated by the lack of gowns, which forced the sick to go naked in the hospital.

As he entered the hospital, each ailing newcomer had to hand over all his clothing to the disinfection unit. The blankets and mattresses were saturated with blood and pus, and often smeared with faeces evacuated involuntarily by patients in the throes of death or suffering from chronic diarrhoea. Because of the lack of bowls, the meals were served in relays, and those whose turn came second or third had to consume their food out of receptacles scantily rinsed in a bucket of cold water. Neither in the *Schonungsblock* nor in the other wards was there any running water, though the bedridden had permission to go and wash whenever they wanted in special *Waschräume*.[26] From time to time the nursing orderlies would pour a litre of water into special basins brought in from outside.

It was in the *Schonungsblock* that the evening bread was left on a bench in the dressings department where patients placed their feet for treatment all day long. This bench too was often fouled by blood and pus, which would be hurriedly wiped off using a rag dipped in cold water.

The next morning, just after reveille, patients admitted the previous day by the duty doctors underwent a brisk inspection by the director of the medical services. If he confirmed their need to be in hospital they were dispatched to visit the showers, and then to have all their body hair shaved off. Summer or winter, they then had to go outside again, clad in just a coat, and retrace the two hundred metres' walk back to their ward.

In the medical wards, the head doctor, assisted by one or two (male) nurses, paid his morning visit without going near the sick men's "beds." It was they who would come to parade in front of him. Only the most seriously ill could be excused. At night, a rapid further check was made.

In the surgical wards, the treatments were administered in the morning. The room was divided into three sections whose patients were treated in daily succession, so that each received treatment on one day out of three. The dressings were fastened with paper bandages that came undone in a few hours, so that most of the time the wounds were exposed to the air. Sticking plaster was in very short supply, and only rarely used.

Medicines were reduced to a minimum: some aspirin, Pyramidon, Prontosil (sole representative of the sulphonamides), bicarbonate of soda, a few bottles of Coramine or caffeine. Absent were camphorated oil, strychnine, opium and all of its derivatives. Also unavailable were belladonna, atropine, and insulin, nor were there any expectorants, bismuth or magnesium salts, pepsin or hydrochloric acid. On the other hand, there were small supplies of hexamethylene-tetramine, medicinal charcoal, and tannalbine. Calcium and restorative preparations were missing. A quantity of Evipan (hexobarbitone) was available for intravenous injection, and bottles of ethyl chloride for local anaesthesia.

In *If This Is A Man*, Primo Levi gave no such thorough medical account, but he did describe the geographical layout of the accommodation Blocks and of the Monowitz *KB*, the infirmary. Block 24 was reserved for infectious skin diseases, Block 7 for the prisoner aristocracy, the *Prominenz* — holders of important posts. Block 47 housed nothing but "Aryan" Germans, the so-called *Reichsdeutsche*, who were either political detainees or criminals. Block 12

119

housed a mixed population of *Reichsdeutsche* and Kapos, and also served as a "*Kantine,*" a kind of trade counter where any smart operator who had the means could get hold of tobacco, insect powder, and sometimes other luxuries. The camp brothel, its Polish *Häftling* inmates reserved for the use of the *Reichsdeutsche*, occupied Block 29.

The standard accommodation Blocks, like Levi's own, were split into two distinct areas. The first, the *Tagesraum*, was a spacious room inhabited by the Block leader and his friends. The furniture consisted of "a long table, seats, benches, and on all sides a heap of strange objects in bright colours, photographs, cuttings from magazines, sketches, imitation flowers, ornaments; on the walls, great sayings, proverbs and rhymes in praise of order, discipline and hygiene; in one corner, a shelf with the tools of the *Blockfrisör* (official barber), the ladles to distribute the soup, and two rubber truncheons, one solid and one hollow, to enforce discipline" (*Man 32/38*).

The other area, reserved for the ordinary prisoners, was a vast dormitory whose 148 bunks, divided by three narrow corridors, were built in three tiers that reached all the way up to the low roof. The bunks were equipped with a thin mattress and two threadbare blankets per inmate. Two hundred to two hundred and fifty men were crammed into each Block, and it was forbidden for a prisoner to enter any Block other than his own.

At the centre of the *Lager* was the immense roll-call square, and a patch of grass, where the gallows were erected on public execution days.

Next to the serial number sewn on to their jackets, the prisoners wore a coloured triangle, point downwards, marked with an initial that displayed their nationality. Political prisoners wore a red triangle; the camps' tough common-law criminals a green one; "asocials" and prostitutes, black; homosexuals, pink; Jehovah's Witnesses, violet; and Jews wore both a red triangle, pointing downwards and indicating their country of origin, and a yellow, upward-pointing triangle that combined with the other to form the Star of David. The institution of this colour-coded hierarchy had a divide-and-rule logic that was explained as follows by Höss, one of the three commandants of Auschwitz,[27] who was sentenced to death by a Polish court in Cracow and hanged on the scene of his crimes on 16 April 1947: "No matter how strong they might have been, a camp's authorities could never have controlled and supervised thousands of prisoners without the help of these oppositions."

Hermann Langbein, who was clerk to Doktor Wirths, one of the chief SS physicians in Auschwitz, explains in his book *Menschen in Auschwitz* that depending on whether the criminals or the political prisoners held the most key posts, the camps were called green or red, and that ten green functionaries were more efficient than a hundred SS men. Even so, no group was altogether homogeneous. Not all of the politicals had been sentenced for acts of rebellion against the Nazi regime — some had been black marketeers. Similarly, some crimes committed by the greens might have had a political complexion, such as forging false papers for use by an underground organization. These were the exceptions, however; the general rule was that reds and greens were opposites, and where it was the reds who held the upper hand, they exerted a moral sway over the life of the camp which alleviated the prisoners' suffering. The Germans and the Poles held most of the positions of authority in Auschwitz, but during the last phase of the war it was possible for Jews to attain these posts in the satellite camps, where they formed almost the entire population.

Levi, who from the moment of arrival had set about observing the world of the camp with a scientist's detachment, very soon realized that one of the most important things was to give the impression of having understood what was said to him. The orders were bellowed in German, and if they were not carried out at once they were repeated in conjunction with a beating, and perhaps an explanation of the beating, because the shouting and the beating were parts of the same speech. Those who did not understand that speech were always the last, always too late, and too easily cheated and deceived. "Language was the first cause of drowning in the camps."[28] In Levi's view there was an enormous difference between a prisoner who could communicate and one who could not: one had a chance to survive, the other had none. Nearly all of the Italians died in the first two weeks because they did not understand that there was no margin of tolerance for anything short of instant obedience. Having said that, in this place that Levi described as "a perpetual Babel" a legion of languages were spoken.

Levi wrote that the Germans treated their prisoners like domestic animals that required only a few familiar signals, a mixture of sounds, prods, and gestures. He had learned some scientific German in order to improve his chemistry and physics — before the war, the serious textbooks were written in that language, such as the famous *Die Praxis des organischen Chemikers* ("The Practice of the Organic Chemist") by Ludwig Gattermann, which he admired so much that he called it "the father's voice." In Auschwitz, he quickly realized that "knowing German meant life" (*DS* 95/74). Failure to understand meant disobedience, and that meant slaps and blows. The orders were translated by those who did speak German, usually Jews whose mother tongue was Yiddish. So Levi decided to study the language of survival with an inmate from Alsace, who in exchange for the currency of survival, which was bread, agreed to give him short whispered lessons in the brief span between evening curfew and sleep. The Alsatian instructed him in the crude and foul-mouthed German of the Kapos and the SS, which had little in common with the German of Gattermann, and still less with the language of Heinrich Heine, whom Levi admired. A German Jewish philologist called it "the language of the Third Reich," and this specific language of the SS Reich was extended by the various jargons of each camp, which also drew on the old German of Prussian barracks. The term *Muselmann* — literally "Muslim" — was common to all the camps.[29] It referred to the moribund *Häftling* in the final stage of exhaustion, the living dead, who no longer fed himself, no longer stood up (though to lie down was a capital offence), and who cared nothing for anything, not even the nearness of death.

In Auschwitz, all language was debased so as to degrade the prisoners too. "To eat" was *"fressen,"* a world applied only to animals in conventional German. The coarse German of the *"Lager* jargon" was enriched, so to speak, by loanwords borrowed from Polish, Yiddish, and Hungarian. Before the arrival of the Hungarian Jews, and before the almost total extermination of the Polish Jews, Yiddish was the principal language spoken by prisoners in Auschwitz. Primo Levi would have liked to have underood it, and his Polish, Russian, and Hungarian fellow inmates were astonished that an Italian Jew did not speak it. To them it was self-evident that a Jew could only speak Yiddish, so much so that one day, a man informed him: *"Reds'tu nicht yiddish, bis'tu nicht kein yid!"* — "If you don't speak Yiddish, you're not a Jew!" There were very few Italian Jews left in Monowitz, and Levi took his linguistic isolation so much to heart that he felt spurned by the Jews from Eastern Europe: "We, the Italian Jews, felt particularly vulnerable; with the Greeks, we were the lowest of the low."

The number of details that had to be urgently assimilated in the first days after arrival in the camp was overwhelming and decisive. A single slip could mean death. Levi lists all of these basic rules in *If This Is A Man.* Always reply *"Jawohl."* Learn to spot the right place to stand in the queue, so as not to get only liquid. "Time to serve the soup," wrote Paul Steinberg. "The queue forms. The trick is to have an eagle eye to arrive towards the bottom of the tub, where the scraps of potato that thicken the soup collect."

Primo Levi did not agree with those who described the soup and bread in Auschwitz as nauseating. "As far as I was concerned, I was so hungry I enjoyed them," he said.[30] The prisoners received a minimum ration, theoretically, of something like 1,600–1,700 calories a day. Theoretically, because organized wastage was widespread, and what finally arrived was far less than the official allocation. According to Levi, a small man could survive on 1,600 calories, provided that he did not work hard and kept out of the cold. In fact, this quota would induce a gradual death by malnutrition. The Germans had calculated that their rations offered a likely survival span of two or three months for a prisoner engaged in hard physical work in the quarries.

The prisoners talked compulsively of food, although to dwell on succulent meats, delicious flavours, and dishes they had never even tasted could only increase their suffering.

Survival was complicated. No opportunity could be lost, and nothing be let slip: wire, rags, paper, and a careful man could tie his shoes, wrap his feet, secretly pad his jacket. All these precious things were systematically stolen from anyone who failed to look out for his possessions, and who did not sleep with his head on his bowl and his boots. One had to learn never to return a blow, how and when to disobey, when to evade the rules, bearing in mind that any infringement of the tangle of *Lager* regulations invited death.

The prohibitions are innumerable: to approach nearer to the barbed wire than two metres; to sleep with one's jacket, or without one's pants, or with one's cap on one's head; to use certain washrooms or latrines which are '*nur für Kapos*' or '*nur für Reichsdeutsche*'; not to go for the shower on the prescribed day, or to go there on a day not prescribed; to leave the hut with one's jacket unbuttoned, or with the collar raised; to carry paper or straw under one's clothes against the cold; to wash except stripped to the waist. (*Man 33–34/39–40*)

As for the obligations, they were even more numerous and absurd than the prohibitions. One daily duty, among many others, was to make one's "bed" in the morning, very fast — because bread was about to be issued — but also perfectly smooth and Teutonically rectangular. Moszek ("Maurice") Reznik, who shared Levi's bunk and worked in the same Kommando for five months, assisted "the little Italian" in this key operation. In *If This Is A Man*, the author paid homage to him in a short chapter entitled "The Work,"[31] but he did not know when he wrote it that his comrade, who spoke French with a juicy Yiddish accent, had survived. This tall, gentle man with red hair resumed his old trade as a tailor in the Marais, where the Paris police had arrested him in the general round-up of Jews staged in mid-July 1942. Not until a fellow deportee, Henri Bulawko, recognized Reznik in Levi's Auschwitz narrative did Reznik realize that his Italian friend had escaped death.

Reznik, who had joined the Foreign Legion when the war broke out, had become a non-commissioned officer in Morocco and Algeria. Demobbed and repatriated after the French defeat, he returned to Paris in the days of the Statute of Jews (issued on 3 October 1940) and the round-ups. As he was physically strong, he found work as a woodcutter in the department of Maine-et-Loire. Having joined a group of 125 workers who included seventeen Jews, Reznik had himself registered as Polish. The woodcutters were helping the Resistance by concealing caches of arms in the forest. When suspicion fell on them they were all arrested, and the seventeen Jews quickly identified. Reznik was sent straight to Drancy internment camp, then transferred to Auschwitz in convoy no. 64, which carried a thousand Jews shipped from the railway station in Bobigny with a chunk of bread and a tin of sardines each. When he reached Auschwitz he was passed fit for work in the first selection, right after getting off the train, then registered as number 167644 and assigned to the "particularly tough" Kommando 85 (transport), "which worked exclusively outside and in all weathers."[32] After coming through the first three months thanks to help from a Kapo and from Georges Wellers, a doctor in the *Krankenbau*, Reznik, who suffered from furunculosis, had the luck to become a *Blockschneider* — the official tailor for his Block.

Thanks to my sewing work, I earned an extra litre of soup a day, and on Wednesdays a double ration of bread. The Aryans in the hut who received parcels also used to give me food when I mended their clothes, which enabled me sometimes to share with a few comrades like Primo

Levi, who arrived about three months after me. We got talking straight away because he spoke French — spoke it a hundred times better than I did, as a matter of fact. He was very reticent, shy, and kind. In such a violent context he was attractive, and I remember how much people in the hut liked him. His physical frailty struck me at once, and I knew that if he didn't get help he wouldn't last long in such a tough Kommando ....

Primo Levi didn't come to occupy my bunk by chance: they always put the big men with the small ones, because there wasn't enough room for two big men together.... He admired the way I made "the bed" every morning. For me it was very easy, I'd gone to the right school. Keeping our disgusting mattress and blanket neat and tidy was extremely important in Auschwitz, whereas not getting it to look like a perfect parallelepiped could cause you real problems, meaning it could get you beaten up and possibly killed. It was rare to find the same person in the bunk for several days running, let alone several weeks. People suddenly came and suddenly went and you never knew their name, and to tell you the truth you didn't notice. They were sick, they'd been selected for the gas chamber, transferred to another Block or another Kommando. Unusually, throughout my time in Monowitz-Buna I stayed in the same Block and in the same Kommando, because I was needed as a tailor. Primo Levi stayed with me in Block 30 until he passed the chemistry examination. Then he left for another Block, about a hundred metres from my own, but I never came across him again. When people ask me why I never tried to find him after the war, I have to say quite frankly that I was convinced that he was dead, because his survival is a real miracle.

When Levi returned, he did not discover that Reznik had survived the evacuation march from Auschwitz in January 1945 — known as the death-march. For Reznik, it ended after a first stage of 60 kilometres on foot in temperatures down to minus 20 degrees, on an open railway platform in the camp at Buchenwald. Then he was transferred to a small camp in Langenstein, where the crumbling Nazis were still busy with their V1 and V2 missiles. On 6 April 1945 the SS drove their prisoners out of the camp and herded them to zones that the Allies had not yet reached. On 2 May they abandoned them near the town of Alt-Grabhoff.

Paul Steinberg — alias Henri in *If This Is A Man* — bore the serial number 157239. He had arrived in Auschwitz not long before Primo Levi, who recalled his colleague in the chemistry Kommando with admiration but with very little affection. Paul Steinberg told me that he had not noticed Levi in Auschwitz. Likewise Jean Améry, interned in Monowitz at the same time as Levi, said that he and Levi had shared the same hut for a while, whereas Levi did not remember him at all, and thought that he might have him confused with the writer Carlo Levi, who was better known than himself in the days when they were exchanging letters. Elie Wiesel, who also lived in the same hut as Primo Levi for several months, observed at the time of their meeting in the 1960s that neither of them had remembered what the other looked like.

Paul Steinberg rehearses in *Chroniques d'ailleurs* his training in "*Bettenbauen*," making beds:

> The bunks were made up of a sacking mattress, into which straw had been inserted through a lateral slit, resting on planks with gaps in between — which meant that the occupants below had their faces dusted with chaff and other bits and pieces — a "pillow" of the same kind, and two blankets, one of them doing duty as a sheet.
>
> In five minutes, timed by a watch, you had to learn to produce a bed with perfect hospital corners. The "mattress" had to be absolutely flat, and the blanket had to fold down at right angles over the pillow arranged in a perfect cube. The *Stubendienst* behind us would undo imperfect productions with a single tug .... It turned out that some of us were allergic to architecture and never did succeed in making a bed properly. Others, on the other hand, were particularly gifted, and pursued careers as specialists, making beds for the incompetent in return for a modest fee in kind.

In every Block there were two monitors, the *Bettennachzieher*, "bed-tighteners," whose job was to inspect all the beds, one by one, and ascertain their perfect alignment. They performed this public service with the help of a piece of string as long as the hut, which they stretched above the flattened surfaces of mildewed, stinking mattresses. A crooked bed meant trouble for its maker.

Another important exercise was the ritual of the salute. New arrivals had to learn the art of *Mützen auf, Mützen ab*, which was compulsory in all the camps. Each time an SS man made his dreaded appearance, the *Häftling* had to stand to attention, then take off his cap — *Mützen ab!* — with a snap against his thigh. During roll-calls, the order *Mützen auf!* meant "At ease!" The wearer had to replace his limp beret on his head. Whenever an SS man looked at or spoke to a prisoner, the prisoner had to salute and recite his serial number.

The initiation went on during a period called "quarantine," which lasted much less than the traditional forty days, and which preceded assignment to a labour Kommando. The newcomers stayed inside without working, and in the evening the veterans would pay them a visit and brief them on the organization of the camp, whose structure was modelled on that of the Blocks. At the apex of the prisoner hierarchy there was the *Lageralteste*, camp elder, chosen from the greens. As Tadeusz Paczula points out, "right from the start, the SS, with the greens, made terror reign. They abetted and vied with each other in crime."[33] The most feared *Lagerälteste* in the history of the Birkenau men's camp was Franz Danisch. He liked to assert that: "On my ground, there are only the workers and the dead."[34]

The first *Lagerälteste* in Monowitz, Jupp Windeck, a German with twenty-three convictions for theft, was a puny dwarf who compensated for his physical defects through violence inflicted especially on the weak and sick, the *Muselmänner*, by beating them to death. Any prisoner who inadvertently splashed mud on his shining boots signed his own death sentence.

In general, the *Lagerälteste* enjoyed living conditions and a real prestige in the camp that he would never have found in ordinary life, as is demonstrated by Paul Steinberg's evidence about the then *Lagerälteste* of Monowitz:

> He was a giant, with hulking shoulders ... a lump of a man, brute strength. He enjoyed the privilege of retaining his hair, and his brass voice, Chaliapin style, effortlessly blotted out the noises round about him. He also wore a black jacket, carrying a badge — in his case, a green triangle — gleaming boots, a peaked cap like a twenties motorist's .... Some said he'd made his living robbing banks, and that he'd killed some uniformed policemen. Others claimed he'd been a gang leader and run a protection racket in some downtown district, just like Chicago. The SS had made the right choice: he was a wild animal, the perfect henchman to carry out their plan. An exterminator. He worked with the pickaxe, truncheon, studded club, bare hands, or boots, not because he was forced to but depending on his moods, not with hatred but as a good professional in crime. He lived in a house, almost a mansion, all spick and span, in the middle of the camp, and held court there in the evenings for the benefit of a few veteran overlords.

Each Block was presided over by a *Blockälteste*, backed up by a *Stubendienst*. The laws were enforced by the *Lagerschutz*, camp guard. *Häftlinge* combined in *Kommandos*, labour crews, were bossed by a *Kapo*, who was assisted by one or more *Vorarbeiter*, foremen. All members of this hierarchy of prisoners in the service of the SS — constituting the caste of "Prominents" — had the power of life or death over ordinary inmates, even though they all displayed the inmate's serial number and coloured triangle. Yet even among the Kapos there were crucial distinctions to be drawn. A small minority, some of whom held key positions in the central administration — the Political Department (a section of the Gestapo), the Labour Service, the punishment cells — men such as Hermann Langbein in Auschwitz, Eugen Kogon in Buchenwald, and Hans Marsalek in Mauthausen, later became the historians of the camps where they worked both inside the system and as members of secret Resistance organizations. Although they were Kapos, they did everything in their power to help their comrades. Unhappily, in most cases the lower-level Kapos, the ones who ran labour Kommandos, were free to commit everyday atrocities, and even kill, with absolute impunity.

How did a man become a Kapo? When the camp commandant or his lieutenants were looking for collaborators, they tended to go for the common criminals, the political prisoners worn down by their years of detention in the concentrationary world, and sometimes for Jews desperate to escape the prospect of the gas chamber, or death by slow starvation. Levi observes that some were looking for social position, others for brute power, like the sadists who could now let their instincts loose without fear. Every one of them ended by identifying with those who delegated a portion of their power of life or death over the other prisoners.

Having established that there was a mimesis between the SS and certain Kapos, Levi was anxious to warn against bracketing killer and victim together, as did the film director Liliana Cavani in her film *The Night Porter* (1973). To draw such comparisons was quite simply to fail to grasp that in the *Lager* there were "grey" inhabitants prone to compromise in order to survive, in the struggle against hunger, cold, violence, and the selection that led irrevocably to the gas chamber and the crematorium. Those who could adapt quickly would survive; those who couldn't would die:

> Dying was simple. You just had to make do with what you were given to eat, and obey every order. Living was more complicated. You had to disobey, stand clear, and not hit back. The common moral law no longer applied. It was an abysmal world. On our side the victims, on their side the butchers, who often belonged to our own group, and who felt all the more separate from us because the privilege earned was great.[35]

After several days of working on a construction site in a cripplingly painful pair of boots, Leonardo De Benedetti, Primo Levi's doctor friend, reported to the infirmary. SS inspections were frequent there, and the merest doubt about a patient's future usefulness had only one solution. De Benedetti was judged unfit for work, and listed for the gas chamber. Four times, his colleagues intervened and managed to have his name removed from the list. As Levi relates, "in the intervals between the sentences and the temporary reprieves, he remained what he had always been: frail, but not corrupted by the inhuman life of the camp, gently and serenely aware, a friend to all, incapable of resentment, showing neither distress nor fear."[36]

Forty years after his return, Primo Levi analysed the relations that grew up between the ordinary prisoners and the privileged. Like all the survivors, he describes how the *Zugang* (newcomer, literally "entry" or "intake") was received with hostility, if not cruel tricks or outright bullying, by the veterans — in Auschwitz, a prisoner went from greenhorn to veteran in three or four months, because the raw detainee seldom lasted much longer. He compared this bullying to the initiation ceremonies practised by primitive peoples; the "we" was reinforced against the "they." The privileged did their utmost to cling on to their advantages, and got even for the humiliations inflicted by their superiors through taking them out on those who lacked *protekcja*, pronounced "protectzia," meaning protection or special entitlement. This presence of the privileged in every human society, including the *Lager*'s, seemed to Levi to be an inevitability that only utopias reckoned to exclude. "Where there exists power exercised by the few or by only one against the many, privilege is born and proliferates, even against the will of the power itself; but on the other hand it is normal for power to tolerate and encourage it" (*DS* 42/27).

Corruption ruled in the *Lager*. This reality took Levi by surprise on his arrival, because he had hardly had any previous contact with Germans, and imagined them to be cruel but incorruptible. Instead, he discovered that the whole camp hierarchy was crooked. For example, each SS man stole four bricks a day via the 10,000 inmates from I.G. Farben — in all, some 40,000 bricks a day. Not only did they steal, they also used the prisoners to carry all this cargo from the construction site to the camp, which was two kilometres away.

In his meditation on the condition and attitude of the men buried deep in the concentrationary world, Levi unearthed a "gray zone" in which good and evil had no sharp demarcation line, and where the victims and their persecutors sometimes found themselves on the same side, the prisoners' side. According to him, the space between the butchers and their victims was not empty: "it is studded with obscene or pathetic figures (sometimes they possess both qualities simultaneously)" (*DS* 40/25). In Primo Levi's view, only Maurice Reznik and his comrades Jean Samuel and Alberto Dallavolta escaped all ambiguity. All responsibility, and all blame lay with those who conceived and created that hideous world, which to the newcomer seemed incomprehensible and mysterious. The slightest solidarity between companions in adversity was very rare. The ordinary rules of society were reversed. The *Lager* had a logic of its own. Sometimes Levi referred to his comrades using the German concentrationary terminology: the prisoner was a *Häftling*, the fellow detainee, "co-man," was a *Mitmensch*. It was not because he identified with the SS aggressor or Kapo that Levi used these terms; rather, it was because no language except the German of the camps had words that could convey their matter-of-fact reality. Similarly, the words *Lager* or *KZ* (*Konzentrations–Zentrum*) evoke the world that took their use for granted, whereas the word 'camp' is out of key. No good could be expected from a *Mitmensch* — he was too busy with his own survival. It was this encounter with aggression where they might have hoped for help, coming on top of the predictable assaults from the SS, that drove some inmates to suicide.

A fatal mistake was made by anyone who sought to preserve his dignity by retaliating against violence from the privileged. *Zurückschlagen*, hitting back, was an act of folly that could cost a beginner his life. Levi cites the case of an

Italian who was drowned in the soup tub after clashing with the man who was saving the best parts for his friends. "It is naïve, absurd, and historically false to believe that an infernal system such as National Socialism was, sanctifies its victims; on the contrary, it degrades them, it makes them similar to itself, and this all the more when they are available, blank, and lack a political or moral armature." (DS 40/25)

At dawn the *Häftlinge* would set off in long columns of five abreast towards the giant chimneys of the Buna, three kilometres' march away, hoping to survive a day each one of whose instants carried deadly risks. At night, after work, those who still lived had to scrape the mud and filth from their clothing, scrape their boots and grease the uppers, display a pair of clean feet, and pass an inspection for lice. The SS conducted a ruthless campaign against lice, with the aim of preventing an epidemic of the highly contagious petechial typhus. The prisoners had to hand their shirts to the specialist *Stubendienst* whose job was to examine the folds and seams where the parasites hid. Bed bugs and fleas were less closely controlled.

> Every night after coming back from work, and with extra rigour on Saturday afternoons — reserved among other things for cropping the hair from inmates' heads, and sometimes also from their bodies — a procedure called "lice control" was practised. Each prisoner had to strip naked and submit his clothing to orderlies specially entrusted with this carefuly examination. If they found so much as a single louse on an inmate's shirt, all the clothes of all the occupants of the room were sent for disinfection straight away, and the men would be sent to the shower, after a rub-down with an insecticide. After that they had to wait naked until the small hours until their clothes came back from being disinfected, thoroughly damp.[37]

Beards and hair were cut on Saturdays, and clothes mended on the same day in Block 30 — this extra job was Reznik's. On Sundays there were checks both on jacket buttons (there had to be five) and for scabies. Its treatment was dispensed every evening outside the *Krankenbau*, where patients waited in the cold with a hundred other cases, to have their bodies smeared in a foul-smelling liquid with a high sulphur content.

> Meanwhile, no steps were taken for the prophylaxis of the contagious diseases that were rife there: typhus, scarlet fever, diphtheria, chicken-pox, measles, erysipelas, etc. ... to say nothing of the many contagious skin diseases, such as impetigo or scabies. Considering the absence of hygienic standards and such severe overcrowding among the prisoners, it is surprising that no fast-spreading epidemics ever broke out.[38]

In Monowitz, I.G. Farben employed the prisoners as a never-failing labour supply that it could exploit to the limit. All of the *Häftlinge* worked, except for the sick in the *Krankenbau*, where a selection might condemn them to the gas chamber at any moment. After roll-call the two hundred Kommandos would go out in all weathers, in columns of five, to the accompaniment of the band that played on a platform by the exit from the camp. Everyone made for the Buna, some in good and some in bad Kommandos. In the Kommandos whose task was to transport equipment, working outdoors, sometimes in snow or rain and sometimes in stifling heat, life-expectancy was short. The man who could wangle a transfer to a less hazardous duty was either resourceful or lucky. For instance, there were squads of skilled building workers, very much fewer in number than the manual labour crews, who worked under the supervision of civilian foremen known as *Meisters*, usually Germans or Poles. Liaising with the Buna management, the *Arbeitsdienst*, the "Labour Service" (a kind of personnel office), chose those who were to work in these less damaging Kommandos. In fact, bribery, generally by means of contraband food skimmed from the supplies intended for the ordinary prisoners, was the fastest route to a soft job in the Buna.

In summer and winter alike, the *Häftling* worked throughout the hours of daylight — in summer from 6:30 to 12 a.m. and from 1 to 7 p.m.; in winter from 8 to 12 a.m. and from 12:30 to 6 p.m. The shorter work hours in winter came from a concern to prevent escapes under cover of darkness and mist. On every other Sunday the *Häftlinge* enjoyed a day off, which was actually spent on maintenance work inside the precincts of the *Lager*. At 5:30 each morning came the ominous summons, spoken in Polish, "*Wstawać!*" — "Get up!" — heralding the ordeals that awaited the sleeper throughout the new day that he could not be certain of surviving.

The light goes on, the bunks are made, the prisoners put their clothes on, their vertical stripes. Moments later they emerge into the biting cold and rush to the collective, open-plan latrines, an affront to modesty, where two hundred inmates must defecate together, harassed by those who wait to take their place so tortured by dysentery that often they cannot contain themselves. Those who retain some strength of will hurry to the unheated washroom Block where they are entitled to "wash" to the waist in ice-cold water, with neither soap nor towels. The washroom floor is thick with mud, and its walls are decorated with frescoes that illustrate the model inmate cheerfully washing, even to his shaven skull, in contrast to the unsound inmate, "with a strong Semitic nose and a greenish colour, bundled up in his ostentatiously stained clothes ... who cautiously dips a finger into the water of the washbasin" (*Man 39/45*). Under the first is the German caption: "This way you're clean;" under the second: "This way you're done for." In addition to these slogans, a third has been added, in French, but in Gothic lettering: "*La propreté, c'est la santé*" — "Cleanliness is health." On the opposite wall, an unknown hand has painted a giant red, white, and black louse, with the inscription: "*Eine Laus, dein Tod*"

("One louse and you're dead"), followed by the couplet

> Nach dem Abort, vor dem Essen
> Hände waschen, nicht vergessen.
> (After the latrine, before you eat,
> Don't forget to wash your hands.)

The water was often cut off; when it was not, it was cloudy and undrink-able. After a week in the camp, Primo Levi, who had always been fastidious, had let his hygiene slide. Yet some men, like his comrade Steinlauf, still acted out the daily bathroom rituals, in an effort to maintain their human dignity and as a personal sign of rejecting barbarism. And it was Steinlauf, scrubbing in dirty water and drying himself with his jacket, who gave Levi a lesson in the power of withholding consent.

After "washing," the prisoners would scramble off again for the distribution of bread. No one let a crumb go to waste, as he swallowed it down with the fetid infusion of stewed herbs called coffee, taken from a 30-litre isothermic urn, the *Kessel*. Each inmate was called by his number, his tattoo checked, the number ticked off on a list, and only then was a ladleful of ersatz coffee poured into the *Schissel*, his bowl. Bread was the unit of exchange for the common Auschwitz prisoner, and as soon as it reached him his creditors would pounce to claim the debt — seconds later, and it would be too late. After that, the *Häftlinge* flocked to the *Appellplatz*, where they grouped together by Block, in rows of five. An SS man came up with his roster, and the Block leader would call out the number of the Block and the total of its inmates. They compared their figures and counted the numbers.

After roll-call the inmates left their Block leader and joined the Kommando to which they had been assinged by the *Schreibstube*, clerks' office. Each Kapo set off for the plant with his Kommando of *Häftlinge*, marching in step, without swinging their arms, in rows of five abreast. They marched past the band of some thirty musicians playing "The March of the Gladiators," and after the Allied bombings of 1944 the elegy "Ich hatt' einen Kameraden." They halted in front of the band, the Kapo shouted "*Häftlinge Mützen ab!*," and they doffed their caps. The Kapo announced the number of the Kommando and the number of men on its strength. The guard shouted "*Los!*," and the music played on while the Kommando left the camp and proceeded to the Buna.[39]

Very quickly, the *Häftlinge* lost their sense of time. It was the minutes that weighed on their minds, and then the hours. Tomorrow did not enter their consciousness, and the previous day's events were fast forgotten. Levi wrote that in the *Lager* there was no time to be afraid. Fear surfaced only when some rare interlude released it, as during his time in the infirmary, or in the last two months of his captivity, when he worked in the warmth of the Buna's heated labs. With all of their senses keyed to seeing out another day alive, the captives

131

lived each moment like an animal, except those who were motivated by a political ideal or by religious faith.

In a few days of quarantine and a few weeks of work, Primo Levi picked up the ground rules of survival in the camp. He knew that he had to snap up and hang on to any item that came his way, because it might become a precious commodity on the Monowitz Exchange. He worked in an excavation Kommando, in the wind and rain, his skinny arms wrestling with heavy shovelfuls of earth. His emaciated body — he weighed no more than sixty kilos when he arrived at the camp — strained to push barrows along rails. His feet were covered in septic sores, his belly swollen with hunger, and his skin flaking.

Most of the prisoners were forced into excavation work not suited to their physical condition; very few men were put to work on jobs that had the slightest connection to their previous trades. They had to handle picks and shovels, carry coal and sacks of cement in all weathers and without adequate protection. This work was carried out on the double, non-stop, except for the hour's food break at midday. Woe betide the man caught resting during working hours.[40]

Facial transformations were so rapid among the prisoners that if a few days elapsed without their meeting, it was hard for them to recognize each other. In the early days, the Italians agreed to meet on Sunday evenings, but they soon gave up, because it did them no good to watch their numbers dwindle each time, their condition decline, or to remember the past.

Assigned to Block 30 after being transferred from one hut to another, Levi was enrolled in Kommando 85 (Maurice Reznik's), which worked out of doors in all weathers. His squad carried cast-iron girders between the railroad and the store. Levi, who was weak, small, and thin, often found himself paired with a callow boy known as "*Null Achtzehn*," Zero Eighteen, whom no one wanted to work with because he always did the toughest jobs. *Null Achtzehn* was slow-witted, and numbed by fatigue and despair. He shambled around in a daze. One day, as they were carrying a girder, he slipped and let go of his end of the girder, which tore loose from Levi's grip. It hit the ground with a thud, and one corner bit into Levi's left foot. The Kapo rushed up, and lashed out at those of his crew who had gathered round, and at *Null Achtzehn* and Levi too. Two workmates picked by the Kapo had to support Levi on the march back to the camp, and when he finally took his boot off he realized that his bloodstained foot was damaged.

After the evening soup, he reported to the infirmary, its eight huts isolated behind barbed wire. The *KB* had a permanent turnover of about a thousand inmates, who could stay there in theory for two weeks, and in a few cases for two months, after which no alternative remained: those who had failed to recover were selected for the gas chamber. Here in Monowitz the conditions were a lot more favourable than in Birkenau or in the main camp, Auschwitz I, where were situated the first gas chambers, the Gestapo torture rooms, and the yard where countless prisoners, Jews and non-Jews, were shot. Levi stood waiting in the darkness in a long line of *Häftlinge* queuing up for medicine or to have sores or wounds dressed, or, in cases of exhaustion, to be hospitalized. They had to take their boots off before they went in, and leave them in the care of a Frenchman whose task and great privilege it was to guard the doors and look after the boots. The patient entered the *KB* barefoot and bare-headed, then stood in line inside, gradually shedding his clothes so as to be naked by the time he reached the male nurse, who stuck a thermometer under his arm. "If anyone is dressed he loses his turn and goes back to join the queue" (*Man 47/53*). Everyone's temperature was taken, to discourage malingerers.

The *Häfling* Levi's temperature was normal, so he was sent back to his hut with instructions to report back to the doctor the next day; he was declared *Arztvormelder*, "applicant to the doctor." After roll-call, those who had to see the doctor were mustered in a corner of the square, where Levi's cap, gloves, spoon, and bowl were confiscated. He did not know that items of value had to be either left with someone reliable or else sold before going to the *KB*, where it was forbidden to bring them. They counted the future patients, then ordered them to undress where they stood, before taking their boots, shaving their faces, heads, and pubic hair, re-counting them, and dispatching them to the showers. After a second re-count they were sent back to shower again, and waited again, still wet, some of them shaking with fever. Levi remained naked for six hours during which no food was provided. The doctor was an inmate in good health, wearing a white coat over the striped uniform labelled with his number. He felt Levi's foot, examined the wound, which was deep, and ordered him to be admitted to Block 23. Before he hobbled the hundred metres to the *Schonungsblock*, someone issued him with a pair of sandals and a coat.

As described earlier, the hospital in Monowitz-Buna had its own operating theatre, laboratory, radiography department and, as Langbein reports, electrotherapy equipment. All of this equipment had been "organized" from Canada by inmates who worked in the Buna — obviously with the full knowledge of the SS. In Auschwitz they operated right next to the crematoria.

Georges Wellers, who was a doctor in the Monowitz *Krankenbau*, reports that late in 1944 the medical team received orders to select their weakest patients for transfer to three Blocks that had been made available to house them during their convalescence. Wary, and fearing that any selection would be for the gas chamber, the doctors listed only the sixty-eight most seriously ill patients out of the eight hundred being cared for in the two Blocks that were under their control. Much to their surprise, the sick were installed in the new huts and enjoyed far better treatment than elsewhere.

In other instances the SS demonstrated calculated sadism, as Hermann Langbein wrote in *Menschen in Auschwitz*. Robert Waitz, an inmate physician in Monowitz, told him how a man who was suffering from a perforated gastric ulcer was given competent surgery, nursed back to health, and then consigned to the gas chamber. Similarly, a prisoner injured during an Allied bombing raid on the Buna received a blood transfusion at the request of the SS doctor, only to be sent to be gassed. "Patients well cared for and put on an invalid's diet were gassed on recovery," testified Doctor Otto Wolken.

Hermann Langbein also recalls the words spoken to the Frankfurt Court by ex-SS *Rapportführer*[41] Oswald Kaduk: "In the hospital, certain inmates had a special diet for two or three weeks after an operation, and then, after six weeks, they were sent to the gas chamber." As for the survivors of selections, apathy often took over completely. As Katalin Vidor wrote: "In the survivors' exhausted imaginations, after a selection only one thought seeped through: 'Tonight we'll have more room to sleep.'"

Discussing the behaviour of the inmates who worked in the *KB*, Langbein mentions in his book that Anna Sussmann "saw nursing auxiliaries steal parcels from the sick who were put in their care."

In Monowitz, a Polish medical student, Stefan Budziaszek, was assigned to the medical service and made his way upwards to become a *Lagerälteste*, first in the Jawischowitz satellite camp and then in Monowitz. He was an anti-Semite, and any Jew who reported to him as a patient was kicked out with gaping new wounds. He was a servile, prompt, efficient organizer on behalf of the Nazis, who even found themselves having to moderate his zeal now and then, because he submitted such long lists of patients selected for the gas chamber that the SS doctor, Fischer, would object. He was not the only doctor who assaulted or otherwise maltreated Jews. The Polish doctor, Zenkteller, sent those who had dysentery to camp BIb, whose victims were kept without food while they waited their turn for the gas chamber.[42] Another Pole, the prisoner surgeon, Wladislaw Dering, who was forty years old when he arrived in Auschwitz in 1940, took pride in the tobacco pouches he made using the tanned scrota of the Jewish prisoners whose testes he had personally removed.

Not all the doctors behaved in this manner, and yet all of them worked in a dangerous double bind, for they had both to retain their posts — by retaining the trust of the SS — and do their duty as doctors. They often did their utmost to get hold of medicines, by stealing them from the SS infirmaries. They managed to have fellow prisoners kept in hospital under false pretences, they falsified records, and they hid sick people selected for the gas chamber. These measures saved only a few: by definition they could not be the general rule. These doctors too had to choose between those they let live and those they let die. Hermann Langbein writes that for this reason the doctors in Monowitz took the decision to administer the very few medicines they had available to the young, who were most likely to survive. Ella Lingens had to face the following moral dilemma: should she "use the few ampoules of cardiac stimulant to give injections to one seriously ill woman who might possibly die all the same, or share them between two less threatened patients who might pull through without them? Was it more proper to help a mother with a large family or a girl at the dawn of her life?" She also describes how Doctor Ella Klein approached the ordeal of selection: "When there was a selection in her Block she herself took the examining doctor to see patients for whom she had given up hope. He would have taken healthier cases who still had a chance to recover. The others would have died in any case, and then the death rate would have doubled." Victims of the selections who were still conscious would often burst into tears, and would scream at the nursing staff: "You too, you're going to die!"[43]

A Jewish gynaecologist, Doctor Maximilian Samuel, had a nineteen-year-old daughter, Liselotte, who was interned in Birkenau. In his efforts to save her, he collaborated zealously in the medical experiments of Professor Karl Clauberg, and even informed on one of his own colleagues, Adelaide Hautval, who had refused to assist with them. When Doctor Samuel wrote to Himmler requesting his daughter's release, the letter, like all correspondence, was passed on to the administrative office, and a few days afterwards came the news of his death. As for Adelaide Hautval, who had been heroic enough to refuse to collaborate with him, she was summoned by the Political Section, the Gestapo, but did not have to appear, because Doctors Wirths and Weber of the SS Hygienic Institute for reasons of their own contrived to have the matter closed.[44]

When he came to the *Schonungsblock* once again Primo Levi found himself naked, hungry, and shivering with cold as he stood at the end of a queue of sick prisoners waiting for admittance to the hospital. His neighbour was a health-looking Pole, not Jewish, and when Levi asked him what would happen next he and the nurse both jeered at him, because he was a relic of the Italian Jews who had arrived in Monowitz a couple of months before, and had been robbed of their bread and beaten ever since, never mind their being doctors and lawyers. They had numbered a hundred when they came, and now they were down to about forty.

Even the strongest had succumbed to hunger, cold, and despair. According to Doktor Robert Waitz, who worked in the camp infirmary, the average life-expectancy for those not working constantly out of doors was six months. Death came in stages. By the time he reached the *Muselmann* stage, the inmate had lost between 15 and 30 kilos. At the moment of death, some weighed as little as 28 or 30 kilos. "The individual consumes his reserves of fat, and his muscles. He becomes decalcified."[45] In the words of Léon Poliakov: 'The *Muselmann* state is characterized by the intensity of muscular wasting. The physical decline is harnessed to an intellectual and moral decline." The able-bodied inmates and the SS despised the dying *Muselmann*, the skeletal figure with empty, staring eyes, who came to be examined knowing that he was doomed. It was all he could do to walk. He no longer washed, no longer sewed his buttons back on, and grovelled for scraps in the mud, if he could reach them before some other creature in the same condition. When he could, he stole bread, soup, a shirt, or a pair of boots from his comrades, and often got caught in the act. He had his gold fillings pulled out in exchange for a piece of bread, and then swapped the bread for tobacco. In the infirmary, he stole bread and soup from the dying, before the selection took him in his turn. Robert Waitz quotes an SS officer who told him: "Every inmate who lives longer than six months is a crook, because he lives at his comrades' expense."

The doctors in the *Krankenbau* could spot a future *Muselmann* in seconds. *Muselmänner* in the advanced stages of malnutrition could not stop talking about food, whereas, as Doctor Berlin explained at the Eichmann trial,

> by way of conditioned reflexes, talk about food increased the production of acids in the stomach, and hence the appetite. It was essential to refrain from talk of food. When someone lost his self-control and started to talk about the food he would eat at home, that was the first sign of Muselmannization, and we knew that after two or three days the man would reach stage two.[46]

For their part, the SS could tell at a glance the difference between the short, stocky morphology they reckoned fit for the camp — *Lagerfähig* — and the slender build they reckoned as unfit — *Lagerunfähig*.

The medical orderly looked Levi up and down then gave his compatriot a point-by-point commentary on his dilapidated state, finally turning to Levi to inform him: "*Du, Jude, kaputt. Du schnell Krematorium fertig.*" — "You, Jew, screwed. You quick ready crematorium." Some hours later (and last, as usual, he remarks) they gave him a shirt and opened a file on his case. After keeping him standing waiting for hours, with an injured foot, now they asked far-reaching questions about his family and professional background. At last he was let through into a heated dormitory, its layout the same as in all the other Blocks. There were 150 pallets for 250 patients. Those on top were so close to the ceiling that they could not sit upright. Levi got bunk number 10, which was empty. In minutes, and in spite of his wound and his empty stomach, he was fast asleep.

In the *KB*, every patient had to get up at four o'clock, then make his bed and wash. They received a ration of bread at 5:30 a.m., and soup at midday. In between they could rest, and they could rest again while they waited for the medical visit and treatment scheduled for around four in the afternoon, when they all had to leave their bunks and wait in line, naked, to see the doctor. The evening soup was taken in bed, just before lights-out at 9 p.m., when only the night guard's light still burned.

Next day at dawn Levi heard the band in the distance, with the brass drum and cymbals, hellishly grinding out "Rosamunda," "The March of the Gladiators," and various German marches while the ten thousand starving and exhausted men in the Kommandos set out from the camp past an SS audience fond of that kind of parade. These marches were "the voice of the Lager, the perceptible expression of its geometrical madness, of the resolution of others to annihilate us first as men in order to kill us more slowly afterwards" (*Man 51/57*).

Levi witnessed the grotesque inspection of those suffering from dysentery, who had one minute to provide evidence of their illness there and then, in a basin. Among those who used trickery in order to stay in the *Schonungsblock* for convalescents was the "Piero Sonnino" of *If This Is A Man* (and the "Cesare" of *The Truce* and *Moments of Reprieve*), whose real name was Lello Perugia.[47] He was twenty-four years old, a lively, quick-witted young Roman with fair hair and blue eyes. Perugia arrived in Auschwitz on 30 June 1944 in an RSHA transport from the transit camp of Fossoli di Carpi, and was registered on 1 July with the number A-15 803. He was a Communist, and had been a member of the international partisan group *Banda Libertà* since 8 September 1943, fighting alongside British, French, and American comrades. He and his four brothers had been taken by the Gestapo in Tufo di Carsoli, not far from Aquila, in the Abruzzi, on 14 April 1944. He was interrogated and tortured for two weeks in the Borgo Colle Fegato prison, then handed over to the SS. They transferred him to the Via Torquato Tasso, where he suffered two more days of the same treatment. He then spent two weeks in the cells of the Regina Coeli prison before being sent to Fossoli di Carpi. From there, he and his brothers travelled for six days in a sealed wagon to Auschwitz-Birkenau, where three of them were murdered. A few days after his arrival, Lello learned what had happened to his brothers by questioning Polish prisoners, who said not a word, but gestured towards the chimneys of the crematoria ovens. Settimio died after the Liberation from gangrene in his leg, contracted in the Auschwitz camp. Only Lello survived.[48]

After a few grim weeks in Birkenau, Perugia was transferred to Monowitz, where he met Primo Levi and Leonardo De Benedetti. In the *KB*, he simulated dysentery and bought diarrhoea from genuine sufferers in return for soup and bread, with the aim of spending the winter in the warm. Even so, as Paul Steinberg recalls,

> in the *KB* one was utterly helpless to resist that diarrhoea that is the combined effect of physical wear and tear, foul water, and soups made of turnips, beet, and cabbage. They dosed the poor basic *Häftling* with a ludicrous product dubbed Bolus Alba, which was nothing but a kind of doughy white substance intended to bind the intestines, but impossible to get down without spasms of vomiting. So scattered around the camp you would see these human wrecks with their mouths made up in white, like clowns.

Levi listened incredulously to one of the men in the next bunk, a Polish Jew called Schmulek, who tried to make him understand what the selections meant.

Faced with the scepticism of *"der Italyener,"* the Italian, Schmulek responded in Yiddish: *"Er will nicht farstein"* — "He doesn't want to understand." Schmulek knew that the selected went to the gas chamber, but the SS never disclosed to the *Häftlinge* the purpose of these procedures, or the fate of the prisoners, many of them naked, that they shipped away in trucks. Sometimes the SS would drop hints about a transfer to another camp, but from the moment the selection took place there could be no doubting its lethal conclusion, because then they dropped all pretence of deception. The following is an account by Hermann Langbein, written late in 1942:

> I walk over to the window. The tangle of barbed wire is right in front of it, separated from the Block by a very confined space. It is there that some men are being assembled. The SS men bellow, the Kapos rush around in all directions, striking haphazardly at the jostling mass with their truncheons. "Get your clothes off!" They all undress in the cold. Yells and blows speed up the process. Most of them certainly know what is in store for them. I see it in their faces. And there is one who hurriedly gets dressed again, thinking that no one is looking, but a Kapo has caught him already. I hear the blows and screams in spite of the closed window. Everyone wants to be the last to undress.... Now they are all naked. Pitiful skeletons. They note down their numbers and push them into the Block. The sun shines, the snow sparkles. The roof is cheerfully dripping. Nothing left outside my window but the heaps of striped muddy clothing strewn along the foot of the wall. Then I hear footsteps and muffled voices on the path. I look outside. There they are, all naked in long lines. The clerk of our Block goes from one to the other, compares the name and number — he is holding the cards in his hand — and uses an indelible pencil to inscribe each of their serial numbers on their chests. In Auschwitz the dead have their number inscribed on their chests. These people here are already considered corpses, and the rules must be observed.... What looks they give me, these skeletons shivering in the cold! ... What can they be thinking, these men naked in the snow, waiting to be loaded on to the lorries that will take them to the gas chamber?
>
> But I don't hear any vehicles. Every time I walk along the street to go to the latrines I see them in the same place. Some are crouching, not reacting, others have eyes that are nervously shifting already.... They were parked outside my window after morning roll-call. Now it is nightfall. They have had nothing to eat all day long, and to drink, only the water used to flush the latrines. Outside my door, three lie side by side. I have to step over them to pass. One is dead, the others still alive. There isn't much difference between them.[49]

For Primo Levi, the illusion lasted until the day of the selection in the *KB*. The SS camouflage had worked. Most of the prisoners believed, or wished to believe, in "transfers to the East." But one evening the door of the hut swung open, a call of "*Achtung!*" sounded, and in total silence two SS men entered and examined the register with the chief doctor, who had already preselected those who would die and those who would be saved.

On what criteria did the choice depend? Did it save the youngest; those who came from the same country, or the same town, as the selector; those who shared his ideas; those designated to him by the secret resistance organization; or those who for some other reason aroused his sense of solidarity? Léon Poliakov wrote in *Auschwitz*:

> When, after 8 or 10 days in camp, a prisoner presents himself to a doctor, it is possible for the doctor to judge whether the prisoner will eventually hold on, or whether he will give way. The prisoner's general demeanour, his tone of voice, the way he speaks, behaves, and so on, are enough to back this judgement.

The chief doctor and the SS officer examined the list of patients and checked off numbers. The inmates had to lift their shirts and expose their nakedness to the officer's eye. Schmulek murmured to Levi in Yiddish: "Watch out." The SS man sauntered between the bunks, swinging his regulation riding crop, and it happened that his eye fell on Schmulek. He noted his number and scribbled a cross beside it. Levi was saved, Schmulek condemned to death. On the following day, two groups left the *Krankenbau*. Those who were cured were shaved, cropped, and sent to the showers before going on to their Blocks. The others were given no treatment, and left unshaved and unwashed. No one would see them again. Among them was Schmulek the blacksmith, who had said to Levi: "*Der Italyener* does not believe in selections?" Schmulek, who had not doubted his fate, gave Levi his spoon and knife as he left for the gas chamber.

On 4 Feburary 1984, forty years after his return, Levi wrote a poem, "The Survivor," dedicated to his friend Bruno Vasari, who survived internment in Mauthausen.

> Once more he sees his companions' faces
> Livid in the first faint light,
> Grey with cement dust,
> Nebulous in the mist,
> Tinged with death in their uneasy sleep.
> At night, under the heavy burden
> Of their dreams, the jaws move,
> Chewing a nonexistent turnip.
> "Stand back, leave me alone, submerged people,
> Go away, I haven't dispossessed anyone,
> Haven't usurped anyone's bread.

No one died in my place. No one.
Go back into your mist.
It's not my fault if I live and breathe,
Eat, drink, sleep and put on clothes."[50]

After twenty days, rated as "cured," Levi left the refuge of the *KB* as naked as he had entered it. Once again he was issued with ill-fitting clothes that would have to be altered, at a cost, and he set off in search of a knife and a spoon, without which he would have to lap up his soup like an animal. Yet it would be false to suggest that there was a shortage of cutlery in Auschwitz. First, there were the hundreds of thousands of knives, forks, and spoons that belonged to those who arrived each day in the transports: these were piled up in the storerooms of Canada. Then again, after the camp's liberation in January 1945, Levi found mountains of new plastic spoons held in store by the SS, who had set out to humiliate their victims by first depriving them of even the most commonplace items, before at last depriving them of life.

Outside, there was no one there to help him. Since it was the practice not to return a patient to his previous Block, the nurse assigned Levi to Block 45, and this was a special stroke of luck, because his friend Alberto Dallavolta lived there. Alberto was a decent, intelligent man, who had the knack of gaining people's respect. In spite of the circumstances he never grew cynical, as many of his comrades did, but adapted perfectly to the rules of life in Monowitz. Primo Levi and he could not obtain permission to share the squalid intimacy of a bunk, where the occupants slept head to foot,[51] but the Kapo had them paired in his mind. The two Italians looked a little like one another, and as the Kapo could not be bothered to tell them apart, he ordered that whenever "Alberto!" or "Primo!" was called, whichever man was closer should respond.

Long winter nights had set in. Late into the evening, Kardos, a former engineer, tended damaged feet in exchange for a slice of bread. A travelling singer slipped quietly into the hut and sang mournful Yiddish songs. Some inmates offered him small rewards. Then came the moment when there was a chance to get hold of better shoes, if you could elbow your way to the front in the stampede for the *Tagesraum*, where they were waiting. The light went out and then on again — a warning of the time. The hut's tailors put away their makeshift sewing equipment, the bell rang in the distance, and the lights went out. In every Block in the *Lager* the men undressed — this was compulsory — and went to bed.

Ties of friendship or solidarity did not develop, but neither did the two tenants of the same bunk get to know or even necessarily recognize one another. They might not have worked in the same Kommando, and anyway the tenants were not necessarily the same from one night to the next. In the rush before lights-out, they might have seen each other's faces for a moment. After leaving the *KB*, Levi inherited an unknown and awkward partner who snored and hogged the space, so that he was forced to sleep half suspended over the bunk's wooden edge. And yet he slept, and dreamed that he heard the puffing of the train he had unloaded in the day, which was in fact nothing but the snores of his companion.

After his arrival in the camp, Levi often had the same recurrent dream, which he told his friend Alberto. In it he would be describing his life in Monowitz to his family and friends, who took no notice; his sister would get up and walk off without speaking, and a deep despair came over him, and would not lift when he woke up. In the gloom of the hut he would listen to his comrades champ their jaws and gulp in dreams of eating, while they slowly died of hunger and exhaustion. Levi woke up every two or three hours. His sleep was fragmented by the need to urinate, because most of his daily nutrition came suspended in a very liquid soup. It was hard for the kidneys to eliminate such volumes of water, and it tended to bloat the bodies of the starving. All through the night they had to relieve themselves into a big drum positioned near the night guard, and a rigid code required the man whose visit filled the drum to take it out and empty it in the latrines a few Blocks away, clad in his shirt and pants, after giving his number to the guard. Assisted by the guard, the privileged — because they were privileged — and the old hands — because they knew how to time their trips to the drum — had ways of dodging the loathsome, humiliating task of stumbling through the dark, clinging to a vessel full to overflowing with 200 litres of urine.

Paul Steinberg gives an account of the container "used as a movable piss-hole," and here there is a striking contrast in tone between Levi, who writes as a moralist, and Steinberg, steeped in black humour. It goes far towards explaining why the streetwise young man, the "Henri" of If This Is A Man, with all his senses tuned to survival, did not even notice Levi, whereas Levi watched, with a disapproval tinged with admiration, the wheeling and dealing of the man he perceived to be an unscrupulous operator.

> This drum was kept continually topped up by the pissers of soup and the dysenterics, in other words the whole population of the Block. When the drum was full to the brim, it had the prerogative of pressing the last client into service to pick it up by means of a pair of carrying poles and take it to the cesspool to be emptied. More than once, I found myself volunteering to lend this drudge a hand. Everyone slept sounder in the absence of physical stress. I put on my sabots, we picked up the tub with these two poles that fitted into lugs attached to the sides and set out through the snow, trying to avoid the splashes. We emptied the contents in the same well-synchronized movement, then went back to the Block where four or five regulars watched out for our return with justified impatience, clenching their buttocks while they waited.[52]

The night dragged on between nightmares and regular trips to the drum made by every occupant of the hut, who would wake up his pallet-mate as he climbed out of the bunk, until the signal for reveille, "*Wstawać!*" which came before dawn, when the *Lager*'s bell rang and the guard put on the lights. Levi notes that this word "*Wstawać!*" was not shouted out loud by the guard, who knew that all of these tense, desperate men were already awake, waiting to start a day whose end they knew they might not see.

Levi was now sharing his bunk with Maurice Reznik, the big Polish Jew from the French camp at Drancy. Levi was alarmed by the size of his new partner, but his fears soon subsided, because Reznik was a polite, clean, delicate man, as well as a master bed-maker.

After roll-call the working day began, and Levi was glad momentarily to notice that Reznik had been posted to the same Kommando as himself, number 85. Reznik recalled: "The first three months were dreadful. I almost became a *Muselmann*, and I developed furunculosis, because of malnutrition. In the *KB*, Professor Georges Wellers found me a sulphur ointment, and the Kapo allowed me to take a warm shower every night. The boils came to a head, burst, and got better."[53]

"Levi had a kind smile," Reznik remembered.

I noticed at once that I wasn't dealing with an ordinary man. He was small and thin, and he couldn't lift the railway sleepers on our construction site, which must have weighed at least fifty kilos. One of us had to volunteer to help him carry them, so I did. Others would have rejected him because he was too small, but this was a matter of life or death. I would rest the sleeper on his shoulder as best I could, and I took nearly all the load. But even then it was an ordeal for him.

As the Kapo of this Kommando was not a Jew, he was not worried about losing his job for lack of zeal. After conferring with a Polish civilian *Meister* on the site, and then consigning his men to the *Vorarbeiter*, he usually took himself off to sleep by the stove in the tool cabin.

One day the members of the Kommando had unloaded an immense cast-iron cylinder from a wagon, and now they had to lay sleepers over the mud, so as to roll the cylinder to the plant. The big strong Reznik guessed the weight of the sleepers at 50 kilos, but the much weaker Levi wrote that they weighted 80. In any event, in spite of Reznik's care and concern, Levi suffered agonies as he fought to keep his balance in the snow and mud that clung to his boots. Reznik's calm voice, a gentle sound in this world of violence, told him: "*Allons, petit, attrape!*" — Come on, little one, grab hold."

For the sake of a few minutes' rest, Levi asked permission to visit the latrines, accompanied by Wachsmann, the *Scheissbegleiter* — "shit escort," in the camp's gross language, which Levi discreetly translates as "latrine companion." This was a rabbi from Galicia, a Torah scholar, who spent his evenings arguing the Talmud in Yiddish with Menahem Haïm Davidowicz, called Mendi, another more modernist rabbi. Wachsmann was a small, frail man who drew on deep reserves of faith for the energy he needed to make his stand against the camp. While some men took only weeks to lapse into *Muselmänner*, he was still on his feet after two years in Monowitz.

It was Wachsmann's job to go and fetch the soup from the kitchens at eleven o'clock. When he returned half an hour later, he was greeted by questions. Is there much soup today? Is it liquid or thick? At midday, the whole crew trooped to the hut with their spoons. No one wanted to be first in the queue and get the most liquid helping. When it came to the turn of a friend, the Kapo would dip his ladle deep so as to dredge a few vegetables from the bottom of the *Kessel*, but it did not happen often, because the bottom of the *Kessel* was his. In the hut where they bolted their litres of soup, the stove roared, and the *Häftlinge* huddled together, dozed, and dreamed for a few minutes. At one o'clock the Kapo turned them all outside, into the wind and the snow. The Polish foreman stood there brandishing his watch, to hurry them back to work, and Levi recorded Reznik's words: "*Si j'avey un chien, je ne le chasse pas dehors*"[54] — "If I had a dog, I wouldn't chase it out of doors" (*Man 70/76*).

In the Monowitz camp, everybody knew that in Birkenau Jews were being gassed around the clock, even though they were out of sight of the vast tongues of flame that flared from the chimneys of the crematoria ovens. Of the Greek Jews from Salonica, a handful of survivors remained. One of them — his name was Felicio — knew Levi, and called out to him: "*L'année prochaine à la maison ... à la maison par la cheminée!*" — "Next year back home ... home up the chimney!" (*Man 72/78*).

Primo Levi used the word "ruthless" to describe the instinct for survival in the Greeks. It was this stubborn insistence, which led to theft, ferocity, and unprincipled behaviour, that Levi the moralist noticed both in the Greeks from Salonica and in Paul Steinberg — "Henri." Steinberg describes how he managed to have a food parcel sent to him through a worker in the French organization, the STO, although half of it was gone by the time it reached him. Now it occurred to him to invest his tin of sardines in his survival, instead of consuming it in private. It was a calculated risk, but the very young Steinberg was a gambler. So he took the tin to the fearsome *Lagerälteste*, who was known to beat *Häftlinge* to death with a spade, to thank him for having granted him permission to go to the *KB* to get treatment for his injured leg. The gamble paid off because the killer had a flaw: he loved flattery, and was to save his protégé's life on several occasions. "It turned out to be the most profitable investment of my life — the dividends fell like rain."

Steinberg also writes:

I had to be very clever, and from the start I watched my subjects coldly, with a clinical eye. I would edge slowly foward, feeling my way. Their intrinsic instability, in fact a genuine madness was a constant danger. It was their common denominator, whose violent symptoms were utterly unpredictable even to those who knew them best. So, psychologically speaking, I practised all the circus arts — animal tamer, tightrope walker, and even conjuror. And at this game, I made rapid strides.

Forty years later, when analysing this type of behaviour and locating it in what he called "the gray zone," Primo Levi sought to trace its roots: "[T]he harsher the oppression, the more widespread among the oppressed is the willingness to collaborate with the power" (*DS 43/28*). And besides, where does collaboration begin or end? How far could it be argued that the fact of slaving under duress, in every kind of weather, on the Buna's construction sites and plant, in the service of the German war machine, was itself an act of collaboration?

It was the very privileges — inevitably won by some kind of collaboration — enjoyed by Hermann Langbein, who worked in the offices of the main Auschwitz camp as a member of the secret resistance organization (founded by Communists), that gave him the power to act. Langbein was half Jewish. He had fought in Spain in the International Brigade, and then had taken refuge in France, like many of his comrades. The Vichy government gave him up to the Germans, who deported him first to Dachau and then to Auschwitz, as one of the earliest prisoners. In *Menschen in Auschwitz* he wrote: "In order to be able to consider a course of action, any organization must first secure tolerable living conditions for the people it trusted. It also had to try its hardest to place its members in positions of influence."

Not all of the prisoners who escaped the first selection for the gas chamber on arrival in Auschwitz had belonged in their previous lives to some anti-Fascist political organization, that would do what it could to achieve a better fate for those members it managed to identify in time, and so feed the germ of secret resistance that had sprung up. In this context Langbein cites Benedikt Kautsky, who was a prisoner in Monowitz: "It benefited the inmates for these posts to be occupied by politicals, but ... they had to have unusual strength of character if they were not to be corrupted either by the power entailed, or by the material advantages."

Those who could not hope for any kind of help attempted to survive by coming to some arrangement with their own idea of good, whose scope was bound to vary hugely from one individual to the next. In *The Drowned and the Saved*, which looks at the circumstances that led some prisoners to collaborate, Primo Levi first makes the point that in cases of this kind "it is imprudent to hasten to issue a moral judgement. It must be clear that the greatest responsibility lies with the system, the very structure of the totalitarian state; the concurrent guilt on the part of the individual big and small collaborators (never likeable, never transparent) is always difficult to evaluate" (*DS 44/28*). The laws of common morality no longer applied. The victims came face to face with their oppressors, who sometimes belonged to the prisoner group, and who felt all the more cut off from their comrades because the privilege they earned was so important. Under this heading, Primo classed the small fry of petty functionaries, "sweepers, kettle washers, night-watchmen, bed smoothers ...

checkers of lice and scabies, messengers, interpreters, assistants' assistants" (*DS 44/29*).

Dealing with the case of the *Sonderkommandos* of Auschwitz and the rest of the extermination camps of Eastern Europe, Levi speaks of an "*impotentia judicandi*" that prohibits judgement. The fate of the members of these Special Kommandos, whose job was to clear the corpses out of the gas chambers and then to burn them, was an abomination beyond all others. Chosen on arrival at the Auschwitz ramp both for their strength and on grounds of physiognomy, these prisoners were taken straight to the crematorium to start work, and were kept in total isolation from the rest of the camp. Those who did not throw themselves into the flames in their horror, and did not refuse to carry out the work (435 Jews from Corfu were gassed on 22 July 1944 immediately after rejecting the duties of the *Sonderkommando*), were incorporated at once into these crews, which worked in shifts round the clock. These men were adequately fed and generously supplied with alcohol. It was they who kept the crematoria ovens working and they who dealt with the deportees dispatched to the gas chambers right after leaving the train, and delivered by trucks to the crematorium complex not knowing what an imminent death awaited them. Jews would emerge naked from the changing room and enter the gas chamber, which was disguised as a collective shower room. After their death, a team of the *Sonderkommando* wearing gas masks and working at high speed under the whips and clubs of the SS had to remove the bloody, tangled corpses, with the help of iron crooks to lever them apart, then extract the gold teeth and bridges, and shear the women's hair. Other teams would sort and stack the clothes, inspect and collect the baggage, move the bodies and then incinerate them in the crematorium furnaces built by Topf und Söhne of Erfurt or in open-air pyres or pits, collect the ashes, use wooden mortars to grind up bones not fully consumed by the flames, and dump the ashes in ponds and fields, along roads, or in rivers nearby. The Auschwitz *Sonderkommando* contained between seven hundred and a thousand men.

Hermann Langbein, often cited by Primo Levi, and who makes use of Levi's work in his book, *Menschen in Auschwitz* mentions the evidence given in 1945 by Sigismund Bendel, a survivor of a *Sonderkommando*, to a British military court: "The prisoners of the *Sonderkommando* had to baste the corpses with the grease that streamed off the pyres so that they burned better.... One hour later, everything is back in order. The men remove the ashes from the pit and make a heap of them. The next convoy is delivered to Crematorium IV."

The members of the special squad were periodically liquidated, and the initiation ordeal for the replacement crew consisted of burning their predecessors' bodies. Seventeen years after the liberation of Auschwitz, searches made at the request of the former inmate electrician Henry Porebski led to the retrieval of documents written by certain members of the *Sonderkommando* and buried in the ground near Crematorium II. Despite their long containment underground it proved possible to decipher some of these carefully stored notes. As the inmate doctor Lucie Adelsberger wrote, the members of the *Sonderkommando* "no longer looked human. These were crazed, ravaged faces."[55] According to the report by Rudolf Vrba and Alfred Wetzler, compiled after their escape from Auschwitz, "they were always disgustingly dirty, unbelievably bedraggled and stupefied, brutal and lost to shame. It was not uncommon for them to kill one another."[56] There were cases of members of the *Sonderkommando* having to escort their own parents to the crematorium. Krystyna Zywulska, a Polish Jew who escaped during the evacuation march from Auschwitz in January 1945, recalled how she asked one of these men how he could possibly bear such a task, and he replied:

> I want to live.... In our job, if you don't got mad on the first day, you get used to it.... They put all my family in the gas chamber, but I want to live so that I can bear witness and be revenged.... Do you think they're monsters, the men in the special Kommando? I tell you they are just like other people, only a lot more unhappy.[57]

The first attempted revolt failed late in 1942. Its authors were denounced by a comrade and gassed in the main Auschwitz camp. In October 1944, after twelve successive special squads had come and gone in Auschwitz, the leaders of the camp Resistance smuggled a message to the latest generation to say that its 663 members were to be liquidated, because new plans for an uprising had come to the ears of a German common-law prisoner who had warned the SS. Other versions claim that it was a member of the Kommando who had given the warning. The fact remains that this badly kept secret prevented the crews in the four crematoria from coordinating and synchronizing their plans. Some of the *Sonderkommando* prisoners blew up Crematorium IV, then some 450 men made a run for the nearby woods, having first cut the wire of the women's camp. They were hunted down and killed. Four SS men were killed and at least twelve wounded. Similar uprisings took place at Sobibor and Treblinka.

Levi, who took Hermann Langbein's *Menschen in Auschwitz* as a main source for his study of the *Sonderkommandos* wrote in *The Drowned and the Saved* that it is impossible for us to imagine what the men of the *Sonderkommandos* went through. He also remarked that the newcomers chosen on the ramp "felt on the threshold of the darkness and terror of an unearthly space" (*DS 51/35*).

The Nazis, exerting all the hatred and all the perversity of which they were capable, set out to compel Jews to participate in the destruction of the Jewish people, reckoning to prove that the *Untermenschen* — "sub-men" — were unworthy to live, because they did not draw the line at destroying one another. According to Levi, the SS in the depth of their wickedness wanted to shift the burden of their crime on to their victims. It was a victory for them to share a foul complicity — even if it was also a forced, imposed complicity — with the members of the *Sonderkommandos*. This principle was put into practice throughout the concentrationary system, where a small number of SS men delegated to their prisoners the infliction of terror and often of death.

In telling the story of a football match played between the "crematorium ravens" and the SS, Levi eavesdrops on the thoughts of the SS: "[Y]ou are no longer the people who reject idols. We have embraced you, corrupted you, dragged you to the bottom with us. You are like us, you proud people, dirtied with your own blood, as we are. You too, like us and like Cain, have killed the brother. Come, we can play together" (*DS* 55/38).

As he pursues his meditation, Levi turns to another atrocious incident also related by Langbein. It concerns the case of a girl of sixteen who was discovered alive on the floor of the gas chamber, in the midst of a heap of dead bodies. At first the men of the *Sonderkommando* hid and warmed her, gave her some meat broth to drink, and asked her questions. She was so utterly at a loss that she did not know where she was or what had happened to her. The men called the doctor attached to their Kommando, and seeing that the girl might live he gave her an injection. Then Muhsfeld arrived — an SS supervisor who was tried, condemned, and hanged in Cracow in 1947. When the case was explained to him he decided that she was too young to be relied on to keep quiet, and therefore she must die. One of his subordinates put a bullet in the back of her neck. With an echo of Hannah Arendt, Levi concluded that Muhsfeld was an ordinary man who deserved his death sentence but who would not have behaved as he did if he had lived "in a different environment and epoch" (*DS* 57/40).

At the end of his commentary on the facts collected by Langbein about the behaviour of the members of the *Sonderkommando*, Levi asks for a suspension of judgement on the "crematorium ravens":

> I repeat, I believe that no one is authorised to judge them, not those who lived through the experience of the Lager and even less those who did not live through it. I would invite anyone who dares pass judgement to carry out upon himself, with sincerity, a conceptual experiment: let him imagine, if he can, that he has lived for months or years in a ghetto, tormented by chronic hunger, fatigue [overcrowding] and humiliation; that he has seen die around him, one by one, his beloved; that he is cut off from the world, unable to receive or transmit news; that, finally, he is loaded on to a train, eighty or a hundred persons to a boxcar; that he travels towards the unknown, blindly, for sleepless days and nights; and that he is at last flung inside the walls of an undecipherable inferno. This, it seems to me, is the true *Befehlnotstand*, the "state of compulsion following an order": not the one systematically and impudently invoked by the Nazis dragged to judgement, and later on (but in their footsteps) by the war criminals of many other countries. (*DS* 59/42)

Cut off in Monowitz-Buna, Primo Levi did not know what had become of Luciana Nissim and Vanda Maestro, who had been taken on foot to Birkenau. Their initiation had been very like his own: they had been shorn, and had passed through the shower with neither soap nor towel, in a room where a freezing draught blew through the window. Luciana Nissim had had her personal toiletries stolen. Then the women were taken to another room, where they put on the worn, striped, ill-fitting clothes. They stayed there all night with nothing to eat or drink. Vanda Maestro rested her head in Luciana Nissim's lap. They were the only ones in the convoy whose families had not been deported with them. The well-dressed, healthy women inmates who had greeted them the previous day had disappeared. One of them had stolen Vanda's attractive shoes. Gruel was dished out, and a small piece of bread like a kind of grey stone. The functionaries they had glimpsed the day before came to register the women and noted down their age, profession, languages spoken, date of arrest, and their family's place of residence. They received a number and a letter indicating their country of origin, inscribed in a yellow star, on a scrap of white fabric, which they had to wear on their left sleeve.

Doctor Bianca Morpurgo, from Genoa, who was correctly dressed, and worked in the *Revier*, the sick-bay, came looking for information about the transport. She herself had arrived on the second transport dispatched from the San Vittorio prisons in Milan. When the women asked her what had happened to those who had been loaded into trucks, she wept as she revealed that by that time every one of them had died in the gas chamber. No one would believe her. They thought she was mad, and advised her to go away and keep her tall stories to herself.

They were lined up five abreast and taken to Block 9, which housed a thousand women. The floor was beaten earth. The prisoners slept in sixes, eights, or tens on three-tier wooden bunks, and the two rows of bunks were separated by brickwork partitions. At the entrance to the hut was the fairly comfortable room that belonged to the *Blockälteste*, the elder of the hut. After that came a space decorated with painted flowers, and on a wall, in big letters, the inscription: "The Block will be your home." The Block was not heated, and the prisoners began their quarantine weeping with hunger and cold. Luciana and Vanda huddled together while the *Häftlinge* looked at the newcomers with indifference or dislike, because they came from the world before Auschwitz. Only a short time ago they had still been free women, with their families, and because of that they encountered a pitiless reception, without a word of comfort. A few Frenchwomen who had arrived a few days previously asked them to be brave and promised them that in two months' time the war would be over.

Vanda and Luciana spent thirty days in the quarantine Block. At four o'clock they would be roused from their sleep by the order "*Aufstehen!*" and would run to the stinking collective latrines. Then they received a drink of ersatz coffee, before lining up on the roll-call square, whether it was raining or freezing. After reporting back to the Block they went straight out again, their wooden sabots sinking into the mud, to perform all sorts of chores. Because they did not understand orders barked in German or Polish, the Italian women were sworn at and beaten. At eleven o'clock they received a floury soup with a few floating vegetables, and took turns to eat because each bowl had to be shared by five or six prisoners. No one had a spoon. After evening roll-call they were given a chunk of bread, twenty grams of margarine, a spoonful of stewed fruit, and a small piece of cheese, or a slice of salami.

The women talked about nothing but food, and the stews they would cook in a couple of months' time, when the war was over, while Luciana and Vanda stared desperately at those who still possessed a piece of bread. In *Lager* A, where Vanda and Luciana spent their quarantine period, there was also the *Revier*. *Lager* B contained the inmates who were already working.

Little by little, as she gleaned scraps of converstaion, Luciana Nissim came to realize that the people judged unfit for work as they stood on the ramp were being gassed and burned in the crematorium furnaces. A *Blocksperre* (hut confinement) was ordered each time a new transport arrived; the *Häftlinge* were forbidden to leave their Block and see the smoke pour from the chimneys. All of them knew what it meant, and everyone shivered.

Luciana Nissim did not have to suffer brutality from her fellow inmates, because they knew that she was a doctor, and they might have need of her when she started working:

> Each woman fights ferociously for life, her poor, desperate, animal life. And in her own eyes that life is worth the sacrifice of all the rest. This moral death, this mockery of all sense of solidarity and neglect of human dignity are much more wretched than physical death. The fact of their having been reduced to the condition of grubs, a shadow of themselves, of having killed within themselves the consciousness of their own humanity, having tainted the divine image, is the abject guilt of the Nazis.[58]

At the end of the quarantine month, Luciana Nissim was posted as a physician to the *Revier* Block, where the sick lay crammed together, suffering from a mixture of diseases, on bare pallets without sheets. The filthy blankets, which were never cleaned or disinfected, spread scabies, and because the infirmary had no medicines to treat this infection the sick were covered in scabs and frantically scratched till they bled. Even then, the situation was much better than during the emergency a few months before, when an outbreak of louse-borne exanthematic typhus had decimated the wards. The infirmary consisted of twelve Blocks, each one housing about two hundred patients. Block 29 was reserved for Aryans; Block 18, where selections took place, for internal diseases; Block 5 was reserved for surgery, but the doctor had no sterile equipment available, and so few dressings that there could only be two operations a week. Jews who suffered from tuberculosis were not entitled to be treated. They were gassed.

Luciana Nissim reports that when people came into her Block they were sickened by the stench of pus, yet in spite of these dreadful conditions some patients came through their illnesses. Block 24 housed women suffering from diarrhoea and gastroenteritis, owing to a diet deficient in protein, fat, and vitamins. Only as a last resort would prisoners come to Block 24, where selections were frequent. Those who enjoyed the extraordinary privilege of a food parcel would recover. The rest would die. For in the *Revier*, where dirt prevailed and there were no medicines, the nurses cared nothing for the patients and would steal bread and soup from those no longer strong enough to respond. This was the ethos of the hospital in the extermination camp of Birkenau, a few metres away from the gas chambers. Doctors Hans Koenig and Josef Mengele required each inmate's hospital chart to be immaculately kept, with temperature and pulse graphs drawn in red and blue pencil, diagnosis, history of the illness, and regular observations. Luciana Nissim had to see to it that serological examinations were performed for abdominal and petechial typhus. She and her colleagues took good care not to enter any diagnosis of cardiac illness or malaria in the records, because that was a death sentence. The admittance procedure was identical to the practice described by Primo Levi in Monowitz.

The naked bodies of patients who died in the night were carried out of the hut and left on the ground outside, sprawled on top of one another and covered with a blanket, until morning. Then the *Häftlinge* of the *Leichenkommando*, corpse squad, came to collect them, threw them into a truck and drove them away to the crematorium. Those whose temperatures had been steady for three days had to return to work in their Kommando. They soon came back, knowing that this time they would not come out alive. Luciana Nissim did not have the heart to discharge them so quickly, and she would falsify their charts so as to keep them a few days longer in the *Revier*. Those whose number had been noted by Doctor Koenig in the course of a selection knew that the gas chamber awaited them. They wept in despair, but when evening came they were loaded naked on to the trucks that made the rounds of the Auschwitz camps to deliver the condemned to the crematorium. One April night in 1944 three hundred women were gassed, not one of them seriously ill. They included about twenty Italians. On their way to the furnaces, the French women sang the "Marseillaise." One Jewish woman sang "Hatikvah."[59]

Luciana Nissim worked at first in the *Durchfall* (diarrhoea) Block, then in Block 12, which replaced Block 18 after the April selection. She had in her care some fifty Jews of various nationalities, but mainly Italians, seriously ill, unaware that they were soon to be murdered.

In Birkenau, where the women prisoners, supervised by SS men with trained attack dogs, did work as arduous as the men's in munitions plants and outdoor construction sites, Luciana Nissim enjoyed the privilege of sharing a bedroom with five colleagues, each with a cot of her own. She was not beaten, and at night, after roll-call, she was free to go and visit Vanda Maestro, who was growing weaker by the day, because she had failed to acquire the slightest of privileges.

Her eyes were fading and her mind darkening. Her legs were bloated and her feet swollen. She moved with difficulty in her enormous sabots. One hard word and she burst into tears. I stayed with her for a while. "What did you eat today? Was the soup good? Did you have enough? Do you really believe, as they say, that Turkey has entered the war? That the Americans have entered Bologna? That here, around the camp, there are thousands of partisans who are going to set us free?" — "No, my dear, you know that none of that news is true. But it's good to believe it because it gives people courage."

Vanda is kind and affectionate. People try to help her because they see her like this, pitiful and good. She grows weaker from day to day, and she is so afraid. I stay a while with her. I give her a piece of advice. Every woman represents family, friends, Turin, for the other. One day she asks me: "If I die, and you have a daughter, will you call her Vanda?" I promise I will.

Other Italians in the same Block looked for help to Luciana Nissim. She fled, because she had nothing to offer. When springtime came, Doctors Bianca Morpurgo and Luciana Nissim did not go straight to bed, but stayed outdoors and sat in a ditch, looking up at the sky. "Even in Auschwitz you see the stars shine." Around them, searchlight beams played over the electrified barbed wire. Both women thought about their families, and the men they loved, and wondered when their turn would come to die. They were frightened as they watched the vast red gush of flame that poured from the crematorium chimney, constantly haunting their thoughts while hunger racked their bodies. Luciana sang a Piedmontese song, a song of the mountains she loved. She thought of the thousands of women who suffered in the camp.

The women in the orchestra were well fed, wore pretty clothes, a blue hat with white polka dots, and played by the exit from the camp, when the long columns of prisoners set off to work. Twice a week the orchestra came to the *Revier* and played Viennese waltzes and love songs for the sick. Its beautiful singer had been a performer in a Viennese café-concert. Her father and everyone she loved had died in the gas chambers.

In May 1944 Luciana saw the arrival of the Hungarian Jews who were deported and murdered *en masse* in a matter of weeks. The trains drew up in the camp, two hundred metres from the crematoria.

We had orders to stay in our Blocks when the convoys arrived, but we managed to see. We saw so many little heads showing a worried face and trying to see what they had coming to them. The first time I saw a transport arrive, I cried. I saw a man lift his child out of the wagon and put him down on the ground. It was so sad. There was so much love for

151

his child, who didn't know what it meant to be Jewish in Auschwitz. I knew. It was all so frightful, and so sad, that I cried with the feeling of all the world's sorrow inside me. One gets used to that too.

Mountains of useful objects and family treasures piled up on the ramp. The men and women were separated at once, and two groups selected. The young and able-bodied to the left, the great majority to the right. The Hungarians waited patiently in line, not imagining that ashes might be all that remained of their families and friends. They thought that they were going for a shower and a medical check. There were so many that the gas chambers could not make room for them all. The crematoria were overloaded, and the SS had big pits dug, where people stunned by gas were burned. The giant flames lit up the night sky of Auschwitz, a dreadful smell of burnt flesh filled the air, and suddenly screams of horror, children's screams, rose from the crowd.

Those who escaped immediate death were taken to camps C and D, still under construction, where there was no piped water and rain had flooded the unfinished huts. Here there were no bunks: the deportees slept in the mud.

An epidemic of exanthematic typhus and scarlet fever broke out among the Hungarians. Doctor Mengele sent all those infected to the gas chamber. Nothing had changed in Auschwitz, although the Allies had landed in Normandy and an attempt on Hitler's life had been tried and failed. Luciana Nissim and her comrades anticipated a rapid end to the war, but did not expect to survive, knowing that now that the Nazis realized they had lost they would do everything they could to wipe out their victims completely, so that none would be left to testify to the enormity of their crimes.

At the end of August 1944 the SS asked for a woman doctor to accompany a transport of *Häftlinge* who were to work in armaments factories in Germany. Luciana Nissim volunteered, and left Auschwitz for a camp attached to Buchenwald, near Kassel, where conditions were hard but there was no extermination camp. Early in April 1945, after the American air raids had begun, the women from this camp were taken by train to a place near Leipzig, and about a month after that, when the Germans abandoned Leipzig, the SS drove thousands of women on an evacuation march. Luciana Nissim and a comrade pretended to collapse by the side of the road, and then made a run for the surrounding forest, where they were joined by a young Slovak girl. They spent four days in the forest, sleeping by day and walking by night, with nothing to sustain them but a hunk of bread and some sugar, until they came to a village. There they stayed with a woman and her children at a nearby farm until one day American tanks reached the village, and Luciana and her comrades went to greet them. It turned out that their commander was also Jewish, and also a doctor. He took the women to a camp in Rima, and Luciana Nissim, who was in reasonable physical condition, started work in a hospital for refugees from all over occupied Europe.

In Auschwitz, all the women who had arrived on the same transport as herself had died, among them Vanda Maestro, who had had the misfortune to be put to work in an outdoor Kommando. Vanda had held out until September 1944. Perhaps, like Primo Levi, she might have been assigned to the Buna laboratories during the final months, but she was already too sick. The last time that Luciana Nissim saw her, she was sitting on the ground outside one of the *Schonungsblock* huts, with her bloated legs tucked under her, and covered with oedemas, sores, and phlegmons.

Vanda Maestro was twenty-five years old when she joined the last selection for the Birkenau gas chambers in October 1944. Her friends had dosed her with narcotics to numb some of the horror of her final dreadful hours.

7   Auschwitz (Part II)

Each morning in Monowitz, Levi and his comrades set out in lines of five abreast for the sinister complex of the Buna chemical plant. Including the German managers and technical staff, the workers in the plant spoke some twenty languages. Each nationality lived in its own *Lager*. Jews were interned in Monowitz, which was a *Judenlager*, and *Vernichtungslager*.[1]

In the middle of the constantly expanding Buna construction site stood the factory — which was never to be completed — and the Carbide Tower, built by slave labour shipped to Poland from all over Europe. Levi wrote that its bricks were "cemented by hate; hate and discord, like the Tower of Babel" (*Man* 73/79). In Yiddish, the Jews called it *Bobelturm*.

Primo Levi worked outside, wielding a shovel with the rest of his starving comrades, who could not prevent themselves from talking about food, and grumbling at each other for doing so. He too yielded to these visions, and thought about the bowl of spaghetti he had been sharing in Fossoli with Vanda, Franco, and Luciana when they heard the news that they were to leave for the East the next day. To think that the spaghetti had been so good, and the help-ings so generous, that it sometimes wasn't finished ...!

Each man had his own way of managing his bread ration. Newcomers made it last as long as possible by splitting it up into portions to be eaten in stages during the day. The low numbers, in other words the "veterans," were so hungry that they wolfed it down in seconds, advancing any number of sound dietary reasons to justify their inability to defer it for more than an hour.

Every now and then the Kommando's master "organizer," Templer, would locate a pot of soup rejected by the Polish workers, or a cartload of turnips left unguarded near the factory kitchens. One day he supplied his comrades in the Kommando with three litres each of extra soup, which they spread out through the day. By staving off hunger for a while, this thick, hot soup revived the human feelings in the *Häftlinge*. With stomachs full, they could think about their wives and families, lost in the gas chambers, and be "unhappy in the manner of free men" (*Man* 76/82)

In all the Nazi camps, and in concentrationary slang, "organize" meant "steal." In order to survive, it was literally vital for the *Häftling* to learn to steal any object, substance, or material that came his way during working hours, then smuggle it back to the camp and barter it for a ration of bread or a litre of soup. "Organizing" consisted in illicitly acquiring anything one needed — and which existed in plenty somewhere in the camp — often by bribing the SS, the Kapos, and the whole pathetic hierarchy of the *Häftlinge*.

Hermann Langbein cites the case of Bernhard Rakers, an SS *Rapportführer* in Monowitz, who allowed the prisoners to break rules and then blackmailed them: "He had the *Häftlinge* steal all sorts of things for him: they had no choice if they wanted to be left in peace. When these items were intended for his wife, he sent them off in truckloads. But quite a lot went to support his many mistresses."

On their side, when those opportunist inmates who not only realized how the camp worked but never missed a chance to do business, "organized" on behalf of themselves and their closest comrades, it was inevitably at the expense of the rest. In a collection of his articles and short stories published in Italy as *Lilit e altri racconti*,[2] Levi recalls the case of a Polish Jew named Rappoport, who had studied medicine at Pisa University and who saw what he must do to survive.

> He lived in the Camp like a tiger in the jungle, striking down and practicing extortion on the weak, and avoiding those who were stronger; ready to corrupt, steal, fight, pull in his belt, lie, or play up to you, depending on the circumstances. He was therefore an enemy, but not despicable or repugnant. (*Reprieve* 3–4/19–20)

Doctor Hans Münch explained in a report written in 1947 that the number of prisoners who were able to eat a normal diet in Auschwitz depended on the scale of corruption, because that was the only way to make up the shortfall in calories.[3] Owing to the inroads made by the diversion of the soup supply at various stages of its production and distribution, instead of the daily 700 calories originally allocated, only 600 reached the prisoners. From a thousand rations of soup, 100,000 calories went missing. Now, even the inmate who was doing light work needed an extra 600 calories. Only the "veterans" managed to get and keep the much-coveted softer jobs, and knew how to "organize," but even so Doctor Münch concluded that, assuming a basic ration of 1,500 calories, only 166 inmates in a thousand could subsist, given the 100 calories that were skimmed off before the food could reach them. Similarly, the evening ration — sausage, cheese, jam, bread, sugar, and margarine — also suffered wastage. Taking his calculations further, Doctor Münch established that, out of a thousand "non-organizing" prisoners, 79 light workers could survive. Ultimately, fewer than 25 per cent of the inmates were adequately fed, while their comrades were condemned to certain death. The higher the number of veterans, the greater their need to "organize," and the faster the rest would die. No one could last for a year without regular extra food, and rarely did anyone who reached the one-year mark become a *Muselmann*.

Levi had the "luck" to arrive in the camp in 1944, when the food ration had been raised for two years running. The average life expectancy had risen from three or four to six and a half months. This improvement obviously did more good to those with light jobs, probably indoors, than to outdoor, all-weather Kommandos.

The moment he returned from Auschwitz, Levi began to write: he had to bear witness to the things he had seen and personally experienced. Forty years later, his conscience had still granted no rest. In his poem "The Survivor" he ordered the shadows of his lost companions to leave him in peace, he who had not "usurped anyone's bread," even when he "organized." Nevertheless, in *The Drowned and the Saved*, his stern meditation took him to the point of impugning his own testimony, on the ground that neither he nor any of those who survived had touched bottom. According to Levi, the true witnesses "have not returned to tell about it." These true witnesses were the *Muselmänner*, together with all those who did not enter the camp but were driven straight into the gas chambers with whips, and the victims of the *Einsatzkommandos* that shot and killed the entire Jewish population of Byelorussia, Lithuania, Estonia, Latvia, and the Ukraine. The "drowned" were the children thrown into and buried alive in the mass graves that the SS made their Jewish victims dig before they butchered them, and the children burned alive in order to economize on hydrogen cyanide.

Levi referred to the sense of guilt and anguish felt by those survivors whose comrades, and often every member of whose families, had been exterminated. He felt shame and grief for the crimes that others had committed. In *If This Is A Man* he wanted both to bear witness and to issue an indictment. The few anecdotes are used to reinforce a reasoned demonstration of the concentrationary system, to elucidate and analyse it. Those memories that did not specifically further that purpose were temporarily set aside. So *If This Is A Man* is a short, clear, sober book, very dense and telling. The reader is spared the scenes of cruelty, the scientific details of diseases suffered by the prisoners, the technical data about the gas chambers. The general tone of the account is less harsh than that of the report produced with Leonardo De Benedetti. It was not till much later that Levi portrayed his comrades in captivity in a series of sketches in which he described daily life in the camp, and the behaviour of exceptional characters projected into a world where madness was the norm.

Of course the camp had barbarous, ruthless laws of its own, but it had also retained distorted memories of the society that produced it. Hence, business went on. There was even a Stock Exchange, where the trader exchanged and bought — and could even sell his shirt. Bread was the inmates' legal tender: half a ration of bread for a litre of soup. Why did a man get rid of his only shirt at a given moment, when he was forbidden to wear his striped jacket without it? If the Kapo found out, you tried to make out that it had been stolen in the washrooms. It finished in a beating, for the Kapo was no fool. All the same, if any prisoner who had been resourceful enough to acquire or steal a spare shirt chanced to see a cartload of washing emerge from disinfection carrying a cargo of new ones from Canada's unending supply, he would try to dispose of the spare as quickly as he could. The appearance of the shirts signalled a

Wäschetauschen, when new shirts were issued for old ones. The sudden glut would cause prices to tumble on the Monowitz Exchange, especially because the shirts from disinfection were likely to be in better condition than those that the inmates had sometimes been wearing for over two months. This was because, in the absence of handkerchiefs, toilet paper, socks, or towels, it was possible to cut up the sleeves or tail of your shirt as a poor substitute. When the washing was due for collection, there was a rush to find needles and thread to camouflage the worst of the damage.

The Stock Exchange was located in the north-east corner of the camp, as far away as possible from the huts of the SS. Dealing took place in the open air in summer, and in the washrooms in winter. Starving prisoners prowled there in search of a windfall, looking for an edge in the transaction. For example, perhaps you would swap a half-ration of bread for a litre of soup, then scoop out the few scraps of potato at the bottom before trying to parlay the remainder into another piece of bread, then that same bread for another litre of soup, and then repeat the whole procedure, keeping the life-prolonging solids, converting warm water into bread.

The trading rate for turnips, carrots, and potatoes varied according to the level of corruption among the storehouse guards. Another product much in demand was mahorka, a low-grade tobacco, always in short supply. In theory, 50-gram packets were available in the canteen in return for bonus vouchers that were supposed to be awarded to "good workers." In practice, these bonus vouchers were more or less monopolized by the Kapos and Prominents, and hence became another kind of money, whose value fluctuated like the other commodities. Aryan voucher-holders were also entitled to the services of women in the *Frauenblock*, the brothel. In general, mahorka served as a currency for those who could sell it to civilian workers in the Buna, who paid with rations of their own bread, more substantial than the camp variety. Levi wrote that the *Häftlinge* ate some of their receipts and invested the rest on a market whose connections reached as far as Cracow.

A more protracted sequence might work like this. In return for a bonus voucher, a *Häftling* would buy a packet of mahorka, swap it for a ration of bread, and barter the bread for a shirt in good or in poor condition. In poor condition, with luck it could be swapped for a shirt in better condition at the next *Wäschetauschen*. A shirt in fair condition could eventually be sold — by taking a considerable risk — to a civilian worker at the Buna, in return for six to ten rations of bread. For these ten rations, the daring *Häftling* might acquire, in this instance, a new shirt, because not to wear a shirt could condemn the offender to the coalmines, and a quick death by exhaustion. Civilian workers convicted of the same crime were liable to serve a sentence in a special section of the *KZ* known as the *E-Lager* — "E" for *Erziehung*, education. The Aryans were segregated and worked in special Kommandos. They kept their hair, did not undergo selections, and were able to collect their stored belongings at the end of their sentence.

Starving and desperate new arrivals often sold their gold dentures for rations of bread on the deferred payment system. The sale of dentures was a serious crime, because Jewish gold was scheduled for the vaults of the Reichsbank. Paul Steinberg describes how he traded in the Buna with two gold teeth pulled from an old man taken to hospital in the *KB*. The deal agreed was twelve rations of bread in return for the two teeth. When the Frenchman in the STO who had pocketed the teeth and given a down-payment of two rations reneged on his promise to deliver the rest by instalments every two days, Steinberg presented the old man with eight rations of bread either bought on his own account or gleaned from his own allowance. The man still died, and Steinberg, who seems to have been a king of organization, with a string of contacts, friends, and protectors, remarks that this was "the sole good deed" he could claim to his credit.

The cleverest traders on the Exchange were the few Greeks from Salonica who had escaped the near-obliteration of their people in the gas chambers. Levi recalled how they had enriched the *Lager* slang with words and phrases such as "*caravana*," bowl, "*klepsi-klepsi*," theft, and "*la comedera es buena*" — "the soup is good." Levi felt a certain admiration for the Greeks who had raised theft to such a fine and systematic art. In his view, they were nevertheless "the most civilized" and cohesive national group in the hell that was the camp, because although they were champion thieves they displayed a deep aversion to violence, and preserved their sense of human dignity.

Levi, who was to become an artful thief himself, describes how the grease used to "clean" the universal wooden-soled boots was brought into the hut. According to the regulations, it was compulsory for boots to be greased every day, but the substance required to do the job was not supplied by the camp administration. The *Blockälteste* got hold of it by swapping some of the extra soup that he received every day, once he had shared a certain amount of it among his friends and "minor officials." Certain prisoners who worked in factories outside the camp used to fill their bowls with machine oil, and then hand it over to the *Blockälteste* with whom they usually did business. Everything was stolen in the Buna: "light-bulbs, ordinary or shaving-soap, files, pliers, sacks, nails; methyl alcohol is sold to make drinks; while petrol is useful for the rudimentary lighters, prodigies of the secret industry of the Lager craftsmen" (*Man 84/90*).

It was common practice for the doctors and nurses to steal precious medicines such as sulphonamides from the *KB*, and the nurses stole food, clothing, and boots from patients selected for the gas chamber. Similarly, the sick had to surrender their spoons when they entered the hospital, and the nurses would sell them on the Exchange, so that those who came out cured had to invest their first bread ration in buying a new spoon. Even though Canada had millions in store, recovered from the baggage of the dead, the administration did not give them out to the inmates. A thriving trade went on in these essential tools, which were hammered out of pieces of sheet metal by the Buna's *Häftling* blacksmiths and tinsmiths, often with an edge put on the handle, for use as a knife to cut bread.

Part of the flow of stolen goods went into the *Krankenbau*, where the doctors would exchange soup for stomach tubes, thermometers, containers, and coloured pencils for use on temperature charts.

Primo Levi never stole at his comrades' expense, but he did learn to steal from the Buna. The scale of his thieving was small, but on several occasions it kept him alive. "And I would not like to be accused of immodesty if I add that it was our idea, mine and Alberto's, to steal the rolls of graph-paper from the thermographs of the Desiccation Department, and offer them to the Medical Chief of Ka-Be [*KB*] with the suggestion that they be used as paper for pulse–temperature charts" (*Man 85–6/91–2*).

Despite such precarious conditions, Primo Levi continued to observe and analyse the behaviour of the men immersed in the *KZ* universe, and it occurred to him to wonder whether the *Lager*, where men of all ages and backgrounds came up against the most extreme conditions, might not be the ideal place "to establish what is essential and what adventitious to the conduct of the human animal in the struggle for life" (*Man 87/93*). His remarks are qualified. He does not go so far as to say that the *Häftling* is a man who has discarded all of the inhibitions instilled by civilization, but he is bound to accept that, under the pressure of hunger, thirst, cold, fear, and physical suffering, most forms of conventional social behaviour are likely to give way to different attitudes. Levi divides the people of the *Lager* into two categories, "the saved" and "the drowned": those who were able to grow and prosper indefinitely and almost unimpeded, and those who went on sinking, inexorably, from defeat to defeat, and down towards death. Both of these courses were possible because no law intervened to moderate the implacable struggle for survival, where it was every man for himself.

As a matter of fact, the weaker you were, the smaller your chance of receiving some kind of help, whereas the more shrewd, wily, and obviously well-fed you were — proud, in fact, to strut down the camp's muddy streets with a comparatively clean uniform in good condition — the more you were respected, and the more likely to gain further advantages from that fact, so that survival became a thinkable prospect. Primo Levi quotes: "[T]o he that has, will be given; from he that has not, will be taken away" (*Man 88/94*), noting that the stronger, smarter individuals might even make contact with the powers that be, whereas no one felt pity for a *Muselmann*. They were good for nothing: they had no important friends in the inmate hierarchy, they worked in the hardest Kommandos, and they found no ways of bettering their diet. Soon they would die in absolute solitude, and not one of their comrades would miss or remember them. And yet it was they who, as transport followed transport, constituted the changing majority — renewed at the urgent pace set by the gas chamber — of the Auschwitz population.

Those who still lived after a year did not belong to the common class of

Häftling. All of them had to have benefited from favourable circumstances. Perhaps they held a position of power, no matter how modest, or had been able to ply their trade or profession in the service of the camp authorities. Perhaps they had agreed to prostitute themselves, or else they had managed to adapt to the camp in just a few days, and then succeeded in finding — and finding ways to keep — material advantages. That does not mean that all *Muselmänner* had been unable to adapt: often it was ill luck that decided against them. The survivors included *Organisatoren, Kombinatoren,* and *Prominenten*: it is because of this that forty years later, when he came to analyse the world of the *Lager*, Levi denied the survivors the status of witnesses. The true witnesses were "the drowned," those whose memory caused him to write: "I haven't dispossessed anyone/Haven't usurped anyone's bread …/Go back into your mist."

The *Prominenten* ("Prominents"), the camp officials, were the Kapos, cooks, nurses, night guards, sweepers, *Scheissmeister* and *Bademeister*.[4] Aryans would automatically obtain some "Prominent" job, whereas for a Jew to reach the same position was an extraordinary feat, achieved at a high cost.

The Aryan "Prominents" — most of them criminals with sadistic tendencies — could more or less do as they pleased. When they killed a prisoner (and this was quite approved of by the authorities), the register stated that number such-and-such had died. The cause and circumstances of the death were unimportant. Hermann Langbein cites Zenon Rozanski's evidence about the way in which the Auschwitz *Blockältesten* were recruited before the construction of the gas chambers. "The people you'll have under you are Jews. In my Kommando I only want Aryans. Got it?" That night, as the chief of the Kommando had instructed, thirty-seven Jews were killed and their bodies dumped in the shower rooms. In fact the *Prominenten* would eventually forget that they were inmates too, and their fellow prisoners feared them more than the SS, so that if ever one of these privileged sadists was stripped of his power for some reason, he could expected no mercy from his comrades.

As the camp population kept growing and the number of Aryan prisoners was relatively constant, the camp authorities had to entrust responsibilities to Jewish detainees. They were especially common in the labour camps that made up Auschwitz III — and therefore in Monowitz, where Primo Levi was.

> If you take a few people who have been leading a life of slavery and offer them a privileged position, some comforts and the prospect of survival, and if in exchange you require them to reject the natural solidarity with their comrades, you are sure of finding someone. If he holds authority over a handful of unfortunates, holds the right of life or death, he will become cruel and tyrannical, because he knows that, if not, some other, more suitable man will take his place.[5]

The political *Prominenten* proved to be just as cruel and brutal as their common-law criminal colleagues, whether they were Poles, Russians, or Germans. In the eyes of the Nazis, black marketeering was just as much a political crime as having sexual relations with a Jew. For Levi, "the true" politicals, interned in other camps, were the ones who frequently died there, although their living conditions were much less harsh than in Auschwitz. On this point, Hermann Langbein criticizes Levi for drawing no distinctions either among the political "Prominents" or among their Jewish colleagues: "In Monowitz, in 1944, Levi did not know about the red triangle officials who quietly used their positions in the common interest; yet there were many, as witnessed by those who knew the prisoner hierarchy in that camp from the inside."

Langbein goes on to name some of the "reds" who behaved in an exemplary way, such as the Austrian Aigner, who headed the electricity Kommando; Felix Amann, the German Kapo of the disinfection unit, who made the prisoners take showers; the German Franz Malz, from Stettin, Kapo of the anthropometry section, who was shot for saying in front of an SS man that the Germans were going to lose the war; and the *Blockälteste* Hans Röhrig, who refused to help the SS to gas prisoners in the Czech "family camp." As punishment, he had his hair cropped like the other inmates. Langbein also mentions Hiasl Neumeir, who died of typhus in the contagious ward, and refused to inflict beatings on his comrades. That said, Langbein concedes that the German politicals did not readily keep their distance from the Reich.

Levi acknowledged that, in the end, the prisoners who were still in a position to do so focused all of their energy and abilities on their struggle against exhaustion, cold, and hunger, which could involve the most shameful, vicious, and brutal behaviour. In general, it was rare to survive in the *Lager* with nothing at all to blame oneself for.

On the subject of blame, Levi cites a particularly painful episode that happened during his internment in Monowitz. The weather was terribly hot in Auschwitz in August 1944. Late in the morning of 20 August, a force of 127 Flying Fortresses and 100 Mustang fighters appeared in the sky above the camp. The meteorological conditions were ideal. The raid lasted for twenty-eight minutes, during which time a Jewish prisoner, Adam Szaller, seized his opportunity to escape from Monowitz. Part of the Buna plant was wrecked, while the local anti-aircraft defences and nineteen German fighters did no damage at all to the Allied bombers, who were tasked solely against economic targets, and had orders not to attack the crematoria and gas chamber installations — eight kilometres away — on the grounds that the bombs might endanger prisoners' lives. In fact, the Allies knew by now that the Germans had condemned all Jews to death. In any case, this sort of scruple did not stay their hand in the case of Monowitz, where the work force contained ten thousand Jews.

On 25 August, American reconnaissance aircraft flying at an altitude of 10,000 metres took photographs to evaluate the damage caused by the bombing of the I.G. Farben plant. On these photographs the Auschwitz I and Auschwitz III camps can be identified. They also show:

> the women's camp at Auschwitz II Birkenau, the fence, guard towers, main gate and guard post, the ramp inside the camp, a goods train of 33 wagons, about 1,500 people, on their way to the gas chambers and Crematorium I, in which direction a gate has been opened in the fence, as well as Crematoria II and III, with the gas chambers and security installations. In the photograph of the KL of Auschwitz I, all the features of the camp can be identified. It is even possible to make out the inmates lined up outside the reception building waiting to be registered and tattooed.[6]

These photographs were not interpreted during the war, but only thirty-five years later, when the results were published in *Courier International*, in an article by Dino A. Brugioni and Robert Porier.

In a smuggled message of 30 August 1944, addressed to Teresa Lasocka, a member of the underground Polish organization, the Assistance to the Prisoners of Concentration Camps Committee (PWOK), the *Häftling* Stanislaw Klodzinski wrote: "In our camp, the bombing had no effect. However, Buna is quite damaged, so production is limited to carbide. Some prisoners were killed and others injured."[7]

A hot wind blew in the afternoon of 20 August 1944, and parched the throats of the slaves sent to clear away rubble after the Allied raid. Primo Levi was working in a cellar when he discovered a length of pipe with a spigot on it, which he managed to turn far enough for a few drops of water to emerge. At the time there was a severe shortage of water both in the camp and on the Buna site. There seemed to be just under a litre of water in the pipe, and three possibilities occurred to Levi: he could drink only part of the precious liquid, and save the rest for tomorrow; he could pass on the secret of his discovery to the whole Kommando; or he could share it with his friend Alberto. He chose the third alternative, and both of them took turns to lie beneath the spigot and catch the falling drips. On the way back to the camp, one of their Italian comrades, Daniele, who was suffering dreadfully from thirst and had seen what they were up to in the rubble, gave them a reproachful look. Alberto did not survive the death-march that evacuated Auschwitz, but Daniele went with Levi after the Liberation when the Russians transferred inmates to Byelorussia, and during that journey he asked the bitter question: "Why you two and not me?" Years afterwards, when they met during reunions for survivors from the camps, Levi still suffered pangs about the "veil" that hung between himself and Daniele because of the water he had failed to share with him. With remarkable honesty, he asked himself: "Is this belated shame justified or not? I was not able to decide then and I am not able to decide even now, but shame was there and is there, concrete, heavy, perennial" (*DS 81/61*). Commenting on the guilt he felt when he recalled his behaviour on the day of the bombing, he wrote that the code of those days differed from today's, and that those who had not gone through the experience of the *Lager* had no right to appoint themselves as judges.

Levi often sought examples in the Bible or the Talmud, taking the sacred texts of Judaism as a yardstick to judge episodes in the catastrophe suffered by the Jewish people during the eleven years the Nazis were in power. In that context, he did not recall the view of the contributors to the Talmud, who said that if two men walking in the desert had a water bottle with only enough for one man to survive, then the owner of the bottle should drink the water, in order to save a human life, because sharing would amount to killing them both.

Levi wrote in 1986:

> Are you ashamed because you are alive in place of another? And in particular of a man more generous, more sensitive, wiser, more useful, more worthy of living than you? ... no, you find no obvious transgressions, you did not usurp anyone's place, you did not beat anyone (but would you have had the strength to do so?), you did not accept positions (but none were offered to you ...), you did not steal anyone's bread; nevertheless, you cannot exclude it. (*DS 81/62*)

Levi concluded that each man is his brother's Cain. Gnawed and tormented by the feeling of having usurped the right to live, Levi swung towards a state of deep depression. Finding no answer to explain why he had survived when others had died, he arrived at the deluded conclusion (to disprove it one has only to examine his own case, which is far from unique) that: "The worst survived — that is, the fittest; the best all died" (*DS 82/63*).

And now the memory of his murdered comrades broke through again. Their faces came to haunt him: Chaim, the watchmaker from Cracow; Szabo, the Hungarian peasant; Robert, the professor from the Sorbonne; Baruch, the docker from Livorno, who hit back at the Kapo and was felled and slaughtered by three Kapos ganging up together.

Levi believed, at the end of his life, that his dead comrades were better men than the ones who got away. The opinion expressed by his teacher, Nicola Dallaporta, who told him that divine Providence had picked him out to become the chronicler of the *Lager*, seemed to him to be a "monstrous" suggestion, one that shocked him into replying that perhaps he, Primo Levi, the survivor, was alive in another man's place. The survivors were the shrewd ones, those who had luck, those who supplanted their comrades and did not touch bottom. Levi had good reason to observe that it was difficult to muse about Providence in a concentration camp. He was not a believer when he took the train to Auschwitz, and the camp had steeled his belief in the non-existence of God. Nevertheless, he had retained his faith in man, and man's capacity to do good. That is why he devoted a great deal of his time to visiting schools and universities so as to testify to what he had seen and experienced in Auschwitz. When he finally lost the appetite for communicating his experiences, feeling that his language was no longer relevant to his young listeners, his optimism crumbled. At the end of a slow transition, the pessimism of the last year of his life broke through to undermine what he had thought in the aftermath of the war, when his first imperative had been to testify, to tell, and keep on telling everyone he met about the events he had endured.

He had acknowledged in *If This Is A Man* that a great many prisoners had not had fate on their side, and had managed to survive thanks solely to their own strength, intellectual resources, patience, and willpower. But that very fact implied a certain number of acts of rejection, deceit, or hostility towards their comrades.

Levi gives examples of those prisoners who achieved their salvation by shrewd manipulation, or by personal traits that made them perfect denizens of the *Lager*, even though, once at liberty, civil society would have locked them up in a psychiatric hospital or put them in prison. A dwarf called Elias Lindzin, a Polish Jew from Warsaw, registration number 141565, caught Levi's special attention, and makes several appearances in his books. Elias possessed an extraordinary animal strength of mind and body; he was crazy, wild, and violent; an acrobat, thief, and informer. In Auschwitz, he seemed to be happy. His exceptional vigour and skills brought him a kind of impunity. He ate his fill, from unknown sources, poured out a torrent of talk and advice all day, and to anyone, and by demonstrating his ability to carry several 50-kilo sacks of cement at a time, paradoxically he exempted himself from the usual labour duties. His face was intimidating. With a single butt of his head to the stomach, he could knock down a man twice his size. Levi describes him as a madman in *If This Is A Man*, but in *Moments of Reprieve* he portrays Elias as callous, obviously, but armed with a fierce black humour. Speaking of a Jew called Wolf, who had scabies but concealed it from everybody by managing not to scratch himself, Elias remarked that "*Krätzewolf*" — "Scabieswolf" in Yiddish — was one of the Just: "[H]e's a strong character: he doesn't scratch. The Just don't scratch themselves" (*Reprieve 36/60*). One day, Elias sprang at Wolf and pulled up his shirt to expose his stomach, inflamed with scabies. The two of them rolled on the ground in an unequal contest that the dwarf was bound to win, and so Wolf became Krätzewolf. But mind regained control over matter. No one knew how he had managed to lay his hands on a violin, but one Sunday found Wolf sitting on a pile of planks in a corner of the camp, playing for his own pleasure, while Elias, the cynical brute, lay on the ground nearby and listened in rapture.

There is some doubt about Elias's identity, for Primo Levi is not the only survivor of Monowitz who remembered him. According to Paul Steinberg, who came from Berlin and claimed to have had the benefit of his protection several times, Elias — who had worked in a circus — was neither Jewish nor Polish, but German. When Steinberg arrived in Monowitz, Elias was *Stubendienst* of the vast quarantine tent, erected and dismantled according to need where each *Zugang*, new *Häftling*, went through the routine of initiation and registration.

After his account of Elias, Levi investigates the case of "Henri," Paul Steinberg, whose evidence has just been quoted. He presents him, in contrast to Elias, as an extremely civilized man. According to Levi, Henri's actions were the product of a very detailed theory concerning the way to survive in an extermination camp. He describes him as a young man of twenty-two, with command of several languages and a high level of general and scientific culture. Ever since the death of his closest friend in the Buna during the winter of 1944, he had put a wall around himself, adapted perfectly inside it, and exploited others through his quick intelligence and good education. In Levi's view, Henri used three methods to ward off death: "organization, pity and theft" (*Man* 98/104). He used his ability to ingratiate himself with the British PoWs interned in another part of the camp to acquire a monopoly on trade with the British, who gave him real cigarettes that he converted into unheard-of luxuries — once, for example, a hard-boiled egg.

Henri was handsome, and reminded Levi of Sodoma's painting of Saint Sebastian, with his languid, tortured body, which decorates the Church of San Domenico in Siena. As greedy as Elias, and agile as a cat — Levi also compares him to a poisonous insect paralyzing its prey — Henri was a cold operator whose achievements were equal to his skills. With the power to stir pity in thugs like SS-*Hauptscharführer* (Sergeant-Major) Rakasch, he could soften and exploit the hardest hearts, and had built up a whole portfolio of protectors among the *Prominenten*, both Jewish and gentile. He also had contacts in the *KB*, who would admit him when he chose, and with the diagnosis he suggested. In spite of everything: "To speak with Henri is useful and pleasant." Levi is quite prepared to grant him human feelings, but moments later he reckons that he has been duped and made a pawn of. The elusive, unfathomable Henri is no longer compared to a figure from Sodoma but to the Serpent in Genesis. When he wrote these lines, Levi knew that Henri was still alive, and was curious to know about his life "as a free man," but added that he did not want to see him again.

Now for what the real Henri remembers. In 1943 Paul Steinberg, aged sixteen, was in the penultimate year of the Lycée Claude-Bernard in Paris. His father had told him that he blamed him for the death of his mother in childbirth. The young Steinberg preferred the gambling table and horse racing to his studies, barely scraped through part one of the *baccalauréat*, and paid his gambling debts with his racing winnings, which were sometimes large amounts. He no longer wore the yellow star, and since the police round-ups had hardly affected the affluent XVIth *arrondissement*, some of his family had had time to go for cover. Unable to find a friend who could hide him, he was betrayed and arrested as he was talking his ration coupons to buy bread from the bakery on the Boulevard Exelmans, near the Rue Erlanger. They took him by *métro* to the

Odéon station, and there Steinberg asked permission to stop for a moment to buy a book on analytical inorganic chemistry at the Librairie Maloine. Like Levi, he had a passion for chemisty. When he left the bookshop, two French officers took him to the police headquarters, then escorted him back to his apartment, to pick up a suitcase. There he could quite easily have made his escape by the service stairs. Instead, he packed his pillow and slippers. The police officers took him to the station on the Boulevard Exelmans, and put him in a cell in the basement, with the door left open. There was an air-raid alert, and again Steinberg might have made his escape, but he did not. He spent the night in the station's cell number 10.

The following day, he was taken to Drancy, where he met the champion boxer Young Perez, who later died in Auschwitz. On 20 October he arrived in Monowitz. In Drancy, Steinberg had made friends with Philippe Hagenauer, six months his senior, whom Levi mistook for his brother, and who was to die of exhaustion in the *Schonungsblock* while Steinberg lay in the room next door and fought for his life against an attack of hepatitis. (When he was given his tattoo, Steinberg and about thirty others were pricked by an infected needle used to mark a predecessor who was suffering from the disease.)

As Primo Levi had done in Italy, when Philippe and Paul left for Auschwitz each of them had thrown a stamped, addressed envelope out of the window of the RATP bus that shuttled between Drancy and the railway station in Bobigny where a convoy of cattle trucks stood waiting. Steinberg's letter reached its destination.

In spite of an injury to his foot that forced him to wear a slipper and qualified him automatically for the gas chamber by the SS rules, Steinberg was allowed to enter the camp because of his excellent Berlin accent, having been born in the capital of the Reich. Thanks to his youth, and fluent German, he had no problem picking up the customs and rituals of the camp.

This very young man quickly realized that "in order to try to survive it was necessary to adapt, but that meant *being able* to adapt .... Those who rebelled were crushed on the spot .... It had to be possible to produce an identikit picture of the deportee best suited to survive. All it took was to list the advantages he should enjoy, and the handicapping defects he should be free from." Not believing — unlike Primo Levi in the last few months of his life — that the deportee who was able to survive was completely bad, Steinberg wrote: "I do not believe in the hard, pure hero who has passed through all adversities without concessions, head held high. If such a man exists, I have not met him, and his halo must make sleeping uncomfortable."

His quick wits were no guarantee against making mistakes that he paid a high price for: the theft of a kilo loaf of bread did not go unnoticed by a ferocious *Stubendienst*. Another day, he slipped and fell while parading in front of an SS man. He suffered a kicking that lacerated his right leg, and the wounds, transformed into deep ulcers, did not heal until the spring of 1946, a year after his return. Later he spent three weeks in the contagious ward for his hepatitis. After the hepatitis came dysentery, scabies, and erysipelas. Admitted to the *KB* again, he benefited from preferential treatment when the doctor twice administered twelve tablets of a sulphonamide, Prontosil. In the *Schonungsblock* he had the good luck to encounter a Romanian doctor who had travelled from Drancy in the same transport as himself. When he left the *KB* he managed to persuade a French STO worker to post a letter for him. Through him, he received the tin of sardines that he used to soften up the *Lagerälteste* who subsequently protected him. It certainly took an exceptionally cool and calculating head, in a young man of seventeen, to gamble his precious supply of protein on his judgement of an unstable character. It was the fact that he accepted the protection of a criminal sadist, who presented him with a sausage in return for the tin of sardines, that Levi condemned. But Steinberg argued that it was thanks to his chosen protectors that he received an extra three to seven litres of soup a day, which he shared with his circle of friends — "the privilege of the rich."

After the parcel with the sardines, Steinberg decided to bluff his way into a safer position when the Kapo of his Kommando asked for chemists to come forward to take an exam. He took the risk, even though apart from the contents of the textbook he had bought at Maloine's, he had made no detailed study of chemisty. Just as Levi was to be, he was questioned by Herr Doktor Ingenieur Pannwitz, the head of the laboratory, and he passed the exam.

His boldness almost cost him his life. The Dutch Jewish Kapo Jupp Lessing, of Kommando 98, the "Chemical Kommando," whom he thought he had won over, reported Steinberg when he caught him translating German war communiqués to the British PoWs. Thanks to his protection, he got away with a lighter punishment than he might easily have suffered: *Hauptscharführer* Rakasch did not kill him.

Yet several weeks later, he committed an act of which he says he felt ashamed. Through his connections, he had been promoted to the post of assistant to the *Stubendienst*, with the ludicrous job of supervising the perfect alignment of the "beds." When he found an old, exhausted Polish Jew still lying on his pallet, he ordered him out of it and raised his hand to slap him. Although he restrained himself in time, his hand still brushed the old man's cheek. By starting to ape the oppressors, he entered the "gray zone" described by Primo Levi. Fifty years later, Steinberg wrote:

> So the contagion did its work, and I was no exception to the rule. In that world of violence I made a violent gesture, and showed when I did so that I had my rightful place there .... The memory of that gesture has pursued me ever since. It remains one of the septic, unhealed wounds that will always stay with me ....

167

Paul Steinberg has read *If This Is A Man*. This is what he says about Primo Levi's account of him:

> The image that comes out of his description is of a rather antipathetic, sterilized character whom he may have found pleasant company, but felt no wish ever to see again .... No doubt he saw straight. I probably was that creature obsessed with survival .... To a neutral observer of my image as he saw it, I was certainly like that, fiercely determined to do all I could to live, prepared to use what means I had available, including the gift of rousing other people's sympathy.

Regretting that he never had the chance to talk with the man who had judged him so harshly, he concluded: "I will never know whether I am entitled to ask for clemency from the jury. Is it so wrong to survive?"

Oddly enough, Paul Steinberg, who worked in the same laboratory as Primo Levi, does not remember him, although the inmates who had the privilege of working there could be counted on the fingers of one hand.

The new Chemical Kommando was in theory reserved for specialists, though Alex, its Kapo, was a common-law criminal, and not at all impressed by the supposed knowledge of the fifteen prisoners under his command. The applicants were to have their credentials checked by appearing in front of Doctors Hagen, Probst, and Pannwitz to answer questions. In the meantime these so-called intellectuals would be working in the Magnesium Chloride store. On the Buna site, it lay on H-Strasse, the warehouse street.

One of Levi's new colleagues was his friend Alberto Dallavolta, who had been a third-year chemistry student before he entered Auschwitz. When they arrived at the Kommando's headquarters, a damp, draughty basement known as the Bude, the Kapo split the Kommando into several teams whose orders were to unload sacks from wagons and transfer them to the basement. In the first three days, three men disappeared without trace, as often occurred in Auschwitz, and five tried to withdraw because they were not chemists, but the Kapo just gave them a kicking and kept them in the Kommando. There was no need to be a chemistry graduate to carry heavy sacks full of corrosive chemicals.

The following account of the skin diseases caused by the kind of sacks that Kommando 98 had to carry comes from the report by Primo Levi and Leonardo De Benedetti:

> In the month of August 1944 the men assigned to the chemistry Kommando were involved in reorganizing a small store containing sacks of a substance with a phenol base. Right from the start, particles of this product mixed with sweat and stuck to the workers' faces and hands. Exposure to the sun at first induced a deep pigmentation of the areas exposed, accompanied by an intense burning. It caused a widespread peeling of the skin. Although the skin thus exposed to the

infecting agent became particularly sensitive and painful, the work went on for twenty days with no protective measures taken. And although fifty men were affected by this painful dermatitis, not one of them was sent to the hospital.[8]

Seven prisoners finally went to be examined in the Polymerization division of the Buna. Among them was Menahem Haïm Davidowicz, called Mendi, already mentioned, a learned rabbi who spoke seven languages. He was not a chemist, but he wanted to try his luck.[9]

While they and the other candidates waited with Alex in front of a closed door, Primo Levi tried to resurrect his former knowledge from the depths of his memory where it was buried. Alex inspected his appearance with a doubting eye. How could a near-*Muselmann* become a chemist? When the door finally opened, Levi learned that he was to be examined last, in the afternoon, because he had the highest registration number. He walked off with Alex, who shot him a look of disgust and wondered how a wasted, grubby little Italian Jew could possibly expect to be allowed to work with German Doktors. Alex felt so sceptical that when Levi was finally admitted to Doktor Pannwitz's office, he came forward cap in hand and explained that this Italian had been in the camp for only three months and yet he was "already half done in." He also doubted whether Levi really was a chemist.

While Alex lurked in a corner, Levi found himself facing Doktor Pannwitz, a tall, blond, blue-eyed Aryan sitting at a clean, orderly desk. Pannwitz wrote for a while, then suddenly looked up at Levi, but with the eyes of a member of the master race confronted by an *Untermensch*. In fact, Doktor Pannwitz did not believe that he and Primo Levi belonged to the same species, but instead of holding a submachine gun ready to dispatch him into a pit, he was there to see what use could be extracted from the "sub-man" who claimed to be a chemist.

Doktor Pannwitz began his interrogation by using the polite, second person plural, "*Sie*" form to address Doctor Levi, who told him that he had taken his degree in 1941, *summa cum laude*. The Aryan cross-questioned the Jew with a sceptical air, but Levi had lost none of his intellect, and the knowledge came when it was summoned. The subject of his thesis, "Measurements of Dielectrical Constants," interested the German, who proceeded to ask whether the *Häftling* knew English, and then held up the well-known work by Gattermann, the one that Levi knew almost by heart, and that he called "the father's voice."

Once the exam was completed, Alex took over again. The unscheduled rest day was coming to an end as the Kapo and Levi walked across a stretch of waste ground strewn with building materials. When a steel cable barred their way, Alex took hold of it to clamber over, and found his hand covered in black grease. As a matter of course, he wiped it on the other man's shoulder. Levi resented this thoughtless insult as one of the most painful that he had to suffer.

In Auschwitz, it was strictly forbidden for Jewish *Häflinge* to write, and they received no mail. To be found in possession of a pencil stub and a piece of paper could mean death, because writing was interpreted as the action of a spy. Yet Levi got his hands on these incriminating items. One day his Kapo, Eddy, a handsome young common-law criminal who had worked as a juggler in civilian life, left him alone in a cellar to stack up some cardboard tubes unloaded from a wagon. In spite of the danger, Levi took his chance and began to write a letter. It might seem like madness for a Jew, the pariah of all the prisoners, to think of sending a letter to his family, and the feat was supposed to be impossible, but chance had intervened.

Primo Levi describes how it happened in the story called "Lorenzo's Return," in *Moments of Reprieve*. In June 1944, after an air raid, he made the acquaintance of an Italian named Lorenzo Perrone, a mason from Fossano. Lorenzo was not a prisoner but a civilian who had worked for an Italian firm in France. When the war broke out, Italians had been rounded up into internment camps, and when the Germans invaded France they revived the firm and moved it to the outskirts of Auschwitz. Lorenzo, who lived not far from the camp, in an army-style barracks, and just as comfortable, had Sundays off and one or two weeks' leave, and his wage was paid in Reichmarks. The Italian workers had the right to send letters and money home to their families, who could send them parcels of food and clothing.

The Buna plant had been hit by the first Allied air raid, and some of the machinery that would have to operate when the factory came on line was damaged by shrapnel and rubble. When the management decided to have their machines protected by brick ramparts, Lorenzo was one of the bricklayers employed by his firm to do the job. It happened that Levi's Kommando was working in the hangar where Italian masons were building these walls around the machines, and by a sheer accident the Kapo ordered him to go and help. Two masons were working there in silence, standing on scaffolding because their wall was already high. One of them told him in pidgin German to fetch a bucket of mortar, but when the totally inexperienced Levi tried to hoist the heavy bucket onto his shoulder, he dropped and spilled it. Now the bricklayer who had spoken turned to his work mate and remarked in the Piedmont dialect that people like this were utterly useless. The man came down from the scaffolding, and even though it was forbidden, Levi started to talk to him. He had some distant relations in Fossano, and it turned out that Lorenzo knew them. That was all, because Lorenzo Perrone was no talker. After the war, Levi learned from his family that he was a bachelor, and that he had a taste for solitude. He liked his trade, but not his bosses, so he moved around a lot. He would not hear a bad word about his work, no matter how politely it was spoken. He used to spend his winters working on the Côte d'Azur, and would cross the border on foot, by mountain footpaths, because he carried no identity papers.

Lorenzo preferred actions to words. Without warning, and at the risk of his life, a few days after meeting Levi he brought him a two-litre Alpine troop mess tin full of soup, and asked him to return it by the end of the day. Then every day, for six months, Lorenzo brought the soup, and sometimes a hunk of bread, to his fellow countryman. As long as Levi was working as his labourer, this was easy enough to do, but later, when they worked some distance apart, Lorenzo had to take great risks so as not to be spotted by the Gestapo. Levi shared the soup with his friend Alberto. As the rations were not very generous even for civilian workers, Lorenzo would get up at three o'clock in the morning and raid the kitchens for supplies. Then he would leave the mess tin at a prearranged spot, so that they should never be seen together and be accused of espionage. But one day the mess tin, which had Lorenzo's name scratched on it, disappeared. Levi had been followed, and the soup stolen. The thief could be a blackmailer, an informer, or both of these, but that did not really worry Lorenzo, who was attached to his mess tin for sentimental reasons, and was not the kind to be intimidated. He identified the thief, a big Pole who made no attempt to conceal his prize, and openly flaunted it in the camp. Then it occurred to Lorenzo and Primo to make a deal with the unstoppable dwarf, Elias Lindzin. If he succeeded, they would give him three rations of bread, payable in instalments. Elias went and found the Pole, who claimed to have bought the mess tin. Elias, true to his reputation, went for the thief and flattened him, to the applause of the prisoners now assembled. He proudly presented the mess tin to his partners, and became their friend.

This was not Levi's first encounter with Elias. Some time previously the two had got into a fight, when for some reason Elias grabbed him by the wrists and shoved him up against a wall, reeling off a barrage of insults. Levi tried to defend himself by kicking Elias in the shin, which caused Elias to cross his opponent's thin arms over his chest, throw him to the ground, and then choke him till he nearly blacked out. After that, he stood up without a word and walked away. Levi promised himself never again to "hit back," to use the words of Jean Améry, who drew his strength from a deep sense of pride and resentment.

Lorenzo Perrone kept Primo Levi fed for no reason but pure altruism. When the grateful Levi offered to arrange to send money to his sister in Italy, he refused to give him her address. He wanted neither thanks nor reward. But he did agree to allow his leather boots to be mended free in the camp, because in the town of Auschwitz the shoemakers were profiteering from the situation. The privileged who wore leather shoes in the camp were entitled to have them repaired at no cost, since the inmates had no money. Primo Levi handed his wooden-soled boots to Lorenzo, put on Lorenzo's leather boots, then took them for mending to the camp shoemakers, who lent him a pair of temporary shoes.

It was through Lorenzo, who could hardly write, that Levi intended to forward a letter, whose contents were anodyne but clear, by getting him to copy it out and then send it to Bianca Guidetti Serra. But Eddy, the juggler

Kapo, moving with the stealth of a cat, caught Levi by surprise. He dropped his sheet of paper and the Kapo picked it up. He slapped him to the ground, questioned him, and did not believe a word of his reply but told him to wait there for an hour. If Eddy had reported him, Levi would have been tortured and hanged.

When Eddy returned he was holding three sheets of paper: the original, and two separate translations made by prisoners who spoke German and Italian. Eddy had warned them that if the two translations did not coincide then they, as well as Levi, would be denounced to the Political Department. The translations tallied, and after telling Levi that he and his unknown accomplice must be crazy, Eddy considered the case closed.

One day a notice written in German and Polish appeared on the door of the Block. It announced, as an exceptional concession, that all the prisoners were to be allowed to write to their families on forms to be provided by the authorities, and in no other language but German. Only those who knew an addressee in Germany, or allied countries like Italy, or in the occupied territories, were permitted to write, and they must not ask for food parcels to be sent. On the other hand, the SS encouraged the inmates to thank their correspondents for imaginary parcels received. This was a crude manoeuvre intended to fool the Red Cross into believing that the Jews were being properly treated in the Nazi camps. There were two schools of thought among the prisoners: those who felt that it was still a good idea to write, and those who opposed colluding with a Nazi deception. Primo Levi decided to try his luck by addressing his letter to Bianca Guidetti Serra, in Turin. For half a ration of bread — his newcomer client was less hungry than himself — he also agreed to write a letter to the fiancée of a young Spanish-born Gypsy picked up by the Nazis in Hungary. Neither letter reached its destination.

His first close shave with Kapo Eddy did not deter Levi from making contact with his family. He asked Lorenzo Perrone to write a postcard addressed to Bianca Guidetti Serra, and when it arrived she took the news to his mother and sister that Primo was alive. Ester Levi's sad response was to remark that the postcard proved only that her son had been alive when it was sent: as it was impossible to learn more, she could not be glad. Nevertheless, with the collusion of Lorenzo and Bianca she ventured a reply. In June 1944, addressed to Lorenzo Perrone, a letter and the priceless resource of a food parcel reached Auschwitz.

Primo Levi could not consume the cakes, the chocolate, and all the other treats that the parcel contained in a single sitting, so he distributed its contents around pockets he had sewn into the back of his jacket, and also kept the letter, taking a considerable risk. Next morning he went for a wash, stripped to the waist according to the rules. After he had hung his clothes on a nail in the washroom he suddenly saw a dangling hook on the end of a string as it snagged in his jacket and was whisked through the window just above.

Someone had been spying on him, and had snatched both his goods and his jacket, which was the property of the camp, with severe penalties for its loss. The supply master issued him a jacket, but if in fifteen minutes he had not removed the registration number from his trousers and sewn it on to the jacket, he would receive an official beating. Some starving, unscrupulous *Häftling* had not only stolen his food but had put him in danger of his life. Fortunately for Levi, he was naturally very thin, and had always had a frugal appetite: he could withstand privation much better than his bigger, stronger comrades, because the shortfall in calories mattered less.

Lorenzo brought his mess tin of soup every day. He also gave Levi one of his mended vests, but would take nothing in return. Levi compares Lorenzo with "professional seducers like Henri," criticizing such men for dressing up their successes in "an aura of equivocal mystery," with the aim of building a reputation as a powerful, influential figure with a lucky streak. Writing in the tone of a stern judge, even a public prosecutor, he declares: "The reputation of being a seducer, of being 'organized,' excites at once envy, scorn, contempt, and admiration. Whoever allows himself to be seen eating 'organized' food is judged quite severely; he shows a serious lack of modesty and tact, besides an open stupidity" (*Man 120/126*). Of Lorenzo, Primo wrote that he was a man, and that his humanity was "pure and uncontaminated." Lorenzo was a "Righteous Gentile." In fact, Elias, Lindzin, Maurice Reznik, Jean Samuel, and Paul Steinberg are all presented in *If This Is A Man* as archetypes of prisoners in the *Lager*.

Jean Samuel[10] was a young student of pharmacy from Alsace, who spoke fluent French and German and belonged to the Chemical Kommando. He and his whole family had been netted in a round-up in Dausse, Lot-en-Garonne. He was in Monowitz with his uncle René, who survived selections, starvation, sickness, and exhaustion, but was to be lost on the death-march that followed the evacuation of Auschwitz. Jean Samuel was the youngest prisoner in Kommando 98, and for that reason he had been appointed *Pikkolo*,[11] apprentice. This post combined the functions of delivery man, clerk, hut cleaner, tool distributor, bowl washer, and recorder of the Kommando's working hours. One of his duties was to collect the soup ration from the kitchens, a kilometre away. Like Primo Levi, Jean Samuel had worked as a labourer on the vast construction site of the Buna. Often they had to unload wagons carrying shipments of bricks, or 60-kilo sacks of betanaphthylamine or magnesium chloride. The chemical products burned the carriers' skin through the mock-protection of the striped Auschwitz jacket. Carrying sacks on their backs, they had to step over rails, make their way across a hundred metres of waste ground, and climb a steep ladder covered by a plank, which acted as a ramp to a platform two metres higher up. Then they had to squeeze through two narrow doors to get down into the basement of Building 940, climb a staircase with two right-angled turnings, and finally lower the sack to the ground — all this while the

Kapo bawled and lashed out at them. One day Jean Samuel fell through the ladder with his load. He landed on his back and twisted his shoulder. That night, when he reported to the infirmary, they gave him an aspirin tablet and warned him of the danger he incurred by having himself admitted to the wards, where the regular selections might feed him to the gas chamber.

In the Chemical Kommando, Jean Samuel witnessed an incident that cost the life of a comrade from Marseilles, a pharmacist like himself. When this exhausted young man fell over, and did not have the strength to hoist the sack on to his back again, the Kapo beat him to death with an iron bar, under an SS guard's approving gaze.

Jean Samuel and Primo Levi had first met on a fine day in May 1944 during an Allied air raid on the Buna industrial complex. Jews were not allowed to enter the shelters reserved for the Germans, and had to fend for themselves or die under the bombs that dug huge craters in the Polish mud. Levi and Samuel had sheltered in a shed on the site, and talked for a long while about subjects seldom discussed in the camp: their families, their studies, and their homes.

One day Levi and five comrades had been put to work to scour out the inside of a deep underground storage tank, in a humid atmosphere thick with powdered rust. When the rope ladder that gave access started to sway in the gloom, they stepped up their efforts, fearing that the *Vorarbeiter* might be on his way. A German technician had first installed an electric light-bulb in the tank, dangling on the end of a flex, and when his boss came to inspect the work he had given his employee a blunt telling-off: "That's very dangerous. If the insulation was faulty, the whole tank would be live and these men could be killed." The *Häftlinge* had suddenly and briefly been transformed into men. After that they were issued with miners' lamps. The I.G. Farben management was not unaware that these prisoners were due to be killed in any case, but it would be inconvenient if it were to happen here, on the Buna site.

Although Jean Samuel had the privilege of being a *Prominent*, he was also liked by his comrades. He dished out the soup (and received an extra half-ration for himself), was exempt from manual work, could warm himself close to the stove, and came in for the cast-off clothing and boots discarded by Alex, the brutal Kapo, whose favour he had gained. Obsequious towards the SS, the near-illiterate Alex had picked Samuel to write out the daily report provided by the detainees, and keep the Kommando's register. Pikkolo had a healthy influence on Alex, and sometimes managed to temper his cruel and violent treatment of his comrades. Levi and Samuel had been unable to speak to each other since the day of their meeting, under the Allied bombardment, but it was Samuel who had set the ladder swaying in the underground tank, as he came to ask Levi to help him collect the soup ration. His usual carrier had lost the privilege after an incident involving the theft of some brooms from the store.

It needed two inmates to deliver the *Kessel* of soup, which they carried by sliding wooden poles through two pairs of lugs. First they had to go and collect the pot from the kitchens, then they would return to dole out the fifty kilos of soup among the *Häftlinge* of the Kommando. As the kitchens were easily a kilometre away from the tank, the two young men walked slowly, and by taking a roundabout route they found the leisure to talk. Levi had suffered from his linguistic isolation, and it was a delight to speak French with a friend.

They talked for a while about their families, and then Jean Samuel asked Primo Levi to give him a lesson in Italian. No better notion could have occurred to him, because the lesson he requested opened the way to a kind of salvation for Levi. The canto of Ulysses, which he had studied in the Liceo d'Azeglio, came to his mind: Dante, *The Divine Comedy: Inferno*, canto 26, lines 76–142. While they walked, Levi tried to remember the poem he had learned in his childhood, and translated it into French as the fragments came to his mind, sometimes a little distorted by his memory.

In the summer of 1944 a young Italian Jew recited *The Inferno* to a young French Jew as they walked the streets of Auschwitz. "The great stock of evil in the universe" was evoked in the words of a poet who had lived six centuries before them. But Dante could not have imagined the scale of the evil that would reign some day on earth. Levi gave a new reading and a new dimension to his poem by reciting it in the streets of an extermination camp. While six kilometres away, in the crematoria of Birkenau, thousands of men, women, and children were dying of cyanide poisoning and then being reduced to ashes, Dante's lines were rising into the clarity of Primo Levi's mind:

> Consider what you came from: you are Greeks!
> You were not born to live like mindless brutes
> but to follow paths of excellence and knowledge.[12]

The lines "Consider what you came from …," learned unenthusiastically at school, so far invaded Primo Levi's mind as to make him forget that he was in Auschwitz. He, the atheist, who sometimes felt envious when he observed the resources faith provided for some of his comrades, wrote that these lines affected him "like the blast of a trumpet, like the voice of God" (*Man* 113/119).

"Consider what you came from … You were not born to live like mindless brutes.…" These two lines of Dante, declaring for eternity, even to the *Häftlinge* of Auschwitz, that they were all part of the uniqueness of the human race, offered a reply to the Nazis, and to the SS in the camp who had divided the world into two species, the race of masters and the race of sub-men. Ulysses' will to know, embraced and reasserted by Levi, emerged to oppose the horror of the camp that could exterminate twenty thousand Jews in a day. Word and thought had not been annihilated in the chaos of Auschwitz.

> when there appeared a mountain shape, darkened
> by distance, that arose to endless heights.
> I had never seen another mountain like it.[13]

After these three lines, Levi found a gap in his memory; he could not fill the space between these last lines and the end of the canto. He tried to use the rhyme scheme to guide him, and felt he would have given his whole day's soup to regain the poem. One line surfaced — "from the new land there rose a whirling wind" — but it was not what he was looking for, and time was pressing because they had nearly reached the kitchens. Levi held Jean Samuel back to tell him three more lines:

> and whirled us round three times in churning waters;
> the fourth blast raised the stern up high, and sent
> the bow down deep, as pleased Another's will.[14]

Levi wanted to explain to Pikkolo the flood of thoughts inspired in him by the words "as pleased Another's will." He wrote in *If This Is A Man* that he had glimpsed a "flash of intuition" that would enable him to understand the meaning of their presence in Auschwitz, in the very heart of the inferno. "As pleased Another's will," Dante wrote. As he spoke these words, Levi suddenly had a vision of "the great stock of evil in the universe." Outside the kitchens, just as they heard the official announcement that today's soup was cabbage and turnips, "*Kraut und Rüben*," Levi retrieved the line he had lost. He explained to Pikkolo what pleased that Other: to swallow men in danger of death, just as the Auschwitz complex swallowed thousands of lives every day:

> And then the sea was closed again, above us.[15]

Thus Levi, as if he were speaking up for the classical high school he had detested, found that he believed in the possibilities of salvation offered by culture, even in the inferno of Auschwitz.

Returning to his quotation from *The Inferno* in an interview with Daniela Amsallem on 15 July 1980, he put forward this hypothesis:

> Auschwitz may be the punishment of the barbarians, of barbarian Germany, of the barbarian Nazis, against Jewish civilization — that is to say, the punishment for daring, just as the shipwreck of Ulysses is the punishment of a barbarian god for human daring.
>
> I was thinking of that vein of German anti-Semitism that struck chiefly at the intellectual daring of the Jews, such as Freud, Marx, and all the innovators, in every field. It was that daring that irked a certain German philistinism *much more* than the fact of blood or race.[16]

In June 1944, Primo Levi was still labouring in the Buna. One of his work mates was Endre Szántó, a young Hungarian who had reached Auschwitz in one of the many transports that began to arrive in May, soon after the Nazi occupation of Hungary on 19 March 1944. Endre called himself a Communist sympathizer and approved, like Lorenzo, of work well done, so it was hard for the veteran to convince the newcomer that when they were supposed to be carrying loads of twenty bricks on a wooden two-man tray it made sense for them to cheat, and save their strength, by arranging seventeen bricks to look like twenty.

Most of the Hungarian Jews were gassed on arrival, yet there were so many of them — about 438,000 were deported to Auschwitz alone between 15 May and 9 July 1944[17] — that the minority that did enter the camp boosted its population, for by now nearly all of the Polish Jews had been murdered. Just like Yiddish, Hungarian now became one of the major languages of Auschwitz. Endre was known as "Bandi," the Hungarian diminutive of his given name. He was a sturdy, fresh-faced young man whom everybody liked and respected. In August, Levi was overjoyed to receive a letter from Turin, forwarded by Bianca Guidetti Serra through the Lorenzo Perrone connection. He trusted Bandi so much that he could not restrain himself from revealing his prize. Inside an underground cistern, by the glimmer of a low-voltage light-bulb, he took the risk of reading him the very cautious message sent by his mother and sister, translating into his rudimentary German. Bandi listened gravely, then fumbled in his pocket and blushed as he pulled out a radish and offered it to Primo. "I've learned," he said. "This is for you. It's the first thing I've stolen" (*Reprieve* 32/54).

Having lasted five months in the *Lager*, Levi had now become a veteran *Häftling*. Thanks to Lorenzo, who continued to deliver the daily bowl of soup that he shared with Alberto, his condition was not desperate. He had not yet caught any illness, and the combination of his small size, natural thinness, and habitual frugality continued to give him a nutritional advantage. Hence his mind stayed sharp. He observed his surroundings and companions, and his exceptional memory enabled him to preserve names and faces, so that years after the publication of his first book, *If This Is A Man*, written in the heat of immediate recollection, the vignettes and anecdotes published in *Moments of Reprieve* threw fresh light on his Auschwitz experience and on some of the people he met there.

The daily Allied bombing of targets in Upper Silesia started in August 1944 and went on into the autumn, decisively damaging the vast installations of the Buna. On 4 April of that year, Allied reconnaissance had taken aerial photos of Auschwitz that show the Birkenau installations very clearly. All requests from the leaders of the Zionist movement asking for the Allies to bomb the railway lines leading to the camp, as well as the gas chambers themselves, met with refusals. But each time the factory was supposed to start production, an aircraft would arrive to bomb the thermal station or power station. Thus, not a gram of synthetic rubber was ever produced. The I.G. Farben bosses stopped expanding the buildings and instead used their slaves to repair the damage caused by the air raids. The plant was found intact at the end of the war.

No shelters were provided for the prisoners. They had to withstand the raids by finding what cover they could on the waste ground of the Buna site, knowing that it would be their job to clear the charred ruins of the walls on fire around them. When they returned to the disrupted camp, there was no water or electricity, and no soup. The resurgent Red Army had crushed the Germans in the Crimea and driven them out of Byelorussia. The Western Allies had landed in Normandy in June, and liberated Paris by 25 August. The Thousand-Year Greater Reich was collapsing. In Auschwitz, tensions rose. More than ever, the camp was divided into two: the Germans, now certain of defeat, and all the rest. Yet among the *Häftlinge* there were also Germans, and the "political" prisoners, as well as the SS, redoubled their hatred and cruelty towards the Jews, the more they feared their vengeance.

Autumn came, and then the mist, snow, and dreadful cold of winter came down across the Polish plains. The cold meant death for most of the underfed, skeletal prisoners who laboured under the open sky, in sub-zero temperatures, wearing nothing but a shirt, underpants, the striped uniform, and an "overcoat" made of the same thin fabric. Any slave caught wearing a layer of paper beneath his shirt to protect him from the blizzard incurred harsh penalties. A pair of gloves cost rations of bread. In *If This Is A Man* Levi wrote: "[O]ur way of being cold has need of a new word" (*Man 123/129*). He added that the same was true of the words hunger, pain, fatigue, fear, and winter. In Auschwitz, they acquired a different dimension; they stood for realities that existed nowhere else but in the extermination camps. Paul Steinberg wrote in his memoirs: "I had grown obsessed with the cold. I used every possible trick to avoid it, at the risk of taking beatings. At evening roll-call the hurt became tangible. Its bite would penetrate the bone, pain enough to scream."

With stiff, numbed limbs, at daybreak the *Häftlinge* had to stand to attention for the interminable roll-call, work till nightfall in the snow and wind, march back to the camp to the Kapo's tempo — "*Links, links, links und links!*" — then submit to the evening roll-call, run to the hut to receive their litre of soup, and possibly emerge again to queue outside the infirmary in the icy darkness, waiting for treatment for their damaged hands. There were too many men in the Blocks, so selections had to be due. The *Muselmänner* were regularly selected for the gas chamber. In Auschwitz slang there was a name for it, part Polish and part Latin, a word of terror: *selekcja*. What the word stood for was common knowledge, but the camp authorities persisted in their policy of never declaring their purpose to their victims.

The veterans were not deceived, but there were newcomers who clung to the hope of remaining alive. Selections affected hardly any but the Jews. Sometimes a final twitch of rebellion might make a man try to escape his sentence of death, but resistance was futile. Hermann Langbein recalls that, according to the reports that passed through his hands, "the victims kept relatively calm. They never neglected to say: 'Do not forget revenge.'" He relates the case of two brothers, one of whom was selected. The other killed him, to spare him the journey to the gas chamber. The Polish Jews were always the first to get wind of a selection, and they would keep the news to themselves, in order to be the only ones who would try out various tricks to elude the procedure. Eventually the rumour would spread throughout the camp, and to the civilian workers. Most *Häftlinge* awaited the SS doctor's visit with resignation and despair. The most exhausted, those with the sunken thighs and buttocks, and wasted chests, had no illusions. They had become *Muselmänner*. Those with protections did all they could to escape. The small fry — the great majority of the inmates — could only console one another.

During his stay in the *Schonungsblock* Paul Steinberg went through several selections:

> We suffered the humiliation of running with our chests stuck out, in our shirts, our buttocks exposed, past the SS doctors in full uniform. Humiliation? Our dignity had said goodbye to that. We made jokes about it among ourselves, it was a humdrum thing. Our self-esteem didn't come back till much later, together with bread, a knife and fork, and freedom.

It was on a "working Sunday, *Arbeitssonntag*" in Monowitz, after the shower, shave and inspection for lice and scabies, that Primo Levi and Jean Samuel went through the autumn 1944 selection.

> The whole camp was closed, and a team made up of an SS doctor and a *Schreiber* moved from Block to Block. We had to get completely undressed, except for our sabots, and pass in front of the SS man who had the power of life and death over us. Imagine this crowd of people, as haggard as I was, with big bellies, because we suffered from that illness that entails retaining water. It was necessary to give the impression to the SS men that we were still capable of working, and so of surviving. Each one stood up straight, stuck out his chest, tried to divert attention from his buttocks, because they were the best indication of a prisoner's state of malnutrition. The prisoner was called by his number, and the SS man decided to have him go either to the right or to the left. You soon knew which side was the right one.[18]

Primo Levi wrote that this selection was carried out in order to make room for a huge transport coming from the Poznan ghetto. Each man dreamed up a reason to be hopeful: the young imagined that the old would be selected; the healthy reckoned on the sick; those with a trade banked on specialists being spared; German Jews told themselves that only the Polish Jews would go to their deaths; the low numbers that it was bound to be the high ones. "You will be chosen. I will be excluded" (*Man 126/132*).

The selection began with a *Blocksperre*. Confining all the prisoners to their Blocks had two useful functions: first, no one could escape the selection; second, no one could witness the departure of the condemned men, bundled into the trucks that would ship them to the gas chambers of Birkenau, where the crematoria chimneys worked day and night, their red flare visible at a distance of several kilometres.

The *Blockälteste* locks the door of the hut and gives each of his charges a file card with details of his record. Naked except for their boots, the prisoners wait for the commission to arrive. When it strides in, the men are jammed together, card in hand, in the *Tagesraum*, which measures seven metres by four. The connecting door between it and the dormitory is shut, the outside doors of both rooms left open. An SS subaltern positions himself between the two doors. Flanking him are two men, the *Blockälteste* and the Block quarter-master. Each prisoner emerging naked from the *Tagesraum* runs towards the dormitory door, handing his card to the SS man as he passes. In the blink of an eye, the SS man assesses him, front and back, and passes the card either to the man on his left or to the man on his right. "In three or four minutes a hut of two hundred men is 'done,' as is the whole camp of twelve thousand men in the course of the afternoon." The *Tagesraum* rapidly empties, and it is Primo Levi's turn. "Like everyone, I passed by with a brisk and elastic step, trying to hold my head high, my chest forward and my muscles contracted and conspic-uous. With the corner of my eye I tried to look behind my shoulders, and my card seemed to end on the right" (*Man 128/134*).

In the nameless stream of men hurrying past him and holding out their cards, the SS man had indeed passed Levi's to his right. Levi returned to the dormitory and dressed. Which was *"die schlechte Seite,"* the bad side? It was the left side, the side of the old, the decrepit, and the *Muselmänner*.

Levi realized that there had been a few "irregularities": prisoners in good health had been selected for the gas chamber. He and Alberto discussed it. Had there been a mix-up with the cards? Young René, condemned to death in perfect physical health, had been just in front of Levi. And a big Transylvanian peasant who had arrived in the camp only three weeks before, and spoke no German, came calmly back from the selection and started to mend his shirt, not realizing that he too had been condemned. The prisoners stayed confined to their Blocks while the selection ran its course throughout the camp. The *Blockälteste* proceeded to dish out the evening soup. As usual in Monowitz, those who had been selected for the gas chamber received a double ration. The condemned received twice as much to eat while they waited, sometimes for several days, for the truck to convey them to be killed.

Among the victims of the October 1944 selection were eight of the twenty-nine Italians who had entered the camp with Primo Levi and survived until that day. Among them was Alberto Dallavolta's father, a man of forty-five. Alberto was Primo's dear friend, sturdy and intelligent, not a man to delude himself. He gave no credence to the rumours that circulated among the prisoners and offered false hopes — that the end of the war was only a matter of days away; that Polish partisans were on the point of liberating Auschwitz. Yet when his father was selected to die in the gas chamber his attitude totally changed. He could not bring himself to accept that his father was about to be murdered, and began to believe in the rumours: the Russians were on their way; knowing that they were so close, the Germans had shut down the gas chambers; those who had been selected were to be transferred to Jaworzno, a camp less harsh than Monowitz. As a matter of fact, that camp was notoriously harsh. The prisoners in Jaworzno worked in the coal mines, where conditions were so appalling that they rarely lived longer than a few weeks.

When Levi returned to Italy in the autumn of 1945, he went straight to see Alberto's mother and brother to tell them what he knew about his friend's sad fate during the death-march from Auschwitz. Signora Dallaporta would not listen. She explained that Alberto had escaped from the immense column of twenty thousand deportees dispatched towards Gleiwitz. Now he was in Russia, and news would soon reach them from there. A year later, Levi paid another visit to his friend's mother. She told him that Alberto must be in hospital in Russia, suffering from loss of memory. When it returned, he would not take long to appear.

When the soup had been dished out and eaten, and every bowl scraped clean, Levi lay in his top-tier bunk, just under the roof, and saw an old man — his name was Kuhn — praying and thanking God for having escaped being chosen. Levi felt a surge of rebellion. He raged in silence against the man at prayer. Didn't he see the young men who had been selected for the gas chamber? Didn't he understand that selection was an act of depravity that nothing — no expiation, no punishment, and least of all a prayer — could put right. "If I was God, I would spit at Kuhn's prayer" (*Man 130/136*).

When he wrote that sentence in 1946 Levi, who was not a believer, nevertheless implied the possibility that there was a God, when he concluded that if he had been that mute God who looked down on Auschwitz, he would have spat at someone who offered up thanks that he, and not some other man, had been spared.

Forty years later, a few months before his suicide, as he reread the typescript of his conversations with Ferdinando Camon, Levi added two sentences in pencil after the one that concluded the book: "If there is an Auschwitz, then there cannot be a God."[19] What he wrote was: "I find no solution to the riddle. I seek, but I do not find it."

In Auschwitz, many Jews retained their faith, and not only those whose lives were spared. They lived through the extermination of their people, yet still believed, and still prayed, until the moment of their death. Some of them even fasted, like Ezra in *Moments of Reprieve*, on the day of Yom Kippur. It was not the fact that a man could still believe in God in Auschwitz that disgusted Levi, but that he could dare to thank his God for having been spared when millions of men, women, and children had suffered a terrible death.

Recalling his arrival in Auschwitz, Elie Wiesel wrote:

Never shall I forget that night, the first night in camp, which has turned my life into one long night, seven times cursed and seven times sealed.

Never shall I forget the little faces of the children, whose bodies I saw turned into wreaths of smoke beneath a silent blue sky.

Never shall I forget those flames which consumed my faith forever.

Never shall I forget that nocturnal silence which deprived me, for all eternity, of the desire to live. Never shall I forget those moments which murdered my God and my soul and turned my dream to dust. Never shall I forget these things, even if I am condemned to live as long as God himself. Never.[20]

After Auschwitz, as Primo Levi said to Ferdinando Camon, it is impossible to imagine an all-powerful, all-benevolent God. Since the Torah asserts that God is intelligible, and his goodness tolerates the existence of evil, it follows that he is not all-powerful. Levi did not deal with this enigma only in his conversations with Camon. He had raised the question of the existence of evil in the world in *La ricerca delle radici* (literally, "the quest for roots," published in February 1981). *La ricerca delle radici* is the author's personal anthology, taking the form of thirty short quotations from obscure or famous, literary and non-literary authors, each with a brief introduction. "I have never exposed myself more fully to my readers than in making the choice of these excerpts. Much more than in writing my books. Halfway through, I felt completely naked."

The volume is preceded by a drawing in the form of a flattened sphere, its northern pole marked "Job," its southern pole "Black Holes."

The Book of Job has been chosen in order to confront the existence of evil in the world. Job is the just man crushed by injustice. He is the victim of a cruel wager between Satan and God. Job is upright, holy, rich and happy. What will he do if he is touched in his goods, in those he loves, then in his body, even to his skin? Well, Job, the just man, humbled like an animal, as usual behaves as any of us would. At first, he bows his head and praises God. Are we to accept the good from God, and not the evil? Then his defences crumble. Poor, robbed of his children, covered in boils, he sits among the ashes, scraping himself with a potsherd, and argues with God. It is an unequal argument. God the creator of marvels and monsters crushes him beneath his omnipotence.[21]

In the month of November 1944, dressed in his striped cotton uniform and standing in a trench full of mud, Primo Levi swung his shovel under a freezing rain. In order to keep his spirits up, he blessed the lack of wind. Although he did not know the Yiddish proverb *"S'volt gekont zaïn erger"* ("It could have been worse"), this way of enduring rain, cold, mud, and hunger by reminding themselves that it might have been windy too was part of the immense power of resistance that helped the prisoners to hold out until the evening, then the following day, and perhaps until the defeat of the Nazis. It was the grain of hope that dissuaded them from throwing themselves on to the electrified barbed wire to escape from so much suffering. At half past four the siren of the Carbide factory announced the end of the working day for the English PoWs. The Jews had to wait until five o'clock before they could return to the camp, marching three abreast, under the Kapo's orders. On the way back, Levi found himself side by side with Kraus, instead of Alberto — the same Kraus who earlier that day had clumsily thrown a shovelful of mud over his knees as they worked together in the trench. To comfort this poor Hungarian Jew, too gentle and decent to survive in the *Lager*, Levi found himself telling Kraus that he had seen him in a dream, looking healthy and well fed, but the dream was an invention.

Snow followed the rain. The Jews were not issued with overcoats. They went to work dressed only in their summer uniform and sabots without socks, while the Germans and the Poles wore thick rubber boots, padded overalls and lined Balaclavas, and the British wore fur-lined jackets.

Levi and his comrades in the Chemical Kommando were humping 60-kilo sacks all day long; they knew that they would not last the winter. After the air raids the sacks of phenylbeta were moved into the Styrene division. Then, when the warehouse was repaired, they had to be shifted back again. A whisper that spread during the summer claimed that the *Häftlinge* who had passed the chemistry exam were soon to be assigned to Doktor Pannwitz's laboratory, which was in the Polymerization division, but on the brink of winter, Building 939, which housed the laboratory, lay half in ruins.

Levi heard about the Warsaw ghetto uprising, and the liquidation of the Lublin ghetto the year before, from Jews arriving from the Lodz ghetto throughout 1944. He wrote: "Three hundred prisoners have arrived in the *Lager* from the Lodz ghetto, transferred by the Germans before the Russian advance; they told us rumours about the legendary battle of the Warsaw ghetto, and they described how the Germans had liquidated the Lublin camp over a year ago: four machine-guns in the corners and the huts set on fire." (*Man 137/143*) By the Lublin camp, Levi must have been referring to the liquidation of the Poniatowa camp, which was part of the Lublin district, and which the German called *Erntefest*, "Operation Harvest Festival." During the single day of 4 November 1943, the Germans machine-gunned 14,500 prisoners, drowning the rattle of the machine-guns and the cries of the victims under fairground music broadcast by loudspeakers. There were two survivors: Esther Rubinstein and Ludwika Fiszer.[22] On some days, when the wind was in the right direction, Levi heard a dull vibration rising out of the ground. The Russians were in Poland. They had taken Lublin, and had halted just east of Warsaw.

In the Chemical Kommando the lethal routine continued. Those who worked in the Magnesium Chloride division had their feet in briny water all day long. It burned their clothes, and their skin was covered in scabs and sores. The others were building a new two-seater latrine for their Kommando, whose number had expanded after the influx of prisoners from Lodz and Transylvania. With its customary elegance, the German administration designated this building as the "two-seater Kommando shit-house." Levi regretted that its creation deprived him and his comrades of a good pretext to break off their work and make contact with the civilian workers. Here he takes another opportunity to have a dig at "Henri," alias Paul Steinberg, whose comment on the inauguration of the *Zweiplatziges Kommandoscheisshaus* was: "*Noblesse oblige.*" Levi does not take these words as a joke; he goes on to say that "Henri" could fend for himself, implying that others could not.

There was a day when all the other squads had left — the brick squad, the tanks squad — and apart from the Prominents only Levi and his comrades in the phenylbeta squad stood waiting for their day's assignment. This was the moment when Alex the Kapo announced that Doktor Pannwitz had chosen his three *Häftlinge* for the laboratory. The three men were 169509, Brackier; 175633, Kandek;[23] and 174517, Levi. There is a discrepancy here. Primo Levi does not mention Paul Steinberg, whereas Steinberg states that he too took the chemistry exam in front of Doktor Pannwitz, and was assigned to the laboratory with the other three. Steinberg readily admits that he was undoubtedly the least competent of the chemists in the Polymerization lab, since his studies had ended in high school. Levi's memory of his term of detention in Auschwitz was extraordinarily accurate, yet he does not put "Henri" in the lab, even though he was paying him particularly close and critical attention. Stranger still, in the late 1960s, Primo Levi corresponded with a German chemist who had worked in this Buna laboratory and whom he called Müller in *The Periodic Table*. From here on Müller shall be referred to as M., or by the initials F.M., in order to protect his anonymity. In his first letter, F.M. asked Levi for news of the companions he had mentioned in his book, but not about Paul Steinberg. When questioned on this point, Steinberg said that he did not have the slightest recollection of Levi in the lab. It is a riddle that is bound to remain unsolved.

From now on Primo Levi would be working under a roof, and in heated premises. Alberto greeted the news with joy. He knew that every material advantage his friend might derive from his new situation would be divided "into two strictly equal parts" (*Man 138/144*). Also, said Levi, Alberto was a free and untamed spirit who did not put up with systems. But in fact the *Häftling* had no choice. No matter what Kommando his fate or his ingenuity assigned him to, he had to put up with it or die.

The Russians were now 80 kilometres away from the camp, and the plant had been badly damaged by Allied bombing. The power station had broken down, the methanol columns were out of action, and only one of the four acetylene tanks was still intact. The Nazis evacuated prisoners from the camps further east, shipped them to Auschwitz, and sent most of them straight to the gas chamber. Food rations were reduced, and epidemics of scarlet fever, diphtheria, and petechial typhus decimated the camp.

Doktor Pannwitz had finally decided to call in the services of Jewish chemists. When he became a specialized worker Levi received a new shirt and underpants, so as not to offend the German lab staff by looking or smelling too repulsive. For the same reason, he had to be shaved not only on Mondays with the rest of the Chemistry Kommando but also every Wednesday. The gas chambers and furnaces of Auschwitz were working night and day, epidemics were raging, and the Russians were driving westward, but the Buna's intact laboratories stayed meticulously clean. Their aim was to produce synthetic fuel and rubber. They did produce methanol, which the prisoners stole as a fermenting agent for their trade in moonshine liquor, even thought methanol was fatal to drink. Auschwitz-Monowitz was a concentration camp, but it was still for the Germans to decide how the prisoners were to die. Numerous signs advised the *Häftlinge* that the absorption of methanol would cause blindness followed by death, but the thefts of the poison persisted, and drinks that contained it were sold, particularly to the Russians, though it killed them.

Levi crossed over from the concentrationary universe into the familiar world of the laboratory. He and his comrades entered it with shaven skulls and clad in their inmate uniforms. At once the smell, the glassware, and all the familiar objects revived his memory of the laboratory in Turin University. It was unbelievably hot — 24 degrees. The head of the laboratory, who was not a chemist at all, addressed the newcomers as "Herr."

The sight of this abundance — petrol, soap, alcohol — at once set Levi thinking about "organizing": stealing these luxuries and selling them for food. He sewed a secret pocket into his jacket to hide the proceeds of his thieving. Now he had grounds for hoping that he might not fall ill, that he might escape the selections. Often, the Polish earth would tremble under his feet; he heard the distant number of the Russian field guns. The end of the war was approaching. Those not scheduled for death — the Poles, the French — held their heads high. The British gave the "V" for victory sign.

The Germans took no notice. They mended the bomb damage, put the factory back in running order, and set 1 February 1945 as the starting date of synthetic rubber production. They went on exterminating Jews, and continued to look forward to victory even when their armies were in flight on every front. Levi, who observed them with the closest interest, remarked that the Germans had a special style of action which was "not meditated and deliberate, but follows from their nature and from the destiny they have chosen. They could not act differently: if you wound the body of a dying man, the wound will begin to heal, even if the whole body dies within a day" (*Man 141/147*).

The three privileged Jews of the laboratory were called before the others every morning. While the men of Kommando 98 set out to labour in the cold, the three chemists would make their way to the overheated Polymerization building. As he worked, Levi "organized" — at no great risk, he said. What he stole was petrol and soap, which were easily available, but bulky and quite plentiful, so they did not fetch high prices. Thirty years later, in *The Periodic Table*, he gave details of the trade that he organized with Alberto so as to stave off the hunger that conditioned their actions and thoughts throughout their waking hours — so much so that it easily eclipsed the fear of death. For Levi, learning to steal required a reformation, almost a change of nature. Without being reckless, the "respectable little university graduate" now stole anything he could, except his comrades' bread. Comparing himself to a dog, he wrote that Darwin's laws of evolution applied to himself; he took some pride in his "involution–evolution" (*Table* 140).

Rather than steal indiscriminately, Levi made a survey of his options. Liquids were difficult to shift, because of the packaging problem. He looked for a good product, portable, solid, not bulky — hence easy to hide in case of a search — and most of all, in demand. Ingenious and persistent, while bombs were falling on the Buna he worked in the laboratory to produce fatty acids by oxidizing paraffin. When he tried out his preparation it eased his hunger but tasted disgusting: no use trying to sell it. Then he made fritters with a base of cotton wool "cooked" on an electric hotplate. They looked so unappetizing that they too never reached the market. Selling the cotton wool direct to the infirmary brought low returns and was risky. He tried it once, then dropped the idea. He used himself as a guinea-pig to test the effects of glycerine, hoping that it would metabolize in the form of calories, but it gave him stomach troubles.

The quest continued. Next, he discovered a single bottle that had no label and contained "about twenty gray, hard, colorless, tasteless little rods" (*Table* 141), roughly 25 millimetres long by four or five millimetres wide. It was too risky to investigate his find in the lab, so he hid three samples in his pocket and took them back to camp that night. To test its resistance, Alberto scraped one with a penknife. It crackled and sparked: "it was iron-cerium, an alloy from which the common flints of lighters are made," but these were not lighter-flints, as Alberto explained. Having worked as a labourer with a welding crew, he recognized the little cylinders used for igniting the jets of oxyacetylene torches. Primo was disappointed: he could not see an outlet for his spoils. Alberto ticked him off. How dare he give up? They absolutely had to market the cerium he had stolen, they had to be astute. This was the magic word, because Primo Levi had no talent for astuteness, except — as he acknowledged — in making friends with someone who genuinely had it. Alberto was shrewd enough to have taken some advantage of his association with the "little doctor," but the thought did not enter his mind.

Alberto knew that there was an illegal trade in manufactured lighters in the camp, and that they were very popular both with civilians and with Prominents. Lighters needed flints. All they had to do was modify the rest of the rods that Primo was going to have to steal from the unlabelled bottle in the lab during the next air-raid alert. Raids were announced by wailing sirens. The Germans would hurry to their shelter, leaving Levi behind. He could rob the shelves at leisure before going out to join his Kommando under the rain of yellow leaflets — a message from the Allies to the Germans:

Im Bauch kein Fett,
Acht Uhr ins Bett;
Der Arsch kaum warm,
Fliegeralarm!

Belly not fed,
Eight o'clock bed;
Arse hardly warm,
Air-raid alarm!

Primo Levi had forty little rods of cerium in his pocket; Alberto had told him that a lighter flint sold for a ration of bread. Now each little rod would make three lighter flints. As bomb loads stamped across the waste ground, Levi calculated that with 120 flints he could buy "two months of life for me and two for Alberto" (*Table* 145). Rescue was possible. Survival was conceivable.

Levi brought the rods back into camp, and Alberto, now armed with a thin copper rod to calibrate their diameter, took the job of paring them to size with his penknife. They had to keep it secret, and the whole operation went on for three successive nights of working blind under the blankets, at the risk of starting a fire if the showers of sparks touched off by the scraping knife happened to set light to the tinder of wooden shavings in the pallets. Just to strike a match in the hut was a hanging offence. When the rods had been whittled down to the required diameter, Alberto and Primo broke them in three and started on the next. Their work went unnoticed, and it earned the two friends the rations of bread they had counted on.

In the laboratory, Primo Levi had a drawer to himself, where he could store his cap and gloves. They also gave him a notebook, a pencil, and a chemistry textbook. Inside the camp, it meant death to be found in possession of any of these precious objects. It turned out that the German Polish foreman, Herr Stawinoga, was not a stickler for punctuality; Levi only had to ask, and he could got out on errands of his own. It was precisely at this moment, when he realized that he was the owner of a notebook and a pencil, working in a refuge free from cold, fatigue, and fear, that he found his feelings as a free man reawakening, and with them his pain.

But in spite of his drawer, his notebook, his pencil, and his chemistry textbook, Levi, no. 174517, was still a *Häftling*. The scornful stares of the women who worked in the laboratory — four Germans and a Pole — left him in no doubt about his status. In contact with these young women he realized how repulsively squalid his clothes were. His teeming fleas made him scratch continually. The very liquid soup dictated frequent trips to the latrines. His boots were foul with mud and grease, and their wooden soles clattered objectionably loudly on the perfectly clean tiled floor of the laboratory. And it was not only his appearance, and his comrades' appearance, that caused his new colleagues to back away. It was his smell. "So young and already he stinks!" prisoners would say to an inmate newly arrived in Auschwitz. The girls in the laboratory felt no compassion for the Jewish chemists. They spent most of their time gossiping, eating bread and jam, filing their nails, smoking, and singing. When they broke glassware, they blamed it on the Jews, but they never spoke to them. One day Levi asked the Pole, Fräulein Liczba, a question. Quite scandalized, she turned to Herr Stawinoga and spoke a sentence in which the only word he could make out was "*Stinkjude*," stinking Jew. Levi felt just as deeply wounded as on the day when Alex the Kapo had wiped his oily hand on his jacket.

The air-raid warnings had grown so frequent that the Jewish specialists seemed to spend all their time assembling and dismantling the laboratory equipment. They were inspected sometimes by an SS man, sometimes by an old soldier of the Wehrmacht, and sometimes by the Doktor F.M. — Müller from *The Periodic Table*.

The circumstances in which Levi made contact with F.M. again after the war were not quite as he described them in the book. After the war Doktor F.M. was in touch with Hety Schmitt-Maass of Wiesbaden, a German friend of Hermann Langbein, who gave her a copy of *If This Is A Man* some time after the first edition had gone out of print. She also knew Jean Améry, and she and Primo Levi corresponded for several years. She recommended Levi's book to F.M., and he expressed his wish to write to Levi. Hety Schmitt-Maass arranged it, and Levi replied to F.M.'s first letter, received on 2 March 1967, and to his subsequent letters, although he would not grant F.M.'s request for a meeting, and for absolution. Eventually, if with some reluctance, Levi did agree to the meeting, although there could be no question of forgiveness, because setting aside the fact that he was not a "forgiver" (despite what Jean Améry had written about him), he claimed no individual authority to judge, even though he insisted categorically that justice must be done:

> Forgiveness is not a word of mine. It is wished upon me, because all the letters I receive, especially from young Catholic readers, take that stance. They ask me if I have forgiven. I believe that I am a just man, in my own way. I can forgive one man and not another. I can only consider justice case by case. If I had had Eichmann in front of me I would have sentenced him to death. Wholesale forgiveness of the kind suggested is not for me.
>
> Anyone who commits a crime must pay, unless he repents. But not in words. Verbal repentance is not enough. I am disposed to forgive a man who has shown by his actions that he is no longer the man he was. And not too late.[24]

Levi was not reluctant to reply to F.M.'s letters because he had always regretted having been unable to find and question the Doktor Pannwitz who had examined him in chemistry in Auschwitz — Pannwitz was dead. He had looked for him not for the sake of revenge but because he wanted to understand how a man like Pannwitz functioned.

Levi's portrait of F.M. in *The Periodic Table* is true to life. He was a tall, thick-set man, "more coarse then refined in appearance" (*Table* 214). In the Buna laboratory he spoke directly with *Häftling* no. 174517 only three times, addressing him with ordinary politeness, which was rare, coming from a German to a Jew. His first question concerned a technical matter. His second was more incongruous in that place: F.M. wanted to know why the Jewish chemist kept his beard in such a state. Levi explained that, like all his comrades, he owned neither a razor nor a handkerchief, and that the regulations allowed shaving only twice a week, on Mondays and Wednesdays. The third time, F.M. handed Levi a *Schein*, a typed certificate stating that *Häftling* no. 174517 was also to be shaved on Thursdays, and that the *Effektenmagazin*, the stockroom — stocked with the looted possessions of Jews murdered in the gas chambers — was to grant Levi the extraordinary privilege of a pair of leather shoes instead of his filthy wooden sabots. On this third occasion, F.M. also asked Levi why he looked so nervous. Levi said to himself in German: "*Der Mann hat keine Ahnung*" — "This man has no idea."

The correspondence between F.M. and Primo Levi covered a short interval: less than a year.[25] For F.M., its purpose was essentially to exonerate himself from his involvement in the genocide of the Jews, even though he had taken no direct part in it. F.M. must have had a sense of remorse for having worked for I.G. Farben in Monowitz, and was hoping to salve his conscience. He died on 13 December 1967, without having received the absolution he expected from ex-prisoner 174517. F.M. referred to memories of his in which he appeared in quite a favourable light. Primo Levi replied — not angrily but firmly, and with a gentle irony — that his own memories did not square with F.M.'s.

In the month of December 1944, Primo Levi and his friend Alberto waited every night for the *menaschka*, a kind of zinc bucket filled with three or four litres of soup, provided by the civilian worker Lorenzo Perrone, at considerable risk to himself. If he had been caught in the act of feeding Jews, he would have suffered a fate like theirs, but that made no difference to Lorenzo. He could barely read or write, but his heart spoke the language of the good. The *menaschka* had been made to order by Silberlust, the tinsmith, with pieces of guttering, in exchange for three rations of bread. Everyone admired it, even some of the Greeks — for Levi, the highest possible praise. Lorenzo used to leave it in a hiding place not far from the site where he worked. The distribution took place twice a day, and Alberto and Primo discussed having a second *menaschka* made, so that they could leave the empty one when they collected the full one. By halving the number of pick-up trips it would reduce their risk of being caught.

At the end of the Monowitz year, Primo Levi's condition had stabilized since his earlier decline. He was working as a specialist, in buildings protected from the cold. There were no beatings in the laboratory, the work was not tiring, and the daily calorie supplement afforded him a margin of safety. Furthermore, better health brought higher status. When describing the improvement, Levi also comments that "Henri" — always the magnet of his disapproval — now took the trouble to speak to himself and Alberto, while Elias the dwarf hung around them, fawning and snooping, trying to find out how they were organizing themselves.

Since the sale of the lighter-flints, Levi had found a new item to market. The "little doctor" had evolved a knack for trade. Knowing that the *Blockälteste* of Block 44 was short of brooms, he stole one on the construction site, detached the head, sawed the handle in two, and smuggled the pieces into camp on successive days, with the lengths of handle tied to his thighs inside his trousers. Then, having organized a hammer, some nails, and a piece of sheet metal, he put the broom back together. This original but risky operation took Levi four days to complete, and the client's approval of the product brought the supplier two new orders.

Alberto was even more ingenious. Twice he drew a large file from the tool store, swapped it with an Italian from Trieste for two smaller files, then returned one file to the store and sold the other. When Alberto gained access to a supply of celluloid tags of several different colours, used to label the various pipes that ran through the Polymerization laboratory, they gave him an idea. He stole several batches of these labels, and Levi used a cork-drill in the lab to cut them into two hundred discs. Then Alberto approached one of the *Blockältesten* and explained what he had in mind. One of the jobs of a *Blockälteste* was to make sure that each of his *Häftling* took a shower during the compulsory visit to the shower block. The showers were unpopular. Sometimes the water was boiling, sometimes cold, no soap or towel was provided, and thieves might steal the users' clothes. As they emerged from the *Badesraum*, the men were inspected by an assistant: only if they came out damp and shivering were they issued with a ticket that entitled them to draw their morning ration of bread. It was this ticket, a scrap of damp paper, that Alberto proposed to replace with his celluloid discs. The *Blockälteste* jumped at the offer, and settled on the exorbitant price of ten rations of bread, payable in instalments. As soon as other *Blockältesten* learned about the new fashion, they wanted supplies of their own, and Alberto manufactured a different-coloured set for every Block.

One night, when they had returned to camp and were mustered on the *Appellplatz*, the prisoners found the gallows lit up by a searchlight and knew that an execution must be due, and that they would be compelled to watch it. Russian artillery rumbled in the distance, on every front the Germans were retreating, the war had to be over soon. Still the Germans refused to accept the inevitable end of their power. Welded to their logic of senseless destruction, they continued to gas, torture, shoot, and hang the remnants of the victims in their camps. The concrete prospect of certain defeat did not abate their cruelty.

Primo Levi had already witnessed thirteen hangings, staged as punishments for attempts to escape and for stealing. This last execution had a very different background. In October 1944, knowing that their liquidation was imminent and inevitable, the members of the Birkenau *Sonderkommando* had risen in rebellion and blown up one of the crematoria. The man to be murdered today was rumoured to have had some connection with the Birkenau rebellion, and to have smuggled weapons into Monowitz with the same objective.

As Hermann Langbein reports in his book *Menschen in Auschwitz*, the first uprising planned by men of the *Sonderkommando* had failed late in 1942. Adolf Weiss, a Slovakian, who worked in one of the squads assigned to build the crematoria, had made contact with the Kapo of the *Sonderkommando* night-shift, who had been in touch with groups outside the camp to prepare for a revolt. The Kapo of the day-shift found out and wanted to join them. When they refused him, he denounced them to the SS. On 3 December 1942, the entire night-shift, who had managed to beat the traitor to death with a spade, was wiped out in the gas chamber of the main camp, Auschwitz I, while the Kapo, the under-Kapo, the foremen, and the day-shift were shot in Birkenau. After that, the SS formed another *Sonderkommando* made up of Jews lately arrived from Sosnowiec.

Some time later, when a new plan took shape, the *Sonderkommando* numbered 952 members, mostly Greek and Hungarian Jews. The Nazis had completed their liquidation of the Hungarian Jews and those from the Lodz ghetto. Having no further need of them, they gassed two hundred members of the Birkenau *Sonderkommando* in the main camp in the utmost secrecy, but the survivors found out, and realized that their fate was sealed. Unable to persuade the camp Resistance to order a general rising, three members of the *Sonderkommando* decided to organize a mutiny, but first they buried various documents — which were retrieved after the war — concerning the mass murders that the Germans had committed in Auschwitz. The leaders of the Resistance in the camp gave support to the originator of the rebellion plan, one Stanislaw Kaminski. It came as a bitter blow to the rebels when the Resistance members refused to join their leaders in support of the rebellion. Some time later, Kaminski appears to have been betrayed. He and a Greek who had attempted to escape were shot by the SS on 8 August 1944, before the outbreak of the rebellion.

Nevertheless, the organizers of the *Sonderkommando* uprising were helped in their preparations by a number of inmates in the camp, in particular a small group of Jewish women, one of them Roza Robota, and some Russian PoWs who had survived the construction of Birkenau. Three of the women worked in the stores of the munitions plant run by Weichsel-Union-Metallwerke. Taking terrible risks, they smuggled out gunpowder that was used to make grenades out of "small lead containers filled with powder, small stones, crumbled bricks, and a fuse."[26]

In August 1944 the *Sonderkommando* crews numbered 874 prisoners whose labours kept the gas chambers and crematoria running round the clock. When the furnaces were unable to keep pace with the rate of gassing, the SS ordered huge incineration pits to be dug, where the corpses were burned to ashes. On 4 October, SS-*Hauptsturmführer* (Captain) Schwarz, the Birkenau commandant, informed the SS guards that four inmates had overpowered a sentry who had turned his back on them, then put his rifle out of action before making their escape.

On the morning of 7 October, a Saturday, the 663 members of the Birkenau *Sonderkommando* learned from the leadership of the Resistance that the camp authorities were getting ready to liquidate them all. The SS had announced that three hundred named members of the squad, working in Crematoria IV and V,[27] were to be "transferred" at the end of the morning. During the midday break, while the members of the *Sonderkommando*'s combat group were holding a meeting, they were surprised by a German common-law prisoner, the Oberkapo of Crematorium III, who threatened to report them. The men of the *Sonderkommando* killed him on the spot. At 1:25 p.m. the same group used hammers, axes, and stones to attack the SS guards who came to take them away. The prisoners set fire to Crematorium IV, then threw the grenades made with the powder stolen by Roza Robota's group, before heading for the woodland near the camp. When the members of the *Sonderkommando* in Crematorium II saw the flames in the distance, they too went into action. They overpowered the Oberkapo, a German of the Reich, disarmed an SS man and threw him into a furnace, killed another SS man, cut the barbed wire that surrounded the crematorium, broke through the fence of the women's camp, and fled.

According to another version of the facts, a stoker under SS-*Kommandoführer* Buch informed on the rebels, betrayed their plan, and so triggered the immediate and premature outbreak of the mutiny. This wrecked the plan to coordinate the actions of the four *Sonderkommando* crews. In the version reported by Hermann Langbein, the crews of Crematoria II and IV were unable to join the insurrection, while the prisoners working in Crematorium I did manage to take part. On the other hand Filip Müller, who worked for three years in the *Sonderkommando*, reports in his testimony[28] that three hundred comrades slated for immediate execution on 7 October 1944 started to throw a hail of stones at the SS men who were rounding them up, while Crematorium IV was set on fire. The sirens sounded an instant alert. Truckloads of shirt-sleeved SS men drove up between Crematoria IV and V, and opened up their submachine guns on the running prisoners who were looking for a way out. Those who were not hit made a dash for the barbed wire and opened up a breach through it. Filip Müller ran towards the blazing Crematorium IV, where he took shelter by getting inside the duct that linked the ovens to the chimney.

Then he crawled to the chimney, and had to make his way along the drainage channel, because the fire department crew (manned by prisoners) were hosing water to put out the fire. He left his hiding place at midnight, crept into the coke bunker, picked up a poker forty centimetres long, then left the bunker and crawled along the crematorium to the looted property warehouse area (Canada), intending to eliminate the SS sentry. But the guard had been reinforced, and Müller had to give up his plan and return to the drainage channel. There he stayed until he heard the sound of a clearance Kommando arriving, and with the help of its Kapo, Schloïme, he joined the group of prisoners sent to collect the bodies of the two hundred mutineers massacred by the SS.

In the afternoon, trucks delivered a further 250 bodies of members of the *Sonderkommando* of Crematoria II and III. When they had seen Crematorium IV ablaze, some Russian PoWs had thrown Oberkapo Karl Konvoent alive into the flames of one of the furnaces. They had cut the barbed wire with insulated pliers, then lobbed grenades at the approaching SS men. Some of them got away in the direction of Rajsko, fought the SS to the last bullet, then took refuge in a barn, which the SS set on fire. Altogether, over 450 prisoners died in the uprising.

Of the ranks of the Birkenau *Sonderkommando*, only 212 were left alive. Four hundred and fifty-five men had died in the rebellion, while the SS had had four men killed and twelve wounded. The organizers of the movement were Polish Jews, of whom four had been deported from Paris. The survivors, fourteen of them, were locked up in Block 11.[28] The leaders of the insurrection, Jankiel Handelsman, deported from France, Wrobel, and Jukl, were tortured to death in the basement of Block 11. Three Jewish women who worked in the Weichsel-Union-Metallwerke were arrested and tortured for helping to smuggle explosives to the members of the *Sonderkommando*. Roza Robota was also arrested, and tortured in Block 11. All four women were hanged on 6 January 1945.

The condemned man who had taken part in the Birkenau uprising and had tried to bring weapons into Monowitz was waiting by the gallows lit by the glare of a searchlight. An SS man delivered a speech in German, not a word of it comprehensible to most of the prisoners, but when another German voice shouted: "*Habt ihr verstehen?*" — "Did you understand?" — Primo Levi heard answers of "*Jawohl.*" Then the condemned man cried out: "*Kameraden, ich bin der Letzte!*" — "Comrades, I am the last one!"

Levi describes the mass of prisoners standing passive and silent to witness the execution — "an abject flock" (*Man* 149/155). These thousands of men with lowered heads, who took off their caps on the order of an SS man before the trapdoor dropped under the feet of the last surviving rebel and the band started playing again, were degraded by the offence committed against one of their fellows, and by the insult done to them. The Nazis corrupted their victims and dragged them down to their own foul level. Levi voiced their thoughts in *The*

Drowned and the Saved: "We, the master race, are your destroyers, but you are no better than we are; if we so wish and we do wish, we can destroy not only your bodies but also your souls, just as we have destroyed ours" (*DS 53–4/37*).

In subsequent meditations on the way in which the Nazis corrupted their victims and pushed them into complicity, into collaborating with them, Levi drew upon the case of Chaim Rumkowski, the elder of the Jewish Council of the ghetto of Lodz, one of Poland's largest industrial towns (called Litzmannstadt by the Germans). Rumkowski ruled his "Jewish kingdom" with almost monarchical power, tolerated by the Germans who appreciated his talent for order. His megalomania found expression in stamps bearing his effigy, in driving through Lodz in a carriage pulled by a skeletal nag, in hymns praising his "firm and powerful hands," and in suppressing Resistance movements, which he regarded as "lese-majesty" against his authority.

However, Rumkowski's zealous and self-aggrandizing embrace of collaboration failed to protect him. In 1944 the liquidation of the Lodz ghetto began: tens of thousands were deported to Auschwitz and eliminated. Rumkowski, too, was sent to Auschwitz, travelling in a special carriage hitched to the last wagon of the cattle trucks carrying the Jews of Lodz to their fate. Mojsze Lewin, a Polish Jew who was deported from Lodz to Auschwitz, reported that Rumkowski was liquidated on arrival by Jews of the *Sonderkommando*, relatives of those he had sent to their deaths. Others claim that he was burned alive in the crematorium; another account has it that he was stunned, then burned.

To Levi, Rumkowski belonged to the "gray zone" inhabited by those who, if not wholly culpable, were nevertheless corrupted by the power which accrued to them under the Nazi regime; he is a grotesque but real example of the "fundamental theme of human ambiguity fatally provoked by oppression" (*DS 60–1/43*). For Rumkowski, as Levi wrote, power was a drug for which "the dependency and need for ever larger doses is born, as are the denial of reality and the return to childish dreams of omnipotence" (*DS 67/49*). And, like Rumkowski, "willingly or not we come to terms with power, forgetting that we are all in the ghetto, that the ghetto is walled in, that outside the ghetto reign the lords of death, and that close by the train is waiting" (*DS 69/51*).

The man who was hanged in Monowitz had preserved his dignity. Levi described the helpless watching crowd as "worthy of the unarmed death which awaits us" (*Man 150/156*). He and Alberto were among these prisoners who returned to their huts with a festering sense of shame.

On 11 January 1945, Levi came down with scarlet fever and entered the camp infirmary, the *KB*. On 12 January, Soviet armoured columns of the 1st

Ukrainian Front advanced from Baranow as the Russians launched their final offensive into Poland and East Prussia. German defences of 600,000 men, 700 tanks and 1,300 aircraft were no match for Russian forces of over 1.5 million men, more than 3,000 tanks and 10,000 aircraft.

At 1:50 in the afternoon of 15 January an American reconnaissance flight took eight photographs of the I.G. Farben installations. They showed that on the Buna site, damage repairs were well under way, and the boiler-rooms necessary for the production of synthetic fuels were still intact. On the evening of 16 January, Soviet planes attacked the Auschwitz camp. Three days before the departure of the 2,530 SS staff, the population of the Monowitz *Lager* and its satellite camps numbered 33,037 male and 2,044 female prisoners.

On 17 January, units of the Red Army approached the suburbs of Cracow from the north and north-west, surprising the Germans, who did not expect an attack from that direction. At 2 p.m. Hans Frank, the governor-general of the *Generalgouvernement* — the Polish territory not incorporated into Germany or the Soviet Union in 1939[29] — convened his final meeting, during which he declared that Cracow, which had been German since the dawn of time, would never be abandoned by the Germans. Half an hour later he left the town and headed for Silesia, as the Russians launched massive air strikes on roads jammed by columns of the Wehrmacht and by the officialdom of the Frank administration, both in full retreat.

The commandant of Auschwitz I, SS-*Sturmbannführer* Richard Bär, took the decision to evacuate the camp. He chose the leaders of the evacuation columns from the ranks of the guards, and gave orders for the ruthless liquidation of all *Häftlinge* who failed to keep up with the columns or who attempted to escape. On the evening of 17 January the weather was very cold, and snow was falling. On the occasion of the final roll-call in the *Lager* of Monowitz, 10,223 inmates were counted, including 110 Italian Jews.

The archives of the *Häftlingskrankenbau* (*HKB*: the camp hospital) and many files were burned overnight in Block 11. The SS officers working in the medical services were also ordered to burn the records in the satellite camps.

In Monowitz the inmate physicians were instructed to make a careful examination of the patients in their care, and to delete from the registers all those who were capable of walking. Those who could walk only as far as the Auschwitz railway station were separated from those who could manage 50 kilometres on foot. It was decided that only the sickest patients, in the care of the sickest inmate doctors, were to be left behind.[30] During the two days that followed, 58,000 prisoners set out on foot from Auschwitz, in freezing weather.

A few days before the evacuation, a hungry Primo Levi had been searching the laboratory, intending to steal some small, unusual object that would buy him a hunk of bread. He came across a drawer full of graduated pipettes and stuffed a dozen into the secret pocket he had sewn inside his jacket. Immediately after roll-call, he hurried to the infirmary and offered his trophies to a Polish nursing orderly who worked in the contagious ward. The Pole replied that he had run out of bread, but he did have some soup, and it was an unusual variety he had to offer — half a bowl of frozen soup, left unfinished by a patient too weak to consume it and probably deceased. The half was semi-circular, because someone had removed the other segment as if it had been a pie.

Levi and Alberto Dallavolta were much too hungry to worry about catching an infection, and they shared the contents of the bowl. Alberto had had scarlet fever as a child. Primo had not. (This was the "small cause" that Levi referred to in the title of his account of this episode in *Moments of Reprieve*.) Some days later, Primo woke up with a high fever, but went to the lab as usual. That day he was told to teach a certain analytical method to a Fräulein Drechsel, a young German lab assistant who displayed a swastika badge on her shirt and refused to speak to Jews. The method involved the use of a pipette. In his demonstration, Levi deliberately put one between his lips, then handed Fräulein Drechsel the contaminated pipette and motioned to her to do the same. Not long after that, on 11 January, Primo Levi entered the *Infektionsabteilung, Stube 8* — infectious diseases ward, room 8, of the infirmary.

The ward was a small room with an area of about 15 square metres, warm, very clean, fitted with ten bunks on two levels, a wardrobe, three stools, and a sanitary bucket. The most seriously ill patients, those too weak to climb on to the top bunks, occupied the lower level. Levi was the thirteenth patient in the ward. Four had contracted scarlet fever, like himself, three had diphtheria, two had typhus, and another was disfigured by facial erysipelas. The last two suffered more than one pathology, and were very emaciated. Six of the patients were Frenchmen: of these, Alcalaï and Towarowski were Jewish, and Cagnolati, Dorget, Ducarme, and Conreau were not. Levi had a bunk to himself. His contagious illness entitled him to forty days' rest and isolation. He had managed to keep his belongings: "a belt of interlaced electric wire, the knife-spoon, a needle [and three lengths of bread], five buttons and last of all eighteen flints which I had stolen from the laboratory" (*Man* 151/157). These were the rods that he and Alberto had learned how to convert into smaller flints, and they now rated six or seven rations of bread.

Levi was fortunate enough to receive heavy doses of sulphonamides, which boosted his chance of recovery. Two of the Frenchmen, natives of the Vosges, had scarlet fever. They had only been in camp for a few days, having been shipped there in a convoy of civilians rounded up in Lorraine during the German retreat. Arthur Cagnolati was the elder of the two, a small, lean peasant; he shared a bunk with Charles Conreau, a 32-year-old primary schoolteacher. As well as scarlet fever, he was also suffering from sinusitis. His face was swollen, and his left eye closed and full of pus. Doktor Coënca finally operated on it by the light of a torch, in a corridor, using an instrument that he had made himself. On the advice of Professor Weitz, he pierced his left frontal sinus through the orbital arch, and applied a wet dressing to the badly infected eye.

Askenazi, a Greek from Salonica, came to shave them all, and told Levi that the camp was to be evacuated the next day. He was not surprised, because rumours had been flying. For several days there had been stories that the Russians were in Czestochowa, a hundred kilometres north of Auschwitz, or in Zakopane, a hundred kilometres south.

Obedient to his orders, in the afternoon of 17 January, Samnelidis, the Greek doctor, came to announce that all patients fit to walk were to receive clothes and shoes and faced a march of 20 kilometres. Just before leaving they would be issued with a triple ration of bread. As for the rest of them, it was obvious that their fate was uncertain. A rumour that the seriously ill were to be liquidated prompted the two young Hungarians in the ward to decide to join the march. Levi could see how weak they were, and he advised them against it, but they were too terrified to stay. The SS killed them the next day, in the early hours of the march.

Levi was running a temperature of 40 degrees (104 degrees Fahrenheit), but he dragged himself out of the ward to look for a pair of shoes, knowing that he was certain to need them. The *KB*'s store of patients' shoes had been raided by some of the prisoners marked for evacuation, but he found a usable pair lying in the corridor. Before he left, Samnelidis, who had got hold of a ruck-sack, told the patients that they would be well advised not to remain in the *KB*, in the hands of the SS. Then he tossed a French novel — *Remorques*, by Roger Vercel — on to Levi's bunk, saying: "Keep it, read it, Italian. You can give it back when we meet again" (*Man 155/161*). This meant never. Levi admitted that for the first time he hated somebody, because Samnelidis was savouring his knowledge of their fate.

The last visitor was Levi's closest friend, Alberto Dallavolta, with whom he had shared everything since their arrival in Auschwitz. He tapped on the window to say goodbye, unaware that it would be for ever. Alberto was glad to be leaving and full of confidence. He never came home.

8   The Last Ten Days

In the afternoon of 17 January 1945 the Block leaders assembled the prisoners on the roll-call square of the Monowitz Lager. The Kapos ordered them to muster by Kommandos. After nightfall, all those who could walk were formed up into columns of a thousand men, with squads of medical orderlies sandwiched between each column. Several thousand prisoners waited, surrounded by SS guards. The evacuation began in the early hours of the icy morning, when the *Lagerführer* gave the order: "Kapos, fall in!"[1] The prisoners marched in close order. Each of them was issued with 500 grams of bread and a finger of margarine.

The retreating Germans evacuated 58,000 prisoners from the three Auschwitz camps and their satellites, aiming to intern them in the concentration camps on German soil. The columns were dispatched towards Gleiwitz (Gliwice), 52 kilometres away, by way of Nikolaï, Bierun, Mikolow, Mokre Slaskie, and Przysowice. Part of the journey was made on foot, to railway stations, in a temperature of 20 degrees below zero. The German escort weeded out the nuisances — those who could not keep up, or who failed to find cover during halts — by shooting them. When they reached the stations the prisoners were crammed into open coal wagons, without food or water. Most of the men and women who set out on the notorious death-march, which lasted in some cases for a week, did not reach their destination. The living threw the bodies of the frozen dead on to the railway track, and licked snow off the ledges of the wagons to ease their thirst and hunger. There were instances of cannibalism, when starving captives were driven to consume parts of their comrades who had died.

About 950 sick men and *Muselmänner* remained in the camp, as well as a few men – either shrewd enough to try their luck, or who had wind of the Nazis' intentions – who at the last minute discarded their clothes and slipped into bunks in the infirmary. In Levi's ward there were eleven men left, each with a bunk to himself, except for Charles Conreau and Arthur Cagnolati, who shared one. A last distribution of soup was made on the morning after the evacuation. Some of the guard towers on the perimeter were still occupied by SS guards.

At dawn on 19 January, Allied aircraft attacked the I.G. Farben factories in Dwory, very close to Monowitz. This raid cut the water and electricity supplies to the town of Auschwitz and all the satellite camps. In the confusion, the remaining Germans made ready to leave. Doctor Mengele collected the records of the "researches" on twins he had conducted, for shipment to Berlin. In the

198

Buna, the heads of I.G. Farben burned their archives. The units of the *Volkssturm* made their escape while waves of Soviet bombers started enormous fires.

On 20 January, SS-*Sturmbannführer* (Major) Franz Xavier Kraus, representing *SS-Obergruppenführer* (Lieutenant-General) Schmauser, had received the order to liquidate sick prisoners in the camps of Birkenau and Auschwitz. An SS detachment set to work by shooting two hundred Jewish women in Birkenau. Then it had crates of dynamite moved into Crematoria II and III, and blew them up.

For Primo Levi and his ten comrades, 18 January was the first of the ten days that still separated them from liberation. An SS officer who came to make an inspection tour of the huts appointed new Block chiefs from the ranks of the remaining non-Jewish prisoners, and ordered them to compile separate lists of Jewish and non-Jewish patients. In the midst of their rout, the Germans fully intended to follow their orders not to leave a single Jew alive. The patients had no doubt that their hours were numbered. Charles and Arthur, who had been in the camp for less than a month and did not know what the officer had said were in a state of panic. Levi expressed his irritation in *If This Is A Man* that these two men, who were not Jews, and likely to survive, should still feel terrified.

There was a last distribution of bread. Levi was so calm that he became absorbed in the novel by Roger Vercel that Doctor Samnelidis had left behind. *Remorques* was an adventure story which had inspired a film by Jean Grémillon, released in 1941, in which Jean Gabin played the part of Renaud, the brave tugboat skipper who battled against the raging elements while his wife was dying in port. This book made such an impact on Primo Levi that he awarded it a chapter in his personal anthology, *La ricerca delle radici*, published by Einaudi in 1981, in which he wrote:

> I feel tied to [Roger Vercel] by a personal factor. In this anthology, here, there ought to be a gap, a discontinuity to match the year I spent in Auschwitz, during which, as well as hunger, I suffered from the craving to read pages of print.
>
> *Remorques* is the first book that fell into my hands after that very long fast. And I read it right through during one dreadful and decisive night when the Germans wavered between killing and running. They opted to run.
>
> I mentioned the book, without naming it, in the final pages of *If This Is A Man*. This unusual novel interests me for its own sake, quite apart from the circumstances of that first reading. It deals with a topical but strangely unfrequented theme: the human adventure in the world of technology....

Now this book shows that adventure still exists, and not only in the antipodes. Man can prove brave and inventive, even in times of peace....

The quest for paternity is always an uncertain adventure. But I would not be surprised if a few genes from Captain Renaud had been transplanted into my Libertino Faussone.[2]

During the afternoon, Levi left his bunk and went foraging for blankets. He found some in the dysentery ward, no longer needed by patients who had left the camp a few hours before. Arthur was disgusted when he saw that they were soiled, but to Levi, who had a year in the camp behind him, the main thing was to be warm.

When night came, the electricity was still working. An armed SS man stood guard at the corner of the hut. Suddenly, around 11 p.m. all the lights in the camp went out and the throbbing engines in the sky signalled the arrival of a massive Russian bomber force. The sound of the bombing was distant at first, as Levi climbed down from his bunk and put his shoes on. Then the camp was rocked by violent explosions. Three bombs had fallen on Monowitz, completely destroying Blocks 1, 4, and 7. Windows shattered. A terrified, naked Cagnolati huddled in a corner and screamed. Some empty Blocks were hit and caught fire. Clusters of naked patients poured out of huts threatened by the flames, some of them trailing loose bandages. Some begged for shelter in the hut occupied by Primo Levi and his comrades, who not only refused to let them in but barricaded themselves inside. The men stumbled off through snow that was melting in the heat of the flames.

When the raid was over, the Germans had disappeared from inside the camp and the guard towers were deserted, but a cordon of soldiers still surrounded it, and detachments of security police would open fire on prisoners who got in their way.

In the chaos of the tottering Reich, Lorenzo Perrone had made up his mind to find his own way home. Primo Levi told the story of "Lorenzo's Return" to Italy several years after the war,[3] because various scruples had prevented him from doing so during his saviour's lifetime. He felt that not even a writer's best intentions could avoid the fact that in re-creating the image of a living person he intrudes on that person's image of himself, and "verges on the violation of privacy" (*Reprieve* 107/149).

On 1 January 1945 the Germans had released the civilian workers in the Italian camp and left them to their own devices. Lorenzo Perrone knew that the Russians were very close, and he wanted to be gone when they arrived. He did not know exactly where he was, and could not even pronounce the name of Auschwitz — according to Levi it came out as "Suíss" — but that did not stop him from deciding to leave the area, together with Peruch, his partner in building the protective brick walls for the Buna machinery. Lorenzo felt no fear, whereas his companion, who squinted, had a nervous temperament. Peruch too had given help to the Italian Jews in Auschwitz, but more sporadically than Lorenzo, because of his terror.

Peruch and Lorenzo took a railway map from Auschwitz station and set off on foot for the Brenner Pass, moving only at night and steering by the elementary map and the position of the stars. They slept in barns, stole potatoes from fields, and offered their services in villages along the way, taking their pay in cash or kind. Their long march lasted for four months, and on 25 April they passed through the Brenner just as the German army straggled by in the opposite direction, crushed by the Allied Fifth and Eighth Armies in northern Italy. A German tank opened fire on them but missed. Peruch came from the Friuli region. When he turned east, Lorenzo plodded on towards Turin, where he arrived after another three weeks' walking.

He had Levi's mother's address, and went straight to see her, telling her bluntly how the Jews of Eastern Europe had been wiped out in Auschwitz and on the evacuation routes. He knew that her son had been ill when the camp was evacuated, and she must not expect to see Primo again. Ester Levi offered to pay his train fare to Fossano, where he lived, but having covered all those thousands of kilometres on foot, Lorenzo wanted to end them on foot. When he met his cousin riding in a cart, near Genola, six kilometres north of Fossano, he refused to take a lift. Lorenzo Perrone, who had been a walker all his life, completed his journey the way he had begun it.

The Germans had fled. In the *KB*'s infection ward hut, the heating was out of action and a window had been broken during the bomber raid. This was the moment when from a convalescent relic of an abandoned extermination camp Primo Levi transformed himself into Robinson Crusoe on his island. As he lay in his bunk he made up a mental list of bare essentials — a stove, coal, wood, and food — and worked out how best to get hold of them. Every item would call for major efforts. Too weak to work on his own, he consulted with Arthur and Charles.

Charles Conreau, the former schoolteacher, now lives in Lusse, a village near Provenchères in the Vosges. In a letter dated 14 December 1993, recalling the ten days he spent with Levi in the wreckage of Auschwitz, he wrote:

> Primo: such a modest man, almost self-effacing, yet able to display real authority as he did after the departure of our sinister guardians. When everything was confusion — the huts without food or water, no light and no heating, temperatures below 20 degrees, those who could still stand seeking to survive without paying too much attention to the bedridden and the dying — Primo organized the life of our "*Stube*" of eleven infectious patients, only three of us able to stand. And all with the greatest calm, with that mild, steady voice of his, that I can still hear

speaking. It was so natural that I failed to put their proper value on those human qualities of his which had withstood the concentrationary life.

On 19 January Charles rose at dawn with Arthur and Primo. Swaddled in blankets, the three of them ventured out into the fog and icy wind, to encounter a vision from a nightmare. Many of the huts were smoking ruins, devastated by the bombing and by fires that had blazed uncontrolled. Ashes swirled and flew in the wind, while walking bags of bones quartered the frozen ground, in search of food and wood. The snow, the only source of water, was fouled by human waste. Small knots of men darted ferocious glances around them as they roasted potatoes in the embers of the blaze, while others melted snow in their bowls. In silos dug in the ground by order of the SS, Levi and his two companions found just enough potatoes to fill two sacks they retrieved from the kitchens, which others had visited before them.

Arthur was left in charge of the potatoes. Primo and Charles scouted around till a search of the ruined *Prominenzblock*[4] unearthed a big cast-iron stove with its flue pipe intact. They loaded it on to a wheelbarrow and Levi began to trundle it back to the hut, while Charles returned to the kitchens to find that Arthur had fainted from the cold. He lugged the sacks back to the ward, before tending to his friend. At this point, Levi was appalled to see an SS man enter the camp on a motorcycle. He terrorized everyone he passed, but he did not notice Levi, wrapped in a blanket, wrestling with his barrow, and he drove on out of sight.

Not without difficulty, Levi manhandled their ponderous prize over the rubble-strewn ground and delivered it to the hut, where Charles helped him to unload it. Their frozen, swollen hands stuck to the metal. They salvaged wood and coal from the burnt huts, and embers to light them. With the window patched and the stove pipe fixed, new warmth seeped into the ward, which was now the only heated room in the entire *Lager* of Monowitz. After this labour for the common good, and as the onset of comfort brought a sense of re-entry into the civilized world, so flickers of solidarity and gratitude were also rekindled. Towarowski, a Franco-Polish prisoner, proposed, and they all accepted, that the patients should give their thanks to each of their benefactors with a slice of bread. Levi wrote: "It was the first human gesture that occurred among us. I believe that that moment can be dated as the beginning of the change by which we who had not died slowly changed from *Häftlinge* to men again." (*Man* 160/166).

Levi managed the division of labour. Arthur, who could not stand the cold, would look after the stove, do the cooking, clean the ward, and tend the sick. Before nightfall, Charles and Primo would go scavenging in the camp. Without delay, Levi the chemist took up his post on the wasteland of the *Lager* abandoned by the SS. He found half a litre of methylated spirits and a tin of brewing yeast dropped in the snow. Yeast contained vitamins; Levi added a spoonful per person to the potato ration. Many sick people from neighbouring wards wanted access to the one source of warmth in the camp, but Charles kept them out.

Here a disturbing premonitory phase stands out from Levi's account in *If This Is A Man*, written in 1946. Remarking that it did not occur to either the would-be guests or the reluctant hosts that close proximity to infected patients made the ward a potentially lethal place to be, he pointed out that to catch diphtheria here, of all places, was "more surely fatal than jumping off a third floor." It is as if that image of dying in a stair-well, perhaps even that particular stair-well, had possibly always been embedded deep inside his mind.

Night had fallen. Russian artillery rumbled in the darkness close by. Charles and Primo sat and talked, and puffed at herbal cigarettes collected in the kitchens. Their taste for conversation had revived. To describe their state of mind as they sat in their enclave of peace in the valley of death, Levi the agnostic spoke in the accent of his ancestors. After that day's achievements, they felt "perhaps like God after the first day of creation" (*Man 161/167*).

According to the book of Genesis, it was not till the end of the second day, when he had created the heaven and the earth, and had divided the light from the darkness and the waters above from the waters below, and when he had created all the plants, that God congratulated himself and saw that his work was good. Genesis says: "And there was evening and there was morning, the second day." To tell the story of the ten days spent at the scene of the crime deserted by the Nazis, in an Auschwitz inhabited by a fraction of all its victims, Primo Levi adopts a style inspired by Genesis. For the day that followed "the first day of creation" he writes: "*20 January*. The dawn came ..."

In returning to an everyday world, Levi behaves like the heroes in the favourite books of his childhood, who battle alone against the hostile elements that they are resolved to understand and master. Weak with fever, he sways when he tries to stand, and like some palaeolithic ancestor he sets out to conquer fire because it is too cold to venture outside the cave. Remembering the flints he stole from the laboratory, he scrapes at one of them with a knife, over a piece of paper soaked in methylated spirits and covered in tinder dust, until a spark sets fire to the tinder and a whoof of flame leaps from the paper.

The fire made it possible to reheat yesterday's boiled potatoes. Everyone got three, but that left only enough for two days more. For water, they had to melt snow into a muddy liquid, and then filter it. Charles and Primo went out foraging again. As they stumbled over the snow, they came across skeletal men who scrabbled through the wreckage picking up anything that they might trade with the Poles who lived in the vicinity of the camp.

In the kitchens, Levi saw a pair of wraiths squabbling in Yiddish and fighting with the little strength they had over some rotten potatoes. Further on, in the courtyard of a storehouse, Charles and Primo took turns with a pickaxe to hack some fifty kilos of cabbages and turnips out of two frozen heaps. Then Charles discovered a packet of salt, and then a 50-litre can of water with its contents frozen solid — "*une fameuse trouvaille*," a marvellous find. They loaded their provisions on to one of the pushcarts used in the old days, less than a week ago, to carry the *Kessel*s of soup from the kitchens to the huts, and hauled it back to the ward. That afternoon they had boiled potatoes, and turnip slices roasted on the stove, before Levi went exploring again. The clinic had been wrecked by looters, and the floor was smeared with faeces and littered with rags and used bandages. A naked corpse lay in this desolation. Even here there were resources to be found: Levi came across a battery from a truck. He tested the poles with a knife, and a spark flew. That night there was light in the sickroom. It was the only place in Monowitz equipped with electricity.

From the window, Levi watched the hordes of the fugitive Wehrmacht flood past — tanks and armoured cars, soldiers on foot, on horseback, and even on bicycles, some of them unarmed. On 21 January, it ended. The bleak Polish plain lay snowbound and deserted. The Nazis who had promised their victims that no one would be left to give evidence were running before the Red Army. Primo Levi felt no joy, or any other kind of feeling. After his struggle to live, he was ready to die.

Filip Müller, a member of the Auschwitz *Sonderdkommando*, found himself in a comparable state when he regained his freedom:

> I was nothing more than a living wreck, a shadow of myself. I was not even capable of feeling an emotion. No tear of joy on my face, no burst of rapture in my heart. Closed to all feeling, I stared into the distance, into emptiness, unable to realize that I had finally escaped from the special Kommando of Auschwitz.[5]

Charles, who was still in good shape, asked Levi to help him to empty "Jules," the sanitary bucket. It was a hazardous task, because three of the patients in the ward had typhus, and there was no water in which to wash their hands. The latrines were blocked, and all the buckets, all the bowls, and all the pots in the *KB* were full of human waste. Levi feared a disaster if the thaw arrived.

While the four men who were able to sit up — Alcalaï, Schenck, Sertelet, and Towarowski — were roped in by Arthur to help prepare the cabbages and turnips, Levi went out to look for wood, and Charles for clean snow to melt. Once there was a practical problem to solve, the chemist in Levi came alive again. He and Charles found a reasonably clean space on the floor of what had been the laundry to light a fire for the soup, then disinfected their hands with chloramine diluted in snow.

Preparing the soup had sapped a lot of strength from them both, and when a crowd of famished inmates besieged the door, Charles shook his ladle and swore at them in French. They drifted away, all except for one man, who claimed to be a tailor from Paris and offered to make warm clothes for them out of blankets left behind in the camp, in exchange for a litre of soup. The man was an expert craftsman. He made a jacket, trousers, and a pair of gloves apiece for Charles and Primo.

That night, as the sound of the Russian artillery crept closer, the taste for living rose again in Levi. He told his comrades that life could still be beautiful, and that meant that there were a number of decisions they had to take if they wanted a chance of survival. He laid down various prophylactic rules. From now on, each one of them must take care of his own bowl and spoon. No one should finish off his neighbour's soup, and they should stay in their bunks, except to visit the latrine. Any other question would be for Primo, Charles, and Arthur to settle. The meek and mild Primo Levi could show authority enough when the circumstances called for it. He delegated tasks to his two French comrades. Hygiene and discipline were Arthur's domain. One of his rulings was that it was better to keep one's own bowl dirty, rather than wash it with the rest and run the risk of cross-infection.

Next morning, on 22 January, Primo and Charles ventured outside the barbed-wire fence and dared to enter the SS compound. In their flight the Germans had abandoned a table laid with plates of soup — now frozen — which the trespassers wolfed down at once. In the SS quarters they found a bottle of vodka, medicines, newspapers and magazines, and four superb quilted blankets. Months later, Levi brought one of these back to Turin, after taking it on his forced expedition into Byelorussia. If it is still possible to follow the example of Nicola Dallaporta and speak of Providence in the context of Auschwitz, then it certainly intervened that day in favour of Primo Levi and Charles Conreau. Half an hour after they left it, a number of SS men entered the abandoned compound and found eighteen Frenchmen sitting around the refectory table where Charles and Primo had feasted on frozen soup. They killed them all with a shot to the nape of the neck[6] and left the bodies lying in the snow, where they remained unburied until the arrival of the Red Army.

Some of the frozen corpses of the sick who had died in all the Blocks were taken to a trench, but it soon overflowed. The dysentery ward was located in Levi's hut, on the other side of a wooden dividing wall. It was a dreadful sight: nearly all the men who were not dead were dying, and the floor was a sea of frozen excrement. Two Italians who were in the ward — one of them was Lello Perugia — heard Charles call Primo's name through the wall, and struck up a chorus of entreaties. Unable to bear their complaints, Levi took the men a little food and some water, and even afterwards the whole ward called his name all day long, each in his own accent. "I felt like crying, I could have cursed them," he confessed (*Man* 166/172).

During the night of 22–23 January, Lakmaker, a young Dutch Jew of seventeen, who had contracted typhus and scarlet fever in succession, threw himself out of his bunk, after soiling his bunk and the floor. Charles Conreau wiped him clean with straw as best he could, cut the worst patches out of his blanket and mattress with a knife, and lifted the dying boy back on to his bed. After that, he scraped and then disinfected the floor with chloramine, and spread some over himself.[7]

On 23 January the SS set fire to the Canada clothing warehouses. In the infection ward the food supplies were running out, but it was rumoured that there was a huge potato store-pit four hundred metres away, on the other side of the barbed wire. When Levi and Conreau left the camp in search of it, Charles said: *"Dis donc, Primo, on est dehors!"* — "Hey, Primo, we're outside!" They reached the spot, and saw that they were not alone. The treasure consisted of tons of potatoes protected by alternate layers of earth and straw, and it was difficult to get at because the ground was iron-hard. An old Hungarian lay frozen in the posture where death had caught him by surprise, his hands reaching out for the vision of plenty. Other searchers pushed the body aside, and dug in the hole he had started. Levi and his comrades now ate nothing but potatoes — boiled potatoes, potato soup, potato fritters. Arthur prepared the fritters by grating raw potato over boiled potato, and roasting the dish on a metal hotplate laid on top of the stove.

Sertelet was suffering from diphtheria, and his condition was worsening. Levi went to fetch a Hungarian doctor who lived in the opposite Block, but the doctor turned him away. In order to lift his comrades' spirits, Levi treated them all with nasal drops of camphorated oil.

The death-toll rose by the hour. The trench where the bodies were thrown became a mound. For Levi and his comrades, their last reserves of strength were dwindling fast. A diet of starch could not relieve exhaustion. Yet every day Charles and Primo ignored their own debility and continued to prepare the 25 litres of soup that Charles shared out, still saving extra rations "for the workers," and something off the bottom for the Italians next door.

Some of the occupants of Block 14 were still in fairly good health, and they ventured out to walk the two kilometres to the English PoW camp, which had been evacuated. They came back wearing khaki uniforms and dragging a cart-load of treasures — "margarine, custard powder, lard, soya-bean flour, whisky" (*Man 169/175*). The poorer inmates racked their brains as to how to lay hands on some small share of the rich men's wealth, and Levi found a way. He had unearthed a block of virgin wax in the electrical stores, and he set about manufacturing a supply of candles with wicks soaked in boracic acid, using cardboard moulds of his own devising. The rich bought every one, and they paid in lard and flour.

During the evening of the 25 January, Charles talked about his life in Provenchères, in the Vosges. Primo told them how he had tried to become a partisan in Piedmont, and how his group had been betrayed and captured. Charles was an attentive listener, and later he wrote that Levi was a "marvellous weigher of souls." Levi's state of mind and morale was fluctuating from day to day and from one event to the next. Of the evening when they talked together, he wrote that he, Charles, and Arthur "felt ourselves become men once again." Recalling the day that followed, he wrote: "We lay in a world of death and phantoms. The last trace of civilization had vanished around and inside us. The work of bestial degradation, begun by the victorious Germans, had been carried to its conclusion by the Germans in defeat." (*Man 171/177*).

The grounds for his judgement show what an ordeal each day had become in the limbo that followed the German departure, as the inmates, still imprisoned by their own helplessness, waited for the Russians to arrive. Levi wrote that while the killer and his victim might both be men, he who could sleep with the dead, or who waited for his comrade to die so that he could eat his ration of bread, was no longer a man, no matter how blameless he might be for the other's collapse. If he was no longer a man in other people's eyes, nor was he human in his own. Then Levi shifts again, and gives thanks to Charles and Arthur for enabling all three to remain men, despite the determination of the Nazis to reduce them all to the state of brutes.

On the same day as Levi and the two Frenchmen had grown animated when speaking about their former lives, on 25 January, eight days after the evacuation, a fifty-year-old Hungarian chemist called Sómogyi entered the last stages of an agonizing death. For two days, he kept muttering the same automatic response to a German order: "Jawohl ... Jawohl," over and over again, thousands of times.

On 26 January there were dog-fights in the sky over Auschwitz, and the sound of bombers droning overhead. That night, Sómogyi died with a last convulsion that sent him crashing to the floor. In Arthur's words: "Death drove him from his bed." Afterwards, they all went back to sleep. They did not know that the fate of the whole camp had hung in the balance that day. In Birkenau, the SS had blown up Crematorium V, but SS-*Obergruppenführer* Schmauser had not implemented the order to liquidate all of the sick prisoners who had been left behind in the Auschwitz camps, because the *SD*[8] unit assigned to carry out the task had been at risk of being cut off by the Red Army, which had reached Libiaz, less than 14 kilometres north-east of Auschwitz. Retreating Wehrmacht units dynamited the railway bridges over the Vistula and Sola rivers, as well as the wooden bridge over the Sola which had been constructed by the prisoners just to the east of the main camp, Auschwitz I.

At dawn, when Levi and his comrades woke, they saw Sómogy's contorted body, but for reasons of hygiene they could not touch him before they had cooked, eaten, and emptied the sanitary bucket.

In a letter sent to Jean Samuel on 23 March 1946, Primo Levi estimated that 25 per cent of the sick prisoners left to fend for themselves in Monowitz died of hunger, cold, and disease between 18 and 27 January 1945.[9] In the same letter, he wrote:

> Conreau was a true comrade to me; I believe that it may well be said that between us we saved each other's lives, and by working together, he with his good sense and strength, me with my experience of the *Lager* (he was a 200 thousand,[10] and hadn't yet learned the art of organizing),

we saved several fellows in our room, who without us would have had nothing to eat.

Of the eleven prisoners who shared room 8 during the ten days before the Liberation, only one man died. Five of them died a few weeks later, in the field hospital set up in Auschwitz by the Russians, and only five men found their way home in the end.

9 Liberation: Detour Through Central Europe

The first Russian soldiers to enter Monowitz were a patrol that arrived around nine o'clock in the morning of Saturday 27 January, 1945, as part of the reconnaissance unit of the 100th Infantry Division of the 106th Corps. They turned up in the camp while Primo Levi and Charles Conreau were moving Sómogyi's body away on a stretcher. An hour later, the whole unit arrived, and found a scene of utter desolation, a theatre of chaos and death. These were "hard men, Mongols, just passing through," wrote Charles Conreau. Of the 850 patients abandoned when the camp was evacuated, 500 died before the coming of their liberators, and 200 more in the days that followed. As soon as they got there, the Russians sent in a doctor with the rank of captain, who started to organize assistance and first aid.

Charles Conreau and Primo Levi saw their first Soviet soldiers around midday, approaching along the road that ran past the camp and overlooked it.

> Later on, [the Russians] gave instructions to put that chaos of a dying world into some kind of order, until the survivors were regrouped into the main Auschwitz camp, where my relatively able-bodied condition automatically qualified me for all the heavy duties, which included moving the night's crop of bodies to Block 11, where we made heaps of the bodies due for autopsy.[1]

Those first soldiers were four young men on horseback, wearing fur hats and carrying Sten-guns. They stared in silence, and as if in shame and guilt, at the sight that met their eyes.

> On the 27th at midday we had the first Russian patrol, and we couldn't believe our eyes. The situation in the camp was desperate: dead bodies everywhere, in the snow and in the beds; a disgusting state of filth, because everybody suffered from diarrhoea and the latrines had been full for a long time; most of the survivors were lying in bed as if paralyzed by cold and hunger.[2]

The few surviving victims were broken men afflicted with a sadness so deadly that it prevented them from running towards their liberators in the way that a well-known Soviet film records. The film is a reconstruction shot a few days later, with survivors turned actors, requested to simulate joy.

After watching the arrival of these four young men, so clearly appalled by what they saw, Charles Conreau and Primo Levi returned to room 8 to

209

announce the news. Levi wrote in *The Truce* that "face to face with liberty we felt ourselves lost, emptied, atrophied, unfit for our part" (*Truce* 18/190).

During the night, Levi felt his illness take hold of him, reinforced by the release of emotions and perceptions that self-preservation had silenced. His limbs hurt, his head seethed with fever, and he could not sleep. Now that the threat of death no longer kept his mind and senses stretched, grievous feelings of solitude and exile broke loose and flooded through him. His free man's consciousness dawned again amongst the ruins of crematoria, ashes, and heaps of corpses. Nearly all of his comrades were dead. His friend Alberto, "so good and so valiant,"[3] had not, in fact, survived the evacuation march. He was seen in the column sent to Gleiwitz, and then nothing more was heard of him. Vanda Maestro had been consumed in the furnace.

An outsider had claimed the bunk of their dead comrade Sómogyi in room 8. Thylle was an old "red triangle" who had been in the camp from the beginning. His status as a German political had conferred certain privileges, of which the most basic was exemption from selection: he had never spent a day in the knowledge that it might bring death in the gas chamber. Just before they ran, the SS had appointed him chief of Block 20, which included the *Infektionsabteilung*. As chief, the final nominee of SS discipline, he had paid inspection visits to room 8, and once had passed a compliment on its cleanliness, earning growling obscenities from Arthur of "*vieux dégoûtant*" and "*putain de boche*" (*Truce* 17/189). Levi said nothing, seeing the German as a potential enemy. On the night of their liberation he heard the sound of weeping in the darkness, then Thylle asked him if he was awake, and came uninvited to sit beside him on his bunk. For ten years, he said, he had been a prisoner in the Nazi camps, and then, in a quavering but solemn voice he started to sing the *Internationale*.

Thylle may have belonged to the Auschwitz Resistance, because it was mainly Communists who ran it. Among its members, the Germans who worked in the administrative offices were in a position to remove a number from the list of those selected for the gas chamber and replace it with another. Therefore in some cases they had the power of life and death over prisoners, for instance when they had a chance to save one of their own people, or to eliminate a particularly vicious Kapo.

Next day, a number of Polish men and women, local inhabitants, were drafted into the camp by the Russians with orders to clear away the corpses and clean up the huts. Around midday, the Russians sent a cow, which arrived at the end of a rope held by a scared little boy. In minutes, there was no cow left. The day after that, more Polish women, disgusted by what they saw, were compelled to wash the sick and dress their sores. They lit a big fire with timber salvaged from the huts, and used it to cook soup.

The thaw came, the snow melted, and now a combination of refuse, excrement, and rotting bodies spread a terrible stench, while the sick went on dying in the huts. Those who were still strong enough, crammed themselves with the meat rations sporadically delivered by the Russians, and collapsed and died soon after. Their shrunken stomachs and weakened systems could not endure or metabolize such a glut of food.

The third day brought Yankel, a young Russian Jew, driving a horse-drawn cart. Starting with the most seriously ill, his job was to collect the survivors in small groups and deliver them to the main camp, now transformed into an enormous temporary hospital.

During these three days Primo Levi, nursed by Charles Conreau, had stayed in his bunk, racked with thirst, more and more feverish, with painful joints, a sore throat, and half of his face swollen and inflamed. When Yankel came to fetch him, Charles and Arthur carried him to the cart, with its cargo of dying men. Rain was falling. Levi saw the huts roll past him, the roll-call square where the gallows still stood, next to a looming Christmas tree, and at last the gateway of the camp, and the same inscription: "*Arbeit macht frei*" — "Work sets free."

He was taken to the main Auschwitz camp, built on the site of a former artillery barracks that the Wehrmacht had taken over in 1939, and which had looked to the *Sipo*[4] and *SD* inspector of Breslau, *Oberführer* (Colonel) Arpad Wigand, like an ideal place for a concentration camp. The town lay on the east bank of the River Sola, at its confluence with the Vistula. The main camp, Auschwitz I, Birkenau, Auschwitz II, each with its own railway spur, were situated on the west bank of the Sola, close to a major railway junction between Silesia, the General Government, and Czechoslovakia. Levi was so impressed by the enormous scale of Auschwitz I, with its rows and rows of three-storey, grey stone buildings, that he felt it made Buna-Monowitz look like a village.

When they arrived in the deserted, silent camp, the sick were bathed by sturdy Russian nurses who laid them on the ground on wooden racks, then briskly soaped and rinsed them from head to foot. Arthur and Charles were also brought to Auschwitz I, just before the Russians split the survivors into national groups. "Arthur and I found [Primo] in the Italian Block, where he was lying in what looked to us like a serious condition."[5]

When they started bathing Arthur, the peasant from the Vosges, he protested on the grounds that he was a free citizen. The Russians gave out clean shirts and underwear, and then the barber, a hulking brute with a Sten-gun slung across his chest, shaved their heads for the last time. To Levi he said: "*Italiano Mussolini*," to Charles and Arthur: "*Fransé Laval*" — showing, said Levi wryly, "how little general ideas help the understanding of individual cases" (*Truce* 24/196). After that, the Italian and the two Frenchmen were dispatched on separate journeys through Poland and Russia.

Levi was now suffering from renal and cardiac complications. His admission record card, with a brief account of his symptoms, is preserved in the Auschwitz museum. After a perfunctory medical examination he was sent to the "infectious ward," in Block 20, a huge dormitory where a single doctor found himself in charge of 800 sick and dying patients. Later Levi estimated that nearly 4,000 of the 5,000 ex-prisoners from all of Auschwitz's thirty-nine camps assembled in the main camp were invalids. There were no drugs or medical equipment, and far too few doctors, most of them as sick as their patients. In the morning, while the dead were removed in their dozens, Levi was moved to a room with twenty beds where, still suffering from a raging thirst and a high fever, he lapsed into a semi-comatose condition.

Five days later, the fever broke and he woke up to the clamour of fellow patients talking, singing and calling out to one another. He realized that during his crisis, most of those who were sick beyond saving had died. Those who remained were coming to life. Snow was falling, but the long straight roads of the camp were no longer deserted. Ex-inmates were exercising their freedom, in a scene of muddle and commotion. It was here that Levi learnt of Vanda Maestro's fate, at a secret meeting with Olga, the Croatian partisan who had given Vanda two sleeping pills as she was taken to the gas chamber in October 1944.

The Russians had taken Warsaw on 17 January 1945. They did not take Poznan until 23 February, Danzig fell on 30 March, Vienna on 13 April, and it was not until the 16th of that month that they launched the final assault on Berlin that led to Adolf Hitler's suicide on 30 April. All their efforts and resources were focused on Hungary, Poland, and eastern Germany as Hitler's armies fought stubbornly to stave off an inevitable defeat. The fighting had moved westward, but it was many months before civic life began to revive in the territories formerly occupied by the Nazis, or serious care could be devoted to the survivors of the concentration camps and the millions of other "displaced persons" from every country in Europe left stranded in the wake of the war. The Russians were hard put to administer their own shattered territories. It was against this background that the survivors of Auschwitz emerged from the concentrationary world only to find that no one was quite sure what to do with them, except to put them where they would not get in the way, and to look after them with whatever personnel and resources could be spared from a fight to the finish waged on a continental scale.

After spending most of February in bed, Primo Levi was still very weak, but he was also restless, and he managed to talk a doctor into discharging him. He wrapped his feet in some strips of a blanket he cut up, put on all the cotton trousers and jackets he could find, one on top of the other, and set off with no particular destination in mind, having no idea where it was possible to go. Outside the door, a Soviet officer took a snap of him and gave him five cigarettes. In the camp, a former Kapo with the habit of not taking No for an answer intercepted him and set him shovelling snow, but he sneaked away, and when he found an occupied Block he asked the old Hungarian who guarded the door whether he could stay. At first the Hungarian refused, but five cigarettes changed his mind. It was warm inside the Block, and in the evening there was soup.

Like the rest of Eastern Europe, Poland was under Russian law. The next morning they put Levi into a convoy bound for a transit camp. Not long after that, he was one of a dozen men who found themselves shipped off to an unknown destination in the middle of the night, on board a horse-drawn wagon driven by a Russian soldier who sang songs "to the stars" and spoke intimate soliloquies to his horses. Snow had been falling, and it was bitterly cold. After a two-hour journey through a frozen landscape the soldier deposited his passengers by a stretch of broken railway line and drove off without a word of explanation. The group included a *Volksdeutsche*,[6] two Jewish brothers from Vienna, a half-crazed man who gabbled to himself in Yiddish, an officer of the Yugoslav army, and "the Greek" whom Levi called Mordo Nahum in *The Truce*. As well as his native language, the Greek also spoke Spanish, French, a little Italian and Albanian, Turkish, and Bulgarian. Levi describes him as a tall man with red hair and red skin, a hooked nose, and very pale, liquid eyes. He carried a big sack, and had on a pair of excellent, almost new, leather shoes.

After waiting there till midday, the group saw a small locomotive come labouring towards them with four goods wagons in tow. Some Polish peasants climbed out, and darted hostile glances before the interlopers boarded one of the wagons and the train went off in the opposite direction. Two peasant women who got on at the next stop explained that the track's two sections from the break ran westwards to Katowice and eastwards to Cracow. The soldier who delivered them must have got his directions mixed up. The situation in Katowice was much better, but he had put them on the line to Cracow, which was teeming with hordes of destitute liberated prisoners sent there by the Russians and crammed into every kind of accommodation — barracks, schools, hospitals, convents. The healthiest had taken to the streets, in quest of any kind of deal or crooked trade that would offer them a living, in a town where even the Russian garrison was starving.

None of the group had had anything to eat for twenty-four hours, the weather was freezing, and their wagon kept bumping and jolting over the gaps in the dilapidated rails. This was nothing like the liberation that Levi had dreamed of. The train crawled on all day, and it was three in the morning before they arrived in a small unlit station. In bitter cold, Levi got down from the wagon and walked into the darkness till he came to the telegraph cabin, which was warm and full of people. No words were exchanged. Levi just flopped in a corner and fell instantly asleep.

At dawn, the telegraphist brought him a big hunk of bread and a piece of cheese, which he stuffed down before rushing outside to find that the train was still there, and his companions half dead from exposure. That night, Levi wrote, had been the worst of all their time in exile. It was after their ordeal that he and the Greek decided to join forces. Why did the Greek choose Levi, and Levi the Greek? Levi respected the Greek's big sack and the fact that he came from Salonica, and therefore was bound to know the ropes, while the Greek had the impression that Levi must have tricks up his sleeve because he had been smart enough not to spend the night in the wagon.

When the train set off again, it took them to Szczakowa, 45 kilometres from Cracow, where the Polish Red Cross ran a twenty-four-hour soup kitchen that fed every hungry mouth that came along. Thin as he was, Levi managed to down such a quantity of soup that the sisters who served him crossed themselves. The journey resumed and continued until dusk, when the engine broke down not far from Cracow, and Levi and the Greek decided to leave their companions and make their way on foot.

It was from here on that the Greek developed a kind of master–pupil ascendancy over a Levi mesmerized by a partner so different from himself. His first display of dominance consisted of loading his sack on to Levi's back, arguing that if he had been clever enough to collect the things inside it, then it was his partner who should carry it. This was his idea of a fair division of labour. Levi's entire assets were confined to a cardboard box which had contained some bread, and the quilted blanket liberated from the SS quarters in Monowitz. The two men walked in single file through the snow, Mordo in front, Primo behind, like Don Quixote and Sancho Panza. Levi was dressed in a shirt, several layers of striped *Häftling* trousers, a *Häftling* jacket, and a pair of thin leather ankle boots rather like those worn by priests in Italy. They didn't last long, and when they gave out on their owner, long before Cracow, the Greek gave him the rough edge of his tongue. A man with no shoes was just a fool, he said, and read him his first lesson in adapting to reality. He too had been ill, but that had not prevented him from giving the slip to a Russian guard and breaking into the store room where shoes were kept. Levi's feet and shoes were wrapped in strips of tough cloth taken from the sack, and so the two vagrants arrived in due course on the outskirts of Cracow, where they boarded a tram at a terminus. The loudspeakers were broadcasting Tchaikovsky's *1812 Overture*.

A French soldier told them how to get to a barracks requisitioned by the Russians, where a whole lot of Italian soldiers had been billeted. It was no easy job to get into the building, which was guarded by a Polish sentry, but they persuaded the Pole to fetch an Italian corporal, and when the Greek extracted from the sack on Levi's back a tin of *Pöckling*, salted herring, it overcame the corporal's reluctance to admit them to the paradise inside, with its roaring stoves, candles and carbide lamps, food in plenty, and straw to sleep on. As for the lack of room, after the grossly overcrowded Blocks of Auschwitz, any accommodation seemed spacious to a former *Häftling*. They received a hearty welcome, and the Greek was a particular hit with the soldiers who had occupied his country for a while. A practical psychologist, he won over his audience with a few shrewd phrases about women, spaghetti, football, opera, war, vene-

Primo Levi at his desk, summer 1986.

Left: The synagogue in Via Pio V where Primo Levi celebrated his barmitzvah in 1932. On 24 April 1996 a small esplanade was created in front of the railings, and named Piazzetta Primo Levi.

Below left: The former Via Roma (later remodelled), where Primo Levi's maternal grandfather kept a fabric store.

Below right: 28 October 1937, the Fascist inauguration of the second section of the new Via Roma.

1936: four anti-Fascist intellectuals from Turin, all members of *Giustizia e Libertà*. Cesare Pavese, Leone Ginzburg, Franco Antonicelli, and Carlo Frassinelli.

The little hotel in Amay where Primo Levi, Vanda Maestro and Luciana Nissim were arrested by the Fascist militia, 13 December 1943.

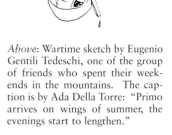

Above: Wartime sketch by Eugenio Gentili Tedeschi, one of the group of friends who spent their weekends in the mountains. The caption is by Ada Della Torre: "Primo arrives on wings of summer, the evenings start to lengthen."

The transit camp at Fossoli di Carpi where Primo Levi was interned at the end of January 1944 and from which he was deported to Auschwitz in a convoy of 650 Jews, 22 February 1944.

Jewish deportees at the I.G. Farben works, Auschwitz–Monowitz, 1942.

Primo Levi at Centro Piero Gobetti, 15 March 1981. *Left to right*: Carlo Mussa Ivaldi, Primo Levi, Giorgio Agosti, Alberto Bianco, Sandro Pertini (President of the Republic) Bianca Guidetti Serra, Giulio Einaudi, Sandro Galante Garrone, Nello Poma.

Natalia Ginzburg received the Strega Prize in 1963. To her right is the publisher Giulio Einaudi and beside him is Italo Calvino, Primo Levi's literary director at Einaudi.

Primo Levi in 1978 at one of Einaudi's annual conferences for their staff and writers.

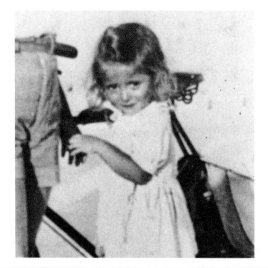

Above, left: Little Emilia Levi who travelled to Auschwitz with her parents and brother in the same convoy as Primo Levi.

Above: Paul Steinberg photographed on his return from Auschwitz, at the reception centre, Hotel Lutétia, Paris. He was aged 19 at the time.

Left: Jean Samuel at Buchenwald when liberated by the Americans. The *Pikkolo*, or apprentice, of the Chemical Kommando, he features in the "Canto of Ulysses" chapter of *If This Is A Man*.

A photograph taken in 1980 at Moncalieri, outside Turin, where Alberto Salmoni and his wife Marcella, Magda Beneyton and her husband Armando Nover shared a house. *Left to right*: Primo Levi, Magda Beyneton, Lucia Levi, Bruno Salmoni (brother of Alberto), Marcella Salmoni, Rina Foglia.

RUDOLF LOEWENTHAL
AVVOCATO
PRESSO LA CORTE D'APPELLO
DI FRANCOFORTE s/MENO

Torino,li 15 Dicembre 1959
via Pastrengo 17 - Tel.580171

Egr.Signor
Lello Perugia
Via degli Equi,70
R O M A

Egr.Signor Perugia,

Sono lieto di poterVi comunicare che la Compensation Treuhand G.m.b.H.
ha riconosciuto la Vs.richiesta contro la I.G.Farbenindustrie ed è pron
ta di farVi un pagamento parziale di
DM 2.500.- .
Di questa somma si deduce le spese dell'avv.Ormond di DM 122,70;cosi
rimangono al Vs.favore DM 2.377,3o.
edotto niente.Il resto Vi sarà rimesso nei

d del 4/12 con conto spese;
tion Treuhand G.m.b.H. del 3/12;
zione di accettare l'accordo con la I.G.Farben
di arbitrario per tutte le differenze che
vvenire;
uli N? 3 e 5 (blue e rosso)sono da Voi da fir-
I Consolato Tedesco o da un notaio per la le-

o di pagamento,da riempire e firmare da Voi
matita,senza legalizzazione.

tre moduli N? 3,4 e 5 al più presto possibile
Francoforte sollecitando il pagamento.

aluti.

R. Loewenthal
(avv.Rudolf Loewenthal

PRIMO LEVI
CORSO RE UMBERTO, 75
10128 TORINO
Tel (011) 884.677

Torino, 3 aprile 1987

Caro Camon,

ho parlato oggi con l'Ufficio Stampa di
Einaudi: mi dicono che I sommersi e i salvati è stato
effettivamente mandato a Gallimard, ma a buon conto
ne inviamo oggi stesso una seconda copia. Mi piacerebbe
molto, naturalmente, se Gallimard lo accettasse e mi è
grata l'occasione per ringraziare Lei di tutto quanto sta
facendo per promuovere i miei libri in Francia. Lei è
straordinariamente gentile e diligente: resto in attesa del
Suo articolo su "Libération", grazie anche di questo.

Buona Pasqua e un cordialissimo saluto

Primo Levi

Pesach

Ditemi: in cosa differisce
Questa sera dalle altre sere?
In cosa, ditemi, differisce
Questa pasqua dalle altre pasque?
Accendi il lume, spalanca la porta
Che il pellegrino possa entrare,
Gentile o ebreo:
Sotto i cenci si cela forse il profeta.
Entri e sieda con noi,
Ascolti, beva, canti e faccia pasqua.
Consumi il pane dell'afflizione,
Agnello, malta dolce ed erba amara.
Questa è la sera delle differenze,
In cui s'appoggia il gomito alla mensa
Perché il vietato diventa prescritto
Così che il male si traduca in bene.
Passeremo la notte a raccontare [...]

Quest'anno in paura e vergogna,
L'anno venturo in virtù e giustizia.

9 Aprile 1982

Primo Levi

Primo Levi at the SIVA laboratory, on the occasion of a colleague's birthday. *Standing, left to right*: Giuseppe Venezia, Aldo Nani, Andreo Carlino, Giuseppe Gilardi, Adolfo Arri, Orsolina Azzario, Primo Levi. *In front*: Giuseppe Cordua, Massimo Palazzoni, and Renato Portesi.

The funeral cortège taking the body of Primo Levi to the cemetery of Corso Reggio Parco, Turin, 13 April 1987. The coffin was placed in the hearse by ex-deportees. Primo Levi was buried in the Jewish sector of the cemetery.

real diseases, wine, the black market, and cars. When Levi drank his first glass of wine his legs turned to rubber and he had to crawl to his bed of straw on all fours.

Early the next morning the Greek shook him awake and hauled him off to "work" in the market — hauled him, because Levi was tired and sick, and longed to be looked after at last. Mordo Nahum's principles were nothing like his partner's; hard work was his religion, but not regular, "servile" work, performed for a wage, which he despised. By work he meant not only trade and barter, but also theft, fraud, and contraband. He would consider anything, as long as it paid. So Levi put on the tatters of his shoes, heaved the sack on to his back, and followed the Greek to the market to observe how he worked.

The market was swarming with buyers and sellers of every age and class; anything saleable was available. Nahum organized the division of labour. He would contribute the raw material and expertise, Levi his knowledge of German and the basic spadework. He had to go and inquire into the price of shirts, say that they were expensive but not be too obvious about it, then come back and deliver his report, on which the Greek would base his prices. After investigating the prices charged by a canteen said to be located behind the cathedral, he decided to sell one shirt and buy some eggs with the proceeds. So timid Doctor Levi was obliged to hold up the shirt and call out: "A shirt, gentleman, a shirt!" When a customer came forward, the Greek haggled at length, concluded the transaction in a gateway, out of sight, and emerged with 70 zlotys, worth seven meals or a dozen eggs. After surveying the stalls, he bought six eggs — the largest, painstakingly chosen — for their evening meal, then decided to go and eat in the canteen.

Levi asked a priest the way to the cathedral, speaking in Latin, the only language they had in common, and enjoying the exchange, while the Greek grew impatient. He was itching to be back on his own feet, and did not intend to be dependent for long on the good will of Italian soldiers, or Russians. Levi was interested in his partner as a human specimen, and was not averse to trying his hand at a different game, playing a part that had nothing in common with his old self, the doctor of chemistry from a strait-laced bourgeois background. Mordo saw nothing but the practical side of things, and wondered out loud whether his associate was "an idiot or an idler."

At the soup kitchen the fuming Greek, acting in a way that Levi might have found obnoxious, but which secretly amused him, ordered two plates of soup but only one portion of beans, to teach the Italian a lesson for his slack attitude. Eventually, though, he relented and gave him a quarter of his own. It was snowing and windy outside, so they sat at a table talking for some time, and the conversation brought further adjustments between the two. The smuggler from Salonica had cooled off and now took a professional line towards his pupil, who was relishing the situation. He explained to him that in wartime shoes mattered more than food. A man with shoes could go looking for food, but not the reverse. Levi objected that the war was over.

"There is always war," replied Mordo Nahum memorably (*Truce 52/224*). His two years in the camp had come as no surprise to him, whereas for Primo Levi, Auschwitz had been a monstrous experience. Years later, he borrowed a phrase from his friend Lidia Rolfi, deported to Ravensbrück for acts of resistance, and said that the camp had been his "university."[7] Nahum spent the afternoon telling Levi about his life in Greece; then they both returned to the barracks, where the Italian colonel in charge almost refused to let them in, and forbade them any soup.

Before daybreak the next morning they each ate two of the hard-boiled eggs from the market, then left for Katowice, 70 kilometres away, because they had heard that there were collection centres there for the various nationalities, where they could depend on finding shelter. The bridges in between had been blown up, all roads and railways were in disrepair, and the trains were moving slowly, and only by day, so it took them three days to reach their destination. The cold was still intense, and they had very little food. When the train stopped in Trzebinia and Levi, still dressed in his Auschwitz stripes, got out to stretch his legs, he found himself surrounded by an inquisitive crowd, among them the first bourgeois civilian he had set eyes on since leaving Italy — a lawyer wearing a felt hat and carrying a leather briefcase.

That was the moment when Primo Levi began to bear witness. He told what he had seen in Auschwitz, and the lawyer translated for the audience of workers and peasants. Levi realized very quickly that the lawyer was not translating absolutely faithfully. He was deliberately avoiding telling his listeners that Levi was a Jew, and described him as an Italian political prisoner. After the crowd broke up, Levi, who had underestimated Polish anti-Semitism, was ingenuous enough to ask his interpreter why he had failed to say that he was Jewish, and the lawyer explained uncomfortably that it was better for him, because the war was not yet over. Levi wrote in *The Truce*:

> I found myself suddenly old, lifeless, tired beyond human measure; the war was not over, there was always war. My listeners began to steal away; they must have understood. I had dreamed, we had always dreamed, of something like this, in the nights at Auschwitz: of speaking and not being listened to, of finding liberty and remaining alone. (*Truce 55/227*)

As the lawyer took his leave, he offered Levi money — which he refused — advised him not to speak German, and confessed that Poland was "a sad country."

The train was ready to leave again, and Levi joined the Greek in the goods wagon. Later on they changed trains to make a detour to Szczakowa, where they visited the Red Cross soup kitchen again, and the sisters recognized the insatiable Italian. That night, when they slept in the station waiting-room, a Polish gendarme came to question them. It happened that he spoke some broken Italian, having worked as a miner near Bergamo. He too warned Levi against speaking German, and then invited both men to spend the night in his warm jail, an offer they jumped at. The next day they left for Katowice, which did contain the collection centres they had been told about, including one for Italians and another for Greeks. Here, Mordo Nahum and Primo Levi parted company, though they would meet again before long. The first time was in May, when a group of a hundred men and women — all the Greeks in Katowice, homeward-bound — paraded through the streets towards the railway station. Mordo Nahum marched at the head of the procession, carrying the blue and white Greek flag. He came to say hello to Primo, and gave him a pair of the coarse linen trousers that prisoners wore in Auschwitz.

Levi reported to the transit camp in Bogucice, situated in a Katowice suburb, which during the war had been a small concentration camp whose inmates worked in a nearby coal mine. Its dozen single-storey concrete huts were still surrounded by barbed wire fencing. By the entrance sat a sleepy Russian sentry with what proved to be an uncertain temperament. He was a big, middle-aged Mongolian with dark eyes and a Joseph Stalin moustache, and carried a submachine gun and a bayonet. Opposite him was a big hole in the fence, where people came and went as they pleased, often to reach the kitchens, canteen, infirmary, or washrooms, which lay outside the fence. Sometimes, when he was cold, the Mongolian would hand his gun to any refugee he chose to take his place, then find a warm dormitory where he could drink vodka and snooze by the stove. The camp housed about a hundred women and four hundred men of many nationalities, some of them deportees, some ex-PoWs, others civilian workers who had worked for the Todt Organization, which coordinated construction work for the German war effort all over occupied Europe.

Levi admired the Russian detachment which had settled in an abandoned primary school by the camp, because he felt that under their sloppy exterior lay a greater, invisible, inner discipline of comradeship which had won them their victory over "the mechanical and servile discipline of the Germans" (*Truce* 60/232).

"We hate in itself our masters' insane dream of greatness, and their contempt for God and men, and for ourselves, as men."

The camp, with its atmosphere of typically Russian chaos and confusion — which seemed to Levi inefficient, inoffensive, and cheerful, more like a squabbling family than a military unit — was managed by Captain Ivan Antonovich Egorov. Three lieutenants worked in boisterous concord with a sergeant, a quartermaster, a *doktorka*, a young medical doctor unable to leave women or alcohol alone, and a female nurse. A band of sturdy women washed, cooked, cleaned, typed, and had affairs with the men. Primo Levi struck up a diffident friendship with the nurse, Marya Fyodorovna.

One of the concrete cabins housed Italians, mostly civilian workers, presided over by a certain accountant called Rovi, who had elected himself

217

their leader because power was his pleasure. Levi, who scrutinized his behaviour like a naturalist in the field, likened him to a spider scuttling round its web — a creature he loathed, which recurs throughout his work and occupies a niche in his imagination. Rovi was no soldier, but he had confected a Ruritanian uniform with boots, cap, and tunic festooned with braid and medals, and on the door of his office, possibly some Block chief's former quarters, he had hung a sign with the inscription "Colonel Rovi." He loved red tape, and kept a crew of keen retainers at the expense of the community.

In Bogucice, Levi found his doctor friend Leonardo De Benedetti, who had arrived there before him and was working in his professional capacity, though he had not practised in Monowitz, and never derived the slightest advantage from his medical expertise. The infirmary, created by Marya Fyodorovna, was located in two small rooms in the school taken over by the Russians. Marya came from Siberia. Leonardo advised Primo to introduce himself to her as a pharmacist–interpreter. She wanted to know whether he was a genuine "*doktor*" — and so he was, if he stretched the point a little. She gave him a *propusk*, an "identity card" — a pass valid at any time of the day or night. Levi spent his time sorting and labelling a miscellany of boxes of medicines salvaged from abandoned Russian and German field hospitals. Marya gave him little gifts, and asked him to tea in her room, where several photographs of uniformed Russians hung above her bed. If Marya's tea was an invitation to anything else, he never explored the possibility.

As well as working with Marya, Levi assisted Leonardo De Benedetti in the surgery, supposedly reserved for the residents of the camp, but also attended by a stream of other patients — soldiers, local people, and various shady migrants who came because the consultations and treatment were free, and no questions were asked. Among other tasks, helping Leonardo required Levi to keep an eye on inmates infested with lice, because of the endemic threat of petechial typhus. He made daily inspection tours of all the huts, examining the folds and seams of shirts, looking for nests and eggs. All such pests had military nicknames. Lice were "also called 'the infantry,' with fleas as the artillery, mosquitoes as the air force, bugs as the parachutists and crab-lice as the sappers" (*Truce* 67/239).

A visit from the drunken Doctor Danchenko led to a request from Marya for Levi to start keeping records of the patients attending the infirmary. He dictated his notes in German to Galina, one of the girls attached to the command post in the school, and she translated them into Russian and transcribed them. Galina was the only woman among the group who appealed to Levi for her qualities of delicacy and grace, but he felt a crippling disadvantage in her presence: "I was painfully conscious of my miserable appearance, of my badly shaved face, of my Auschwitz clothes; I was acutely conscious of Galina's glance, still almost infantile, in which vague compassion was mixed with definite repulsion" (*Truce* 65/237). Yet despite these barriers, a friendship developed between them. She told him how she had come to join the command post in the Caucasus, far to the east, where a request to help with secretarial work had turned into a nomadic life with her friends in the group, and a commitment to the war. He watched her flirtations, and enjoyed and envied her faith in herself and the future, until in May she set off again, this time for the east, with no money and no train ticket, a few days after the German surrender.

Like the rest of the inmates, Levi was entitled to the standard Russian food ration, which was not small, but Marya also gave permission for him and Leonardo to take midday meals in the infirmary. The cooks were two women of the French Resistance, sad-faced and prematurely aged, who had lost their husbands in a camp where they too had been detained. Although they served generous helpings, and disapproving seconds and thirds when pressed, Levi would keep on eating far past the limits of his physical requirements with all the compulsion of his Auschwitz reflexes.

Slowly, his strength and health recovered, and he could summon up the energy to leave the camp, and to make trips into Katowice by tram. He even went to the cinema a few times, accompanied by "Cesare" — the same Cesare, alias Lello Perugia, who in Monowitz-Buna had exhibited diarrhoea bought from genuine sufferers, so as to spend some of the winter in the warmth of the *KB*. It was he who had heard Charles Conreau calling Levi's name through the partition wall in the *Infektionsabteilung*, after the SS had abandoned the camp. Every day after that, Levi had brought water and a little soup both to Lello and to another Italian called Marcello, a Jew from the ancient Venice ghetto, whom he had met in Fossoli and who had been deported in the same transport as himself. Marcello had died. Lello, who weighed 35 kilos when he was liberated, had made an excellent recovery.

After the ten last days in Monowitz-Buna, the war had had one more ordeal in store for Lello Perugia. He had been settled in the collection camp in Bogucice at the time when the Germans attempted a last desperate counter-thrust from Breslau in the direction of Silesia. The Russians had press-ganged every able-bodied man in the Katowice area to help construct an emergency anti-tank ditch, and had herded the inmates of Bogucice at gun-point to make a 30-kilometre route march to Gleiwitz, where they were housed in barns and stables and compelled to work sixteen hours a day with picks and shovels. Three days of this, and Lello had decided to fall ill. He swapped his bread for two cigars, ate one of them, soaked the other in water, then stuck it under his armpit for a night. Next day's genuine symptoms got him sent to bed, and a stealthy departure had restored him to Bogucice, where he and Levi shared the same room and became friends.

One spring day, Primo and Lello left the camp by the main gate in quick succession, Lello using the same *propusk* that Primo had just handed back to him through the wire. The sentry did not mind that two Primo Levis came past him. They went to Katowice, where amid the chaos and desolation left behind by the bitter street-fighting which had captured the town, life was flourishing

219

again. The trams were working and the cinemas had opened their doors. Levi and Perugia were hungry and penniless, so they headed for the market place, which was bustling with people, and there Lello worked his way through all the food stalls without paying, by first sampling their wares, and afterwards pretending that they were not worth buying. Then he urged Levi to do the same.

Lello already had a business partner, Giacomo Pavoncello[8] — whom Levi called "Giacomantonio" in *The Truce* — but if Primo felt like joining in, he was welcome to work with them both. Levi had fallen in with another "Greek," except that Lello's warmth and free-wheeling nature were in utter contrast with the tight-lipped obsessiveness of Mordo Nahum. Levi took the job of apprentice, interpreter, and porter because Lello was a life-enhancing character. Giacomo Pavoncello used to hang about the railway station in Katowice waiting for the trainloads of soldiers who were passing through on their way home from Germany, and could easily be tricked into selling off some of the loot they carried at cheap prices, because they did not know the going rate and needed cash in hand. He had paid some Russians 50 zlotys for a fountain pen, a shirt with a hole in it, and an hourglass. Primo and his two companions went off to sell them in the market, which by now was overflowing with fresh produce from the local farms. Lello, who spoke the dialect of the Roman ghetto, sold the fountain pen straight away: the Poles were spell-bound by his sales talk. Then came the shirt. Lello kept his fingers over the hole, and started to bait and make mock of his audience, among them a likely customer whom he addressed as "Big Belly." When he squeezed a hesitant bid out of this man, Lello shouted in Yiddish that Big Belly was "*meshuge*" — crazy — a word that all the Poles understood. He made merciless fun of Big Belly, but the fish took the worm and paid out 150 zlotys. Then Perugia tugged Primo off on a leisurely retreat to the nearest street corner, followed by a dash for the camp when they reached it, for fear that the hole would be found.

Under the surface, Levi was growing bored in the Bogucice camp, in spite of some colourful times spent with Lello Perugia, who now had a regular pitch in the market, and was thriving. Lello had broken up with his first business partner, Pavoncello, but many others had replaced him, and did not ask for contracts when they entrusted him with goods to sell. But one morning Lello dropped out of sight, and did not reappear till four days later, at dawn, looking like a cat worn out by amorous nights and skulking back to its owner. Lello had found a girl in town. Many Italians had done likewise, and were replacing lost husbands in the beds of Polish widows.

Lello told Primo that his "*pagninca*" was young, beautiful, and well dressed. She spoke only Polish, and the help he wanted from his partner was to teach him to say a number of things in Polish or German that Primo was at a loss to translate. So Lello stormed off to the market, bought a dictionary for 20 zlotys, threw it at Primo, and told him to get busy. Much to his chagrin, he learned that the words he was looking for did not appear in the dictionary. Primo Levi wrote in *The Truce* that Lello spent most of his time with his *pagninca*. Lello, who now lives in Rome, puts a different spin on his encounter with the "Polacca":

> I had been asked to lunch by this lady, and I wasn't thinking about an affair. She asked her sister to see me to the tram that took us back to the camp in Bogucice. We came to the terminus, but the curfew declared by the Russians had begun, and no one was allowed to drive. The sister took me back to her house. As she worked at night, she offered me her bed. Later we had dinner, then I went off to sleep in the single bedroom. At a certain moment I went to the "Polacca" and told her I was cold. She invited me to come and get warm in her bed. I thought it over, and decided to try to make love to her. And so I did. The men and women who had been deported no longer felt like making love. The women lost their periods. We used to wonder whether the Germans were putting some substance in the beet-and-water soup they gave us so as to turn us impotent and sterile. When I returned to camp I told the story to Primo. It wasn't boasting, or showing off. I said to him: "Everything's working!" I simply wanted to let him know about my experience. I wanted to show him that we were still men, and encourage him to do likewise; show him that it just took a little time to gather his strength, to get back to normal. Primo thought I was showing off about my conquest.[9]

The Allied victory ended the period of semi-liberty for Primo Levi. On 30 April Captain Egorov sent for the holders of passes and confiscated them with an awkward air that made the Italians feel uneasy. Yet there was a party atmosphere over the next few days. At some point during that time Lello came back to camp, looking the worse for wear. Returning one evening to his *pagninca*'s house, he had found himself replaced by a Russian. One look at the military greatcoat, belt, and bottle of vodka in the hall, and he had grabbed the bottle and run, but the Russian had trailed him all the way to a local dance hall where they were celebrating the end of the war. After decanting the vodka into another bottle, then smashing the original to pieces, Lello invited his friend Primo to help him drown his sorrows.

On 7 May 1945, at Allied headquarters in Reims, General Alfred Jodl signed the unconditional surrender of all German forces. The following day, the Russians insisted on the Germans attending a second signing ceremony in Berlin, and it was on 8 May that frenzied rejoicing broke out in Bogucice and all across Poland and beyond. All over the camp, the Russians shouted, hugged, danced, fired shots into the air (but sometimes lower down, and dangerously), sang, and got drunk. Then they put on a big celebration for the refugees, to greet the victory properly.

After the German surrender, Primo Levi started to look forward to going home. No news had reached him from Italy, and he did not know that his family had come out unscathed from the war. That night he and all the other Italians attended the show that the Russians had spent the last few days organizing in the school gymnasium. The master of ceremonies was Captain Egorov, drunk, swaying, wearing a pair of huge baggy trousers and a tail coat. He was a tearful drinker, and sobbed as he announced the performers. All of the Russians did a number. There was a choir, some wild Caucasian dancing, and an imitation of Charlie Chaplin.

Some days later there was a memorable football match between the Italians and a well-trained Polish team, refereed by a young captain in the NKVD[10] who had come to inspect the camp some weeks before, and liked it so much that he stayed. Rain put a stop to the match, and it turned into a heavy downpour that soaked Levi to the skin on the way back to the camp. The next day he woke up feeling ill, with stabbing pains in his chest and back, and hardly able to breathe. He lay in bed for several days, unable to move, or to swallow more than a few spoonfuls of soup. Leonardo De Benedetti had no equipment but a stethoscope, but by sounding Levi's back and chest he diagnosed a dry pleurisy, located in between his lungs.

Leonardo and Lello Perugia combed the streets of Katowice looking for black-market sulphonamides and intravenous calcium, but without success. What they did find was the well-equipped office of an Italian colleague, Doctor Hainor, who appears in *The Truce* under the name of Gottlieb.[11] Hainor was working illegally in full public view. Primo Levi wrote that the doctor, who came from Fiume, had a paralyzed arm and spoke fluent German, Hungarian, Italian, Polish, and Russian. He had lived in Vienna and Zagreb, and had been through Auschwitz, though Levi never learned in what capacity. He lived with a brother and brother-in-law who by some miracle had come through Auschwitz with him and had also survived. According to Lello Perugia, who corroborates the rest of Levi's account, it was Doctor Hainor's legs that were semi-paralyzed, so Perugia's memories of the doctor's physical condition differ from Primo Levi's story — perhaps because the writer wanted to preserve the doctor's anonymity.

Hainor had managed to get out of the transit camp and was now the most popular doctor in Katowice. He was not only a mysterious, shrewd, and outstandingly intelligent man, but also a first-class practitioner, who had confidence in his own abilities. He showed unusual devotion to Primo Levi's case, and paid several calls to the camp to examine him, bringing his patient medicines and administering injections. According to Levi, on his final visit he ordered him to: "Rise and walk" (*Truce* 97/269). We do not know whether this injunction really was spoken by Hainor, but it is reminiscent of the order to "Follow me" that Levi attributes to the physics lecturer Nicola Dallaporta in

The Periodic Table, remarking that the words came from the Gospel. Citing the call of the Apostles made Dallaporta a Christ-like figure, and Levi his disciple, for Matthew is called Levi by Mark and Luke.[12] As for "Rise and walk," it too belongs to the New Testament. Christ heals a paralytic — "a man sick of the palsy" — then orders him to get up and walk. In this case, according to Lello Perugia it was Hainor, the doctor, who was paralyzed.[13]

Although the patient was no longer in pain, and was breathing freely, he still felt very weak, and had to stay in bed for another three weeks. He spent his time reading the very few books available in the camp: an English grammar in Polish, a textbook of trigonometry, a Nazi propaganda novel, *Die grosse Heimkehr* ("The Great Homecoming"), *Marie Walewska, le grand amour de Napoléon*, *The Convicts of the Cayenne*, and *Rouletabille à la rescousse*.

Lello and Leonardo took care of Levi, who observed the human specimens occupying the dormitory with his usual keen and humorous eye. He took a special interest in "the Moor," a towering old man, perpetually angry, cursing all the time. Then there was Ferrari, infested with lice, and Ambrigo Trovati, nicknamed "Dusk," both of them professional thieves usually to be found in Rome, in the San Vittore quarter. Trovati had once been tried and acquitted of manslaughter, in a case he was always reliving; he would stage re-enactments of his trial, in which he forced his room mates to play the parts of the various court officials. Another room mate was old Mr Unverdorben from Trieste (whose name means "pure" in German), a survivor of Birkenau, and a teller of tall tales. He was a former conductor and composer who had forsaken music for a career as a cook on ocean liners when his enemies accused him of plagiarism after discovering that four bars of an opera he had written were identical with four from *I Pagliacci*.

Levi described Cravero, a thief from Turin, as "one of those rare beings in whom the abstract criminal hypothesis of the penal code seemed to take flesh and human shape" (*Truce 101/273*). Cravero, according to Levi, had worked for the Todt Organization in Berlin, then dropped out of sight and put a German woman on the streets. His job was to pimp for her, collect her fees, and sort out problem clients with a knife. Cravero had found his niche in the Berlin underworld, but when the Russians neared the city he decided that it was high time to ditch his woman and go back to Italy under his own steam. Events had forced him south-east to Katowice, but he still aimed to find his own way home, and Levi was weak or gullible enough to accept his offer to deliver a letter to his family. This out-and-out crook set off on foot from Katowice in the middle of May and arrived in Turin a month later. He found Levi's mother, and handed her the letter in the presence of her daughter.

Cravero told the two women that Primo was very ill, but if they would let him have 200,000 lire there and then he undertook to fetch him home safe and sound in three weeks. Signora Levi and Anna Maria were not taken in. They listened, then asked him to come back in a few days' time because they didn't keep that much cash in the house. Cravero could not leave empty-handed.

Anna Maria had been a courier in the Resistance, and it happened that she had been looking after a Beretta submachine gun on behalf of a comrade who no longer needed it. He caught sight of the gun, where it lay half hidden under her bed, and made her a "cautious offer" that she chose to refuse.[14] On his way out, he stole the bicycle that Anna Maria kept in the entrance to the building. Theft came so naturally to him that two years later he sent Levi a cheerful Christmas card from his prison in the Nuove Carceri in Turin.

Primo Levi wrote in *The Mirror Maker* that following the visit from Cravero, Anna Maria went to enquire about her brother at the Military Command centre in Turin run by the "Anders Army," a Polish force made up of soldiers released by the Russians late in 1942 and now serving under General Wladyslaw Anders, appointed as their commander-in-chief by the Polish government-in-exile. The frosty reception given by the Poles to a young woman whose surname was Levi did not deter Anna Maria. Two days later she visited the Soviet command centre, to no effect, though the reception was more cordial. On her way out, she noticed that she was being followed by an Italian policeman, no doubt acting on information from the Poles. At once she thought about the Beretta submachine gun, but she had no intention of parting with such a "sacred" weapon. It was not long before the policeman rang the door-bell of the attic where she was living at the time, but it turned out that his interest was chiefly in Cravero, suspected of being a Soviet spy.

"Rise and walk," Doctor Hainor had said, after prescribing injections of insulin to help his patient's body to metabolize blood sugar. Early in June, the convalescent Levi started to make trips outside the camp, driven by the need to walk like a free man again and to breathe in the smells of woods and fields. In the morning he would gather his strength and venture out into the countryside around Katowice. But his blood-sugar levels were low, and when the insulin found no more fuel left to burn, his legs would give way and he had to sit down fast. Fortunately Marya kept him supplied with packets of glucose, which he carried in his pocket, and swallowed when the earth began to sway.

One morning in mid-June, when he returned from his walk, Levi saw Captain Egorov standing in the camp square surrounded by Italians, waving a big revolver and bawling at the crowd. None of them spoke Russian, but every-one had realized that the Italians were to be repatriated by way of Odessa. After four months' waiting, the news caused universal jubilation, and some started packing straightaway.

On the eve of their departure, which took place on the first of July,[15] Leonardo and Primo returned the keys of the surgery to Marya and said goodbye to the Russians. At Danchenko's request, and with some reservations, Levi described himself as a "Doctor of Medicine" when he signed a statement about his good treatment by the Russians. In return, he was presented with a certificate written on a sheet of lined paper torn from an exercise book, and which declared that he had "merited the gratitude of all the workers of the world" (*Truce 110/282*).

On the following day, the eight hundred rejoicing Italians boarded the battered goods wagons of a long freight train bound for Odessa, where the Russians promised that there were boats waiting to take them to Italy. Just before leaving, each wagon was issued with a loaf of bread and a tin of American soya margarine, very hard and salty. The train left Katowice with no escort and not a single Russian on board. Doctor Hainor was part of the group, and took charge of the convoy. For six days they travelled in fits and starts, constantly having to wait in sidings till the line was clear because military convoys had priority. No one had been warned that it was due, and it caused "doleful surprise" in the stations along the way. But the amazing Doctor Hainor unravelled every bureaucratic tangle with a virtuoso display of quick wit, cheek, and humour. If asked for a signed authority that could not be produced because it did not exist, he did not disappoint the official but manufactured an impressive-looking fake that was just as effective. When he asked for rations for his starving group in the name of Comrade Stalin, he got them at once.

During the journey, Levi fell ill again. Every night he suffered a bout of violent fever that left him barely conscious in the morning, and suffering from searing pains in the elbow, knee, or wrist. Past huge expanses of dense, dark forest, the train ran eastward through Rzeszów and Przemysl and arrived in Lvov, ceded by Poland to the Soviet Union in 1945. The town had been shattered by air raids. It was pouring with rain, and the roof of the wagon was leaking, so Levi and a few companions had to look for shelter in the muddy, draughty subway of the station. When the train set off again, it ran on through Ternopol and Proskurov, where the locomotive was uncoupled and Primo, Leonardo, Lello, and Daniele (one of the Italians Levi knew in Auschwitz) settled down in the outsize waiting-room. Lello went off to look for food, and when he returned with some eggs, lettuce, and tea they lit a fire on a floor littered with the remains of previous fires, cooked the eggs, and drank strong tea.

The tea kept them lively and wakeful. Levi wrote that it must have been this that etched that night so sharply on his memory. As daylight faded, he felt restored to life, despite his illness. He watched the sky turn to night, and was admiring the moonlight that followed when he realized that the two teenage girls dressed in black sitting next to him were speaking Yiddish. Lello appointed Primo their ambassador, and the usually shy young man turned to the girls and spoke to them in German, trying to mimic their pronunciation of Yiddish and explaining that he was Jewish, and so were his three companions. That made them laugh, and their answer echoed words he had heard in Auschwitz: none of them could possibly be Jews, because they didn't speak Yiddish. In *The Truce*, Levi attempted to reproduce the girls' reply. He made some errors, and the sentence came out as a mixture of German and Yiddish.

He wrote that their words to him were: "*Ihr sprech keyn yiddish; ihr seyd ja keyne Jiden!*," whereas the girls must surely have told him: "*Ihr redt nicht keyn yiddish; ihr seydt nicht keyne Yid'n!*" They could not conceive that there could possibly be Jews in the world who did not speak Yiddish. Before the war, eleven million Jews had spoken that language, chiefly in Eastern Europe.

In order to convince them, Levi started to recite the *Shema Israël*[16] in his Italian accent, which they found even funnier. The two girls came from Minsk. Their parents had had the good sense to ask to be moved to the interior of the Soviet Union as the *Einsatzgruppen* approached, and they had been sent to Uzbekistan while the girls were still small. Their mother had died, and their father had been drafted to work on the frontier. After the German defeat they had decided to return, starting their journey from Samarkand and travelling on foot, and by lorry, bus, train, and boat, with not a kopek in their pockets. While they were speaking, Lello started to fret. When was the action going to start? Eventually he gave up, and went in search of less platonic pursuits.

Before the night ended, Levi relapsed into fever again, and Doctor Hainor dosed him with half a litre of moonshine vodka which smelled musty and burned like fire. He woke up next morning buried beneath a blanket of other sleepers who had not found room on the floor. Caught between the fire of the vodka inside him and the human warmth around him, his body had sweated the fever out. It never returned, nor did the stabbing pains.

When the train stopped in Zhmerinka, 350 kilometres from Odessa, Doctor Hainor learned that the convoy was to travel no further. The passengers had to leave their wagons and bed down in the station for the night. It was the first time that Hainor had failed, and it proved to be a bad omen. The next morning, he and his brother and brother-in-law were nowhere to be found. They had managed to persuade a Russian railwayman to let them board a military train to Poland, together with all their luggage.

The ex-deportees remained in Zhmerinka, which Levi described as "a large agricultural village," for three days, during which they grew more and more worried by the trickle of information about their future that they managed to squeeze from the Russians. They heard talk about convoys leaving for the north, and for the Far East. On the third day a passenger train arrived from Romania carrying about six hundred well-dressed Italian nationals, with plenty of baggage, who had paid for tickets home. These were civilian and military staff from the Italian legation in Bucharest, together with former members of the ARMIR,[17] some of them travelling with their families. The "Romanians" had money and could afford to pay high prices for food, whereas Levi and his comrades were forced to go begging, as Lello Perugia confirms.[18]

Both convoys camped in the station and went looking for supplies in the village, where the scene described by Levi might have come from the paintings of Chagall's Russian period. The walls of one of the station latrines were plastered with German banknotes, meticulously stuck there with excrement. Some families of very primitive nomads, dressed in goatskins, were camped in the main square. They travelled in a massive wagon with solid wooden wheels, drawn by four shaggy carthorses.

Elsewhere in the village, near the railway line, Levi and his friends came upon a dozen German soldiers, still dressed in tattered Wehrmacht uniforms, and so hungry that they begged for bread from this group of Jews. They all refused, except for Daniele, whose entire family had been deported and murdered. He put a piece of bread on the ground and told these specimens of the "master race" that it was theirs if they would go on hands and knees for the sake of it. The pure Aryans crawled in front of Daniele to collect the chunk of bread.

In the rejoicing that followed the Liberation, a triumphal arch of foliage had been put up in the railway station, as well as giant portraits of the victors — Stalin, Churchill, and Roosevelt. While the Italians were there, the portraits came down. The wall of the station had carried the slogan: "Workers of the world, unite!" During their stay, they saw a sign painter put a coating of white-wash over these words, and replace them with another, more ominous slogan: "Onwards to the West."

Some trains were travelling south, carrying Ukrainian women, some with their children, who had gone to work in Germany, in harsh conditions. Now they were being shipped back home in cattle trucks, destitute and in disgrace.

At the end of June, the Russians packed all 1,400 Italians and "Romanians" — ragged ex-deportees and affluent diplomatic staff — on to a convoy of thirty goods wagons and sent them northwards, away from Odessa and Italy, towards an unknown destination. For reasons it could not or would not explain, Russian officialdom was taking them ever further from home, yet it was also the Russians who had liberated Auschwitz, and that gave them great prestige in Levi's eyes, even as he confronted "the inscrutable Soviet bureau-cracy, an obscure and gigantic power, not ill-intentioned towards us, but suspicious, negligent, stupid, contradictory and in effect as blind as the forces of nature" (*Truce* 117/289). He found a reason for hoping that the journey would not last long in the fact that no food was issued to the passengers.

For two days and a night the train drove on across a landscape of steppes, rivers, forests, and secluded villages. During a halt on the first night, Primo Levi and Lello Perugia noticed that the front of the train contained several empty passenger carriages and a hospital car, which Lello decided to board. Its fixtures and luxury amazed them: running water, soap, beds complete with sheets and warm blankets. On the bed he had chosen, Levi found an Italian edition of the novel *The Paul Street Boys* by Ferenc Molnár, a Jewish Hungarian author who fled when the Second World War broke out, and who was to end his days in the United States.

After crossing the River Beresina, the train came to a stop in the middle of the night, during a heavy storm. The passengers had to jump down and set off over muddy ground in total darkness and pouring rain, each of them clinging to the one in front. Half an hour later the bedraggled column arrived at an enormous bomb-damaged building. Under its leaking roof, they waited until the light of a radiant dawn showed them that the building was a ruined theatre, and that it lay in the wreckage of a Soviet military camp abandoned by the army. The retreating Germans had methodically looted the place, tearing out every nail, the water pipes, electric wiring, footlights, radiators, and heating plant. They had also wrecked the railway lines that led to the camp, using a purpose-built machine. Levi remarked of this systematic destruction that it represented "the mystique of barrenness, beyond all demands of war or impulse for booty" (*Truce 123/295*).

The Germans had left intact the crude but vivid frescoes on the inside walls, with their giant figures of Stalin, Lenin, and Molotov. Hitler was portrayed there in the form of an enormous spider wearing a swastika on its rump, and beneath it the caption: "Death to Hitler's invaders." The frescoes also showed a tall blond Russian soldier, raising handcuffed hands to accuse hundreds of "insect-men" who cowered before the chained hero.

The assembly camp of Slutsk, 100 kilometres south of Minsk, inhabited by ten thousand men, women, and children from all over Europe — Jewish, Russian Orthodox, Muslim; white, black, yellow; German, Polish, French, Greek, Dutch, Italian — quartered in and around its roofless barracks with their gaping windows.

On the day they arrived, a summer warmth drifted in the misty air. Levi had set out on a walk, looking for a place to remove his worn damp clothes to dry out in the sun, when in the middle of a meadow he came upon "the Greek," the rogue moralist Mordo Nahum, always big, now sumptuously fat, and wearing a kind of Soviet uniform. At once, Mordo wanted to help. He could get Primo food, clothes, even a woman. Primo Levi, who was very inexperienced with women, although he was nearly twenty-six, saw that lying in the meadow around Mordo were a score of rugged girls with bovine looks. The Greek explained to Primo that these "white and substantial" creatures, who came from Bessarabia, appealed to Russian tastes. They worked under his orders — hygiene and discretion guaranteed — and he too took his pleasure with them. Levi declined Mordo's free offer, they talked for a while, and he never saw the Greek again.

In Slutsk there were no facilities to accommodate all these people, and they slept on the ground, but Levi felt at ease during the ten days he spent there, because the weather was warm, there was no compulsion to work, and the food was not only plentiful but deliciously unusual. The Russians had arranged for each of the major nationalities to take charge of the cooking on a weekly rota system, and the meals were served in a big, clean, airy dining-hall, at tables laid for eight. For ever after, Levi savoured the memory of the platefuls of hot, spicy goulash and sugared spaghetti served up by the Hungarians while a Gypsy orchestra dressed in traditional costume played the Soviet and Hungarian national anthems, *Hatikvah*,[19] and csárdáses. All over the camp's huge parade ground, bordered by dilapidated one- and two-storey barracks, the residents slept, deloused themselves, mended their clothes, cooked extra food, even played football or skittles. In the centre of the square a building of respectable proportions housed the latrines, distinguished by its three separate entrances for men, for women, and for officers. Levi described the interior: a rickety wooden floor pierced by a hundred square holes in rows of ten, and with no partitions for any of the three categories.

The print-starved Levi dipped into a German textbook on obstetrics that he found in an attic, or slept for hours in the grasslands that surrounded the camp. When he went walking outside the barracks complex, the level immensity of the Russian plains made him feel giddy. Thirty-seven years later he described these treeless expanses in his only work of fiction, *Se non ora, quando?*[20] (*If Not Now, When?*) which tells the epic story of a group of young Jewish partisans who make their way to the Promised Land across the vast forests and plains of wartime Russia.

One morning some of the Italian inmates heard from the Russians, and the news then spread around the camp, that on 20 July their contingent was to leave for Starye Dorogi, 70 kilometres east, where there was a special assembly camp for Italians. When the day came, the women and children, and the men in the know, boarded a train in the morning. After some chopping and changing by the Russians, the rest set out on foot around midday, down a highway of beaten earth that ran geometrically straight through steppe and forest to Starye Dorogi, with only one slight kink along the way. This was the region of the Pripet Marshes, where Levi was later to set some of the action of *If Not Now, When?* The country was monotonous and empty — not a single village, or even a house, no milestone, not a living soul. After some hours of walking it seemed to Levi as if the column, three kilometres long, had made no progress.

A horse and cart driven by a Russian soldier who had lost the lower half of his face in combat brought up the rear and collected the belongings dropped by exhausted marchers on the way. They were never returned to their owners. That is how Levi came to lose both volumes of the obstetrics textbook which had helped him pass the time in Slutsk. He walked in a group with Leonardo, Daniele, who suffered from thirst, Mr Unverdorben, and a friend of his from Trieste, and Lello Perugia. By nightfall they were worn out, and suffering from sore and blistered feet, so they stopped at the only bend in the road, near a ruined hut with a well behind, where they could quench their thirst. Levi had replaced his priest's shoes with a pair of cycling shoes that were too tight, so that he kept on having to remove them and walk barefoot. Now that they had water and some sort of shelter, the six of them decided to leave the column for a while and go on to Starye Dorogi the next day.

They were not watched or guarded by the Russians. It was easy to hide by the wayside and wait for the last stragglers to go by. But when they had their blankets spread, and were ready to eat a frugal meal of bread, tinned peas, and *kasha*, a porridge made of millet, Lello rebelled and insisted that tonight he would dine on roast chicken. Even in the middle of the Pripet Marshes, a village must mean chicken, and he intended to find both. The group would afford him only six earthenware plates to barter with, but Primo volunteered to join him, and they explored a promising path through the woods that led them to a light shining out of the mosquito-ridden darkness ahead. Lello hailed the unseen inhabitants with shouts that he was *"Italienski,"* and a bullet sang over their heads. (The last foreign visitors had probably been German.) But Lello kept talking, and they ventured cautiously closer till they came upon a cluster of five or six wooden houses around a tiny square where the whole village stood waiting, led by a patriarch with a beard and a rifle.

It was up to Levi to do the talking, and he tried the words for "chicken" in every language he knew, but drew a blank. Lello offered a very poor mime of a chicken, and a sound like *"coccoday,"* but Russians say *"coucaricou,"* and the mystified villagers began to suspect that their midnight visitors were dangerous lunatics. Finally, Primo drew a chicken on the ground, and an egg beside it, and light dawned on an old peasant woman who called out: *"Kura! Kuritsa!"* To roars of laughter, the deal was done: six plates for a plump plucked chicken. Primo and Lello returned to their sleeping companions, and they ate roast chicken with their fingers before falling very soundly asleep.

When they woke up, the sun was shining, and they still felt cheered by the thought of the previous day's adventure. They were free men, and nobody wanted them dead. They picked wild strawberries and mushrooms in the woods, smoked a cigarette, and decided that they had better get moving again, because they had only eight roubles between them, and their provisions were exhausted. Lello and Primo returned to the hamlet with the money, to see what they could buy, but on the way there it occurred to them that they might hire a horse and cart from the peasants to take them to Starye Dorogi. When friendly faces greeted them, Levi drew on his boyhood reading to quote Jules Verne's *Michel Strogoff*[21] and announce: *"Telega, Starye Dorogi,"* displaying the eight roubles. No one understood him, so he pointed at a farm cart parked beneath a roof, till the old man with the gun corrected his pronunciation: *"Tyelyega."*

The offer was instantly accepted. The old man harnessed a mule to the cart, waved them on board and loaded some sacks. They collected their comrades back at the road. Viewed from the cart, the plain looked less monotonous and dreary as it undulated gently across a patchwork of pools and marshes, and Levi saw the burnt-out wrecks of tanks, abandoned guns, helmets, drums, and barbed wire. Towards nightfall, they were overtaken by a long-striding walker who proved to be "the Moor" — his real name was Avesani — who had been with them in the sick room in Bogucice. He carried a sack on his back, with an axe lashed on to it, and when they invited him to join them on the cart he only growled: "Disgrace to humanity! Inhuman old swine!" as he passed by.

Starye Dorogi means "Old Roads" in Russian; there was a hamlet of that name in the woods near the road, which Levi was to describe, together with the landscape around it, in *If Not Now, When?*. The 1,400 Italians were housed in an enormous building called Krasny Dom ("the Red House"), a gigantic warren of a place, which stood next to the road but seemed to Levi to be out of this world. It too was a former military establishment, and its facilities included a lecture room, a big theatre, several classrooms, a gymnasium, kitchens, sick bay, and wash houses, all tacked crazily together in a maze of random accretions, with all kinds of mysterious Gothic stairways, some of considerable proportions, some leading nowhere. The state of the Red House was ruinous: as in Slutsk, the Germans had gone to great lengths to wreck all of the electrical fittings and wiring, furniture, and pipes.

The Russians may have run the Red House in an anarchic fashion, but they continued to enjoy the sympathy and fondness of Primo Levi. The site was not enclosed, nor was it supervised by the Russian soldiers and officers who lived in a wooden hut not far away. A number of Italian officers, former PoWs, had been put in charge of the civilians — a bizarre development, to place these former enemies of the Soviet Union in command of men and women who had been sent to their probable deaths by the Fascist regime these officers had fought for. They looked down on the civilians, because they themselves dined in the Russian officers' mess, slept on comfortable camp beds, and wore brand-new Russian boots and uniforms, though without insignia.

As for the disparate and complex community of the new arrivals, their food and conditions were exactly the same as those of the ordinary Russian soldiers. They slept on beds of plants, spread with straw mattresses 70 centimetres wide. Each person received a kilo of poorly made rye bread a day, as well as a *kasha* that was an indigestible block of lard, millet, beans and, very spicy meat, which could only be improved with hours of boiling. Every two days or so, each of them also received a big fish called a *ryba*, raw and not very fresh. The Russian soldiers ate it as it came, but the disgusted Italians preferred to sell it either to the local peasants or to passing soldiers. Lello, who recalls that the fish in question was a kind of herring, became a skilled fishmonger, and a rich one. He collected the herrings in big sacks, then threaded them on to a wire and went off into the country to peddle his heavy brochettes in exchange for cheese, eggs, and chicken. The scales he bought with the first proceeds gave him a professional air.

Primo Levi gives an instance of the business acumen of Lello Perugia in *The Truce*. One day Lello came to see him in the sick bay asking to borrow a syringe. When Levi asked what he intended doing with it, he answered: "What do you care?" Levi gave him a big syringe in poor repair. He could not prevail on Lello to let him into his trade secrets, but he pieced together evidence from various sources. Lello was seen fetching water in a bucket, then sitting with his fish and the bucket, then selling some altogether plumper-looking fish. In the end he had to fill in the rest of the story. He was injecting the fishes with water to make them look firm and fresh. He had got the idea when he swapped two limp fishes in the village for a big fat chicken that turned out, when killed and plucked, to have been afflicted with a big watery cyst. He sold the fowl to a rival, and then it came to him that what nature could do to a chicken, a salesman could do to a fish. Water poured into their mouths would just pour out again, but after some experimentation and dissection, he established that the proper procedure was to inject it into the swim-bladder. Perugia sold his inflated herrings only to soldiers who were passing by the Red House, and who would not notice the deception until they had driven several kilometres down the highway.

According to information from Lello Perugia, Primo Levi tended to embroider and exaggerate his exploits. In fact, he says, he confined his activities to washing the herrings in a basin because they smelled so bad that they were otherwise unsaleable. He also explains that he went into this business in order to improve on the diet provided for himself and his comrades from Auschwitz.

Most of the guests in the camp were left to their own devices. No one was obliged to work, except for those who came forward to run the kitchens, the baths, and the electric generator. Leonardo De Benedetti had volunteered his services as a doctor, Primo Levi as a nurse, but illness was rare. There was nothing to stop the occupants from leaving the camp and trying to find their way home, but in practice the aim was not achievable. All those who tried it were turned back at the frontiers. The Russians were indifferent to this micro-society in which Communists rubbed shoulders with monarchists, Fascists, a handful of deportees liberated from Auschwitz, former collaborators with the Todt Organization, criminals, and prostitutes.

Levi was a resident of the Red House until 15 September 1945. When the season of mushrooms and bilberries arrived, they all spent their days in the woods, where bilberries grew in lush and inexhaustible profusion, and where Lello discovered that there were two kinds of mushrooms. He tested a kind that were supposed to be edible and looked like ceps on some of their number who could not forget "the Auschwitz hunger" and suffered an indiscriminate greed for anything that could be eaten. The food that the Russians provided was too little for the permanently famished, and the more affluent among them bought supplementary rations from the peasant women of Starye Dorogi, who came every day to sell their produce — bilberries, strawberries, mushrooms, milk, cheese, eggs, poultry, and vegetables — to the inhabitants of the camp. Levi describes them sitting waiting for the rain to stop with their skirts flung up above their heads. He never fails to show his fellow feeling for the Russians, whose lackadaisical attitude offered such a radical contrast to the thoroughness, efficiency, violence, and blind obedience he had witnessed in the Germans. Having seen the Nazis at work, the Russian disorder, casual inefficiency, and lack of organization earned Levi's abiding affection.

Time passed, and still there was no knowing when the Italians were going to be sent home, or if they would ever go home at all. The soldiers of the Red

Army were returning, no longer by rail and many on foot. Primo Levi watched them pass by, often in tattered clothes and without their weapons, but carrying some piece of loot — a saucepan, a chair, a standard lamp, a clock. These homeward-bound Russians also travelled by motor cycle, on horseback, in horse-drawn carts, and crammed into German buses still displaying the name of their last destination in Berlin. American trucks towed damaged trailers limping along on spectacularly clumsy makeshift repairs. Broken-down vehicles were hauled by what seemed to Levi to be the entire population of Germany, and in the end the traffic consisted of nothing but horses, hundreds of thousands of them, plagued by gnats and horseflies.

Now that his strength had returned, the role of amused observer began to grow tedious for Levi: "As always happens, the end of our hunger laid bare and perceptible in us a much deeper hunger" (*Truce 156/328*). With the frontiers hermetically sealed, those who set out in search of variety would return in the end, having nowhere better to go, but only to resume the more and more frustrating sameness of endless summer days. Levi and some of his comrades tried to make acquaintance with local people, but those who spoke English or German proved to be very wary of foreigners: rather than be spied on and possibly disciplined, they broke contact.

Four months after the end of the war, the Italians were still being held by the Russians, and could not even write to their families. When Levi approached "the Lieutenant," a Russian officer who spoke fluent Italian and seemed to be respected and even feared by his superiors, he was rebuffed. The tight-lipped Lieutenant shunned his fellow Russians no less than the Italians. He did not drink or smoke, nor did he accept invitations. He seemed to know his way around Turin and Milan, but when asked if he had been to Italy, he brushed away the question. Levi concluded that he probably belonged to the *NKVD*.

At long last, early in September, signs of movement began to be noticed. A detachment of young Russian soldiers arrived from Austria, with instructions to escort a group of foreigners — they did not know who — to some distant destination — they did not know where. New shoes were given out to those who needed them. The surly Lieutenant vanished, and did not reappear. No doubt this meant departure, but for what destination? By this time there was a chill in the air. It crept in through the windows, whose panes were all broken, and the beds grew damp with rain from the leaky roofs. No one had any winter clothing. While the roads turned to mud, the peasants collected cartloads of wood from the forest and readied their houses for the bitter Russian winter. They lit fires indoors, and they all wore their boots. It was the third successive autumn that found Primo Levi far from home, but this time the coming of September cold and rain brought news of an end to wandering.

The "Romanian" Italians had taken to organizing theatrical performances to while away the time, a variety show with songs, tap-dancing, clowning, and mime, and an allegorical sketch called "The Shipwreck of the Spiritless," which was an obvious satire on life in the castaway existence of the camp, complete with a cannibal chief impossible to mistake for anybody except the Comrade Colonel in charge of Starye Dorogi. One night, when there was nothing better to do than watch possibly the tenth performance of "The Shipwreck," whose script changed every night, the cannibal chief completed the final scene by tearing off his costume and shouting: "Tomorrow we leave!" Seeing that the audience was at a loss, he shouted again: "I'm telling the truth, this is not theatre, this time it's real! The telegram has arrived, tomorrow we're all going home!" (*Truce* 177/349). The Colonel confirmed the news, and the camp broke out in celebration, talking and singing for the rest of the night round bonfires blazing in the woods.

The following morning, the battered wreck of a Fiat 500 "Topolino" ("Mouse") — a tiny car — drew up outside the Red House and disgorged, with a struggle, the colossal form of Marshal of the Soviet Union Semyon Konstantinovich Timoshenko. Pausing to don a vast black cloak that almost swept the ground, he stalked majestically into the Red House to speak to some of the Russians. After that, he strolled out onto the open ground where people were bent over cooking pots, and told them: "War over, everybody home." For Russians, the word "tomorrow" meant nothing quite so urgent as the day after today, but "soon" was good enough, and no one took offence.

Now that departure was certain, Primo Levi realized how attached he had become to the landscapes and people of Russia. He also knew that he was coming to the end of an extraordinary interlude, an adventure whose attractions he was often to look back on with nostalgia from the sheltered perspective of a bourgeois existence in Turin.

On 15 September 1945 an Italian procession set out for the station of Starye Dorogi, where a big locomotive stood waiting in a siding, coupled to a convoy of sixty shabby goods wagons, 500 metres long. Here they could settle down in comfort — no more than twenty-five people to a truck — grouping themselves according to community of origin, "profession," sex, civil status, and affinities. The groups of travellers listed by Levi were: the "Romanians," who occupied a dozen wagons; single women; couples, married or unmarried; families with children; the "orchestra-car," housing all those who had taken part in the show, together with their instruments and a piano, the gift of the Russians; the San Vittorio thieves; and lastly the "hospital-car," a purely notional title, since the entire medical kit available to Leonardo De Benedetti and Primo Levi consisted of a stethoscope and a syringe. On the other hand, no one was ill. As well as the "staff," this wagon also contained Lello Perugia, Daniele, Avesani, Mr Unverdorben, the Moor, Lello's former partner Pavoncello, and some ex-PoWs. They waited all night, and then next morning the engine got up steam and the convoy set out into the solitary steppe, with no official presence except the engine-driver and the escort of seven Russian soldiers from Austria, all aged eighteen.

On the evening of 16 September the train reached Bobruysk, and the following day Ovruch. Primo Levi attempted to follow their progress on one of the few maps available in the train; he soon realized that their return had not been scheduled at all, and no advance arrangements had been made. The only certainty was that they were creeping southwards, very slowly, at the expense of exasperating halts and detours. In their growing anxiety, Primo and his comrades kept on pressing the engine-driver to keep them informed, but all he could say was: "Where are we going tomorrow? I don't know, dear friends, I don't know. We are going where we find railway tracks" (*Truce 184/356*).

According to Lello Perugia, Primo Levi took some creative liberties in *The Truce* with the episode that follows. In order to allow for his objections, we shall give both men's versions of the facts, starting with Levi's.

As Levi tells it, Lello was at his wits' end. He could not handle being cooped up in the wagon with nothing to do. As the train was on its way to Zhitomir, he noticed that Pavoncello was wearing a brass ring on his finger, and he offered to buy it. Both men enjoyed the haggling that followed, which ended with Lello uncharacteristically coughing up the considerable sum of 4 roubles for an object worth much less. He spent the rest of the day polishing the ring, first with bits of cloth, then with cigarette paper. When the train stopped at a small town, he jumped down and prowled along the platform with the ring hidden under his jacket, sidling up to peasants and muttering: "*Tovarishch, zloto, zloto*" ("Comrade, gold, gold!").

Lello prolonged the bargaining so as not to hand over the ring till the convoy was leaving, and the blast on the whistle found him stuffing some 50 roubles into his pocket, then making a jump for the train just as it pulled out of the station. But the train had covered barely a few metres when there was a screech of brakes and it stopped again. He peered through a crack in the closed wagon to find out what was happening outside, and saw that the buyer had realized that he had been had, and he and his friends were coming to find the swindler. This was not difficult, because Perugia was hiding in the only wagon whose doors were closed. When the searchers came closer, he curled up in a corner and had his friends pile all the blankets, sacks and clothing there on top of him. Levi heard snatches of muffled prayers as the Russians banged on the doors. It was a scene worthy of the *commedia dell'arte*, and it finished with the triumph of the culprit when suddenly the train moved off, and this time kept on going. When he emerged from his hiding place, white as a sheet, Lello said: "Now let them look for me!" (*Truce 186–7/358–9*).

According to Lello Perugia, this is what happened. A woman travelling in the same wagon as himself had found a small ring of no value. She readily gave it to Lello, and he used bicarbonate of soda to polish it up. When they stopped at a station in the Soviet Union, he tried to sell the little ring by shouting "Goldo! Goldo!" from the wagon, to make out that it was gold. He asked for 300 roubles, and found a taker for 150. In Lello's words, these roubles were "transformed into good roast chickens" that he shared with his comrades, including Primo Levi.

The next morning, in brilliant sunshine, the train arrived in Kazatin, and to Primo's delighted surprise he saw a face that he recognized on the platform. It belonged to Galina, the same Galina who had worked as a typist and translator in the Russian HQ in Bogucice. He jumped off the train to embrace her, but they hardly had time to exchange a few clumsy words in German before the train began to move. Levi smelled "the cheap perfume" left by her hand on his own, the perfume of a woman he had not dared to make a pass at. He wrote that he felt "sad at the memory of the hours spent in her company, of things unsaid, of opportunities unseized" (*Truce* 187/359).

The train passed through Zhmerinka, where in the early summer the Italians had spent three days waiting to leave for Starye Dorogi. After a fast journey through Bessarabia, on the evening of 19 September it reached the River Pruth, at the Romanian border. Here the railway gauge changed from Russian to western, and the Italian contingent was transferred into another set of equally dilapidated wagons. At last, the convoy came to the station of Iasi, where the train was divided into three sections (four, according to Lello Perugia). At this stage of the journey Levi records two events: the disappearance of the "Romanians" and the reappearance of two young German women who had lived as prostitutes in the woods near the Red House, having stayed there ever since the German defeat. He learned that they had crossed the Soviet frontier hidden between the axles of the wagons, with the help of some Italian soldiers. Now that they were safe they ventured on to the platform, dressed in Soviet uniforms, covered in dirt and grease, but wrapped once again in smug insolence.

During the long halt, Perugia visited the town. He had heard that there was an office of the Joint Distribution Committee (JDC)[22] there, the American–Jewish organization that gave assistance to Jewish survivors all over Europe. It seems that Perugia — more enterprising than his fifteen comrades — had decided to go looking for food supplies. Having made contact with some JDC officials, who promised to help, he returned to the station only to find that the train had left. The station master told him that its next stop was only 6 kilometres away from Iasi, and Lello broke into a desperate run along the track, arriving just in time to board the train, and so exhausted that Leonardo De Benedetti gave him a sedative to pull him round.

After leaving Iasi the convoy went on south in short stages through Ciurea, Scantea, Vaslui, Piscu, Brăila, and Pogoanele. On 23 September they came through Ploiesti, and the following day turned northward past the royal castles of Sinaia. In freezing weather the train crossed the Transylvanian Alps through the Predeal Pass, the continued to Brasov, where the locomotive was uncoupled. This was bound to mean a long wait, and led to an exodus from the wagons of people looking for water, or a chance to trade with the local people. The children pilfered where they could, while the women washed clothes or bathed themselves. As always in such circumstances, cooking fires were lit.

When it left Brasov, the convoy headed for the Hungarian border, and on 26 September they reached Curtici, near Arad, and stayed there for a week while the Romanian authorities tried to hand them over and the Hungarians stalled about accepting them. Those were seven days that the people of Curtici can never have forgotten. The thousand inhabitants of the village were outnumbered and almost overwhelmed by the 1,400 Italians, who descended from the steppes with an unquenchable greed. They drained all the wells, burned all the timber then vandalized the station for more, and turned the station latrines into swamps it was safer not to enter. As long as it could afford to, the stranded horde paid for its provisions; from then on, it stole them. Soon there was not a goose to be seen in a village whose flocks had been its pride. All that can be said in mitigation is that they were suffering from hunger and cold, and that it rained every day.

It was at the end of the sixth day that Lello Perugia ran out of his small reserve of patience and deserted the convoy — or so Levi says in *The Truce*. Returning to this episode in *Moments of Reprieve*, he explains that Lello went off with "a mafioso from the north, by profession a fence" (*Reprieve 100/140*), because he had had enough of the train, the Russians and his comrades, and was able to fend for himself. More than that, he had decided to return to Rome by plane. No one else was bold enough to follow them when they caught the first train for Bucharest. Levi claims to have heard this and the rest of the story from Lello's own lips.

According to Lello, that is not exactly how it happened. Levi wrote that Lello's partner, a native of Milan, was a Signor Tornaghi. We have it from Perugia that his true name was Massimo Bini. Perugia recalls that when he heard that there was a possibility of flying straight home instead of crawling across the frontiers of a shattered south-east Europe, he passed on the information to Primo Levi, Leonardo De Benedetti, and a few other comrades among the sixteen former deportees to Auschwitz. Primo and Leonardo replied that they would not abandon the convoy. Perugia and five others caught the train to Bucharest, where they went to see the consul, Signor Dominici, and demanded to be repatriated. The answer was no, because the Ferruccio Parri government had come to an agreement with the Allies by whose terms every Italian subject — even a deportee — who wished to be repatriated had to pay for the privilege. So Lello Perugia and Massimo Bini bought train tickets and travelled through Hungary and Czechoslovakia, staying at a series of addresses that the Italian consulate had given them. Though liberated from Auschwitz, the ex-deportee Lello Perugia was considered an ex-prisoner. He was finally repatriated by plane, at his own expense. How did he find the money for the flight? According to him, through Romanian bankers in Curtici, consulted on the consul's advice. His group had now expanded, and contained eleven people.

In Levi's story, Lello and "Tornaghi" (alias Bini) got to Bucharest and begged enough money from charitable sources to buy new clothes. After that they split up. Lello found himself a rich girl whose father was either a banker or an owner of oil wells in Ploiesti — here too, Levi says that he is passing on the story as told to him by Lello — and the couple got engaged. When Lello told his future father-in-law that he was returning to his country from a concentration camp, he received an advance on the dowry. The girl had no more intention of marrying than did Lello himself, but she colluded in the charade, and as soon as Lello got his hands on the money he made the mutually agreed exit. He bought a plane ticket to Bari, and a crowd of his friends turned out to greet him.

When questioned about this wayward episode, Lello Perugia informed us that Levi's account in *Moments of Reprieve* was the product of the writer's imagination. It was true that he had met a Romanian girl, but her parents were poor. The money for the ticket came from a different source. Documents provided by Perugia prove that he flew from Bucharest to Bari on 16 November 1945 in an aircraft of the Royal Air Force. The transport document, for which he paid the sum of £16 sterling, is made out in his name and bears the number 10355. An express letter dated 10 May 1945 had informed his parents that he had been liberated from Auschwitz by the Russians.

What is clear is that Lello Perugia arrived in Italy four weeks after the train that carried his destitute comrades. In Levi's apparently fictionalized version, as soon as his feet touched the ground Lello was arrested, because he had bought his ticket with dollars provided by his "father-in-law," and the dollars were counterfeit. Levi wonders whether the Romanian had found a neat way to get rid of his "son-in-law" and also get his own back at the same time. He describes how Cesare-Lello was taken to Rome, interrogated, and then released. According to Levi the counterfeit dollars began to be manufactured in 1942 in the camp of Sachsenhausen, where the Germans had housed the "Kommando Bernhard," a secret workshop of high-class forgers.

After his return to Rome in 1946, Lello Perugia, who had practised as an accountant before the war, took a competitive examination to enter the National Stationery Office, where he was employed as a graphic artist until his retirement in 1975. In the same year, the mayor of Rome awarded him the gold medal of the Resistance. In 1947 Primo Levi dedicated copy no. 3 of the original edition of *If This Is A Man* to his friend Lello Perugia. They met on several occasions after that, when Levi went to Rome to visit his sister, Anna Maria, who lives there. For a long time, Lello did not speak about his ordeal. "I was disgusted with the whole world. All of them, from the Vatican to the French, the British, and the Americans, knew that the camps existed."

In autumn 1945 Primo Levi was stuck in the Romanian mud in a detached railway wagon, but the convoy left Curtici at last and entered Hungary, where he took pleasure in station names such as Hódmezövásárhely and Kiskunfélegyháza. Primo and the other occupants of the wagon felt bored, now that Lello Perugia had gone. The train passed Budapest without entering the city, but it made several stops in Ujpest and in other suburban stations, all of them in ruins. It followed the course of the Danube northward, and stopped at Szób on market day. Levi was terribly hungry. Having hung on to his striped jacket all this time, in the market place of Szób he bartered it for a plate of *körözöt*, a mixture of fermented cheese and onions.

When the train moved off again, there were two new passengers in the goods wagon. The first was Vincenzo, a Calabrian shepherd, a wild, shy, silent boy of sixteen, with fine blue eyes. No one knew why the Germans had deported him. He had come all the way from Starye Dorogi, never staying long with any wagon. Vincenzo was an epileptic, and when he felt an attack coming on he would climb on to the roof of a wagon to avoid prying eyes. The second fellow traveller was a Hungarian orphan of fourteen, whose parents had been killed in an air-raid. His name was Pista and he was a cooper by trade. He made himself useful in the wagon, ran errands, and did odd jobs with enthusiasm, and quickly learned Italian. The community in the wagon had become his family.

On 7 October the train reached Bratislava, in Slovakia, some 250 kilometres south-west of Auschwitz and Katowice. The following day it arrived in Leopoldau, in the suburbs of Vienna, which had been flattened by heavy bombing. Food was rationed, and it was impossible to buy anything. The next day they moved a few kilometres from Leopoldau to Jedlersdorf. Levi went for a walk that took him to the banks of the Danube, where all the bridges had had their middle spans blown out. In a big square, he came upon a free market that reminded him of the one in Katowice, where Lello Perugia had taught him the ABC of business. Here there was a furtive, urgent trade in bread, potatoes, and single cigarettes. Levi wrote that at this point he felt anguish rather than compassion — the sensation of "an irreparable and definitive evil which was present everywhere, nestling like gangrene in the guts of Europe and the world, the seed of future harm" (*Truce* 202/374).

After three days of manoeuvring, the convoy found itself in Nussdorf, over the Danube from Jedlersdorf. At last, on 11 October, it left again at greater than usual speed to travel westward through St Pölten, Loosdorf, and Amstetten. Later that day, as Levi was looking out at the road that ran parallel to the track, he saw a sight that came to him and all his comrades like landfall to a seafarer. The omen was a black man driving along in a jeep while one of its passengers windmilled his arms and shouted in Neapolitan dialect: "You're going home, you guys!" The line of demarcation between the Russians and the Americans was at St Valentin, not far from Linz. There they got down from the train, with all their baggage, and said goodbye to the engine-driver and to the escort of young Russian soldiers.

The Americans took the travellers to a squalid transit camp in St Valentin, where there was no heating or light, no beds, and the floors of the huts were covered in mud. However, the baths and the disinfection procedures were efficiently organized. The GIs brought their charges first to some well-equipped cabins with showers and the pleasures of warm water, then to an enormous shed where the whole convoy was crammed together with no separation of the sexes. This was the disinfection unit, where ten men clad in white overalls, helmets, and gas masks blew DDT powder into all the openings in people's clothing, using tubes attached to pneumatic bellows. Everything went smoothly until one of the masked operators approached the fiancée of a naval officer, who intervened at once to stop her being touched. The operator removed his overalls, helmet and mask, a space was cleared, and the two men fought a very orthodox boxing match that ended when the officer was floored and the anxious young woman duly powdered and purified, American style.

After thirty-one days cooped up in bare wagons, shunted and jolted, repeatedly stopping and starting along the circuitous route necessitated by the ravages of war and the administrative confusion of postwar Eastern Europe, the 1,400 exhausted Italians felt nothing but loathing for travel and trains. Yet although St Valentin is only 200 kilometres as the crow flies from Tarvisio, in Italy, their new train was heading westward, across the German border. On 15 October it arrived in Munich, of all cities, chosen by Adolf Hitler as the headquarters of the Nazi Party. It was less than eight months since Levi had left Auschwitz. To enter Germany was a nerve-racking experience, a source of conflicting tensions:

> We felt we had something to say, enormous things to say, to every single German, and we felt that every German should have something to say to us; we felt an urgent need to settle our accounts, to ask, explain and comment, like chess players at the end of a game. Did "they" know about Auschwitz, about the silent daily massacre, a step away from their doors? If they did, how could they walk about, return home and look at their children, cross the threshold of a church? If they did not, they ought, as a sacred duty, to listen, to learn everything, immediately, from us, from me; I felt the tattooed number on my arm burning like a sore. (*Truce* 204/376)

It was while he was roaming the ruined streets of Munich that the need to testify took shape in Levi's mind, an urgent, sacred duty that was to consume his time, once he arrived home. He testified orally by telling his story anywhere at all, to anyone he met. At the same time he began to record his memories, just as they came to mind, in no set order. It was later, when he resolved to combine these unstructured sketches into a coherent narrative, that he linked and organized them into the book that became *If This Is A Man*.

240

Levi paced the obliterated streets in a state of mind akin to that described by Jean Améry in *Jenseits von Schuld und Sühne*, when he wrote that he saw in each German an insolvent debtor who refused to pay what he owed (*Truce* 204/376). In a chapter called "Resentments," Améry analysed "the subjective state of the victim" who survived.[23] This cold bitterness no doubt led him to his suicide in 1978. He rejects the arguments of moralists and psychologists out of hand, the former because they view his feelings as a defect, and the latter because they view them as a sickness. Améry considered that Nazism and the Holocaust were the collective crime of the German people, because only the tiniest minority had stood up against Hitler during the twelve years of his rule over Germany. In a tone of black humour, Améry cites, in his book, a south-German businessman he met in a hotel in 1958, who informed him that: "The Germans no longer had any hard feelings towards the Resistance fighters and Jews. How could these still demand atonement?" And Améry comments: "But to my own distress, I belonged to that disapproving minority with its hard feelings."[24]

Levi looked hard at the few men, in pitiful condition, that he passed in the street. He wished that every one of them could read on his face the stigmata of the *Lager* that he had survived. He wanted to be recognized and heard, but nobody wanted to hear what he had to say. The Germans, he wrote, were "deaf, blind and dumb ... still capable of hatred and contempt, still prisoners of their own tangle of pride and guilt" (*Truce* 205/377). As he stared into the faces of those who had not seen his otherness and yet his likeness to themselves, Levi found himself searching for faces he remembered, men who would have to remember, because they themselves had "commanded and obeyed, killed, humiliated, corrupted." But he went on to call this "a vain and foolish search," and concluded that only "the few just ones" were capable of answering for all the rest.

It is precisely in that conclusion that Levi's thinking diverges from the position reached by Jean Améry, with whom he held a posthumous debate in his final book, *The Drowned and the Saved*. Resentment bound Améry to the torture he had endured, the sufferings he had undergone in Auschwitz, and to the destruction of the Jewish people. He required that the irreversible should be reversed, that the event should never have happened. Wajs, his SS torturer in Fort Breendonk, was tried and executed. Améry was thankful — "It is not a matter of revenge, nor one of atonement."[25] He believed that only in front of the firing squad did Wajs grasp the "moral truth" of his actions. That was the sole condition by which the SS man could become his fellow man once again. Améry could have slept in peace if all those who took part in the "final solution" had also been tried and condemned. But the SS man from Breendonk was only one criminal among his common kind, and ever afterwards Améry felt categorically hostile to any propensity towards conciliation between the victims and the butchers, which could stem "only from insanity and indifference to life, or the masochistic conversion of a suppressed *genuine* demand for revenge."[26] Améry even went so far as to consider Levi as a "forgiver," a verdict that the latter vigorously denied, saying instead that it was not his role to take human justice into his own hands.

In Szob, an extra wagon had been added to the sixty in the convoy. It had been bought, and coupled to the train, by a group of very young Jewish men and women, still in their teens, refugees from Eastern Europe, who had decided to go to British-run Palestine and build the Jewish state. Levi was staggered by their nerve, independence, and strength of mind: it amazed him that they could have hitched their wagon without asking anyone's permission. When he expressed this to their leader, "with his intense hawk-like glance," his answer was: "Hitler's dead, isn't he?" (*Truce 205/377*). Levi was fascinated by these young Jews who, having fought as partisans against the Nazis, were making their escape from Eastern Europe, the graveyard of European Jewry, to create a new country where they intended to become the masters of their fate. For many years their memory lingered in his mind, and their special story blended with the account that he heard from his friend Emilio Vita Finzi,[27] of the arrival of another such group in a reception centre in the Via Unione in Milan for Jewish refugees from all over Europe. In fact Italy had become the main transit centre for Jews intending to emigrate illegally to Palestine, where the British were doing everything in their power to keep them out. After crossing the Alps on foot, the refugees were driven by night in lorries to La Spezia, where they boarded ships such as the *Dov Hoz* and the *Eliyahu Golomb*, which in May 1946 unloaded a thousand refugees at the port of Haifa, after they went on hunger strike.

As he listened to his friend Emilio, Levi scribbled a few notes that he later put away in a drawer. One day, while he was tidying up his desk, he found them again and rang Emilio to refresh his memory about the episode with the young Polish and Russian Jews in the Via Unione. In a mood of jubilation, he decided that he would write his first novel about these young Jews who had refused to be taken to their deaths. He wanted to know everything about them — their language and customs in particular. He bought a dictionary, and a Yiddish grammar. He, the assimilated Jew from Turin, learned to read Yiddish in order to bring himself close to those Jews whose civilization had been destroyed. He wanted to write the odyssey of a handful of partisans who had put up a resistance, when he and his companions had been captured in Piedmont before they had had their chance to fight. This was the inspiration of his novel *Se non ora, quando?* (*If Not Now, When?*), published in 1982.

One evening the train arrived in Mittenwald, on the German border with Austria, not far from Garmisch-Partenkirchen. The next morning the convoy stopped at Innsbruck, where Italian smugglers gave out chocolate, tobacco, and *grappa*. Then they set off again for Italy, and some hours later a coupling snapped between two wagons, cutting the train in two and causing several injuries. Late that same night Primo Levi crossed the Brenner Pass, which he had last crossed in the opposite direction, in a goods wagon taking him to Auschwitz. While some of their companions rejoiced, Primo and Leonardo stayed silent. Twenty months before, the thought of their return had already entered Levi's mind:

> We passed the Brenner at midday of the second day and everyone stood up, but no one said a word. The thought of the return journey stuck in my heart, and I cruelly pictured to myself the inhuman joy of that other journey, with doors open, no one wanting to flee, and the first Italian names ... and I looked around and wondered how many, among that poor human dust, would be struck by fate. (*Man 17/23*)

Six hundred and fifty Italian Jews had set out from Fossoli. There were three survivors on the train that ran on into Italy that night. Primo Levi still did not know whether any of his family had survived. He and Leonardo had "the Auschwitz poison" in their veins. They could not tell what lay ahead, or how they would summon the energy to face it. "We felt the weight of centuries on our shoulders, we felt oppressed by a year of ferocious memories; we felt emptied and defenceless" (*Truce 206/378*). They looked back with gratitude on the months since Auschwitz, their summer on the steppes of Byelorussia, the period of aimless wandering. It had been a convalescent interlude, a "truce" offered by fate before they were required to reassemble the pieces of their lives.

The train passed through the Adige Valley, and on 17 October the convoy reached its final station, Pescantina, near Verona. The 1,400 travellers who emerged from the ruins of Eastern Europe were housed in a transit camp for the night. Signor Avesani, "the Moor" of Verona, came to say goodbye to Leonardo and Primo, and to give them his blessing, because his village, Avesa, was only a few kilometres away.

After thirty-four days of travelling, Primo Levi waited for a train in Verona until the following evening. In the passenger carriage that took him to Turin, he told his story to his unknown fellow travellers, who listened in disbelieving silence in the semi-darkness of their third-class compartment, while the train chugged into the night on damaged tracks, through war-wrecked stations.

Part Two

10   The Return

Primo Levi arrived at Porta Nuova station on the morning of 19 October 1945 with Leonardo De Benedetti, who was also arriving home. From the train, he saw the apartment buildings on the Corso Sommeiller, a short walk away from his house. The trams were sporadic, the streets bare of cobblestones, the shops empty. The block where he had lived since his childhood had come through the bombing undamaged. When he entered the hall of the building, the concierge took some moments to recognize him, then rushed up the staircase, triumphantly chanting: "*Il dottore! Il dottore! Il dottore!*" The door on the third floor opened, and Primo Levi made his entrance, a bearded, ragged figure, so puffed up by six months' solid diet of potatoes that they hardly knew him.

Every member of his family had been spared. He wrote in *The Truce* that "no one was expecting me" (*Truce* 207/379). Does that mean that they had stopped expecting him? Were they resigned to his loss? Obviously not, but there had been no news of Primo since Cravero, the petty crook from Auschwitz, had told his mother and sister that he was alive, before trying to squeeze them for money, then stealing Anna Maria's bicycle.

When they saw who it was, there were no shouts or tears. It was October, and his mother told him: "It's cold, put a sweater on." Levi refused. He would not wear a pullover, and besides, he didn't have one.

As soon as she heard the news, Primo's cousin Giulia hurried to the Corso Re Umberto. She remembers:

> He was dirty and bloated, and he had a beard. He carried everything he owned on his person, even his bowl. He had thought that he might not find anybody, not even the house. When the concierge recognized him she went upstairs and rang his mother's doorbell to warn her. He arrived at the door not knowing what had happened to the family. Naturally, five minutes later the news was all over town. They talked about it for a week. His mother kept saying: "Get some rest." "No," he told her, "these last two years I've lived with the sole obsession of returning and telling the story." He told it over and over, because everyone who came asked him questions. He talked and talked, in an edgy kind of way. He said: "You can't know how much good it does me to bring out everything I've been keeping inside me. My only thought was to survive and tell."[1]

His closest friends were informed at once. Eugenio Gentili Tedeschi travelled straight over from Milan, and Alberto Salmoni and Bianca Guidetti Serra came running to the house. In Piedmont, it is not the custom to put feelings on display.

> We knew that he was going to return, but when? One evening I had a telephone call. "Primo is back in Turin!" It was marvellous. I ran all the way to his house. It was he who opened the door. He held out his hand. "*Ciào! Ciào!* How are you?" We didn't even hug each other. It wasn't done in those days. He added "Thank you" too, and in that thank you he meant to express his affection, and his friendship.
>
> Primo was not particularly run down. In fact, none of us were very presentable. He was almost the same. Very balanced. He talked a lot, obsessively. He didn't stop. We were the closest, we knew the whole story, all the characters. He wanted us to understand what had happened to him.[2]

Alberto Salmoni, who was married to Bianca at the time, felt that Primo had changed:

> I was upset, because his face was swollen. He had eaten everything that came his way on the journey. I understood that he had many things to reveal. He wanted to bear witness. He talked a lot in the days and months that followed his return. We often got together with a few friends, and he told the story endlessly about everything that had happened to him.[3]

What Levi noticed most was the sheer vitality of his friends. He felt no sense of victory. In the first weeks that followed his return he was depressed, and spoke "with a purpose of inner liberation." Relief came with "the liberating joy of recounting my story" (*Truce 207/379*). Soon he would yield to the urgent need to write down what he had hardly stopped expressing orally to his family, his friends, and soon to Lucia Morpurgo, the girl to whom he would become engaged in 1946, and whom he married in September 1947. His audience listened. They allayed the fear that had haunted his dreams in Auschwitz:

> This is my sister here, with some unidentifiable friend and many other people. They are all listening to me and it is this very story that I am telling ... [I speak] of our hunger and of the lice-control, and of the Kapo who hit me on the nose and then sent me to wash myself as I was bleeding. It is an intense pleasure, physical, inexpressible, to be at home, among friendly people and to have so many things to recount: but I cannot help noticing that my listeners do not follow me. In fact, they are completely indifferent: they speak confusedly of other things among themselves, as if I was not there. My sister looks at me, gets up and goes away without a word. (*Man 60/66*)

Giulia remembers that in fact the apartment on the Corso Re Umberto became "a port of call" whose door was always open to all who wanted to listen to Primo and spend nights of endless talking.

At the same time, he found himself fearing, even as sleep approached, that his return was only an illusion:

> It is a dream within a dream, varied in detail, one in substance. I am sitting at a table with my family, or with friends, or at work, or in the green countryside; in short, in a peaceful relaxed environment, apparently without tension or affliction; yet I feel a deep and subtle anguish, the definite sensation of an impending threat. And in fact, as the dream proceeds, slowly or brutally, each time in a different way, everything collapses and disintegrates around me, the scenery, the walls, the people, while the anguish becomes more intense and more precise. Now everything has changed to chaos; I am alone in the centre of a grey and turbid nothing, and now, I *know* what this thing means, and I also know that I have always known it; I am in the Lager once more, and nothing is true outside the Lager. All the rest was a brief pause, a deception of the senses, a dream; my family, nature in flower, my home. (*Truce* 207/379)

On the first night, Primo Levi went to bed in his room, the room where he was born, and where he was to place his writer's desk. He stretched out on the bed, made with clean sheets and warm blankets, and suffered "a moment of terror" when he felt the mattress gently give beneath his weight. His cousin Giulia recalls that for several days he slept on the floor because he could not accustom himself to his own bed.

In January there was a party given at the Jewish Brigade[4] centre in the De Benedetti house in the Via Francesco Mordosini. Primo and Giulia attended it. Primo asked his cousin: "Teach me to dance," but Giulia could not dance either. They had never had the chance to learn, because the passage of the racial laws had turned their lives upside-down when they were not yet twenty years old.

So ended the great adventure of Primo Levi's life, twenty months during which he had suffered the ordeals of a Nazi extermination camp, and then gone on to breathe the air of freedom, and to lead a brief anarchic life in the open spaces of Russia. And so he began, by returning to his home and his room, a new and rather sedentary existence, unobtrusive, predictable and peaceful, yet shaped by the tensions of a duty that he consented to bear for the rest of his life. Even though the adventure had been forced upon him in the horror of Auschwitz, there was a sense in which he would come to miss it. He told Philip Roth when they met in Turin in September 1986: "Family, home, factory are good things in themselves, but they deprived me of something that I still miss: adventure."[5] This unfulfilled taste for adventure was to influence his literary choices much more than his ideological affinities or aesthetic leanings. It underlay the love he felt for authors as varied as Joseph Conrad, Herman Melville, Roger Vercel, Homer, Saint-Exupéry, Marco Polo, Isaac Babel, and Mario Rigoni Stern.

He lived his year in Auschwitz in a state of exceptional intellectual alertness. The camp, his "university," taught him a great deal. In spite of the dreadful conditions of his imprisonment in Monowitz, he never stopped observing people and analysing the world around him with the intensity and curiosity of a naturalist.

Like Job, whose fate he explored in *La ricerca delle radici*, he had suffered unjustly, and saved himself by attempting to understand the meaning of evil in the world. Before Auschwitz, knowledge meant power. In the *Lager*, understanding made it possible to overcome the horror and make ready to give evidence. Levi gave his evidence a collective significance. With scrupulous honesty, he always spoke solely about what he himself had seen, but his voice was raised in the name of all those — he called them "the true witnesses" — whom the *Lager* submerged. He testified in order to put evidence before the judges, in the hope that they would punish the guilty.

The joy of being reunited with his family and his quiet home — a hope he had not dared to indulge in Auschwitz, and then had felt so deeply during the months of wandering in Poland and Byelorussia — did not have the power to alleviate the infinite anguish engendered by his death year in the *Lager*:

> Now this inner dream, this dream of peace, is over, and in the outer dream, which continues, gelid, a well-known voice resounds: a single word, not imperious, but brief and subdued. It is the dawn command of Auschwitz, a foreign word, feared and expected: get up. "*Wstawać*." (*Truce* 207–8/379–80)

With these two sentences, Primo Levi concluded *The Truce* in November 1962, seventeen years after his return, as if his passage through devastated Europe and his stay in the havoc of Byelorussia had been an extended illusion, a "truce" beyond whose limit the sole reality was the memory of Auschwitz.

Like Coleridge's ancient mariner — a comparison that he himself wanted to make — in Turin, Levi "waylaid" his friends, and everyone he met, with the story of his "adventure." He spoke, he says, "in a kind of giddiness." As he gathered notes together, and started to write, he felt himself becoming a man

like other men again. On 11 January 1946, three months after his return, he
began with a poem, "Reveille:"

> In the brutal nights we used to dream
> Dense violent dreams,
> Dreamed with soul and body;
> To return; to eat; to tell the story.
> Until the dawn command
> Sounded brief, low:
> > "*Wstawać*":
> And the heart cracked in the breast.
>
> Now we have found our homes again,
> Our bellies are full,
> We're through telling the story.
> It's time. Soon we'll hear again
> The strange command:
> > "*Wstawać*."[6]

As he wrote, he thought about all those who had not come home again, and
who had died by human hands. He remembered Vanda Maestro, the young
Jewish chemist dear to his heart, and lost for ever. He dreamed of the camp
every night, and in his waking hours he suffered a fear of the sudden return of
barbarism. He wrote in the grip of his urgent need to free himself from his
experience, believing that such a release — never to be achieved — was a moral
and civic obligation. Several times over, Levi relapsed into the "grey nothing"
that Auschwitz bequeathed in perpetuity.

In haphazard order, as they came to him, Primo Levi wrote down "the most
important, heaviest, biggest things,"[7] the short chapters that would form the
basis of *If This Is A Man*. In preparing the case against the torturers and killers,
acting in the spirit of a public prosecutor, his purpose was to convey his indignation to his future readers. It was no part of his agenda to stir up hatred, or
to incite retaliation against the Germans, but the indictment had to be drafted,
and the guilty put on trial. Nor were his intentions literary. He modelled his
account on what he later described as "the weekly report commonly used in
factories."[8] His ambition was to write in a language accessible to all, and this
scrupulous requirement was to shape his whole career as a writer. Levi is a true
man of Piedmont, a lover of "work properly done." "It is up to the writer to
make himself understood by those who wish to understand him: it is his trade,
writing is a public service and the willing reader must not be disappointed"
(*Trades 171/159*). When he writes, he addresses a reader whom he sees as
entering into a "contract" with him. Writing in a way that the reader did not
understand would be "an act of rudeness, a commercial fraud."[9] In Levi's

words, these are the duties of the writer, stated like the laws of the Ten Commandments:

> You will write concisely and clearly.
> You will avoid embellishments and convolutions.
> You will say of each word you have used why you have used that one and not another.
> You will love and imitate those who have followed this same path.[10]

He derived this need for clarity and exactitude from his experience as a chemist. Every word is weighed in the precision balance of the laboratory. The chemist observes reality with delicacy, and mistrusts the "almost identical" that is often the cause of confusion. He had been able to observe that a verifiable relationship exists between the formula written down on paper, and what happens in the test tube during an experiment. Scientific rigour is for him the surest means to understand and reveal the world's secrets. He assembles phrases on paper just as, in the laboratory, he assembles the "slothfully hostile" molecules of *hyle*, "Matter," personified as Melville's white whale. *If This Is A Man* is written in the good Italian of the author taught in the classical Liceo d'Azeglio. The critic Cesare Cases said that this "marble Italian" had become his *Heimat* — his homeland.

Clarity was commanded by the overriding need to communicate. Levi wanted the order of words to match the order of the world. He wished to be understood, and could not let go of that wish. In the camp, he had discovered that understanding, and the ability to communicate, were a question of life or death. He loathed all obscurity in language, and was not afraid to say so. He could not stand Nietzsche, and reproached Georg Trakl and Paul Celan for their obscurity, daring to liken their poetry to the death rattle of a dying man. In Levi's view, the facts tended to support his conviction that obscurity was a proto-withdrawal from the world, because both men had committed suicide. Though not unaware that there are elements of the unknowable and irrational in each of us, nevertheless he made the mistake of believing that clarity of speech could somehow ward them off.

Four months after his return, Levi still suffered from an irresistible urge to eat whenever there was food available, no matter what the circumstances, he always carried spare provisions in his pocket. He considered his feet with surprise and fascination — the feet with which he had done so much walking, and that were still attached to his legs.

He looked for a job in ravaged postwar Italy. That winter in Turin there was a severe shortage of coal and firewood, and food and meat were rationed. Many houses that had not been destroyed in the bombing had lost all their window panes. The shops were still empty, shoes were unobtainable, people were starving, and work was scarce.

Elections to a Constituent Assembly — the first national elections in which women took part — were held on 2 June 1946, and in a referendum held on the same day a majority of 54 per cent voted to abolish the monarchy. King Victor Emmanuel III had abdicated in May in favour of his son, Umberto II, who then followed him into exile. A coalition government led by Alcide De Gasperi excluded the Communists and socialists in May 1947.

When the new constitution came into force on 1 January 1948, the first president of the Italian Republic was Luigi Einaudi, a Liberal, and former governor of the Bank of Italy, who was not a Christian Democrat. De Gasperi, who remained prime minister until 1953, established the ascendancy of the Christian Democrats in a period of economic reconstruction, with the help of United States aid provided under the Marshall Plan. Italy had lost all its possessions in Africa, except for Somalia, as well as the Dodecanese, Dalmatia, Fiume, and Istria, but it kept the French-speaking Valle d'Aosta and the German-speaking South Tyrol (Alto Adige), despite the ambitions of France and Austria respectively.

On his return, Primo Levi had found a letter waiting for him from Charles Conreau, the elementary school teacher from Lusse. When Charles told Jean Samuel — the "Pikkolo" from Buna-Monowitz — that Levi had survived, Samuel sent a letter to Turin early in March 1946. The reply, written in French, in Avigliana, where Levi had found work as a chemist with the varnish manufacturer Duco-Montecatini, is dated 23 March 1946. In one passage of his six-page letter, Levi writes:

> It is a miracle that I am still alive, in good health, with my family. I have made a vow never to forget that, and I repeat it to myself every day, like a prayer. It is not that I thank Providence, because if there really was a Providence, Auschwitz and Birkenau would never have existed; but this way, from now on I can genuinely enjoy all the little things in life that usually go unnoticed, and not grumble too much about everyday worries, great or small.

Levi wrote to Jean Samuel, who was to remain his friend throughout his life, that he had vowed never to forget. "I repeat it to myself every day, like a prayer" — that Jewish prayer, the *Shema*, that he had learned when studying for his *bar-mitzvah* ceremony, and to which he dedicated a poem on 10 January 1946. In the last verse he borrowed the *Shema*'s style and solemn character, its commandments, and its curses in the event of disobedience:

> Consider that this has been:
> I commend these words to you.
> Engrave them on your hearts
> When you are in your house, when you walk on your way,

When you go to bed, when you rise.
Repeat them to your children.
Or may your house crumble,
Disease render you powerless,
Your offspring avert their faces from you.[11]

The full text of the *Shema* is in Deuteronomy, chapter 6, verses 4–9. Levi drew on verses 6–7:

And these words, which I command thee this day, shall be in thine heart:
And thou shalt teach them diligently unto thy children, and thou shalt talk of them when thou sittest in thine house, and when thou walkest by the way, and when thou liest down, and when thou risest up.

In Deuteronomy 28, there follow the curses incurred by the sons of Israel should they fail to respect the divine commandments:

But it shall come to pass, if thou wilt not hearken unto the voice of the Lord thy God, to observe to do all his commandments and his statutes which I command thee this day; that all these curses shall come upon thee, and overtake thee. Cursed shalt thou be in the city, and cursed shalt thou be in the field. Cursed shall be thy basket and thy store. Cursed shall be the fruit of thy body, and the fruit of thy land, the increase of thy kine, and the flocks of thy sheep. Cursed shalt thou be when thou comest in, and cursed shalt thou be when thou goest out .... Thy sons and daughters shall be given unto another people, and thine eyes shall look, and fail with longing for them all the day long: and there shall be no might in thine hand. (Deuteronomy, verses 15–19, 32)

Levi wrote again to Jean Samuel a month later:

Whether we like it or not, we are witnesses and we carry the weight of that fact.

When you come to think about it, the friendship that binds us is something quite amazing and unique. We became acquainted in particular circumstances, in more or less the sorriest condition that a man can be thrown into; we found ourselves joined in our struggle against *Vernichtung* — not only material but above all spiritual — by the *Lager*. We were saved by chance, by two extremely improbable processes, and beyond all hope we found one another again. For all that, we know practically nothing about each other, which makes it especially amusing and moving to write, and to read each other's letters. As it would be rather awkward and uncomfortable to describe at length who Mr Primo Levi is, I am sending you two poems and one of the stories I've written, as a sample of myself. It's not of the best, but I'm sending it to you because it is about you. I wrote it when I hadn't the least suspicion that you were alive and would have the chance to read it, and I do assure you that I haven't changed a word: I apologize for the inaccuracies and for anything that might shock you in any way. I hope you'll understand my Italian. About the atom of Carbon, I hadn't at all forgotten, not the idea, but having talked to you about it. I haven't abandoned the plan, but I now find myself too involved in material concerns, and the recent memories are weighing on my mind; perhaps when I'm older, if I'm not too worn out by life ....[12]

Levi is referring to a plan for a story dealing with the life of a carbon atom, the same story he had thought about in his cell in the Aosta barracks less than three years before. Twenty-nine years later, his account of episodes in the carbon cycle — the atom passes through the synthesis of chlorophyll, and enters the brain of the author to fuel an instant of the routine that ends with his hand placing the last full stop on the last page of his book — became the final chapter of *The Periodic Table*, the book that was to establish his international reputation.

Not long after his return, Primo Levi had written to Nicola Dallaporta, to inform him that he had survived. Dallaporta, the lecturer who had welcomed him so readily into the Physics Institute after the promulgation of the racial laws, and to whom he had sent a letter during his internment in Fossoli di Carpi, caught the next train to pay him a visit. He found his former pupil very little changed physically, and remarkably self-possessed, and he was struck by his quasi impersonal and impartial manner in relating all that he had seen and endured.[13] He told Levi then: "You must write all this down! These things are so dreadful, so unbelievable, that no one would have imagined them," and he added that he saw "in his miraculous salvation a transcendental meaning, an indication that he had a mission."[14] In Dallaporta's view, God had chosen Levi to tell people the things he had witnessed. The idea outraged Levi, and he rejected it vehemently, but the reunion between the teacher and mystic and his former pupil had been very affectionate. In the intervals between the few times they met later on, Levi never failed to send copies of his books dedicated to the man who had welcomed and protected him when all the rest treated him as a pariah.

In January 1946 Primo Levi was engaged at 7,000 lire a month as a colour technician at Duco-Montecatini, an Italian subsidiary of Dupont of Nemours, which made paints using alkyd resins. The factory, which had been damaged during the war, stood on the shore of Lake Avigliana, 25 kilometres from Turin. Twice a week, Levi left the guest house where he was staying to go home to his family.

In the Duco factory he had a rickety desk in the corner of a not very comfortable lab where other people went about their business while he had nothing at all to do. He used the desk for writing down his memories of Auschwitz, while his colleagues, to whom he had told his story, watched him with an indulgent, knowing air. He never stopped writing, and very fluently — whether in the tram, the laboratory, or in the train that took him home on visits. As he often remarked, the memory of Auschwitz "burned" inside him. But he was not simply the chronicler of the camp, casting the eye of a scientist and moralist over humanity, even though he was still totally unknown. His intense need to write was connected to the threat of psychic disruption that he had undergone in Auschwitz. He responded to it by putting himself in order, and with his own weapons: the clarity and verbal precision that the study of chemistry had brought him. He knew that science presupposed the organized knowledge of the real. With the help of his concise and exact language, he would also restore order to the chaotic world of Auschwitz, and present it to his reader in an intelligible way. The young chemist who wrote on a wobbly desk at the back of the laboratory had already become a writer.

He drafted the last chapter first. The book grew with no effort, and no preconceived plan, sustained by the sheer necessity to testify. "The need to eat and to tell were situated at the same level of primal necessity."[15] The tone is neither lyrical, like Elie Wiesel's, nor vengeful, like Jean Améry's. No curses are called down. In an utterly human fashion, Levi describes an inhuman world; with that calm, poised tone that belongs to him alone, he wakes in every reader the indignation of the judge. Ferdinando Camon, to whom he gave several interviews, wrote: "He forgoes his own reaction, in exchange for the reaction of all. He thinks long term. He advances as if treading on enemy territory."[16]

From time to time, Levi would come and knock at the door of the factory's director to ask if there was something he could do, but there never was. At best he would suggest that Levi might go to the library and translate a few articles from German. However, the day came when the director sent for him and took him outside into the yard, where thousands of blocks of a softish, gelatinous, orange substance were heaped along the foot of a wall. The substance was "livered" paint — the director explained that "livering" is a process that turns some kinds of paint into a softish solid with the consistency of raw liver, hence the name. These blocks of paint produced in the factory and mysteriously transformed, had had to be cut out of their cans and dumped. He wanted Doctor Levi to tell him how all this paint had been spoiled, and whether he could devise a solution to prevent it from happening again, or even reverse the process.

It was on the following day, a Sunday, that Primo Levi met Lucia Morpurgo and fell instantly in love with her. He married her in September 1947. Lucia was a year younger than Primo. In *The Periodic Table* he recalls:

> the encounter with a woman, young and made of flesh and blood, warm against my side through our overcoats, gay in the humid mist of the avenues, patient, wise and sure as we were walking down streets still bordered with ruins. In a few hours we knew that we belonged to each other, not for one meeting but for life, as in fact has been the case. (*Table* 153)

Levi needed to tell his story and to be listened to. "I returned from the camp with an absolute, pathological narrative charge."[17] Lucia never grew tired of listening as he spoke about what he had seen in Auschwitz. This experience did not appear to him in an entirely negative light, because — surprisingly — he associated it with the fact of having met Lucia, as he acknowledged years later to Ferdinando Camon: "Among other things, before Auschwitz I was a man without women; after, I met the woman I was to marry .... Before, I was inhibited — I don't know why. Maybe because I was Jewish."

Levi was infinitely grateful to Lucia for having consented to love him — an ex-deportee, a shy and repressed young man. His inability to establish relationships with the girls he felt attracted to was painful to him; despite his cool exterior, his desires were no less powerful than his inhibitions. The effect of the racial laws had been to intensify the puritan upbringing imposed by the Jewish families in Turin; schoolmates had jeered that circumcision equalled castration. He whose mission on entering a laboratory was to tame and control matter could not venture close to a woman. Understanding matter, "fornicating with matter" (*Table* 179), had been a kind of compensation for his disabling diffidence. His meeting with Lucia swept away years of pain in a matter of hours. Thanks to her, who was as shy as he was, he was reborn to life: she brought him joy. His love for Lucia is expressed in the poem he wrote for her, whose title is the date that they met: "11 February 1946." Thanks to her, he felt that he had found his place in a world that no longer appeared to him as the fruit of a divine mistake.

> I kept searching for you in the stars
> When I questioned them as a child.
> I asked the mountains for you,
> But they gave me solitude and brief peace
> Only a few times.
> Because you weren't there, in the long evenings
> I considered the rash blasphemy
> That the world was God's error,
> Myself an error in the world.
> And when I was face to face with death —
> No, I shouted from every fibre.

I hadn't finished yet;
There was still too much to do.
Because you were there before me,
With me beside you, just like today,
A man a woman under the sun.
I came back because you were there.[18]

Although Levi saw Judaism as a purely cultural fact, he agreed to a religious ceremony. The racial laws and the *Lager* had made him a Jew. "Since then, I am Jewish. They sewed the star of David on to me, and not only on to my clothes."[19]

Out of the love they shared he drew a new energy for writing. No longer would he go begging for the compassion of his future readers. The testimony he prepared would be a logical structure in which every word would be weighed and assayed "with the greatest rigor and the least clutter" (*Table* 153). Out of his dreadful memories of the *Lager* he drew the substance of his indictment, which now that Lucia had entered his life had found its exemplary reader. As a man of the Enlightenment, he did not doubt for a moment that his mother tongue, Italian, could portray an event such as the extermination of the Jews. His words sprang up out of the cold damp ashes of Auschwitz. Primo Levi had come to offer an account to those who were still living men. He drew up the case for the prosecution, but without illusions, so that those who had wanted the death of man might be judged.

In one of his first letters to Jean Samuel, Primo Levi, who was looking around for a better job, had described his poor situation as a chemist in Avigliana. His mother and sister very much needed his salary, but he was earning so little that he could not marry Lucia. Nor could he afford a train ticket to visit his friend in Alsace. He wrote to Jean Samuel that he was ready to come and work in France if the opportunity arose. Another impediment to their getting together again was that despite all their travels, neither of them owned a passport. In the end they arranged to meet on the Italian frontier, between the border posts of Ventimiglia and Menton. One day in July 1947, after giving up their papers to the customs officers, the two young men with their hair grown back and their civilian clothing had trouble in recognizing one another. Primo had brought Jean some oranges. Overjoyed to be meeting again, they settled on a bench in no-man's-land and were able to talk for three hours. It was the first time that Jean Samuel had seen the sea.

Some time later Levi went to Paris to investigate the possibilities of finding work there, but the journey came to nothing.

When he left the Duco-Montecatini factory, once again Primo Levi was in a very precarious position. But he was free. Each page of his book had been shown to Lucia, and the manuscript was complete. He also gave chapters to read to his cousin Giulia, and to Bianca Guidetti Serra, Alberto Salmoni, and Silvio Ortona, his closest friends. When it was finished he sent the manuscript to Eugenio Gentili Tedeschi, who lived in Milan. He listened humbly to advice and criticism. Most of all he wanted to be clear, accessible to any reader. In order to be certain of this, he was to keep up the habit of having his work read by his little circle of friends, modestly slipping copies of the chapters typed on poor-quality onionskin paper into their letter boxes as he wrote them. Then he would collect his judges together, listen to their comments, and go back to work until they had no objections left to raise.

Finding himself out of work, Levi decided to set up his own laboratory with Alberto Salmoni. Alberto's cousin, Cesare Cases, had managed to spend the war in Switzerland, where his studies had taken him. Now he was living in Milan, and when Primo turned up Cesare gave him his bed, considering him more a relation than a friend. Cases and Levi used to meet on Sundays at Bianca Guidetti Serra's house, who had married Alberto. Levi, a keen student of etymology, gave Cases, a distinguished Germanist, the very rare German dictionary in three volumes compiled by Heine.

Primo Levi said that success and failure are the two great experiences of adult life. After working as a badly paid technician, he now tried to create his own business by going into partnership with his good friend Alberto Salmoni. "Making mistakes and correcting them, taking blows and hitting back, facing a problem and either solving it or coming out defeated and starting the struggle again, all that has a symbolic impact. The chemist with his successes and his failures is like Conrad's sailor who measures himself against the sea."[20] He went into battle as an optimist. "You can't go to war, convinced you will lose," he used to say. Salmoni and Levi, who were very close neighbours, set up their laboratory in Alberto's parents' fourth-floor flat. To make the thing official they had their own headed paper printed: "Laboratorio Salmoni–Levi, 42 Via Massena."

The basic income of the business came from converting tin into stannous chloride, which is used to make mirrors. It was a shoe-string operation. Alberto's wonderfully selfless parents allowed their son and his friend to take over their bedroom and sometimes their bathroom and kitchen too. As well as meals, the kitchen stove had to cook up stannous chloride in various receptacles, filling the place with nauseating fumes. The lab overflowed on to the balcony, which contained the dismantled parts of a motorbike that Alberto had bought in that condition. In this scene of utter chaos, the partners installed a big extractor hood of wood and glass to protect them all from hydrochloric acid fumes that attacked the wallpaper, paint, doorknobs, and window catches in the flat. As they were short of equipment, they crystallized their stannous chloride in any non-metallic container that came to hand, which included a soup tureen, a chamber pot, a cooking pot, and even one of the glass component parts of an Art Nouveau-style standard lamp.

In an extended metaphor, Levi — who led an unusually home-bound, stable life, and never willingly left his mother or the family apartment — compared the "militant" chemist to the primitive hunter. When he sat in his laboratory and designed a molecule that he would then have to build, he declared that he was performing the same propitiatory ritual as the hunter painting, on the walls of his cave, the bison he meant to kill the next day.

The partners' lab was cramped. Their cave bore some resemblance to a junk shop. To get their work done, the two rogue chemists used not only the traditional tools of the trade — retorts, beakers, condenser coils, Bunsen burners — but also pots and pans, a coffee grinder, and Allied army surplus petrol cans. They tapped into the power line upstream of the electricity meter to run four 1,000-watt resistors. In addition, for a handful of clients they did what amounted to menial work, compared with the level of their studies at the Chemical Institute. Small traders and industrialists brought samples of their products — sugar, wine, milk, spaghetti, soap, ravioli — for analysis, in quantities much greater than the few grams needed, a fact that Primo and Alberto refrained from pointing out in those days of postwar rationing. Levi drew on all his knowledge, his insight, and his "nose." On one occasion he detected arsenic in a package of sugar brought to him by an old cobbler from the Via Gioberti whose language and manner Levi describes with a vivid relish. A young competitor had left the package among some shoes to be repaired, in an attempt to poison him.

However, their analytical work earned very little money, and what Primo and Alberto longed for was to be hired as consultants. This was "the ideal work, the sort from which you derive prestige and money without dirtying your hands, or breaking your backbone, or running the risk of ending up roasted or poisoned: all you have to do is take off your smock, put on your tie, listen in attentive silence to the problem, and then you'll feel like the Delphic oracle" (*Table* 175). When this ideal customer arrived, he was a very vulgar, hirsute man, a cosmetics manufacturer. He made a lipstick that was causing him problems, and he invited the *dottore* to visit his premises the next day.

Levi recalls in *The Periodic Table* that in honour of the occasion the newly married consultant wore the better of his two suits. Perhaps it was the one that he wore on the day of his marriage to Lucia in September 1947: in a traditional ceremony, celebrated at his house, Lucia's father, Giuseppe Morpurgo, had united them religiously as they stood beneath the *chuppah*, the bridal canopy, in the presence of friends and witnesses. The couple had then gone to live for a few months in a small house that belonged to Lucia's sister, who taught literature in a school.

When Levi visited the new client's factory, it proved to be a draughty shed staffed by a dozen cheeky, lazy girls, all wearing too much make-up. The client demonstrated his problem by grabbing one of the girls, who stood chewing gum while Levi examined her mouth. One side was made up using the house product, the other with a good French lipstick. On the right-hand side, the lipstick ran into the tiny lines of the skin around the girl's mouth, making an ugly smear. On the left-hand side, the lipstick had remained in place. The owner explained that he had all his girls make up half and half every morning, and kissed them eight times a day to test the product. Levi took away a sample of both lipsticks, and the formula for the home-grown one. It did not take long to solve the problem. The recipe used a soluble dye in a mixture of waxes and fats. When body heat melted the mixture, it spread, and the dye spread with it.

Levi wrote out and delivered his report, and collected his fee. Now his shady customer made him a proposition. He would pay well for a supply of alloxan: he had heard that it had the property of colouring mucous membranes durably red, and he had visions of revolutionizing the cosmetics business. Levi's researches informed him that alloxan was an organic compound present in tiny quantities in the uric acid of mammals, but in much higher amounts in the excrement of birds and especially of reptiles. There followed a farcical episode in which Primo and Lucia scouted the local farms "in search of chicken shit," which didn't come cheap because it turned out to be much prized as a fertilizer. Still, they managed (with their own hands) to collect about a kilo of the stuff, not pure, but mixed with stones, feathers, and chicken lice. Before he attempted to extract alloxan from this unpromising material by a process of oxidizing demolition, Levi paid a visit to a reptile exhibition that had just opened in the gallery of the Turin underground. Did they have any reptile dung for sale? The director's reception was frosty. Pythons ate only twice a month; their dung was rare, extremely valuable, and sold only to the major pharmaceutical companies. That left Levi with his chicken dung mishmash, which gave him several days of frustrating work, some obnoxious smells, but not a gram of alloxan. The client lost his new cosmetic, and the Levis the prospect of an income that would have been welcome at the time.

Though the partners tried their hardest, the business was failing, and a saddened Levi informed his friend that he could no longer afford to continue. He needed a safer job and a higher income. But the failure of the laboratory was not his only setback. A much more bitter experience concerned the book that he had now completed. Giulio Einaudi, which had emerged from the days of the Resistance, was the publishing house Levi approached and Einaudi turned it down. The book had passed through several hands, including Cesare Pavese's. The worst blow was that it was the professional reader Natalia Ginzburg, whose husband Leone had died under torture in the Regina Coeli prison in Rome, who rejected the manuscript, on the grounds that the time was "not right for its publication."[21] She was unmoved by its beauty. In those days, the firm was taking more interest in crude attempts at experimental literature than in the classical perfection of a young author who was not an insider. In that immediate postwar period, even those who had fought against Fascism and Nazism were not prepared to give a hearing to a survivor of Auschwitz.

The medical review *Minerva Medica* had published the ten-page report produced by Primo Levi and Leonardo De Benedetti in 1945 at the request of the Soviet authorities of the camp in Katowice. Its tone was much blunter and tougher in its account of the Auschwitz camp, the gas chambers, and crematoria, and the hunger and diseases that afflicted the prisoners, than the pages soon to be read by the originally small group of readers who bought the first copies of *If This Is A Man*.

After the very restricted appearance of *Minerva Medica*, Silvio Ortona had had some chapters of *If This Is A Man* published in several successive issues of the Communist Party weekly *Amico del popolo*, in Vercelli, in 1946. But all the major publishers who were approached rejected the manuscript submitted by the unknown author. What he had to say to the world, the world did not want to hear. The lucid prose of this survivor, which rendered all eloquence obscene, resounded in a void. Levi's nightmare was coming true. Was he not witnessing the death of man?[22] As the Nazi executioners had predicted, there were few who were ready to hear and believe the survivors. George Steiner wrote: "Where language is still human, in the fundamental meaning of that word, it is spoken by survivors, people who remember, and by ghosts. Its haunted music is the music of the embers that continue to crackle in the cold ashes of a dead fire."[23]

It was Anna Maria, Primo's sister, who broke through the barrier, as a result of the friendships she had made as a liaison officer with the CLN (Committee of National Liberation). In particular, she had come to know Alessandro Galante Garrone, a young judge whose refusal to join the Fascist Party had prevented him from becoming a history teacher. Both of his mother's brothers — "*i fratelli Garrone*" — had been killed during the war. Galante Garrone was one of the ten men who had led the insurrection in Turin on 26 April 1945. After working as a magistrate for thirty years, he finally sat the competitive examination that enabled him to teach history at the university.

Alessandro Galante Garrone, who still lives in Turin, had joined the fight against Fascism when the racial laws were passed. Using his position as a magistrate, he had done everything in his power to defend the Jews: he sheltered some of them in his house, and had the audacity to write an article in a legal journal attacking the laws at the moment of their publication. When he met Anna Maria in the ranks of the Resistance she had heard no news of either her brother or her fiancé, who was never to return from the concentration camp to which he had been deported. This frail young woman took considerable risks. She made deliveries for the underground press, took messages by bicycle, bought food on the black market, and harboured exhausted wounded partisans. She rarely spent two nights consecutively in the same place, as she moved between the countryside, where her mother was in hiding, and Turin, where friends gave her shelter.

A few months after the end of the war, Anna Maria told Galante Garrone that her brother had written a book describing his time in Auschwitz, and that not one publishing house, including Einaudi, was willing to publish it. She asked him to read the manuscript. He realized that he was looking at a master-piece, "a book of great poetry, profound morality, and a poignant, irresistible beauty." He was struck by the perfect balance between evidence and analysis. Each short chapter, narrated in the present tense (because in the heart of the author Auschwitz was always present) with its evocative power, dealt with an aspect of life in the camp.

Galante Garrone took the manuscript to Franco Antonicelli, an ex-comrade in the CLN and co-leader of the Turin insurrection, who was also a lover of literature. Under Fascism, before the creation of Einaudi, Antonicelli had been involved with a small publishing house, Frossinelli, founded in a spirit of commitment to European anti-Fascist culture. He had published the first Italian translation of Kafka's *The Trial*, and Galante Garrone's book on Gracchus Babeuf. In 1946 he had started the short-lived publishing house of Francesco De Silva, named after one of the first Italian publishers of the Renaissance. When Galante Garrone brought him the manuscript of a book called *The Drowned and the Saved*, written by a young chemist, Antonicelli read and accepted the book at once, but asked the author to change the title. He preferred the fifth line — "Consider if this is a man" — of the poem "Shemà," written on 10 January 1946, which Levi had chosen as the epigraph to his book. It took thirty-nine years before the original title of Primo Levi's first book appeared on the jacket of his last.

Franco Antonicelli printed 2,500 copies of the book in the autumn of 1947, in a series dedicated to the memory of Leone Ginzburg. In his preface to this first edition, Levi wrote that he had been driven by the need to describe the inhuman by the use of human words, to enable those who had stayed at home to apprehend the kingdom of death. The man whose very existence had been questioned in the title of his book had survived to bear witness.

It happened that the first novel published by Italo Calvino, *Il sentiero dei nidi di ragno* (*The Path to the Nest of Spiders*), came out at the same time as *If This Is A Man*. The books were reviewed in the same issue of *La Stampa* by Arrigo Cajumi, who saw long careers ahead for both their authors. But Levi's book sold hardly any copies. Italo Calvino, who was one of the few readers to perceive its importance, published an admiring critique in *L'Unità*. In it he saluted the exceptional balance that combined factual evidence and evocation with insight to make *If This Is A Man* the best book written on the theme of the concentrationary world.

Primo Levi sent copies of his book, each with a brief dedication, to his family and friends. The fact is that the little volume was distributed rather than sold. Six hundred copies stored in a warehouse in Florence were destroyed when the River Arno flooded in the autumn of 1966.

The indifference that greeted his story came to Levi as a disappointment so severe that he gave up writing and decided to return to his trade as a chemist. Apart from a few short stories published in *Il Giorno* he wrote nothing more till 1961.[24] He started to look for work again, and very fortunately, through an old chemist friend, Signor Ganotti, in December 1947 he met Federico Silla Accati, the owner of a small paint business, who was looking for a chemist to help him with the manufacture of special varnishes. A practical, prickly man, with a modest education, Accati came from a family of small builders. His factory in Turin, the SIVA, had just started up after the disaster of the war. So began an association that was to last for thirty years.

Although they were very different characters, Accati and Levi got along perfectly together. At first they worked in a garage owned by Accati's parents. Accati then bought a small house on a vacant lot in Settimo Torinese, in the north-east suburbs of Turin, just off the highway to Milan. They overhauled the house, and established a laboratory there. They started by producing waterproof paints and varnishes for the building industry, but owner and chemist quickly discarded ordinary paints to concentrate on synthetic wire enamels, on which Levi was to become one of the forty leading specialists in the world. This technology had already existed in Germany but the products that SIVA soon developed were Levi's own creation. The varnishes he invented were deposited in very thin layers on copper wire, then baked in a kiln where they became practically rigid insulating coatings. Some were capable of bearing considerable mechanical or electrical stresses. Others, designed to withstand a saline atmosphere or particular temperatures for many years, were used to coat the insides of the condensors of transatlantic liners. At that time, nobody else in Italy was producing insulating coatings for electrical conductors, required in particular in electric motors. Till then they had been available only in Germany and the United States.

Philip Roth gave the following description of the SIVA factory after a guided tour by Primo Levi in September 1986:

> Altogether the company employs 50 people, mainly chemists who work in the laboratories and skilled labourers on the floor of the plant. The production machinery, the row of storage tanks, the laboratory building, the finished product in man-sized containers ready to be shipped, the reprocessing facility that purifies the wastes — all of it is encompassed in four or five acres a seven-mile drive from Turin. The machines that are drying resin and blending varnish and pumping off pollutants are never distressingly loud, the yard's acrid odour — the smell, Levi told me, that clung to his clothing for two years after his retirement —

is by no means disgusting, and the skip loaded with the black sludgy residue of the anti-polluting process isn't particularly unsightly. It is hardly the world's ugliest industrial environment, but a very long way, nonetheless, from those sentences suffused with mind that are the hallmark of Levi's autobiographical narratives.[25]

SIVA grew fast, and two new plants were built: the SICME and the SCET, one to produce copper wire of various diameters, the other to bake the varnish-coated wire in the house kiln. SIVA was the smallest structure in the little complex. Primo Levi, originally engaged as a chemist, quickly became the technical manager and then the general manager of the plant in Settimo Torinese, which still produces the varnishes he created. He hired and fired workers, and negotiated with customers and suppliers. He was liked and respected in SIVA, even in the period in the 1970s when trade unions and employers in Turin were caught up in violent confrontations.

Paola Accati, Federico's daughter, became a chemist and eventually succeeded her father when he died (some time after Levi). When she was a little girl, Primo Levi used to take her on early morning tours of the factory. She remembers a small, slender, not very talkative man who would push his glasses up above his forehead and say: "Well then, let's see what we can do." He seemed cold, but when they got to know each other better he ventured occasional jokes. He explained that the factory had a kind of beauty, and that chemistry was not the enemy of nature, and to prove it he showed her the moss that grew in the cooling pond, inhabited by frogs.

Primo Levi and Federico Silla Accati were very close to each other, but in the style of Piedmont, which requires its adherents never to talk about personal matters, or only in a very roundabout way. This is Federico Accati as described by his elder daughter Luisa: "Words were never to be too loud. He seldom opened his mouth; a quarter of an hour's silence to say four words. My father spoke short, significant, immortal sentences. He was quiet, untruthful, and enigmatic."[26] Accati called everyone a fool, except Primo Levi, whom he secretly admired. A very conservative man, he worked to make money, whereas Levi, who did not love money for its own sake, preferred to earn it by using his wits. When Levi became a best-selling author, Federico Accati made shrewd investments with his general manager's royalties. Every six months he paid him the interest, and in order to earn his esteem he would even cheat a little. As for Levi, he would sometimes ask for his employer's advice when he had an appointment with his publisher.[27]

Primo Levi practised his trade as a chemist with a sense of exaltation. He never entered his laboratory without the feeling that he was, like the God of Genesis, coming to restore order to the "*tohu-vavohu*"[28] of the universe. Far more than textbook abstractions, it was his daily, solitary work in the laboratory that yielded his knowledge about matter. There he confronted matter heroically, with his hands and his reason. This clash with *hyle*, "Matter," which Levi was so attached to, and whose key metaphors enrich his work, would no longer be possible today, because the procedures he used to build molecular structures have become obsolete, replaced by a sophisticated technology that uses computerized modelling.

To go to the plant in the morning he had to drive all the way through town by way of the Via Cigna, where some SIVA production units were housed at no. 114. In the poem "Via Cigna," written on 2 February 1973, he described the endless street:

> There isn't a shabbier street in this whole city.
> Fog and night; shadows on the sidewalk ...
> Maybe it will be dark for ever.

The words used in these sinister lines read like metaphors of the camp, always present in his mind, coming to displace the reality: night and fog, shadows and darkness.

At noon, Levi lunched in the SIVA restaurant, where he tended to bristle at critical remarks about the standard of the food. To a guest who complained one day that the meal was not much good, he replied: "You can eat a lot worse than this." Here again, this terse remark shows how the memory of Auschwitz, never far from his thoughts, adhered to every moment of his life.

Levi saw nothing at all alienating in his work, although alienation was a stock image in contemporary Italy. As general manager of SIVA he did his job without reluctance, but also unassumingly, with no liking for power. He never lost his temper, never raised his voice, but his controlled reserve made a strong impression on the people who worked for him.

Primo Levi often spoke with Renato Portesi, a chemical engineer who worked with him in the laboratory. He would puff out the smoke from his mentholated cigarettes, slide his glasses up above his head, and talk about books he had been reading. He loved Machiavelli and T.S. Eliot, and he made Portesi read Thomas Mann, admitting that whereas he had no real affinity with Russian literature, including Dostoevsky and Tolstoy, it seemed to him that *Joseph and His Brothers* was one of the high points of world literature.

His only objection was to an additional responsibility assigned by Federico Accati, which meant that he had to provide technical assistance to customers. It irked him because he disliked paying visits. He wrote some vivid accounts of this extra duty in *Vizio di forma* — literally, "breach of procedure."

One day a representative of the Bayer pharmaceutical company, interested in the varnishes produced by SIVA, arrived from Germany to propose a collaboration. Not daring to raise the subject directly, Federico Accati mentioned the visit to Levi as if it had happened some time ago. To his surprise, Levi was not at all put off by the thought of going to Germany. He simply answered: "I'm curious to see." Accati made contact with Bayer again, and so began Primo

Levi's travels to Germany. When they took place in summer, during the school holidays, Accati used to bring his daughter Luisa, who was studying German, and drop her at the Goethe Institute of a chosen city. He would pick her up again at the end of their journey, during which he and Levi visited customers and purchased basic products from the Bayer headquarters in Leverkusen, near Cologne.

Luisa Accati was eleven years old the first time she travelled with Primo Levi, in July 1953. Levi wore a short-sleeved shirt, and she saw the number 174517 tattooed on his arm. She remembers a lunch at a *Gasthaus* in Leverkusen with some important executives, when one of them noticed the number and asked what it stood for. Primo Levi replied: "It is the number I had in Auschwitz." A total hush descended on the table. There was the sound of spoons clinking on plates. No one said a word until the end of the meal. "When my father and Primo Levi made trips to Germany I sometimes heard them say: that one looks like a Nazi and that one doesn't. Do you think he was, or not? Primo Levi was calm and self-controlled. When he started talking to the Germans they were tongue-tied and ill at ease. He was quite the opposite — very interested, without hatred."[29]

On one visit Levi took Luisa to Cologne by himself, when she was thirteen. The train was pulled by a coal-fired locomotive, and flakes of soot came in through the open windows. The water tasted like coal, and Luisa told Levi that she wouldn't drink it. "Drink," he said, "it will do you good. You can drink this water quite safely."

SIVA was a source of inspiration for Primo Levi. The "sick tube" in *La chiave a stella*[30] refers to the acetic acid extraction tower which was visible from the Turin–Milan motorway, just after the right-hand toll gate, before its demolition in spring 1996. Levi had switched it on, and had shown the workers how to operate it. An engineer from Milan had designed it by copying the features of an existing tower, but the ceramic rings inside the SIVA had ground themselves to pieces under their own weight when the tube filled with steam and the pressure rose. Levi solved the problem, which took him several nights to work out, by having a series of steel distillation plates fixed inside the tube.

In the eyes of the Marxists who called the tune in the working-class Turin of the 1960s, work was pure alienation. That was not the case for Levi. He who had passed through the *Lager* (he preferred this word to the word "camp," but we do not know whether he said it in German or Yiddish: the same meaning, but with different emotional connotations) loved work, and rejected comparisons between factories and concentration camps. The Nazis, with those "three derisive words," *Arbeit macht frei*, displayed above the gates of all the camps, had wanted to destroy a work ethic that Levi embraced.

> Loving your work represents the best, most concrete approximation of happiness on earth. Competence is an experience of the most accessible freedom, and the most useful to mankind.[31]
>
> ... I believe in work. I need to have courage, and to stand up to the rhetoric of platitudes about work as a negative reality, even at the risk of offending. The love of work is not as rare as people think. A man who loves work is not necessarily a reactionary. Certainly there is such a thing as repetitive, degrading work, but that can be avoided by organizing it differently.[32]

The received wisdom among the drawing-room trade unionists of the 1960s and 1970s, by which the world was peopled by slaves chained to their assembly line by wicked bosses seemed to him both abstract and false. He had found in his SIVA laboratory a Conradian image of life, a metaphor for the saving grace of work. In Levi's view, this implied acceptance of responsibility, a step towards growing up. Putting it bluntly, he added that if everybody refused to work, humanity would starve. To put forward such opinions in Turin at the height of the passion for Gramscian ideas amounted to a kind of sacrilege.

Levi observed and admired intelligent workers who had "their brains at the tips of their fingers." In the "Sulphur" chapter of *The Periodic Table* he describes how Lanza, the night worker, mixed the ingredients in the SIVA kettle — including sulphur — whose transformation by fire and vacuum gave rise to resin.

He marvelled to see workers intuitively solving problems in a few minutes that a desk technician would have spent hours examining. It was these men who provided the models for Faussone the rigger, the hero of *The Wrench*. Levi started this book after a career of thirty years with SIVA. He compared himself then with Conrad, who started to write after twenty years in the merchant navy, and modelled his characters on colleagues and shipmates. The factory and the world of chemistry and technology were just as inspiring for the Italian chemist as the sea had been for the Polish master mariner. Seeing that our universe was intelligible through science and technology, it was not rational to ignore them, and literature had to make room for them. There was a time when there was only one culture, the culture of Leonardo da Vinci, Galileo, Lazzaro, Spallanzani, and Lorenzo Magalotti, and when a painter like Piero della Francesca was also a mathematician and geometer. Had not Kant studied astronomy before he wrote books on philosophy?

But for eleven years, from 1947 to 1958, Primo Levi did hardly any writing: literature was no longer a part of his life. He had entered it so briefly and unobtrusively that he did not imagine that one day he would be considered as one of the major writers of his time. He and Lucia, and their daughter Lisa, had gone back to live with his mother Ester because they did not want to leave her alone in the big apartment on the Corso Re Umberto. Ester looked after Lisa, and later their son Renzo, and did the housework. Lucia taught Italian literature and Latin at the Regina Margherita school, where she was looked up to both by her pupils and by her colleagues. They spent their holidays by the seaside, in their apartment in the Via San Domenico, in Pietra Ligure.

Dottore Levi led the comfortable bourgeois life of a senior executive running a large factory. Every day he drove through Turin in the rush hour to get to SIVA, where, clad in his white lab coat, he supervised the running of the plant, and also dealt with customer relations and suppliers. Every night he came home to a quiet family life. Yet at bed time he never knew whether he would sleep through the night in peace. He could be called at any time because a valve had burst, a storm had flooded a conduit, or a fire had broken out.

On Sundays he was pleased to welcome the few friends who had free access to his home. This intimate circle extended, in a limited way, the family atmosphere — which was both protective and repressive — that he had known in his childhood and in which he lived until the end of his life. In summer he allowed himself a few days' rest. In 1950 Jean Samuel, who had just got married and was on his honeymoon, stopped in Tredici Laghi for a couple of days, to join Primo Levi, Lucia, and little Lisa, who were holidaying in this village perched high in the Alps.

In 1951 Levi paid a visit to Charles Conreau, who had been his companion during the last ten days after the evacuation of Auschwitz by the Nazis. He found him sad, marked by the horrors he had witnessed. He had resumed his profession as a teacher in the small primary school in Provenchères, in the Vosges, and taught the children about bee-keeping and planting pine trees.

Their daughter Lisa Lorenza was born in 1948. Her second name was dedicated to the memory of Lorenzo Perrone, the semi-illiterate Italian mason who had saved her father's life in Auschwitz, Lorenzo who walked all the way home from Auschwitz to his village in Italy. A son was born in 1957; they called him Renzo, again in memory of a good man.

Primo Levi had gone looking for Lorenzo Perrone in Fossano when he himself returned, but he deliberately refrained from giving further information about his benefactor in *If This Is A Man* because, he wrote: "the task of transforming a living person into a character ties the hand of the writer. This happens because such a task, even when it is undertaken with the best intentions and deals with a respected and loved person, verges on the violation of privacy and is never painless for the subject" (*Reprieve* 107/149). However, several years after Lorenzo's death Levi expanded on his portrait of the individual who had come to his aid out of pure altruism in the pitiless world of the camp.

When Levi had travelled to Fossano to visit Lorenzo, he had brought him a woollen winter sweater. They went to the local inn, where it was all Primo could do to squeeze a few words out of this simple man who had never had many to spare. Even so, Lorenzo did tell Primo that he was not the only man he had helped in the camp, because, he explained, "we are in this world to do good, not to boast about it" (*Reprieve* 118/160).

After witnessing Auschwitz, Lorenzo had lost his love of life, and had given up working as a mason. He became a scrap-metal dealer, and spent what little money he managed to earn in the tavern, where he shut out reality by drinking himself into a stupor. Primo felt that he should get away from Fossano, and found him a job as a mason in Turin, but Lorenzo turned it down. He had lost all his moorings, and refused to be tied. As he was sleeping out of doors in the depth of winter, it was not surprising that he fell ill. Primo Levi got him into hospital with the help of some doctor friends, but wine was not prescribed there, and he made his escape. Soon after that he was found dying, and he died by himself in hospital. Levi responded to the death of Lorenzo Perrone as if he were foreseeing his own, as if his own scant taste for life at this point had begun stealthily to sap his resistance. "He had seen the world, he didn't like it, he felt it was going to ruin. To live no longer interested him .... He, who was not a survivor, had died of the survivors' disease" (*Reprieve* 117–18/159–60).

If This Is A Man had been utterly forgotten outside his circle of friends, and Primo Levi was no longer writing when the Italian translation of Robert Antelme's *L'Espèce humaine* came out in 1957. In those postwar years Levi seems to have retained his confidence in man's capacity to understand the universe, to give form to the formless, and to explain the inexplicable. After spending twelve months in the kingdom of the dead, he still believed that the tradition of the Enlightenment was capable of leading humanity closer to reason and further from pain.

In Turin, a group of intellectuals with links to the Resistance had gathered around the president of the Piedmont Liberation Committee, Franco Antonicelli, publisher of *If This Is A Man*. They explored a whole range of ideas about the relations that had to be established between culture and politics, and between men of culture and the masses. They founded an association, *l'Unione Culturale* (the "Cultural Union"), which held meetings and organized lectures in the fine salons on the ground floor of the Palazzo Carignano. In the course of endless arguments they debated the question of whether the new culture ought to be popular, and responsive to the needs of those who were not cultivated, or whether instead they should push for an avant-garde culture, which Fascism had stifled. These debates soon gave way to cultural and political conferences, usually organized by Antonicelli. A centre for methodological studies also started up in 1946, under the influence of Ludovico Geymonat, whose books were published by Antonicelli's publishing house, De Silva. The circle included mathematicians, physicists, and biologists, and it was joined by the philosopher Nicola Abbagnano. In the cultural landscape of postwar Turin, the Communist Catholics also enjoyed a short-lived influence, with their philosopher Felice Balbo, who considered himself close to Piero Gobetti and wrote for the publishers Einaudi.

In the broader circle of Italian intellectuals, outside Turin and the friends of Franco Antonicelli, Primo Levi was still an unknown. He lived a life apart from the world of letters, and was seen as a survivor of the camps, a man of science, and a spare-time writer. The fact that he had belonged to the *Giustizia e Libertà* movement during the war cut no ice with the writers who revolved around the house of Einaudi, which had rejected his book. Those ties Primo Levi had were with the friends of his youth, all of them close to the *Partito d'Azione* spawned by *Giustizia e Libertà*. As he was outside the literary establishment, and did not really feel like a man of letters, he followed a solo path. He never gave a moment's thought to leaving SIVA to concentrate on full-time writing. During the period of the racial laws he had been "a grain of mustard," an "impurity" in Italian society; now he was a grain of mustard in the world of Italian letters.

To Levi, chemistry was a battle, "a trade, which is only ever a particular instance, a bolder version of the trade of living."[33] The chemistry that interested him was not the kind practised in big companies where the finished product is an anonymous piece of corporate work. He loved the odyssey of the solitary chemist who transmutes matter in his laboratory with nothing to help him but the skill of his hands and the power of his reason and imagination. As an optimistic man of science, he gropes his way forward through the darkness, and in spite of the hostility and malice of stupid matter, "inclined to evil," when he finds the right direction he finally glimpses a light that grows stronger, "and order at last succeeds chaos."[34]

The chemistry whose vocabulary he cherished also provided him with a hoard of poetic metaphors. "Distilling is beautiful" (*Table* 57). "The words 'pale,' 'dark,', 'heavy,' 'light,' or even 'blue' cover a range of meanings both wider and more concrete. For me, blue is not only the colour of the sky, I have five or six available ...."[35] Thus his language as a writer is precise and rich, even though he stated that his style was modelled on "the 'weekly report' commonly used in factories."[36]

Not only did the trade of chemist save Levi's life when he was in Auschwitz, it also brought him other gifts, as well as a comfortable living. In fact he considered that he owed his trade of writing to chemistry, which he defined as "the art of separating, weighing and distinguishing: these are three useful exercises also for the person who sets out to describe events or give body to his own imagination" (*Trades* 187/175). Thus, to anybody who expressed surprise that he was both a chemist and a writer, he replied that it was precisely because he was a chemist that he wrote. The trades that he practised had somehow fused together.

At weekends, Levi often made trips into the mountains of Piedmont with his friends: Alberto Salmoni, now married to Bianca Guidetti Serra, and Silvio Ortone, who had married Primo's cousin, Ada Della Torre. It was they who were soon to become the first readers and judges of his manuscripts. Once more he climbed the peaks he loved. A keen naturalist, he would often stop to identify plants for his friends, or to explain the life cycle of some animal or insect.

Primo Levi read the first book by Mario Rigoni Stern, *Il sergente nella neve* ("The Sergeant in the Snow") published by Einaudi in 1953, which dealt with the retreat of the German army through the vast expanse of Russia. Rigoni Stern had served with the ARMIR, the Italian army in the Soviet Union. Captured by the Germans after Italy signed the armistice, he had crossed the frozen steppes on foot, then managed to escape from a camp in Austria and had walked back to Italy, arriving home on 5 May 1945. Rigoni Stern was born on the Asiago plateau in 1921, and lives there to this day. He built his stone house in the hamlet of Rigoni di Sotto with his own hands, and started to keep bees there. Knowing that Levi shared his passion for the mountains, he invited him to stay. On a Christmas evening in the 1950s he wrote to Levi: "Come, we shall go walking in the virgin snow, in the mountains. We will climb, we will light a camp fire, and we will stay quiet and watch the flame. We won't need wine or bread. The company of the fire will be enough for us."

Levi did not take up that invitation because work and the family prevented his leaving Turin, but one spring day he arrived with Lucia. Stern the keen bee-keeper showed them his hives. Levi observed the bees at work, the larvae, and the honey-combs. They walked on a footpath used by roe deer, and Levi asked questions about the mountain flowers, trees, mushrooms, and animals. On 12 April 1987, the day after Levi's suicide, Stern wrote him a posthumous open letter in *La Stampa*, remembering his visit:

> All that was fine, but from time to time an unexpected silence fell between us, which had not descended to let us hear the sounds of nature, but because your presence and my own were mutually tuned to the phantasms of another distant spring that we had endured in similar circumstances. Thus, now and then, a snatch of a phrase, a word in German, Russian, Polish, or Yiddish, would come between us and induce a kind of shy reticence.

By 1955 the first edition of *If This Is A Man* had been totally forgotten. In the special issue of the Jewish review *L'Echo dell'educazione ebraïca* commemorating the tenth anniversary of the Liberation, Levi had written:

Nowadays it is indelicate to mention the camp. One risks being accused of setting up as a victim, or of indecent exposure. Is this silence justified? Should we put up with it, we the survivors, we the people of the survivors? Should we withhold this collection of testimonies that, despite our enemies, history appears to have preserved? There is only one answer. It is forbidden to forget, it is forbidden to be silent. If we are silent, who will speak? Certainly not the guilty and their accomplices. Our evidence will be lacking, and in some near future, because of its very enormity, the history of Nazi bestiality will be consigned to legend. So it is absolutely necessary to speak, and to keep on speaking.

In 1956, an exhibition on deportation drew masses of visitors to Turin. Primo Levi spoke there, and was besieged by groups of young people who wanted to ask him questions about his experience as a deportee. It was then that he suggested to Einaudi that they should reissue *If This Is A Man*. During a seminar devoted to Levi, Giulio Einaudi maintained that there were no clues in the house archives that could account for the rejection of his book. The legend has it that Natalia Ginzburg rejected the manuscript. Giulio Einaudi attempted to play down his publisher's reader's blindness by his suggestion that: "No doubt, in those hard postwar times, people did not want to hark back to the painful years that were only just over." It was a flimsy explanation, given that a number of personal stories by deportees were published after the war. Nevertheless, on 11 July 1955 Primo Levi signed a contract for Einaudi to bring out a new edition of his book, though his pleasure was short-lived, when he came to realize that a contract did not ensure publication.

To justify the delay that did indeed ensue, and the sceptical attitude taken towards a book which had gone almost unnoticed when it first appeared, Giulio Einaudi has said that 1955 was a bad year for the firm, which had been converted into a joint-stock company, and had to make an appeal for new capital in order to survive and expand. Levi became a subscriber when he agreed to invest the royalties the book might earn. In fact, no one at Einaudi believed that *If This Is A Man* could possibly do well, because De Silva in Florence had been left with unsold copies on their hands. In the meantime they had published books that made a better impression on the editorial board. Levi was a patient man. Every now and then he would jog Einaudi's memory in an effort to get things moving, but to no effect. His professional work certainly offered a kind of cure for the disappointment caused by Einaudi's apathy, and in fact the publisher's indifference was so far-reaching that even after a great deal of pleading from Levi, it was not until three years later that the new edition was published, in June 1958.

Primo Levi and Lello Perugia had presented a demand for compensation to I.G.

Farben Industrie for having been used as slaves in their Auschwitz factory. On 8 November 1957, Levi had written to Lello informing him about the routine to be followed, and enclosing the forms he would need to fill out and send to the German lawyer in charge of the procedure: Henry Ormond, Rechtanwalt, Schillerstrasse 15/17, Frankfurt am Main. According to the French documents made available by Lello Perugia, the proceedings between the complainants and I.G. Farben Industrie developed as follows:

After the signature of an agreement on 6 February 1957 between, on the one hand, I.G. Farben Industrie, and on the other the Claims Conference and Mr Norbert Wolheim, it had been decided that:

I — Those entitled to make a claim were all those ex-prisoners of a KZ who were persecuted because of their race or political commitment, or who were coerced during the war into forced labour in one of the following I.G. Farben establishments: Buna-Monowitz, Heydebreck, Fürstengrube, Janingrube.

II — In exceptional cases, the heirs (only their sons, parents, husbands, or wives) hold the entitlements of those ex-prisoners of KZs who, while they were alive, notified their claims against I.G. Farben, but who are now deceased. No rights pertain to the widows or other heirs of prisoners deceased in KZs.

III — This right is not transferable.

IV — I.G. Farben has put up a sum of DM 30 million. Of this sum, DM 27 million is allotted to ex-prisoners persecuted for racial reasons, who make up the majority. The remainder, that is to say DM 3 million, is allotted to political persecutees.

V — Any claimant constrained to forced labour on behalf of I.G. Farben in any of the above-named establishments for six months or more will receive a fixed sum of DM 5,000. Any claimant who worked for I.G. Farben for less than six months will receive a lesser sum, but a minimum of DM 2,500.

VI — The terms of this agreement will be carried out through the intermediary of a trustee company founded for that purpose.

VII — Settlement of these sums cannot be relied upon before the year 1958, because:

1 — The entitlement of every prisoner has to be established.

2 — The effectiveness of the agreement depends on two conditions:
a) that the general meeting of I.G. Farben called for 5 April 1957 gives its consent;
b) that a new law is published by the Federal German Republic which — in the interest of such a procedure — will limit the date for making the claim (for all those who have not already done so) to only six months.

3 — The two parties have the right to terminate the agreement within a

period of three months after the end of the six months during which the claims may be registered.

A letter dated 7 May 1958 informed the ten thousand claimants, among them Lello Perugia, Giacomo Pavoncello, and Primo Levi, that a final agreement had been signed with I.G. Farben in April 1958. It stated that:

I.G. Farben and the Claims Conference did not invoke the right of withdrawal from the agreement of 1/2/1957 by 31 March 1958. The agreement between I.G. Farben and the Claims Conference has therefore come into effect. By the terms of this agreement, I.G. Farben is obliged to make available to those Jews who were put to work as forced labour in the Buna-Werke near Auschwitz a sum of DM 27 million, and for non-Jews a sum of DM 3 million.

As of 31/3/1958, 10,000 claims have been submitted, which will decrease — for juridical reasons — by some thousands.

Excluded from this agreement are the claims of Hungarian women and those of the heirs of the slave workers of Auschwitz. Some hundreds of claims have been filed in error, and thus, in well-informed circles, it is believed that the number of eligible parties will come to between five and six thousand, a figure that about corresponds to the original estimates.

Claims will be examined by the commissions created by the persecutees that already exist in the United States, Israel, and West Germany. Another committee is also to be formed for the Benelux countries. These commissions will be responsible for distributing the sums to those who are genuinely entitled to receive them.

The Paris lawyer Eugène Ayache wrote to the claimants on 28 September 1959 on behalf of the "Compensation Treuhand GmbH Benelux, France, Italy, Switzerland Advisory Committee" to inform them that their claims were awaiting investigation. Lello Perugia was invited to attend a further inquiry at the Hotel Hassler, Villa Medici, in Rome, on 18 October 1959 at 10 a.m. precisely.

Perugia and Primo Levi had their claims granted in October 1960. Before they received their rightful compensation of DM 2,500, they had to pay DM 122.70 to Henry Ormond, lawyer of Frankfurt am Main. Yet the writer and his friend did not draw the same conclusions:

Myself and Primo, who was always a gentle man and never laid the blame directly on the German people, we think differently. In my view, the Germans and the free world have an enormous responsibility.

In the early 1960s, Levi's friends did not perceive him as the writer of international standing that he was gradually to become. They often used to meet at Alberto Salmoni's, who had separated from Bianca Guidetti Serra and married

Marcella Garino. Levi belonged to Franco Antonicelli's Cultural Union, and attended meetings with Bianca, Alberto Salmoni, and Magda Beyneton, the wife of Armando Novero, in those days an avant-garde poet. Magda Beyneton, Bianca Guidetti Serra, and Lucia Levi belonged to *l'Unione Donne Italiane* (*UDI*) ("Organization of Italian Women") and to the teachers' organization *Federazione Nazionale Italiana Scuola Media*. Although his wife was an activist, Primo Levi was not affiliated to any party. He was openly sympathetic to the left, but wanted to preserve his freedom to criticize the Communist Party.[37]

Marcella, Alberto, his son, Magda, Armando and their children decided one day to found a kind of close-knit community in Turin, then opted instead for the Moncalieri district for political and practical reasons. They bought some apartments in a recently constructed building out in the countryside, in the Turin hills. Primo Levi used to visit them, and the group was welcome in the Corso Re Umberto. Primo continued to love and admire Alberto, his absent-minded friend who prospered in business and was always so successful with women.

11 Witness

After three years of waiting, *If This Is A Man* was republished in 1958 with a cautious print run of 2,000 copies. Primo Levi had made some changes to the version published by Franco Antonicelli in 1947. The first edition had started the story in the camp at Fossoli di Carpi, where Levi was transferred after his detention in Aosta. The opening did not make it clear that the narrator was both a Jew and a partisan. The version published by Einaudi gave a brief account of Levi's arrest by the Fascist militia, his internment in Fossoli, near Modena, and deportation in a convoy bound for Auschwitz. New characters make their appearance: little Emilia, who travelled with her brother and their parents in the same sealed wagon as Levi; Schlome, who welcomed him "on the threshold of the house of the dead" (*Man 31/37*); Flesch, the interpreter whose face was scarred in a fight with the Italians on the Piave (*Man 24/30*); Chaim the watchmaker, the pious student of the Torah; Alberto, the dear friend who vanished in the havoc of the evacuation, who held his head high in the camp, and never did harm to his comrades.

The sales stayed very low during the first six years. Reprints of 2,000 copies each were issued in 1960 and 1963 — an average of a thousand copies a year. In 1960 the book was published in Britain, translated by Stuart Woolf, who had just graduated from Oxford when he met Primo Levi by chance in 1956. He had come to Turin, where he did not know anybody, to carry out historical research, but after reading a copy of the original and now unobtainable De Silva edition of *Se questo è un uomo* given to him by Franco Venturini, an editor with Einaudi, he decided to translate it into English. He went in all innocence to put the idea to Primo Levi, even though he knew no publishers in Britain. Levi agreed at once, though he wanted to work with Woolf in order to avoid errors. They met twice a week in Levi's apartment, on Tuesday and Friday evenings, setting to work after a simple meal. Every Friday, Woolf would bring Levi the pages he had translated since Tuesday, and they would read them together. Levi had a phenomenal memory: he would quote whole sentences from books he had read in English, such as Melville's *Moby Dick*. He was also at home with seventeenth-century English, and knew passages of the Authorized Version of the Bible by heart. He checked Woolf's work meticulously and slowly, but he was not complacent about what he had written, and was willing to discuss every word. Stuart Woolf's impression was of a man who was both confident in his own ideas on literature, and also thoroughly modest.

The English translation of *If This Is A Man* came out in 1960, and *The Truce* in 1965. In spite of its excellent critical reception in major newspapers such as the *Observer*, the *Sunday Times* and the *Guardian, If This Is A Man* was a publishing failure. The two books had to wait until 1979 to be reissued in paperback as Penguin Modern Classics. Until then, *If This Is A Man* vanished into a black hole, just like the first Italian edition. When Orion Press published it in the United States in 1960 it was completely ignored by the critics, and sold only a few hundred copies.

Two years after its English publication, *If This Is A Man* was published in German by Fischer Verlag of Frankfurt, translated by Heinz Riedt, who was a very unusual figure among the younger generation in his country.[1] He was born in the same year as Primo Levi, into an anti-Nazi family. His mother was French, his father a German diplomat stationed in Italy. Their son, who grew up speaking German, French, and Italian, spent his childhood in Naples and Palermo, where he attended primary school. His parents sent him to prepare for university entrance of the monastery of Ehel, near Munich, run by the Benedictines, who channelled Italian culture into Germany. He went on to attend the university in Munich. He was called up in 1942, and after a few months of military service succeeded in having himself sent to hospital, with the collusion of a doctor, and then declared unfit for service owing to an internal illness. Having wangled himself out of the Nazi army, he wanted to leave Germany, so he sat a competitive examination for permission to go and study in Italy during his convalescence. He passed with the highest mark, and enrolled at Padua University to study political science and history of art. A musician and pianist, he also met the great pianist Arturo Benedetti Michelangeli.

At the university he made contact with "the anti-Fascist groups led by Concetto Marchesi, Meneghetti and Pighin" (*DS 170/140*), and carried out undercover missions under the name of Marino. When Badoglio signed the armistice of 3 September 1943, announced by the Allies on the 8 September, the Nazis invaded northern Italy. In order to escape the SS, who were looking for him but did not know his real name, Heinz Riedt went underground with the partisans of *Giustizia e Libertà*, in the Euganean Hills, west of Padua. When he returned to Bavaria in 1950 he was regarded as a traitor.

Violent emotions surfaced in Levi when he heard the news in 1959 that *If This Is A Man* was to be translated into German, the language of the murderers of the European Jews. He wrote in *The Drowned and the Saved* that the book had been aimed essentially at the Germans, like a loaded weapon. Only fifteen years had elapsed since Auschwitz, and many of those who had voted for Hitler and brought him to power were still alive. Most of the SS men who had been members of the *Einsatzgruppen* or helped to run the extermination camps had not been made to answer for their crimes. Those who had played no active part in genocide had been passive bystanders, silent accomplices.

It goes without saying that Levi felt no spontaneous trust for his German publisher, because he did not know that Fischer Verlag had been a Jewish company before the war. He wrote Samuel Fischer quite a frosty letter at first, warning him that he expected to receive and vet the manuscript chapter by chapter as the work progressed, and he forbade him to change the slightest word of his text. Heinz Riedt, an expert on Goldoni, and who was later to translate Collodi, Gadda, D'Arrigo, and Pirandello, sent him a well-translated first chapter, and introduced himself in an accompanying letter written in fluent Italian.

Heinz Riedt had settled in Berlin, where he earned a moderate living as a literary translator from Italian, which he spoke without a trace of a foreign accent. He was delighted to be translating Levi, and exchanged many letters with him while he worked on the book. Although Riedt was extremely well-read, for obvious reasons he did not know the squalid jargon of the extermination camps. His German was much more refined than the language that Levi had learned in Auschwitz. So every word was weighed and debated at length, once Levi had informed him of the way that he remembered sentences being spoken in Auschwitz. Usually, Heinz Riedt would tell him that what he suggested was not good German, and Levi would reply that all the same, it was how they had talked in Auschwitz. He did not want to lose any of the coarseness of that special strain of German that suffered a mutation in the death camps. No doubt Heinz Riedt wanted to speak a different language by using the same words: he wanted to purify Nazi German. But Levi succeeded in preserving intact his samples of the language of death.

Levi was very satisfied by his collaboration with Riedt, and called it not so much a translation as a "restoration." He spoke of a "retroversion to the language in which things had taken place and to which they belonged. More than a book, it should be a tape recording," (*DS 173/142*). The result, in the opinion of Levi and all the critics, was excellent. When the publisher asked him for a preface, Levi suggested that he should publish the letter he had written to Heinz Riedt in May 1960 to thank him for his work. Here is the text of that letter, used as a preface to the first German edition:

And so we are finished: I am glad of it and satisfied with the result, grateful to you, and also a little sad. You understand, it is the only book I have written, and now that we are finished transplanting it into German I feel like a father whose son has reached the age of consent and leaves and one can no longer look after him.

But it is not only this. Perhaps you have realised that for me the Lager, and having written about the Lager, was an important adventure that has profoundly modified me, given me maturity and a reason for life. Perhaps it is presumption, but there it is. Today I, prisoner No. 174517, by your help, can speak to the German people, remind them of what they have done, and say to them: "I am alive, and I would like to understand you in order to judge you."

I do not believe that man's life necessarily has a definite purpose; but if I think of my life and the aims I have until now set for myself, I recognise only one of them is well defined and conscious, and it is precisely this, to bear witness, to make my voice heard by the German people, to "answer" the *Kapo* who cleaned his hand on my shoulder, Dr Pannwitz, and those who hanged "the last one," and by their heirs.

I am sure that you have not misunderstood me. I never harboured hatred for the German people. And if I had felt that way, I would be cured of it after having known you. I do not understand, I cannot tolerate the fact that a man should be judged not for what he is but because of the group to which he happens to belong.

[…]

But I cannot say I understand the Germans: now, something one cannot understand constitutes a painful void, a puncture, a permanent stimulus that insists on being satisfied. I hope that this book will have some echo in Germany, not only out of ambition, but also because the nature of this echo will perhaps make it possible for me to better understand the Germans, placate this stimulus. (*DS 173–4/142–3*).

It cannot be said that the book scored a great success when it was first published in Germany. In spite of complimentary reviews, it sold no better than when it first came out in Italy. However, Levi received about forty letters between 1961 and 1964, the year when *The Truce* appeared in Germany, published by Christian Wegner Verlag under the title *Atempause*.

Among the letters from German readers that Levi discusses in Chapter 8 of his last book, *The Drowned and the Saved*, he quotes some of those written by Hety Schmitt-Maass, who put him in touch with F.M., the German chemist in Auschwitz whom Levi writes about in *The Periodic Table*. He also mentions Hety Schmitt-Maass in his conversations with Anna Bravo and Frederico Cereja, published under the title "The Duty of Memory."[2] She and Levi exchanged about fifty letters in the sixteen years from October 1966 to November 1982, although they were never on close personal terms. However, Hety sent him copies of her relevant correspondence both with her children and with certain German intellectuals whom she dealt with in the course of her work at the Ministry of Culture of the state of Hessen. Hety had caught Levi's attention when she told him in her first letter: "You will certainly never be able to understand 'the Germans:' even we are unable to do so, because at that time there happened things that, under no circumstances, should have happened" (*DS 190/159*).

Hety Schmitt-Maass's father had been a teacher, and an active member of the Social Democratic Party, who had lost his job in 1933 when Hitler came to power. The family moved to a smaller apartment, police searches followed, and Hety, who had refused to join the Hitler Youth organization, was expelled from her secondary school. In 1938 she married an engineer who worked for the firm of I.G. Farben. In 1944 her father was deported to Dachau. Every week she took him a parcel of food at the gate of the camp.

Hety's husband opposed this, and after the war, when his father-in-law came home, he objected to Hety's continuing her father's work in the Social Democratic Party. Their relations deteriorated, and the husband requested a divorce and married a refugee from Eastern Prussia, who had taken the same route back to Germany as the prisoners evacuated from Auschwitz by the Nazis in January 1945.

In 1967, Hety Schmitt-Maass had attended the euthanasia trial where doctors who had poisoned or gassed their German mental patients had to answer for their acts. People she knew gave her hostile responses when she mentioned the trial. She told Levi in a letter that many people in Germany did not condemn the attitude of soldiers who had taken part in the extermination of Jews, on the grounds that they had been obeying orders.

It was also Hety Schmitt-Maass who gave Primo Levi's address to Jean Améry, and Améry's to Levi, on the odd condition — and odder still, they accepted it — that the two send her copies of the letters they exchanged.

After the war F.M., who had been a colleague of Hety's husband at I.G. Farben, worked in a firm that sold chemical products to SIVA, where Levi was the general manager, so it appears that the circumstances in which Levi and F.M. came into contact after the war were slightly embroidered in the "Vanadium" chapter of *The Periodic Table*.

Just as she had done with Améry, Hety Schmitt-Maass asked for copies of the correspondence between Levi and F.M. to be sent to her. In the mission of "*Wieder gut Machung*," ("making things good again"), in 1975 she even ventured to visit Albert Speer, Hitler's architect and minister for armaments, who had been released from Spandau war crimes prison in 1966 and had just published his Spandau diaries. She spent two hours with Speer, during which she gave him Hermann Langbein's and Primo Levi's books, and he gave her a copy of his Spandau diaries to send to Levi. Levi wrote to Hety "with a trace of irritation" to ask: "What impelled you to visit Speer? Curiosity? A sense of duty? A 'mission'?" She wrote in reply:

I hope you understood the correct meaning of the gift of that book. Your question is also correct. I wanted to look into his face: look at how a man is made who allowed himself to be the succubus of Hitler, and became his creature. He says, and I believe him, that for him the Auschwitz slaughter is a trauma. He's obsessed by the question of how he could "not want to see or know," in short, block everything out. I do not think he's trying to find justification; he would like to understand what, for him too, it is impossible to understand. He appears to me as a man who does not falsify, fights loyally, and torments himself over his past. For me, he has become "a key": he is a symbolic personage, the symbol of German aberration. He read Langbein's book with great pain, and he promised me that he would also read yours. I will keep you informed of his reactions. (*DS 196/164*).

Hety paid a second visit to Speer, and was disappointed to realize how intrinsically narcissistic he still was, and how proud of his past. Speer died in 1981, and Hety Schmitt-Maass in 1983, after a brain operation.

In F.M.'s first letter to Primo Levi, which arrived on 2 March 1967, he informed Levi that Hety Schmitt-Maass had given him *If This Is A Man* to read, and offered the possibility of his writing this letter. Adopting an unduly casual tone, given the circumstances, he first says how glad he is to learn that Levi has survived, and then suggests that it would be useful for both of them to meet "for the purpose of overcoming that terrible past," never doubting whether Levi would wish to meet one of the functionaries of the industrial empire of Auschwitz. He proceeds to say that he has often thought about Primo Levi and his comrades, and would like to know what had become of Brackier, Kandel, the doctor from Breslau, and Doktor Goldbaum. Lastly, F.M. gets to the heart of the matter: the circumstances that brought him to work in the extermination camp. He arrived in Auschwitz in November 1944 with the rank of sergeant in the Wehrmacht, not knowing so much as the name of the camp. When he read Levi's book he had been glad to learn that the stay in the Polymerization lab had brought him some relief. F.M.'s chief mission had been to install the Polymerization laboratory. He claimed not to have known that Levi had been examined in chemistry by Doktor Pannwitz. He had left Auschwitz on 25 January 1945, with the last Germans, and had the utmost difficulty avoiding being conscripted by the SS into the *Volkssturm*, the rag-tag army of old men and adolescents that was supposed to block the advance of the Red Army.[3] Taken prisoner by the Americans, he was released in mid-June of that year. Since 1950 he had been working in Ludwigshafen as a chemist with BASF — another firm that used slave labour from the camps — and now lived near Heidelberg. In signing off his letter he assured Levi of his sincere friendship, which was jumping the gun.

Primo Levi replied very politely, on 12 March, and sent Hety Schmitt-Maass a German translation of his letter, as she had requested. Although this is the only copy we possess, it is likely that Levi kept his promise and sent her copies of the whole of his correspondence with F.M.

Levi excuses himself for writing in Italian, but tells F.M. that his German is poor, and limited mainly to what he picked up in Auschwitz. Afraid that he might not be understood, he has therefore chosen his mother tongue, because what he has to say to him requires clarity and precision. F.M. may go on writing in German, and must let Levi know whether he is able to read French or English.

Levi's letter starts in a friendly way. He is pleased to be in communication with F.M., he says, because as he must know from Frau Schmitt-Maass, he has a good memory of him, and good memories about Auschwitz are rare. Then Levi moves on to the key questions, and here a touch of irony appears. He explains to

F.M. that, just like him, he is persuaded that every civilized man must aim to master the past; at the same time, he does not conceal the fact that he writes with some suspicion, because for the first time since the end of the war he is about to converse with a man who was on the side of the butchers, even if, as F.M. is claiming, it was against his will. Levi writes that he wants to believe in his correspondent's good faith when he claims in his letter that he came to work in Auschwitz against his will, but he implies that he has his doubts.

F.M. was set on a meeting, and when he wrote to ask Primo Levi if he might pay him a visit, Levi raised no objection to the idea. He travelled to Germany once a year for professional reasons, generally to Leverkusen and to Höchst, so he could easily make a detour — unless F.M. were to come on holiday to Italy, or his work for BASF brought him there.

Levi went on to answer the questions put to him by F.M., before asking questions of his own. He did not know what had become of Brackier and Kandel, his workmates in the laboratory. Goldbaum had died of cold and hunger during the evacuation of Auschwitz to Buchenwald.[4] Levi told F.M. that as F.M. had read *If This Is A Man* he already knew the basic things about him. He also wrote that after the Liberation, instead of repatriating him the Russians had transferred him to Byelorussia. He told F.M. about his family and professional situation. Since 1948 he had been technical director of SIVA, a varnish company in Settimo Torinese, which bought products from BASF.

Levi explained that he had no pretensions to being a professional writer. He had written his book in order to bear witness. But now he would like to put a few questions to F.M. In *If This Is A Man* he had drawn a portrait of Doktor Pannwitz because he wanted to analyse the type of human being he represented. Levi, who had stood on the other side of the fence, wanted to know whether F.M. thought his portrait seemed accurate or distorted. He knew that Doktor Pannwitz was dead, but not in what circumstances. Did F.M. know?

There followed some searching questions that must have given pause to F.M. Was it credible that the I.G. Farben management had taken on the prisoners they hired from the concentration camps with the aim of making their future less uncertain? Had their work been useful or not to I.G. Farben? Had the top management of I.G. Farben known about the existence of gas chambers in Birkenau?

Levi was not unmoved by the fact that F.M. had remembered his name, and those of his comrades. Here was a German for whom the *Häftlinge* had not been merely numbers. He asked F.M. what kind of image he retained of the Jewish chemists in the laboratory, and of himself in particular. For his own part, Levi recalled F.M. as a tall man — he would even say strong — aged about thirty-six years.

Then suddenly Levi introduces a doubt about the facts as represented by F.M. in his letter. It seemed to Levi that F.M. had been Doktor Pannwitz's superior in the management structure, not his subordinate. He met him only once in the laboratory of Building 938. As Levi recalls in *The Periodic Table*,

F.M. had asked him why he was unshaven, handed him a chit that allowed him to shave more often, and had given him permission to draw a pair of leather shoes and a clean shirt. He had also asked why Levi seemed so nervous. Levi wrote that he could not remember his reply, but that he did remember thinking that F.M. had absolutely no idea of his and his comrades' situation. Levi believed it was possible that F.M. might have felt pity and shame when he looked at them.

Writing with formal politeness, Levi asked whether F.M. would give him a few days' sight of the notes he had mentioned having taken in Auschwitz. Were they private remarks, or had they been meant for publication? He concluded by telling F.M. that he was glad to be in touch with him, and that he viewed their contact — by letter for the moment — as a gift of fate from which he had good hopes.

In his letter of 5 April, F.M. opened his heart to Primo Levi. According to him, in writing his book, Levi's intention was to tell the truth, and to put forward proof concerning the extermination of the Jews, so that young people should know and understand what had happened. If This Is A Man showed what horrors men were capable of committing. Here he was offering Levi a rather ponderous explanation of his own book: according to F.M., Levi had not meant to condemn men, so much as to stigmatize the enormity of genocide. Levi's was a nobler, higher goal, for he believed in man and in his future. Yes, said F.M., you believed that men who were worthy of that name existed even in the night of Auschwitz.

After praising the humanity of If This Is A Man, F.M. confided that he had been deeply touched by its account of individuals like Alberto and Lorenzo, who did good in a world of darkness. He then proceeded to tell his own story at greater length than in his first letter, hoping to gain his reader's understanding.

In 1933, after Hitler came to power, F.M. joined a National Socialist students' association, which became affiliated with the SA after a few months, without consulting its members.[5] In 1942 he was drafted into the Luftwaffe, and until 1944 he served as a private in the anti-aircraft corps in Duisburg. He felt angry and ashamed, he said, about the scale of the destruction and number of people killed. In 1944 he was released from armed service and posted to Auschwitz as a chemist. Till then, he claimed, he had no idea what the camp at Auschwitz was. Employed at first by BASF, he took a training course in Ludwigshafen, then left in mid-November for Auschwitz, together with fifteen young Ukrainians who had trained in the same establishment as himself. F.M. was an executive, and he took charge of their transfer to the camp. Levi remembered having seen them there.

F.M.'s meeting with the technical director in Auschwitz was brief, but during it he learned that the Jews who worked on the construction sites of the Buna Werke were required to do the hardest work, and no pity was to be shown to them. He took no notice of these instructions, he wrote, and when he suggested to his superiors, Doktors Hagen and Pannwitz, that he personally should choose the Jewish chemists who were to set up the Buna lab, his request was granted. As in his first letter, he stated that he knew nothing about the chemistry examination organized by Pannwitz, though it can be surmised that Pannwitz gave F.M. his list of the men selected and that he then took them on. It is obvious that F.M., writing twenty-three years after the events, is trying to claim the credit for the three appointments, as if the examination conducted by Pannwitz had not occurred.[6]

F.M. was greatly affected by the news of Goldbaum's death. He had found Doctor Goldbaum an interesting man, and a skilful and meticulous worker. He had not managed to trace him, but had always hoped to see him again, because a bond of friendship had developed during the brief spell he was working in the lab. He had even tried to get him a better job, but Goldbaum had chosen to stay in the laboratory rather than to accept a "promotion."

According to F.M., the laboratory was an "oasis" where he loved listening to the "joyful and melancholy" songs sung by the Ukrainian girls who worked there as assistants. He recalled how, a few days after his arrival, Levi had broken a piece of glassware and annoyed one of his bosses, who had sent for F.M. The reason he had told Levi not to worry was that the expression on his face belonged to a man in fear for his life. This episode had struck him so forcibly, he wrote, that he had told his wife and children about it. He said that he also remembered conversations with Levi during which they had discussed scientific problems. It was then, he remarked, that he had realized that men of inestimable worth were being coldly and brutally destroyed.

The tale of his achievements included the time when, as he made one of his daily tours of inspection on a bitterly cold day, he noticed a team of Jews who were unloading a wagon, and asked for them to be supplied with some of the sheepskin jackets that the Buna had in its stores. The Kapo issued the jackets, but when F.M. returned after half an hour, to see how things were going, he noticed that the prisoners were back in their striped summer uniforms again. A slavish superior had insisted that Jews were forbidden by the rules to wear fur-lined jackets.

Continuing his generous survey of his own good deeds, F.M. told his correspondent about the time when the technical director, accompanied by Doktor Pannwitz, came to inspect the laboratory and asked how it was going with the three Jewish chemists. He had been good-natured enough to inform his superiors that everything was fine. In the shambles of the German retreat, he had even found time to worry about Levi, having learned to his sorrow that he had contracted scarlet fever. But he knew that it was possible for him to be treated in Birkenau, because there was even a radiology department there. They had to take good care of prisoners who were still capable of working. F.M. wrote that when the decision was made to evacuate Auschwitz he had been very worried about Levi, knowing that he could not stand up to such an ordeal.

When the last train had gone, there were only 2,000 Germans left in Auschwitz, the majority of them women. F.M. had spent the last days in the

Bunker, because of the fire from the Russian artillery. On the Sunday at midday the order came to stop operating the plant, and that evening he had to drop everything and leave by bike. The next day, the 2,000 Germans were surrounded by the SS, who proceeded to select which among them was to be allowed home. When F.M. had asked Pannwitz, while they were sheltering in the Bunker, whether they were to receive an *Ausweis*[7] and a travel warrant when they left, the question went unanswered. As they waited in the frozen snow, half of the Germans, as well as Doktors Probst and Hagen, the senior managers, and laboratory assistants, took from their pockets the *Ausweise* that entitled them to board the last train home. On the other hand, F.M. and another chemist, both of them detached from the Wehrmacht and assigned to the ranks of the *Volkssturm*, faced a dangerous situation. So they went to see the technical director, and he authorized them to join the group picked out to return to Germany, to the surprise of those who, unbeknown to F.M., had already been granted that privilege.

F.M. told Levi that in 1946 Doktor Pannwitz had died of a brain tumour. F.M. did not seek to excuse him, but he explained to Levi that Pannwitz was not the only man whose cold ambition prompted him to obey criminal orders. The lesson was that vigilance was necessary, if such tragedies were not to happen again.

With a crass bad faith that verged on stupidity, F.M. answered Levi's question about I.G. Farben's reasons for employing a labour force of Jewish deportees on the Auschwitz site. He dared to maintain that the purpose of the Buna, which was built two years later than Birkenau, was to help at least some Jews to survive the war. There was no doubt at all in his mind that the order to have no compassion for them was a cover story. Knowing the enormity of what he was asserting, nevertheless he added that this had at least been the case during his own brief stay in Auschwitz, during which he did not recall a single action aimed at the murder of Jews.

Not content with falsifying history, F.M. proved equally unable to condemn his employer, and for a very good reason: he worked for a firm that was descended from it. With a pitiful wish to alter the past, F.M. turned instructions to be ruthless into compassion disguised. He dared to write that he did not remember anything done with the purpose of exterminating the Jews, even though it seems that the flames from the crematoria could have been visible from the Buna works during his posting there. He lived in Monowitz, where 10,000 Jewish slaves were exploited, starved, beaten, and sent to the gas chamber once they had passed the point of physical exhaustion. In his own laboratories he employed skeletal figures, terrorized, filthy, covered in sores, infested by parasites, dressed in stinking rags, and all this was camouflage for good intentions. In his reply, Levi showed extraordinary forbearance in the face of such clear repression of both the memory and the feeling of guilt.

Shortly before the end of the war, F.M., dressed in shabby civilian clothes, had found himself a prisoner of the Americans in a makeshift open-air camp. He was interrogated by an American officer who spoke fluent German and whom he identified as a Jew — how he made the identification he did not say. (Who but a Jew was going to ask a German to account for himself?) When this officer examined the contents of F.M.'s wallet he found his military identity papers, which recorded his transfer to Auschwitz. Very warily, he asked F.M. what his duties had been: did he make "soap," or did he "light the ovens"? F.M. said that he had answered that he could swear before God and men alike that he had nothing to hide about what he had done in Auschwitz. The officer dismissed him with a gesture, after throwing his wallet on the floor. His briefcase fell over, and the water ration that he kept in a can without a lid spilled over the floor.

F.M. returned to his family in Heidelberg at the end of June 1945. It was his first sight of his baby daughter, born the previous month. When he wrote to Levi, F.M. was the father of three daughters, two of them already married, and one son, Thomas, aged fifteen, who was a student in secondary school.

Having read an article on the writer Jean Améry in the *Frankfurter Allgemeine Zeitung*, F.M. then ventured a few observations about Améry's book *Jenseits von Schuld und Sühne*, in which he wrote: "No bridge led from death in Auschwitz to *Death in Venice*."[8] The soldier dies like a hero or a victim, whereas the prisoner selected was killed like a beast in the slaughter-house, so Améry maintained. F.M. cannot acknowledge this crossing over into a different dimension. Having quoted Rilke — "O Lord, give each his own death!" — he ties himself up in generalities about the aesthetic portrayal of death, and its power to offer intellectuals a partial awareness of their aesthetic of the art of living.

Tormented by his past, F.M. finally comes to the heart of the matter. According to him, men — he uses the word "we" to bind butchers and victims together — became neither wiser nor more profound in Auschwitz. He adds that, in an extermination camp, a man did not become either more human or more mature. He reveals that the *Lager* called into question the notion of human dignity. F.M. feels entitled to write "we" when he refers to himself and Primo Levi in the same breath. When he writes the sentence, "We came home from the camp," no warning voice seems to ask him whether his casual phras-ing is not obscene. He writes as if he, the German working in Auschwitz on behalf of I.G. Farben, and men like Primo Levi or Jean Améry could be equated with one another, could talk about the same return, or could conceivably be making the same statement if they spoke of coming home from the camp feeling ravaged, drained, and lost. Imagining that he speaks with the same voice as *Häftling* 174517, and so has crossed over the divide, in his rambling, F.M. proceeds to assert the idea that the transcendent spirit of man is a mere illusion once one has experienced Auschwitz. Straying into feeble ruminations about Sartre, he discards "philosophy." He asks Levi to reply in French if possible, but will accept some Italian, which he says he is ready to learn. He encloses a recent photograph with his letter, offers his "sincere friendship," and signs off with "yours, F.M."

Primo Levi replied on 13 May 1967. He began by explaining that he earned his living as a chemist, and only had time to write in the evening after work and on Sundays, so he did not see himself as a fully-fledged man of letters, and had very little spare time to answer the letters he received. Many years later, in his interviews with Anna Bravo and Federico Cereja, Levi summed up the reply he wrote to F.M.: "I, a layman, do not know what forgiveness signifies, I don't really know the meaning of the word, what it means to say: I absolve you of your sins, if you committed them. But you, tell me what you did."

The truth is that Levi was in a quandary, and made no secret of the fact to his correspondent. Germany inspired him with conflicting feelings. Towards Nazi Germany, his attitude amounted to "stern condemnation." As for his stance towards present-day Germany, he described it as "distrustful interest." He rejected collective judgements about the Germans, and preferred to judge one case at a time. Then he raised the case of his correspondent, and having duly expressed his sense of respect and gratitude, at the risk of wounding F.M. he ventured to help him to settle his score with the past — because Levi himself was in no doubt that there was a score to be settled. He added that every man — not only the Germans — had to submit himself to this kind of examination. In this context he used a Yiddish word he had learned in Auschwitz. It comes from the German, and F.M. would be able to understand it, but it was Yiddish that invested a moral significance in saying that a person was, or was not, a *Mensch*. A *Mensch* was a decent human being, one who was worthy of the name. Levi gave F.M. a subtly ironic lesson: every man, he wrote, must fight against "his neighbour's bad conscience and stupidity." The prescription may be debatable at the legal level, but at the moral level there is no verdict to debate. The Germans, and F.M. in particular, cannot evade their responsibility. F.M., through passivity, did nothing to prevent genocide. He never opposed National Socialism. In a tone neither aggressive nor full of hate, Levi recalls what the true law is. Recent or ancient, unfortunately a crime can go unpunished, but it cannot be forgotten.

Then he takes up F.M.'s use of the quotation "*Diligite inimicos vestros,*" "Love your enemies." It is a noble and heroic commandment, Levi observes, and he would love to live in a world and at a time when it would be conceivable to love one's own enemies. With blunt irony, he tells the man who is trying to rebuild and rehabilitate his own past that it is generous of him to have wished to ascribe such a sentiment to him, Levi, but frankly, he does not feel it. He feels capable of forgiving, even loving his enemy, only if he perceives genuine repentance in him. Jean Améry, who imagined loving his — Nazi — enemy only once, on the scaffold, or at the foot of the gallows, reproached Levi for being a forgiver. Levi replied:

For forty years I have tried to understand the Germans. To understand how that could have happened is a goal of my life. ...Forgiveness is not a word of mine. ...Wholesale forgiveness of the kind suggested is not

for me. Who are the Germans? I do not believe in God. For me, absolution has no meaning. No one, not even a priest, has the power to make
and to unmake. ... Anyone who commits a crime must pay, unless he
repents. But not in words. Verbal repentance is not enough. I am
disposed to forgive a man who has shown by his actions that he is no
longer the man he was. And not too late.[9]

Levi makes it clear to F.M. that repentance after the event is not repentance. If
such a man exists — one who meets the conditions that he has just set — then in
Levi's view he would no longer be an enemy. On the other hand, the man "who
persists in his will to destroy, to harm, and to create suffering" remains an
enemy still. It is out of the question to forgive that man, and more than that, he
has to be prevented from doing harm. As Levi aims to be an equitable judge, he
explains that this man does not necessarily have to be killed, or made to suffer.

In his letter to F.M. — written before the interview given to Anna Bravo
and Federico Cereja, quoted above — Levi stated his opposition to the hanging
of Eichmann. There was no doubt at all, Levi wrote, that Eichmann had to be
captured and put on trial. The Jews had done well to kidnap him, since the
legal systems of Germany and Austria were letting him live with impunity. Did
he want Eichmann to be sentenced to death, and the sentence commuted to life
imprisonment? What he wished for Eichmann, he wrote in a poem, "For Adolf
Eichmann," dated 20 July 1960. The last verse reads:

Oh son of death, we do not wish you death.
May you live longer than anyone ever lived.
May you live sleepless five million nights,
And may you be visited each night by the suffering of everyone who saw,
Shutting behind him, the door that blocked the way back,
Saw it grow dark around him, the air fill with death.[10]

Levi explained to F.M. that he had no longing for vengeance, even where the
Germans were concerned. On the other hand, he found himself in a state of
distrust towards everything that smelled of Fascism both in Germany and elsewhere. F.M. was not one of those who had resisted the system in any way, and
Levi informed him that he deeply respected those who had had the courage to
resist. Here he cited the case of a *Meister* in the Buna's Polymerization division, a
man named Gröner, who for several months brought bread in secret to a Dutch
Jew, one of Levi's comrades in captivity. In November 1944 Gröner suddenly
disappeared, and the rumour spread in the camp that he had been caught by the
SS and sent to the Russian front. For all his unspoken remorse and craving for a
good conscience, F.M.'s good deeds had never gone so far as to give a single
hunk of bread to the starving Jews who worked for him. Just as he had overlooked the project to exterminate Jews in Monowitz, so he had not noticed that
the three Jewish chemists in his laboratory were dying of hunger.

Levi offered further illumination to his correspondent by asking for news of

Stawinoga, the laboratory manager who during an air raid in December 1944 had taken him to a bunker, where prisoners were not allowed to go. Stawinoga told the *Häftlinge* chemists: "You three come with me." A guard admitted Stawinoga but told the three Jews to clear off. Stawinoga replied that it was all of them or no one, and he and the guard came to blows while the sky grew thick with Allied bombers. Here it must be noted that there is a slight divergence between two accounts of this episode written twenty years apart. In his letter to F.M. in 1967, Primo Levi refers to a German "green triangle" barring the way to Stawinoga; in *The Drowned and the Saved*, first published in 1986, the man at the entrance to the bunker is described as "a guard with a swastika on his armband" (*DS 169/139*). He was still wrestling to fend off Stawinoga and his protégés when the all-clear sounds and the planes droned further northward.

Levi continues his letter by asking F.M. if he knows what has become of Sina Rasinko, a Ukrainian girl from the laboratory, the only one who was kind and gentle, and who made no show of loathing the presence of the three Jewish chemists. Although he had not known until now that it was F.M., and not Pannwitz, who had chosen him to work in the laboratory, he tells him that he is inclined to accept his account. If it is true that he owes his survival to F.M., then he thanks him from the bottom of his heart. It would mean that he had considered the three Jews in the laboratory as *"Mitmenschen"* — fellow human beings. (There is every reason to believe that F.M. exaggerated his role in their conscription, as it was certainly Pannwitz who examined them.) Primo Levi ends his letter by offering to meet F.M. either in Italy or in Germany, so as to converse at their ease, and he signs off with a "friendly hand-shake."

F.M. writes again on 29 June 1967. His letter opens with some naive and pretentious compliments on Levi's work. F.M. is not the only one to have recognized his gifts as a writer: when he went to a conference which was attended by Hety Schmitt-Maass and Hermann Langbein, everyone agreed that *If This Is A Man* was the best eye-witness view of Auschwitz. Then he embarks on a bumbling analysis of the themes he has discovered in Levi's account.

He wonders whether Nazism exists in human beings in general, or whether it flourishes only in Germany. Is Nazism rooted in the nature of the German people? Does it have a history? Can Nietzsche and German idealism be linked to this movement?

Is the extermination of the Jews solely the work of a madman and his accomplices?

F.M. then turns to the work of Jean Améry. Améry has failed in his undertaking, he learnedly declares, and offers to send Levi his reflections on the subject. According to him, the debate between Herr Langbein and Fräulein Schmitt-Maass was a fruitful one: a sincere dialogue is always useful. There follow some right-minded considerations about population growth, the social order, and respect for others.

F.M. does not seem to have grasped that Levi's recommendations about people needing to examine their consciences were addressed in particular to him. He draws assurance from the fact that he is corresponding with a man of Levi's standing and integrity, but neglects to examine his own case, choosing instead to make some pronouncements about capital punishment. Considering that his views go further than Levi's, he explains that he is not in favour of the death penalty.

According to him, man aspires to wage a permanent struggle for mastery over history, but does not achieve it. There is another life he lives, and some synthesis of these two options is the highest that he can hope to rise. Then F.M. goes on to practical matters. He is still a chemist with BASF, and works as group manager in the laboratory where Carl Bosch adapted the preparation of ammonia for industrial production. His specialities include condensation, phenolic resins, malamine resins, foam materials, and varnishes. In other words, F.M., like Levi, is a specialist in resins, and believes that they have things in common in that field.

Levi had asked in his previous letter whether F.M. knew what had become of Gröner and Stawinoga, who had both given help to prisoners. He did not recall either one of them. On the other hand he did remember Sina Rasinko, who had supervised the other Russian lab assistants. As he was to spend his summer holiday in Germany that year, he could not expect to go to Italy before winter time. He assured Levi of his sincere attachment, and sent greetings to his family.

F.M., his conscience perhaps not salved after all through his exchange of letters with Primo Levi, phoned him a few months later to ask if he might pay him a visit. Levi named a distant date: a meeting the next summer in Pietra Ligure, where he owned a holiday home. He heard nothing more, until an announcement dated 18 December 1967, and sent by Gabriele G., one of F.M.'s daughters, informed him of her father's sudden death on 13 December. She enclosed a brief letter in which she referred to Levi's influence on her father. Because of it, she said, the whole family had often talked about him. Gabriele thanked him for the letters which had thrown light into a world of darkness. So if Primo Levi's words had not assuaged his sense of guilt, at least they had given F.M. a kind of moral boost with his wife and children.

———————

In *The Periodic Table* Levi presented his "reunion" and correspondence with F.M. — alias Doktor Lothar Müller — as the outcome of a discreet inquiry sent to representatives of a German firm that did business with SIVA. Levi embroidered only the circumstances of his crossing F.M.'s trail again. In the book he said that it was he who sent a copy of the German edition of *If This Is A Man* to the man he had identified, whereas it was Hety Schmitt-Maass and Hermann Langbein who put F.M. on to reading Levi's book. On the other hand, the date of 2 March 1967 given by Levi for his receiving F.M.'s first letter is accurate.

Writing in *The Periodic Table*, Levi makes it much clearer than he does in his quite lenient response to F.M. that he was not at all taken in. In the "Vanadium" chapter, he compresses two of F.M.'s letters, dated 2 March and 5 April 1967, into one. He also says that the first of his replies was written in Italian, which is true, and mentions having received an eight-page letter and a photo from F.M., which is also true. He wrote in *The Periodic Table* that he was "afraid" of the meeting suggested by F.M. — he did not want to see him. Rather than spell this out in his letter, he agreed to the possibility, but deferred it till some later date. Even if he did not view Müller as "the representative of the butchers," he was not prepared to let himself be manipulated by him.

What was Levi's retrospective verdict on F.M. in his book? His response to F.M.'s first letter was that: "It was visibly the work of an inept writer: rhetorical, sincere only by half, full of digressions and farfetched praise, moving, pedantic, and clumsy: it defied any summary, all-encompassing judgment" (*Table* 219). He rates as "improbable" the role that F.M. professes to have played in his survival, and grows more sceptical still, in the face of F.M.'s claim to have had conversations with him not only about scientific problems but also about "what precious human values are destroyed by other men out of pure brutality" (*Table* 220). Levi's only too detailed and indelible memories of the year he spent in Auschwitz contain no conversation with F.M. In any case, he points out, any such conversation was quite unthinkable in the Auschwitz world. He explains these false memories — so often reiterated that F.M. came to believe them, and which he also related to his family — as wishful thinking brought on by F.M.'s need to improve upon his image and his past. Only one man in the world can disbelieve his tale, and in his blindness and smug stupidity he tells it to that man. Levi comes to see him as "a typically gray human specimen, one of the not so few one-eyed men in the kingdom of the blind" (*Table* 221–2).

In one of his letters, F.M. had proposed to "overcome the past." There was no doubt in Primo Levi's mind that in contemporary Germany this "*Bewältigung der Vergangenheit*" was a euphemism that stood by common consent for "redemption from Nazism." In order to evade his own guilt, F.M. tried to take refuge in a pious fabrication, and more than that, to squeeze a favourable verdict out of the former *Häftling*. Even so, Levi gave him credit for the fact that he did feel guilty, and emphasized that it was not all Germans who would go so far.

The epilogue of the "Vanadium" chapter does not correspond with the true sequence of events. Levi says there that he did not send F.M. the critical letter he had drafted. The fact is that he did send the letter, and it was not until December, seven months later, that he learned of the death of the former chief of the Buna laboratory, who had sought for inner peace and respectability.

In 1960, Levi and Hermann Langbein, who had been deported to Auschwitz for acts of resistance, started to engage in a long correspondence that lasted till

1983. In his first letter, Langbein asked Levi for his permission to include a chapter of *If This Is A Man* translated by Heinz Riedt in a collective work, *Das Auschwitz Buch*, which was to be published by the Europäische Verlagsanstalt in autumn 1961, and launched at the Frankfurt Book Fair. Levi wrote back on 17 December 1960 accepting his request and saying that he had chosen the penultimate chapter, "The Last One," which describes the hanging of a resister. He informed him that the translation was in the hands of S. Fischer Verlag in Frankfurt. He wanted the text to be preceded by the poem "Shemà," which opens the book. After all sorts of difficulties, this anthology of texts was finally to appear in 1962, under the title *Auschwitz*. It contained two chapters from Levi's book, both "The Last One" and the final chapter, "The Story of Ten Days," about the long spell of waiting in Monowitz before the arrival of the Russians. Each testimony was preceded by a biographical note about the author.

In his letter of 5 December 1961, Hermann Langbein informed Levi that he had written an account of his book that he would send him as soon as it appeared in the review *Die Furche*.

Later on, Langbein made several requests for his friend to take part in various conferences and commemorations of deportation. Most of the time, Levi refused, pleading pressure of business. He could not leave SIVA and his family to attend so many events. He was so overworked that it took him several months to write to Langbein agreeing to join the International Committee of the Camps.

In the 1960s, Italy's economic take-off brought rapid prosperity. Turin, the town of Fiat and other major industries, saw its population double in ten years. Workers arrived in their thousands to join the production-lines, particularly in the car industry, where the many strikes and demonstrations were met by violent police repression. At the same time the masses of young people now attending university were organizing student protests in collaboration with the trade unions. Six months after May 1968 in Paris, Turin witnessed the upsurge of a violent radical movement in which students joined with workers in open warfare against the consumer society, capitalism, and private property. Turin lived through the era of *Lotta Continua*, *Potere Operaio*, and the Red Brigades, while far-right neo-Fascist groups with Mafia links developed their "strategy of tension" by organizing murderous terrorist attacks.

In 1961, the name of Primo Levi appeared for the first time in the world of French publishing. In its May issue, *Les Temps modernes* published a section of thirty-seven pages from the first French translation of *If This Is A Man*, "soon to be published by Editions Côrrea." The text, which consisted of four extracts, carried the botched translation, *J'étais un homme* — "I was a man" — which Levi was soon to insist on having withdrawn. Three chapters were presented under their original titles — "Our Nights," "This Side of Good and Evil," and "The Last Ten Days." The translator had converted "The Drowned and the Saved" into "The Victors and the Vanquished."

In 1962, Canadian radio produced a radiophonic adaptation of *If This Is A Man* which Primo Levi had very much admired. No doubt that is what gave him the idea of submitting to RAI, the Italian broadcasting corporation, his own version, different from the Canadian adaptation. In it he preserved the episodes best suited to radio, while retaining the form of the polyphonic, multi-lingual dialogue that was to be adopted in the stage production created by Gianfranco De Bosio in 1966. RAI accepted the radiophonic abridgement of *If This Is A Man*, and chose as director Giorgio Bandini, who assembled in the studio a cast of German, Polish, French, Yiddish, and Italian speakers. The production was broadcast by the RAI Third programme on the night of 24 April 1964, to commemorate the anniversary of the Liberation.

Being published by Einaudi, the prestigious publishing house in the Via Biancamano, had revived Levi's relish for writing after fourteen years of silence and an affluent urban life shared between the factory, business trips, home, and family.

One December day in 1961, Alessandro Galante Garrone invited Primo Levi to dinner with a few friends. During the evening, Garrone took him aside to ask some questions about his return from Russia, and this launched Levi into a description of that extraordinary experience so moving and expressive that Garrone broke in to tell him: "You've got to write this." Levi answered: "No, it's not possible," because he was afraid of publishing something that would fall short of *If This Is A Man*. Nevertheless, it would seem that Garrone's pleading made a powerful impression, because a few days later Levi embarked on the story of the haphazard adventures which had brought him by a round-about route from Auschwitz home to Turin in October 1945. Since he only wrote in the evening after work, on Sundays, and during holidays, he completed *The Truce* in November 1962. He had passed each chapter, as he produced it, on to the little committee of his old friends Bianca Guidetti Serra, Alberto Salmoni, and Silvio Ortona, and, listening to their advice, continually revised his text.

> When I wrote *The Truce* I chose the clearest possible language, in the hope that the information would come through without distortion to the reader, who by buying my books is making a contract with me. It would be a commercial fraud not to give him what he expects, and a discourtesy to write in a way that he did not understand. For these reasons, I impose a maximum clarity and the greatest concision upon myself.[11]

Levi would sometimes stop off at the Einaudi office in the Via Biancamano around seven o'clock in the evening, on his way home from the plant. He would ask Ernesto Ferrero, Italo Calvino, and Guido Davico Bonino to give him their frank opinion of his text, not wanting to leave anything to chance. The manuscript of *The Truce*, which took as its epigraph his despairing poem about Auschwitz, "Reveille," written on 11 January 1946, went at first to Ernesto Ferrero, who had just returned to Einaudi. After him it was read by Giulo Bollati, Italo Calvino, and Guido Davico Bonino. The enthusiastic decision to publish it was made during one of the traditional Wednesday afternoon readers' meetings.

The book came out in April 1963 and scored an immediate success. In Turin, it is usual for publishers to launch a new book in a bookshop or cultural venue and Alessandro Galante Garrone, who was present on this occasion, went up to his friend to congratulate him on his success. Levi replied: 'This book was born in your house!'

The greatness of the book, which tells the story of Levi's epic return to Italy from the forests and marshlands of Byelorussia to Turin, by way of the Ukraine, Romania, Hungary, Austria, and Germany, expresses itself in the artistry with which he revives and retraces the wind of freedom and anarchy that inspired and exhilarated him after the year of slavery in Auschwitz. All through the summer of 1945 he had observed his comrades in captivity, and the people of Russia. In *The Truce*, he recreated the excitement and fascination of his encounters with the unknown immensity of Russia, and with the soldiers and civilians whose anarchy and zest for life had so delighted him. The unfolding of those adventures, and of that liberating flight through a devastated Europe, is the story of a formative season. Twenty years later, Levi was to feel the need to revisit that world and that experience in *If Not Now, When?*. After all, *The Truce* was only a truce. The escape, the nomadic existence, and the far horizons receded when he returned to the comfort and security of his home base on the Corso Re Umberto. Yet the book does not end with the memory of that epic journey; it closes with the voice of the true reality of the world, as the *Lager* had revealed it, that "single word, not imperious, but brief and subdued. It is the dawn command of Auschwitz, a foreign word, feared and expected: get up, '*Wstawać*.'"

The success of this new book galvanized the sales of *If This Is A Man*, which reached 29,000 copies in a year. According to Giulio Einaudi, *The Truce* had sold over 320,000 copies by May 1989. The translation rights were also sold, but the book attracted little attention abroad. When it was published in Britain in 1965 it received respectful reviews, but sales were not significant. The French translation went unnoticed in 1966. On the other hand, in Italy, *The Truce*, which was nominated for the seventeenth Strega Prize in June 1963, was listed third among the finalists, behind Natalia Ginzburg's *Lessico famigliare* and Tommaso Landolfi's *Rien va*. The prize was awarded to Ginzburg's book on 4 July 1963. When *La Stampa* gave thumbnail sketches of the nominees, it described Primo Levi as a chemist, a description which placed him apart from the traditional definition of a writer.

Yet those who admired the author of *The Truce* — too little known and marginal a figure to receive his country's best-known literary prize — did not give up. On the night of 3 December 1963, on the isle of San Giorgio, a jury that consisted of readers chosen in secret from all over Italy, as well as nine writers who included Bonaventura Tecchi, Giovanni Comisso, and Michele Prisco, unanimously awarded the first Campiello Prize to Primo Levi, who was forty-four years old.

One day in September 1961 Primo Levi paid a visit to Alessandro Galante Garrone, who had been a contributor to *La Stampa* since 1955, to show him a document written in German. It was the patent filed by the house of Topf & Sons, the German firm that had built the crematorium furnaces in Auschwitz, and that now had the audacity to publish a brochure for crematorium furnaces designed for the use of those who wished to be incinerated after natural death. Topf & Sons, which stayed in business till 1975, dared to write: "This company, with a reputable name in its field, has been able to perfect its technique, which assures the utmost rapidity in this operation, and, in the humanitarian interest, thus reduces the waiting time for the parents and family, with a perfection ...."

These are the terms of a letter sent on 14 July 1941 by Topf & Sons (whose engineer Kurt Prüfer had already built the Buchenwald crematorium) to its customer, the *Zentralbauleitung* (Central Construction Office), in Auschwitz:

> With reference to your letter, in accordance with your request we are forwarding the model specifications for the Topf double-muffle, coke-burning crematorium furnaces. They are capable of burning 30 to 36 corpses in approximately ten hours. This target can be met every day, without malfunctioning of the furnace, and without damage. In addition, as you require, cremations can be effected continuously, day and night, without difficulty. We hope herewith to have rendered an excellent service, and we remain yours faithfully ....

Garrone was on the point of leaving with his wife for Malcesine, on Lake Garda, to celebrate their twentieth wedding anniversary. They arrived on the evening of 27 September 1961. The weather was glorious, the hotel was swarming with prosperous German tourists, but Garrone could still hear Levi's voice, and the terms of cold simplicity in which he had spoken. Through the open window he could also pick up conversations among the German tourists strolling in the street. He went to the window, watched them passing by, then went and sat down at his table with "the impression of writing under Primo's dictation." Garrone told me that as he wrote the article he phoned through to *La Stampa* that day, and which appeared in the next day's issue, he felt as if he were inhabited by a mind that was not his own. The following is part of what he wrote:

The Crematorium Furnaces of the Company of Topf & Sons

From one generation to the next, an extraordinary continuity in the application to work, in brilliant inventiveness and technical improvement, and in an active, ever faster and more economical rate of production; a mass industry that floods the markets thanks to its unbeatable prices and the good quality of its products: this is the most obvious aspect of the "German economic miracle."

My attention has been drawn to an astonishing example of that unshakeable fidelity to the past, that total selflessness in the service of the wonders of technology, that infinite capacity for undertaking what two lost wars, destruction, and catastrophe have failed to smother. I refer to patent no. 861,731 (class 24 d; group I) developed by the firm of J.A. Topf & Sons of Wiesbaden, published on 5 January 1953 by the Patents Office of the Federal Republic of Germany. It has to do with an invention — or, to be precise, an inventive improvement — concerning "a process and a device for the cremation of remains, cadavers, and parts of human bodies."

This will seem odd or simply disconcerting, but this firm, whose head office was then in Erfurt, was considered from the viewpoint of industrial mass production as one of the most gigantic enterprises in contemporary history, since it had attached its name to the rapid elimination, in gas chambers and crematorium furnaces, of millions and millions of human beings.

The documents of the Nuremberg trials, the various commissions of inquiry on war criminals, the Höss autobiography, and the Eichmann trial speak plainly. It has been demonstrated that similar prodigies of inventive simplicity, forceful organization, and perfect synchronization were achieved in the extermination camps. Things started on a cottage industry scale. The first, very amateur, slaughters were tiresome and expensive, given the ever-increasing number of the victims. The method, devised by a physician in the Auschwitz camp, Doktor Entress, and consisting of injecting phenol, first intravenously, then directly into the heart, although it was very fast and ingenious, rapidly proved inadequate.

It was necessary to "invent" something else, while the endless convoys of Jews and political opponents converged from all over Europe on those dismal labour and extermination camps. Just at that moment, when the gas chambers were being prepared, came the discovery of Zyklon B, originally meant for killing vermin, rats in cellars and in the holds of ships. This substance was produced by a firm belonging to the great complex of I.G. Farben Industrie. As Primo Levi said in Turin on 23 February 1961, in his memorable evidence, I.G. Farben carried out the orders very promptly, cashed the invoices, and paid no heed to anything else. Had there been an invasion of mice? It was better not to ask, so as not to know. The German industrialists shielded their consciences and made profits on the sale of their poison.

In reality, those industrialists and wholesalers knew very well. Doktor Peters, general manager of the company that provided Zyklon B to the SS, tried eight times and finally acquitted, stated in order to exonerate himself that he had acted in all good faith, in the conviction that, after all, the poison "might be a comfort for people already condemned to death in any case." In 1955 the Frankfurt court, unable to accept Doktor Peters' excuse, acquitted him because — it wrote this verbatim in its verdict (even though all doubt had been dispelled by thousands of documents and the evidence of Höss) — there was a lack of proof to certify that the deportees had actually been killed with Zyklon B!

The gas chamber was complemented by a highly efficient crematorium furnace. J.A. Topf of Erfurt was a firm with a respectable past that went back for several decades, which produced furnaces for cremations in Protestant cemeteries. It had built up a solid reputation, and had made new improvements in its equipment all based on the extremely practical principle of "recycling," using the heat produced by the combustion of the bodies.

Its finest hour came in 1942, with Himmler's order to implement the "final solution." To this day there are plaques that bear the name of the firm on the Buchenwald furnaces, but not on those in Auschwitz-Birkenau, which the Germans blew up when they abandoned the camp. But in Auschwitz it is still possible to consult part of the correspondence exchanged between the Topf managers, the SS, and the police command. What emerges is that Topf was snowed under with requests to build bigger and better furnaces. In order to install and get them working, the Topf technicians and staff paid several visits to Auschwitz. So they knew what those furnaces were used for.

To salve their consciences, no doubt the directors told each other that, really, it was not they who exterminated; they only provided the post-mortem service, hygienic, beneficial, and pious, thus preventing the build-up of decomposing corpses and the contamination of the air, they reduced everything to quintals of cinders that the waters of the Vistula carried away. But under pressure from the SS they built ever more "colossal" furnaces, to speed up the work rate (the requirements were such that the firm asked for a rise of 6 per cent on the price agreed) .... Those who built these crematorium furnaces therefore knew that they were playing a key role in an enterprise of mass extermination.

But obviously, for the firm of Topf, formerly of Erfurt, now of Wiesbaden, what mattered then and matters today was and still is its love of the art, work well and conscientiously done, continual improvements in the methods of production, and comfortable profits .... [12]

After reading the article by Alessandro Galante Garrone, Augusto Monti — who had taught Norberto Bobbio, Cesare Pavese, and Massimo Mila in the Liceo Massimo d'Azeglio — sent a letter to the author to tell him that from now on he belonged to "La Banda," the group of his disciples, which he took as a great honour.

By way of adventures, Levi now had to content himself with business trips in Italy, and to Germany, and Britain on behalf of SIVA, when he and Federico Accati would pay visits to customers and suppliers: Ciba-Geigy in London, and Bayer in Leverkusen.[13] Signor Accati sometimes took one of his daughters along, and when he himself could not make the trip he would entrust one or the other of them to his right-hand man. Luisa Accati was fascinated by the ethnological detachment that Levi maintained in his relations with the Germans.

When Paola Accati lived in England, she looked after the contacts between SIVA and her father's British customers. One night, while drinking in a pub with one of them, it surprised her to hear Primo Levi, merry after a glass or two of wine, tell a slightly risqué joke that he had heard in Russia in 1971. There was nothing improper about the story, but merely to have told it struck her as out of the ordinary for Levi. When he had put a few hundred kilometres between himself and his everyday life, it seems that he felt a little more free and easy.

In the 1960s, Primo Levi, Lucia, and their children sometimes made summer visits to the Valle d'Aosta, where the Levi family used to spend the summer when Primo was a child. They stayed in Brusson, not far from St Vincent, where he was arrested by the Fascist militia in 1943. There he ran into Hugo Sacerdote, now an engineer in Turin working for the European Space Agency, whom he had known since his teenage years, when he used to holiday in Courmayeur with the Artom family.

In 1965 Einaudi published a textbook edition of *The Truce*, intended for schools and colleges. *If This Is A Man* became part of the curriculum in 1973, with notes by Primo Levi and a historical appendix. Both books scored an immediate success with their young readers, and there were numerous reprints. In this connection it is interesting to note that the house of Einaudi, represented by Fabio Coccini, the head of its educational department, had to defend itself in 1992 against accusations published in *L'Unità* by some fourth-year pupils at a college in Bergamo who felt offended because the edition of *If This Is A Man* that was issued to them apparently had had some supposedly obscene passages about homosexuality and natural functions removed. Einaudi replied that this edition had been prepared in 1973 by Primo Levi himself, and Fabio Coccini defended it on the grounds that "we are dealing with young people in mid-adolescence who might misunderstand the meaning of a sentence." Finally, Coccini conceded that his concern had been not so much with what the young might think as with the attitudes of certain teachers who would never have accepted the book without these cuts. This censorship affected not only Primo Levi but other famous writers published by Einaudi, among them Leonardo Sciascia, Italo Calvino, and Mario Rigoni Stern, who explained that there was a time when no headteacher would ever have opened his doors to a book published under that imprint.

In December 1965, in the auditorium of the Romano cinema, Massimo Scaglione's young *Compagna del Teatro delle Dieci* ("Company of the Theatre of the Ten") staged versions of three short radio plays by Levi — *La bella addormentata nel frigo, Il versificatore*, and *Il sesto giorno* — commissioned by RAI and recorded in September 1965, and published in Italy in the following year in Levi's story collection *Storie naturali*.[14]

The *Storie naturali* are not mainstream science-fiction stories. Levi had shown some of them to Italo Calvino, his favourite reader at Einaudi, and Calvino wrote to him on 22 November 1961:

> I've read your stories. This science fiction, or rather biological science, always appeals to me. Your fantasy mechanism that's always set in motion by a scientific–genetic fact has for me an intellectual and even poetic power of suggestion akin to the morphological and genetic writings of Jean Rostand. Your humour and subtlety save you from the danger of lapsing into the sub-literary, the danger that threatens anyone who uses literary works in order to perform intellectual experiments of this kind. Some of your notions — such as the Assyriologist who deciphers the tapeworm mosaics — are first-rate, and the evocation of the origin of the centaurs has a credibility enhanced through its poetic strength.
>
> Naturally, you still lack the sure hand of the writer who is in full possession of his stylistic personality; like Borges, who uses the most disparate cultural suggestions and transforms each invention into something exclusively his own, and whose rarefied atmosphere is like the signature that identifies the works of all great writers. You move in a dimension of intelligent prospecting on the margins of a cultural–ethical–scientific panorama that should be the view of the Europe we live in. Without doubt, your short stories please me most of all because they imply a common civilization markedly different from the one that is presupposed in so many Italian works. And the underlying background of tenuous provincialism, of "Piedmontese eccentricity," also adds a special fascination to the minor elements of the collection, like

the story of the old doctor who collects smells — almost a story by a Mario Soldati converted to positivism.

Altogether, it's a direction I encourage you to work in, but most of all so as to find a position from which things like this can with a certain continuity establish a dialogue with a public capable of appreciating it. No doubt we could put together a small collection of unpublished stories and publish them in the *"Nuovi Argomenti"* collection.

For the stories of a different inspiration, the prospects are not so good. The ones about the camp are fragments of *If This Is A Man*, which detached from a broader narrative have the limitations of a sketch. And the attempt at a Conradian epic about mountain climbing gains all of my sympathy, but so far remains an intention.

We'll talk in person soon. Best wishes,

Calvino

Will you write me a book for young people?[15]

In spite of Calvino's encouragement, the twenty or so stories by Levi inspired by his work in the factory and by science are not his best writing. Calvino preferred them to the series of sketches set in and around the *Lager* world that appeared in *Lilit e altri racconti*,[16] which drew its inspiration from various sources: Auschwitz, chemistry and science, nature, and a kind of ironic and fantastic fiction that recurs in *Storie naturali* and *Vizio di forma*. Levi himself believed, with justification, that his stories about his experiences as a young man, about the camp, and his return to the Jewish tradition — in other words those that came from his other half — were more successful. That said, the Turinese literary critic Giovanni Tesio, who met Levi several times towards the end of his life in the course of writing an authorized biography, points out that in reading his short stories one has to look behind the lucid and rational public persona that he kept turned towards his readers.

Levi said that he felt awkward about having written short stories inspired by his life as a chemist, so much so that when Einaudi agreed to publish them in September 1966 he chose to use a pseudonym. Fearing that the author of *If This Is A Man* and *The Truce* might be considered to have demeaned himself by turning to lighter themes, he chose the pen-name Damiano Malabaila from the front of a shop in his district, on his way to work. He behaved as if offering the serious readership of his first two books a collection of entertainments in the form of fables was some sort of "minor transgression." Yet in Levi's view there was a link between the *Storie naturali* and the world of the camp, because that world was "the greatest of the vices, the most threatening of the monsters generated by reason."

I said to myself that between that name and these stories a connection exists. An allusion fostered by one of the deep levels of consciousness.

Malabaila means "cattiva baila" — bad nurse. It seems to me that from many of my stories there wafts a vague odour of milk gone sour, food not fresh, in other words of contamination and malediction.[17]

In spite of everything, Levi claimed a close link between his short stories and his first two books, because both showed man reduced to a state of slavery, whether by man or by technology. All the same, he was afraid to present himself to his ex-deportee friends "wearing a different skin." He felt, he said, "like a deserter," and when he had published science-fiction stories in newspapers, some people had sent him letters telling him how angry it made them feel. Levi had answered by explaining the liberating joy he experienced in the act of writing. He had made them understand that he refused to be "labelled solely as a writer about the concentration camps."

Because of the pseudonym, the sales of *Storie naturali* were low, but in the literary world the incognito lasted no longer than a few days. These stories had to wait for fifteen years to be widely read, when they were republished under the author's real name. Even so, on 14 January 1967 the thirty-first Bagutta Prize, chaired by Riccardo Bacchelli, and with a jury that included Eugenio Montale and Dino Buzzati, was awarded to Damiano Malabaila, alias Primo Levi, chosen as "writer of the year." To a storm of applause, he received the sum of 100,000 lire, a substantial amount at the time. But the critical response was dismissive. One anonymous critic, writing in the review *Quaderni*, saw no originality in Levi's stories, which he found disappointing after his excellent first two books. Only the caustic wit of Cesare Cases dared to come to Levi's defence in an article entitled *"Difesa di 'un' cretino"* ("Defence of a Cretin"):

> Honoured editor! May an old reader and contributor to your esteemed review be permitted to add a codicil to the excellent defence of a cretin by Franco Fortini published in your issue 29. The "cretino" I would like to defend is Primo Levi, liquidated for his *Storie naturali*. I do not want to discuss the verdict on the book. Personally, I find the standard of the stories variable, but some of them are really good.
>
> Levi has carved himself an Italian zone of science fiction in which, instead of the cruelty of the best American science fiction, he offers a humanist melancholy, and instead of a bare, immediate style, a linguistic awareness linked to a vast cultural background. Instead of skyscrapers and astronauts, an atmosphere of scientific practice, the old professor and traveller. It is precisely the authenticity and modesty of the enterprise that make me fond of the results, and I much prefer them to any other venture in the genre that I know of ....[18]

12   Chemist and Writer

On 19 November 1966, the public at Teatro Carignano gave a long ovation to the author of *If This Is A Man*, whose theatre version, written in collaboration with a young actor, Pieralberto Marché, had just been staged by the Teatro Stabile of Turin, in a production by Gianfranco Bruno, Giovanna Bruno and Marta Egri, with décor by Gianna Polidori.

Levi had worked for two years on this adaptation, in collaboration with Marché and De Bosio. The cast had rehearsed for six weeks in Rome, followed by another three in Lucca. It was made up of fifty-two actors, some of them foreigners recruited by the Company of the Seven Nations: among others, there were two Frenchmen, three Poles, three Hungarians, three Israelis, and a German. The Israelis, French and Italian actors played prisoners; the Poles and the Hungarians, the Kapos; the German, the SS. Some Italians were included in the chorus. The few women in the production did not appear as prisoners, but as voices in the oratorio. Influenced by Julian Beck's and Judith Malina's Living Theatre, the producers had decided to condition the actors by making them crawl under heaps of tables and chairs, before starting work on the text itself. Most of the elements in the camp were represented: the Blocks, bunks, kitchen. The actors, with shaven heads and clad in striped uniforms, carried heavy 50-kilo beams that made a fearful crash when dropped on the stage. The actor who played the part of Primo Levi was on stage all the time. The scenes, made up of long monologues, succeeded one another without telling a linear story.[1]

The production, staged in the Metastasio di Prato, was to have been the main event of the prestigious International Theatre Festival in Florence, but the disastrous floods of 4 November 1966 — the same floods that destroyed the unsold warehoused copies of the first edition of *If This Is A Man* — forced the group to transfer the production to the Teatro Carignano in Turin.

Levi, who had been very nervous about this new departure, wrote in the preface to the stage text:

It seemed to me that *If This Is A Man* had already been rehashed too often, and there was a risk of it boring the public. I was also afraid of the theatre itself. The theatre audience is there, it judges you. The aim was to pass on our experience as immediately as possible to a vast and varied public. I feared that they might think of it as a kind of personal exhibition. For this reason I have changed the name of the chief protagonist, who is called Aldo in the stage version, so as not to make it an autobiography. The stage version is not the story of a single victim but

303

the voice of a people, of millions of victims of the ideology of death. I wanted to write a European play, and several theatres have responded to it. In so far as it was clear to me, I accepted Marché's central idea. This ought not to be an exercise in horror. The drama of the prisoners in the camp was not to be performed with an excess of realism.

We have tried to show the drama of the lack of communication among the deportees. Auschwitz was a hostile world whose people knew nothing about it because they had no common language. When I arrived, the standard languages were Polish and Yiddish. Then it was Hungarian. Dutch, French, and Russian were also spoken. The guards spoke a jargon of their own. To communicate with the SS, there were Kapos of all nationalities. For the Italians, it was a situation that gave rise to very great suffering. I was afraid of not managing to establish a dialogue, or remaining dumb. I was aware that there was an intention to destroy me as a man.

Each actor speaks his own language. The aim was to recreate in the theatre, with the greatest possible authenticity, the anguish of the prisoner unable to either understand or to make himself understood. There are those who may be capable of bearing solitude. I needed to prove to myself that I was not yet an object. Whatever happened, one had to be capable of responding very quickly to orders, and failing to understand them could be fatal.

It was difficult to achieve a theatrical balance between what was said in Italian and what was said in the foreign languages. We have, I hope, succeeded in reconstructing that Tower of Babel atmosphere that made our existence even more monstrous, without lapsing into excessive realism as a result.

The SS orders come through loudspeakers. They are impersonal, their ferocity is cold. What needs to be understood is said in Italian. The other speeches function purely as sound, and the audience should make no attempt to understand them. Our aim is to convey the absolute isolation of a man in Auschwitz.

It can happen to many individuals and peoples to think that every foreigner is an enemy. This conviction infects the soul, and usually expresses itself only in an unpremeditated way. But when this way of seeing becomes an organized system, the major premiss of a syllogism, then at the end of the chain there is the *Lager*.

The book crystallized stories that the survivors had told dozens of times when they returned. As with Coleridge's ancient mariner, to present such inflammable material in the theatre required channelling, bringing out a universal meaning, inducing the spectator to arrive at a verdict, without dishing it up ready made.

One of our preoccupations was to avoid a sentimental adherence to the victims, and to convey the tragic essence of each instant. We have also introduced a chorus that is not a Greek chorus. These are monologues for several voices. We have included even the marginal episodes of life in the *Lager*, the moments of repose, of reverie. Which enabled us to show the resources that survived among the victims. I hope to have prompted the audience to condemn the ideology that made possible the destruction of man. Our work is intended for that generation that does not like to mention these things because it feels obscurely responsible. I would rather that no one should be able to leave the theatre saying: "Poor them!"[2]

The critical reception was excellent, and Einaudi published the text of the adaptation. By an odd coincidence, the performances of *If This Is A Man* had been given at the same time of those of *The Investigation*, Peter Weiss' documentary drama account of the first Auschwitz trial in Frankfurt of 1963–65. The Italian Theatre Institute awarded *If This Is A Man* its prize for the best production of the year. Levi was deluged with letters from members of the audience, and wrote brief replies to every one. Yet despite its success, the piece received only fifty performances in Turin; it would have been prohibitively expensive to go on tour with a company of fifty-two actors.

In 1965 Levi returned to Auschwitz for the first time on the occasion of a Polish ceremony held to commemorate the liberation of the camp. "The return was less dramatic than it might seem. Too much noise, little time for reflection. Everything has remained in good order; the façades are clean. Too many official speeches." But although he "didn't feel anything much" in Auschwitz I, his visit to Auschwitz II, Birkenau, where nothing had changed, caused him "a feeling of violent anguish."[3]

It was at this time that Levi started to do regular educational work with school and college students, which involved him in two decades of travelling around Italy to describe what he had seen and endured in Auschwitz. He listened indulgently to the naive, offensive, or superficial questions that were bound to be asked by pupils incapable of imagining the barbarous world of the *Lager*, and did his best to answer them. What struck him in particular was the fact that the young talked about the extermination of the European Jews as if it were ancient history, and were taken aback not to find themselves listening to a very old man.

Levi felt that he had a good relationship with his own children, Renzo and Lisa, yet both of them refused to raise the subject of his Auschwitz experiences with him. He thought that they had absorbed it all, because his house was full of books, documents, and photographs of the camps, but they did not want to hear their father talk about it, though they had read his books. He himself would have liked to tell them about what had happened to him, but when he tried to do so, with a nine-year interval in between, each of them turned pale and burst into tears. They gave their father's books to their friends to read, but could not bear to hear him talk. They wanted to have a "normal" father.

In June 1967, when the Six-Day War broke out between Israel and the Arab states, Primo Levi issued no public statement, as he was to do during the invasion of Lebanon in 1982. But he was photographed with other Jews from Turin waiting to give blood for the Israeli wounded.[4]

On 25 January 1970 Primo Levi agreed to sign a statement timed to coincide with a demonstration organized by the International Committee of the Camps and by the Union of Jewish Deportees and of their Beneficiaries, in Belgium. Hermann Langbein, the leading light of the International Committee of the Camps, never failed to invite Levi to the conferences he organized, but Levi was unable to travel to the Palais des Beaux-Arts in Brussels, pleading, as usual, that SIVA, his family, and his writing took up all his time. Langbein sent his friend the text of an appeal issued the year before, when Wladyslaw Gomulka, first secretary of the Polish Communist Party, had launched an "anti-Zionist" campaign, then proceeded to expel most of the last surviving Jews from Poland.

> Twenty-five years ago in Auschwitz, the largest National Socialist concentration camp, was liberated.
>
> In the course of the quarter of a century that has passed since the day of 27 January 1945 when the first Russian troops went into it, mankind has only slowly come to learn what happened in that extermination camp: the mass murder, organized with bureaucratic precision and indifference, using modern technological methods, of men whose only "crime" was their origin, which offended the masters of the hour. In their millions, they were taken to Auschwitz, and only a few tens of thousands of them returned....
>
> ...We make it our duty to raise our voice today, although we know that no party, no political tendency, no nation, and no religious community has the right to speak in the name of the victims of Auschwitz, for those who were taken to the gas chambers had very diverse fundamental beliefs for as long as they still drew breath. Anyone who speaks in the name of the victims of Auschwitz must abide by what was the common will of all those who were consigned to that factory of death: must see to it that such a tragedy can never happen again. And the fundamental lesson to be drawn is this: that we must fight at any time and in any place where attempts are made to persecute people because of their origin, and we must unmask all allegations under which such intentions may be camouflaged. In the present age, it is only too easy in

fact for racial hatred to culminate in extermination achieved by technological means and reaching unimaginable proportions, as Auschwitz
clearly showed. Therefore it is necessary to oppose every anti-Semitic
tendency, and any contempt shown towards Gypsies or any other
human group, before it is too late and it reaches the point of murder.

We, the survivors of Auschwitz, feel that it is our obligation to call
this imperative to the attention of each individual.

We know that, twenty-five years ago, anti-Semitism was a widespread attitude deliberately fostered among both the Germans and the
Austrians, and that it did not disappear with Hitler's suicide. The point
is therefore to thoroughly condemn any tendency that works in that
direction, and to urge and encourage the Germans and the Austrians to
oppose all generalizations and all discriminations made about human
groups.

Yet nor must we overlook the fact that other peoples too harbour
anti-Semitism. We cannot be silent when we see, twenty-five years after
the destruction of the Auschwitz gas chambers, the Polish authorities
driving from their country, in shameful conditions, the few surviving
Jews, and solely because they are Jewish.

What is frightening is the fact that these anti-Semitic measures
should be taken by the authorities of the very country where the vilest
of the Nazi extermination camps were located, to which the vast majority of the Jews were deported and murdered, and where for these
reasons the murderous consequences of racial hatred ought to have been
felt more intensely than in any other country.

Today, on the anniversary of the liberation of Auschwitz, we raise
our voice, in the name of the millions of our people harried to their
deaths, against the fact that Jews, among them veterans of Auschwitz,
should be expelled from Poland. That is a disgrace to the Polish
authorities.

At the same time, we pay tribute to all of our friends from the cruel
era of the camps who live in Poland or in other countries where it is
forbidden to protest against these shameful expulsions, and in this
connection we raise our voice against any misapprehension that might
tend to blame the Polish people as a whole for these disgraceful and
infamous measures.

In launching this appeal, we believe that we carry out our duty
towards the victims of Auschwitz.

Levi travelled to Germany quite often, and sometimes to Britain, but in 1968
he went to Moscow for the first time. He went back again in November 1971,
en route to Tolyatti, where during a long visit he worked on a resin for car
brakes for Fiat, who were building a plant on the bank of the Volga. It

delighted him to return to the great expanses that he had crossed after his liberation from Auschwitz. As he watched the skilled Italian labour force at work on the enormous site, he marvelled at the prevailing atmosphere of carefreeness and anarchy. Describing the trip (in French) to Charles Conreau, he wrote on 22 June 1972:

> It's really funny: a lot of the characteristics I noticed among the Russians at the time of "the truce," and that I put down to the historic moment, are in fact absolutely ingrained; their muddle, their indifference to passing time, their *joie de vivre* and rowdy warmth broken by unexpected silences. Under the surface structures, which have undeniably been shaped by the Revolution, one has the clear impression of an eternal Russia that neither the tsars nor Stalin were able to suppress, and which has its roots in the earth itself, the frightful distances that separate the towns, the climate, and the distant history.

Levi was equally struck by the respect with which the Russians treated the skilled Italian workers. This attitude aroused his curiosity, and he had every opportunity to observe them, since he ate his meals "elbow to elbow with them" every day, in the site canteen. Little by little, the idea of a book evolved in his mind. He wanted to pay homage to these inventive, cheerful characters who without him were fated to remain anonymous. That was the source of *La chiave a stella* (*The Wrench*), which relates the adventures of Libertino Faussone, a rigger from Turin, a specialist in complex metal structures.

Back in Turin, Levi satisfied his dream of adventure at his desk. By writing several books whose action was set in distant places, he appeased a longing for travel kept constantly repressed. "As for my travels, since I haven't done them, well, I've invented them," he told Giorgina Levi in an interview for the monthly magazine of the Jewish community in Turin given when *The Wrench* was published in 1978. "I also had in mind the idea of producing a linguistic entertainment." The book, which uses the dialect of Piedmont, created a political storm in Italy. Its English translation in 1986, by William Weaver, went almost unnoticed, although Bernard Levin wrote in the *Sunday Times*:

> This is not a book for journalists. Civil servants, too, will feel uneasy while reading it, and as for lawyers, they will never sleep again. For it is about a man in his capacity as *homo faber*, a maker of things with his hands, and what has any of us ever made but words? I say it is "about" the man who makes; truly, it is more a hymn of praise than a description, and not only because the toiler who is the hero of the book is a hero indeed — a figure, in his humanity, simplicity, worthy of inclusion in the catalogue of mythical giants alongside Hercules, Atlas, Gargantua and Orion. He is Faussone, a rigger.[5]

Introduced to *La Stampa* by Arrigo Cajumi, who had reviewed his first book there, Primo Levi began to contribute to "La Terza Pagina," "Page Three," the cultural page of the great Turinese daily, owned by Fiat. He started with articles concerning persecutions of the Jews, and in particular a text about the Warsaw ghetto, but he did not want to be labelled solely as a specialist on the Nazi camps.

When he had written something for *La Stampa* — it could be a poem, a story, or a column — he would put it in a folder and bring it to the office of Lorenzo Mondo, then editor-in-chief of the cultural pages. There he would sit down unobtrusively, and if Mondo was busy on the telephone he would leaf through a few of the books sent for review. His eyes were full of kindness, Mondo remembers. "He smiled, not with his mouth, but with his eyes. He would offer me this article, and say: 'If you don't think much of it, you can throw it away.'"[6]

After that, he would drop by to exchange a few words with his other acquaintances among the journalists in the office. A particular friend was Gabriella Poli, who joined *La Stampa* in 1966. She used to make a selection of the articles she thought likely to interest him, and after 1975 he gave her his manuscripts to read. "He asked specific questions. He wanted to know if the text was interesting, and if it was clear. Writing, for him, was a procedure just as rigorous as the one that governs the making of a telephone, for example. Everything had to work."[7]

Levi took notice of the advice and criticisms of this experienced journalist. For instance, when she pointed out that he had killed off Dov, one of the heroes of *If Not Now, When?*, too soon, he resurrected him. He called the press cuttings chosen by Gabriella "the Friday cuttings," because that was the day she sent them. He was also on close terms with Giorgio Calcagno, and after his death Calcagno and Poli collaborated on a book dedicated to the memory of Primo Levi, *Echi di una voce perduta*. Two other friends were Alberto Sinigalia and Carlo Casalegno, the assistant editor of *La Stampa*, who was shot and fatally wounded by the Red Brigades in November 1977.

While he was contributing to *La Stampa*, Levi was also writing a series of cautionary tales heralding the potential threat to civilization posed by technological disasters — ideas that would often occur to him during his work in the SIVA laboratories in Settimo Torinese. They appeared in his short story collection *Vizio di forma*. One of them, "*Versio occidente*," ("Westward"), puts forward a theory of suicide, showing that this idea had been in his mind for some time, even though as a good Piedmontese rationalist he condemned it.[8] "Westward" tells the story of a pair of ethnologists, Anna and Walter, who are intrigued by the collective suicide of the lemmings. After witnessing their drive to the place of their voluntary death, and capturing six for investigation, Anna and Walter attempt to understand the behaviour of the rodents. Anna asks Walter:

"Why would a living being want to die?"
"And why should it want to live? Why should it *always* want to live?"
"Because...well, I don't know, but we all want to live. We are alive because we want to live [...] Life is better than death: that seems an axiom to me." (*Sixth Day* 146)

Walter reminds Anna of her months of postnatal depression after the birth of their daughter, and she remembers:

"That hole. That void. That feeling ... useless, with all around me useless, drowned in a sea of uselessness. Alone also in the middle of a crowd: buried alive amidst everybody else buried alive." (147)

A little later, Walter remarks:

"Now I also wanted to tell you that between a person who possesses the love of life and a person who has lost it there exists no common language." (147)

He goes on to say:

"Life does *not* have a purpose; pain always prevails over joy; we are all sentenced to death, and the day of one's execution has not been revealed; we are condemned to watch the end of those dearest to us...." (148)

At the time when Levi wrote these lines, his mother was already very old. Perhaps he was not reconciled to the idea that some day she was bound to die before him. These lines also show that the memory of Auschwitz was constantly present in his mind. The metaphor of collective death as a force more powerful than the will to live permeates this story, possibly presented as a metaphor of the camp.

At first, the laboratory investigations of the blood, urine, and other samples taken from the two groups can find no biological difference between the lemmings that have committed suicide and those that have chosen to live. The pharmacology department steps up its efforts "to identify or synthesize the hormone that inhibits the existential void" (*Sixth Day* 150).

Anna and Walter embark on a journey up the River Amazon, and then along a tributary of the River Cinto, in search of an Indian tribe, the Arunde, that they have seen mentioned in an anthropological journal. These people, once widespread in the region, have dwindled to a single village, owing to their abnormally high incidence of suicide. Walter questions the village elder, who informs him that his people have never had metaphysical convictions, and that they value individual survival very little, and national survival not at all.

When they return, the two ethnologists learn that the biologists have discovered a "factor L," an alcohol present in minute quantities in the blood of "all healthy mammals, including man," but absent from that of the migrating lemmings, and which proves able to restore the will to live in humans who have lost it. It turns out that the Arunde metabolism does not secrete this compound, so Walter sends the Arunde elder "a small package which contained a dose of factor L sufficient for one hundred persons and for one year" (*Sixth Day* 153). He also decides to spray a solution of factor L over columns of lemmings scurrying to their deaths through a gorge that leads to the sea, but their momentum is too great, and he dies in the gorge under their desperate tide. A few days later, Anna reads a message from the Arunde people, addressed to Walter and returning his package because "we prefer freedom to drugs, death to illusion" (*Sixth Day* 154).

Seen with hindsight, the story is a sinister omen, though it rang no alarm bells at the time. This profession of faith by which the truth of death supplanted the illusion of life, and even the instinct to live, showed that Primo Levi remained essentially the prisoner of the camp, together with the masses of the drowned who had been reduced to ashes.

Levi published *Vizio di forma* in 1971, under his own name, but its critical reception was lukewarm, and it was the only book of his that failed to collect an award. Its sales were modest, and the publisher could not sell the translation rights. It was reissued fifteen years later, and in January 1987, three months before he died, Levi added a preface sending an ironic letter to the publisher:

> Your proposal to reprint *Vizio di forma* after more than fifteen years both saddens and delights me.... It delights me because it thus revives the least appreciated of my books, the only one not to have been translated, not to have received a prize, and which the critics turned up their noses at, accusing it of not being sufficiently catastrophic.[9]

He sounds fairly resigned in a letter written on 22 June 1972 to his friend Charles Conreau, the schoolteacher from Provenchères and his former companion in the infectious ward in Auschwitz. In it he writes that, in concrete terms, not much has changed in his life: for twenty-four years he has worked at SIVA designing varnishes. "It's almost a life!, which always annoys me, but why change? Retirement is not so far away." He goes on to say that he published a volume of stories in 1966 and another the previous year. "Neither has met with the success of the two books you know about, and with good reason. They haven't been translated into French. More generally, for me the great wave of literary adventure is receding, which gives me a little sadness sometimes, but not despair." Just when he was on the verge of writing three more major books, one of which, *The Periodic Table*, was finally to bring him international recognition, Levi imagined that his literary career was over.

Reflecting on the other aspects of his life, he confesses that he cannot really complain about them: he has no money worries, everyone is well, his children — Lisa is twenty-four, Renzo fifteen — are grown up, but, he adds: "I often have the feeling that the 'colour' period of my life is over and gone, and what remains is only 'black and white'."

311

Levi believed that his literary career was in decline, at a time when the controversy over *The Wrench* and the success of *The Periodic Table* and *If Not Now, When?* were still to come. Already he was talking of sadness, "but not despair," and yet he thought that what he had in store was "black and white." His life in "colour," covering his professional and family life, the year in Auschwitz, and the time in Byelorussia and Eastern Europe, was at an end.

It is interesting to note that the image used by a doctor friend who described his past life as episodes in "colour" and even "Technicolor" should have struck Levi so forcibly. This metaphor made such a deep impression that he mentioned it to Risa Sodi in the interview he gave her for the *Partisan Review* published in 1987, and also in his interview with Philip Roth, published in the *London Review of Books* in 1986.

He said to Risa Sodi:

A very intelligent friend of mine told me one day: "That period [in Auschwitz] was in Technicolor and the rest of your life has been in black and white."... It was certainly painful, but also — it may seem cynical to say so — it was also the most interesting moment in my life. It was an adventure.[10]

And to Philip Roth:

A friend of mine, an excellent doctor, told me many years ago: "Your remembrances of before and after are in black and white; those of Auschwitz and of your travel home are in Technicolor."

Levi passed through several cycles of depression, and the melancholy tone of his letter to Charles Conreau suggests that even when it seemed to be dormant the depression was always ready to break out. In fact his work, and particularly his poetry, is transfused with a vein of deepest gloom that runs entirely counter to the optimistic, didactic current, derived from the Enlightenment and from Piedmontese positivism, with which he identified himself until the end of his life.

Primo Levi had paid an impromptu visit to Charles Conreau one day in September in the early 1970s, *en route* for one of his frequent business trips to Germany. He arrived in the small village of Lusse, near Provenchères, in the company of his employer, Federico Accati, and Accati's daughter Luisa. He made the detour specially to see his friend again, and caught him by surprise in his garden, picking pears:

Without thinking, I gave him the fine golden pears I was holding, and they set off again leaving me slightly dazed by such a marvellous and unexpected visit, my head full of memories after that quick look-in from Primo, that elegant man, full of life, whom I had left, many years before, sick and skeletal on his pallet in Auschwitz.[11]

In April 1972, Primo Levi wrote to Hermann Langbein to say that he had been reading and rereading his *Menschen in Auschwitz*. Yet in spite of his urging, it was proving impossible to persuade Einaudi to bring out an Italian edition of the book which was being published in Vienna that year. This rejection may be compared to their equally inflexible refusal, more than twenty years before, to publish *If This Is A Man*. Once again, although by now the reality of the extermination camps was no secret to anyone, Einaudi felt that the time was not right to publish a book about Auschwitz. The decision is all the more mysterious because the firm was founded by three intellectuals deeply opposed to Fascism, including Leone Ginzburg, later tortured and murdered in German hands. It is puzzling that the publishing house should have been so reluctant to enlarge on the memory of the genocide of the European Jews, at a time when they were in fact publishing all manner of political texts.

Primo Levi was tied to Hermann Langbein by his memories as a veteran of Auschwitz; he usually addressed him as "caro amico." He continued to fight for the publication of his friend's book, and refused to be discouraged by the setback with Einaudi. Of course, Levi was not acting for the sake of their shared experience in the main camp and in Buna-Monowitz. He was utterly convinced of the need for the book to be published, and many letters passed between them both as part of their efforts to reach an agreement with the publishing house of Mursia in Milan, which stalled for a while before asking for substantial cuts in order to keep the sale price down. Levi did all he could to keep them to a minimum, but in the end they had to settle for a compromise.

Levi read *Menschen in Auschwitz* slowly, between two business trips. "I haven't yet had time to finish your book at a time when my work in the plant has grown frantic, and leaves me little free time; I travel, work, and fume." In fact the equipment and staff relations manager at SIVA had been killed in an accident, and until he was replaced Levi had to take on his late colleague's job as well as doing his own. He was constantly on call, always on the move around the store yards and offices in the plant. In cases of emergency — never to be taken lightly in a chemical plant — they would wake him in the middle of the night. This pressure of work made him long for retirement, and he confided to his correspondent that he had been through "a new phase of depression that only lasted for two months, however, and that stopped abruptly just a few days ago in an amazing way (it was a matter of hours! isn't that strange!)."

He added at the end of his letter that he had recently returned to Tolyatti for a couple of weeks. It was a boring town. "In Russia, everything is uncomfortable and makeshift." But the forests and the river were as silent, beautiful and untouched as on the day of creation. How much longer could this miracle last?, he wondered.

Levi finished reading *Menschen in Auschwitz* in December 1972, just when Einaudi rejected the book. He felt bitter, but not really surprised. In a letter to Hety Schmitt-Maass dated 28 December 1972 he confesses that, despite what he has been through, he has read Langbein's book with "the painful feeling that the time to talk about the Nazi camps, Nazism and Fascism in such a detached, 'historical' way has not yet arrived: we are still (at least in Italy) — worse, we are *once again* — in the state of mind not of talking about Fascism, but of fighting against it."

Levi went on to list some of the terrorist attacks that had cost many lives in Italy over the past three years. He noted with bitterness that Peitro Valpreda, the anarchist accused of having planted a bomb in the Banca Nazionale d'Agricoltura in Milan on 12 December 1969, killing sixteen people, had still not been brought to trial. Three days after the bombing in Milan, another anarchist, Giuseppe Pinelli, had suffered a fatal fall from the fourth floor of Milan's main police station. No case was brought against the senior police officers implicated, but a few months later one of them was found murdered in front of his house. In November 1972 the publisher Giangiacomo Feltrinelli, the friend of Fidel Castro and Che Guevara, had blown himself up while trying to sabotage an electricity pylon. A wave of arrests had followed his death. Levi talks about the Fascist "strategy of tension" whose aim was to spread a sense of fear and insecurity intended to open the way to the man of the hour. And he adds that, very fortunately, in Italy strong men have too close a link with the Fascist past to be credible.

13 "You Will Write Concisely and Clearly"

In the month of March 1968 Primo Levi had made a brief but important visit to Israel with a group of about twenty Jews and intellectuals associated with *Giustizia e Libertà* who wanted to understand the political situation in the country in the year that followed the Six-Day War. Remarkably, the Italians chose to stay, not in the Jewish part of Jerusalem, but at a hotel in the Arab quarter. They met political leaders in the Knesset, and drove to Eilat through the Negev by night, escorted by tanks that patrolled along the frontier with Jordan. Levi took advantage of his stay to telephone one of his former comrades from Monowitz who had immigrated to Israel, and whom he had not seen since 1945. They made an appointment to meet in the lobby of a hotel, and although the place was full of people, they knew each other at once.

Back in Turin, on 2 April Levi wrote to his cousin Paola, who lived in Israel and whom he had seen there. The brief visit was fading "already into the darkness of the past, as generally happens with all 'heteronomous' memories." He had come back with a deep nostalgia, and a sense of regret for not having seen and understood enough. He spoke of a wish to return soon, and yet he never returned. He added that he had much preferred being guided through the country by his cousin and her husband than by "the very efficient [woman] colonel" who had been the official guide of their group.

Vizio di forma, the collection of stories that came out in 1971, was coolly received by the critics, who blamed the author for his failure to offer a clear political message. Levi took no notice, and continued to stand by his very classical ideas about literature. He told a journalist from *La Gazzetta del Popolo*:

> The novel is alive. It can still be alive today. The novel informs in a stealthy fashion, unknown to the reader. Each of us harbours at the bottom of his heart the childish desire to have someone tell us a story. It is not important to know whether a novel is classical or experimental, as long as the experimentation is not so reckless that it harms comprehension, and the conveying of the facts.[1]

The controversy that surrounded the publication of the stories — whose inspiration was so different from that of the first two books that it disconcerted some professional readers — took Levi by surprise. The critics were inclined to perceive these short stories as some sort of allegory about Auschwitz, but Levi disagreed. More than that, he responded to their arguments by rejecting their definition of the politically committed writer.

Indifferent to the critical objections, Levi went calmly to work again. He started a new book, *The Periodic Table*, whose broadly autobiographical inspiration derived its structure, its organizing principle, from a key feature of his knowledge as a chemist, namely Mendeleev's table of the elements. He recalled the history of his family and the events that had shaped his life in twenty-one chapters, each of them bearing the name of one of the elements in the Russian chemist's classification system. They give a framework to the story of a series of trials suggesting oppositions — matter and mind, reality and fiction, order and chaos. The characters of the people in the book are often associated with the chemical and physical properties of the element whose name heads the chapter in which they appear. In other cases the element itself becomes a kind of character, and makes a concrete intervention in the story.

Levi describes his trade as a chemist, his victories and defeats, and realizes his long-standing dream of building a bridge between the classical and literary culture of the traditional high school and the culture of science. When the man who taught him literature in the Liceo d'Azeglio stated that the sciences had merely an informational value, Levi's hair had stood on end. The narrative and scientific themes fuse in *The Periodic Table* to present a kind of mirror of man at war with evil and with hostile matter, and Levi is convinced that the condition of the chemist reflects the human condition in general. Throughout the book, he glorifies the nobility of work and the grandeur of scientific culture. Presented in this light, the idea so dear to his heart, which sees work neither as a sentence of punishment in the biblical sense nor as a kind of alienation in the Marxist sense, no longer offended the critics.

> I have tried to show that a science or technique can be not only the subject of a book, but a school of thought and even of literature. I would be happy for a physicist or biologist to imitate me. As for the doctors, they have already been aware of it for a long time.[2]

Wishing to prove that it is not only Greco-Latin culture that can give meaning to literature, in answer to questions about *The Periodic Table* he replied:

> I write because I am a chemist. My trade has provided my raw material, the nucleus to which things join.... Chemistry is a struggle with matter, a masterpiece of rationality, an existential parable.... Chemistry teaches vigilance combined with reason. When reason surrenders, Nazism and Fascism are not far away.[3]

No only was Levi a militant chemist, it was chemistry that taught him how to describe the world without a rhetorical gloss.

He, the sheltered bourgeois living with his wife and children, mother, and mother-in-law, in the house where he was born, confessed that he wrote with two images present in his mind: those of the prehistoric hunter setting out to kill bison, and of Conrad's sailor, confronting the gigantic forces of the raging sea.

He submitted his manuscript for the critical approval of Italo Calvino, his literary director at Einaudi, who lived in Paris most of the time. Calvino liked the book in general, but suggested some changes that Levi eventually decided not to pursue:

Paris, 12 October 1974

Dear Primo

I've looked at the new version of *The Periodic Table*, and I feel that it's going very well. I've read the new chapters "Iron," "Phosphorus," "Nitrogen," "Uranium," "Silver," and "Vanadium," which enrich the "chemical" (and moral) biography.

Putting carbon at the end and appointing it as the symbol of the writer's experience is a good idea. It reinforces the heterogeneity of lead and mercury, which don't disrupt the whole.

As for "Argon," I still have the same reservations to bring up about the fact that it is to open the book (in spite of its value as a prologue), because it is the only chapter in which the chemical element is metaphorical; here too the structural distortion would be less glaring if the chapter was placed in the middle of the book. (For instance: return from deportation, reunion with surviving family, reflections on what this family continuity has been.)

But if the chapters follow one another in the order of the atomic weight of the elements (which some exceptions, it seems to me), I say no more. Altogether, to my mind, the book now exists and I'm happy with it.

I hope to see you soon.[4]

Calvino's most emphatic reservation had to do with the positioning in the book of the "Argon" chapter, which tells the story of Levi's ancestors, but there was nothing coercive in Calvino's remarks, and the book came out with the "Argon" chapter quite logically opening the narrator's autobiography, even if, to the regret of the literary director, strict formality was flouted because the gas argon was only metaphorically present in these pages.

The writing of *The Periodic Table* was very slow, because Levi had only Sundays to devote to it. In fact the chemical industry had suffered the full impact of the oil crisis that followed the Yom Kippur War, and the author wrote to Hermann Langbein in January 1974 that his work had assumed such "a frantic rhythm" that he felt compelled to turn down the other's invitation to visit him in Berlin.

After the rejection from Einaudi, he had sent *Menschen in Auschwitz* to Mursia the Milanese publishers. A month later, on 10 and 15 February, Levi wrote twice in five days to Hermann Langbein to tell him the good news that the editor Roberto Tozzi had contacted him to say that he was recommending the book for publication. However, he had also said that cuts would be required. Levi then confided in his friend about his worries as plant manager: he was having to fight hard at a time of economic crisis to preserve the jobs of the SIVA staff — himself included. He added, in a manner that is unusually abrupt for Levi: "It is for this reason that my attention at this moment is rather diverted from the 'Auschwitz' side, which is our past, to the 'chemistry-factory-everyday job' side, which is my present." Before the letter closed, an anguished sentence escaped him: "I know that you understand me: since 1945, never have I found myself in such a critical situation."

In April 1974 he had to inform Langbein that Mursia was proposing to cut no fewer than a hundred pages from *Menschen in Auschwitz*. He considered this a poor response, but suggested that his friend should come to some arrangement, because "in this time of Fascist restoration, testimony like yours would be very topical and important."

During the summer Levi's mother, now eighty years old, fell ill. He wrote to Langbein saying that the operation originally planned for June had been deferred until October, which meant that once again he would be unable to attend the commemoration, this time of the thirtieth anniversary of the Liberation. There had been little progress with the publication of Langbein's book, except that the editor considered that the author's suggested cuts did not go far enough. He was now asking for its length to be cut from 550 to about 400 pages, and suggested that Levi might do the job — an offer he had refused. Levi was very upset, and no longer knew how to advise his friend. He awaited his instructions.

The public launch of *The Periodic Table* took place on 4 June 1975, in a room in the Cultural Union, in the Palazzo Carignano. The book was an instant public and critical success. A spate of articles greeted it as a major achievement. On 12 September 1975, Arrigo De Benedetti, Mario Tobino, Diego Valeri, and Geno Pampaloni awarded *The Periodic Table* the twenty-sixth Prato Prize. Two days later he made a television appearance in a programme devoted to his life and work.

In the decade from 1965 to 1975, the sales of *If This Is A Man* had reached the 200,000 mark. In addition, between 1973 and 1976 Einaudi published six editions of the version for schools, a total of 70,000 copies.

In 1975, after working there for almost thirty years, Primo Levi decided that it was time to leave SIVA and retire. The parting was friendly, and he accepted a post as consultant for two years, to enable Federico Accati to find and induct his successor. During these years he did not break contact with the plant, but his hours were now more flexible and his work more creative. For example, he built up an index of 10,000 file cards, arranged in three long boxes, covering SIVA's products and chemical patents — some of them his own inventions. To make them easy to consult, he used a punched-card retrieval system.

He revelled in those early days of freedom, for it was this that he had dreamed about while he pursued his duties as a father, manager, and chemist. Merely to be able to wander at random through the streets of Turin reminded Levi how much he had loathed having to crawl through traffic jams in the mist and cold of the early morning to go to work in Settimo Torinese. Now he could stroll in the Via Po, where his paternal grandmother had lived, or in the Via Roma, remembering the Via Roma Vecchia where his legendary maternal grandfather had sat in state in his textile store. He would push on as far as the Parco Valentino, and walk the wooded pathways on the hill.

And there was more to his new freedom than being able to come and go as he pleased in the city he loved. There was also the prospect of long days spent as a man of letters — a status he had never dared to claim in the past, and which the Italian literary world had been reluctant to concede, although a narrow circle of true admirers had seen to it that almost all of his books were nominated for literary awards. All the same, these had been spare-time achievements, fitted into evenings, weekends, and vacations. How much new ground he would be able to cover, now that his hours were no longer restricted! But things did not turn out exactly as he had imagined.

In the last interview he gave to Roberti Di Caro, for the weekly literary supplement of *La Stampa*,[5] in January 1987, he admitted that he was not the person his readers believed him to be:

> The truth is that I live a neurotic life with woeful blanks between books.... Before, writing was, so to speak, a need that filled all of my evenings. I wrote at least three books while practising the trade of a chemist. I fail to understand how I found the time to do all that at once. Now I write less than I did then, and with less intensity.

However, in 1975 he was not yet facing the writer's block he feared so much, and that he complained about during the final months of his life. Even though he had felt that the pressures of his work at SIVA constricted his life as a writer, it had also provided opportunities to escape from a family situation overshadowed by his mother's state of health. The days of his travels with Federico Accati were over. Now he was forced into a home-bound routine. His mother had suffered a stroke that left her paralyzed down one side and completely dependent, while his eighty-three-year-old mother-in-law had gone blind. The two old ladies had to be cared for night and day, so much so that even though Levi and his wife had nurses to help them, they were seldom able to leave Turin.

The idea of taking retirement in order to find freedom, and to answer the calls he received on his time, had been a delusion. He found himself sharing house arrest with a bed-ridden mother who demanded his presence, especially at mealtimes. Travel was out of the question. His obligations were to make no plans, and to stay at home and write.

In autumn 1975, Scheiwiller of Milan published a book of twenty-seven poems by Levi, written since his return from Auschwitz, under the title *L'osteria di Brema*. The first three poems in this slim collection of sixty-six pages were familiar from other contexts. "Shemà" had been the epigraph to *If This Is A Man*; "Alzarsi" ("Reveille") to *The Truce*; "Erano Cento" ("There Were a Hundred") to *Vizio di forma*.[6] The other poems, known only to his friends, had been published in Turin in 1970 in a small, untitled, private edition of three hundred copies.

All through his life, Primo Levi had occasionally written poems, prompted by an impulse he did not understand. He could go for years without writing any, then suddenly he would produce five or six poems in three days — starting, as he explained, with the "nucleus" of a line. There were to be eighty in all. Some which had first been published on the "Terza Pagina" of *La Stampa* were republished together with those in the first collection by Garzanti Editore of Milan in 1984, under the title *Ad ora incerta* ("At an uncertain hour"), which is a translation of a line from Coleridge's *The Rime of the Ancient Mariner*, to whom Levi liked to compare himself because of his own irrepressible wish to tell his story to everyone he met. His favourite lines came from part VII, verse 16:

> Since then, at an uncertain hour,
> That agony returns:
> And till my ghastly tale is told,
> This heart within me burns.

The publication of his poems in *La Stampa* brought Levi many letters and occasional phone calls. He explained to a reader from Zurich who had read *L'osteria di Brema*:

> I wrote my first poem after the period I spent in Balangero, near Turin, in 1943. I wrote about fifteen others in 1946, after my first book came out.... The others I wrote between 1949 and 1974. Why? Well, writing poetry belongs to a mental process that I do not know very well, and have little control over. My rational side represses all the rest. The poems are the fruit of emotionality that I find difficult to analyse. As a writer, I have tried hard to be clear. What lies behind our rationality we do not know. Our own depths are unknown to us. It may be that poetry is the fruit of two left hands.[7]

Levi did not consider himself to be a great poet, but he did not shy away from his impulse, which he thought of as reflecting his genetic inheritance. He knew little about prosody, and described his occasional need to write poems as an illness. Dark and morbid themes pervade them. The collection *Ad ora incerta*, tragic in its tone, derives from the tradition of the classical moralists. The first poem on Auschwitz, written on 28 December 1945, portrays the Buna factory, with smoke rising from its innumerable chimneys, and starving shadows that once were free men and women trudging through mud to go to work. Other poems recall the dawn reveilles in the camp, the Jews of Eastern Europe lost in the gas chambers, and the transit camp of Fossili di Carpi. Not all the poems are sombre: a tender one recalls an evening in June 1946, when he was alone in Avigliana, where he was working for Duco-Montecatini. Lucia, his fiancée — whose name resembles the Italian for fireflies, *"lucciole"* — was not with him.

> I've left the fireflies alone
> (There were lots of them all along the path),
> Not because their name resembles yours,
> But they are such gentle dear little creatures;
> They make every care vanish.
> And if someday we want to part,
> And if someday we want to marry,
> I hope the day will fall in June,
> With fireflies all around
> Like this evening, when you are not here.[8]

Brian Swann and the poet Ruth Feldman (who also translated the stories collected in *Moments of Reprieve*) translated Primo Levi's first privately printed collection of poems for Menard Press, a small London publisher, under the title *Shemà*. In 1976 they received the John Florio Prize, awarded for the best translation from Italian. Ruth Feldman came across the poems when Hannah Jona, a cousin of Levi's, who taught Italian language and literature at the Centre for Adult Education in Cambridge, had recommended them to Ruth Feldman, who attended her course. Feldman was moved by the poems. She wrote to the author and travelled to Turin to meet him, and a friendship developed from that evening. Ruth Feldman loved his "long unwrinkled face, and his bright and smiling eyes."[9] She found no devastating traces there of past experiences. Levi later wrote many letters to Feldman, who became a confidante of his. When she first met him in Turin, his books had not yet acquired an international readership, so that when she tried to publish his *La Stampa* article, "Why Auschwitz," in the United States, no editor was interested.

A number of the poems that Primo Levi sent to Ruth Feldman were written in a vein of desperation. Some of them expressed violent feelings of rage and hatred against the Nazi butchers, which do not appear in the rest of his work.

The collection *Ad ora incerta* had contained all the poems in *Shemà*, plus a number of others. Einaudi included these, together with a group of later poems, in volume II (published in 1988) of their edition of Levi's complete works. Ruth Feldman later translated the additional poems in *Ad ora incerta* on her own, as well as the later poems and others previously uncollected. They appear beside the poems translated in collaboration with Brian Swann in the *Collected Poems* published by Faber and Faber in London and Boston in 1992.

Ruth Feldman, who spent part of the year in Rome, saw Levi again when he came to receive the first Strega Prize, the fifth prize awarded to his work. When they met he gave her his short story collection *Lilit e altri racconti* (literally, "Lilith and other short stories"), which included a number of episodes dealing with the camp of Buna-Monowitz that he had deliberately left out of *If This Is A Man*. "Here are my stories," he told her. "Do as you please with them."[10] She translated the stories, and tried to find a publisher, but again without success, because *If This Is A Man* and *The Truce* had failed to find a readership when first published in the US a few years before, with their titles changed respectively to *Survival in Auschwitz* and *The Reawakening*. Ruth Feldman's translation of the Auschwitz stories from *Lilit* was eventually published in 1986, under the title *Moments of Reprieve*.

On 10 April 1976 Levi wrote to his friend Langbein to tell him that he would not be able to attend the rally in Riva to which he had been invited because of new worries about his mother's health. He added: "Here in Italy we are passing through weeks of extreme distress and uncertainty." In fact the campaign for the national elections of 1976 had been fought in a climate of violent clashes between neo-Fascists and revolutionary groups with considerable student memberships, such as *Lotta Continua* (literally, "the struggle continues"), during which several people died. The result of the elections highlighted a growing tension between the parties of the left — the PCI, with 34.4 per cent of the votes, and the PSI, with 9.6 per cent — and the Christian Democrats, who maintained their vote at 38.7 per cent, just as in 1972. Giulio Andreotti reached a compromise with the PCI by forming a "government of national solidarity," and the revolutionary groups, which had suffered a severe defeat in the regional and local elections of 1975, launched into a spiral of terrorism, while the police displayed an inexplicable laxity. The Red Brigades stepped up their attacks on the police, journalists, and magistrates, and killed some dozens of people before and after their notorious kidnapping of the former prime minister, Aldo Moro, on 16 March 1978, and his murder on 9 May of that year.

On 11 December 1976, quite unintentionally, Levi sparked off a sharp public controversy with the writer and literary critic Giorgio Manganelli when he published an article in *La Stampa* entitled "On Obscure Writing."[11] Two key passages read as follows:

> Therefore emphatically renouncing any regulative, prohibitive or puni-
> tive claim, I would like to add that in my opinion one should not write
> in an obscure manner, because a piece of writing has all the more value
> and all the more hope of diffusion and permanence, the better it is
> understood and the less it lends itself to equivocal interpretations.
> (*Trades* 170/158)

> But then the howl is an extreme recourse, good for the individual as
> tears, inert and uncouth if understood as a language, because that by
> definition it is not: the inarticulate is not articulate, noise is not sound.
> For this reason I am fed up with the praises of texts which (I quote at
> random) "sound at the limit of the ineffable, the non-existent, the whine
> of the animal." I'm tired of "dense magmatic imposters," of "semantic
> refusals," and stale innovations. White pages are white, and it is best to
> call them white; if the king is naked, it is honest to say that he is naked.
> (*Trades* 172/160)

An indignant Giorgio Manganelli replied in the *Corriere della Sera* issue of 3 January 1977. He accused Primo Levi of harbouring a terrorist ambivalence in his heart, under a smooth and civilized veneer, and wrote:

> I wonder how a writer can brag about being a typical case of rational-
> ity triumphant. I am deeply dismayed by the use of the word irrational
> in a solely negative or inaccessible sense. Primo Levi maintains that the
> healthy is preferable to the unhealthy, and clarity to the ineffable. That
> sounds like a typical case of existential terrorism.

Levi answered Manganelli at length, but as his reply was published on the letters page of *La Stampa* it passed almost unnoticed:

> The belief that the written page is the symbol of the ultimate chaos to
> which we are doomed is an idea typical of our century.... I prefer to
> read someone who writes in a clear and luminous way. I prefer clarity
> to confusion ....
>
> It grieves me that Manganelli has got himself into this state because
> of my article in *La Stampa* "On Obscure Writing," and I thank him.
> This is the first time I have let myself be dragged into a controversy. It
> is not an even match, that is easy to see. In fact, Manganelli is perfectly
> entitled to be obscure, and he is. Whereas in my case I have a duty to be
> clear, or rather naked. Manganelli describes me as an existential terror-
> ist. That is an apposite example of contradiction in terms, and of
> obscurity. But there it is, he has that ability, and I have not. Because I
> prefer the healthy to the unhealthy, among other things, I am asked

what it means to be healthy. Let us assume that the two words are equivalent. I used them in referring to Ezra Pound, who seemed to me to be unhealthy in all the usual senses of the word. On the other hand I would define as healthy someone who uses the full range of the proper physical and mental functions, hoping that Manganelli will not ask me, because if he does I will play him the following trick: that he mustn't ask me for explanations. So I hope that Manganelli will not ask me what the full range of the functions means. And I insist on my preference for what is healthy. In fact, the unhealthy, as I have defined it above, suffers, and I don't like suffering. Either my own or other people's. So I am existential, I admit it, but why a terrorist? I believe that I have never practised terror towards anyone, least of all in the article in question. I admit just as readily that I was wrong to identify clear with rational. However, it seems better to me to be clear, because an obscure message can be violent, as happens with Nietzsche. The obscurity of politicians is one of our national afflictions. It is fine and strange that Manganelli and I should find ourselves agreed about a proposition that states that "no author deeply understands what he has written"; but for him, that incomprehension seems normal, and even desirable, and for me it is a failing and a cause for concern.[12]

This was not to be the last time that Levi was attacked for his rejection of obscure writing. Two years later, during a public debate at the *Unità* festival, Paolo Volponi disputed the validity of the clarity deliberately chosen by Levi because, he said, of what he called his "internal clarity."

Levi could not bring himself to accept that it was necessary to write obscurely in order to express the confusion of the world. As an heir of the Enlightenment who professed to be an atheist but whose atheism was subverted by his fondness for quoting from the Bible, the *Pirkei Avot*,[13] the *Shulchan Aruch* and the Talmud, it was Levi's view that the writer must try to rise above his own intellectual conditioning to develop a broad and organized vision of the world.

In 1977 Primo Levi wrote the preface to the Italian edition of the long poem by Yitzhak Katzenelson, *The Song of the Murdered Jewish People*, begun in October 1943 and completed in 1944 at the Vittel concentration camp in France.[14] The poet thought that he had found a refuge with his eldest son Zvi, after managing to get out of the Warsaw ghetto with the help of a Honduran visa. His wife and two other sons had been murdered in the gas chambers. For him and his son, Vittel was only a stay of execution. On 29 April 1944 both of them were deported, by way of Drancy, to Auschwitz, where they were gassed on arrival. The manuscript of the poem was discovered in three sealed bottles buried at the foot of an old tree in the camp in Vittel.[15]

14   Man of Letters

After serving his term as a consultant, Levi broke his ties with SIVA and set out to realize his dream of a writer's career. Although he was highly respected, and his work had been honoured by a number of literary awards, he had yet to achieve the status of a full-time man of letters. He did not belong to the publishing world, and did not venture into fashionable experimentalism; consequently there were some Italian critics who did not consider his work important. In their view he was merely a chemist who had written two books, in too conventional a style, about his successive experiences in the Auschwitz camp and in Byelorussia.

In the beginning, Levi found a promising theme that drew on the memories of his long journey to Tolyatti, and on two other trips to the Soviet Union. He dug out an exercise book that contained his outline of a book about a rigger called Libertino Faussone, whose professional skills took him all over the world. Levi had met many of the workers sent by Fiat from Piedmont, and who spoke the same graphic factory dialect as Faussone, in the town that sprang up out of the Russian forest in the space of a few months. He loved to hear them talk about their lives.

Levi started by doing comprehensive research in specialist journals on the technical problems a rigger had to deal with. Certain episodes related in *The Wrench*, such as the "sick tube" in the second chapter, drew on his fund of experience at SIVA. The tube was part of an acetic acid extraction tower based on a design by a Milanese engineer, and it caused Levi several sleepless nights after he first switched it on and showed the workers how to operate it. The tower could be seen from the Turin–Milan highway till early 1996, when it was condemned as obsolete, and pulled down. Its remains now lie rusting in a scrap yard in the plant littered with redundant monsters that were all installed and operated in the days when Levi worked there. With the exception of Paola Accati, the founder's daughter, who manages the three production units, today there is only a single chemist, Renato Portesi, who has sad memories of Primo Levi. The laboratories are equipped with sophisticated apparatus and computers; aside from a few relics, nothing remains at SIVA of the heroic age of chemistry that inspired the writer.

In order to create the forceful and loquacious figure of Libertino Faussone, Levi fused together aspects of the dozens of men he had met on the construction site in Tolyatti, where Fiat specialists were building the Zhiguli automobile factory. In a kind of euphoria, he uses the Piedmontese dialect — "the Fiat idiom, a poor dialect, like a sort of metaphor of the world of industry" — to write up the stories of his life as a working chemist that Faussone

325

supposedly inspired him to remember. Tino Faussone comes from Turin, where so much revolves around the giant FIAT company. He belongs to the working population that is heir to the craft traditions of the nearby valleys. The book is a kind of oral history retranscribed, made up of fourteen stories — eleven told by Tino Faussone and three by the narrator. Levi saw it as deriving from the age-old tradition of the popular storytellers of Africa and Asia. All of the stories told by Faussone are based on reality. The father assigned to him by Levi really existed, in the person of the father of a boilermaker who worked at SIVA, and who gave his permission for the portrait.

Levi wrote this book with tremendous fluency. He told Giuseppe Grassano, a critic who took a great interest in his work, that he had typed the manuscript practically from beginning to end without a single deletion, as if it had been dictated to him.[1] And in an interview with Giorgina Levi for *Ha-Keillah*, the magazine of the Jewish community in Turin, he told her that he was glad to have taken on a work of fiction, and to have shed the exclusive label of a writer on the concentration camps that others had pinned to him.[2]

He did not foresee the scandal that was soon to break over a book written in the hope of throwing a bridge between the two cultures, the worlds of the intellect and of technology. And in fact, away from its immediate context it is hard to understand the commotion it caused. Primo Levi published *La chiave a stella*[3] (*The Wrench*) in a particular climate; at the moment when, in Europe, the fact of having a job had not yet become a privilege. In the heyday of the Red Brigades of Italy, it was politically common and correct to condemn work as the worst of alienations, and not unusual for the extreme left newspaper *Lotta Continua* to assert that there was nothing to choose between a factory and a concentration camp. Levi, who had known the Auschwitz camp, and seen the slogan above the gate, *Arbeit macht frei* ("Work sets free"), could not accept the spurious comparison between a factory and a concentration camp where the function of work was to cause the death by exhaustion of the inmates. So he did not hesitate to confront the "rhetoric of platitudes" of the revolutionary groups that portrayed work as a negative reality. "The love of work is not as rare as people think," he explained to Giuseppe Grassano. "A man who loves his work is not necessarily a reactionary."

As soon as the book was published, Levi was called upon to justify himself to a hostile audience of journalists, trade unionists and students, but he refused to be put off by the chorus of opposition, and was not afraid to take on the "drawing-room trade unionists for whom the world is peopled by slaves tied to the assembly line and by wicked bosses. The world is more articulate than that. Work is neither punitive nor alienating, like the work that I performed for thirty years .... If everybody refused to work, we would die of starvation. My position does not rule out struggles for work."[4]

This did not prevent the journalists from asking Levi why his hero Faussone was not a keen trade unionist. Surprise was expressed that in dealing with the world of work in his first piece of full-length fiction he had no political project to put forward. Why was Faussone not involved with Italian political reality, *Lotta Continua* complained, and would not grant Levi the right to write about a worker, because he himself was middle-class. How was it possible, his critics wondered, for Levi, once a member of *Giustizia e Libertà*, to have written "a right-wing book"? The journalists of *Lotta Continua* urged him to examine and criticize himself.

In fending off the questions and aggressive demands of *Lotta Continua*, Levi asserted the absolute freedom of the writer. He argued that the saving grace of work was an integral part of human civilization — this was the idea of work that he had found in Joseph Conrad. He overturned the rhetoric of the time when he informed his detractors: "I simply wanted to have my character say that, in life, one needs to have a trade, to be in control. Fear and rage are not good enough. It is dangerous to expect from a welfare state solutions that it cannot provide."

In a town where the working class and the trade unions were adopting the language of terrorist groups, Primo Levi suggested to Giuseppe Grassano that "Loving one's work constitutes the best, most concrete approximation of happiness on earth. Competence in one's own work is without doubt the most accessible kind of freedom, the most subjectively agreeable, and the most useful to mankind."[5]

Unlike his contemporaries, Levi had found in work a metaphor for the Conradian adventure. To pass it off as a negative reality seemed to him to be a rejection of responsibility, a refusal to grow up. In a debate organized by *La Stampa*, at one point he became so exasperated that he declared: "When you hate work, you end up by hating life."[6] He repeated that pride in work had long traditions, rooted in the countryside, where craftsmen respected work well done. His character Faussone was the heir to these traditions when he took pride and pleasure in putting up a crane or other complex metal structure. Levi's thirty years with SIVA had left him with a great admiration for such people: "I've seen men just like him, very intelligent and not cultured. You might say that he has his brains at the tips of his fingers."

After Levi had given a talk in San Mauro Torinese, he was approached by a young man with a Piedmont accent, who introduced himself as the real Faussone. "What's your job?" the writer asked him. "Rigger," he said. Primo Levi immediately invited him to appear with him in a TV broadcast, but the real-life rigger turned him down and disappeared.[7]

Levi, whose two children were close to some of the far-left student groups, maintained a careful distance from the currents of thought inside the Communist Party. He was wise enough to remain a critical observer of what was happening in Turin, a city which ever since the early days of Fascism seems to have been a proving ground for generations of political ideas in Italy. His friend Armando Novero, who admits to not having taken Levi's books very seriously as literary creations, thinks that he would have found success much faster if he had not lived in Turin.

Primo Levi returned from a trip to Rome in spring 1979 and found that his mail contained a request from *La Stampa* to review a novelization by Gerald Green based on the TV series *Holocaust*. He wrote in his review that:

> The facts the book describes are all established. If some of them do not seem to be, it is because of their enormity, which is so great that it raises doubt. Some killers and some cynics try to take advantage of this, but the millions of dead really existed, and their death weighs down today on the world. It is a terrible thing to remember that forty years ago, in Europe, a civilization was destroyed. It happened .... The film does not misuse the incandescent material on which it is based .... Its makers have shown restraint, and have not given in to the macabre temptations of horror. No doubt we would rather have seen something less discursive, with greater historical precision, and more purposeful. But even so, it still remains an ally.[8]

In spite of the polemics it incurred, on 16 May 1979 *The Wrench* was awarded the thirty-third Strega Prize, ahead of seventeen novels chosen by 440 voters, while the sales of *The Periodic Table* rose to 120,000 copies. Paradoxically, twenty-two years after the publication of *If This Is A Man* Primo Levi was still perceived as a "second-class" writer, although the thought was never voiced in public. His name did not appear in any contemporary dictionary or encyclopedia of literature.

When Antonio Debenedetti interviewed him for *Corriere della Sera* after the announcement of the winner's name, Levi declared:

> It is commonplace to reject one of the two mutually exclusive cultures. For Galileo, there were not two cultures, nor were there two for Einstein. It seems to me that it is a typical European aberration to put up a barrier between humanist culture and scientific and technical culture. This book and its predecessor, *The Periodic Table*, were intended to lower or demolish that barrier. In *The Wrench* I have done my best to show that even the work of an ordinary technician can be a source of inspiration and material for a novel. In that sense, *The Wrench* is evidence.[9]

The official presentation of the prize took place on 6 July, and Levi rose to the summit of cultural society when the minister of national education offered him his congratulations and attended the gala cocktail party and dinner. But though it was a glittering occasion, a tense atmosphere surrounded the reception of the prize. Assassination attempts carried out by the Mafia, the Camorra, and 'Ndrangheta against prominent public figures, prevented the attendance of the president of the Council of Ministers, Giovanni Spadolini, whose life had been threatened.

Despite the prizes regularly awarded to Levi's books, in 1979 the Strega laureate had yet to achieve recognition as a literary author, a fact confirmed by the young critic Giovanni Tesio, who had contributed a portrait of him to the university magazine *Belfagor*:[10]

> In 1979 nobody in the literary world was interested in Primo Levi. I was the first to consider him as a writer, rather than as a witness and chronicler of the *Lager*. It grieved him not to have obtained that recognition.

Levi did not understand why the fact of having written an account of the Auschwitz camp and having had a scientific training should bar him from the literary world. His view, as we have seen, was that the true writers were men such as Spallanzani or Galileo, whose culture was not divided. He loved to point out that Kant had studied astronomy before going on to write his philosophical works. He believed that the modern man of letters, brought up in a narrow cultural world and experienced only in the field of publishers' offices, knew very little about the wider universe.

Yet he did not feel indifferent to what was written about his books. He kept all the reviews, wrote down the names of the reviewers and the titles of the papers that published them, and entered marks from 1 to 5 in two parallel columns for the value of the critique and its rating of his book.

The success of the Strega Prize did not go to Levi's head. Back in Turin he went on leading his modest, reticent life. At the same time he was beginning to tire of delivering talks in colleges and schools. After visiting more than 130 of them, he had reached the conclusion that evidence about the camps was becoming an anachronism, even if the audience was impressed by the presence of authentic eye-witnesses. Feeling that his dialogue with the young had gone stale, he decided, if not to stop, then at least to taper off. At the same time he was deeply affected by the publicity given to the revisionist theories of Robert Faurisson, in particular by the newspaper *Le Monde* in a "case file" published in the issue of 29 December 1978, under the heading of "The Gas Chambers." Galled by *Le Monde*'s attitude, he wrote in *La Stampa*:

> It is true that the rector of his university has suspended Faurisson from teaching, and expressed doubts about his mental balance. But *Le Monde*, which for four years had been receiving letters from a man who must have appeared to the senior editorial staff to be suffering from a

monomania that verged on paranoia, has ended by giving way, and has admitted into its issue of 29 December 1978 some leading pages on "The Rumour of Auschwitz," in which he maintains that the genocide of the Jews is a legend, a hoax.[11]

In an interview given to Silvia Giacomoni for *La Repubblica*, Levi expressed his sense of outrage that a major newspaper like *Le Monde* should have given such extensive coverage to Faurisson's ideas. The article was headed by what Levi described as a "curious" introduction to the denial allegations. Part of it said:

Absurd though M. Faurisson's argument may seem, it has raised a few doubts, particularly among the younger generation, disinclined to accept established ideas without proof. For several of our readers it was essential to judge for themselves. We therefore publish the text that has been repeatedly circulated by the lecturer at the university of Lyon-II, with its title and notes.

On the same page, opposite Faurisson's article "The Problem of the Gas Chambers — The Rumour of Auschwitz, Abundance of Proof," *Le Monde* published a reply by Georges Wellers, a veteran of Auschwitz. In other words, the most reputable daily paper in France seemed to be putting the lies of a charlatan like Faurisson on a par with the first-hand evidence of Georges Wellers, director of research at the National Centre for Scientific Research, general representative of the Centre for Contemporary Jewish Documentation, and editor of *Le Monde juif*.

Levi voiced his indignation in *La Stampa* on 19 January 1979:

There is no doubt that, when brought up against the survivors, Faurisson's obscenities conflict with the reality of things seen. The lecturer knows that it is possible to brutally compress 2,000 people into 200 square metres. This is told to him by a deportee who, while waiting for selection for death by gas, was shut up with 250 others in a space of 7 metres by 4. He knows that, in order to kill Jews, prussic acid was used. His fatherly solicitude declares that this was not dangerous because, he says, too slow a dispersion of the gas would also have killed the Germans in attendance. But those in attendance were not Germans but prisoners. In the conditions in which it was used, in chambers full of human beings, at a temperature of over 37 degrees, the gas was extremely volatile, as it starts to boil at 24 degrees — take the word of a chemist.

The widespread press coverage given to Faurisson's claims followed a notorious interview, published in the French weekly *L'Express* in November 1978, with Louis Darquier de Pellepoix, former commissioner-general for Jewish Affairs under the Vichy regime, and as such in charge of the deportation of

Jews to death camps. Levi responded in an interview given to *Corriere della Sera* on 3 January 1979.

The operation has succeeded: it is not enough to read the horrors of Darquier de Pellepoix in *L'Express* last November, not enough to allow the murderers of those days space and a voice in respectable magazines, so that they may dictate their truth with impunity: the truth that the millions of dead in the camps never died, that Genocide is a fable, that in Auschwitz they only used gas to kill lice. All that is obviously not enough. Obviously the time is ripe, and from his university chair Professor Faurisson comes to put the world at ease. Fascism and Nazism have been denigrated, slandered. We don't talk about Auschwitz any more: that was a sham. We talk about the lie of Auschwitz, the Jews are cheats, they have always been cheats, and liars, liars enough to concoct the gas chambers and the crematorium ovens all by themselves, *after the event*. I don't know who Professor Faurisson is. Perhaps he is only a fool, even if he does hold a university office. Another hypothesis is more likely. Perhaps he himself was one of those in charge at the time, as Darquier was, or perhaps he is the son, or friend, or mainstay, of people in charge, and is striving to exorcize an episode that, in spite of modern permissiveness, weighs on his conscience. We are familiar with certain psychological mechanisms. Guilt is corrosive. In times now long since gone in Italy and France, it was also dangerous. People start by denying in court, in public, then in private, then more and more to themselves. The trick succeeds. Black turns to white. The dead are not dead, there is no murderer, there is no more guilt. There never was. It wasn't me who did something. That thing itself no longer exists.

No, Professor, life is not like that. The dead are truly dead. Even the women, and even the children, tens of thousands in Italy and France, millions in Poland and the Soviet Union. That's not so easy to conceal. You don't have to wear yourself out to find the evidence. If you really want to be informed, ask the survivors — there are enough of them in France. Listen to them. They saw themselves dying day after day, one by one, after their comrades who walked the dark path to the crematoria. They returned (those who did return), and they found their families wiped out. The path to avoiding guilt is not that one, Professor. Even for chair-borne professors, facts are stubborn. If you deny the slaughter organized by your friends of that time, you must explain why, from 17 million in 1939, Jews were reduced to 11 million in 1945. You must deny the hundreds of thousands of widows and orphans, and you must deny us, the survivors. Come and debate with some of us, Professor, and you'll find it harder to teach your pupils. Are all of them so badly informed that they accept this stuff? Has none of them raised a hand to protest? Then what have the university authorities done in France, and the law? By letting you deny the dead, they have tolerated your killing them a second time.

Infuriated by seeing the deniers given a sympathetic hearing by the press, Primo Levi gave another interview to *La Repubblica*. The duty of memory towards those who did not return must not remain an empty slogan. He looked on with anguish, while little by little the remaining witnesses disappeared, and his recurrent dream in Auschwitz was becoming true. Those who heard the survivors who communicated what they had seen and endured did not listen and did not understand. His was the voice of a chorus of six million murdered human beings. He could have borrowed the words of Itzhak Schipper, killed in Majdanek in 1943, who suggested to Alexandre Donat[12] that:

> Everything we know about murdered peoples is what the killers wanted to say about them. If our killers are victorious, it is they who write history ... they can erase us from the memory of the world. ... But if it is we who write the history of this time of blood and tears — and I am convinced that we will — who will believe us? No one will want to believe us, because our disaster is the disaster of the entire civilized world.[13]

Primo Levi already had in mind the subject of what was to be his final book: a sombre meditation on the condition of the prisoner in the ghettos and extermination camps, and on the difficulty of judging the behaviour of the victims. This scrutiny also covers the attitude of the executioners, and the relationship between oppressors and oppressed engendered by the machinery of extermination. Levi wished to make an impartial examination of the *Lager* structure designed to destroy human beings morally as well as physically. He also wanted to correct some of the squalid images propagated by "Nazi porno films" that deeply shocked him. He detested Liliana Cavani's film *The Night Porter*:

> Please, you film producers, leave the women of the camps alone .... They were not sexy actresses: people suffered there, but in silence; and the women were not beautiful, on the contrary they aroused an infinite compassion, like defenceless animals. As for the SS, they were not monsters or idiots or perverts. They were functionaries of the state. They were more pedants than brutes, intrinsically insensitive to the daily horror in which they lived, and which they seemed to get used to very quickly.[14]

Gnawed by despair, and tortured by a sense of guilt for having survived, Levi was sometimes to pass verdicts on the victims that the survivors could not possibly accept. He would reach the point of writing that all those who came out alive had something to reproach themselves for, and that only "the best" had been murdered, a judgement that many see as both absurd and untrue. It is common knowledge, and an obvious fact, that among the survivors there were not only the *Lager* elite but also many more ordinary *Häftlinge* whose survival came down to nothing but luck.

In 1980, the Polish government decided to restructure the museographic design of the Auschwitz main camp, and in particular to assign huts to every nationality. This had the effect of obscuring the fact that the overwhelming majority of the prisoners in Auschwitz were Jews. However, in the so-called "Italian" Block it was decided to create a monument dedicated to the Jews who had been murdered there, and Primo Levi was invited to write an introductory text. He drafted eight brief paragraphs intended as guides towards understanding the material exhibited. The Auschwitz museum kept only the greater part of paragraph eight. Here they are in full:[15]

1. The history of the Deportation and the extermination camps, the history of this place, cannot be separated from the history of the Fascist tyranny in Europe: a continuous thread runs from the first arson attacks on trade-union labour exhanges in Italy in 1921 to the burning of books in German squares in 1933 and on to the hideous flames of the crematoria in Birkenau. An ancient wisdom affirms the forecast made by Heinrich Heine, a Jew and a German: "Where books are burned, men too are burned in the end. Violence is a seed that does not die."

2. It is a sad admission, but we have to tell ourselves, and tell other people, that the first European experience of destruction of the labour movement and sabotage of democracy was born in Italy. Fascism was born in the immediate postwar crisis, in the myth of the "mutilated victory," and was fuelled by ancient miseries and guilts. Out of Fascism came a spreading delirium, the cult of the providential man, enthusiasm organized and imposed. All decisions were abandoned to the judgement of a single man.

3. Not all Italians were Fascists. We can testify to that for those who died here. As for Fascism, another unbroken thread was spun in Italy before anti-Fascism responded to it. All those who fought against Fascism and who suffered under Fascism bear witness with us: the martyred workers of Turin in 1923, the men imprisoned, and our brothers in all the political movements who died to resist the Fascism restored by the National Socialist invader.

4. Other Italians testify with us. Those who died on all fronts in the Second World War, fighting against their will and hopelessly against an enemy that was not their own, and who saw the trap too late: they too are victims of Fascism, victims unaware.

5. We are not unaware. Some of us were opponents and partisans. Some were captured and deported in the last months of the war, and died here while the Third Reich was collapsing, tortured by the thought of Liberation close at hand.

6. Most of us were Jews. Jews from every town in Italy, and even foreign Jews, Poles, Hungarians, Yugoslavs, Czechs, Germans, who in the Fascist Italy of the racial laws had encountered the hospitality and generosity of the Italian people. They were rich and poor, men and women, healthy and sick.

7. There were many children among us, and there were old people on the point of death, but all of us were shipped like freight in wagons, and the fate of those who passed through the gates of Auschwitz was the same for all. Even in the darkest centuries it was unheard of for millions of human beings to be exterminated like insect pests. It was unheard of for children and the dying to be sent to their deaths. We, the sons of Christians as well as Jews (but we dislike these distinctions), from a country that had been civilized and that became civilized again after the night of Fascism, here we bear witness.

8. In this place where we innocent people were put to death, barbarism touched its deepest level. VISITOR, OBSERVE THE REMAINS OF THIS CAMP AND CONSIDER: WHATEVER COUNTRY YOU COME FROM, YOU ARE NOT A STRANGER. ACT SO THAT YOUR JOURNEY IS NOT USELESS, AND OUR DEATHS NOT USELESS. FOR YOU AND FOR YOUR SONS, THE ASHES OF AUSCHWITZ HOLD A MESSAGE. ACT SO THAT THE FRUIT OF HATRED, WHOSE TRACES YOU HAVE SEEN HERE, BEARS NO NEW SEEDS, EITHER TOMORROW OR FOR EVER AFTER.[16]

In March 1979 Primo Levi wrote to Fischer Verlag, the German publisher of *If This Is A Man* in 1961. Heinz Riedt, his translator, had informed him that in Frankfurt am Main they had "almost decided" to republish the book. To give some incentive for the reissue, Levi wrote to inform Fischer that in Italy his book was still selling at the rate of 30,000 copies a year, with total sales of 350,000. It had been translated and published in the United States, Britain, France, Holland, Finland, Romania, and Poland, and the school edition published by Einaudi had enjoyed a wide circulation in Italy. There had been adaptations for radio and the stage. Lastly, Levi reminded Fischer that the German edition had brought him a large number of letters from readers. All this seemed to him to justify the republication of the book "without too great a delay," for obvious commercial reasons, and for the instruction of the younger generation.

On the same day, Levi also wrote to his friend Hermann Langbein. Reflecting on his four years' retirement, he confessed that things were not the way he had imagined them: "I am a pensioner now, which leaves me with plenty of leisure. However, I have discovered that it is not so easy to spend *all* one's spare time writing: not for me, at least. I write, but not a lot." He enclosed a copy of his letter to Fischer Verlag, and suggested to Langbein that he should back him up either by writing an article himself or by "commissioning" a supportive piece from Theo Sommer, who was a contributor to *Die Welt*.

In April 1980 Primo Levi visited the pipe-laying vessel *Castoro Sei* off the southern coast of Sicily. He spent thirty hours on board, marvelling at the sophisticated technology and automated systems, but also reminded of his reading of Coleridge, Conrad, Verne, and Melville. The work of the sailor–engineers whose mission was "to deposit on the bottom of the sea, from Tunisia to Sicily, a rigid steel pipe covered with cement, by manipulating it as if it were as light and flexible as a rubber tube" inspired him to write an article that was to appear in *L'altrui mestiere* (*Other People's Trades*), published by Einaudi in 1985.

It was in 1981 that Guido Davico Bonino and Giulio Bollati, who edited various series published by Einaudi, suggested to Primo Levi that he should write an account of the books that had influenced his life. In fact, Giulio Bollati planned a whole collection in which authors including Italo Calvino, Leonardo Sciascia, and Paolo Volponi would tackle the same subject. Levi alone expressed enthusiasm. "In the first place I liked the idea for narcissistic reasons. To open and show off my sources was an act of exhibitionism that appealed to me."[17] So here was the chronically shy Primo Levi ready to bare his secrets through the medium of a personal anthology. The result was unexpected, since in *La ricerca delle radici* Levi combines literary sources with others of a different kind.

The first surprise is that it is not the memories of Auschwitz that guide his preferences. The bipolar spheroid that precedes his choice of extracts, each with its own preface, displays four meridians, four itineraries, four lines of resistance against the despair felt by those who suffer unjustly, as Job does in the Bible. What is striking in this anthology is its rigorous restraint. The extracts chosen by Levi are longer than his commentaries: he reveals himself through the juxtaposition of the two.

Italo Calvino said that *La ricerca delle radici* was an encyclopedia before it was an anthology, because it was structured on the basis of experience. In Levi's choice of authors, Calvino saw his faith in the powers of the human mind, able to find its salvation in an unjust world through a process of awareness, a stoical resistance which did not exclude humour or understanding. At the two poles of the sphere are Job — man confronted with injustice, evil, and the silence of God — and the "Black Holes" — Auschwitz. On the meridian of "salvation through understanding" Levi places Lucretius, Darwin, Bragg, and Clarke. On the second meridian, "the stature of man," are Marco Polo, Rosny, Conrad, Vercel, and Saint-Exupéry. On the meridian of "man suffers unjustly" stands T.S. Eliot, Babel, Celan, and Rigoni Stern. The last meridian offers a loophole from suffering in the form of Rabelais, Porta, Belli, and Sholom Aleichem.

Freed from the burden of the plant, where he had often felt "close to neurosis," Levi would often call in at the Einaudi offices, which were not far away from where he lived. There he met Ernesto Ferrero, Guido Davico Bonino, and sometimes Italo Calvino. He also used to visit Agnese Incisa; he felt a deep friendship for her, and sometimes told her about his worries. Giulio Einaudi, who in the words of Natalia Ginzburg made very shrewd use of his own timidity,[18] rarely emerged from his office to greet an author. Levi was not a close friend of his. Even though the public success of his books and the prizes awarded to them had enhanced his status as a writer, the literary world still considered him as the author of two great books about the concentrationary world and the liberation of the Auschwitz camp.

After the war, the house of Einaudi no longer resembled the tiny concern founded by Leone Ginzburg, Giulio Einaudi, and Cesare Pavese during the dark years of Fascism. A branch had been opened in Rome. In Turin, the firm had moved to new headquarters in the Corso Re Umberto, the same Corso Re Umberto where Vittorio Foa, Leone Ginzburg, Sion Segre Amar, and Felice Balbo used to stroll, and where the adolescent Primo Levi must have crossed their paths, not knowing that these young men deep in conversation were the flower of the city's intelligentsia and of its anti-Fascist publishing world.

The publishing house where Cesare Pavese, Felice Balbo, and Natalia Ginzburg worked now occupied several office doors. Outside his door, Pavese had put up a sign saying "Editorial Manager." The room next to his was occupied by Giulio Einaudi, who hung a portrait of Leone Ginzburg on his wall. Einaudi no longer summoned his secretary by shouting out her name into the corridor; his desk was festooned with telephones and buzzers. The scowling Pavese, with his pipe clamped between his teeth, staved off visitors with his constant complaint of: "I have things to do! I don't want to see anybody! Let them go hang! I don't give a damn!"[19] He also liked to say: "We don't need ideas here, we've got enough and to spare!" Pavese committed suicide in the summer of 1950, when all his friends were out of town. According to Natalia Ginzburg: "He had planned and calculated the circumstances of his death, the way you plan a walk or a party. ... For years, he had talked about suicide. No one took him seriously."

15   Returning to Jewish Roots

In 1981 Primo Levi published *Lilit e altri racconti*, a collection of short stories most of which had been published in *La Stampa* between 1975 and 1981. The first twelve cover memories of Auschwitz, and deal with themes explored in *If This Is A Man* and *The Truce*. Several of these episodes could have been included in the first book, but Levi considered that their anecdotal character would mar the rigour of the indictment he was writing. The other "tales," as he liked to call them, were in the same vein as those collected in *Storie naturali* and *Vizio di forma*.[1]

In the same year, Levi embarked on a project that broke new ground in his literary career. *If Not Now, When?* was a full-scale novel that absorbed him completely and gave him more pleasure than any of his other books. This epic story about a band of young Jewish partisans in the forests of Byelorussia during the Second World War, his first work of narrative fiction, took him eight months to plan and research and a year to write — time spent in a mood of euphoria quite untypical of his usual low-key temperament. He told Philip Roth:

> I had made a sort of bet with myself: after so much plain or disguised autobiography, are you, or are you not, a fully-fledged writer, capable of constructing a novel, shaping characters, describing landscapes you have never seen? Try it![2]

The book has its roots in the past. *The Truce* had been the odyssey of an eventful homeward journey made in constant jeopardy, the story of an exceptional and liberating adventure, a tale of growing up, and of metamorphosis. It is not surprising that twenty years later Levi felt the need to travel that landscape and explore that experience once again, in *If Not Now, When?*

Levi had never forgotten the hard-bitten young Jews, none of them over twenty, who in October 1945 had hitched their wagon to the train of the homeward-bound Italians, without asking anyone's permission. The new passengers, who came from all the countries of Eastern Europe, were Zionists, heading for Palestine. A ship was waiting for them in Bari. Levi was astounded by their air of freedom and by their daring. Here he had come across a small group of survivors who belonged to a shattered civilization, "Yiddishland," but who felt that they were masters of their fate, and capable of changing the world. Certainly, neither before his capture nor in the immediate postwar era did Levi ever consider settling in Palestine, but once it was founded he viewed the State of Israel as the natural haven for those who had escaped extermination, and felt a powerful bond with the land and its inhabitants.

The second seed that sprouted in the book was the story once told to him by his friend Emilio Vita Finzi (a close relation of Leonardo De Benedetti), a member of a partisan network operating between Venice and Rome, whose task was to collect information on deportee shipments by rail, in order to support sabotage operations. Vita Finzi had realized that there was something fishy about their schedule. Later on he went into hiding in Switzerland, but kept making secret trips back to pursue his resistance activities. During the summer of 1945 he had volunteered to help the displaced Jews who were flooding into Italy from Eastern Europe in the hope of boarding a ship bound for Palestine, in spite of strong opposition from the British under their League of Nations Mandate.

Emilio Vita Finzi was secretary-general of the Milan *Hechalutz*,[3] whose headquarters were at 5 Via Unione, the reception centre for survivors of the Holocaust. The third *aliyah* (1919–23), or emigration to the Promised Land, encouraged by the Balfour Declaration in 1917,[4] had been organized by the *Hechalutz* movement, which shipped 35,000 immigrants to Palestine. In 1920 some of them had founded the *Histadrut*, or General Federation of Labour.

In 1945, the fine Renaissance stairways of the *palazzo* in the Via Unione were crammed with refugees. Sheets were hung in the corridors so that women could give birth away from prying eyes. They did not always know who the father was, for many had been raped, and did not want their newborn children.

One day Emilio Vita Finzi told Primo Levi that a group of Jews staying in the Via Unione had turned up fully armed at the hospital where one of their number was to be operated on for appendicitis. These young people, who had lost every member of their families, refused to be considered as refugees. They had carried out guerrilla and sabotage operations against the retreating German army in the forests of Byelorussia. They were so wary that they had refused to put down their weapons at the door to the operating theatre when the surgeon asked them to. It took a lot of patience to convince them that the doctor was there to save their comrade's life. While Emilio was talking, Primo Levi made some notes that he later put away in his desk. One day he came across them again, and phoned Emilio to ask him to repeat the story.

Levi could not help being fascinated by these young men and women, all in their teens, their parents butchered by the Nazis, yet who had managed not only to survive but to put up resistance to their people's murderers. Their actions exploded the notion that the Jews had offered no resistance and had let themselves be herded like cattle to the slaughter. There is no doubt that Levi, who had been captured before he could learn how to handle a weapon or had taken a single action, would have wanted to follow their example. Those young people proved that, where it was possible, the Jews had resisted, as they did in Warsaw, Vilnius, Bialystok, Riga, Minsk, and even inside the extermination camps: in Auschwitz, Sobibor, and Treblinka.

Ten years had passed when Levi listened to the story again, and conceived the idea of a historical novel on a grand scale that would pass on the legacy of those young Jews who had stood against the Nazis in an unequal fight. To pay them homage, he resolved to study the language and culture of those who had struggled "for their love of freedom and for their people's dignity."

Primo Levi's encounter with Polish Jewry in Auschwitz had come as a tremendous cultural shock. In deciding to write this story, he was setting out on a long process of regaining his roots by identifying himself, not with the assimilated Italian Jews who had shed so much of their original culture, but with the civilization of the Yiddish world that had vanished into the ovens of the crematoria or had fallen under the machine-guns of the *Einsatzgruppen.*

Levi's page of notes, and the memories of his Russian journey, did not provide nearly enough material for the ambitious novel he had in mind. He started to do detailed research into Jewish resistance to the Nazis, aiming to confirm whether such movements really had existed, and he found that there had been far more of them than was usually assumed. In order to interpret certain documents, and to enter the mental and linguistic universe of his future heroes, there was a handicap he had to overcome: his ignorance of the Yiddish language. He decided to study it.

> I intended to be the first (if not the only) Italian writer to describe the Yiddish world. I intended to "exploit" the success I had had in my own country to impose on my readers a book about the Judaeo-Germans, their culture, their history, their language, their way of thinking, all practically unknown in Italy.[5]

He bought a grammar, a textbook, and a dictionary and, knowing the Hebrew alphabet, he learned to read quite quickly. Emmanuel Ringelblum's *Notes from the Warsaw Ghetto,*[6] recording the death of 500,000 Jews inside the walls of the ghetto, was not the only testimony to the annihilation of Polish Jewry to be written in Yiddish. Several documents on Russian partisan bands in the forests of Byelorussia had also been written in that language. Primo Levi went to Paris, where he came across Moshe Kaganowic's full-length study, *Di milkhomeh fun di Jiddische Partisaner in Mizrach-Europe* ("The War of the Jewish Partisans in Eastern Europe"), published by the Central Union of Polish Jews in Buenos Aires in 1956. He also read a collective testimony, *Oïfn weg zum zieg* ("On the Way to Victory"), composed under the supervision of Djadja Misza and published in Paris in 1950 by the Organization of Polish Jews in France. He had read and partially translated them in order to understand "how one reasoned, how one thought, how one wrote in Yiddish." Learning to read a language he knew nothing at all about required a considerable effort that brought Levi great satisfaction. For a whole year he did nothing and read nothing that did not relate to the book he was writing. Emmanuel Ringelblum's diary became his bedside reading. From it he borrowed the phrase: "To conquer three lines in History's journal."

In these works he found the history of the few handfuls of fugitives from the liquidated ghettos and the mass murders perpetrated by the

Einsatzgruppen, who had managed to reach the forests of Byelorussia and the Pripet Marshes, there to form groups driven by the urgent need both to survive and to defend themselves. They sought to join up with formations of Soviet partisans who took their orders from Moscow and had mastered the rules of guerrilla warfare. Sometimes they were accepted, sometimes rebuffed. They marched westward in the footsteps of the German rearguard. They had no home, no family, and no country, but they hoped to start new lives in the land of Israel, having built up a mythic image of the place. Totally destitute, they prowled in woods and marshlands, hunted by the Nazis, and striking back whenever they could.

Thus, the characters in this book, even if they are invented — except for Polina, the young pilot of the P2 plane, assigned to bring them food and medical supplies — were all inspired by partisans whose profiles Levi discovered in works published in Yiddish after the war, pages where a breath of Jewish life still remained. Of course, as he himself admitted, his Yiddish — "a paper Yiddish" — was somewhat clumsy, but Italian readers did not notice.

If Not Now, When?, the title of the book, is taken from the *Pirkei Avot*, the "Sayings of the Fathers," or the ninth tractate of the *Nezikin* order of the *Mishnah*,[7] which collects and codifies rabbinical aphorisms and sayings that depict the advice of the wise man, steeped in his knowledge of the Torah. Here it refers to the final passage (paragraph *aleph*, verse 14) in the meditation of Rabbi Hillel:

> Im ain ani li mi li?
> Oukhshe ani le atzmi ma ani?
> Ve-im lo achshav eimataï?

> If I am not for myself, who will be for me?
> And being for myself, what am I?
> And if not now, when?

The narrative teems with biblical allusions and Hebrew expressions. Thus, when the band of young partisans wipes out the SS men who have been compelling a few survivors living on borrowed time in a small extermination camp to burn some bodies, they decide to sign this execution by writing on the wall with a piece of charcoal the Hebrew letters "VNTNV" — "*Vnatnou.*" This palindrome, made up of five Hebrew consonants — *vav, nun, tav, nun, vav* — is taken from a psalm, and can be read from right to left as well as from left to right. It signifies "And they will give back" — in other words: "What you have done, we too can do."

Levi also pored over the texts that make up the biblical and post-biblical literary corpus: the Pentateuch, the *Mishnah*, the Proverbs, the *Midrash*,[8] the *Aggada*,[9] and even the *Shulchan Aruch*, the study written by the Spanish-born rabbi Joseph Caro which contains "the rules, customs and beliefs of the Judaism of his time."[10]

In writing *If Not Now, When?*, Primo Levi assumed a cultural heritage, an identity, by choosing roots that were not those of his own antecedents. They gave him a link with the language and culture of the murdered Jews of Eastern Europe. Behind his heroes stood the ghostly presence of the Yiddish language; it held the footprints they left behind. His arrival in Auschwitz had brought him face to face with the very different Jewish civilization of Eastern Europe when a Polish Jew informed him in Yiddish: "If you don't speak Yiddish, you're no Jew." In Auschwitz, he had felt himself welded to the history of the Jewish people when they sewed a star of David on his deportee's jacket and marked his flesh with his registration number 174517: "My Jewish identity took on a great importance following my deportation to Auschwitz; it is very likely that without Auschwitz I would never have written, and would have given only a little weight to my Jewish identify."[11] His and all his comrades' arrival in the camp seemed to him to belong to an episode "from a new Bible" (*Man* 66/72).

In *If Not Now, When?*, there are so many quotations taken from the Bible and rabbinical texts that they seem to compose the frame in which the story is inlaid, even to the heroes' hymn, "Gedale's Song,"[12] in which the meditation of Rabbi Hillel is quoted several times:

> Do you recognize us? We're the sheep of the ghetto,
> Shorn for a thousand years, resigned to outrage.
> We are the tailors, the scribes and the cantors,
> Withered in the shadow of the cross.
> Now we have learned the paths of the forest,
> We have learned to shoot, and we aim straight.
> > If I'm not for myself, who will be for me?
> > If not this way, how? And if not now, when?
> Our brothers have gone to heaven
> Through the chimneys of Sobibor and Treblinka,
> They have dug themselves a grave in the air.
> Only we few have survived
> For the honor of our submerged people,
> For revenge and to bear witness.
> > If I'm not for myself, who will be for me?
> > If not this way, how? And if not now, when?
> We are the sons of David, the hardheaded sons of Masada.[13]
> Each of us carries in his pocket the stone
> That shattered the forehead of Goliath.
> Brothers, away from this Europe of graves:
> Let us climb together towards the land
> Where we will be men among men.
> > If I'm not for myself, who will be for me?
> > If not this way, how? If not now, when?

(INNW 168–9/127)

341

This hymn of the partisans in *If Not Now, When?*, inspired by the *Pirkei Avot*, is not the only reference to the basic texts of Judaism. Thus there is this passage, quoting Deuteronomy, chapter 25 verses 17–19:

> Remember what Amalek[14] did to you on the way, after you had come out of Egypt. He attacked you while you were on the road, he killed all the weak, the sick, the weary, who were straggling behind; he had no fear of God. And so, when your God grants you peace from your enemies, you will extinguish even the memory of Amalek; don't forget it. (*INNW 161/121*)

And later on, spoken by young Rokhele, each night comes the same prayer: "Let the Merciful break the yoke that oppresses us, and lead us, heads high, into our land."

Primo Levi, who had not chosen, as his heroes did, to go and build the State of Israel, used to explain that he had regained his fatherland, his home, and his family on his return from Auschwitz. Yet he believed that the Jews of Poland, the land where they were hated, those rare survivors who had lost everything, had good cause to make their way to the Promised Land. The mayor of a Polish village tells the group:

> Jews and Poles lived together for I don't know how many centuries, but there was never any friendliness between them ... in church, the priest said they were the ones who had sold Christ and crucified him. We never shed their blood, but when the Germans came in nineteen thirty-nine, and the first thing they did was strip the Jews, and mock them, and hit them, and shut them up in ghettos, I have to say truly ... we were glad ... we thought they had come ... to take the Jews' money away from them and give it to us. (*INNW 212/163–4*)

In *If Not Now, When?*, Levi narrates the exodus of a small group of Jews who have escaped extermination, and who retrieve their dignity in combat. Their long and hazardous migration, which can be read as a metaphor of the flight from Egypt, leads them with a messianic drive towards the construction of a new state in mandated Palestine. The fervour of the heroes, and their faith in the goal they have set themselves, are an enigma, considering the writer's manifest attitude towards both religion and Zionism. Levi always said that he was interested in the cultural fact of Jewishness, and the existence of the State of Israel, but that he was no believer and no Zionist. Yet the Zionism of his characters seemed to him a political necessity. They imagine a country peopled by exalted, noble farmers who worked the land, which has nothing in common with present-day Israel — something that Levi, very naively, often regretted. Gedaleh, the leader of the band, tells the mayor:

> We will fight until the end of the war, because we believe ... that killing Nazis is the most just thing that can be done today on the face of the

earth; and then we'll go to Palestine, and we'll try to build the house we've lost, and to start living again the way all other people live. (*INNW 215/166*).

Gedaleh describes to a Polish resistance fighter an idealized image of the kibbutz "where there's no money, but everybody does what work he can and is given what he needs. It sounds like a dream, but it isn't: this world has already been created by our brothers, more farsighted and courageous than us, who emigrated down there before Europe became a *Lager*" (*INNW 249/195*).

Levi, who had written "we don't want to become landowners: we only want to make the sterile soil of Palestine fertile, plant orange trees and olive trees in the desert, and make it bear fruit," portrayed Israel as an ideal — a land "which in reality does not exist," he declared in an interview after his book came out.

Primo Levi admitted to the many journalists who asked him questions that he identified himself with the character of Mendel the watchmaker, the partisan, because he would have liked to be a real partisan. His novel enabled him to project onto his heroes the life of active resistance that his premature capture did not allow him to lead. Having himself endured the fate of the prisoner in a concentration camp, he wanted to tell the world that not all Jews had followed that path, and that some had achieved the feat of "making their own future with their own hands."

Beneath the joy of writing a true historical novel, a novel of adventure, constructed along traditional lines and set against landscapes where the author had found himself in conditions very different from those of his characters, there was a vein of gloom that almost undermined his happy epilogue — that of the young partisans setting off to build the State of Israel, after a child has been born in the refugee centre in the Via Unione in Milan. The true story of the young armed Jews besieging the operating theatre, told by Emilio Vita Finzi, had been transformed by Levi into a nativity. But the symbolic redemption of the Jewish people heralded by the birth of a child occurring on the way to the Promised Land was darkened the very same day by a tragedy: the bomb exploding over the city of Hiroshima.

Levi considered himself a Jew returning to his roots from a strictly cultural viewpoint. His Judaism had been gradually imposed on him by the race laws, captivity in Fossoli, and then his deportation to Auschwitz, where he was suddenly immersed in an almost exclusively Jewish environment, and the fact of being stamped as a Jew was a preliminary to annihilation. He had never been a believer, and Auschwitz, where every moment confronted him with evil, had strengthened his conviction that the heavens were empty. He had wobbled for just a few moments when he faced the selection in October 1944 at the same time as Jean Samuel and Alberto Dallavolta, and almost went so far as to pray to God to spare his life, but he pulled himself together with the thought that of all the times to appeal to him, this one was the least noble.

Written with a sense of freedom seldom experienced by its author, *If Not Now, When?* scored an immediate public success. In the weeks that followed its publication, Einaudi reprinted 50,000 copies of this heroic story, which went on to sell more than 100,000.

In this traditionally structured novel, Primo Levi tackled the theme of love for the first and last time. It was so new to his work that a critic asked him why he did not write a love story. Levi replied that the idea would have very much appealed to him, but he didn't feel up to it, because he experienced love "in a very private, intimate way. If I wrote a love story, people would see too many personal things."[15]

If Not Now, When? was a popular success, and it was awarded the Viareggio Prize in June 1982 and the Campiello Prize in September. But it cannot be said that the literary world greeted Levi's novel as a major work. His publisher kept his distance, and did not follow the usual custom of launching a new book in a bookshop or cultural centre. The fact is that, as Cesare Cases has often remarked, the literary world continued to consider Primo Levi as a less than first-class writer. It is true that in the end he was honoured for his testimony as a deportee, but there was no question of giving him a place in the history of Italian literature. It was only after his death that Levi would make his appearance in Italian literary histories and reference books.

For the moment, Cesare Cases accepted Einaudi's request to launch *If Not Now, When?* on the premises of a branch of the Communist Party in Lingotto, the centre of the Fiat empire. Einaudi's commercial director, not its literary director, put in an appearance. 11 July 1982 was a stifling hot day, and the town was crammed with celebrating football supporters, because the Italian football team had just won a match in the World Cup. Israel was engaged in a major land operation against the PLO in Lebanon, and in the hall at the launch venue, two Palestinians had come to heckle Levi about his support for the existence of the State of Israel. Cases and Levi tried in vain to persuade them that this was not the subject of the evening, but the two men went on shouting, and the noise inside the hall combined with the din outside it to make the launch impossible.

Cesare Cases wrote a perceptive account of *If Not Now, When?*, in which he says of Levi that:

> The idea of a Jewish people unique in faith and idiom has always been with him, and finds its expression in *If Not Now, When?*, which in my view, apart from its obvious objective as an apologia for the possibility of Jewish self-defence, serves a curious function of transference. The wonder of the western Jew confronted with eastern Jewry is projected into the wonder of the Polish Jewish partisans, who in the closing pages arrive in Italy and discover the existence of their co-religionists. The

shame of the persecuted is perfectly integrated into the economic, social, and cultural fabric of the Christian ascendancy. It seems that the transference failed. Levi wishes to see with the eyes of a people that was only too little known to him, and which was dying. It is certain that his encounter with it was instrumental in making his sense of exclusion, the consequence of anti-Semitic persecution, a little less absurd and solitary. The Italian Jews were not a people; the Jews of Eastern Europe were. After the camp, Levi never ceased to harbour a deep interest in Jewish life and culture that he certainly lacked before it. In the sphere of religion and ideology he was and remained a strict agnostic, even though he sometimes regretted the fact. In Auschwitz, that faith represented a great reserve of strength, because it was necessary in order to comprehend the incomprehensible, as Levi explains in a moving passage where he says, among other things, that the believers finally experienced a different fate from his own. Auschwitz was in their eyes a divine punishment, an expiation, or else the fruit of capitalist putrefaction.[16]

Levi had not chosen to live in Israel. He had found his mother and sister in good health when he returned, and the family's apartment, sequestrated during the period of the race laws, had been restored. Italy was in ruins, but he had never felt like an outcast there. Yet his feelings for the land of Israel were not neutral:

> My relationship with that land is out of the ordinary, for emotional and personal reasons. It is a State founded for those who were with me in the camps. A country of old companions, people who are dear to me. Statistically, they are only twenty, out of three million, but those twenty were in Auschwitz with me, and then they found their home, their land. I will say that for me it is an unacceptable thought, the idea that Israel might some day be destroyed.[17]

Primo Levi was in two minds. He felt an unshakeable attachment to the survivors of Auschwitz who had found refuge in Israel and fought in the war of independence, but his approach to the Middle Eastern conflict was similar to the analysis of the Italian socialists, to whom he was close without being politically active.

In this connection it is relevant to report a story told by the French journalist and editor Claude Glayman, who, during the war in Algeria, was forced to go underground because he was giving help to the Algerian resistance, the FLN (*Front de Libération Nationale*). Wanted by the French police, he took refuge in Italy for a time. One day he found himself in a living-room where some Italian intellectuals were talking to a member of the FLN to whom they had given their backing. Among those present, Glayman recalls noticing a silent, dignified man who suddenly intervened to inject some terse but softly-spoken comments into an awkward silence. The man was Primo Levi. He had come to remind this gathering that although the FLN were fighting in a just cause, there was no overlooking the fact that the Arab countries were calling for the destruction of the State of Israel, and were broadcasting anti-Semitic propaganda. Later he took Glayman to one side and explained in an undertone that he had been deported to Auschwitz and that Israel was the refuge of the Jews who had survived extermination.

While "Operation Peace for Galilee" continued in Lebanon, to the general disapproval of the international community and the Israeli left, Primo Levi put his name to a petition calling for a ceasefire, signed by 150 Jewish and non-Jewish personalities — the former including Natalia Ginzburg, the historian Ugo Caffaz, and the psychoanalyst David Meghnagi — and published in *La Repubblica* on 16 June 1982:

APPEAL FOR ISRAEL TO WITHDRAW FROM LEBANON

We sign this petition as democrats and Jews to ask the Israeli government to withdraw its troops from Lebanon at once. We reaffirm the necessity of a solution to the conflict that recognizes the right to sovereignty and to national security of all the peoples of the region. Those who in other circumstances have trembled because of the threat of destruction that hung over the State of Israel must find the courage today to oppose the policy of Mr Begin's government, and everything it represents for the democratic future of the State of Israel and for the prospects of peaceful coexistence with the Palestinian people. Mr Begin likes to present himself as the most convincing interpreter of Israel's requirement for security. On the contrary, his policy is very damaging to the democratic aspect of Israeli society, which is already pervaded by dangerous exclusivist trends. Trends that, in the case of the annexation of the West Bank, peopled by more than a million Palestinian Arabs, will turn out to be mortally dangerous. All those who considered the restoration to Egypt of the Sinai peninsula as a significant step towards a peaceful solution to the conflict in the Middle East will see it as a heavy blow to their hopes. The fate of democracy in Israel is in fact totally bound up with the prospect for peace and for mutual recognition with the Palestinian people. That people is paying an atrocious price not only for the tragic events in the West, but also for the past and present attacks aimed by Arab nationalism and Islamic ideology against the Jews. The military solution adopted against the PLO, which calls to mind a language that carries grim memories for every Jew, is happening with the complicity of the political forces connected with the parties in the Israeli opposition. It is a policy whose sole possible outcome is to force the entire Palestinian resistance organization back on to positions which led to the Munich disaster and the Entebbe hijack. We are bound to believe that the collusion between anti-Semitic terrorism and Islamic fundamentalism ... will emerge from the present invasion reinforced. There is also the risk of seeing public opinion, which is more and more bombarded by the news of war arriving from so many different points on the globe, now increasingly indifferent to the new manifestations of anti-Semitism, as could be seen after the attack on the synagogue in Vienna. For all these reasons, fighting the policy of the Begin government in this tragic moment for the Palestinian people is more than a gesture in favour of the withdrawal of the Israeli troops from Lebanon and of the right to self-determination of the Palestinian people; it is also a means of fighting the potential seeds of a new anti-Semitism joining forces with the old anti-Semitic tendencies that never went away, and which can be observed in the civil society of countries in the grip of totalitarian regimes. The present appeal is intended to offer a framework for bringing together political positions that may still be very different from each other, but that all have an interest in a just peace between the peoples of the region. We invite all those who are living through the agony of these hours to sign it by sending their messages of support to *La Repubblica*.

The appearance of the appeal brought an immediate flood of letters to the paper, addressed to Primo Levi. Italian Jews blamed him for taking a critical stand at a time when Israel was in trouble on its northern border. His friend Sion Segre Amar told him in person, and then in a letter published in *Shalom*, the journal of the Jewish community in Milan, in June 1982, that his stand was mistaken.

On 25 June, when half a million workers marched through the streets of Rome in a demonstration against government policy organized by the left-wing trade unions, a small ultra-leftist group broke away to lay a coffin in front of the main synagogue in Lungotevere Sanzio as a symbolic act against Israel played out against the Jews of Rome.

In Italy, Israel was the object of an extremely violent press campaign which became intolerable when certain journalists compared Israel to Nazi Germany.

Primo Levi agreed to an interview with Alberto Stabile that was published in *La Repubblica* on 28 June 1982. The journalist told him that some people saw an analogy between the plight of the Palestinians and the tragedy of the Jews during the Second World War. Levi commented:

I don't want to push things too far, but it seems to me that the analogy is as follows. This has to do with a *nation* — because in the Arab world these things are always hard to define — that has found itself without a country. This is a point of resemblance to the Jews. There is a recent Palestinian diaspora that has something in common with the Jewish diaspora of two thousand years ago .... Two peoples the victims of excessively powerful neighbours. All the same, I refuse to compare what Hitler called *the final solution* to the more or less violent and terrible events that the Israelis are causing today. There is no plan to exterminate the Palestinian people. That is going too far.

To the question: "What is the deepest wrench felt by Jews, and not only by Jews, faced with what is happening in Lebanon?," Primo Levi replied:

> For me and for my friends, and aside from the image of the State of Israel that we had created for ourselves — at least in terms of what we wished for, and what the facts already implied (that it was the haven of the Jewish nation, and the country of its reconstruction) — what worries us is its development in the opposite, militarist direction, an incipiently Fascistic direction. The issue was to restore not only a geographic but also a cultural centre to world Judaism. Now we are seeing power falling to nationalist authorities with aggressive tendencies, while the internationalist aspect of Judaism is passed over. ... Israel has pressure on its borders, it has been that way since 1948, but this initiative strikes me as excessive and unfounded. There is a disproportion between the provocations of the PLO and the reaction to them. It seems to me ... that Israel has gone too far ....
>
> Everyone has to come to terms with his own conscience and his own feelings. We must be democrats first, and Jews or Italians, or anything else, second.

After his second journey to Auschwitz with members of the Jewish communities of Rome and Florence, Levi published an article in *La Stampa* on 24 June 1982 on the war in Lebanon under the title "Who Is Afraid in Jerusalem?"

> It so happens that the news of the Israeli attack on Lebanon coincided for me with a return to Auschwitz, acting as the guide for a group of visitors. The two experiences have overlapped in a painful way, and I am still trying to sort out the reasons why I feel tormented. The signs of the slaughter forty years ago are still there in the place where it happened. They cut like a machete. One cannot be surprised that Hitler's slaughter should have strengthened the ties among the survivors, making them potentially a nation, and conferring the depth of will with which, in the space of a few years, they defeated the combined Arab countries and the hostility of the British, and miraculously built a new state. To a certain extent, the terrible violence endured justified the violence inflicted. In fact, Israel was recognized immediately by all the great powers, including the Soviet Union and the countries of the Eastern bloc. Most of the Jews of the diaspora recognized and identified themselves with Israel; it was the country of the Bible, the heir to all the strands of Jewish culture, and the redemptive

land and ideal homeland of all Jews.

The decades that followed have sapped and distorted that image. After its several defeats on the battlefield, the Arab world has built up an intense hatred towards Israel, seeing the new State as the guilty party responsible for centuries of troubles, and hardening their position of rejection. As usual, rejection was answered by rejection. Israel, less and less the Holy Land and more and more militarized, took on the behaviour of the other Middle Eastern countries, their radicalism, and their distrust of negotiation.

The present attack in Lebanon is not ungrounded; there was extensive provocation by the PLO. The PLO has never consented to start negotiations, and has stubbornly refused to recognize Israel (which it continues to call "the Zionist entity"), but the violence with which the attack has been conducted has astonished the world. I am not ashamed to admit that I feel torn. My ties to that country remain. I feel it in a way as my second country, and I would like it to be different from all other countries. And that is precisely why I feel anguish and shame about this action. I distrust successes won by the wrongful use of arms. I feel contempt for those who compare the Israeli generals to the Nazi generals, and yet I must admit that Begin is bringing these accusations down on his own head. It very much disturbs me to see the solidarity of the European countries fading. I claim that this initiative, dangerously costly in terms of blood shed, is spoiling the image of Judaism and has done damage that it will be difficult to repair. Rather to my surprise, I retain a close sentimental tie with Israel, but not with this Israel.

The Palestinian problem exists. It cannot be changed, and cannot be solved the Arafat way, by denying Israel the right to exist, but nor will it be solved the Begin way. Sadat was neither a genius nor a saint. He was just a man endowed with imagination, good sense, and courage, and he was killed for having opened up a path. Is there no one in Israel or elsewhere who feels able to pursue it?

Events took a tragic turn with the Sabra and Shatilla massacre of 17 September 1982, committed by the Lebanese Christian Phalange, which the Israelis failed to stop. A commission of inquiry was appointed, and hundreds of thousands of Israelis demonstrated in Tel Aviv. Primo Levi signed a second petition published in *La Repubblica*, which opened with the words: "Tormented by the outrage suffered by the whole country, and anguished for its future. ..." and on 25 September he demonstrated outside the Israeli embassy with other Italian Jews. A few days earlier he had been approached by Giampaolo Pansa, of *La Repubblica*, for an interview that he hesitated to give. It was finally published on the front page on 24 September: "I hesitated for a personal reason. The civil war, I carry in my guts. These days I am receiving a large number of letters because of what I have written and said about the war in Lebanon."

The reporter asked him if he was afraid. "In what sense?" he replied. "Fear is a profound phenomenon, and I do not feel it. I am not afraid as a Jew. For us Jews, I see neither a second genocide coming, nor an imminent outburst of Hitlerian Fascism. I do feel grief. This Israeli war and this siege of Beirut are troubling the imagination of Jews throughout the world."

Levi told Giampaolo Pansa that he would like to see Menachem Begin resign.[18] He chided Israel like a stern father threatening to cut off his allowance — of love — to a delinquent son. He added that he did not believe in the olive branch offered by Arafat, and accused Begin of having given him "the political victory and the stature of leader of the Palestinians that he did not have till now." He suggested some solutions to "help Israel to regain its European origins, and the balance of the founding fathers, Ben Gurion and Golda Meir," and confessed that some of his friends living in Israel, whose sons had been killed in one or another of the wars that followed the founding of the state, had written to reproach him for being blind to the Jewish blood spilled during all these years. Levi was distressed and wounded by these poignant letters from his former comrades, "people with an Auschwitz number tattooed on their arms, without a home, without a country, survivors of the horrors of the Second World War, who found a home and a country there." Yet because this was an argument also invoked by Menachem Begin, he instantly denied its validity.

Levi maintained a public silence for a while, and then agreed to meet Gad Lerner for *L'Expresso*. He was convinced that the Jews of the diaspora had the right to steer the Israelis on to the paths of wisdom and tolerance. He saw an Israeli withdrawal from the West Bank and the Gaza Strip, and negotiation with the PLO, as the radical solution to achieving normality in the region. Then he wondered: "Where is the centre of Judaism today?" He saw it in the diaspora, and was glad that it was so. "I would say that the best of Jewish culture is connected to the fact that it is polycentrist."

Finally he took stock of the history of the Jews in Italy and pronounced himself satisfied with their integration, even while he regretted that it had led to their assimilation, and to the disappearance of their culture. In fact, Primo Levi never attended the services held in the synagogue in the Via San Pio V, but he came there to buy *matzah* for Passover. He also wrote occasional articles for the magazine *Ha-Keillah* ("The Community"), and attended cultural events organized by the community, as Dan Vittorio Segre recalled. In those days Dan Segre was living in Israel, where he taught international relations at the university of Jerusalem, but he had kept his flat in Turin and his house in Govone. One day when he came to give a lecture in the Hebrew Library, he caught sight of a small man wearing rather a long grey overcoat as he emerged from the synagogue, who came up and reminded him: "I'm Primo."

When Dan Segre read the manifesto signed by Levi appealing to the Israelis to withdraw from Lebanon, which was published in *La Repubblica* on 16 June 1982, he called him on the telephone. Levi invited him to his house, and they argued for three hours.

> I found the man, who had an extraordinary reach of knowledge, very remote from politics, and extraordinarily ingenuous and innocent. I explained certain things to him. The basic elements of the Israeli situation were unfamiliar to him. Having said that, I did not support the right-wing view, I was against the war. He was totally candid about admitting the fact that he did not know the answer. In the end, we did not talk about the war, or his position on the subject. We reviewed some different aspects of Israel. I thought that Levi had signed that appeal because the people around him had asked him to. He had done some reading, but in fact he was a stranger to Jewish culture. No experience, but great interest — a detached interest. He had landed on a Jewish planet in Auschwitz with no preparation and no Jewish upbringing, like many Italian Jews. I always had the impression that his attitude to the Jews was committed because of his life, but as I say, detached.
>
> He did not come from the Jewish middle class. The Jews of Piedmont were very few in number, but generally rich. They belonged to high finance, high politics, and the university. Levi was a Jew who did not count. He had nothing in common with that society of Jews who considered themselves as the cream, the cream that used religion the way the Catholics do.[19]

Shalom, the monthly magazine of the Jewish community in Milan, published an interview with Albert Nirenstain, in which Nirenstain rejected the terms of the appeal published in *La Repubblica* in its June 1982 issue, with the text of the appeal printed in parallel.

As for Cesare Cases, who was also Jewish, this is how he saw the Jew in Levi:

> Levi rejects Judaism as a normative religion, but defends it as the disinterested game of the creator. He thinks that the punctilio of the rite conceals an ironic attachment, laughter. Religion interests him as a cultural phenomenon, and besides that, his writings attest to a familiarity with the Bible quite rare in Italian Jews and Christians, who share a general ignorance, both about the new testament and the old. After his death, there was an attempt to transform Levi into a kind of Jewish saint.

Saint or not, Levi was a generous man. Some time after his conversation with Dan Vittorio Segre he went to see Segre's son, who ran a travel agency in Turin, to ask for his father's telephone number in Jerusalem. He called him straight away, and told him: "I'd like to send you what I've written about your book[20] before publishing the whole article in *La Stampa*."

> The title of this intelligent, long-considered book is subtly ironic. In order to call oneself happy, is it enough to have escaped slaughter and avoided suffering? In a relative sense, yes, certainly. In an absolute sense, I leave the judgement to the reader — in this case, to the counterpart of the author, that is, to the young Italian of today, whose life is safe and identity secure ....[21]

Although he was convinced that Israel had made a grave mistake by embarking on its military operation in Lebanon, it hurt Levi to see so much importance attached to his signing the manifesto that condemned it. The accusations both in the Italian and in the international press quickly took on a disproportionate and sometimes hateful tone. When reporters asked him for more comments, he replied: "I no longer want my name to be linked to this war." He felt shocked by the demonization of Israel, and deeply wounded when the press had no scruples about using words like genocide, extermination, and racism in its chronicle of the events in the Middle East. However, he broke his silence on the day of the attack on the synagogue in Rome on 9 October 1982, killing a two-year old boy and leaving thirty-four people wounded: "The mistakes made at the other end of the Mediterranean in no way justify these actions, which are true crimes."

After this interview, Levi refused to issue another public statement on the Middle Eastern conflict. However, his interventions had their repercussions: in 1983, the Union of Italian Jewish Communities, which had invited him to make the opening address at its annual congress, decided to cancel the event that year; in 1984, another speaker was invited.

In Italy, the atmosphere was poisonous. When the Maccabi Tel Aviv Israeli basketball team came to play against Emerson Varese, on 7 March 1979, spectators in the gymnasium stood up and chanted: "Ten, a hundred, a thousand Mauthausens!" Immediately the Federation of Young Italian Jews organized a national congress to which it invited Umberto Terracini, Primo Levi, and a group of ex-deportees, two of whom, Lidia Rolfi and Edith Bruck, were friends of Levi's. In his speech to the congress Levi declared: "To wish, as was done in Varese, 'ten, a hundred, a thousand Mauthausens' to the Israeli athletes is evidence in itself of one consoling fact: that neo-Nazism or neo anti-Semitism, for reasons hard to clarify, seems inclined to find its new recruits among idiots."

It was also in 1982 that Levi started being interviewed by Ferdinando Camon, a writer from a Catholic family who was interested in Levi because he asked himself why man does evil, who should judge that evil, and how. Camon thought that Levi had played, in the twentieth century, the part of questioner that Dante and Manzoni had played in their own time; "It is the culture of crime and punishment, of God and Hell."[22] These interviews went on sporadically until 1986. In May of that year, Camon submitted the complete typescript to Levi. Between them they chose a dozen pages for publication in the weekly *Panorama*, timed to coincide with the appearance of Levi's book — his last book, and personal testament — *The Drowned and the Saved*. The theme of these conversations was located between two poles: "the presence of 'the devil' in German history, and the absence of God in the universe." In the Christian tradition, God guarantees victory over evil. At the end of his reflections, Levi came instead to the conclusion that the victory of evil implied the absence of God, although this conclusion was not quite categorical. In fact Levi added in pencil on the manuscript: "I find no solution to the riddle. I seek, but I do not find it."

A week after their first interview, Ferdinando Camon sent Levi a series of questions that were intended to provide a framework for their conversations. Levi added all the details he thought relevant, and requested control over the final text of the interview. He made a large number of hand-written alterations, which Camon respected without exception.

The first working session took place in Turin, in a corridor on the top floor of the Palace hotel, opposite Porta Nuova railway station, where Camon was staying. While he waited for Levi on the pavement outside, he watched the scene on the street, and saw the police stopping and searching young people who were lined up against a wall with their arms raised — a sight not unusual in those days of terrorist attacks. Levi finally arrived, "small, pale and agreeable." He wanted us to go straight into the hotel and start the interview in a quiet corner.

"His hair and beard were white, the beard more than the hair. He had a rather ironic expression and a slightly mischievous smile. A very methodical mind, with precise, detailed memories."[23]

The two men settled down in armchairs not far from Camon's room, for an interview that lasted for over three hours. There were to be three more meetings between them, two in small restaurants near the station, and the last in Levi's apartment, when they chose the excerpts for *Panorama*.

The initiative had come from Ferdinando Camon, who, having been brought up in a family of partisans, had posed questions to himself about the innocence or guilt of the culture of Christian Western Europe in the extermination of the Jews.

> There is something in Christian culture that recommends relations with the other, with the sole purpose of achieving his conversion. Any relation that is not finalized by conversion is considered as useless and dangerous. The fate of the other, including his death, or execution, is

considered as nothing compared to his conversion. If you look into this assertion, at the end of a certain time you can see extermination.[24]

Primo Levi was very surprised by Camon's approach, and had reservations about this idea. The fact remains that the Holocaust was not the only campaign of extermination to have been perpetrated by Christian civilization. "The conquest of America caused the almost total genocide of the Indians, The missionaries blessed the Indians they had murdered. The possibility that before their execution they might show a semblance of conversion was well worth putting them to death."[25]

Primo Levi did not share Camon's idea that the German people were collectively responsible for the Holocaust. For Levi, the history of the deportation and extermination of the Jews was closely bound up with the history of Fascism.

> Violence is a seed that does not die. It is painful to recall this to other people and to ourselves. The first European experience of destruction of the labour movement and sabotage of democracy was born in Italy. And Fascism arose out of the immediate postwar crisis, out of the myth of the mutilated victory, and was fuelled by ancient miseries and guilts. From Fascism was born a delirium that extended to the cult of the providential man, to enthusiasm organized and imposed. Every decision was left to the caprice of a single man.[26]

Ferdinando Camon remembers that Primo Levi looked at him with a smile of good will on his lips. He told him that a single man — Hitler — had held in his hands the power of speaking to his people. "If you have seen in the cinema or on television Hitler's dialogues with the crowd, you have witnessed a frightening display. A mutual induction built up, as between a cloud charged with electricity and the ground. Lightning was exchanged."[27] Camon, convinced that the guilt did not lie with a single man, and that Germany's culture did not improvise extermination out of nowhere, answered that the leading Nazi figures tried at Nuremberg had hidden behind the very same argument when they claimed to have obeyed their leader's orders. Levi thought — because the German people also included Goethe and Beethoven — that the Germans had somehow become anti-Semites with the advent of Hitler to power, knowing his ideas and knowing the plans he had repeatedly proclaimed. Camon believes to this day that Levi was mistaken, and that he suppressed his entitlement to pass judgement on German guilt. Like Raul Hilberg and Daniel Goldhagen,[28] he is convinced that a murderous hatred of the Jews was first expressed by Luther. Camon and Levi could only agree to differ. However, we shall see that the debate was not closed in Levi's mind, since he returns to the question in *The Drowned and the Saved*, reproaching Jean Améry — who committed suicide in a hotel in Salzburg on 17 October 1978 — for having called him "the forgiver": "I consider this neither insult nor praise but imprecision. I am not inclined to forgive, I never forgave our enemies of that time ... because I know no human act that can erase a crime" (*DS 137/110*).

Camon had wanted to see Levi because he had come to the conclusion that the Christian world could not understand the grief, and the sum of sufferings, endured by the Jews. He also said to him that the Christian world, by affirming that only "its" God died for the salvation of men, felt protected by this small and eternal conviction. When the pope made an official journey to Africa, Camon, who is convinced that guilt lies at the heart of Christian civilization, submitted an article to *L'Osservatore Romano* in which he argued that the Holy Father ought to have told the Africans that the black slaves had been sold to the Christian world, and that the Christian world was guilty, and carried the burden for it. The Roman Catholic newspaper rejected the article.

16　Famous and Marginal

Primo Levi was burdened by the growing responsibility, shared with his wife, of caring for two old ladies day and night. To his mind, it prevented him from making any kind of journey away from Turin, even though he would have liked to accept a few of the invitations that reached him from abroad. But the fact is that it would have been unthinkable for him to entrust his mother to any kind of nursing home, no matter how excellent. The idea would have horrified him. He had lost the protection of his father while still a young man, when he died of stomach cancer. Now he saw death coming close to the woman who had brought him into the world, and whom he had never voluntarily left. In Auschwitz, death had been his companion at every moment, and corpses a commonplace sight, but the prospect of facing his mother's death was a very different matter. Even in frail old age, she still embodied his ultimate protection against a world no less barbaric and enigmatic for all his faith in science. Ester Luzzati might die at any time, and her son must not deprive her of a single moment that he could, and should, devote to her.

He was trapped in an immensely painful double bind, caught between his fear of losing a mother old enough to die, and his duty of care. But Primo Levi, the prisoner in Turin, inflicted further duties on himself. Was it in expiation of having survived Auschwitz? He saw himself as an exception, and could not explain to himself why it was that, being a good man, he had nevertheless survived, when the conviction that had gradually overtaken and obsessed him was that the best had died, and that only those best adapted to the *Lager* — and therefore the worst — had survived.

One of his self-imposed tasks was to improve on the German that he had picked up in Auschwitz of an extremely impoverished, brutal, vulgar standard. Levi had a great respect for the German language, because it had once been the language of chemistry. He had studied from textbooks written in German, in particular the standard text by Gattermann, and there is no doubt that Gattermann, "the father's voice," played some part in Primo Levi's stubborn refusal to condemn the German people as a whole, or at least to hold them responsible. He resisted those who tried to influence him in that direction. Thus, as we have seen, he held on to his position under questioning from Ferdinando Camon, who adopted the even broader perspective of the responsibility of the Christian world for the extermination of the Jews. His bookish knowledge of German had helped Levi to come through Auschwitz, and that seems to have given him a sense of gratitude to the language. He took an interest in the responses of German critics and readers to his books, and regularly attended the courses given at the Goethe Institute.

Cesare Cases, a distinguished Germanist, remembers being asked by the teacher one day whether the word *Männin* existed in German, because Primo Levi maintained that, in the German Bible, this word means "woman." Cases knew that Luther had in fact coined the neologism *Männin*, which he had used to translate the Hebrew word *isha* meaning "woman," taken from the word "*ish*," "man" (Genesis, chapter 2, verse 23). Because he was a stickler for accuracy, and determined to acquire good German, one that was not stained with blood, Primo Levi had managed to embarrass his German teacher.

It was thanks to this twofold knowledge of German, both vulgar and bookish, that he started to translate Franz Kafka's *The Trial* during the summer of 1982. He also translated two books by Claude Lévi-Strauss, *La Voie des masques* and *Le Regard éloigné*, because despite his retirement pension and substantial royalties the high cost of medical care for his mother and mother-in-law forced him to take on extra work to supplement his income.

Giulio Einaudi had a project in mind: to commission new translations of foreign classics from Italian writers. He had suggested *Lord Jim* to Italo Calvino and *Madame Bovary* to Natalia Ginzburg. It was also his idea to give *The Trial* to Primo Levi to translate. The project was an onerous one for Levi, and the result less than successful. Cases places the blame on Einaudi himself, for assigning this book to Levi:

> He had said to himself, Kafka anticipated Auschwitz, Levi lived through Auschwitz, so it's going to be brilliant. And it wasn't at all! Levi was a basically optimistic man. In spite of his suicide, Kafka's pessimism was completely foreign to him. He actually said so in the afterword to his translation. Kafka is enigmatic and Primo was a philosopher of the Enlightenment, a positivist, a man of science. He believed in the Truth that can be demonstrated and established. Kafka was not for him. I'll give you an example: in the opening lines of *The Trial*, Joseph K wakes up and notices that Anna, the servant, hasn't brought his breakfast yet. Kafka writes: "*Das war noch niemals geschehen.*" Primo Levi translated it into Italian as: "It was the first time it had happened." Which means that he still had faith in the continuity of time, whereas Kafka wants to indicate a break after which time no longer exists. Levi almost got the meaning wrong, and there are many other instances in his translation.[1]

In an interview published in *La Stampa*, Primo Levi had stated:

> I like and admire Kafka because he writes in a manner that is totally foreign to me. In my writings, for better or for worse, knowingly or unknowingly, I have always made an effort to move from dark to clear, like a filtration pump that sucks in cloudy water and expels it clarified, if not sterile. Kafka takes an opposite path; he pours out an endless stream of the hallucinations dredged up from levels unbelievably deep,

and never filters them. The reader feels them swarming with seeds and spores: they are burning with meaning, but he is never helped to tear down or bypass the veil, so as to see things in the place where they are hidden. Kafka never touches ground, he never deigns to offer you the clue to the maze.[2]

Primo Levi's new translation of *The Trial* reached the bookshops at the end of April 1983. He said that he had tried to soften the text, and had felt himself grow ill as he worked. To his eyes, *The Trial* was a "sick book." "Faced with Kafka, I discovered unconscious defences in myself ... my defences crumbled in translating him. I found myself involved in the character of Joseph K. I accused myself, as he did."[3] In fact, Joseph K does not know what he stands accused of, while Primo Levi blamed himself for being among the few survivors.

Levi was perplexed about the reasons for Joseph K's arrest. In its obscurity, the book seemed incoherent. "I am Italian, and a lot less Jewish than he. I try to take a rational view of the world."[4] Yet while he taxed Kafka with obscurity, he thought highly of his "smooth and aseptic" German. If Kafka's Jewishness is always a background presence in his writings, the word Jew, for example, is never once spoken in *The Trial*. Levi had strong reservations about psychoanalysis, but he expressed his surprise that Kafka, a contemporary of Freud, had taken no interest in a scientific approach to the human spirit and to the rules that guide its behaviour.

But what keeps Levi further removed from Kafka is his conviction that literature is the instrument of a dialogue between the one who reads and the one who writes. Even if Levi is essentially an optimist and positivist, and Kafka a pessimist, it is most of all the absurdity of Kafka's universe that Levi rejects. In the end, he admitted that if his publisher had given him the choice he would have much preferred to translate Thomas Mann or Joseph Conrad, with both of whom he felt a great affinity.

Early in 1983 Primo Levi undertook to resume his talks to schools, even though a sense of utter exhaustion had caused him to interrupt his dialogue with young people for a while. But almost at once he had the feeling "of being a survivor from a bygone age, an old soldier, an old fogey, nothing more. ..."[5]

Without having read the work of deniers of the Holocaust such as Robert Faurisson or apologists such as Ernst Nolte, the young doubted the reality of what they heard from Levi, the survivor. They did not believe it simply because their knowledge of the media had accustomed them to thinking that everything could be fantasy. The line between fact and fiction had been eroded. For example, they had seen the same familiar actors playing in the television miniseries *Holocaust* and in a series about King Arthur. Levi told a delicious, funny, frightening story about a ten-year-old schoolboy who listened to his description of the camp, then solemnly told him what he should have done to get away — cut a guard's throat, switch off the power to the electric fence — and urged him not to forget his advice if it should happen again (*DS 157/127–8*).

As a believer in the persuasive power of language, Levi was depressed by an encounter that took place in July 1983. An anti-Fascist friend asked if he would speak to his teenage son, who had got himself involved with the new right and denied the existence of the extermination camps. Levi agreed, but when he described his experience the young man claimed not to believe him, and denied the existence of the gas chambers, though he also displayed a suspicious interest in the effects of Zyklon B. Levi rolled up his sleeve, showed him the number tattooed on his forearm, and said to him: "Eight thousand Italian Jews were deported to Auschwitz, six hundred returned. Where do you think the rest of them are?" Nothing could change his visitor's convictions.[6]

Faced with the attitude of schoolboys who listened to his evidence with apathy or even hostility, Levi had felt "a sense of inferiority towards them,"[7] even though he never for a moment doubted the value of the books he had written. With great honesty, he admitted that he was at a loss to reply when children at junior or high schools asked for his opinion about the existence of God and the reason why He had allowed such horrors to be perpetrated in the twentieth century. They tended to put the Stalinist camps and the war in Korea or Vietnam into the same category. Adolescents would often ask Levi to explain why it was that the Jews had been exterminated, as if there was bound to be a reasonable answer.

Levi was so discouraged that he completely abandoned his visits to schools. He said to Anna Bravo and Federico Cerejo:

> And now I would like to ask you, could you answer this question: Why do people make war? Why do they torture their enemies, as the Romans did, and the Nazis? Although they ceased for half a century, the lull didn't last; at present we are living in a cruel period. Well, I don't know how to answer, except with vague generalities about the fact that man is bad, he is not good.

Levi had believed in the superiority of Enlightenment thought over an irrational world. Once this bad world, inexplicably bad, was no longer accessible to the light of reason, he had no course left except but to despair.

Having published very little for a while, Primo Levi emerged from his isolation. He was concerned about the future of the earth. The air we breathe is polluted, he declared. Isn't there a symmetry between the moral fate of the world and its material fate? "Thanks to our failure to believe in almost everything, it has become really difficult to mobilize people for the ecological rescue of the world. Whether it has to do with making war or with achieving some other purpose, good or bad, we no longer have faith in the future."[8]

For a left-wing man like Primo Levi, this was a grievous loss of confidence in the ideals of justice. He contended that young people, born into a world he perceived as physically doomed, harboured a deep distrust towards the past. "The world is one," he said. "Ever smaller, ever more fragile."

On 28 and 29 October 1983, Levi took part in a congress organized in the Palazzo Lascaris by the Regional Council of Piedmont and the National Association of Ex-Deportees. The speakers addressed a central theme: "The duty to bear witness. So that the memory of the extermination camps, the culmination of the Nazi criminal doctrine, may not be lost." Primo Levi took the floor on 29 October. This is his speech, whose content is close to the first chapter of his final book, *The Drowned and the Saved*:

The Camp and Memory[9]

Human memory is a marvellous instrument, but a deceptive one. This is a truth that is known not solely by the psychologists who focus their attention on the behaviour of the people around them and on their own behaviour. The memories that exist inside us are not written in stone. Not only do they tend to fade with time, but often they change or grow by incorporating extraneous features. Judges are well aware of this. It hardly ever happens that two eyewitnesses of the same event describe it in the same way and with the same words, even if the event is recent and if neither of the two has any personal interest in distorting it. This scant trust we accord our memories will not be explained satisfactorily until we know in what language and alphabet they are written, on what material and with what pen. Today we are some distance from that. We know some mechanisms that put memory into particular states — traumas, not only of the cerebral kind; interference from other "rival" memories. Abnormal states of consciousness, repressions, shocks. However, even under normal conditions a slow dissipation is at work. An erasure of memories, a virtual physiological forgetting, that few memories withstand. It is probable that this can be recognized among the great forces of nature, the same forces that break down into disorder and bring life into death. It is certain that, in this case, practice and frequent recollection refresh the memory in the same way as a muscle is refreshed when often called upon. It is equally true that a memory too often recalled and expressed in the form of a story tends to solidify into a stereotype, a crystallized, perfected form of experience that supersedes the original memory.

It is interesting to examine the memories of our extreme experiences as deportees. In this case, practically all of the factors that can obliterate or distort the recording of memory are at work. The memory of a trauma received or inflicted is itself traumatic because to recall it is painful, or at the very least disturbing. The one who suffered the wound tends to eliminate its memory so as not to revive the pain. On the other hand, the one who inflicted the wound on somebody else will hide its memory deep down inside himself in order to be released from it, to alleviate his feeling of guilt. Once again we come upon a paradoxical analogy between victim and oppressor, and once again anxiety takes hold. They are in the same trap, but it is the oppressor, and he alone, who made it, and if he suffers from it, then it is just that he should suffer. On the other hand it is iniquitous that the victim himself should still suffer, decades later. Once again, it is painful to have to observe that the offence is incurable. It propagates through time, and the Furies, whom we have to believe in, do not afflict the torturer alone (if they do afflict him, with or without the help of human punishment), but also perpetuate his work by withholding peace from the tortured. Not without dread do we read the words bequeathed by Jean Améry, the philosopher tortured by the Gestapo because he belonged to the Belgian Resistance, and then dispatched to Auschwitz because he was a Jew: "Whoever was tortured, stays tortured. ... Whoever has been subjected to torture can no longer feel at home in the world. ... Faith in humanity, already demolished by torture, is never regained." The oppressor remains what he was, and so does the victim. The former is to be punished and loathed, but if possible understood; the latter is to be pitied and helped. Both of them, faced with the brutal reality of the act that was irrevocably committed, need refuge and defence.

We now have many confessions, depositions, and statements made by the oppressors of that time. Some related in trials, others during interviews, others in books and memoirs. As I see it, these are documents of the utmost importance. In general, the descriptions of things seen and acts committed have little interest. They broadly coincide with what has been told by the victims. They have gone to trial, and now they are part of History. They are taken as read. The motivations and justifications are important. Why I did it. Did you realize that you were committing a crime? The answers to these questions and to others like them are very similar, irrespective of the personality of the man interrogated, whether he is an ambitious professional like Speer, an icy fanatic like Eichmann, or a dull brute like Boger and Kaduk, torturers in Auschwitz. They are expressed in different wording and with more or less stubbornness or arrogance, according to the mental or cultural level of the speaker, but they all come down to much the same assertion: I did it because I was ordered to; others, my superiors, committed acts more serious than mine; given the upbringing I received and the surroundings I lived in, I could not do otherwise. If I had not done it, another would have done it in my place, and more harshly.

For anyone who reads these justifications the first impulse is one of horror: they're lying, they can't possibly hope to be believed, they can't not see the imbalance between their excuses and the amount of pain and death that they have caused. They lie, and they know that they lie. They speak in bad faith. Now, anyone who has enough experience of people knows that the distinction — the opposition, a linguist would say — between good and bad faith is optimistic and illuminist. It is all the more so, and for a number of important reasons, if it is applied to men like those we have just named. It presupposes a mental clarity that few people have, and that even those few lose at once when for some reason reality past or present causes anxiety or trouble. In those circumstances, the deliberate liar coolly falsifies reality itself, but more common are those who distance themselves for the moment or for ever from real memories and manufacture a more convenient reality for themselves. Even in this case, the victims and the oppressors have a common fate, because for both groups the past is a burden. In both cases it often happens, for similar but opposite reasons, that they feel repugnance for things done or suffered, and tend to replace them with others. The substitution may start consciously with an invented, untruthful, or restored scenario, but anyway less vexing than the real one. They repeat its description to others, but also to themselves; the distinction between true and false gradually loses its sharpness, and the teller ends up by believing the story he has told so often, and that he goes on telling, touching it up here and there with incongruous or unbelievable details out of context from the events that took place. The original bad faith has become good faith. The silent shift to the lie turned self-delusion is useful: he who lies in good faith lies better, he speaks his part better. He is more easily believed by the judge, or historian, or reader. The further back the events recede, the more the construction of the convenient truth expands and is perfected.

I believe that only by way of this psychological mechanism is it possible to interpret, for example, the statement made to L'Express in 1978 by Darquier de Pellepoix, the former commissioner-general for Jewish Affairs under the Vichy government in 1942, and as such, personally responsible for the deportation of 70,000 Jews. Darquier denies everything: the photos of heaps of dead bodies are montages, the statistics of millions of dead were fabricated by the Jews, always greedy for publicity and commiseration. The deportations happened (it is hard to deny them: his signature appears on too many documents that give orders concerning deportations of children), but he did not know where to, and with what outcome. In Auschwitz, the gas chambers were used only for killing lice, or then again (note the consistency!) they were built for propaganda purposes, after the end of the war. I do not mean to justify this base and stupid man. It offends me that he should live a quiet life in Spain. But I believe that I see in him the typical case of a man who, having had to lie in public, finishes by lying even in private, even to himself, and identifies himself with a convenient truth that enables him to live in peace. To distinguish between good faith and bad necessitates a profound sincerity with oneself, a continual effort, both intellectual and moral, and how can one ask such an effort of men like Darquier?

If one reveals the statements made by Eichmann during his trial in Jerusalem, and by Rudolf Höss, the commandant of Auschwitz, the inventor of the gas chambers, in his autobiography, one observes a subtle process of elaboration of the past. In substance, both of them defended themselves in the classic manner of the grassroots Nazi, or better, of all the privates in the ranks: we were brought up in absolute obedience, in hierarchy, nationalism, the religion of blood and soil; we were steeped in slogans, demonstrations, and ceremonies. We were taught that the only justice was what served the German people, and the only truth the orders of the leader. What do you want from us? How can you think of expecting from us anything else but what we did, or behaviour different from what ours and our fellows' was? The decisions weren't ours because the regime that we lived in did not permit autonomous decisions to be taken. Others took decisions for us, and it could not be otherwise, because we lacked the ability to decide. Not only was it forbidden to take a decision, but we had become incapable of doing so. For all these reasons we are not responsible and cannot be punished.

Even if it is projected on to the backdrop of the chimneys at Birkenau, this argument cannot be taken at face value, innocent of all impudence. The pressure on the individual that a modern totalitarian state can exert is appalling. Basically it has three weapons: direct propaganda camouflaged by upbringing, education, and popular culture; bans imposed on pluralism of information; and terror.

Nevertheless, it cannot be conceded that this pressure is irresistible. Least of all during the brief period of the twelve years of the Third Reich. In the affirmations and vindications of men like Höss and Eichmann, the exaggeration is obvious, and the omissions in their memories even more so. Both of them were born and grew up long before the Reich became truly totalitarian. Their support was by choice. The reconstitution of their past was a later operation, slow and probably not methodical, not systematic. To ask oneself whether it was done in good or bad faith is naive, even if they say themselves were not. They too, facing the death they deserved, and facing their judges, constructed a convenient past for themselves, and ended by believing in it: especially Höss, who was not a subtle man. What comes through in his autobiography shows a character given so little to self-examination and introspection that he was incapable of admitting the crude anti-Semitism apparent in the very way he denied and disowned it, or of realizing how utterly slimy his self-portrait as a good functionary, father, and husband made him appear.

One comment on these reconstructions of the past (but not only on these: it is an observation that applies to all memoirs): one must note that the distortion of the facts is often limited by the objectivity of the facts themselves, on which there are testimonies, documents, and historically accepted accounts. It is generally difficult to deny having committed a given action, or that the action was committed, but on the other hand it is very easy to falsify the motivations that led to an action, and the passions within ourselves that accompanied the action itself. This is an extremely fluid matter, liable to be skewed by even the weakest forces acting on it. To the question, "Why did I do it?" "What was I thinking when I did it?," there is no reliable answer, because the memory of the facts is liable by nature. Total suppression is the extreme instance of distorting the memory of a crime committed. There too, the boundary between good and bad faith can be vague. Behind the "I don't know" and "I don't remember" heard in many courts, there is a precise intention to lie in the one case, but in others there is a fossilized lie, set into a formula. The one who remembers wishes to become a man without memories, and he succeeds: by dint of denying their existence, he expells the harmful memories as if he were expelling excreta. Lawyers for the defence are well aware that the memory blanks, or the possible truths that they suggest to their clients, tend to become things actually forgotten, or actual memory sequences. We need not confine ourselves to mental pathology to find human examples whose statements leave us baffled. They are certainly false, but we are at a loss to tell whether or not the subject knows that he is lying. Supposing, absurdly, that the liar turned honest for a moment, he himself would be unable to resolve the dilemma; in the act of lying he is an actor totally merged with his character.

He can no longer distinguish himself from it. The best way to protect oneself from excessively painful memories is to exclude them from consciousness, putting a buffer zone along their borders. It is easier to keep a memory out than to rid oneself of it after it has been recorded. That, in substance, was the purpose of the devices invented by the Nazis to defend the consciences of their followers when they were doing dirty work, and to secure their services, which were unpleasant even for the most hardened thugs. To the *Einsatzkommandos* who paraded with automatic weapons against Jews standing by the side of common graves, in the rear of the Russian front, they issued all the alcohol they could drink, so that the slaughter was clouded in drunkenness. The well-known euphemisms ("final solution," "action"; the very word *Einsatzkommando*, which means "action unit," disguised a frightful reality) were not used only to deceive the victims and prevent defensive reactions. They did not want the public to get to know what had happened in all the territories occupied by the Third Reich.

In the much vaster camp of the victims, one observes that memory is falsified in various ways. But here, fraud is obviously absent. Someone who falls victim to an injustice or a crime has no need to make up lies to exonerate himself from a guilt he does not feel. But that does not rule out the possibility that his very memories may be altered. It is known, for example, that many survivors of the camps, or of other complex and traumatic experiences, tend unconsciously to filter their memories: when they mention them among themselves, or relate them to third parties, they prefer to linger on the truces, the grotesque, strange, or distorted interludes, and to skim over the more painful episodes. The latter are not willingly dredged up from the reservoir of memory, and yet they tend to disappear with time, to lose their outlines. The behaviour of Count Ugolino is psychologically credible; he feels reticence about relating his dreadful death to Dante, and finally forces himself to do so, not out of courtesy, but in order to take a posthumous revenge on his eternal enemy.

With the aim of defending oneself, reality can be distorted, not only in memory but also in the very action in which it is verified. During the whole of my captivity in Auschwitz, I had Alberto D[10] as my fraternal friend. He was young, strong, and braver than the average, and quite critical in examining the many illusory happenings fabricated for their consolation value — "The war will be over in two weeks, there won't be any more selections, Polish partisans are going to liberate the camp," and so on. Alberto had been interned with his father, who was forty-five years old. As the big selection of October 1944 drew near, Alberto and I commented on the event with anger, and resignation before the inevitable, but without seeking refuge in convenient truths. The selection came, Alberto's father was chosen for death by gas, and from that moment on, within hours, Alberto changed. He had heard bits of news around us that seemed to him plausible: the Russians were close, the Germans would not dare to continue the slaughter. This selection was not like the rest, it wasn't gas. It had been done to select the weak but redeemable prisoners — just like his father, who was weak, but not sick. On the contrary, he knew where he had been sent — not very far away, to Jaworzno, to a special camp for convalescents, adapted for light labour. Naturally his father never reappeared, and Alberto himself died in the evacuation march of January 1945.

Strangely, though they knew nothing about Alberto's behaviour, his relations, who had remained in Italy, responded as he did, by rejecting too bitter a truth. When I returned to Italy I made it my mission to go at once to Alberto's home town[11] to tell his mother and his brother what I knew about him and his father. I was greeted with affectionate courtesy, but I'd hardly begun my story when his mother interrupted.

They already knew everything, at least where Alberto was concerned. There was no use my repeating these horrible stories. They *knew* that Alberto had miraculously managed to slip away from the column, without being killed by the SS. He was safe and sound, in the hands of the Russians. He hadn't yet been able to send news, but he soon would, I could be certain of it. And now, would I please change the subject and tell them how I had survived. A year later I happened to be passing through the town, and I paid another visit to the family. The truth had changed slightly. Alberto was in a Soviet clinic. He was well, but he had lost his memory, he didn't even remember his name, but he was alive, and he would soon be coming home. Alberto never returned. Thirty-five years have gone by, and ever since then I have not had the courage to go back to that town and pit my painful truth against the consolatory truth that Alberto's family had concocted for itself.

The phase of pessimism subsided, and Levi again agreed to meet journalists, and some students who were preparing a thesis on his work. He went to Camerino to collect a literary prize for a work about mountain climbing. The award went to the "Iron" chapter in *The Periodic Table*.

He made more trips to the mountains near Turin with his old friends Bianca Guidetti Serra, Magda Novero Beyneton, Alberto Salmoni and his wife Margaret, and sometimes the philosopher Norberto Bobbio, a close neighbour and one of the founders of the *Partito d'Azione*. He also saw something of Francesco Ciafaloni and Nuto Revelli, the great memorialist of the war in Russia, who fought in the Resistance.

Marginalized in the Italian literary world, which still viewed him only as a "memorialist," Levi's work was starting to gain ground abroad, in particular in the United States, where the English manuscript of *The Periodic Table* was ready for publication by Schocken Books. At about the same time, *If Not Now, When?* was being prepared for publication by Summit Books in a translation by William Weaver, one of the best-known American translators from Italian; other titles were to follow. A tide of fame was flowing from the United States, while sales of the Italian edition of *The Periodic Table* had now reached over 150,000 copies.

Levi attained instant international stature as a writer with the publication of *The Periodic Table* in English by Schocken Books in 1984. Raymond Rosenthal, an American-born translator who lived for many years in Italy and had befriended Levi, offered his translation of *The Periodic Table* to Emile Capouya, who was then Schocken's Editorial Director. With early advance praise from Saul Bellow and Rosenthal's award-winning translation, the book received wide acclaim in reviews and was subsequently translated into over a dozen languages. The unusual format of the book, combining science with scenes from the life of a working chemist, created a new image for Levi, who was welcomed as a literary celebrity when he visited the United States in 1985. The success of *The Periodic Table* paved the way for the reissue of his first two books, more or less forgotten in the twenty years since their first appearance in English, and aroused intense interest in his other books as well. Raymond Rosenthal subsequently translated *Other People's Trades*, *The Drowned and the Saved*, *The Sixth Day*, and *The Mirror Maker*.

In September Primo Levi met Elie Wiesel again, when he came to attend the Congress of Ex-Deportees in Turin. They had corresponded in the 1960s when both of them agreed to join a literary jury created by survivors of the Bergen-Belsen camp.[12] Their first meeting had taken place during the 1970s in Milan, at a conference devoted to Wiesel's work. They were to meet again in October 1983, at the Congress on Jewish Literature in Italy organized by the community of Venice. It was during their conversations that Wiesel and Levi deduced that they must both have been in the same hut in Buna-Monowitz. Wiesel had worked in Kommando 1 for I.G. Farben, but neither of the two had any recollection of the other. They spoke about prisoners' behaviour in camps, and about the denial of the Holocaust. Their long conversations did not grow heated, although they did not share the same ideas about the attitude to Israel of the diaspora, and the role of the survivor in society. Elie Wiesel and Primo Levi came from different worlds. Primo Levi had a late and bookish knowledge of the sacred texts. Elie Wiesel had lived with them in the community of Sighet before being deported to Auschwitz, where his rebellion had broken out, and brought him into basic agreement with Levi's indignation, and his inability to pronounce himself on the existence of God. Here is Elie Wiesel in *Night*:

> This day I had ceased to plead. I was no longer capable of lamentation. On the contrary I felt very strong. I was the accuser, God the accused. My eyes were open and I was alone — terribly alone in a world without God and without man. Without love or mercy. I had ceased to be anything but ashes, yet I felt myself to be stronger than the Almighty, to whom my life had been tied for so long. I stood amid that praying congregation, observing it like a stranger.[13]

17 "Old, Am I?"

A second collection of poems by Primo Levi was published by Garzanti in Milan at the end of October 1984, under the title *Ad ora incerta* ("At an Uncertain Hour"). All the rest of Levi's books up to that point had been published by Einaudi. He went to Garzanti because the famous Turinese publisher was in compulsory liquidation.

The book contained the twenty-seven poems published by Scheiwiller in Milan in 1975, under the title *L'osteria di Brema*, plus thirty-four new ones that had appeared in *La Stampa*, a few translations of Heine and Kipling, and an anonymous Scottish ballad. Levi had chosen Heine and Kipling, but he claimed that he was no great reader of poetry.

The title of the collection is a phrase borrowed from his poem "*Il superstite*" ("The Survivor"), whose epigraph is a verse from Coleridge's *The Rime of the Ancient Mariner*, beginning with an Italian translation of the first line:

> *Dopo di allora, ad ora incerta,*
> Since then, at an uncertain hour,
> That agony returns:
> And till my ghastly tale is told,
> This heart within me burns.[1]

"The Survivor," written on 4 February 1984, is dedicated to his friend Bruno Vasari, who was deported to Mauthausen for acts of resistance.[2] In this poem, Levi expresses the feeling of guilt for having survived his comrades. He was to examine this issue at length in *The Drowned and the Saved*, where he asks himself: "Are you ashamed because you are alive in place of another?" (*DS 81/62*) But he did not quote Coleridge solely because of his theme of a man haunted by an experience that he can never forget and feels compelled to tell. Levi loved quotations — he called them "a rabbinical vice" — and like many other secular Jewish intellectuals, he nevertheless enjoyed studying and quoting sacred texts.

Primo Levi did not make great claims for his poetry:

> I am a man who has little belief in poetry, and yet goes in for it. There is certainly a reason. For instance, when my verses appear in *La Stampa*'s "*La Terza Pagina*" I receive letters that express agreement or disapproval. When I publish short stories, the reactions are less sharp. I have the impression that poetry in general has become a vector of human contact. Adorno wrote that after Auschwitz there could be no more poetry, but my hope has been just the opposite. In 1945–46 it

seemed to me that poetry would be better suited than prose to explain what was weighing inside me. When I say poetry, I have nothing lyrical in mind. In those days, I would have reformulated Adorno's remark like this: After Auschwitz, there can be no more poetry, except about Auschwitz.[3]

This is what Adorno wrote:

Even the most radical awareness of the disaster risks degenerating into gossip. The critique of culture finds itself confronted by the final stage of the dialectic between culture and barbarity: to write a poem after Auschwitz is barbarous, and this fact affects even knowledge, and explains why it has become impossible to write poems today.[4]

And, as Denis Trierveiller observes in his study *Paul Celan. Poésie après Auschwitz, ou comment traduire?*, "the highest degree of culture is henceforward fouled beyond redemption by barbarity, and in accordance with an irreversible, irreparable, negative dialectic."

When he wrote *If Not Now, When?*, Primo Levi was aware that in fact the "poetry of annihilation" had been written in the language of those who had been exterminated — Yiddish. The poets who launched that cry into the indifference and silence of the world voiced it before they were put to death in the ghettos of Bialystok, Lodz, Vilno, and Cracow, and in the extermination camps of Auschwitz and Treblinka. The language in which death was administered was German. A great many of those who received the death sentence spoke Yiddish. And no doubt that is the only language that could construe the kingdom of the dead. Some writings have been found sealed inside tins or rolled up in bottles buried beneath the ruins of the ghettos, or next to the gas chambers.

Primo Levi wanted to give the Italian language the power to talk about extermination. He thought that clarity and transparency of language had the paradoxical capacity to give expression to darkness. And in fact a number of his poems are devoted to the extermination of the Jewish people: "Buna," "Shemà," "Reveille," "Ostjuden," and "For Adolf Eichmann."

The last poems in the collection were written in 1983 and 1984, after the publication of *If Not Now, When?*. When a journalist questioned Levi about Pliny, to whom he refers in one poem, thinking about what will become of the atoms of his old body, he answered without hesitation:

I am not thinking of anything metaphysical. It is an idea as old as the world. It is found in Pythagoras and Lucretius. And besides, the fathers of chemistry in the last century taught that the oxygen we breathe comes from plants, and that the substance that plants and woods are made of comes from the carbon dioxide that we, and all the other animals, produce during our life and after our death.[5]

In June 1984 Primo Levi met the astrophysicist Tullio Regge, who taught the theory of relativity in the theoretical physics department at the university of Turin. Regge had invited the mathematician Corrado Bohm to dinner, whose parents had perished in the Holocaust. At the last minute, Bohm called to ask if he could bring Primo Levi too. During the meal, Levi suddenly announced to his host: "By the way, during the war I was in a concentration camp." Of course, everybody knew that. Then Levi rolled up his shirt sleeve, displayed the number tattooed on his forearm, and told his host that in Turin there were three or four people alive who had a number on their arm.

Levi had arrived at Regge's house carrying a box full of strange flowers with transparent coloured petals supported on a tracery of steel wire. Regge had seen the same kind of confections on sale as a do-it-yourself kit in the United States, and he said to Levi: "So you bought them, too." It came as a blow to Levi, who had created these exotic flowers himself and believed that he was the first to use a solution of a particular kind of resin that formed a film like soap bubbles over a lacework of delicate, transparent wire, and dried with a very lifelike look. Regge turned the screw still further by informing his guest that these materials could be bought for a couple of dollars in every novelty store in Princeton.

Levi quickly banished his disappointment, and proceeded to ply the astrophysicist with questions about cosmology, which Regge answered at length. "I convinced him to come and see a curious computer animation wherein a visiting American mathematician attempted to visualize the fourth dimension. He seemed to like it, but later admitted that he was not quite sure that he had seen the extra dimension."[6]

Some time later, Tullio Regge was asked by RAI to organize a series of twelve educational programmes in the form of conversations about physics. He invited Primo Levi to take part with the philosopher Carlo Augusto Viano in the introductory programme on the history of science.

One day Ernesto Ferrero, who had been literary director at Einaudi before it went bankrupt, and who was working now for a small Milanese house, Edizioni Comunità, asked Tullio Regge if he would be prepared to be interviewed for a book, because Regge had not found time to write the book he had agreed to deliver. Regge turned down every one of the specialist science writers on the list submitted by Ferrero, but responded with enthusiasm when Ferrero suggested Primo Levi. The idea of a broad-based conversation was born.

The first interview session took place in Franco Debenedetti's apartment in the huge grey building on the Piazza Castello built by Mussolini in the city centre. The two men dropped the formalities at once, and after that they met at Regge's house. Their exchanges were more a series of wide-ranging monologues than a discursive dialogue, each man painting a verbal self-portrait for the other through reminiscences about his formative years, his profession, and his vision of the future of science. All were published in full in *Dialogo* (*Conversations*).[7] In the brief interventions that Levi permitted himself, he confided quite freely in Regge, although he was not a close friend. He spoke about childhood memories — in particular about the intellectual influence of his father — that do not appear in such detail elsewhere in his work.

For Primo Levi, 1984 was a year of international recognition. *The Periodic Table* came out in the United States, translated by Raymond Rosenthal, after he proposed a translation to Emile Capouya of Schocken Books, a friend of Nobel Laureate Saul Bellow. Capouya sent the manuscript to Saul Bellow, whose verdict was quoted on the jacket: "We are always looking for the book it is *necessary* to read next. After a few pages I immersed myself gladly and gratefully. There is nothing superfluous here, everything this book contains is essential. It is wonderfully pure, and beautifully translated." A chorus of enthusiastic reviews came from Neal Ascherson in the *New York Review of Books*, Alvin Rosenfeld in the *New York Times Book Review*, and John Gross in the *New York Times*. Twenty years after the muted reception abroad of Levi's first two books, several countries expressed interest in translation rights.

Levi, who had just celebrated his sixtieth birthday, wrote in *La Stampa*:

Old, am I? In absolute terms, yes, if I am to believe the registry office, long-sightedness, greying at the temples, and grown-up children. Last week, for the first time, somebody gave up their seat for me in a tram, and that felt really funny. Subjectively, I don't feel old. I haven't lost my curiosity in the world around me, or my interest in my family and friends, or my taste for fighting, playing, and problem-solving. I still enjoy nature; it brings perceptible pleasures to my five senses, and I love to study it, and describe it with words. My organs, limbs, and memory still serve me well, although I am very aware of the grave implications of that word that I have just written but that I have uttered twice: "still."[8]

He bought a computer, which was to be shared between him and his son Renzo, and as soon as it arrived he phoned his cousin, Paolo Avigdor, to ask for his help with installing it. He was so pleased with his purchase that during a short interview on Italian television for the *Italia Sera* programme he referred to it humorously as his "concubine." In honour of the first anniversary of their living together he wrote an essay, "The Hidden Player," in which he confided that he had started to play chess with it.[9] Elsewhere he described some of the pros and cons of keeping such a companion: "The simplicity of deleting, correcting, inserting, and cancelling puts the mind at ease with the medium. It even puts it too much at ease. ... The fact of being able to erase things at once, and leave no scar on the paper, is easy and painless. Unluckily for them, the philologists of the future will not find manuscripts, with their record of successive approximations."

In 1985 the house of Einaudi found itself in financial straits again. In order to try to save it, the publisher offered his authors and contributors worthless shares. It was a kind of alms collection. When the situation worsened, the authors were asked to give up the royalties due to them from their previous books, and to sign a kind of agreement to stave off the bankruptcy. They left the sinking ship *en masse*, but not Primo Levi, who would never have abandoned his publisher, and to whom he was very attached. He discussed the matter with Federico Accati, his former employer, but by then it was really too late. He told Luisa Accati: "As long as I was with your father, I was never cheated. Now that I'm on my own, I've been had." Although the publishing house was now deserted, Levi often looked in because he liked to talk to Agnese Incisa, Giulio Einaudi's editorial secretary.

Every year the literary editors at Einaudi used to meet in a secluded place for ten days or so to confer among themselves and take stock of the publishing year that ended in June. The meeting took place in July in the little valley of Val di Rhêmes, about 65 kilometres north-west of Turin, and not much frequented by tourists. Writers and editors crowded into two small hotels and a few cottages, to work in perpetual committee, with sessions in the morning and afternoon. They talked about the various series, the back list, and the books from abroad to be acquired. Levi enjoyed his visits to what had become a legendary meeting place where journalists, smarting at their exclusion, were not allowed to stay. In particular he was glad of the chance to spend time with Italo Calvino, who was always the first to receive his new manuscripts.

It was in Rhêmes-Notre-Dame, in 1985, that Calvino was looking over the translation by Sergio Solmi of Raymond Queneau's *Petite Cosmogonie portative*, which he was not entirely happy with. Levi offered some suggestions to Calvino, who was working on Solmi's manuscript in the presence of a cat that would sit on his desk and amuse itself by turning pages over. Levi admired Queneau, even though he did not write "with order and clarity." He felt so dazzled and so bowled over when he read the book that he was obliged to revise his principles, to the point of regretting that he was not a high-wire artist like Queneau, balancing literary with spoken language, and verbal invention with puns and slang.

In 1985 Einaudi was ruined — among other things by its grandiose project for a massive encyclopedia. Agnese Incisa made special arrangements for the authors to draw their royalties, so that Natalia Ginzburg — who was owed a lot of money — and Primo Levi were able to be paid in September by virtue of a contract that provided for them to receive an advance payment greater than the sum they were owed. But Italo Calvino, who in June had asked the company accountant for money because he owed taxes, was not paid. The accountant had hit on the very cunning plan of telling him that he could give him nothing, and that he was going to consult the ministry of finance in Rome, to see what could be done. Agnese Incisa then proposed to pay Calvino the money in the form of an advance on his future books, but the accountant refused, and Calvino moved to Garzanti.

Levi was worried. Yet he had found success in Italy with *If Not Now, When?*, whose rights had been acquired by Summit Books in the United States, *The Periodic Table* had sold 250,000 copies in its English translation, and the Americans were now inviting him to go there to give a series of lectures and to meet the press. He had visited the RAI offices in Turin to record answers to eight questions put to him by the *New York Times*. But he was anxious and depressed because his mother, now ninety years old, was deteriorating in health, and tyrannizing her son. He said that he could not write any more, and that he even no longer felt interested enough to write another book. Agnese Incisa made an office available at Einaudi, but he never went to work there. One day as he was telling her how despondent he felt, she suggested that he should put his mother into the care of a nursing home close to where he lived. Levi blanched with shock, and was trembling as he told Agnese: "It would kill her." Agnese tried to convince him that he had to go on writing, and that if this deadlock continued he would fall ill himself. Levi told her: "You've really shaken me, talking this way!," and she poured him some brandy to restore him.[10]

L'altrui mestiere (*Other People's Trades*), a collection of nearly fifty articles first published in *La Stampa*, had come out in January 1985. Its subtitle was *Notes Towards a Redefinition of Culture*, a theme on which Levi continued to express his regrets that culture was no longer one, as it had been during the Renaissance when in Urbino the Duke of Montefeltro had been able to assemble men who were at once painters, mathematicians, and artists, in order to build an ideal city. *Other People's Trades* contains reflections on the most varied fields and subjects, from science and technology to literature and religion, through which the author provides an intellectual portrait of himself that is both grave and full of humour. A subject especially close to his heart was language and its use, and we have already examined the controversy that followed his severely critical essay "On Obscure Writing," in which he refers to the last writings of Paul Celan as "the last inarticulate babble ... of a dying man," and complains — in terms unusually strong for Levi — that: "If his is a message, it gets lost in the 'background noise': it is not a communication, it is not a language, or at most it is a dark and truncated language precisely like that of a person who is about to die and is alone, as we all will be at the point of death" (*Trades* 173–4/161).

In the same collection Levi also spent several pages writing about the fear of spiders. This was not the first time he had referred to these creatures, and his last article for *La Stampa* reverted to the subject. This essay is open to interpretations that throw an odd light on his last fatal act. Levi reports that he owes one of his earliest childhood terrors to a spider, and confesses that: "All of them, from the minuscule scarlet spiders which live in the porosity of rocks to the obese, crossbearing spiders stationed head-on at the centre of their geometric webs, inflict on me a revulsion–horror which is totally unjustified and highly specific" (*Trades* 154/142).

On 29 October 1981 he had dedicated a poem to "Arachne":

> Patience! I'll weave myself another web.
> My patience is long, my mind is short;
> Eight legs and a hundred eyes,
> But a thousand spinner breasts.
> I don't like fasting;
> I like flies and males.
> I'll rest for four days, seven,
> Holed up in my lair,
> Until I feel my abdomen heavy
> With fine shiny, sticky thread.
> And I'll weave myself another web,
> Like the one you tore when you passed by,
> According to the plan printed
> On my memory's little tape.
> I'll seat myself in the center
> And wait till a male arrives,
> Wary but drunk with desire,
> To fill my belly and my womb
> At one fell swoop.
> Nimble and fierce, as soon as it gets dark,
> Quickly, quickly, knot upon know,
> I'll weave myself another web.[11]

Although his horror of spiders and their frequent appearance in his work offer a fruitful field to specialists, Primo Levi strongly distrusted the psychologists of the unconscious. As for his phobia, it was connected, as we have seen, with the engraving of Arachne by Gustave Doré that illustrates Canto XII of Dante's *Purgatory*, which shows a beautiful girl half transformed into a spider, and Dante kneeling to look up at her crotches, "half disgusted, half voyeur." In the writer's imagination this "metamorphosis" was to be completed a few days before he died in a story entitled *"Amori sulla tela,"* ("The Marital Web").[12]

Zoology, astronomy, and linguistics, which were Levi's special interests, all make their appearance in *Other People's Trades*. Here again he campaigned against the division between humanities and the culture of science that he branded as a taboo of the Counter-Reformation.

In February 1985 Levi wrote the preface to a new edition of the autobiography of Rudolf Höss, written on the advice of his lawyers and of some of the key figures involved in the investigation of Nazi war crimes in Poland. Höss had written his memoirs during his detention in Cracow prison, before he was sentenced to death on 2 April 1947, and hanged in the Auschwitz main camp two weeks later. As the following extract shows, Primo Levi brings a scientist's precision to his portrait of a dedicated war criminal:

> During the summer of 1941 Himmler informed [Höss] "personally" that Auschwitz was to be more than a place of punishment: it must become "the biggest extermination centre of all time," and it was up to him and his colleagues to invent the best technique. Höss did not flinch; it was an order like any other, and orders are not for debating. Experiments were carried out in other camps, but mass machine-gunnings and lethal injections were not proving adequate. He had to find something faster and more reliable. In particular he needed to avoid a "blood bath" answer, because it demoralized the executioners. After the bloodiest actions, some SS men committed suicide, while others got drunk. Some aseptic, impersonal method was required to protect the soldiers' mental health. Collective gassing done by piping exhaust fumes into sealed vans was a good start, but it could be improved upon: Höss and his assistant had the inspired idea of using Zyklon B, the poison used for moles and cockroaches, and everything now fell into place. Höss felt extremely satisfied after the pilot exercise carried out on 900 Russian prisoners. In terms both of quantity and quality, the mass murder procedure worked well. No blood, no trauma. Between machine-gunning people standing naked on the edge of their own burial pit and dropping a small pellet of poison into an air duct, the difference is fundamental. His highest ambition had been achieved, his professionalism had been demonstrated, he was murder's finest technician. Envious colleagues were very put out.
>
> The most repugnant pages of the book are those in which Höss dwells on the brutality and indifference with which the Jews assigned to remove the bodies carried out their work. They contain a vile indictment, an accusation of complicity, as if these wretched men were not "executors of orders" who had to shoulder the guilt of those who had devised and issued them.

In April 1985, after some hesitation because of the problems of caring for his mother and mother-in-law, Primo Levi decided that he would make a three-week visit to the United States, while his sister came up from Rome to relieve him.

Levi was a man in love with perfection. His knowledge of the English language was excellent, but knowing that he would have to speak in front of an audience of students at several American universities, in December 1984 he asked Gretchen Chiari, who taught his son Renzo English, to give him some conversation lessons and to look over the text of his speeches. Gretchen went to the Corso Re Umberto every week until June, to talk exclusively in English for two hours with Levi, who wanted to learn the English equivalents of Italian idiomatic expressions.

The first time she crossed the threshold of Primo Levi's apartment, Gretchen had to put felt slippers on her feet so as not to spoil the parquet floor. On the second visit, her host excused her from this custom, which seemed to belong to another era. Levi was a lively, brilliant, timid "pupil." One day, when Alan J. Pakula's film of the William Styron novel *Sophie's Choice* (1984) was showing in Turin, Gretchen asked Primo if he would like to see it with her. He accepted at first, then changed his mind because the film started at the time he had to put his mother to bed.

While two American publishers competed for the rights to *If Not Now, When?*, William Weaver translated *La chiave a stella* (published in the US as *The Monkey's Wrench*, 1986, and in Britain simply as *The Wrench*, 1987) and Ruth Feldman was translating a number of the previously untranslated poems from *Ad ora incerta* that eventually appeared in the *Collected Poems* (1992).

"*Tutto Libri*," the literary page of *La Stampa*, organized a survey in which readers were asked to name the book that they had most loved and the one they had most detested. With *If This Is A Man*, Primo Levi took fifth place in the first category, behind Italo Svevo, Giuseppe Tomasi Di Lampedusa, Carlo Levi, and Pirandello. Despite his fame, Alberto Moravia collected the most votes in the latter category.

Invited by the New York Institute of Italian Culture and the B'nai Brith, Primo Levi arrived in April 1985 in the US with Lucia, and was immediately caught up in a whirlwind of lectures and meetings in New York, Boston, Los Angeles, and Bloomington. He accepted the Kenneth Smilen Award at the Jewish Museum in New York for *The Periodic Table*. At the City University of New York, he participated in an evening programme with Professors Howe and Yosef Yerushalmi. In three weeks he was booked on to nine air flights to take in five different towns, where he gave twenty-five interviews and delivered six lectures. The speech he made to his American audiences was the text he had written at the request of the Rockefeller Foundation on the occasion of the Congress of Jewish Authors that he had attended in Bellagio in 1982.

> In Italy, but even more abroad, I am now considered as a Jewish author. I accepted this definition with good grace, but not at once and not without reluctance. In fact, I accepted it quite late in my life .... I adapted to the status of a Jew when the racial laws were promulgated in 1938, when I was nineteen years old, and then when I was deported to Auschwitz in 1944. I adapted to the status of an author later still. ... Among Italian Jews, the awareness of Judaism was not very great.

Levi gave patient answers to the students' questions. "In three weeks I had to juggle with three labels [Italian author, Jew, and chemist] .... The Americans were interested in this funny sort of Jew who was an Italian."[13] Every night he returned exhausted to his hotel, and took his telephone off the hook to get away from the journalists who kept badgering him for interviews.

Embarrassed and surprised by the scale of his success, he was also tired by so many receptions, and found it hard to shed his habitual reserve. During an interminable cocktail party given in his honour at the Jewish Museum in New York, and attended by Saul Bellow, he could not take his eyes off some drawings by an ex-deportee.

> At a party you keep standing for an hour or maybe two, with a canapé in one hand and a glass in the other, so there's nothing left to make gestures or shake hands with people when you're pointlessly introduced.
>
> You're attacked from the rear and on your flanks by chatterers or whiners, while the serious people that you'd like to talk to are surrounded by chatterers of their own. Everybody talks, and talks in English; to make yourself understood you have to raise your voice, but as everybody else is doing the same the result is nil, and acoustic exhaustion increases. It is a kind of tiredness that I'd never previously experienced; when it gets on top of you, speech paralysis sets in: you're reduced to pretending to understand and replying with grimaces and nods of the head, and instead of speaking you make do with grunts, but it makes no difference to the outcome in any event.[14]

Levi expressed surprise that the organizers of his tour arranged for him to meet only prominent Jews, and to speak only to Jewish audiences. In the interview he gave to the *Partisan Review*, he told Risa Sodi that, not having met a single Christian during her stay, his wife asked at one point: "But where are the others?" Certain American Jews were curious enough to ask him what kind of Jew he was. After his return he was to write: "It is very remarkable to realize how little Americans know about Europe. It is small and distant, and adds up basically to Poland, Italy, Greece and Spain. ... I aroused curiosity about Italy, and about that sub-species, the Italian Jew."[15]

Invited by Alvin Rosenfeld, professor of English and director of Jewish Studies at the University of Indiana at Bloomington, Levi answered questions from students in the literary faculty, and he did the same at Claremont College, near Los Angeles. On that occasion he expressed his indignation concerning the visit made near the time by President Ronald Reagan, at the invitation of Chancellor Helmut Kohl, to a German military cemetery at Bitburg where SS men were buried.

Levi collected his impressions of the trip in an article called "On the Heights of Manhattan," published in *La Stampa* on 23 June 1985. In it he tells us that he was surprised by the number of people of all shapes and sizes to be seen running through Central Park with their Walkmans and headphones, and that he tried on some jogging shoes, which he found ugly but wonderfully comfortable. He also noticed how little importance Americans attached to their clothes, with their unpretentious fondness for slopping about. He was hugely impressed by the bay, the islands, canals, isthmuses, Manhattan, "proud and gigantic," the skyscrapers, temples of efficiency, and the World Trade Center, with its "lyrical, cynical, insolent beauty."

In October 1985, *Commentary*, the monthly literary and political journal, published a long piece by Fernanda Eberstadt entitled "Reading Primo Levi" which was a critique of both the writer and his books. The essay began with an overview of Italian Jewry as well as of Levi's personal history as part of this comfortable and largely assimilated community. Levi is characterized as "a survivor without Jewish — or more specifically, without East European — inflections ... a man who is more at home in Dane and Homer than in the Bible." What seemed to be an objective observation soon took the form of criticism as Eberstadt remarked on "a lack of familiarity with Jewish history or religion ... typical of his generation of Italian Jewish writers." Particular criticism was reserved for his novel, *If Not Now, When?*. The author argued that Primo Levi had tried to write an ambitious book that had failed in its objective. She judged that the characters lacked psychological depth and had no real pasts. Each of them seemed to her to be a vehicle for an idea or type of behaviours, and taken as a whole they made up a kind of catalogue of Jewish nationalism: Marxism, religious orthodoxy, anarchism, egalitarianism, and a "Tolstoyan" return to the soil. "Unfortunately, although he has chosen a most engrossing and important subject, *If Not Now, When?* must be judged a failure. ... For all his hard work and good will, the distance between Turin and the forests of Eastern Europe proves too far to be bridged by so fastidious and uncertain an imagination as his."

Levi felt so deeply hurt by the cutting tone of Eberstadt's account that he wrote a reply which appeared in the issue of February 1986. Raymond Rosenthal, who had translated several of his books, wrote another angry letter, and a third protest came from Alan Viterbi, a councillor from West Hollywood, California, himself a descendant of Italian Jewry.

Levi opened by expressing his support for freedom of criticism in the United

States as in Italy. He stated at the outset: "I neither wish to nor am I able to discuss Miss Eberstadt's opinions on the literary merit of my books .... I would like, however, to comment on several passages in the article." He was writing to remind Fernanda Eberstadt of certain things, and to re-establish the truth, which she seemed to have either ignored or distorted.

Levi took particular offence at Eberstadt's statement that "It was only with the first signs of a decisive Allied victory and with the collapse of the Fascist regime on July 25, 1943, that Levi found within himself the will to resist."

In his reply he wrote:

This assertion amounts to an accusation of opportunism, and it strikes me as insulting. I was not the only one to take up arms so late. I am not speaking here of the minuscule Italian Jewish community, but the entire Resistance movement against the Nazis, in all of Europe, did not begin until after the German invasion; before that, it would not have made sense. A soldier, even if animated by the best will in the world, does not mobilize alone, spontaneously, against an enemy who is not there. The decision to fight militarily was taken when it was possible to take it, but my anti-Fascist commitment, and that of my family and the group of friends I belong to, goes back many years earlier (see, for example, the chapters "Zinc" and "Iron" in *The Periodic Table*), in fact, to the years of my adolescence.

Levi also bristled at an implied lack of Jewish consciousness. Concerning his arrest prior to his detainment at Fossoli, Eberstadt wrote: "Levi ... mistakenly thought it safer, if caught by Italian Fascists, to declare himself a Jew rather than a member of the partisans. ..."

In his letter, he replied: "That was the least important part of the motives that led me to declare myself a Jew. I expressed them clearly in *The Periodic Table*: 'Partly because I was tired, partly out of an irrational digging in of pride.'"

Later, Fernanda Eberstadt accused him of not having attempted to demonstrate that the slaughter of the Jews was provoked by the Nazi terror and Hitler's ideology. In writing about *If This Is A Man*, as a "brilliant and stunning" book she admires for its detached and ironic style, Eberstadt takes issue with Levi for failing to note the specific nature of the Nazi genocide: "By adopting, however ironically, this denatured pseudo-scientific prose, Levi deliberately glosses over the plain fact that the 'experiment' of which he speaks was designed by a particular group of people, the Nazis, ... to wipe another particular group of people, the Jews, off the face of the earth."

Levi answered this charge directly:

Such a drastic statement can spring only from an extremely superficial reading of my books, especially *If This Is A Man*. ... Even if one simply relies on the narrated facts, the revulsion against and condemnation of

Nazism leap from every page. Moreover, the explanation which Miss Eberstadt seems to put forward — that Jews are persecuted where and when they tend to assimilate — seems to me false, or at least not generally true. They weren't assimilated in Spain in 1500, and yet they were burned or expelled. They were assimilated in Italy, where they would have remained undisturbed or almost so if it had not been for the German invasion in the course of the Second World War. They were and are assimilated in Bulgaria, whose (pro-Fascist) government opposed their deportation. They rejected assimilation in Poland and Russia in the last century and were paid back in pogroms. In short, I see no correlation between assimilation (desired or attained) and anti-Semitism. The anti-Semite hates the Jew no matter what: if he assimilates, because he "tries to hide himself," if he remains faithful to tradition and religion, "because he is different."

As a Jewish writer, Levi is criticized by Eberstadt for a lack of familiarity with Judaism and Jewish life, colouring his depictions of it based on what he witnessed among the Eastern European Jews in the camps: "Levi is simply cursed with a tin ear for religion, and is incapable of representing imaginatively the life of the people who practise their faith ... he unwittingly reduces that tradition's central component — the Jewish faith — to the status of an archaic cult ..."

To this criticism, Levi replied:

I am accused of irreligion. I am not religious; furthermore, the experience of Auschwitz led many religious people, Jewish and not, to doubt. I profoundly respect, and sometimes envy, those who have the support of faith. The pious Lithuanian Jew [this is "Mendel" in *If Not Now, When?*] on whom Miss Eberstadt dwells is plainly a positive character, and the episode described in the story in which he appears really happened. The line of reasoning has been misunderstood; it is known to everyone (including me) that "cooking" on Yom Kippur is prohibited, but the discussion described hinges on whether it is permitted to "keep the soup warm," that is, not let it get cold. Whether this is allowed or not I personally do not know; my character Ezra, maintains that it is not ....

In none of my books does there appear a malevolent representation of religious zeal; however, the way in which quotations taken from my books are used does seem inexplicably malevolent.

Even the characters in *If Not Now, When?* are not very religious. This fact should not surprise or scandalize anyone; most of them were born or raised in the Soviet Union, where all religions, and the Jewish religion in particular, were openly discouraged.

I am implicitly criticized for being assimilated. I am. There do not exist Jews in the diaspora who are not, to a greater or lesser degree, if nothing else than for the fact that they speak the language of the country in which they live. I reassert, for myself and for everyone, the right to choose the level of assimilation that best suits their culture and their environment.

Finally, Levi rejected Eberstadt's comparing him to Ausonius, a retired Roman gentleman of late antiquity who wrote anagrams and cultivated roses. This was one assertion Eberstadt was willing to retract.

Raymond Rosenthal demanded apologies to Primo Levi both from Fernanda Eberstadt and from the editors of *Commentary*, writing "I know a hatchet job when I see it." There followed the angry letter from the town councillor in Hollywood. The editors of the best Jewish literary review in the United States were content to publish the whole polemic in the readers' letters pages, together with a self-justifying reply from Fernanda Eberstadt, who persisted in her argument, with the help of selective quotations taken out of context from various books of Levi's.

Levi's honest admission that before Auschwitz he had not been truly conscious of his identity was neither understood nor approved of in the United States, and he was irked by this response, though he did not lose his sense of humour.

> *If Not Now, When?* was not a great success in the United States, and it is Jewish circles in particular that criticized the book. In fact they sensed that my knowledge of the Jewish world (language, quotations, customs, proverbs, etc.) was a "second-hand knowledge," which really is the case. Disguised as an Ashkenazi Jew, I certainly succeeded in deceiving my fellow countrymen, and perhaps I will succeed in deceiving the Germans (those of today), but when it comes to the American Jews, who nearly all originate from Eastern Europe, I don't succeed, worse luck.[16]

While he was transferring the 140 articles about his work that appeared in the United States on to his computer files, he also reread the translation of *The Wrench* sent to him by William Weaver, and was slightly disappointed. It seemed to him too clean and asepticized. The English spoken by Faussone made him rather too distinguished a gentleman.

In Italy, though he was snubbed in literary circles, Levi was awarded the Aquila Prize for *Other People's Trades* and the Marina di Pietrasanta Prize for his book of poems, *Ad ora incerta*.

When Italo Calvino died in 1985[17] Primo Levi wrote his obituary for *La Stampa*, after submitting the text to Calvino's widow, Ester.

With The Key of Science

We do not choose our parents, but we do choose our fellow travellers.

My ties to Italo were delicate and deep. As near-colleagues, and with a common, formative experience in the Resistance, we achieved the rank of authors together in the same (for me memorable) review by Arrigo Cajumi in these columns, which dealt with his *The Path to the Nest of Spiders* and my own *If This Is A Man*. We never spoke at length to one another, we had no need to. A quick mention of the "work in progress," and there was instant understanding.

And not only understanding. I owed a lot to Italo. When he was literary director at the Einaudi offices in Turin, it was natural for me to consult him. I felt him as a brother, and rather as an elder brother, even though he was four years younger. Unlike me, he was in the trade: he had it in his blood. As the spiritual heir to Pavese, he had inherited editorial experience and a keen, quick severity of judgement. His comments were never unfounded.

Other things also connected us. As the son of a scientist, a rare specimen on the Italian literary scene, he was hungry for science, cultivated it, revelled in it as a critical amateur, and the most mature of his books were nourished by it. For him, nature and science were one and the same thing. Science as a means of seeing better, a key to penetrating, a code for understanding nature. Nothing in his temperament was lyrical or idyllic, and yet he was a great poet of nature, even in a negative manner, when he was describing its essence, its absence in the city. He was being only half ironic when he said that he envied me my decades of working as a chemist in laboratories and factories. We discussed and shared vague, grandiose programmes for a mediating, revelatory literature, straddling "the two cultures" and belonging to them both. From this standpoint he succeeded better than I, armed as he was with a vast and varied literary culture and his acquaintance with the greatest intellectuals of our time. As an admirer and disciple of Raymond Queneau, he invited me to revise a few passages in the Italian translation of the *Cosmogonie portative* with him, and for me it was a spiritual feast: I was fascinated by his philological finesse, to which my modest experience as a technician had no great contribution to offer.

His premature death leaves a void full of anguish: he was at the height of his powers, and still had so many things to build, things that belonged to him and him alone, that no one will ever be able to say in his inimitable manner — a light, incisive, never gratuitous manner, sometimes joyous, never facile, never content with the mere appearance of things.

18   "I Find No Solution to the Riddle"

Early in 1986, Levi had been visited by two young historians, Anna Bravo and Daniele Jalla, who were compiling a major work of oral history devoted to two hundred survivors of the camps in Italy who were talking about their experiences for the first time. The region of Piedmont was financing their research, which was published under the title *La vita offesa* ("Insult to Life"); the subtitle was "History and Memory of the Nazi Camps Related by Two Hundred Survivors."[1] Levi contributed the preface to the book, in which he writes:

> We are many (but every year our numbers diminish) .... If we die in silence as our enemies desire ... the world will not know what man could do and what he can still do: the world will not know itself, and it will be more vulnerable to a return of National Socialist barbarity or of any other barbarity, of any other political origin.

In November *La Stampa* published a collection of articles by Levi printed in the daily between 1960 and 1986.[2]

After his visit to the United States, Primo Levi started a book about his experience of the camp, a bitter meditation that had been brewing in his mind for a long time. He had spoken about it to Giorgina Levi, in an interview for *Ha-Keillah*, the magazine of the Jewish community in Turin:

> It seems to me that the subject of the camps is topical. To re-examine the experience of the camp thirty-five years after. To judge it with the eyes of the indifferent, the eyes of the young man who knows nothing about these things, and even with the eyes of the opposition. The outcome may be a sociological study, already attempted by others, no doubt, but in which I believe that I have something very personal to say. It has to do with assuming a position on the edge of ambiguity.[3]

Forty years after his return, Levi was writing in torment about the fact that he had survived when most of his comrades had died. The anguish caused by the silent reproach that seemed to reach him from the vast arena of the lost came to the surface in his poems. He ordered the countless shades of the dead who came to visit him to disappear, to fade back into their mist. He had taken no one's bread, he wrote. "Stand back, leave me alone, submerged people. ..."[4]

In *The Drowned and the Saved*, Levi took the risk of rejecting the interpretation — which he considered shallow — that saw the pure oppressor on the one hand and on the other the victim, "sanctified in his role of victim." According to him, things did not really match this description: it was too simplistic. Man was a more complex creature. Those who became killers and torturers were ordinary men, each of whom assumed the role of killer and torturer for a reason of his own. It is the sum of those reasons that Levi set out to analyse in his deeply sombre book, which hurt the feelings of certain veterans of the extermination camps who owed their survival to sheer chance. Until then, Levi had believed in man, in *homo faber*, as he liked to remark to Ernesto Ferrero. A year before his death, it seems that his convictions wilted, and gave way to a pessimism which was occasionally unjust when he wrote, for instance, that in the camps "the best all died" (*DS 83/63*). So this is the pain that eats away at him: he knows very well that the deportees were innocent, but if "the worst" escaped death, how can he, who never harmed a soul, account to himself for the miracle of his own survival? And even as he writes this, he asks himself more questions about the value of his own testimony: the true witnesses are those who touched "the bottom," those who breathed their last breath in the gas trucks and gas chambers, or died under machine-gun fire in Babi Yar, Riga, Minsk, or Ponary.

> At a distance of years one can today definitely affirm that the history of the Lagers has been written almost exclusively by those who, like myself, never fathomed them to the bottom. Those who did so did not return, or their capacity for observation was paralysed by suffering and incomprehension.
>
> On the other hand, the "privileged" witness could avail themselves certainly of a better observatory, if only because it was located higher up and hence took in a more extensive horizon; but it was to a greater or lesser degree also falsified by the privilege itself. (*DS 18/6–7*)

One chapter of this final book takes up the theme of "shame": a sense of anguish laced with guilt, an unjustified sense of guilt linked to the fact of appearing among the few survivors. "What guilt? When all was over, the awareness emerged that we had not done anything, or not enough, against the system into which we had been absorbed" (*DS 76/57*). Then again: "Self-accusation is more realistic, or the accusation of having failed in terms of human solidarity" (*DS 78/58–9*).

A long section is devoted to the status of the intellectual in Auschwitz, in which Levi takes issue with Jean Améry. Améry, whose original name was Hans Mayer, was an Austrian intellectual born in Vienna in 1912 into a totally assimilated Jewish family. Améry had fled from Nazi Austria to Belgium in 1938, and later joined a resistance movement there. He fell into the hands of the Gestapo in July 1943 for the minor crime of putting out leaflets. He was told that if he refused to give the names of the members of his network he would suffer torture. But he did not know them. In *Jenseits von Schuld und Sühne*, the story of that episode of torture and the reflections inspired by his experiences in Nazi prison camps, Améry confessed that if he had known their true identity, not being a hero, he would "perhaps, or probably" have talked. Améry's wrists were shackled behind his back, and the shackle hooked to a pulley that raised him a metre above the floor. With the balls of his shoulder joints torn from their sockets, and his dislocated arms twisted up above his head, he hung from the hook while one of his torturers lashed him repeatedly with a horsewhip. He was then taken unconscious to a cell in Fort Breendonk, now a Belgian national museum. Améry recovered from his injuries but was then identified as a Jew and sent to Auschwitz, to the same Block as Primo Levi, although Levi had no recollection of him.

Améry's book, published in Germany in 1966, is a cold meditation, full of the "resentment" inspired by his passage through several Nazi prisons and concentration camps: Breendonk, Auschwitz, Buchenwald, and Bergen-Belsen. He begins by considering whether the fact of being an intellectual in Auschwitz constituted an advantage or a disadvantage. In *The Drowned and the Saved*, Levi considers Améry's definition of the intellectual unnecessarily restrictive, but agreed that cultivated inmates had a definite disadvantage when it came to manual labour:

> At work, which was prevalently manual, the cultivated man was gener-
> ally much worse off than the uncultivated man. Aside from physical
> strength, he lacked familiarity with the tools and the training which his
> worker or peasant companion often had; in contrast, he was tormented
> by an acute sense of humiliation and destitution — of *Entwürdigung*,
> that is, precisely, lost dignity. (*DS* 132/106)

Not without wry humour, Levi observes that he himself had only a moderate feeling of humiliation about doing manual labour, and he adds ironically:

> [E]vidently I was still not "intellectual" enough. And after all, why not?
> I had a degree, true enough, but mine was an undeserved piece of luck.
> My family had been rich enough to send me to school: many contem-
> poraries of mine had shovelled dirt since adolescence. Did I not want
> equality? Well, then, I had got it. I was forced to change my opinion a
> few days later, when my hands and feet became covered with blisters
> and infections ... (*DS* 133–4/107)

Levi and Améry also suffered from the absurd and vicious rules and customs that governed the barracks routine, just as they suffered from "the mutilation of language," even though Améry had grown up speaking German. Levi suffered through not understanding, and through being "a philologist who loved his language." The intellectual Améry was not only a deportee but "a stranger in his own country."

When it came to the ability to "hit back" — *zurückschlagen* — Levi

385

confesses his absolute inferiority compared with Améry, who in order to retrieve his dignity had the courage to aim a punch at a Kapo, a gigantic Polish common criminal, knowing perfectly well that he was risking a ruthless beating. Levi admired Améry for his courage and intransigence, but pointed out the consequences of his taking his attitude to its ultimate conclusion:

> "Trading punches" is an experience I do not have, as far back as I can go in memory; nor can I say I regret not having it … I admire Améry's change of heart, his courageous decision to leave the ivory tower and go down into the battlefield, but it was, and still is, beyond my reach. I admire it: but I must point out that this choice, protracted throughout his post-Auschwitz existence, led him to positions of such severity and intransigence as to make him incapable of finding joy in life, indeed of living. Those who "trade blows" with the entire world achieve dignity but pay a very high price for it, because they are sure to be defeated. (*DS* 136/109–10)

Améry had called Levi "the forgiver" but he did not forgive. Both men observed with anguish the onward march of time that took them further from the events that tortured them and allowed many of the perpetrators to live peaceful lives.

In September 1986 Milvia Spadi came to interview Primo Levi on behalf of West Deutsche Rundfunk about the motivations that had led him to write his book about the camps, forty years after his return from Auschwitz. This interview was later to be published by *L'Unità*.[5]

> I realized, especially through the reactions of my younger readers, that we are living at an anti-historic moment. My first two books are very widely read in Italy. I know even through the letters I receive, and I receive a lot, that they stir up feelings, and a sense of participation. But it is as if it concerned an event that no longer involved us, no longer involved Europe, or our century. … On top of that, we have seen the attempt to deny the truth of genocide altogether. So this process of the dissolution and annihilation of the facts is intensifying […]
>
> Today it is hard to understand how Hitler could have mobilized the masses by such absurd means, and yet he did it. It is very hard to tell the difference between the good prophets and the false. All prophets are false. I don't believe in prophets, even though I come from a lineage of prophets […]
>
> I insist on the fact that even the oppressors of those times were creatures like us. It is a kind of extreme simplification that my young readers perform when, reading my books, especially the first, they think of a humanity cut in two. On one side, there are supposed to be the

butchers, who are monsters. And we are the innocents. That is why I believe that the second chapter of this latest book is the most important. It is called "The Grey Zone."

In that chapter, Levi gave a discerning and detailed analysis of the way the Nazi system managed to induce a large number of prisoners to enter the cycle of collaboration and take part in the persecution of their comrades in captivity. This view of things, which argues that there was no solidarity among the prisoners in the camps, is highly controversial. Hermann Langbein established, for example, that the members of the Communist Party did their utmost to save the lives of their comrades in danger. In her book *L'exercise de vivre*, Simone Alizon gives numerous instances to confirm Langbein's claims. Many survivors have told how they owed their lives to a comrade's solidarity, but Levi had examined the camp as a sociologist, on a vaster scale. He was convinced that, far from being an ally, the comrade was an opponent, even though this conclusion contradicts a part of his evidence concerning Maurice Reznik, Jean Samuel, Leonardo De Benedetti, and Alberto Dallavolta. Would he go so far as to describe the ties that once united him with these men as "selfishness extended to the person closest to you"?

In his scrutiny of the text written by Rudolf Höss, Levi observes that even in the shadow of the gallows, Höss did not understand. He did not change his credo one iota. He had done his duty as a German, and brought to perfection the work required of him, which happened to be the organizing of an extermination camp. Levi believed that Höss was not what his young readers called a monster. Execution was Höss's trade. How could a man accept the profession of killing 15,000 people per day? Levi found no alternative explanation to "the myth of the fatherland above all."

Lastly, writing about the way that memory preserves the facts, and about his status as a witness, Levi makes some more measured statements: "I have become a professional, a survivor by trade, practically a mercenary. All in all, the memory of my experience of that time is very much modified by a mass of subsequent conversations and reflections. All this comes between the experience and the present day."[6]

Levi delivered his manuscript to his publisher in the early weeks of 1986. After the American success, his works were being widely translated. *If Not Now, When?* was now available in German in an excellent translation by Barbara Kleiner, who had worked in close collaboration with him, and *If This Is A Man* would appear in French at long last in 1987, though without attracting critical attention.

In April 1986, Primo Levi and Lucia made a visit to England, where the author took part in a conference devoted to Italian Jewry. It was on this occasion that he met the family of Gerhard Goldbaum, one of his comrades in the chemical Kommando, who died on the evacuation march from the camp. Goldbaum was an expert on sound, and after receiving the stamp of official approval from Doktor Pannwitz he was assigned to an acoustics laboratory. When *The Periodic Table* came out in England some members of his family had read the book, and then written to Primo Levi to ask whether by any chance the Goldbaum mentioned in his book was their relation: they did not know the circumstances of his death. Seven members of the family kept the appointment to meet Levi in London. They gave him a photo of Goldbaum taken in 1939, and even though more than four decades had elapsed, he recognized his former comrade at once. He learned from the niece that after the annexation of Austria Goldbaum had sought refuge in Holland, where he had worked at Philips until the Nazis came. Then he had joined the Resistance, was arrested as a partisan, identified as a Jew, and deported to Auschwitz.

In 1986 Primo Levi entered a new cycle of depression, and his cousin Giorgio Luzzati, who was a doctor, prescribed some antidepressants. Though Levi complained that he had trouble concentrating and writing, he started a new book, *Doppio legame* ("The Double Bond"), in a literary genre quite new to him, but linked in spirit to *The Periodic Table*. It was an epistolary novel. The narrator writes to the lady of his thoughts, Gisella, to reveal the mysteries of physics and organic chemistry in everyday life. Thus he proposes to explain the phenomena that control, for example, the successful making of a mayonnaise or a vinaigrette. When Levi asked Ernesto Ferrero to look over two or three of these sections of five to fifteen pages each, Ferrero was delighted by the freshness, tenderness, and humour of the letters, which reminded him of the correspondence between Abélard and Héloïse. He encouraged Levi to keep on writing in the interval before his book *The Drowned and the Saved* was published.

On 28 March Levi wrote a letter to his friend Hermann Langbein in which he referred to his mother's decline and its effect on his domestic life. "No, we still can't breathe: this isn't the moment to relax. Our filial duties grow more and more heavy and oppressive. The 'interior minister' isn't very well, and our life is difficult." (The "interior minister" was Levi's humorous reference to his inner state of mind.) Langbein had told him that he would be coming to Turin in October, and Levi looked forward to seeing him again. He marvelled that his friend was still so dedicated and energetic, and that he continued to visit schools. He himself no longer felt like going. "It is more and more difficult for me to find a language in common with the young. They are (rightly) concerned with very different things — basically unemployment and academic problems. They ask me if I am religious, and as I'm not, they ask why, which leaves me lost for words."

From now on, Levi preferred to express his views through writing. He informed his friend that in a few months' time he would be publishing a book of nine essays dealing with questions about the camps.

> For example:
> — How and to what extent, in forty years, the memories of the victims and the oppressors have changed;
> — Why some of those who came back suffer from a paradoxical sense of shame;
> — How, in an inevitable way, a very complex class of collaborators was born and took shape;
> — How, for non-Germans like myself, the lack of comprehension (of the language) was a major threat to life, etc.

> The title will be *The Drowned and the Saved*: this is no accident — the title corresponds to one of the chapters in *If This Is A Man*. So as you can tell, I'm a second offender. I don't know yet whether Hanser Verlag will be interested, but there is already some mention of an English translation, possibly this year.

A reading of Chapter 9, "The Drowned and the Saved," of *If This Is A Man* reveals that it contains, in an extremely concentrated form, the themes that Levi was to enlarge on forty years later. In 1946 he had already written:

> We would also like to consider that the Lager was pre-eminently a gigantic biological and social experiment.
>
> Thousands of individuals, differing in age, condition, origin, language, culture and customs, are enclosed within barbed wire: there they live a regular, controlled life which is identical for all and inadequate to all needs, and which is more rigorous than any experimenter could have set up to establish what is essential and what adventitious to the conduct of the human animal in the struggle for life. (*Man* 87/93)

For Levi, the camp would remain the measure of every other experience that followed this fundamental trauma. Yet he also made the unequivocal statement: "That poison is exorcized; it no longer flows in my veins."[7]

Later in 1986 Levi was in a sombre mood, but he had not yet abandoned all activity, as he was to do in the final weeks of his life. He made a trip to Switzerland, met Philip Roth in London, and travelled on to Stockholm. He gave a lecture in Pesaro, and on his return received visits from Barbara Kleiner, his German translator, and from his German publisher, who came to tell him that he planned to reissue all his books in a new translation.

At the end of May, Levi received the "*Leone d'oro*" ("Golden Lion") award in the splendid eighteenth-century Palazzo Cisterna, the regional administrative centre of Piedmont. He also agreed, though rather reluctantly, to visit several Italian towns to launch his book.

In *La Stampa*, he informed Giorgio Calcagno:

> I have chosen this theme out of a need for truth, and to stand up against

rhetoric. We ex-deportees are compared to ex-partisans, and that is right. I am prepared to tolerate a certain amount of rhetoric, which is indispensable in life. We have a need for monuments and celebrations: something that is monumental, in the etymological sense of the word, indicates an admonition, a warning. Yet there is a counterpoint, a prose response to rhetoric. I decided to make that response, knowing that I was going to hurt a few feelings.[8]

One Sunday in May, Ferdinando Camon saw Primo Levi at home for what was to be their final interview. At the end of the conversation, Levi related how his teacher, Nicola Dallaporta, had come to see him a few weeks after his return from Auschwitz, and told him that he had been "chosen to survive in order to write *If This Is A Man*. And I have to admit that it seemed like a blasphemy to me: it would mean that God had granted privileges, by saving some and condemning others. I am obliged to say that the experience of Auschwitz hit me so hard that it drove out any remnant of religious education that I might have received."[9]

In other words, Camon asked him, Auschwitz is the proof of the non-existence of God? "If there is an Auschwitz, then there cannot be a God," Levi replied. (Although as he was rereading and correcting the manuscript a few days later, he added in pencil: "I find no solution to the riddle. I seek, but I do not find it.")

Ten pages of interviews with Ferdinando Camon, selected and revised by Primo Levi, appeared in the weekly *Panorama* on 28 May 1986, to mark the publication of *The Drowned and the Saved*.

One Friday in September, Philip Roth arrived in Turin, accompanied by Claire Bloom. He had talked to Primo Levi in London, and now he was to interview him for the *New York Times Book Review*. Levi received him at home, and Roth later wrote a detailed description of the apartment and the writer's office, where their conversation took place. On the wall hung a sketch of a barbed-wire fence at Auschwitz, and Levi had preserved a piece of rusty wire that he had brought back to Turin. Also on the wall was an old election poster with a reproduction of a letter written by Garibaldi, sent from Caprera on 6 February 1880.

Primo Levi took Philip Roth to visit the historic centre of Turin, with its luxurious covered galleries and long geometric avenues lined with arcades, and they sat for a while looking at the Palazzo Carignano. Roth asked to visit SIVA, now SICME–SIVA–SCET, the factory where the writer–chemist had worked for thirty years. Levi phoned Paola Accati, and told her: "I'm coming to the factory, but I'd like you to accompany me, because I'm not capable of driving and speaking English at the same time."[10] They picked up Roth, took him to the plant, and after the visit drove him back to his hotel. Then Levi and Paola

Accati went for a drink together, laughing about the incongruous presence of the author of *Portnoy's Complaint* in the laboratories in Settimo Torinese. They laughed because Levi had advised Paola on no account to mention the book to its author, having heard tell that Roth no longer liked it.

In June, Primo Levi agreed to be visited at home by Risa Sodi, to whom he granted a long interview. At the end of their conversation, when she asked whether he was thinking of returning to the United States in the near future, he replied:

> "Allow me to tell you that my wife and I find ourselves in a disastrous situation, here in Italy. We have to look after two people: my mother is ninety-one years old (she is in the next room); my mother-in-law, who is ninety-five, is blind. We cannot go anywhere, even though we have help: the women who help us out go on vacation in summer. That is why, for us, instead of bringing rest, summer is always a source of problems. I am invited to go to the United States this coming November for the launch of *The Wrench*. I have replied that it will not be possible for me to accept. If I did go, I would be leaving the entire burden on my wife's shoulders. By a miracle, we managed to get away for twelve or thirteen days in April, but only by asking my sister to come up from Rome, and she has problems of her own. We can't go anywhere. I spend my time turning down the invitations I receive."
>
> "Your mother and mother-in-law are exceptionally long-lived."
>
> "My mother-in-law is ninety-five years old, but she has two sisters in the United States. One of them is ninety-seven, and the other ninety-six. The youngest, who is eighty-nine, lives here. It is an extraordinarily long-lived family."
>
> "That's a good omen for you!"
>
> "It all depends on the way one grows old. My mother-in-law has been totally blind for fifteen years. We need someone here for twenty-four hours a day. My mother is not blind, but she is senile. We also have to do everything for her. Consequently I can't make any plans. I can only write. I receive invitations from all over the world. I've had an invitation to go to Germany. I'm very interested in Germany because a publisher there is going to reissue all my books. The dialogue with the Germans would be very interesting. But for the moment I've said no. I have received an invitation to go to the United States. My publisher is frantic. He has suggested the following timetable (which I wouldn't have accepted anyway): to come for two weeks with stops in New York, Chicago, Boston, Houston. ... I don't recall the rest — something like eight towns on the east coast, and the whole Pacific Ocean coast, plus an unspecified number of interviews."[11]

In 1986, *The Monkey's Wrench* and *Moments of Reprieve* appeared in the United States. *If Not Now, When?* was published in Germany. Twenty-four translations were under way. For a man whose peers still looked down on him in his own country, international recognition was an established fact. Primo Levi had become a famous writer, and he was certainly his country's most prize-winning author. In October he received the Acqui "Witness of Time" Prize for *If Not Now, When?*. He turned up to collect it with his cousin, Vittorio Foa, both of them cheerful, and kissing all the women's hands. A few days later a photographer from *Time* magazine came and took a hundred photographs of him in his apartment.

On 21 October he published an article in *La Stampa* under the title *"Covare il cobra"* ("Hatching the Cobra"), in which he called for a greater moral awareness on the part of scientists, whose discoveries could be used for purposes of destruction. The members of university science faculties must "absolutely insist on one point: that what you do when in the practice of your profession can be useful to the human race, not useless or harmful." He went on to say:

> Do not fall in love with suspect problems. Within the limits that you will be granted, try to know the end to which your work is directed. ...
>
> Whether you are a believer or not, if you are given a choice do not let yourself be seduced by material or intellectual interests, but choose from the field that which may render less painful and less dangerous the journey of your contemporaries, and of those who come after you. Don't hide behind the hypocrisy of neutral science: you are educated enough to be able to evaluate whether from the egg you are hatching will issue a dove or a cobra or a chimera or perhaps nothing at all.[12]

Primo Levi had been impressed by the decisions taken by two physicists to resign from their positions. One of them, Peter Hagelstein, an American, had left his laboratory, set up by the Department of Defense, which was studying the medical applications of laser beams. The other, the Englishman Martin Ryle, winner of the Nobel Prize for physics in 1974, had founded a movement to "stop science now," because its discoveries — including his own in the field of radioastronomy — could be used for military purposes. Levi was convinced that it was the duty of scientists to integrate their knowledge and the lessons it implied into their personal ethics. He approved of Hagelstein's decision without reservation, but considered Ryle's viewpoint "both extremist and utopian."

In November, Editrice La Stampa published a collection of Levi's articles under the title *Racconti e saggi di Primo Levi*. The author wrote a preface in which he begged his readers to excuse the diversity of the themes he had tackled in articles spanning a quarter of a century. But the world is beautiful because it is varied, he explained. He asked people not to look for messages in these essays, and added: "I am a normal man, equipped with a good memory, who was caught in a whirlwind, escaped more through luck than through virtue, and who since then has retained a certain curiosity about whirlwinds great and small, metaphorical and real."

It was the autumn of 1986. A demoralized Levi told his friends that he was having difficulty writing, and could get no further with his epistolary novel, having as usual given out a few chapters for his closest friends to read.

He accepted an invitation to address an international conference on the theme of "Living History," organized by the region of Piedmont and the National Association of Ex-Deportees, to be held at the Palazzo Lascaris on 21 and 22 November. In the crowded hall, he was surrounded by young people ingenuously asking for autographs. Sceptical by now about the possibility of conveying the message of the survivors to the present generation, he went to the rostrum to deliver his final speech, "The Duty to Bear Witness," of which the following is a brief extract:

> I have been invited because of my dual role as witness and author. ...
> Ever since my first book, *If This Is A Man*, I have wanted my writings,
> even though it is I who sign them, to be read as collective works, as a
> voice representing other voices that offer an opening, a bridge between
> us and our readers, and particularly the young. Among us ex-deportees,
> it is pleasant to sit back and tell the tale of our now distant adventures
> to the people around us, but it doesn't do much good. For as long as we
> live, it is our duty to speak, yes, but to the others, to those who were
> not yet born, so that they may know how far "things can go." So it is
> no accident that a fair amount of my present work consists of a kind of
> running dialogue with my readers. I get a lot of letters fully of whys ....
> I'm always asked two basic questions: "How could the horror of the
> camps have occurred, and will it happen again?" I don't believe that
> prophets exist, readers of the future. Those with such pretensions have
> failed miserably, and often in a ridiculous way. So I don't see myself as
> a prophet, or as an authorized interpreter of recent history. Yet these
> two questions are so urgent that I feel obliged to try to give an answer,
> and even a number of answers .... We, the survivors, are witnesses, and
> every witness is bound, and bound by law, to answer both fully and
> truthfully. For us, this comes down to a moral duty. Because our group,
> which was always tiny, is dwindling fast.

Giovanni Tesio, a young critic from Turin who has already been mentioned as one of the first to give serious consideration to Levi's work, asked his permission to write an authorized biography.[13] Levi agreed at once, and with enthusiasm, even though he had already entered a cycle of severe depression. Tesio recalls that when he went to see him the writer had injured his foot, and was worried because the wound was slow to close. He was also suffering from shingles, which is not unusual in people under mental stress.

Tesio thought that by working with him Levi would find an outlet for his melancholy. They decided to work on Mondays, twice a month, and met four times in Levi's apartment, where Tesio taped their long conversations. He switched off the recorder during intimate sequences. What the interviews revealed above all else was the extent of Levi's depression: he regretted no longer having anything to say. When Tesio sought to console him by pointing out that he had a considerable body of work behind him, Levi replied that everything he had written had been useless.

However, he did agree to write the preface to *La vita offesa*, the collection of survivors' memories mentioned earlier, and he also gave a lecture at the university on the way that the mind filters and organizes memories.

If Primo Levi told Giovanni Tesio that everything he had written had been useless, the reason was that he had been deeply affected by the press coverage given to the latest claims made by those who denied the Holocaust. He had agreed to write prefaces, speak in public, and give a lecture at the university in order to reply to the revisionists. He never gave up his fight against the rewriters of history, and as late as 22 January 1987 *La Stampa* published an article by Levi entitled "*Buco nero di Auschwitz*" ("The Black Hole of Auschwitz").

Levi identified two lines of argument in Germany: one that the Holocaust was unique, and the other that mass slaughter was not unusual in history, and had been practised in the Soviet Union, for example, against "class enemies." Those who took the second line argued that the only innovation introduced by the Germans had been technological: they had invented the gas chamber. (Here Levi pointed out that this was the very fact that was flatly denied by the disciples of Robert Faurisson, who claimed that the gas chambers were a myth, a Zionist invention.)

The new German revisionists presented Hitler's wholesale slaughter as "a preventive defence against an 'Asiatic' invasion" by the Soviet Union. Levi saw no evidence of any such invention. Nor could it be said that Stalin's use of murder as a political weapon was reflected in Hitler's treatment of the Jews, since before the rise of Hitler it was common knowledge that the Jews had been good Germans, fully and willingly integrated into the national fabric. Hitler's obsession with the Jews as agents of Bolshevism was particularly misplaced in Germany, where the overwhelming majority belonged to the bourgeoisie.

That "the gulag existed before Auschwitz," Levi acknowledged, but the gulag had been murder among equals: it had no racial basis, and assumed no division of mankind into supermen and subhumans, the latter liable to extermination by any means available. He identified the special contempt exemplified by symbolic details such as the Nazis' practice of tattooing, the use of a lethal gas originally designed for killing rats in the holds of ships, and vilest of all, the economic exploitation of the corpses of the dead. Nothing in Solzhenitsyn resembled camps such as Treblinka and Chelmno, "black holes" that required no labour and did not operate as concentration camps, but whose

394

sole function was to kill Jewish men, women, and children. The Russians had been thirsty for revenge "when they invaded Germany after the martyrdom of their country," but they brought no *Einsatzkommandos* to machine-gun civilians and bury them in mass graves. There was no question of exterminating the German people. There were no "selections" in the gulag, no doctors choosing new arrivals either to work or to die.

Nor were the gas chambers a marginal "innovation," the "only" different feature. They were linked to a systematic, and thoroughly German process. The gas was produced by famous German chemical firms, German industry used the hair of murdered women, German banks dealt in gold from the teeth of corpses. "No German should forget it." There had been failures on the part of the Allies, sins of omission, fear of giving asylum and having to care for millions of refugees, refusal to bomb the railway lines to Auschwitz. But this did not amount to collusion. If Germany wanted to resume its place among the nations, then it must not whitewash its past.

Levi appeared on television as the guest of a new cultural programme, *Focus*. He also granted two interviews to the press: one to the literary magazine *Uomini e Libri*, the other to a local cultural periodical, *Piemonte vivo*. They were the last he gave.

One of Levi's preoccupations during the final months of his life was with the human treatment of the environment. He wanted scientists to take the equivalent of the Hippocratic Oath.

> The neutron bomb was certainly the outcome of a request to a physicist from a politician. "Can you conceive a bomb with the power to destroy only human beings and leave buildings intact?" The physicist tried, and then said: "Yes, I can." It's obvious that we cannot prevent this, yet I would like to bind the future scientist in the way that a doctor is bound, so that he should abstain from such things. He may not abide by his oath, but if so he will be a traitor. He will have a sense of guilt. Obviously not everybody will feel this, but someone will say no, I can't do that, because I have sworn that I would not. I am well aware that all this is naive, but I also know how many other naive ideas have made their mark.[14]

Levi's pessimism tended to concern his inner life, "the interior minister," as he joked to Hermann Langbein. His faith in man and in democracy remained intact, and when a "Club for Science and Peace" was founded, whose members included Edgar Morin, Cesare Segre, Giulio Carlo Argan, Franco Fortini, Freeman Dyson, and Akira Ishida, Primo Levi joined at once. Nor did he do so in pursuit of a vacuous pacifism. In January 1987, in the course of a televised interview, he pointed out that the frontiers of Italy were no longer disputed by its neighbours, and that it was a member of NATO. He knew that Italy kept dangerous weapons in the hope of not having to use them. All the same, he wanted his country "to set an example, with a culture intent on peace and the repudiation of war." In the field of science, he hoped that Italy's physicists, chemists, and biologists would pay heed to "their sinister power."

In 1987 Primo Levi and others agreed to support the candidacy of his friend Bianca Guidetti Serra in the municipal elections to represent *Democrazia Proletaria*, a grouping of the far left. She was elected with 8,000 votes, and duly sat on the town council. Levi's consent to have his name appear on the list of her supporters had been grudgingly given. Before he signed, he phoned Bianca to ask her: "Does it really mean that much to you, Bianca?"[15] He told Pier Franco Quaglieni that he had been both vexed and saddened by the way that certain electioneering tactics had been employed to "capture" intellectual support for, as he put it, hopeless exercises in political cosmetics. Quaglieni was taken aback by the harsh tone of the remarks spoken by a man who seldom strayed far from his habitual reserve and moderation.

During the months that preceded his death, two women were in Primo Levi's confidence. It is a fact that while he was a Jew he was also a man of Piedmont, and that in Piedmont it is not done for men to talk to other men about their personal lives, let alone complain about them. Levi took antidepressants, but did not consider a psychoanalytical approach, because he utterly distrusted specialists in depth psychology. He found an outlet from his pain and isolation by writing to a distant listener, Ruth Feldman, the translator of his poems, who lived in the United States. She understood that all of the rage and despair that Levi kept so closely confined in his prose broke out in his poetry, as in the poem "Eichmann," which resonates like a biblical curse. Ruth Feldman was a warm-hearted, comforting person whom he had first met in 1976, on the occasion of his receiving the Strega Prize in Rome, where she liked to spend part of the year. Two months before he died he wrote to tell her about his sleepless nights, and days spent full of anguish by the side of his bedridden mother, and in the constant presence of nurses who worked shifts around the clock. His final letter contained an extraordinary remark. In a sense, he wrote, the period he was living through was worse than Auschwitz, because he was no longer young and no longer had the ability to react, and take a grip on himself. While he hoped to emerge from it all, after his usual greetings — *"Cara, ti saluto"* — he signed *"De Profundis."* This letter took a month to reach its destination. Ruth Feldman answered at once, but given the slow pace of the mail, she did not know whether it reached Turin before Saturday, 11 April 1987.[16]

Primo Levi also continued to pay frequent visits to his publisher's offices to talk to Agnese Incisa, who had proposed that he should write the preface to the Italian edition of Jean Améry's book, *Jenseits von Schuld und Sühne*. He told this young woman about his weariness with living. She listened, and tried to comfort him. He had never come to work in the office she set aside so that he could concentrate in peace, away from the torments he endured at home. In fact he forbade himself ever to be very far away from his mother who never stopped summoning him to her, and made it impossible for him to work. On the rare occasions when he did allow himself out on parole, his friends noticed that he would dart worried glances at his watch, then slip away when meal times came.

He still went walking now and then in the hills around Turin, with Silvio Ortona, whose wife, Levi's cousin Ada Della Torre, was seriously ill, and dying.

Until the autumn of 1986 Primo Levi's condition gave no cause for alarm, but he was incarcerated in his own home, held in a prison where a very old lady, who was not strictly speaking ill, but who had grown totally dependent in her slow journey towards death, was dragging her son down with her, who had only ever briefly lived away.

Primo Levi had stopped writing, and had the impression that he was losing his memory. He who had lived to bear witness said that apart from a few details, nowadays he had to reread his books to bring to mind the year he had spent in Auschwitz. He was now spending whole days at a time playing chess with his computer. On 7 February he wrote to David Mendel, an English cardiologist: "I have fallen into a quite serious state of depression. I've lost all interest in writing and even in reading. I am extremely low, and I don't want to see anybody. I ask you, as a 'Proper doctor', what I must do."[17] The unusual circumstances of their meeting are worth while recording.

David Mendel retired as a doctor in 1986, planning to devote himself to literary translation. One day that year he walked into a bookshop just as it was closing, and bought a book of Primo Levi's by mistake, having confused him with his namesake, Carlo Levi, the author of *Christ Stopped at Eboli*. In discovering his error, he remembered that he had already read *If This Is A Man*, in the translation by Stuart Woolf, and was fired with new enthusiasm for its author. He recommended it to one of his friends, who ran the obituary columns of a newspaper, and the friend asked him to write an obituary for Levi. Mendel was shocked at first, because writing the obituary of a living person felt to him like conducting an autopsy on a conscious patient, but he was so eager to meet Primo Levi that he asked for his phone number from International Inquiries, got it, and phoned at once to suggest an interview. Levi was not keen on the idea. Mendel, who had not disclosed the purpose of their possible meeting, then sent him a copy of his book, *Proper Doctoring*. Levi replied in English: "My mother, aged ninety-one, has had a stroke and is paralysed down her left side. My wife is already nursing her mother who is ninety-five and blind ... it would seem wise for you to call me when you arrive in Italy. ..."

Mendel, who had never been a journalist, arrived in Turin. Levi gave him a cordial welcome to his study, and told him that he had been born in this room. As their conversation progressed, Levi complained that Mendel spoke English too quickly and they agreed that Levi would speak English and Mendel Italian.

Levi wanted to know how Mendel had come to hear of him. Mendel thought for an instant, then told his host frankly what had brought him to Turin. Levi made a wry grimace as he listened, and finished by joking that he supposed he might feel flattered. The following is an extract from David Mendel's article in *L'Indice*:

> He was short and slight, but wiry. Inquisitive eyes were the dominant feature in a pleasing, puckish, bearded face. He had an air of goodness about him. He looked like an intellectual although, as he once wrote "the word gives me a vague uneasiness." He sat as compact as a cat, considering what I said and asking me questions. He seemed to find me much more interesting than anyone else had ever done. When I told him I'd been in the army during the war, his eyes opened in admiration for what was after all a common fate at that time. He clearly felt that being in a concentration camp was nowhere as remarkable as what I'd done. He didn't exaggerate when he wrote of his "curious confessional gift"; I was forced to point out that I was the one who was supposed to be doing the interviewing. He strove untiringly to stop me being deferential. He would concentrate on whatever I said, however trite, as if he were solving some philosophical riddle, examining my off-the-cuff statements under the microscope. Open-minded — but not enough to allow the truth to fall through — if he found my view wanting he made no bones about condemning it, but he did it gently.
>
> I thought he was delightful. My obvious infatuation with him failed to set him against me; we got on like a house on fire.[18]

After that first encounter, the two kept in touch with each other. Levi gave Mendel a list of his favourite books by contemporary Italian authors, and a copy of a book by Italo Calvino sent to him by the author. When Mendel suggested that he should inscribe it "from Italo Calvino to Primo Levi, and thence to David Mendel," Levi grinned but declined. Later on, he found a shopping list on the flyleaf jotted down in Levi's hand.

In one letter Levi wrote to David Mendel: "The main reason for my writing to you in Italian is that it gives me the chance to use [the friendly] "tu" when I address you. I am touched beyond any expression by your compliments, and the way you have read my books." He told him how his classmates at school used to mock their Jewish fellow pupils: "Aryan schoolmates jeered at us, saying that the circumcision was nothing else but castration, and we, at least at the inconscious [sic] level, tended to believe it."

He told Mendel that he was convinced that his professors had granted him his doctorate more to demonstrate their anti-Fascism than to reward the excellence of his thesis. He also said that he had been a disastrous partisan, that his knowledge of chemistry was of a merely average standard, and that his books made him seem wiser, braver, calmer, and more collected than he really was.

David Mendel showed Levi the article he had written about him, and asked if he saw himself as a guru. Levi replied: "I am not a guru. I would be glad to be one for myself and those around me, but there's one essential thing that I lack — self-assurance. I have more doubts than firm convictions. Besides that, I do believe that I lack charisma, and will always lack it, because I have too great a tendency to laugh both at others and at myself." Mendel wanted to know if he had a hero or heroes. Levi said he admired a certain number of people, but hero-worshipped no one. Finally, when the English doctor asked him why, in his books, he did not mention the women in his life, Levi's answer was: "Everybody else writes about that, why should I?"

When he received Levi's letter of 7 February mentioned earlier, in which he asked for advice about his depression, Mendel phoned him to ask for detailed information about drugs he was being prescribed. Levi explained to Mendel that he had come through a similar bout of depression twice before, with the help of antidepressants; today he was taking the same drugs, but in higher doses. He had also consulted a new psychiatrist, even though he denied psychiatrists the right to exercise their skills on those who had survived the Nazi extermination camps. He doubted whether they could understand and help patients like these. Mendel advised Levi to get away from the family atmosphere for a while, and invited him to come and stay at his house in Italy for a few days. Levi replied that it would probably make sense for him to get away, but that he lacked the energy to do it. The tone of the letter perturbed David Mendel, but he hesitated to interfere in the treatment of another doctor's patient, and at such a distance.

Primo Levi's reservations about psychoanalysis also extended to Bruno Bettelheim and his work. Bettelheim had been briefly detained in Dachau and Buchenwald, but was released thanks to the intervention of influential friends, and emigrated to the United States in 1939. He described his internment as an experience of degradation and infantile powerlessness. It was precisely this diagnosis of the deportee's behaviour as comparable to infantile regression that offended Primo Levi, who himself had learned a lot in Auschwitz. Moreover, the SS could not conceivably be compared to parents trying to bring up their children; parents did not usually behave towards their offspring like an SS commandant, even if they give them orders, and feed them at set times.

In March 1987, Primo Levi learned that he needed to undergo a prostate operation. He broke off his interviews with Giovanni Tesio and stopped taking antidepressants. The news signalled that he too was entering the cycle of illness and experiencing the first symptoms of old age, having for so many years endured and observed at close quarters and in intimate detail his mother's long decline.

In the hospital where he was operated on, only his closest circle were allowed to visit, among them his lifelong friend Alberto Salmoni, the inventor of a formula for a resin that had made his fortune: Alberto, whom he had admired in his youth for his free spirit — it took tremendous nerve to arrive on roller skates at the Chemical Institute of Turin in the 1930s — and for all his successes with women.

A minor post-operational haemorrhage prompted a brief return to the operating theatre. Convalescence was painful. Levi was troubled by discomfort caused by inflammation in the affected area, and the re-adaptation necessary to restore its normal functions. After he came home, he confided to Bruno Vasari in a telephone conversation that he dreaded the effects of the operation. He had pains in one leg, and telephoned Federico Accati, who was suffering from a carcinoma of the prostate.[19] Accati invited him to stay at his home in the country for a few days, "away from the women," but Levi never came. The household seemed to have him completely in its power.

The Periodic Table was published simultaneously in France and in Germany. Having remained unknown for forty years, Levi's work had taken off in the United States, in the last three years since the publication of *The Periodic Table*. All of his books received wide review attention.

Hearing that Levi was in crisis, Alessandro Galante Garrone phoned him and ventured to take an almost chiding tone. "You mustn't give way to despair," he told him. "We need you. What you do, only you can do for us." Softly and wearily, Levi kept answering: "*Grazie … Tu sei molto gentile*" — "Thank you, you're very kind" — and this riled Galante Garrone into barking: "You mustn't say that. It isn't kindness. It's an insult to tell me that!" But Levi would only repeat: "*Grazie … Tu sei molto gentile*." It was a refusal to reply. He wanted to end it. That is how the two men took their leave of one another.[20]

Against this background of melancholia, Primo Levi's moods fluctuated, and those who are determined to reach a clear-cut verdict on his final action can find arguments on the side both of despair and of hope in the future. Some will point out that he shut himself away inside his home, others that he gave an interview to Roberto Di Caro for *L'Espresso* a few days before he died. (It was published posthumously.) He told the journalist that he had written at least three books — *If This Is A Man*, *The Truce*, and part of *The Periodic Table* — while practising the trade of a chemist. It amazed him that he had squeezed so much writing into his working life. Now that he was released from the pressure of having to earn a living, he was writing "less than I did then, and with less intensity." He added: "I have the feeling that I have run out of things to say, and stories to tell." When Di Caro inquired whether he had another book in mind nevertheless, he replied that he was working, but "against his will."[21] Then suddenly Levi, who was usually so reticent, confessed to this man who had certainly interviewed him several times, but could not be counted as a close friend: "The truth is that I live a neurotic life, with woeful blanks between books, as at the moment after *The Drowned and the Saved*." He went on:

> I have finished up by internalizing my duties, and these days it is very hard for me to travel, for family reasons …. In the past, when the trans-

lation of one of my books arrived in my house, it was a cause for celebration. Now it doesn't matter to me. Even the process of revising the
translations into languages I know — English, German, French — has
turned into nothing but one more boring job to be done. I've been
immunized.

When Di Caro followed up by asking him to account for the way he presented
himself in his books, Levi's uncharacteristically confessional mood persisted:

In my books I have sometimes presented myself as brave or as faint-
hearted, and sometimes as thoughtful or naive, but always as a stable
person, which I'm really not. I've been through long phases of instability, no doubt tied up with my experience in the extermination camp. In
the end, I stand up badly under strain. And that is something that I've
never written about. ... In fact, I am not a strong character. ... I'm
considered as a sort of guru. Perhaps there is a wisdom in my books,
which I don't think I have. For me, it is nothing more than moderation
... that is a Piedmontese virtue.

The journalist insisted that it took strength to relate the experience he had lived
through. Levi summed up his position: he wrote because he felt a compelling
need to tell the story, to bring order out of "a chaotic world."[22]

On 2 January, Levi had written his last poem, "Almanac," for *La Stampa*,
on the occasion of the New Year. He had just been awarded the Marotta Prize
in Naples. "Almanac" is a farewell to the world, a farewell in the form of a
prophecy, proclaimed by a follower of the Enlightenment who detested both
prophets and their prophecies:

> The indifferent rivers
> Will keep on flowing to the sea
> Or ruinously overflowing dikes,
> Ancient handiwork of determined men.
> The glaciers will continue to grate,
> Smoothing what lies beneath them,
> Or suddenly fall headlong,
> Cutting short fir trees' lives.
> The sea, captive between
> Two continents, will go on struggling,
> Always miserly with its riches.
> Sun, stars, planets and comets
> Will continue on their course.
> Earth too will fear the immutable
> Laws of the universe.
> Not us. We, rebellious offspring
> With great brainpower, little sense,
> Will destroy, defile,

Always more feverishly.
Very soon we will extend the desert
Into the Amazon forests,
Into the living heart of our cities,
Into our very hearts.[23]

On 20 January Primo Levi put in a brief appearance at a conference organized to commemorate the Wannsee Conference, held on 20 January 1942, at which the SS announced its plans for "the final solution of the Jewish question in Europe." His presence was not scheduled in the programme, but his entrance into the hall of the Palazzo Lascaris brought an immediate ovation, and a request for him to mount the platform and speak, which he refused to do. He could only stand and look back at the audience in surprise and embarrassment. Bruno Vasari, who had just read his paper, remembers: "Primo had to go home, so he put his hand on my shoulder to say goodbye. When the chairman of the session saw him leaving he said: 'Excuse me, I can't let Primo Levi leave without wishing him well.' I stood up and embraced him, and said to him: 'Remember that I love you.'"

The next day, La Stampa printed an article setting out the denialist claims of Andreas Hillgruber, who argued that the gas chambers were "a simple technological invention" — a proposition that caused a favourable stir in Germany. On 22 January, Levi refuted the lies put forward by the denial propagandists in his article "The Black Hole of Auschwitz."

In February, Primo Levi wrote in La Stampa a review of A.G. Cairns-Smith's book Seven Clues to the Origins of Life.

When he received a phone call from Edith Bruck, one of his friends who had been deported to Dachau, he told her that he felt he was losing his memory, and that he had to reread his own books in order to remember what he had written.

If thoughts of suicide occurred to Primo Levi, both in his youth and at the end of his life — though for quite different reasons — this does not justify the assumption that it had been a permanent presence in his mind.

———————————

A week before he died, he agreed to go walking with Alberto Salmone in the hills above Turin. They had just got out of their car, and were looking at the town spread out below them, when suddenly Levi remarked to his friend, as if saying farewell: "How many things we've seen and done together."

For years, Francesco Rosi had been thinking of adapting The Truce for the cinema. It was a project he had dropped and revived more than once. Only weeks before Primo Levi died, he phoned to inform him that he intended to go ahead, and Levi answered: "This news about a film of The Truce is the one thing that has cheered me up a bit, these last few days. It is a great joy in a moment of sadness."[24]

A few days later, Giulio Einaudi made his first visit to Primo Levi's home in twenty years. At this time, the house of Einaudi was in a state of financial crisis. Giulio Einaudi walked up the Corso Re Umberto bringing an offer to make Primo Levi the honorary chairman of the firm — a belated gesture that Levi politely refused.

Ernesto Ferrero admired and respected Levi, and it was concern about his state of health that prompted him to phone and pass on some good news, in the hope of restoring his taste for life. The news was that Levi's name had appeared on the list of writers in line to receive the Nobel Prize. On hearing these words, Primo Levi broke in to say: "You're joking!"

Levi was very attached to his endangered publishing house, and had phoned Norberto Bobbio, his near neighbour in the Via Sacchi and his companion on walks in the mountains, to discuss its future. But his friend was not at home, so Levi told Signora Bobbio that he would call later.

He also made a call to Rome, to speak to Lello Perugia, who had inspired the truculent character of Cesare in *The Truce* and in the story "Cesare's Last Adventure." It is relevant to recall that Lello Perugia was not only the man who had fascinated and inspired Levi in the months after leaving Auschwitz. He was also a partisan, a comrade in captivity, and a fellow survivor with whom he had joined forces in 1953 to demand compensation from I.G. Farben Industrie, exploiters of slave labour in the camp of Auschwitz-Monowitz. For I.G. Farben had survived the collapse of Nazism. While it is true that twenty-four of its top managers were brought to trial in August 1947, the verdicts concluded on 12 May 1948 were staggering in their clemency. Twelve of the twenty-four men accused were sentenced to light terms of eighteen months to six years in prison, and not one of them served his full sentence. During that call Levi told Perugia that he had the impression that the content of his books had not been grasped, and that Nazism still existed in the world.

Some days before his death, Levi mustered strength enough to write a final *Storia naturale* intended for the May issue of the review *Airone*, and which *La Stampa* was to publish with *Airone*'s permission on Sunday, 26 April 1987. Its theme is linked once more to his childhood phobia, spiders, in this case the black spider, hairy and menacing, a negative metaphor rich in implications for psychologists of the unconscious.[25] But Levi had anticipated their interpretations in another essay, "The Fear of Spiders," also published in *La Stampa*, in which he wrote:

> Their hairiness is supposed to have a sexual significance, and the repulsion we feel supposedly reveals our unconscious rejection of sex: this is how we express it and at the same time this is how we try to free ourselves of it ... [T]he spider is the enemy–mother who envelops and encompasses, who wants to make us re-enter the womb from which we have issued, bind us tightly to take us back to the impotence of infancy, subject us again to her power .... (*Trades* 156/143–4)

Bianca Guidetti Serra, Giovanni Tesio, and David Mendel had the opportunity to see Primo Levi or to speak to him on the telephone during the last few days of his life.

On 7 April, Lucia, Levi's wife, made a very anxious phone call to Bianca Guidetti Serra, asking her to come to the Corso Re Umberto and try to persuade her husband to go out. The following morning, Bianca phoned Levi to tell him that she would be calling to take him for a short walk in town. He replied: "No! No! No!" She persisted. "I'm coming over, and we'll go for a stroll." She picked him up in her car, and took him to the Parco del Valentino, on the banks of the Po. Bianca tried to divert him by talking about her work and her plans, but Levi was too downcast to respond, except when he suddenly told her:

"You're probably right, but I don't feel any interest any more."

"All right, you have no interest," she replied. "Then tell me the cause of the trouble."

"You think I feel depressed because of Auschwitz? I don't think so. I survived, I told the story. I testified."

Bianca had failed to make a dent in his despair when she brought him back to the Corso Re Umberto. She saw him go into his apartment, still at his lowest ebb. She did not know that she was never to see him again.[26]

On 8 April, Primo Levi and Elie Wiesel had a brief conversation on the telephone. Knowing the state he was in, Wiesel suggested that he should come over to New York for a few days. Levi could only sigh: "Too late."[27]

On the same day, Primo Levi wrote to Ferdinando Camon. There is nothing in his letter to show that it was written by a man in despair. On the contrary, it looks forward to the future:

Dear Camon
I spoke today to my publishes Einaudi: they tell me that *The Drowned and the Saved* has in fact been sent to Gallimard, but for good measure they are sending a second copy this very day. I would be very pleased, naturally, if Gallimard took it, and this gives me the opportunity to thank you for all you are doing to promote my books in France. You are extraordinarily kind and active. I look forward to your article in *Libération*, thank you for that too. Happy Easter and good wishes.[28]

Three days before his death, Primo Levi phoned the office of the Jewish community to ask if the *matzah* had arrived. On 10 April, Giovanni Tesio phoned Levi to wish him well for Passover. Levi sounded almost cheerful when he answered: "I'm glad you phoned me. We'll be seeing each other to start our work again." Perhaps he was trying to persuade himself that he was still interested in this biography.

Knowing how low he was feeling, his sister Anna Maria came from Rome to visit him.

On Friday 10 April, Primo phoned his cousin Giulia at three o'clock in the afternoon. Her husband, Teodoro Diena, picked up the telephone; Levi and his cousin then had a very ordinary conversation. Levi asked her: "Don't you feel well? Are you sleeping?" She told him that she had just prepared the delicacies for the Passover meal; she had been standing up to work, and had felt tired, and had now been lying on the sofa to rest. They talked about special cakes for Passover, and she promised to bring him some the next morning. Then Levi told Giulia that he had been having trouble with his health and had had an operation. She advised him not to worry, things would soon sort themselves out. "Why do you say that?" he asked her. "Have you had personal experience?" She attempted to reassure him by saying that friends in similar situations had recovered in a few weeks. The conversation went on like this for half an hour, and ended with Giulia promising again to look in the next morning and bring the Passover cakes.

On the same day, Primo Levi also made a phone call to Cesare Cases, one of whose close relations had died of a carcinoma of the prostate that had produced bone metastases. Levi asked him for information about the development of the disease.

David Mendel, the British doctor whom Levi had asked for advice, felt so concerned about him that he arranged to take the plane to Turin on 10 April. He had written to inform Levi that he would arrive on the 10th, and proposed to take him away for a few days' holiday. Although Levi had not replied, Mendel did not postpone his flight, but the plane was four hours late, and as he felt tired on arrival he decided not to call Primo Levi till the next day. When he woke up, he heard the news of Levi's suicide over the radio.

On the morning Primo Levi plunged down the stairwell of his home to his death, Cesare Cases, Bianca Guidetti Serra, and Luca Baranelli were strolling in the Parco della Rimembranza, where Levi sometimes went walking with Bianca, even in the depths of his depression. This vast park, situated on the hills that overlook the city of Turin and the banks of the Po, houses the graves of hundreds of soldiers who died in the First World War.

As they walked on that wooded hillside, Bianca talked to her friends about the terrible depression that had overtaken Primo, whom she had seen three days before. They told her: "But after all, he's very strong, he'll pull through." Bianca explained that it wasn't as easy as that: this time, things were really serious. She said "this time" because she knew it was not the first bout of depression that her friend had faced since the days of his youth, or since his return from Auschwitz.

On the morning of Saturday 11 April, between 10:20 and 10:30 a.m., Primo Levi telephoned the chief rabbi of Rome, Elio Toaff, and told him: "I don't know how to go on. I can't stand this life any longer. My mother has cancer, and each time I look at her face I remember the faces of the men lying dead on the planks of the bunks in Auschwitz." Elio Toaff kept secret this brief conversation until the tenth anniversary of Levi's death, revealing it on the occasion of a homage paid to the writer.

That morning, at ten o'clock, the concierge of the building, Jolanda Gasperi, rang *Dottore* Levi's doorbell, as she did every morning, to bring him the mail. He was alone with his mother. Lucia had gone shopping in the neighbourhood. The concierge noticed nothing special about Levi's attitude when he opened the door: as usual, he smiled and said "*Grazie.*" A few minutes after returning to her lodge, she heard an ominous muffled noise. She went outside and found the broken, bleeding body of Primo Levi sprawled behind the lift cage. Some minutes later, Lucia Levi returned from her errand to find her husband's dead body lying at the bottom of the stairs.

Primo Levi left no message for his friends and family. The autopsy carried out at the Medical–Legal Institute confirmed the reality of death from the fall, although Rita Levi Montalcini and David Mendel have always refused to believe it was suicide.

In *The Periodic Table* Primo Levi wrote of the difficulty he had in living since his return from captivity. The things he had seen and suffered burned within him. Like Coleridge's Ancient Mariner, he felt compelled to inflict his story on every passer-by. He wrote it down "at breakneck speed, so much so that gradually a book was later born: by writing I found peace for a while and felt myself become a man again, a person like everyone else, neither a martyr nor debased nor a saint" (*Table* 157).

Pliny

Don't hold me back, friends, let me set out.
I won't go far; just to the other shore.
I want to observe at close hand that dark cloud,
Shaped like a pine tree, rising above Vesuvius,
And find the source of this strange light.
Nephew, you don't want to come along? Fine; stay here and study.
Recopy the notes I gave you yesterday.
You needn't fear the ash; ash on top of ash.
We're ash ourselves; remember Epicurus?
Quick, get the boat ready, it is already night:
Night at midday, a portent never seen before.
Don't worry, sister, I'm cautious and expert;
The years that bowed me haven't passed in vain.
Of course I'll come back quickly. Just give me time
To ferry across, observe the phenomena and return,
Draw a new chapter from them tomorrow
For my books, that will, I hope, still live
When for centuries my old body's atoms
Will be whirling, dissolved in the vortices of the universe,
Or live again in an eagle, a young girl, a flower.
Sailors, obey me: launch the boat into the sea.

                                        23 May 1978

— From *Collected Poems*, Faber and Faber, 1992.

Appendix I: "The Jews of Turin"
Preface by Primo Levi

On the occasion of the centenary of our synagogue ... we, the Jews of Turin, have decided just this once to abandon our traditional twofold reserve. The Piedmontese reserve, tied to geographic and historical roots, is well known; because of it there are some who see in us the least Italianate of Italians. And subject to the age-old reticence of the Jews of the diaspora, we have always had to live in silence and suspicion, to listen a lot and talk a little, not to draw attention, because "you never know."

We have never been numerous: just over four thousand in the thirties, and that was the greatest number we have ever reached; just over a thousand today. And yet we do not feel that we exaggerate if we say that we have counted for something, and still do count for something, in the life of this town. Paradoxically, our history as quiet folk is tied to this grandiose Turinese monument which is not humble and does not reflect our nature. We have run the grave risk of sharing with Alessandro Antonelli the responsibility for the presence right in the city centre of the Mole, that outlandish exclamation mark.[1] Like all Turinese, of course, even we ourselves have a certain affection for the Mole, but it is an ironic, polemical love, which does not blind us. We love it as we love the walls of our house, even thought we know that it is ugly, overbearing, and not very functional; that it has wasted public money, and that after the cyclone of 1953 and the restoration of 1961 it stays upright only by virtue of a metal prosthesis ... [W]e owe a debt of posthumous gratitude to the assistant to Mayor Malvano, our coreligionist, who in 1875 managed to sell to the town the money-guzzling building which had been commissioned and remained unfinished. If the deal had fallen through, today we would have to witness the sad spectacle of the few hundred Jews who go to the temple for solemn festivals and of the few dozen who attend the daily services, practically invisible in the vast space bounded by the Antonellian dome.

When our fathers (for the most part not Turinese, but mainly dwelling in the small community of Piedmont) came to live in the town towards the end of the last century, they brought with them the great strength — undoubtedly, unique, and a specific gift — that history has bequeathed to the Jews: literacy, religious and secular culture understood as a duty, a right, a necessity, one of life's delights; and this in the era when the population of Italy was almost

---

[1]The Mole Antonelliana (completed in 1884) was to be the gigantic synagogue of the tiny community of the Jews of Turin, only recently emancipated.

entirely illiterate. For that reason, emancipation did not catch them unawares, as the history of many families shows. In a couple of generations the Jews just out of the ghetto moved quite easily from crafts and small-scale business into the early days of industry, administrative posts, public service, the army, and the university. It is precisely in the academic sphere that the Jews of Turin have left illustrious traces totally out of proportion to their number, and here their presence has been significant ever since. In their rise, which parallels that of a section of the Christian lower middle class, they also benefited from the fundamental tolerance of the population. It has been said that every country has the Jews it deserves; post-Risorgimento Italy, a land with an ethnically homogeneous, ancient civilization, unscathed by serious xenophobic tensions, gave its Jews a status as decent, law-abiding citizens, loyal to the state.

From this point of view, the integration of Italian Jewry is unique in the world; but the balance achieved by Piedmontese–Turinese Jewry, which integrated easily without giving up its own identity, is surely even more remarkable. Except for a few rare and marginal cases such as the centres in Yemen and the Caucasus, the Jewish communities of the world bore (and still bear) the scars of the troubled history of the people of Israel, laden with massacres, expulsions, humiliating discrimination, odious and arbitrary taxation, forced conversions and migrations. The Jews expelled from one country (England in 1290, France throughout the fourteenth century, the Rhineland during the Crusades, Spain in 1492, the more recent migrations to the US) sought refuge elsewhere by joining existing communities or founding new ones. Hence they were doubly foreign, both by their religion and by their origin. For this reason, the majority of the communities were stratified and heterogeneous, with occasional tensions and splits. Israel Zangwill gave a vivid portrait in his famous story *The King of Schnorrers,* in which he describes the impossible meeting, [situated] in eighteenth-century London, between a learned, stubborn, mendicant 'Spanish' Jew and a Jew of German 'tedesco' origin, integrated and *nouveau riche*. In Amsterdam, the local-born Jews of German origin took in the Jews expelled from the Iberian peninsula, but the two communities never really merged. Today there are five synagogues in Venice that were originally built for Jews with different origins and rites. The present situation is identical to the one in Paris, where Jews of old-established French origin live side by side with Algerian, Egyptian, Polish, Russian, German, and other Jews. The most complex, and historically most important case is that of Israel, where the presence of Jews from every branch of the Diaspora causes insoluble internal problems. The most recent case concerns the community of Milan, in which the massive influx of refugees from the Arab states and Iran is causing disturbances and collisions and an unexpected rise in population.

On the other hand, the Turinese Jews of distant Franco-Provençal and Spanish origin have never experienced sizeable intakes from other regions. Trickles, yes, in different periods, as witness a few names of obviously German origin (Ottolenghi, Diena, Luzzati, Morpurgo, and of course Tedeschi)[2], and, if nothing else, the dialectal and liturgical term *"ij ursài,"* the anniversary of a death, which is a corruption of the Yiddish *"yorzeit,"* "time of the year." But the influences were quickly absorbed by a social fabric that remained ethnically stable for forty years (1880–1920) and to which this exhibition is dedicated. There is a clear contrast here with what is happening today in Turin, which in the days of the economic boom absorbed five or six hundred thousand immigrants in only two or three years, causing a transformation in its structures and superstructures.

The fact that Turin's is a small Jewish community conscious of its own identity and endowed with a strong physiognomy — as it were, a village embedded in the capital of Savoy — is demonstrated by the widespread endogamy, rarely practised beyond the boundaries of the region, and by the curious Judaeo-Piedmontese dialect, now an object of study for linguists and sociologists, but already described by that shrewd observer of Piedmont, Alberto Virgilio. In order for this linguistic hybrid to grow up and survive, it was essential for there to be a close integration with the majority population, an adquate memory of the liturgical tongue (the sole vector through which Hebrew and Aramaic rode the currents of the Diaspora), and a climate that lacked strong tensions between the majority and the minority. When these tensions exist, hybrid languages do not spring up. No Judaeo-Polish dialect ever developed, for example, and there is no Italian–German dialect in Alto Adige, whereas in spite of poor phonetic compatibility the Italian emigrants to the United States developed among themselves a specific language well explored by Giovanni Pascoli in a famous short poem.

Our fathers, and above all our mothers, spoke Judaeo-Piedmontese every day, as a matter of course. It was the idiom of home and family. At the same time they were aware of its intrinsic comical effect, which sprang from the contrast between the fabric of speech, which was the rustic and laconic Piedmontese dialect, and the Jewish accretions, derived from the language of the patriarchs, which was ancient, but whose memory was rekindled each day in public and private prayer, and by the reading of texts polished smooth by the millennia like the bed of a glacier. But this contrast had no less respect for a particular otherness, basic to Jewry dispersed among the "goym" (just so, the "goym"), torn between the divine vocation and daily poverty, and a much greater otherness, inherent in the human condition because man is divided in two, an amalgam of heavenly spirit and earthly dust. After its dispersion, the Jewish people lived out this conflict painfully, and drew a kind of wisdom from it — the laughter that is missing from the Bible and the Prophets ...

This exhibition is dedicated to our fathers, decent, shrewd and hardworking, not heroic, and neither saints nor martyrs, not too far removed in time and space. We are conscious of its limits, which we have deliberately

[2]*Tedeschi*, plural of *Tedesco*, means "Germans" in Italian.

411

imposed. Other things could be said — much darker things — about the history of the Jews of Turin through successive decades. Their early anti-Fascist commitment was paid for by long years of prison and isolation, and induced by that thirst for liberty and justice that pervades Jewish history. The example of men like Umberto Terracini, Leone Ginzburg, Emanuele and Ennio Artom, Giuseppe, Mario and Alberto Levi; the dead partisans, Sergio, Paolo and Franco Diena; the Jewish contribution to the Resistance, once again proportionally greater in number compared to the rest of the population; the eight hundred deportees of whom nothing remains but a stone slab in our graveyard. But on this occasion we did not wish to speak of victory, defeat, struggle, and massacres. Here we intend to recall and bring to mind, to make known before it is too late. There exists in fact, for every human group, a critical mass below which stability ceases; its drifts towards an ever more thorough dilution, a silent, painless disappearance. Short of unforeseeable events, our own community seems to be embarked along that path. With this exhibition, we mean to perform an act of filial piety, to enable our Turinese friends and our children to see who we are and where we come from.

Primo Levi, 1984, from the preface to *Ebrei a Torino — Ricerche per il centenario della sinagoga 1884–1984*. Archivo di arte e cultura piemontesi, Umberto Allemandi & C., 1984, now out of print.

Appendix II: "The Marital Web"

"Good evening, Mr Spider," said the journalist, "and good evening to you too, Mrs Spider."

"Are you edible?" replied the male, in a shrill voice.

"Yes, I suppose so, but the question has never crossed my mind."

"Do you know that we have many eyes, but are very short-sighted, and we're always hungry? For us, the world is divided into two: the things you can eat, and the rest."

"I'm not here as a potential victim but to conduct an interview."

"An interview? Can you eat interviews? Are they nourishing? If so, give me one right away; it's what I'm most interested in. I've eaten a bit of everything in my time, but never an interview. How many legs do they have? Have they got wings?"

"No, actually, you can't eat them, but they are consumed, in a different way. How can I put it? Well, I suppose they have readers, and sometimes they're a little bit nourishing."

"Well, then, the subject is not much good to me; but if you could give me some small reward — a fly or some mosquitoes ... Did you know that with hygiene so important nowadays, you hardly see any around? Are you brave enough to catch mosquitoes? Being the size you are, it can't be very hard: who knows how big your web is ...?"

"As a matter of fact, we have other ways of catching flies and mosquitoes but it's not a very worthwhile occupation for us. We eat them against our will and by mistake. All right, it's a deal, I'll do my best. So, can I begin? Tell, me, why do you always hang upside down?"

"To concentrate: I have very few thoughts and that way they all fall down towards my brain, and I see things more clearly. But don't come so close, and be careful with that instrument you're holding: I wouldn't want you tearing my web. It's newly woven this morning. It only had one little hole, you know; beetles don't notice anything, but for us it's perfection or nothing. The first flaw, and I eat my web up, digest it, and then I've got new material all ready to make another. It's a question of principle. We're not much on brains, but there's no end to our patience. I've been known to weave my web as many as three times in a single day, but that was an unbelievable effort. After the third web, which luckily no one spoiled for me, I had to rest for three or four days. That takes time, and so does replenishing the silk-producing glands in the belly; but as I was saying, we have a lot of patience and waiting doesn't bother me at all. When you're waiting, you don't expend much energy."

"Your webs are works of art, but do you weave them all alike? Is there never some improved version, some innovation?"

"Don't ask too much of us. You see, I'm already making an effort to answer your questions; we have no imagination, we aren't inventors, our cycle is simple: hunger, web, fly, digestion, hunger, new web. So why should we rack our brains — sorry, our ganglions — trying to work out new patterns? Far better to trust in our imprinted memory, the good old model, and at the very most adapt it to the prevailing conditions. That's already almost too much for our intelligence. If I remember rightly, I spun my first web only a few days after I'd hatched. It was as big as a postage stamp, but apart from the size, it was identical to the one in front of your nose ..."

"I understand. [*Turning to the female*:] Now, tell me: there are rumours going around about your ... let's say, your matrimonial behaviour. These rumours ... you understand, I personally have never seen anything wrong with it, but you know how people gossip ..."

"Are you referring to the fact that we eat our males? Is that all? But of course, we certainly do — it's a kind of dance. Our males are thin, weak and timid, and not even brave enough to weave a decent web. When they feel their desire coming on, they venture onto our web, step by step, uncertain, hesitant, because they themselves know how it can all end up. We wait for them, we don't make the first move, both sides know how the game is played. We females like males as much as we like flies, if not more. We enjoy them in all senses of the word, as husbands (but only for the minimum time necessary) and as food. Once they fulfil their function, they lose their attraction for us, except as fresh meat. So they fill our stomachs and our wombs in one go."

"Do your marriages always end in that way?"

"Not always. There are some provident males who know about our constant hunger and bring us a wedding gift — not out of affection or respect, but simply to keep us fed. A fly, a daddy-longlegs, sometimes something more substantial. Then everything goes well, and it's time for an anxious retreat. You should see the males as they check-up to see whether their gift is satisfactory. If they suspect it's not enough, they sometimes run back to their own web to collect another mouthful."

"It sounds like an ingenious system, and come to think of it, it does have a certain logic, I'd do the same in their place. But you must understand that my wife has a smaller appetite and a much more friendly attitude. Our marriages last a long time. And we think it a shame to make do with mating just once."

"Each to his own, naturally. But I wanted to tell you that it's not the only method the males have invented so as not to get eaten. There are others. Some of our distant cousins perform a dance of praise around their chosen female. They gradually tie her up, carefully criss-crossing their threads. Then they impregnate her and go away. Still others are afraid of our strength: they carry the female off when she's only just hatched, not developed and not so dangerous, and they shut her up in some little nook or cranny until puberty. They feed her, but as little as possible, so that she stays alive but doesn't get too strong.

Then they do their job, release the females, and make a quick getaway."

"Thank you very much, that ends the interview."

"Just as well, I was starting to get tired. Brain work is not my strong point. But don't forget the flies: a promise is a promise."

This piece, Primo Levi's last contribution to *La Stampa*, was published posthumously on 26 April 1987.

Notes

Full bibliographic details of Primo Levi's major works and their translations are given on p. x. Please refer to the Select Bibliography on p. 439 for details of other works.

Introduction

1   Primo Levi, *The Drowned and the Saved, (I sommersi e i salvati*, 1986). Citations in this book are taken from Vintage Books, 1989 (US) and Abacus, 1989 (UK) editions. Subsequent references to this title will be shortened to *DS* with the page numbers to the US edition given in *italic* — (*DS 76/57*).

2   Italian writer to whom he had given a series of interviews published as *Conversazione con Primo Levi*, 1987.

3   *Il sistema periodico*, 1975, translated as *The Periodic Table* in 1984 (US) and in 1985 (UK). Subsequent references to this title will be shortened to *Table*. Citations in this book are taken from Schocken Books, 1995 (US) and Abacus, 1986 (UK) editions; only one set of figures for page reference numbers is given, as pagination in both US/UK editions is identical — (*Table 5*).

Prologue

1   *Se questo è un uomo*, 1958, translated as *Survival In Auschwitz*, 1960 (US) and *If This Is A Man*, 1965 (UK). Citations in this book are taken from the Touchstone, 1996 (US) and Abacus, 1987 (UK) editions. Subsequent references to this title will be shortened to *Man* with the page numbers to the US edition given in *italic*. *La tregua*, 1963, translated as *The Reawakening*, 1965 (US) and *The Truce*, 1965 (UK). Citations in this book are taken from the Touchstone, 1995 (US) and Abacus, 1987 (UK) editions. Subsequent references to this title will be shortened to *Truce* with the page numbers to the US edition given in *italic*.

2   "The Set Table," the title given to the classic codification of Jewish religious law compiled in the sixteenth century by Joseph Caro of Safed in Palestine.

3   Robert Faurisson, a French professor of literature, began a campaign in 1978 to deny that the Holocaust occurred, claiming that the "alleged gas chambers and the alleged genocide are one and the same lie ... which is largely of Zionist origin."

4   The street has been divided to make room for the Piazzetta Primo Levi outside the gates of the synagogue. It was inaugurated on 24 April 1996.

5 *Ebrei a Torino — Ricerche per il centenario della sinagoga 1884–1984,*
1984.
6 The full text of Levi's preface is given in Appendix I of this book, "The
Jews of Turin", see p. 409.

see p. 409.

1 **Corso Re Umberto**
1 Ernst Nolte is a German scholar whose defence of the Nazi regime is based
on the necessity of crushing Communist Russia.
2 From *The Drowned and the Saved.*
3 Jean Améry, *Jenseits von Schuld und Sühne: Bewältigungsversuche eines
Überwältigten,* 1966, translated as *At the Mind's Limits,* 1980.
4 Paolo Spriano, "*L'avventura di Primo Levi,*" *L'Unità,* 14 July 1963.

2 **A Jewish Childhood under Fascism**
1 Primo Levi published some of these essays in 1985 under the title *L'altrui
mestiere.* The English translation of the collection was published as *Other
People's Trades* in 1989 by Summit Books (US) and Michael Joseph (UK).
Citations in this book are taken from the Summit, 1989 (US) and Abacus,
1991 (UK) editions. Subsequent references to this title will be shortened to
Trades with the page numbers to the US edition given in *italic.*
2 Philip Roth's interview with Primo Levi first appeared in *The New York
Times Book Review* on 12 October 1986 and in *The London Review of
Books* on 26 October 1986.
3 *Il sistema periodico,* 1975.
4 From an interview with Stefano Jesurum who met and interviewed Primo
Levi on a number of occasions. The quotation appeared in a book by
Jesurum on Jewish identity entitled *Essere ebrei in Italia,* 1987.
5 Primo Levi, *La ricerca delle radici — Antologia personale,* 1981.
(Literally, "the quest for roots — a personal anthology".)
6 The quotation comes from a book on Levi that Stefano Jesurum co-
authored with Massimo Dino, entitled *Primo Levi, Le opere dei giorni,*
1992.
7 From "*Ranocchi sulla luna*" in *Racconti e saggi di Primo Levi,* 1986.
8 Interview with the author, 24 April 1986.
9 In a story printed in *Other People's Trades,* under the title "Love's Erector
Set."
10 The families of Rita Levi Montalcini — Levi's friend, and winner of the
Nobel Prize for Medicine in 1986 — and Carlo De Bendetti lived in the
Crocetta district.
11 Literally "son of the Commandment," the ceremony by which a boy, on
reaching the age of thirteen, enters the religious community as a responsible adult.
12 Rosh Hashanah (Hebrew, "the head of the year") is the Jewish New Year.
Purim (Hebrew, "lots") commemorates the deliverance of the Persian Jews

from the destruction planned by Haman, the favoured minister of King Ahasuerus.

13 Giorgio Bassani, *The Garden of the Finzi-Continis*, 1965, p. 36.

14 The word *"ras"* originally meant a chief in Ethiopia. It came to be attached to the Fascist chiefs, such as Roberto Farinacci, Dino Grandi, and Italo Balbo, who organized terror in major Italian towns before Mussolini seized power.

15 Quoted in Pierre Milza and Serge Bernstein, *Le fascisme italien 1919–1945*, 1980.

16 From Primo Levi and Tullio Regge, *Dialogo*, 1984, translated as *Conversations* in 1989, p. 14.

17 Levi, *La ricerca delle radici*.

18 Levi and Regge, *Conversations*, p. 13.

19 Piedmontese dialect for: "You're just snot-noses drowning in the stock-pot!"

20 The Abbé Henri Grégoire, the Constitutional bishop of Blois in 1791, was elected to the French Convention, where he was active in passing the decrees that granted civil and political rights to the Jews.

3 **The Chemical Institute**

1 Gabriella Poli and Giorgio Calcagno, *Echi di una voce perduta*, 1992.

2 Levi and Regge, *Conversations*, p. 19.

3 Most of the quotations from this chapter are taken from Primo Levi's *The Periodic Table*.

4 Renzo De Felice, *Storia degli ebrei italiani sotto il fascismo*, 1961.

5 *Ibid.*

6 *Ibid.*

7 *Ibid.*

8 Raul Hilberg, *The Destruction of the European Jews*, 1985, p. 662.

9 *Ibid.*

10 De Felice, *Storia degli ebrei italiani sotto il fascismo*.

11 *Ciano's Diaries*, 1952, 30 July 1938, p. 141.

12 The historian Renzo De Felice (author of *Storia degli ebrei italiani sotto il fascismo*) is also the author of a monumental biography of Mussolini published by Einaudi, and director of the review *Storia contemporanea*.

13 Susan Zuccotti, *The Italians and the Holocaust — Persecution, Rescue and Survival*, 1987, pp. 60–1.

14 The planned encyclical was to be called *Humani Generis Unitas* ("the unity of the human race"), see Georges Passelecq and Bernard Suchecky, *L'Encyclique cachée de Pie XI. Une occasion manquée de l'Eglise face à l'antisémitisme*, 1995.

15 *Ibid.*

16 Michele Sarfatti, *Mussolini contro gli ebrei*, 1994.

17 *Ibid.*

18 *Ciano's Diaries*, p. 40.

19 Alessandro Galante Garrone, *Amaleke, Il dovere della memoria*, 1989, p. 197.

20 Levi and Regge, *Conversations*.

21 From correspondence between Ettore Delmastro and the author, February 1994.

22 Quoted in Alberto Cavaglion, *La scuola ebraica a Torino (1938–1943)*, 1993.

23 *Ibid.*

24 Galante Garrone, *Amaleke, Il dovere della memoria*.

25 Quoted in Cavaglion, *La scuola ebraica a Torino (1938–1943)*.

26 Interview with Primo Levi in Poli and Calcagno, *Echi di una voce perduta*.

27 *Ibid.*

28 Mount Herbetet is a high peak in the Valle d'Aosta.

29 Roth interview, *The New York Times Book Review*, 12 October 1986/*The London Review of Books*, 26 October 1986.

30 All quotations from Nicola Dallaporta are from an interview with the author, on 1 May 1993.

31 *Einsatzgruppen* ("killing squads") were active in the Soviet Union, following on the heels of Operation Barbarossa. *Einsatzkommandos* were smaller units of the *Einsatzgruppen*, or individuals in them. *Einsatzkommando*-style actions took place in the *Generalgouvernement* in Poland while most of the murders were in death camps.

32 From here on, referred to by her true name, Gabriella Garda Aliverti.

4   The Era of the Racial Laws and the Nazi Occupation

1 Primo Levi, "Week-End," in *Lilit e altri racconti*, 1981.

2 All quotations here from Eugenio Gentili Tedeschi are from an interview with the author, on 22 April 1993, and from letters and documents sent subsequently to her.

3 Primo Levi, "The Pharaoh with the Swastika," *La Stampa*, 9 September 1983.

4 Carlo Levi, *Christ Stopped At Eboli*, 1967.

5 Primo Levi, "The Pharaoh with the Swastika."

6 Primo Levi, *If This Is A Man* and *The Truce*, published as a combined volume by Abacus, 1987, p. 19.

7 Primo Levi, "The Pharaoh with the Swastika."

8 Piedmontese dialect word, of Hebrew origin; "*baït*" means "house" in Hebrew.

9 Guido Bachi's words throughout the book come from a number of conversations between Bachi and the author.

10 Luciana Nissim, "*Ricordi della casa dei morti*," in *Donne contro il mostro*, 1946.

11 In Camon, *Conversazione con Primo Levi*, Primo Levi describes this scene

slightly differently in *The Periodic Table*, where he attributes these words to Cagni, his interrogator, in the Aosta prison.

12 *Ibid.*

5 From the Mountains to the Fossoli di Carpi

1 Poli and Calcagno, *Echi di una voce perduta.*
2 Hilberg, *The Destruction of the European Jews.*
3 Camon, *Conversazione con Primo Levi.*
4 Primo Levi, "Remembrance of a Good Man," *La Stampa*, 21 October 1983.
5 Bernhard Lösener, expert adviser on Jewish affairs to the Nazi state secretary of the interior ministry, Wilhelm Stuckart, had defined several categories of *Mischlinge*, "half-breeds." See Hilberg, *The Destruction of the European Jews.*
6 Gitta Sereny, *Into That Darkness*, 1974.
7 *Ibid.*, p. 9.
8 *Ibid.*, p. 202.
9 *Ibid.*, p. 101.
10 Testimony of Primo Levi and Leonardo De Benedetti, published in 1946 by the journal *Minerva Medica.*
11 Hilberg, *The Destruction of the European Jews*, p. 410.
12 *Ibid.*, p. 411.
13 *Ibid.*
14 *Ibid.*
15 Nissim, *Ricordi della casa dei morti.*
16 Details of the journey to Auschwitz by Primo Levi, Luciana Nissim and Vanda Maestro that are not based on Primo Levi's book, *If This Is A Man*, come from the evidence of Luciana Nissim, whom the author met in Milan in 1994.

6 Auschwitz (Part I)

1 Nissim, *Ricordi della casa dei morti.*
2 Plural of German *Häftling*, prisoner.
3 *Kommando* — all-purpose German term for section, squad, crew, unit, work detail. The term is retained in this book.
4 Hermann Langbein, *Menschen in Auschwitz*, 1972. (In Auschwitz slang, to "organize" was to steal, scrounge, or otherwise procure forbidden goods, whether to barter them for other goods or privileges, or for personal use.)
5 For further information on Auschwitz and the Polish resistance movement, see Langbein, *Menschen in Auschwitz.*
6 Primo Levi says ninety-six men were tattooed but these are the tattoo numbers he gives.
7 Quoted in Léon Poliakov, *Auschwitz*, 1964.

8   Quoted in Lucy Davidowicz, *The War Against the Jews*, 1986, p. 139: "Resettlement for work in the East" was the fundamental lie used to deceive the Jews concerning their fate..." "Resettlement" became the euphemism for transporting Jews to the gas chambers.

9   Hilberg, *The Destruction of the European Jews*, p. 923.

10 *Ibid.*, p. 924.

11 In August 1941, five hundred Soviet prisoners of war were brought to Birkenau, so that Zyklon B, the creation of I.G. Farben, could be tested on them.

12 Hilberg, *The Destruction of the European Jews*, p. 935.

13 *Ibid.*

14 Kapo (from Italian "*capo*", chief) prisoner in charge of a work squad; Block leader ("*Blockälteste*," literally "Block elder") prisoner in charge of a Block; *Stubendienst* ("barrack room duty") subordinate to the Block leader. Most of these powerful underlings were Germans or Poles (though it was not unknown for a Jew to be appointed), and usually they were criminals. For a thorough account of the entire Auschwitz system, its hierarchy and conditions, see Yisrael Gutman and Michael Berenbaum (eds), *Anatomy of the Auschwitz Death Camp*, 1994, p. 22.

15 Paul Steinberg, *Chroniques d'ailleurs*, 1996.

16 Levi and De Benedetti, in *Minerva Medica*.

17 *Ibid.*

18 See Primo Levi, "The Memory of the Offence," Chapter 1 of *The Drowned and the Saved*.

19 Jean Améry, as quoted in Primo Levi's *The Drowned and the Saved*, p. 12. The passage appears in the translation of Améry's book, *Jenseits von Schuld und Sühne*, entitled *At the Mind's Limits*.

20 These details are taken from the evidence compiled by Levi and De Benedetti and published in *Minerva Medica*.

21 Langbein, *Menschen in Auschwitz*.

22 First published in 1982. Translated into English as *If Not Now, When?* in 1985 (US) and 1986 (UK). Citations in this book are taken from the Penguin, 1995 (US) and the Abacus, 1987 (UK) editions. Subsequent references to this title will be shortened to *INNW*; US page numbers are given in *italic*.

23 Roth interview, *The New York Times Book Review*, 12 October 1986/*The London Review of Books*, 26 October 1986.

24 Primo Levi, "Ostjuden," in *Collected Poems*, 1992, p. 14.

25 Evidence of Levi and De Benedetti, *Minerva Medica*.

26 Literally, wash-rooms; here, sinks.

27 Rudolf Höss was appointed commandant on 1 May 1940, and ran Auschwitz until promoted away on 11 November 1943. His successors were SS-*Obersturmanbannführer* Arthur Liebehenschel (to May 1944) and SS-*Sturmbannführer* Richard Bär, who commanded until the liquidation of the camp.

28 Poli and Calcagno, *Echi di una voce perduta.*

29 The adoption of the term *"Muselmann"* or *"Muselmänner"* to denote prisoners in the last stages of exhaustion has been attributed to a Polish doctor, Fejkiel, who apparently compared a group of prisoners to a group of praying Arabs.

30 Poli and Calcagno, *Echi di una voce perduta.*

31 Levi spells his name "Resnyk."

32 Moszek (in French: Maurice) Reznik told his story to the author in an interview which was published in *Nouveaux Cahiers* no. 114 (Autumn 1993), and in *La Stampa*, 31 October 1993.

33 Tadeusz Paczula, *"Die ersten Opfer sind die Polen,"* in H.G. Adler et al., *Auschwitz — Zeugnisse und Berichte*, 1962.

34 Langbein, *Menschen in Auschwitz.*

35 Lecture given by Primo Levi in Settimo Torinese, quoted in Poli and Calcagno, *Echi di una voce perduta.*

36 Primo Levi, "Remembrance of a Good Man," *La Stampa*, 21 October 1983. Published on the death of Leonardo De Benedetti.

37 Levi and De Benedetti, report in *Minerva Medica.*

38 *Ibid.*

39 Testimony of Jacques Zylbermine, deported to Monowitz at the age of sixteen, interviewed by the author in February 1995.

40 Levi and De Benedetti, report in *Minerva Medica.*

41 SS efficiency required the compilation of a daily *Rapport*, a report on the number of prisoners held in the camp. Its compiler was the *Rapportführer*. He was responsible for the daily roll-calls, and also reported on the quantity of rations issued, and the punishments awarded. His immediate subordinate was the *Blockführer*, the SS man who commanded each Block: for the prisoners, the most familiar face among the SS.

42 For an explanation of the precise nature of the different camps within Auschwitz-Birkenau, see Hilberg, *The Destruction of the European Jews.*

43 Langbein, *Menschen in Auschwitz.*

44 *Ibid.*

45 Poliakov, *Auschwitz.*

46 *Ibid.*

47 Lello Perugia was born in Rome on 20 October 1919, the son of Israel Perugia and Emma Della Ricola.

48 Interviews with Lello Perugia, published in *L'Unità*, 3 September 1992 and in *La Repubblica*, 24 January 1995.

49 Langbein, *Menschen in Auschwitz.*

50 Primo Levi, "The Survivor," in *Collected Poems*, p. 64.

51 Alberto Dallavolta and Jean Samuel did share the same bunk for a while.

52 Paul Steinberg, conversation with the author.

53 Georges Wellers was a trained physiologist. A Russian Jew, he was arrested late in 1941, interned first in Compiègne and then in Drancy, and

deported to Auschwitz in July 1944. His testimony — which also constitutes the best study of Drancy published to this day — was reissued in
1991.

54 Primo Levi also recorded Reznik's Yiddish accent.

55 Lucie Adelsberger, *Auschwitz — ein Tatsachenbericht*, 1956.

56 Rudolf Vrba and Alfred Wetzler, "*Ein geflüchtener Häftling berichtet,*" in
H.G. Adler et al., *Auschwitz — Zeugnisse und Berichte*, 1962.

57 Langbein, *Menschen in Auschwitz*.

58 Nissim, *Ricordi della casa dei morti*.

59 Luciana Nissim's evidence concerning this event is confirmed by Simone
Alizon's account in *L'Exercise de vivre*, 1996.

7   Auschwitz (Part II)

1 Jew camp, extermination camp.

2 Some of them were published in English as *Moments of Reprieve* in 1979
(US) and 1986 (UK). Citations in this book are taken from the Penguin,
1995 (US) and the Abacus, 1987 (UK) editions. Subsequent references to
this title will be shortened to *Reprieve*; US page numbers are given in *italic*.

3 Report by Hans Münch quoted in Poliakov, *Auschwitz*.

4 Literally, "shit masters and bath masters," which Levi discreetly translates
as "superintendents of the latrines and showers" (*Man 90/96*).

5 Langbein, *Menschen in Auschwitz*.

6 Danuta Czech, "Auschwitz" (doctoral thesis) and in APMO,
Bearbeitungen Luftaufnahmen, t. 64, f. 50–69.

7 In APMO, Bearbeitungen Luftaufnahmen, Mat. RO., T.II, f.125.

8 Levi and De Benedetti, *Minerva Medica*.

9 Like Elie Wiesel, Menahem Davidowicz came from Sighet, a small town in
Transylvania. He married Haya Cilli Davidowicz in 1941, and they had
two children. In spring 1944 the Hungarian police shipped the Jews of
Sighet to a ghetto. From there, the Davidowicz family was deported to
Auschwitz, where both children were murdered on arrival. Menahem and
Haya survived the camp, and after the war they settled first in Prague and
then in Dortmund. They had two more children. Mendi and Primo Levi
were in touch by letter, and were able to meet during Levi's frequent business trips to Germany. Mendi Davidowicz died in 1986. (This information
comes from the author's interview with Haya Cilli Davidowicz, on 20 June
1996.)

10 Jean Samuel's story comes from conversations and correspondence with
the author.

11 Primo Levi spells it "Pikolo," in *If This Is A Man*.

12 Dante, *The Divine Comedy: Inferno*, Canto XXVI, lines 118–20 (*The
Portable Dante*, 1984).

13 *Ibid.*, lines 133–5.

14 *Ibid.*, lines 139–41.

15 *Ibid.*, line 142.

16 *Université de la Sorbonne Nouvelle*, no. 31/32, 1992.

17 The figure comes from Randolph L. Braham, "Hungarian Jews," in Gutman and Berenbaum, *Anatomy of the Auschwitz Death Camp*, p. 466.

18 Jean Samuel, conversations and correspondence with the author.

19 Camon, *Conversazione con Primo Levi*.

20 Elie Wiesel, *Night*, 1981, p. 45.

21 Primo Levi, *La ricerca delle radici*.

22 Sam Hoffenberg, *Le Camp de Poniatowa*, 1988.

23 "Kandel" in *If This Is A Man*.

24 Primo Levi, writing in *La Stampa* on the occasion of the publication of *If This Is A Man*, as reported in Poli and Calcagno, *Echi di una voce perduta*.

25 For a full account of this correspondence, see Chapter 11, pp. 282–92.

26 Langbein, *Menschen in Auschwitz*.

27 The four crematoria in Auschwitz II-Birkenau were numbered from II to V. Crematorium I was located in the main camp, Auschwitz I.

28 Filip Müller, *Sonderbehandlung: Drei Jahre in den Krematorien und Gaskammern*, 1979.

29 Hilberg, *The Destruction of the European Jews*, p. 195: "East and south of the incorporated territories, the Germans created a new type of territorial administration, first known as the "General Government in Poland" and later referred to simply as the "General Government" (*Generalgouvernement*)." Hitler appointed Hans Frank as governor-general of the *Generalgouvernement* in 1939. In addition to Auschwitz, the territory also contained the death camps of Belzec, Sobibor, and Treblinka. Hilberg says that the region held approximately 1,400,000 Jews. In *Hitler's Willing Executioners*, Daniel Goldhagen puts the number of Polish Jews killed by 1943 at two million, while Davidowicz gives a figure of 3,300,000 Polish Jews killed by the end of the war, but that includes Polish Jews living outside the region. Frank was sentenced to death at Nuremberg, and hanged in October 1946.

30 Danuta Czech, *Kalendarium der Ereignisse im Konzentrationslager Auschwitz-Birkenau 1939–1945*, 1989.

8   The Last Ten Days

1 Maurice Reznik in *Notre volonté*, November/December 1992 to January 1993.

2 Libertino Faussone is the hero of Primo Levi's book *La chiave a stella*, 1978, translated as *The Monkey's Wrench*, 1986 (US) and *The Wrench*, 1987 (UK). Citations in this book are taken from the Penguin, 1995 (US) and Abacus, 1988 (UK) editions. Subsequent references to this title will be shortened to *Wrench*; only one set of figures for page reference numbers is given, as pagination in both US and UK editions is identical.

3 The story appears in *Moments of Reprieve*.

4 Accommodation Block reserved for those top members of the inmate functionary hierarchy who enjoyed special privileges.

5 Filip Müller, *Sonderbehandlung: Drei Jahre in den Krematorien und Gaskammern.*

6 This killing technique was called the *Genickschuss.* The SS, and particularly the practised killers of the *Einsatzkommandos*, worked out a way to do it without being splashed by blood and bone.

7 In a letter to Charles Conreau dated 1 January 1985, Primo Levi wrote that in December 1984 he had received a letter from Lakmaker's brother, "who came across his family name when he happened to read my first book, and so had the news, forty years later, about his brother's final days. He writes that he is coming to Turin on a business trip, but on the subject of that poor boy I don't remember anything more than what I wrote. What about you?"

8 *SD: Sicherheitsdiendst* — Security Service.

9 These statistics may not be quite accurate, as Levi himself writes (*Truce* 15/187) that out of 800 prisoners, around 500 died before the Russians arrived and another 200 in the following days.

10 200,000: the "high numbers" were newcomers to the camp.

9 Liberation: Detour through Central Europe

1 Letter from Charles Conreau to the author, dated 14 December 1993.

2 Letter from Primo Levi to Jean Samuel, dated 23 March 1946.

3 *Ibid.*

4 *Sipo: Sicherheitspolizei* — Security Police.

5 Letter from Charles Conreau to the author, dated 14 December 1993.

6 Ethnic German citizen of a country other than Germany. An ethnically German full German citizen was a *Reichsdeutsche.*

7 See Levi's Afterword (*Truce* 230/398). Interview with Lidia Rolfi, 27 April 1993, at her home in Mondovi. She is the author of *Le donne de Ravensbrück*, and the reluctant inspiration of Liliana Cavani's film *The Night Porter*. She very much resented the way that Cavani had exploited her memories without bothering to consult her.

8 Lello Perugia reports that Pavoncello, who was also a survivor of the camp, returned to Italy, and has since died.

9 Lello Perugia, telephone conversation with the author.

10 *NKVD: Narodnyi Kommissariat Vnutrennikh Del* — People's Commissariat for Internal Affairs — the enormously powerful Soviet Security Service, headed by Lavrenti Beria.

11 This information, including the real name of "Dr Gottlieb," was provided to the author by Lello Perugia.

12 "And as Jesus passed forth from thence, he saw a man, named Matthew, sitting at the receipt of custom: and he saith unto him, Follow me. And he arose, and followed him." (Matthew, chapter 9, verse 9)

13 "But that ye may know that the Son of man hath power on earth to forgive sins, (then saith he to the sick of the palsy,) Arise, take up thy bed, and go unto thine house." (Matthew, chapter 9, verse 6)

14 Primo Levi, "The Tommy Gun under the Bed" in *The Mirror Maker: Stories and Essays*, p. 77. *The Mirror Maker* includes the translation of portions of *Racconti e saggi*, 1986. Citations in this book are taken from the Schocken, 1989 (US) and Methuen, 1990 (UK) editions.

15 These journey dates, which differ slightly from those which appear in *The Truce*, were given to the author by Lello Perugia.

16 First words of the verse that expresses the fundamental profession of faith of Judaism: "Hear, O Israel: The Lord our God, the Lord is One." (Deuteronomy, chapter 6, verse 4.)

17 Italian Army in Russia, which had fought on the side of the Germans.

18 Telephone conversation with the author, 25 May 1996.

19 Now the Israeli national anthem, "Hatikvah" ("The Hope") was written by N.N. Imber in 1878, and adopted as the Jewish national anthem by the first Zionist Congress in 1897.

20 Primo Levi, *Se non ora, quando?*

21 Full title, *Michel Strogoff, Moscou-Irkoutsk* (1876), translated into English by W.H.G. Kingston as *Michael Strogoff, the Courier of the Czar* (1877).

22 The American-Jewish Joint Distribution Committee is a relief and rescue organization founded in 1914 to aid Jewish refugees during the First World War. Known as the JDC or "the Joint," it was the primary source for financial support of the US War Refugee Board during the Second World War. At the war's end, it provided food, clothing, and assistance to Jewish DPs ("displaced persons").

23 Améry, *At the Mind's Limits*, p. 64.

24 *Ibid.*, p. 67.

25 *Ibid.*, p. 70.

26 *Ibid.*, p. 71.

27 Emilio Vita Finzi was a relation of Leonardo De Benedetti.

10 The Return

1 Giulia Diena, interview with the author, 24 April 1993.

2 Interview with Bianca Guidetti Serra in Turin, March 1993.

3 Interview with Alberto Salmoni in Moncalieri, March 1993.

4 The Jewish Brigade was a force of Jewish volunteers who fought on the Allied side in the British army.

5 Roth interview, *The New York Times Book Review*, 12 October 1986/*The London Review of Books*, 26 October 1986.

6 Primo Levi, "Reveille," in *Collected Poems*, p. 10.

7 Primo Levi, interview of 27 January 1983, with Anna Bravo and Federico Cereja, in Anna Bravo and Daniele Jalla (eds), *La vita offesa*, 1987.

8 Roth interview, *The New York Times Book Review*, 12 October 1986/*The London Review of Books*, 26 October 1986.

9 Poli and Calcagno, *Echi di una voce perduta*.

10 Debate organized in spring 1977 by the review *Hommes et livres*, on the condition of the writer in the Italian political context.

11 Primo Levi, "Shemà," in *Collected Poems*, p. 9.

12 Jean Samuel was kind enough to send the author a copy of this letter, which he read out in public at a conference devoted to Primo Levi that took place in Metz in 1992.

13 Interview with Nicola Dallaporta, 1 May 1993.

14 Interview with Nicola Dallaporta in Padua, April 1993.

15 Poli and Calcagno, *Echi di una voce perduta*.

16 Ferdinando Camon, *Libération*, 13 April 1987, pp. 23–4.

17 Primo Levi, interview with M. Grassano (1979) in Giuseppe Grassano, *Primo Levi, Il castoro* (La Nuova Italia, Florence, 1981).

18 Primo Levi, "11 February 1946," in *Collected Poems*, p. 16.

19 Poli and Calcagno, *Echi di una voce perduta*, p. 282.

20 Poli and Calcagno, *Echi di una voce perduta*.

21 Alessandro Galante Garrone, interview with the author. The same story of the Italian publishers' rejection of Primo Levi's book, in particular that of Einaudi, was told by Cesare Cases, in his interview with the author, 23 April 1993.

22 George Steiner, "*La Longue Vie de la métaphore. Une approche de la Shoah*," *Ecrit du temps*, February 1987.

23 *Ibid.*

24 The stories were included in the collection *Storie naturali*, 1966 by Einaudi. Together with the stories in *Vizio di forma*, 1971, these were translated into English and published in 1990 as *The Sixth Day* (US/UK). Citations in this book are taken from the Summit, 1990 (US) and Abacus, 1991 (UK) editions.

25 Roth interview, *The New York Times Book Review*, 12 October 1986/*The London Review of Books*, 26 October 1986.

26 Luisa Accati, interview with the author, 23 March 1993.

27 Interviews with Paola and Luisa Accati in February and March 1993.

28 The chaos and utter confusion before the Creation.

29 Luisa Accati, interview with the author, 23 March 1993.

30 Primo Levi, *La chiave a stella*. For the story of the "sick tube" see *Wrench* pp. 14–28.

31 Primo Levi, interview with Giorgio Manzoni, "*Elogio del libero lavoro*," *Paese Sera*, 11 December 1978.

32 Primo Levi, interview with Giorgio de Rienzo, "*All'eroe dell'ultimo romanzo di Primo Levi lavorare piace*," *Famiglia Cristiana*, January 1979.

33 Poli and Calcagno, *Echi di una voce perduta*.

34 From *The Periodic Table*.

35 Levi and Regge, *Conversations.*

36 Roth interview, *The New York Times Book Review*, 12 October 1986/*The London Review of Books*, 26 October 1986.

37 Interviews with Magda Beyneton and Armando Novero, April and May 1996.

11 Witness

1 Heinz Riedt now lives on the isle of Prócida, in the Bay of Naples. The author interviewed him on 26 June 1996.

2 First published in Italian as a research paper in 1983 and in *Rassegna mensile di Israele*, 1989. It was later published in France as *Le Devoir de mémoire* (Mille et une nuits, 1995).

3 The *Volkssturm*, "People's Militia," was a last-ditch German defence force made up of teenage boys and older men (aged up to sixty), created by a Hitler order of 25 September 1944.

4 Jean Samuel was a witness. He now lives in Strasbourg. He and Levi used to meet quite regularly.

5 The SA — *Sturmabteilungen*, Storm Troopers, also known as Brown Shirts — were originally strong-arm squads and street fighters organized by Major Ernst Röhm as the private army of the Nazi Party in opposition. Once Hitler was in power the SA's job was done, but Röhm had higher ambitions. In the "Night of the Long Knives," 30 June 1934, Hitler wiped out both him and most of the SA leadership, together with various other opponents.

6 F.M. claimed to have picked out Brackier, Kandek, and Levi from a possible thirty candidates. His story is shaky, but the situation is further complicated by the fact that whereas F.M., like Levi, does not mention Paul Steinberg, both Steinberg and Levi concur that the selection was made by Doktor Pannwitz.

7 *Ausweis*: identity card, or pass.

8 Améry, *At the Mind's Limits*, pp. 16–17.

9 Poli and Calcagno, *Echi di una voce perduta.*

10 Primo Levi, "For Adolf Eichmann," in *Collected Poems*, p. 24.

11 Primo Levi, interview with Paolo Spriano, "*L'avventura di Primo Levi*," *L'Unità*, 14 July 1963.

12 Reprinted in Galante Garrone, *Amalek, il dovere della memoria*, 1989.

13 Bayer is one of the three companies created by the token dismantling of I.G. Farben after the war.

14 The first two pieces were published in English in the Primo Levi collection *The Sixth Day*, (1990) as *The Sleeping Beauty in the Fridge: a Winter's Tale* and *The Sixth Day*.

15 See Italo Calvino, *I libri degli altrui*, 1991.

16 The Auschwitz stories published in *Lilit e altri racconti* appear in English in *Moments of Reprieve*.

17 Poli and Calcagno, *Echi di una voce perduta*.
18 In *Quaderni*, IV, 1967, no. 30.

12 Chemist and Writer
1 Interview with Jean-François Chaix, who played the part of Jean Samuel (Pikkolo) in the stage adaptation of Levi's book.
2 Primo Levi, preface to the stage version of *Se questo è un uomo* (Collezione di teatro, Einaudi, 1966); and cited in Guido Boursier, "*Primo Levi rievoca in teatro la barbarie dei Lager nazisti*," Gazzetta del Popolo, 17 November 1966.
3 The last two phrases come from Levi's Afterword to *The Reawakening* (Touchstone, New York, 1995) and in the combined edition of *If This Is A Man* and *The Truce* (Penguin, London, 1979).
4 *La Stampa*, 7 June 1967.
5 Bernard Levin, *The Sunday Times*, 17 May 1987.
6 Lorenzo Mondo, interview with the author, 29 March 1993.
7 Gabriella Poli, interview and correspondence with the author, 1993.
8 Primo Levi, "Westward," in *The Sixth Day*.
9 *Il sesto giorno*.
10 Risa Sodi, interview with Primo Levi, *Partisan Review*, vol. 54, no. 3, 1987.
11 Letter from Charles Conreau dated 14 December 1993.

13 "You Will Write Concisely and Clearly"
1 Primo Levi, interview with Piero Bianucci, "*Tanti atti de fede nel romanzo*," La Gazzetta del Popolo, 20 November 1971.
2 Primo Levi, interview with Gabriella Poli, "*Primo Levi come chimico puo diventare uno 'scrittore'*," La Stampa, 20 November 1976.
3 Primo Levi, interview with Gabriella Poli, "*Primo Levi, l'alfabeto della chimica*," Tuttolibri, 4 December 1976.
4 Italo Calvino, *Il libri degli altri*, 1991.
5 *Uomini e libri*, no. 112, 1987, p. 13.
6 See Primo Levi, *Collected Poems*, pp. 9, 10, 23.
7 Quoted in Poli and Calcagno, *Echi di una voce perduta*.
8 From Primo Levi, "Avigliana," *Collected Poems*, p. 18.
9 Ruth Feldman, interview with Deborah Ford for the television documentary, *The Memory of the Offence* (Fine Art Productions for BBC Television). The author is grateful to Deborah Ford for providing a transcript of that interview.
10 *Ibid.*
11 "On Obscure Writing" appeared in *La Stampa* on 11 December 1976, and is included in *Other People's Trades*.
12 Reprinted in Poli and Calcagno, *Echi di una voce perduta*.
13 The *Pirkei Avot* ("Sayings of the Sages") are a collection of moral and reli-

gious sayings contained in the ninth tractate of the fourth order of the Mishnah.

14 Vittel in France was one of the camps for Jews with foreign passports who were hoaxed into believing that they were being held for exchange. Almost all of them were sent to extermination camps where they were murdered. See Davidowicz, *The War Against the Jews*.

15 Yitzhak Katzenelson came from a long line of rabbis and intellectuals. He was born in Korelichi in Russia, in 1886, and arrived in Lodz as a child. He was part of Y.L. Peretz's circle in Warsaw, and became a poet and playwright in Hebrew and Yiddish. In the Warsaw ghetto, he led a Hebrew cultural society and also joined the combat group *Hashomer Hatzaïr*. A Holocaust research institute at the Ghetto Fighters' Museum in Israel is named in his honour.

14 Man of Letters

1 Grassano, *Primo Levi, Il castoro*.
2 Ha Keillah *("The Community")*, February 1979, p. 6.
3 Primo Levi first called it *Vile meccanico*, but Einaudi persuaded him to change it. (See Guido Gerosa, *"Santa Lucia per 'Se questo è un uomo'," Il Giorno*, 24 November 1981.
4 Primo Levi, quoted in an article by Silvia Gicomoni, *"Il mago Merlino e l'uomo fabro," La Repubblica*, 24 January 1979.
5 Grassano, *Primo Levi, Il castoro*.
6 The debate was organized by Stefano Reggiani, and published under the title *"Difenda sfida il lavoro ben fatto," La Stampa*, 14 January 1979.
7 This anecdote, which took place most probably in autumn 1978, can be found in Enrico Boeri, *"Quattro chiacchiere con Primo Levi," Tecnologie chimiche*, December 1983. Sometime later, another Piedmontese rigger, Mario Maccagno, saw himself so exactly portrayed in Faussone that he went on to write his own life story, *Costruire uno motore*.
8 *"Un olocausto che pesa ancora sulla conscienza del mondo," La Stampa*, 28 April 1979.
9 Antonio Debendetti, *"Vincitore il romanzo," Corriere della Sera*, 4 July 1979.
10 No. 6, November 1979.
11 From *"Buco nero di Auschwitz," La Stampa*, 22 January 1987. This was Primo Levi's third response to Faurisson, his first two responses appeared in *La Stampa* on 3 and 19 January 1979.
12 Author of *The Holocaust Kingdom* (Holt, Rinehart and Winston, New York, 1965).
13 Rachel Ertel, *Dans la langue de personne — Poésie yiddish de l'anéantissement*, 1993.
14 *La Stampa*, 12 February 1977.
15 See Poli and Calcagno, *Echi di una voce perduta*.

16 Only those words in capitals in paragraph 8 appear today in the "Italian" Block in Auschwitz.

17 *La ricerca delle radici.*

18 Natalia Ginzburg, *Lessico familiare,* 1966.

19 *Ibid.*

20 *Ibid.*

15 Returning to Jewish Roots

1 *Lilit e altri racconti,* 1981/85 (most of which is included in *Moments of Reprieve* in English) drew inspiration for its series of sketches from wide-ranging sources, including: Auschwitz; chemistry and science; nature; and a brand of ironic-fantastic fiction that recurs in *Storie naturali* and *Vizio di forma.*

2 Roth interview, *The New York Times Book Review,* 12 October 1986/*The London Review of Books,* 26 October 1986.

3 From the Hebrew *Chalutz* — pioneer.

4 In 1917 Chaim Weizmann, the Russian-born Zionist who replaced Theodor Herzl and who later became the first president of Israel, persuaded Great Britain to issue the Balfour Declaration, which stated that "HM government view with favour the establishment in Palestine of a national home for the Jewish people."

5 Primo Levi, address to the Congress of Jewish Authors organized by the Rockefeller Foundation in Bellagio from 29 November to 2 December 1982.

6 Emmanuel Ringelblum, *Notes from the Warsaw Ghetto,* 1958.

7 Refers to the Oral Law in all its aspects.

8 Rabbinical commentary on the Bible that sets out to clarify various juridical points or to expound a moral teaching by appealing to various literary genres: stories, parables, and legends.

9 Literally "story." Non-juridical part of the classical rabbinical texts. Rabbinical literature is divided into two great collections, the *Halachah* and the *Aggada.*

10 Primo Levi, "Ritual and Laughter," in *Other People's Trades.*

11 Interview with Raffaello Manzini and Brunetto Salvarini.

12 A translation of this song appears in *Collected Poems,* p. 75.

13 Mountain-top fortress in Israel where Jews sustained a heroic siege against the Romans in AD 71–73. The Masada garrison committed collective suicide in AD 73, as reported by Flavius Josephus in *The Jewish War.*

14 Refers to the nation of the Amalekites — the archetype of evil in the Jewish tradition.

15 Primo Levi speaking in an interview on *Canale 5,* published under *Prima Pagina* in *La Stampa,* 13 June 1985.

16 From the Introduction to *Primo Levi, Opere I,* 1987 and more recently in *Primo Levi: un'antologia della critica,* ed. Ernesto Ferrero, 1997. The full

text of Cases' review, entitled *"L'ordine delle cose e l'ordine delle parole,"* is printed in *L'Indice*, December 1987.

17 Primo Levi, interview with Stefano Jesurum, quoted in Poli and Calcagno, *Echi di una voce perduta*.

18 Begin resigned on 15 September 1983, following his wife's death.

19 Interview with Dan Vittorio Segre in his house in Govone, 8 May 1994.

20 *Storia di un ebreo fortunato*, 1985. Translated by the author in 1987 as *Memories of a Fortunate Jew*.

21 *La Stampa*, 15 June 1985.

22 Ferdinando Camon, *Conversazione con Primo Levi*.

23 *Ibid*.

24 Ferdinando Camon, interview with the author, May 1994.

25 *Ibid*.

26 *Ibid*.

27 *Ibid*.

28 Hilberg, *The Destruction of the European Jews*, and Goldhagen, *Hitler's Willing Executioners*, 1996.

16 Famous and Marginal

1 Cesare Cases, interview with the author, 23 March 1993.

2 *"Tradurre Kafka," La Stampa*, 5 June 1983. Reprinted in *The Mirror Maker*, pp. 106–9. The interview was with Luciano Geuta, *"Cosi ho rivissuto 'Il processo' di Kafka"*, *La Stampa*, 9 April 1983.

3 Giuseppe Bernadi, *"Primo Levi traduce Kafka," Il Giornale*, 22 May 1983.

4 Primo Levi, *"Kafka col coltello nel cuore," La Stampa*, 5 June 1983.

5 Primo Levi, interview with Bravo and Cereja.

6 Poli and Calcagno, *Echi di una voce perduta*, p. 311.

7 Primo Levi, interview with Bravo and Cereja.

8 Interview with Edgardo Bartoli, *"Prima che il sole ci ingoi," La Repubblica*, 16 August 1983.

9 The text of Primo Levi's speech was provided by Sion Segre Amar, who attended the conference.

10 The reference is to Alberto Dallavolta.

11 Alberto's family lived in Milan.

12 Elie Wiesel, interview with the author, 21 June 1996.

13 Elie Wiesel, *Night*, p. 79.

17 "Old, Am I?"

1 See also pp. 320–1.

2 *Il revier di Mauthausen. Conversazione con Giuseppe Calore*, preface by Norberto Bobbio, Edizioni Dell'Orso, 1992.

3 Primo Levi, interview with Giulio Nascimberi, *"Levi: l'ora incerta della poesia," Corriere della Sera*, 28 October 1984.

4 Theodor Adorno, "Critique of Culture and Society," written in 1949 and published in 1951 in *Soziologische Forschung in unsere Zeit.*

5 Primo Levi, *Conversazione e interviste 1963–1987*, ed., Marco Belpoliti, Einaudi, 1997.

6 Levi and Regge, *Conversations.*

7 *Dialogo*, 1984.

8 Primo Levi, "Vecchio io?," published in *Stampa Sera*, 15 November 1982.

9 The article appears in *Trades*, pp. 205–8/192–5.

10 Agnese Incisa, interview with the author, 9 May 1994.

11 Primo Levi, "Arachne," in *Collected Poems*, p. 49.

12 This story, Levi's last contribution to *La Stampa*, published posthumously on 26 April 1987, is translated as "The Marital Web" and is reproduced in Appendix II of this book.

13 Primo Levi, interviewed by Giorgio Bocca on the *"Prima Pagina"* programme, *Canale 5*, 13 June 1985.

14 Primo Levi interviewed by Risa Sodi for the *Partisan Review*, vol. 54, no. 3, 1987.

15 Bocca interview, *Canale 5*.

16 Letter to Hermann Langbein, 28 March 1986.

17 He was born in Cuba in 1923.

18 "I Find No Solution to the Riddle"

1 *La vita offesa.*

2 *Racconti e saggi*, 1986.

3 *Ha-Keillah*, February 1979.

4 From "The Survivor." The poem is quoted in full on pp. 139–40.

5 *"Giovani, rifiutate tutti i profeti," L'Unità*, 7 November 1992.

6 Levi, interview with Milvia Spadi.

7 Interview given to Lucia Borgia (*"Rifarsi una vita"*), cited by Poli and Calcagno, *Echi di una voce perduta.*

8 *"Tuttolibri,"* 26 July 1986.

9 Ferdinando Camon, *Conversazione con Primo Levi.*

10 Primo Levi as quoted by Paola Accati during her interview with the author at SIVA on 20 April 1993.

11 Sodi interview.

12 Reprinted in *The Mirror Maker*, pp. 175–6.

13 The preparatory interviews are in the possession of Giovanni Tesio. At the request of Primo Levi's widow, their contents have not been disclosed.

14 Interview given on 22 December 1986 to *Focus*, and quoted in Poli and Calcagno, *Echi di una voce perduta.*

15 Article by Anna Maria Guadani, *L'Unità*, 7 February 1988.

16 Ruth Feldman wrote two letters to the author in 1993.

17 David Mendel published an account in Cesare Cases' literary review, *L'Indice*, in May 1994, from which some extracts are here reproduced.

18 *"Un incontro con Primo Levi,"* *L'Indice*, May 1994.
19 In spite of his illness, his former employer managed to live an almost normal life for seven or eight years, but died after the tumour produced bone metastases.
20 This exchange was related by Alessandro Galante Garrone on 29 April 1993.
21 He was referring to *Doppio Legame*.
22 The above quotations are from Di Caro's interview published in his article entitled *"La fatica di scrivere,"* *L'Espresso*, 26 April 1987.
23 Primo Levi, "Almanac," in *Collected Poems*, p. 98.
24 Francesco Rosi's film was released in the United States in 1998.
25 See the discussion concerning spiders in Chapter 17, and Appendix II for a translation of Levi's last story.
26 Bianca Guidetti Serra, interview with the author, 19 April 1993.
27 Elie Wiesel, letter to the author, 21 June 1996.
28 The text of this letter was communicated to the author by Ferdinando Camon.

Glossary of Concentration Camp Terms

There is a full and excellent glossary of concentration camp jargon in Wolfgang Sofsky, *The Order of Terror*, Princeton University Press, 1997.

Appellplatz main square and parade ground where roll-call was held

Arbeitsdienst "labour service," a kind of camp personnel office

Aufräumungskommando an der Rampe "clearing Kommando on the ramp," whose job it was to clean out the wagons and collect the baggage left behind on the platform when a new transport arrived

Bademeister "bath master": in charge of the showers

Bettennachzieher "bed-tightener," whose job it was to inspect all the beds, to ascertain their alignment

Blockälteste prisoner in charge of a Block

Blockfrisör official barber

Blockschneider official tailor for a Block

Blocksperre hut confinement

"Canada" Auschwitz jargon for a specialized warehouse area of the camp, where inmates were given the task of sorting and storing Jewish belongings for shipment to Germany

Einsatzkommandos action unit, task force, in particular, execution squads operating in the occupied eastern territories

E-Lager (E for *Erziehung*) education camp, special section of the *KZ* where civilians served a sentence for an offence

Frauenblock the brothel

Häftling/Häftlinge prisoner/s

Judenlager Jew camp

Kalendarium Auschwitz log-book

Kantine a kind of trade counter where a smart operator could get hold of any luxuries available

Kapo prisoner in charge of a work squad

Kommando all-purpose German term for section, squad, crew, unit, work detail

Konzentrations–Zentrum (KZ) concentration centre

Krankenbau (KB) infirmary and dispensary in Auschwitz-Monowitz, consisting of eight Blocks

Lager camp

Lagerälteste camp elder, in charge of the prison population, chosen from the "greens," the common-law criminals

Lagerschutz camp guard

Leichenkommando "corpse squad" who collected the dead bodies and drove them to the crematorium

Meister civilian foreman, usually German or Polish

Mischlinge "half-breed," meaning half-Jewish

Muselmann (pl. *Muselmänner*) literally "Muslim": a prisoner in the final stage of exhaustion, the living dead who no longer cared for anything

Obergruppenführer SS rank equivalent to lieutenant-general

Prominenten "Prominents," the camp officials
Prominenz prison aristocracy, holders of important posts
Prominenzblock accommodation Block reserved for the top members of the inmate hierarchy

Rapportführer compiler of the daily camp report on the number of prisoners, rations issued, punishments awarded, and so on
Reichsdeutsche a German national as distinct from a *Volksdeutsche*, an ethnic German born outside the Reich
Revier sick-bay

Scheissbegleiter the "shit escort," who accompanied the working prisoner to the latrines
Scheissmeister "shit master": in charge of the latrines
Schonungsblock recuperation ward
Schreiber "scribe" who tattooed the serial number on the prisoner's forearm

Schreibstube clerk's office
Sonderkommando Special Kommando whose job it was to clear the corpses out of the gas chambers and then to burn them, after removing any gold teeth
SS *Wirtschafts-Verwaltungshauptant (WVHA)* the economic–administrative main office
Stubendienst barrack-room orderly, subordinate to the Block leader

Tagesraum spacious room of accommodation Block, inhabited by the Block leader and his friends

Untermensch (pl. *Untermenschen*) "sub-man"
Untersturmführer SS rank equivalent to second lieutenant

Vernichtung annihilation
Vernichtungslager extermination camp
Volkssturm "People's Militia," last-ditch German defence force
Vorarbeiter foreman

Select Bibliography

For details of the works of Primo Levi and their translations, please see p. x. Readers seeking something more comprehensive are referred to the Institut de Memoire de l'Edition Contemporaine (IMEC), 25 rue de Lille, 75007 Paris; telephone +1 42 61 29 29, fax +1 42 27 03 15, and/or the bibliography of the original French edition of this book.

Adelsberger, L., *Auschwitz — ein Tatsachenbericht*, Lettner Verlag, Berlin, 1956.

Adler, H.G., H. Langbein, and E. Lingens-Reiner, *Auschwitz — A Doctor's Story*, Northeastern University Press, Massachusetts, 1995.

Alizon, S., *L'Exercise de vivre*, Stock, Paris, 1996.

Améry, J., *Jenseits von Schuld und Sühne: Bewältigungsversuche eines Überwältigten*, Szczesny, Munich, 1966. Translated into English by S. Rosenfeld and S. P. Rosenfeld as *At the Mind's Limits*, Indiana University Press, Indiana, 1980.

Bassani, G., *The Garden of the Finzi-Continis*, translated by William Weaver, Harcourt Brace Jovanovich, Florida, 1996/translated by I. Quigly, Faber and Faber, London, 1965.

Berenbaum, M., and Y. Gutman, (eds), *Anatomy of the Auschwitz Death Camp*, Indiana University Press, Indiana, 1994.

Bravo, B., and D. Jalla, (eds), *La vita offesa*, Franco Angeli, Milan, 1987.

Calcagno, G., and Gabriella Poli, *Echi di una voce perduta*, Mursia, Milan, 1992.

Calvino, I., *I libri degli altrui*, Einaudi, Turin, 1991.

Camon, F., *Conversations with Primo Levi*, translated by John Shepley, Independent Literary Publishing Association, Illinois, 1989.

Cavaglion, A., *La scuola ebraica a Torino 1938–1943*, Pluri-Verso, 1993.

Ciano's Diaries, translated by Hugh Gibson, Doubleday, New York, 1946/translated by A. Mayor, Methuen, London, 1952.

Czech, D., *Kalendarium der Ereignisse im Konzentrationslager Auschwitz–Birkenau 1939–1945*, Rowohlt Verlag, Reinbeck bei Hamburg, 1989. Translated as *Auschwitz Chronicle 1939–1945*, Henry Holt, New York, 1990.

Dante (Alighieri), *The Divine Comedy*, in *The Portable Dante*, translated, edited, and with notes by M. Musa, Penguin Books, New York/London, 1984.

Davidowicz, L., *The War Against the Jews*, Bantam Books, New York, 1986.

De Felice, R., *Storia degli ebrei italiani sotto il fascismo*, Einaudi, Turin, 1961.

Dino, M., and S. Jesurum, *Primo Levi, Le opere dei giorni*, Rizzoli, Milan, 1992.

Ebrei a Torino — Ricerche per il centenario della sinagoga 1884–1984, with preface by Primo Levi. Archivo di arte e cultura piemontesi, Umberto Allemandi & C., Turin, 1984, now out of print. See Appendix "The Jews of Turin", p. 409 in this book, for the text of Levi's preface.

Ertel, R., *Dans la langue de personne — Poésie yiddish de l'anéantissement*, La Librairie du XXᵉ siècle, Le Seuil, Paris, 1993.

Galante Garrone, A., *Amaleke, il dovere della memoria*, Rizzoli, Milan, 1989.

Ginzburg, N., Family Sayings, Little, Brown, New York, 1996.

Goldhagen, D., *Hitler's Willing Executioners: Ordinary Germans and the Holocaust*, Alfred A. Knopf, New York/Little, Brown, London, 1996.

Grassano, G., *Primo Levi, il castoro*, La Nuova Italia, Florence, 1981.

Guidetti Serra, B., *Storie di giustizia, ingiustizia e galera*, Linea d'ombra, 1994.

Hilberg, R., *The Destruction of the European Jews*, 3 vols, Holmes and Meier, New York, 1985.

Hoffenberg, S., *Le Camp de Poniatowa*, Editions Bibliophane and CDJC, Paris, 1988.

Jesurum, S., *Essere ebrei in Italia*, Longanesi, Milan, 1987.

Langbein, H., *Menschen in Auschwitz*, Europa Verlag, Vienna, 1972.

Lanzmann, C., *Shoah: The Complete Text of the Acclaimed Holocaust Film*, Da Capo, New York, 1995.

Léon, P., *Auschwitz* Archives, Julliard–Gallimard, Paris, 1964.

Levi, C., *Christ Stopped At Eboli*, translated by F. Frenaye, Farrar Straus, New York, 1967; Penguin, London, 1982.

Milza, P., and S. Bernstein, *Le fascisme italien 1919–1945*, Le Seuil, Paris, 1980.

Müller, F., *Sonderbehandlung: Drei Jahre in den Krematorien und Gaskammern*, Munich, 1979.

Nissim, L., *"Ricordi della casa dei morti,"* in *Donne contro il mostro,* Turin, 1946.

Paczula, T., *"Die ersten Opfer sind die Polen,"* in H.G. Adler et al., *Auschwitz — Zeugnisse und Berichte*, Europäische Verlaganstalt, Frankfurt, 1962.

Rendall, S., trans., *The Hidden Encyclical of Pius XI*, Harcourt Brace Jovanovich, Florida, 1997.

Pittocto Fargiorne, L., *Il libro della memoria — ebrei deportati dal Italia 1943–1945*, Mursia, Milan, 1945.

Regge, T., and P. Levi, *Dialogo*, Edizioni di Comunità, Milan, 1984. Translated by Raymond Rosenthal as *Conversations*, Princeton University Press, New Jersey/I.B. Tauris, London, 1989.

Ringelblum, E., *Notes from the Warsaw Ghetto*, translated and edited by J. Sloan, McGraw-Hill, New York, 1958.

Sarfatti, M., *Mussolini contro gli ebrei*, Silvio Zamorani, Turin, 1994.

Segre, D., Vittorio, *Storia di un ebreo fortunato*, Gruppo Editoriale Fabbri SpA, Milan, 1985. Translated into English as *Memories of a Fortunate Jew*, Peter Halban, London, 1987.

Sereny, G., *Into That Darkness*, McGraw-Hill, New York, 1973/André Deutsch, London, 1974.

Sofsky, W., *The Order of Terror*, Princeton University Press, New Jersey, 1997.

Steinberg, P., *Chroniques d'ailleurs*, Ramsay, Paris, 1996.

Stille, A., *Benevolence and Betrayal: Five Italian Families Under Fascism*, Vintage, New York, 1993.

Vrba, R., and A. Wetzler, *"Ein geflüchtener Häftling berichtet,"* in H.G. Adler et al., *Auschwitz — Zeugnisse und Berichte*, Europäische Verlagsanstalt, Frankfurt, 1962.

Wiesel, E., *Night*, translated from the French by S. Rodway, Bantam, New York, 1982/Penguin Books, UK, 1987.

Zuccotti, S., *The Italians and the Holocaust — Persecution, Rescue and Survival*, University of Nebraska Press, Nebraska, 1966/Peter Halban, London, 1987.

Index

The life of Primo Levi is arranged under the headings: Auschwitz; Beliefs; Chemist; Childhood; Nazi Occupation; Postwar Years; Wanderings; Writings